1,001 Low-Fat RECIPES

Third Edition

SUE SPITLER

with Linda R. Yoakam, R.D., M.S.

Surrey Books
Chicago

1,001 LOW-FAT RECIPES
is published by Surrey Books Inc.,
230 E. Ohio St., Suite 120, Chicago, IL 60611.

Third edition: 1 2 3 4 5

This book is manufactured in the United States of America.

Library of Congress Cataloging-in-Publication Data

1,001 low-fat recipes / edited by Sue Spitler with Linda Yoakam.
—3rd ed.
p. cm.
Includes index.
ISBN 1-57284-048-X
1. Low-fat diet—Recipes. I. Title: One thousand one low-fat recipes.
II. Spitler, Sue. III. Yoakam, Linda R.
RM237.7 .A184 2002
641.5'638—dc21 2002013328

Editorial and production: *Bookcrafters, Inc., Chicago*
Art Direction and book design: *Joan Sommers Design, Chicago*
Nutritional Analyses: *Linda R. Yoakam, R.D., M.S.*
Cover illustrations: *Patti Green*

For prices on quantity purchases or for free book catalog, contact Surrey Books at the above address.

This title is distributed to the trade by Publishers Group West.

CONTENTS

ACKNOWLEDGMENTS

The publisher wishes to thank the many talented, creative people who contributed to this fine book:

Food Consultant Sue Spitler, who selected and compiled the delicious recipes with Chef Pat Molden, Managing Editor Gene DeRoin, Copy Editor Leona Pitej, Art Director Joan Sommers, and Editorial Assistants Mildred Kwan and Mary Kushiner.

INTRODUCTION

In 1993, when we began putting together the first edition of *1,001 Low-Fat Recipes*, healthy cooking was primarily an interest of people who had heart conditions, high blood pressure, or diabetes—in other words, people who were told to "eat right" by their doctors and health professionals. Much of the common wisdom at that time told readers to cook plain and simple meals; fat-free and salt-free was the ideal. The result was lots of taste-free dishes, a diet of deprivation that was very difficult to stick to. We opted for flavor over convention and selected recipes that reflected the new thinking about fat and cholesterol.

The research we've done for this new edition has shown that millions of us are now aware that healthy eating is for everyone, not just for those who have no choice. Our goal has been not only to make everyday cooking healthy, but to make everyday cooking interesting and delicious so that healthy eating becomes an enjoyable daily habit, hopefully one that's easy to stick to and hard to break. Our quick-and-easy recipes, each complete with nutritional information and diabetic exchanges, make it a pleasure to plan a week's worth of healthy meals.

More than half the recipes are new, including many from Europe, Latin America, India, and Asia. Most others have been revised to reflect new cooking methods and styles, following current food trends. The Vegetarian Entrées chapter, and the five dessert chapters boast completely new recipes, and the Memorable Menus, Chapter 19, now lists nutritional data for each meal as well as each recipe. Every recipe in the book has been tested to make sure the average cook can prepare it in less than an hour, using ingredients that are available at the local supermarket.

Italian, Mexican, and Asian recipes are among the offerings that reflect popular cooking styles and flavors from many countries, regions, and cultures—all easy to prepare and certain to delight and satisfy. Clever ideas for appetizers and pizzas will inspire festive gatherings, planned or impromptu. Comfort foods, those old-fashioned favorites, will evoke fond memories and pleasures. You'll also savor hearty soups and stews that bubble and simmer to unbelievable goodness.

Fabulous seafood dishes and creative offerings featuring chicken, beef, pork, and lamb highlight the flavors and versatility of these foods. New ideas for rice, grain, and vegetable side dishes will inspire taste buds, and homemade breads will enhance any menu. Desserts are so sumptuous you'll want one with every meal. There are recipes for every occasion, and most are just as appropriate for casual entertaining as for family dining.

If your goal—for your family as well as yourself—is to eat less fat without sacrificing flavor or variety, this cookbook is for you. We have tried to cover every major recipe category—appetizers, soups, salads, seafood, poultry, meats, vegetables, grains, pasta, breads, sauces, desserts, and beverages—and to bring every single recipe into line with the overwhelming consensus of diet and health professionals: *keep portions reasonable and eat less fat.*

Healthful Ingredients

In order to achieve good taste with optimal nutritional value and low fat percentages, we emphasize fresh rather than processed ingredients throughout. We also call for many of the excellent low-fat, fat-free, and "light" products now available.

Vegetable nonstick cooking spray is a boon to today's cook. It contains no fat, cholesterol, sodium, or calories, and it can be used for sauteing, eliminating some of the high-calorie oils usually found in pan-fried recipes. Herbs and spices further enhance flavors and create new taste combinations without loading dishes with fat, sodium, and cholesterol. In a few recipes we list "bouquet garni" as an ingredient. This traditional French combination of herbs consists of a few sprigs of parsley, thyme, and basil or tarragon—plus a bay leaf—all in a cheesecloth bag that is discarded before serving.

Substitutions

On occasion you might wish or need to substitute "regular" ingredients for the reduced-fat or "light" products listed. These will work just as well, but, of course, the nutritional data will be affected. Again, we might list a sauce or soup stock and refer you to this book's recipe for that item; a canned or reconstituted substitute may be used, though this will change the nutrition data.

When herbs and spices are called for, dried products are intended unless the context obviously indicates a fresh item or the recipe specifically lists the ingredients as "fresh." Even then a dried version of the herb may be substituted, but you should use only half as much for equivalent flavor. Reversing the situation, if you substitute fresh for dried herbs, use about twice as much. Fresh parsley is always intended unless specifically stated otherwise.

Nutritional Data

None of the recipes in this third edition of *1,001 Low-Fat Recipes* exceeds 35% calories from fat. Specific nutritional information is provided for each recipe (not including variations), but remember that nutritional data are not infallible. The nutritional analyses are derived by using computer software highly regarded by nutritionists and dietitians, but they are meant to be used only as guidelines because results may vary slightly depending upon the brand or manufacturer of an ingredient used.

Ingredients noted as "optional," "to taste," or "as garnish" are not included in the nutritional analyses. When alternate choices or amounts of ingredients are given, the ingredient or amount listed first is used for analysis. Similarly, data is based on the first number of servings shown, where a range is given. Nutritional analyses are also based on the reduced-fat or fat-free cooking methods used in recipes; the addition of margarine, oil, or other ingredients will invalidate data.

Other factors that can affect the accuracy of nutritional data include variability in sizes, weights, and measures of fruits, vegetables, and other foods. There is also a possible 20% error factor in the nutritional labeling of prepared foods.

If you have any health problems that impose strict dietary requirements, it is important to consult a physician, dietitian, or nutritionist before using recipes in this or any other cookbook. Also, if you are a diabetic or require a diet that restricts calories, fat, or sodium, remember that the nutritional data may be accurate for the recipe as written and tested but not for the food you cooked due to the variables explained above.

We hope that you will find this book useful and that it will soon become the cookbook you turn to every day. We've enjoyed selecting and testing all the new recipes, and we wish you "Bon Appétit!"

—Sue Spitler and Linda Yoakam

ONE

Appetizers AND Starters

SPICY POPCORN

8 servings

- 1/3 cup popcorn
- Butter-flavored cooking spray
- 1 teaspoon paprika
- 1 teaspoon chili powder
- 1/2 teaspoon garlic powder

Per Serving
Calories: 15
% Calories from fat: 5
Fat (gm): 0.1
Sat. fat (gm): 0
Cholesterol (mg): 0
Sodium (mg): 3
Protein (gm): 0.6
Carbohydrate (gm): 3
Exchanges
Milk: 0.0
Vegetable: 0.0
Fruit: 0.0
Bread: 0.0
Meat: 0.0
Fat: 0.0

1. Pop popcorn in hot air popper or microwave popper. Spray popcorn lightly with cooking spray. Sprinkle combined flavorings over hot popcorn, mixing well to coat.

HOT STUFF

16 servings (1/2 cup each)

- 2 cups oyster crackers
- pita chips (purchased)
- 1/2 cup dry-roasted smoked almonds
- 1 cup coarsely chopped mixed dried fruit
- 1 cup dried pineapple chunks
- Butter-flavored cooking spray
- 1 teaspoon dried oregano leaves
- 1 teaspoon garlic powder
- 1 teaspoon chili powder
- 1-1 1/4 teaspoons cayenne pepper
- 1-1 1/4 teaspoons black pepper

Per Serving
Calories: 120
% Calories from fat: 22
Fat (gm): 3.2
Sat. fat (gm): 0.2
Cholesterol (mg): 0
Sodium (mg): 160
Protein (gm): 3.2
Carbohydrate (gm): 21.7
Exchanges
Milk: 0.0
Vegetable: 0.0
Fruit: 0.5
Bread: 1.0
Meat: 0.0
Fat: 0.5

1. Mix crackers, pita chips, almonds, and fruit on large jelly roll pan. Spray mixture generously with cooking spray; sprinkle with combined herbs and peppers and toss to coat.

2. Bake at 350 degrees 15 to 20 minutes, stirring after 10 minutes. Cool; store in covered container at room temperature.

GORP, BY GOLLY

16 servings (about 1/2 cup each)

- 3 cups low-fat granola
- 2 cups pretzel goldfish
- 1/2 cup sesame sticks, broken into halves
- 3 cups coarsely chopped mixed dried fruit
- Butter-flavored cooking spray
- 1 teaspoon ground cinnamon
- 1/2 teaspoon ground nutmeg
- 1/4 teaspoon ground allspice

Per Serving
Calories: 172
% Calories from fat: 13
Fat (gm): 2.6
Sat. fat (gm): 0.2
Cholesterol (mg): 0
Sodium (mg): 82
Protein (gm): 2.7
Carbohydrate (gm): 37.8
Exchanges
Milk: 0.0
Vegetable: 0.0
Fruit: 2.0
Bread: 0.5
Meat: 0.0
Fat: 0.5

1. Mix granola, pretzel goldfish, sesame sticks, and dried fruit on large jelly roll pan. Spray mixture generously with cooking spray; sprinkle with combined spices and toss to coat.

2. Bake at 350 degrees 15 to 20 minutes, stirring after 10 minutes. Cool; store in covered container at room temperature.

STUFFED CELERY

6 servings

- 1 cup low-fat cottage cheese
- 1/4 cup chopped scallions
- 2 teaspoons fresh lemon juice
- 1/2 teaspoon Tamari soy sauce
- 1 teaspoon prepared mustard
- 1/4 cup chopped pimiento
- 1/4 cup chopped fresh chives
- 1 clove garlic, minced
- 6 ribs celery

Per Serving
Calories: 52
% Calories from fat: 10
Fat (gm): 0.6
Sat. fat (gm): 0.3
Cholesterol (mg): 1.7
Sodium (mg): 233
Protein (gm): 5.9
Carbohydrate (gm): 6.5
Exchanges
Milk: 0.0
Vegetable: 1.0
Fruit: 0.0
Bread: 0.0
Meat: 0.5
Fat: 0.0

1. Place all ingredients except celery in a food processor or blender. Process until smooth. Stuff celery with cheese mixture. Cut each rib into 6 pieces.

MARINATED BROCCOLI

8 servings

- 2 pounds broccoli, cut into bite-size pieces
- 3 tablespoons fresh lemon juice
- 1/2 cup low-calorie Italian dressing
- 1/2 cup sliced red onion
- 1 teaspoon capers
- 1 tablespoon grated lemon rind

Per Serving
Calories: 54
% Calories from fat: 27
Fat (gm): 1.9
Sat. fat (gm): 0.3
Cholesterol (mg): 1
Sodium (mg): 154
Protein (gm): 3.5
Carbohydrate (gm): 8.3
Exchanges
Milk: 0.0
Vegetable: 2.0
Fruit: 0.0
Bread: 0.0
Meat: 0.0
Fat: 0.0

1. Simmer broccoli in lightly salted water in large saucepan, covered, 3 to 5 minutes until crisp-tender. Rinse in cold water; drain well.

2. Arrange broccoli in glass mixing bowl. Toss with remaining ingredients. Cover and chill 24 hours, stirring occasionally. Drain broccoli and serve with toothpicks.

HERB-MARINATED MUSHROOMS

12 servings

- 1 tablespoon vegetable oil
- 2/3 cup tarragon wine vinegar
- 2 cloves garlic, minced
- 3 tablespoons sugar
- 1/2 teaspoon salt
- 2 tablespoons water
- 3 tablespoons chopped fresh basil
- 2 teaspoons dried tarragon leaves
- 3 green onions, minced
- 1 1/2 pounds mushrooms, trimmed
- 2 tablespoons chopped parsley

Per Serving
Calories: 39
% Calories from fat: 28
Fat (gm): 1.4
Sat. fat (gm): 0.2
Cholesterol (mg): 0
Sodium (mg): 100
Protein (gm): 1.8
Carbohydrate (gm): 6
Exchanges
Milk: 0.0
Vegetable: 1.0
Fruit: 0.0
Bread: 0.0
Meat: 0.0
Fat: 0.5

1. Whisk all ingredients, except mushrooms and parsley, in medium bowl until blended; add mushrooms and toss gently to mix. Cover with plastic wrap and refrigerate 3 to 4 hours. Toss mushrooms, drain and spoon into serving bowl. Sprinkle with parsley.

MARINATED MUSHROOMS

8 servings

- 1/4 cup balsamic vinegar
- 2 tablespoons olive oil
- 2 tablespoons granulated sugar
- 1 teaspoon dried basil leaves
- 1 teaspoon dried thyme leaves
- 1 teaspoon dried oregano leaves
- 1/8 teaspoon pepper
- 1 pound medium mushrooms, washed, stems trimmed
- 1 small red onion, thinly sliced
- Lettuce leaves
- 1/4 cup minced chives

Per Serving
Calories: 37
% Calories from fat: 31
Fat (gm): 1.4
Sat. fat (gm): 0.2
Cholesterol (mg): 0
Sodium (mg): 3
Protein (gm): 1.4
Carbohydrate (gm): 5.7

Exchanges
Milk: 0.0
Vegetable: 1.0
Fruit: 0.0
Bread: 0.0
Meat: 0.0
Fat: 0.5

1. Whisk vinegar, oil, sugar, basil, thyme, oregano, and pepper in large bowl until blended; add mushrooms and onion, tossing to coat. Cover and refrigerate for at least 8 hours, stirring occasionally. Drain before serving. Arrange on lettuce-lined platter; sprinkle with chives.

STUFFED MUSHROOMS

10 servings

20 large mushrooms
Vegetable cooking spray
1 small onion, finely chopped
1/4 cup chopped parsley
2 tablespoons white wine
2 tablespoons chopped pimiento
1/2 cup dry bread crumbs
1/4 cup (1 ounce) grated Parmesan cheese
Salt and pepper, to taste

Per Serving
Calories: 80
% Calories from fat: 18
Fat (gm): 1.6
Sat. fat (gm): 0.6
Cholesterol (mg): 2
Sodium (mg): 158
Protein (gm): 3.4
Carbohydrate (gm): 12.7
Exchanges
Milk: 0.0
Vegetable: 0.5
Fruit: 0.0
Bread: 1.0
Meat: 0.0
Fat: 0.0

1. Remove mushroom stems and chop; reserve caps. Spray large skillet with vegetable cooking spray; heat over medium heat until hot. Add chopped mushroom stems, onion, and parsley and saute until onion is tender. Stir in wine, pimiento, bread crumbs, and Parmesan cheese. Season to taste with salt and pepper.

2. Arrange mushroom caps in shallow baking pan. Spoon cheese mixture into mushrooms. Bake at 350 degrees until mushrooms are tender and cheese mixture is heated through, about 15 minutes.

MUSHROOM ROLLS

12 servings

12 thin slices nonfat white bread, crusts removed
Butter-flavored vegetable cooking spray
1 pound mushrooms, minced
3 tablespoons flour
1/2 teaspoon salt
3/4 cup evaporated fat-free milk
3 green onions and tops, minced

Per Serving
Calories: 77
% Calories from fat: 9
Fat (gm): 0.8
Sat. fat (gm): 0.2
Cholesterol (mg): 0.5
Sodium (mg): 213
Protein (gm): 4.2
Carbohydrate (gm): 15.3
Exchanges
Milk: 0.0
Vegetable: 0.0
Fruit: 0.0
Bread: 1.0
Meat: 0.0
Fat: 0.0

1. Roll each slice of bread with rolling pin until very thin; set aside.

2. Spray 12-inch nonstick skillet with cooking spray. Add mushrooms and saute 4 to 6 minutes or until soft. Partially cover if necessary. Blend in flour, salt, and milk. Continue stirring over medium heat until mixture begins to thicken. Stir in green onions.

3. Spread mixture evenly on each slice of bread. Roll up jelly-roll style. Arrange, seam side down, on cookie sheet. Bake at 400 degrees 10 minutes or until beginning to brown. Slice rolls in thirds and serve.

CHUTNEY CHEESE SPREAD

8 servings (2 generous tablespoons each)

1 package (8 ounces) fat-free cream cheese (block, not tub, type), softened
1 cup (4 ounces) shredded reduced-fat Cheddar cheese
1/2 cup chopped mango chutney, divided
1/4 cup finely chopped onion
2 tablespoons chopped raisins
1-2 teaspoons finely chopped gingerroot
1 clove garlic, minced
1/2-1 teaspoon curry powder
1-2 tablespoons chopped dry-roasted cashews
Thinly sliced green onion tops, as garnish
Pita chips, *or* whole wheat lavosh, as dippers (purchased)

Per Serving
Calories: 116
% Calories from fat: 21
Fat (gm): 2.6
Sat. fat (gm): 1.1
Cholesterol (mg): 7.6
Sodium (mg): 367
Protein (gm): 7.4
Carbohydrate (gm): 14.6
Exchanges
Milk: 0.0
Vegetable: 0.0
Fruit: 1.0
Bread: 0.0
Meat: 0.5
Fat: 0.5

1. Mix cheeses, 2 tablespoons chutney, onion, raisins, gingerroot, garlic, and curry powder until blended (do not beat or fat-free cream cheese will become thin in texture). Refrigerate 1 to 2 hours for flavors to blend.

2. Mound spread on plate; spoon remaining 6 tablespoons chutney over or around spread. Sprinkle with cashews and onion tops; serve with pita chips or whole wheat lavosh (not included in nutritional data).

ROASTED GARLIC AND THREE-CHEESE SPREAD

12 servings (2 generous tablespoons each)

- 1 small garlic bulb
- Olive oil cooking spray
- 1 package (8 ounces) fat-free cream cheese, softened
- 1 1/2-2 ounces goat cheese
- 1/4 cup (1 ounce) grated fat-free Parmesan cheese
- 1/8 teaspoon white pepper
- 2-4 tablespoons fat-free milk
- Minced parsley, *or* dried tomato bits, as garnish
- Assorted vegetables *or* crackers, as dippers

Per Serving
Calories: 43
% Calories from fat: 28
Fat (gm): 1.3
Sat. fat (gm): 0.9
Cholesterol (mg): 3.8
Sodium (mg): 142
Protein (gm): 4.7
Carbohydrate (gm): 2.5
Exchanges
Milk: 0.0
Vegetable: 0.0
Fruit: 0.0
Bread: 0.0
Meat: 0.5
Fat: 0.5

1. Cut off top of garlic bulb to expose cloves. Spray garlic lightly with cooking spray and wrap in aluminum foil; bake at 400 degrees until very tender, 35 to 40 minutes. Cool; gently press cloves to remove from skins. Mash cloves with fork.

2. Mix cheeses, garlic, and white pepper in medium bowl, adding enough milk to make desired spread consistency. Refrigerate 2 to 3 hours for flavors to blend.

3. Spoon mixture into serving bowl; sprinkle with parsley or dried tomato bits. Serve with vegetables or crackers (not included in nutritional data).

GOAT CHEESE SPREAD

16 servings

- 1/2 cup goat cheese, softened
- 1/2 cup fat-free ricotta cheese
- 2 tablespoons minced parsley
- 2 tablespoons chopped scallions
- 2 tablespoons chopped radishes
- 1 teaspoon chopped fresh, *or* 1/2 teaspoon dried, tarragon leaves
- Crackers, French bread slices, *or* baked bagel chips

Per Serving
Calories: 92
% Calories from fat: 22
Fat (gm): 2.2
Sat. fat (gm): 1.2
Cholesterol (mg): 4.5
Sodium (mg): 193
Protein (gm): 4.3
Carbohydrate (gm): 13.5
Exchanges
Milk: 0.0
Vegetable: 0.0
Fruit: 0.0
Bread: 1.0
Meat: 0.0
Fat: 0.5

1. Mix all ingredients, except crackers, in small bowl. Refrigerate overnight to blend flavors. Use as spread on crackers, French bread, or bagel chips.

YOGURT CHEESE

16 servings

- 1 quart plain low-fat yogurt
- 1 clove garlic, finely minced
- 2 tablespoons minced parsley
- 1 teaspoon dried thyme leaves
- 1 teaspoon dried oregano leaves
- 1 teaspoon dried tarragon leaves
- 1/2 teaspoon salt
- 1/4 teaspoon pepper
- Crackers, *or* fresh vegetables

Per Serving
Calories: 28
% Calories from fat: 22
Fat (gm): 0.7
Sat. fat (gm): 0.4
Cholesterol (mg): 2.6
Sodium (mg): 30
Protein (gm): 2.3
Carbohydrate (gm): 3.3
Exchanges
Milk: 0.5
Vegetable: 0.0
Fruit: 0.0
Bread: 0.0
Meat: 0.0
Fat: 0.0

1. Rinse a 1-foot length of cheesecloth in cold water and wring out. Place yogurt in center, wrap cloth around it, and set in strainer or colander in a bowl. Refrigerate until thick, 8 to 14 hours or up to 24 hours. Discard drained liquid, and unwrap yogurt cheese.

2. Mix yogurt and remaining ingredients; refrigerate several hours for flavors to blend. Serve with crackers or fresh vegetables.

SWEET-SOUR COCKTAIL DOGS

8 servings

- 2 tablespoons cornstarch
- 2/3 cup apple juice
- 2/3 cup red wine vinegar
- 1/4 cup frozen pineapple juice concentrate
- 1/4 cup chopped pimiento
- 2 tablespoons soy sauce
- 1/2 teaspoon garlic powder
- 1/2 teaspoon ground ginger
- 2-3 tablespoons sugar
- 1 pound low-fat turkey hot dogs

Per Serving
Calories: 120
% Calories from fat: 12
Fat (gm): 1.5
Sat. fat (gm): 0.7
Cholesterol (mg): 21.3
Sodium (mg): 812
Protein (gm): 7.7
Carbohydrate (gm): 17.6
Exchanges
Milk: 0.0
Vegetable: 0.0
Fruit: 1.0
Bread: 0.0
Meat: 1.0
Fat: 0.0

1. Combine cornstarch and apple juice in small saucepan. Stir in remaining ingredients, except hot dogs. Cook over medium heat, stirring until thickened and bubbly. Add hot dogs and simmer until warm, 2 to 3 minutes.

MICROWAVE POTATO CHEEZEES

4 servings

- 2 medium Idaho potatoes (about 1 pound)
- 1/2 cup (2 ounces) shredded low-fat Alpine Lace or mozzarella cheese
- 1/4 teaspoon garlic powder
- 1/4 teaspoon chili powder
- 1/4 teaspoon dried basil leaves
- Pepper, to taste

Per Serving
Calories: 143
% Calories from fat: 10
Fat (gm): 1.6
Sat. fat (gm): 0
Cholesterol (mg): 5
Sodium (mg): 84
Protein (gm): 6.4
Carbohydrate (gm): 27
Exchanges
Milk: 0.0
Vegetable: 0.0
Fruit: 0.0
Bread: 2.0
Meat: 0.0
Fat: 0.0

1. Wash potatoes and pierce each with a fork. Microwave potatoes on High until tender, 4 to 7 minutes. Cool; refrigerate until chilled.

2. Cut potatoes into 1/4-inch slices. Arrange on paper towel-lined microwave safe platter. Sprinkle with cheese, combined spices, and pepper. Microwave for 30 to 40 seconds, just until cheese melts.

BAKED SPINACH BALLS

12 servings (2 balls each)

2 cups herb-seasoned bread stuffing cubes
1/4 cup (1 ounce) grated fat-free Parmesan cheese
1/4 cup chopped green onions and tops
2 cloves garlic, minced
1/8 teaspoon ground nutmeg
1 package (10 ounces) frozen chopped spinach, thawed, well drained
1/4-1/3 cup Vegetable Stock (see p. 48)
2 tablespoons margarine, melted
Salt and pepper, to taste
2 egg whites, beaten
Mustard Sauce (recipe follows)

Per Serving
Calories: 86
% Calories from fat. 24
Fat (gm): 2.4
Sat. fat (gm): 0.4
Cholesterol (mg): 0
Sodium (mg): 271
Protein (gm): 4.2
Carbohydrate (gm): 13
Exchanges
Milk: 0.0
Vegetable: 1.0
Fruit: 0.0
Bread: 0.5
Meat: 0.0
Fat: 0.5

1. Combine stuffing cubes, Parmesan cheese, onions, garlic, and nutmeg in medium bowl. Mix in spinach, stock, and margarine; season to taste with salt and pepper. Mix in egg whites.

2. Shape mixture into 24 balls. Bake at 350 degrees until spinach balls are browned, about 15 minutes. Serve with Mustard Sauce for dipping.

Mustard Sauce

makes about 1 cup

3/4 cup fat-free sour cream
3-4 teaspoons Dijon-style mustard
1 1/2-2 tablespoons honey
1 tablespoon chopped chives

1. Mix all ingredients; refrigerate until ready to use.

POTATO SPINACH BALLS

8 servings

1 package (10 ounces) frozen chopped spinach, thawed, drained
3 cups mashed potatoes
2 egg whites, slightly beaten
4 cloves garlic, minced
1/2 cup minced parsley
1/2 teaspoon ground mace
1/2 teaspoon dried marjoram leaves
Olive oil, *or* vegetable, cooking spray
2-3 tablespoons grated Parmesan cheese

Per Serving
Calories: 86
% Calories from fat: 10
Fat (gm): 1.1
Sat. fat (gm): 0.6
Cholesterol (mg): 2.7
Sodium (mg): 314
Protein (gm): 4.4
Carbohydrate (gm): 16.7

Exchanges
Milk: 0.0
Vegetable: 0.6
Fruit: 0.0
Bread: 0.9
Meat: 0.2
Fat: 0.0

1. Squeeze spinach dry between sheets of paper toweling, and place in large mixing bowl. Mix in mashed potatoes, egg whites, garlic, parsley, mace, and marjoram. Using wet hands, shape mixture into 1 1/2-inch balls; place on tray or plate.

2. Spray nonstick skillet with olive oil or cooking spray and fry potato balls until cooked crisp and golden brown. Remove to serving plate; sprinkle with Parmesan cheese.

BAKED ARTICHOKE DIP

16 servings (about 3 tablespoons each)

1 can (15 ounces) artichoke hearts, rinsed, drained
1/2 package (8-ounce size) fat-free cream cheese, softened
1/2 cup (2 ounces) grated fat-free Parmesan cheese
1/2 cup fat-free mayonnaise
1/2 cup fat-free sour cream
1-2 teaspoons lemon juice
1 green onion and top, thinly sliced
2 teaspoons minced garlic
2-3 drops red pepper sauce
Salt and cayenne pepper, to taste

Per Serving
Calories: 39
% Calories from fat: 2
Fat (gm): 0.1
Sat. fat (gm): 0
Cholesterol (mg): 0
Sodium (mg): 190
Protein (gm): 3.5
Carbohydrate (gm): 6.8

Exchanges
Milk: 0.0
Vegetable: 1.5
Fruit: 0.0
Bread: 0.0
Meat: 0.0
Fat: 0.0

Assorted vegetables, bread sticks, *or* crackers, as dippers

1. Process artichoke hearts, cream cheese, Parmesan cheese, mayonnaise, sour cream, and lemon juice in food processor until smooth. Stir in onion, garlic, and red pepper sauce. Season to taste with salt and cayenne pepper.

2. Spoon dip into small casserole or baking dish. Bake, uncovered, at 350 degrees until hot through and lightly browned on the top, 20 to 25 minutes. Serve warm with assorted vegetables, bread sticks, or crackers (not included in nutritional data).

ARTICHOKE PÂTÉ

16 servings (about 2 tablespoons each)

- 1 can (15 ounces) artichoke hearts or bottoms, drained
- 1/2 package (8-ounce size) fat-free cream cheese, softened
- 1/3 cup (1 1/3 ounces) grated fat-free Parmesan cheese
- 2-4 tablespoons fat-free mayonnaise
- 1-1 1/2 teaspoons minced roasted garlic (see pg. 8, Step 1)
- 2 tablespoons finely chopped parsley
- 1-2 teaspoons lemon juice
- Salt and cayenne pepper, to taste
- 2 tablespoons chopped black olives
- 2 tablespoons chopped roasted red bell peppers
- Assorted vegetables, lavosh, *or* melba toast, as dippers

Per Serving
Calories: 31
% Calories from fat: 13
Fat (gm): 0.5
Sat. fat (gm): 0.1
Cholesterol (mg): 0
Sodium (mg): 142
Protein (gm): 2.7
Carbohydrate (gm): 4.7

Exchanges
Milk: 0.0
Vegetable: 1.0
Fruit: 0.0
Bread: 0.0
Meat: 0.0
Fat: 0.0

1. Process artichokes, cream cheese, Parmesan cheese, mayonnaise, and garlic in food processor until smooth. Stir in parsley, season to taste with lemon juice, salt, and cayenne pepper. Refrigerate several hours for flavors to blend.

2. Spoon mixture into a crock, or mound it on a serving plate. Garnish with olives and red peppers. Serve with vegetables, lavosh, or melba toast (not included in nutritional data).

ROASTED GARLIC AND HERB CANNELLINI DIP

6 servings (about 1/4 cup each)

- 1 can (15 ounces) cannellini, *or* Great Northern, beans, rinsed and drained
- 1 teaspoon minced roasted garlic (see pg. 8, Step 1)
- 1 tablespoon olive oil
- 1 tablespoon prepared horseradish
- 2 tablespoons minced chives
- 1/2 teaspoon dried oregano leaves
- 1/2 teaspoon dried basil leaves
- 2-3 drops red pepper sauce
- 2-3 teaspoons lemon juice
- Salt and white pepper, to taste
- Pita chips, *or* assorted vegetables, as dippers

Per Serving
Calories: 75
% Calories from fat: 25
Fat (gm): 2.8
Sat. fat (gm): 0.3
Cholesterol (mg): 0
Sodium (mg): 167
Protein (gm): 5.3
Carbohydrate (gm): 13.1
Exchanges
Milk: 0.0
Vegetable: 0.0
Fruit: 0.0
Bread: 1.0
Meat: 0.0
Fat: 0.5

1. Process beans, garlic, olive oil, and horseradish in food processor until smooth. Mix in chives, herbs, and red pepper sauce. Season to taste with lemon juice, salt, and white pepper. Refrigerate 1 to 2 hours for flavors to blend.

2. Spoon dip into bowl; serve with pita chips or vegetables (not included in nutritional data).

TOASTED ONION DIP

12 servings (2 generous tablespoons each)

- 3-4 tablespoons dried onion flakes
- 1 package (8 ounces) fat-free cream cheese
- 1/3 cup reduced-fat plain yogurt
- 1/3 cup fat-free mayonnaise
- 2 small green onions and tops, chopped
- 2 cloves garlic, minced
- 1/4 teaspoon crushed vegetable bouillon cube

Per Serving
Calories: 32
% Calories from fat: 4
Fat (gm): 0.1
Sat. fat (gm): 0.1
Cholesterol (mg): 0.4
Sodium (mg): 223
Protein (gm): 3.3
Carbohydrate (gm): 3.9
Exchanges
Milk: 0.0
Vegetable: 0.0
Fruit: 0.0
Bread: 0.0
Meat: 0.5
Fat: 0.0

2-3 tablespoons fat-free milk
1/2-1 teaspoon lemon juice
2-3 drops red pepper sauce
Salt and white pepper, to taste
Assorted vegetables, *or* bread sticks, as dippers

1. Cook onion flakes in small skillet over medium to medium low heat until toasted, 3 to 4 minutes, stirring frequently. Cool.
2. Mix cream cheese, yogurt, mayonnaise, green onions, garlic, and bouillon in medium bowl until smooth, adding enough milk to make desired dipping consistency. Season to taste with lemon juice, pepper sauce, salt, and white pepper.
3. Spoon dip into serving bowl; serve with vegetables or bread sticks (not included in nutritional data).

CURRY DIP

12 servings (2 generous tablespoons each)

1 1/2 cups fat-free mayonnaise
1/2 cup fat-free sour cream
1/4 cup thinly sliced green onions and tops
1 1/2-2 teaspoons prepared horseradish
1 1/2-2 teaspoons curry powder
2-3 teaspoons sugar
2-4 teaspoons lemon juice
Salt and white pepper, to taste
Assorted vegetables, or pita chips, as dippers

Per Serving
Calories: 34
% Calories from fat: 1
Fat (gm): 0
Sat. fat (gm): 0
Cholesterol (mg): 0
Sodium (mg): 393
Protein (gm): 0.7
Carbohydrate (gm): 8
Exchanges
Milk: 0.0
Vegetable: 0.0
Fruit: 0.0
Bread: 0.5
Meat: 0.0
Fat: 0.0

1. Mix mayonnaise, sour cream, green onions, horseradish, curry powder, and sugar. Season to taste with lemon juice, salt, and white pepper. Refrigerate several hours for flavors to blend.
2. Spoon dip into bowl; serve with vegetables or pita chips for dipping (not included in nutritional data).

ROASTED ZUCCHINI AND GARLIC SPREAD

12 servings (about 2 tablespoons each)

Olive oil cooking spray
1 1/4 pounds zucchini, cut into 1-inch pieces
1 small onion, cut into wedges
2 garlic cloves, peeled
1/3 cup fat-free plain yogurt
2 tablespoons finely chopped parsley
Lemon juice, to taste
Salt and cayenne pepper, to taste
Sliced vegetables, baked tortilla chips, *or* pita chips, as dippers

Per Serving
Calories: 14
% Calories from fat: 6
Fat (gm): 0.1
Sat. fat (gm): 0
Cholesterol (mg): 0.1
Sodium (mg): 7
Protein (gm): 1
Carbohydrate (gm): 2.6
Exchanges
Milk: 0.0
Vegetable: 0.5
Fruit: 0.0
Bread: 0.0
Meat: 0.0
Fat: 0.0

1. Line jelly roll pan with aluminum foil and spray with cooking spray. Arrange zucchini, onion, and garlic in single layer on pan. Bake at 425 degrees until vegetables are very tender, about 15 to 20 minutes for garlic, 25 to 30 minutes for zucchini and onion. Cool.
2. Process vegetables in food processor, using pulse technique, until coarsely chopped. Stir in yogurt and parsley; season to taste with lemon juice, salt, and cayenne pepper. Serve with sliced vegetables or chips (not included in nutritional data).

EGGPLANT CAVIAR

6 servings (2 generous tablespoons each)

1 large eggplant (1 1/2 pounds)
1/2 cup chopped tomato
1/4 cup finely chopped onion
3 cloves garlic, minced
1/4 cup fat-free yogurt
2 teaspoons extra-virgin olive oil
1/2 teaspoon dried oregano leaves
1-2 tablespoons lemon juice
Salt and pepper, to taste

Per Serving
Calories: 59
% Calories from fat: 28
Fat (gm): 2.1
Sat. fat (gm): 0.3
Cholesterol (mg): 0.2
Sodium (mg): 19.1
Protein (gm): 1.8
Carbohydrate (gm): 10.1
Exchanges
Milk: 0.0
Vegetable: 2.0
Fruit: 0.0
Bread: 0.0
Meat: 0.0
Fat: 0.0

2 ripe olives, sliced
Lavosh, *or* pita bread wedges, as dippers

1. Pierce eggplant in several places with fork, place in baking pan. Bake at 350 degrees until eggplant is soft, 45 to 50 minutes. Cool.

2. Cut eggplant in half, scoop out pulp with spoon. Mix eggplant, tomato, onion, garlic, yogurt, olive oil, and oregano in bowl; season to taste with lemon juice, salt, and pepper. Refrigerate 3 to 4 hours for flavors to blend.

3. Spoon eggplant into bowl; garnish with olives. Serve with lavosh or pita wedges (not included in nutritional data).

EGGPLANT-MUSHROOM SPREAD

8 servings

1 eggplant
1 cup minced onion
2 cloves garlic, minced
4 stalks celery, chopped
1/2 cup chopped mushrooms
1 tomato, peeled and chopped
2 tablespoons fresh lemon juice
6 tablespoons tomato juice
1/2 teaspoon salt
1/2 teaspoon pepper
1 tablespoon chopped fresh basil leaves
1/2 teaspoon dried oregano leaves
8 slices dark rye bread

Per Serving
Calories: 115.6
% Calories from fat: 10
Fat (gm): 1.4
Sat. fat (gm): 0.2
Cholesterol (mg): 0
Sodium (mg): 407
Protein (gm): 3.9
Carbohydrate (gm): 23.1
Exchanges
Milk: 0.0
Vegetable: 1.5
Fruit: 0.0
Bread: 1.0
Meat: 0.0
Fat: 0.0

1. Pierce eggplant with fork; place on aluminum foil-lined baking sheet. Bake at 400 degrees about 30 minutes or until tender. Cool.

2. Cut eggplant in half and scoop flesh with a spoon; mince flesh and place in large mixing bowl. Mix in remaining ingredients except bread. Cover and chill. Serve on slices of dark rye bread.

MEDITERRANEAN EGGPLANT DIP

8 servings

- 2 medium eggplant
- Salt
- Vegetable cooking spray
- 4 cloves garlic, minced
- 1 tablespoon paprika
- 2 teaspoons dried oregano leaves
- 1 teaspoon ground cumin
- 1 1/2 teaspoons olive oil
- 2 tablespoons lemon juice
- Pita bread *or* crackers, as dippers

Per Serving
Calories: 39
% Calories from fat: 25
Fat (gm): 1.2
Sat. fat (gm): 0.2
Cholesterol (mg): 0
Sodium (mg): 3.7
Protein (gm): 1
Carbohydrate (gm): 7.3
Exchanges
Milk: 0.0
Vegetable: 1.5
Fruit: 0.0
Bread: 0.0
Meat: 0.0
Fat: 0.0

1. Remove 3 vertical strips of skin from each eggplant, leaving it striped, then cut eggplant into 1/2-inch-thick slices. Sprinkle with salt and leave to drain in colander 30 minutes. Rinse well, squeeze gently, and pat dry with paper towels.

2. Spray large slices. Sprinkle skillet lightly with cooking spray; heat over medium heat until hot. Saute eggplant slices a few at a time over medium to medium-high heat until golden brown, 3 to 4 minutes on each side. Drain on paper towels.

3. Mash eggplant with fork; stir in garlic, herbs, and olive oil. Cook puree in greased skillet until all liquid evaporates, stirring often to avoid scorching. Season with lemon juice to taste. Serve at room temperature with pita bread or crackers (not included in nutritional data).

HUMMUS

8 servings

1 can ($15^1/_2$ ounces) garbanzo beans, rinsed, drained
2 tablespoons fresh lemon juice
2 cloves garlic, minced
2-3 tablespoons tahini (sesame seed paste)
Pita bread, cut into triangles

Per Serving
Calories: 90
% Calories from fat: 25
Fat (gm): 2.6
Sat. fat (gm): 0.3
Cholesterol (mg): 0
Sodium (mg): 117
Protein (gm): 3.4
Carbohydrate (gm): 13.8

Exchanges
Milk: 0.0
Vegetable: 0.0
Fruit: 0.0
Bread: 1.0
Meat: 0.0
Fat: 0.5

1. Process all ingredients, except pita bread, in food processor until smooth; spoon into serving dish. Serve at room temperature with pita bread triangles (not included in nutritional data).

SUN-DRIED TOMATO HUMMUS

8 servings (about $^1/_4$ cup each)

1 can ($15^1/_2$ ounces) garbanzo beans, rinsed, drained
$^1/_3$ cup fat-free yogurt
2-3 tablespoons tahini (sesame seed paste)
3 cloves garlic
3 tablespoons sun-dried tomato bits, *or* 4 sun-dried tomato halves (not packed in oil, finely chopped)
1 teaspoon dried oregano leaves
1 teaspoon dried mint leaves
2-3 teaspoon lemon juice
Salt and white pepper, to taste
Pita bread, cut into wedges as dippers

Per Serving
Calories: 73
% Calories from fat: 21
Fat (gm): 1.7
Sat. fat (gm): 0.2
Cholesterol (mg): 0.2
Sodium (mg): 256
Protein (gm): 3.6
Carbohydrate (gm): 11.4

Exchanges
Milk: 0.0
Vegetable: 0.0
Fruit: 0.0
Bread: 1.0
Meat: 0.0
Fat: 0.5

1. Process garbanzo beans, yogurt, tahini, and garlic in food processor until smooth. Stir in sun-dried tomato bits and herbs; season to taste with lemon juice, salt, and white pepper. Refrigerate 1 to 2 hours for flavors to blend.

2. Spoon hummus into serving bowl; serve with pita wedges (not included in nutritional data.)

EASY CHICKEN SALAD SPREAD

8 servings

- 1½ cups chopped cooked chicken breast
- 1 cup chopped apple
- ½ cup fat-free sour cream
- ¼ cup chopped green onions
- Assorted crackers and melba toast

Per Serving
Calories: 55
% Calories from fat: 15
Fat (gm): 0.9
Sat. fat (gm): 0.3
Cholesterol (mg): 20.6
Sodium (mg): 24
Protein (gm): 8.2
Carbohydrate (gm): 3.4
Exchanges
Milk: 0.0
Vegetable: 0.0
Fruit: 0.0
Bread: 0.0
Meat: 1.0
Fat: 0.0

1. Mix all ingredients, except crackers and melba toast, in small bowl. Serve with crackers and melba toast (not included in nutritional data).

DILLED SALMON SPREAD

10 servings

- 1 can (15½ ounces) salmon, skin and bones removed
- 1 tablespoon lemon juice
- 1 tablespoon prepared horseradish
- 1 package (8 ounces) fat-free cream cheese
- 2-4 tablespoons fat-free mayonnaise
- 1 tablespoon dried dill weed
- 4 green onions and tops, chopped
- ½ cup finely chopped parsley
- Assorted crackers and cucumber and zucchini slices

Per Serving
Calories: 91
% Calories from fat: 28
Fat (gm): 2.8
Sat. fat (gm): 0.9
Cholesterol (mg): 19
Sodium (mg): 369
Protein (gm): 13
Carbohydrate (gm): 2.8
Exchanges
Milk: 0.0
Vegetable: 0.0
Fruit: 0.0
Bread: 0.0
Meat: 2.0
Fat: 0.0

1. Combine all ingredients except parsley, crackers, cucumber, and zucchini in medium bowl. Shape into ball and roll in parsley. Place on plate and serve with crackers and cucumber and zucchini slices (not included in nutritional data).

SMOKED SALMON CREAM CHEESE ROLLS

4 servings

- 1 package (4 ounces) fat-free cream cheese
- 2 tablespoons chopped capers
- 4 thin slices (4 ounces) smoked salmon
- 4 large romaine lettuce leaves
- Lemon wedges
- 8 mini bagels

Per Serving
Calories: 179
% Calories from fat: 11
Fat (gm): 2.1
Sat. fat (gm): 0.5
Cholesterol (mg): 8.8
Sodium (mg): 1028
Protein (gm): 14
Carbohydrate (gm): 26.2
Exchanges
Milk: 0.0
Vegetable: 0.0
Fruit: 0.0
Bread: 0.0
Meat: 0.0
Fat: 0.0

1. Mix cream cheese and capers in small bowl. Spread smoked salmon slices with cream cheese mixture; roll up jelly-roll fashion. Cut rolls into sixteen 1/2-inch slices.

2. Place a romaine leaf on each serving plate. Place 4 salmon rounds in a row down the center of each leaf. Garnish with lemon wedges. Serve with bagels.

MUSHROOMS IN VERMOUTH

6 servings

- 1 pound medium mushrooms
- 1/2 cup dry vermouth
- 1 tablespoon olive oil
- 5 tablespoons red wine vinegar
- 2 tablespoons lemon juice
- 1 clove garlic, minced
- 2 tablespoons chopped shallots
- 1 tablespoon chopped fresh basil leaves
- 1 teaspoon sugar

Per Serving
Calories: 69
% Calories from fat: 31
Fat (gm): 2.7
Sat. fat (gm): 0.3
Cholesterol (mg): 0
Sodium (mg): 5
Protein (gm): 1.8
Carbohydrate (gm): 6.4
Exchanges
Milk: 0.0
Vegetable: 1.5
Fruit: 0.0
Bread: 0.0
Meat: 0.0
Fat: 0.5

1/2 teaspoon dry mustard
1/2 teaspoon pepper
Salt, to taste

1. Place mushrooms in a large jar with a tight-fitting lid. Process remaining ingredients, except salt, in blender until smooth. Pour mixture over mushrooms; season to taste with salt. Seal jar and refrigerate 1 or 2 days for flavors to develop.

SALMON-FILLED MUSHROOM CAPS

6 servings

1 can (7 1/2 ounces) salmon, bones and skin removed
2 tablespoons dry unseasoned bread crumbs
2 tablespoons chopped green onions and tops
2 tablespoons chopped parsley
18 medium mushroom caps (1 1/2 to 2-inch)
2 tablespoons diced pimiento
3 tablespoons low-fat chicken bouillon

Per Serving
Calories: 71
% Calories from fat: 25
Fat (gm): 2.3
Sat. fat (gm): 0.6
Cholesterol (mg): 13.8
Sodium (mg): 205
Protein (gm): 8.9
Carbohydrate (gm): 3.9
Exchanges
Milk: 0.0
Vegetable: 0.5
Fruit: 0.0
Bread: 0.0
Meat: 1.0
Fat: 0.0

1. Combine salmon, bread crumbs, green onions, and parsley in medium bowl; fill mushroom caps and place in a baking pan. Garnish each with pimiento and drizzle with bouillon, and bake at 350 degrees 15 to 20 minutes, or until tender.

TOMATO-HERB BRUSCHETTA

6 servings

- 12 slices French bread
- 2 large cloves garlic
- 2 tablespoons olive oil
- 1 1/2 cups fresh plum tomatoes, peeled, seeded, chopped
- 1/2 cup chopped fresh basil leaves
- 1 tablespoon chopped fresh, *or* 1 teaspoon dried, oregano leaves
- Salt and pepper, to taste

Per Serving
Calories: 86
% Calories from fat: 12
Fat (gm): 1.2
Sat. fat (gm): 0.3
Cholesterol (mg): 0
Sodium (mg): 177
Protein (gm): 2.8
Carbohydrate (gm): 16.1
Exchanges
Milk: 0.0
Vegetable: 0.5
Fruit: 0.0
Bread: 1.0
Meat: 0.0
Fat: 0.0

1. Grill or toast bread slices. Rub each slice with garlic, and brush with olive oil.

2. Mix tomatoes and herbs in bowl; season to taste with salt and pepper. Top bread slices with tomato mixture and serve immediately.

ROASTED PEPPERS WITH HERBS

12 servings

- 3 large red bell peppers
- 3 large yellow bell peppers
- 2 large green bell peppers
- 3 cloves garlic, minced
- 2-3 tablespoons olive oil
- 1 tablespoon Italian seasoning, *or* herbes de Provence
- Salt and pepper, to taste
- 24 slices French bread, toasted

Per Serving
Calories: 186
% Calories from fat: 19
Fat (gm): 4
Sat. fat (gm): 0.7
Cholesterol (mg): 0
Sodium (mg): 307
Protein (gm): 5.4
Carbohydrate (gm): 32.8
Exchanges
Milk: 0.0
Vegetable: 1.0
Fruit: 0.0
Bread: 2.0
Meat: 0.0
Fat: 0.5

1. Cut peppers into scant 1/2-inch slices; cut slices in half. Combine peppers and garlic in 13 x 9 x 2-inch baking dish; drizzle with oil and toss to coat. Bake at 400 degrees 35 to 40 minutes, or until peppers are tender and begin to brown, stirring occasionally.

2. Sprinkle with Italian seasoning or herbes de Provence; season to taste with salt and pepper. Spoon onto toasted bread.

MARINATED TORTELLINI VEGETABLE KABOBS

12 servings

24 cooked small spinach, *or* cheese, tortellini
24 medium mushrooms
6 artichoke hearts, cut into quarters
12 cherry tomatoes, halved
Tortellini Marinade (recipe follows)

Per Serving
Calories: 74
% Calories from fat: 18
Fat (gm): 1.5
Sat. fat (gm): 0.7
Cholesterol (mg): 7.9
Sodium (mg): 64
Protein (gm): 3.6
Carbohydrate (gm): 11.7
Exchanges
Milk: 0.0
Vegetable: 1.5
Fruit: 0.0
Bread: 0.5
Meat: 0.0
Fat: 0.0

1. Alternate tortellini, mushrooms, artichokes, and tomatoes on 6-inch skewers; place in a 13 x 9 x 2-inch glass baking dish. Pour dressing over kabobs, turning to coat. Cover and marinate in refrigerator 4 hours, turning occasionally. Drain before serving.

Tortellini Marinade

makes about 1 1/4 cups

2/3 cup water
1/2 cup wine or cider vinegar
1 teaspoon dried basil leaves
1 teaspoon dried oregano leaves
1/2 teaspoon dried dill weed
1/2 teaspoon dry mustard
1/2 teaspoon dried thyme leaves
1/4 teaspoon onion powder
1/4 teaspoon garlic powder
1/2 teaspoon salt
1/4 teaspoon pepper, freshly ground

1. Combine all ingredients.

VEGETABLE ANTIPASTO

8 servings

Per Serving
Calories: 276
% Calories from fat: 24
Fat (gm): 7.5
Sat. fat (gm): 1.1
Cholesterol (mg): 0
Sodium (mg): 636
Protein (gm): 11.1
Carbohydrate (gm): 41.5

Exchanges
Milk: 0.0
Vegetable: 2.0
Fruit: 0.0
Bread: 2.0
Meat: 0.0
Fat: 1.5

2 cups cauliflower florets, blanched, *or* raw
24 asparagus spears, cooked, cut into 1-inch pieces
1 can ($15^1/_2$ ounces) artichoke hearts, drained
1 small red onion, thinly sliced, separated into rings
1 cup canned, drained garbanzo beans
8 cherry tomatoes, cut into halves
Antipasto Dressing (recipe follows)
Salt and pepper, to taste
Lettuce leaves
2 ounces fat-free mozzarella cheese, cubed
$^1/_4$ cup halved small black olives

1. Combine cauliflower, asparagus, artichoke hearts, onion, garbanzo beans, and tomatoes in large bowl. Pour Antipasto Dressing over vegetables and toss to coat; season to taste with salt and pepper. Cover and refrigerate for at least 1 hour, tossing several times.

2. Line platter with lettuce. Spoon vegetable mixture into center of platter. Sprinkle with mozzarella cheese and olives.

Antipasto Dressing

makes about $^1/_2$ cup

$^1/_4$ cup olive oil
2 tablespoons onion, diced
2 tablespoons red wine vinegar
1 tablespoon lemon juice
1 tablespoon fresh chives, minced
1 garlic clove, minced
$^1/_4$ teaspoon basil
$^1/_4$ teaspoon oregano

1. Mix all ingredients.

ARTICHOKES WITH GREEN SAUCE

4 servings

- 1/4 cup dry white wine
- 2 tablespoons lemon juice
- 1 tablespoon finely chopped parsley
- 1/2 teaspoon dried marjoram leaves
- 1/4 teaspoon dried tarragon leaves
- 1 can (8 1/2 ounces) artichoke hearts, drained

Per Serving
Calories: 43
% Calories from fat: 4
Fat (gm): 0.2
Sat. fat (gm): 0
Cholesterol (mg): 0
Sodium (mg): 58.8
Protein (gm): 2.2
Carbohydrate (gm): 7.7
Exchanges
Milk: 0.0
Vegetable: 1.5
Fruit: 0.0
Bread: 0.0
Meat: 0.0
Fat: 0.0

1. Combine wine, lemon juice, and herbs. Pour mixture over artichoke hearts.

MARINATED ARTICHOKE HEARTS AND PEPPERS

12 servings

- 3/4 cup water
- 1/4 cup balsamic vinegar
- 1 tablespoon drained capers
- 2 teaspoons Dijon mustard
- 1/2 teaspoon dried basil leaves
- 1 tablespoon chopped fresh parsley
- 2 cloves garlic, minced
- 1 can (20 ounces) artichoke hearts, drained
- 1 large red bell pepper, cut into strips
- 1 large yellow, *or* green, bell pepper, cut into strips
- 4 large black olives, sliced
- 1/4 cup diced pimiento
- 1/2 cup chopped parsley
- Boston lettuce leaves

Per Serving
Calories: 52
% Calories from fat: 9
Fat (gm): 0.6
Sat. fat (gm): 0.1
Cholesterol (mg): 0
Sodium (mg): 79
Protein (gm): 2.5
Carbohydrate (gm): 11.4
Exchanges
Milk: 0.0
Vegetable: 2.0
Fruit: 0.0
Bread: 0.0
Meat: 0.0
Fat: 0.0

1. Shake water, vinegar, capers, mustard, basil, parsley, and garlic in a large bottle with tight-fitting lid. Pour mixture over artichoke hearts, peppers, olives, pimiento, and parsley in a bowl and mix well. Refrigerate 2 hours before serving.

2. Arrange lettuce leaves on a platter and spoon marinated vegetables over.

ARTICHOKE-STUFFED APPETIZER BREAD

8 servings (2 pieces each)

- 1 package (8 ounces) fat-free cream cheese, softened
- 1 can (14 ounces) artichoke hearts, drained, chopped
- 1/2 cup red bell pepper
- 1/2 cup chopped celery
- 1/4 cup chopped pitted green, *or* black, olives
- 2 teaspoons drained capers
- 1 clove garlic, minced
- 1/2 teaspoon dried basil leaves
- 1/2 teaspoon dried oregano leaves
- 1-2 teaspoons white wine vinegar, *or* lemon juice
- Salt and white pepper, to taste
- 1 loaf French bread (8 ounces, about 15 inches long)

Per Serving
Calories: 151
% Calories from fat: 29
Fat (gm): 5.1
Sat. fat (gm): 0.3
Cholesterol (mg): 0
Sodium (mg): 600
Protein (gm): 6.9
Carbohydrate (gm): 20.9
Exchanges
Milk: 0.0
Vegetable: 1.0
Fruit: 0.0
Bread: 1.0
Meat: 0.0
Fat: 1.0

1. Mix softened cream cheese with artichoke hearts, bell pepper, celery, olives, capers, garlic, and herbs; season to taste with vinegar, salt, and white pepper.

2. Slice bread lengthwise in half. Remove bread from centers of bread halves, using paring knife or serrated grapefruit spoon, leaving 3/4-inch shell of bread.

3. Spoon filling into each bread half; press halves together firmly and wrap in plastic wrap. Refrigerate 2 hours or until serving time. Cut into 16 pieces.

MINI CHEESE QUICHES

30 servings (2 appetizers each)

- 1 egg
- 16 ounces low-fat small curd cottage cheese
- 3 tablespoons fat-free yogurt
- 1 cup (4 ounces) shredded reduced-fat Swiss cheese
- 1/2 cup baking mix
- 3/4 teaspoon dried dill weed
- 1/2 teaspoon pepper
- 1 tablespoon margarine, melted

Per Serving
Calories: 34
% Calories from fat: 34
Fat (gm): 1.2
Sat. fat (gm): 0.6
Cholesterol (mg): 3.7
Sodium (mg): 141
Protein (gm): 3.1
Carbohydrate (gm): 2.1
Exchanges
Milk: 0.0
Vegetable: 0.0
Fruit: 0.0
Bread: 0.0
Meat: 0.5
Fat: 0.0

1. Combine all ingredients in medium bowl. Spoon mixture into lightly greased miniature muffin cups, filling each cup 2/3 full. Bake at 375 degrees until set, 25 to 30 minutes. Cool in pans before removing.

Tip: Quiches can be made several hours in advance; cook and refrigerate on a cookie sheet. Reheat 10 minutes at 350 degrees before serving.

SPINACH AND CHEESE MINI-QUICHES

1 1/2 dozen (1 per serving)

- 1 1/4 cups fat-free cottage cheese
- 1/4 cup (1 ounce) grated fat-free Parmesan cheese
- 2 tablespoons fat-free milk
- 2 tablespoons flour
- 1/2 cup finely chopped fresh spinach
- 1/2 teaspoon dried oregano leaves
- 1/4 teaspoon dried thyme leaves
- Salt and white pepper, to taste
- 2 eggs
- 1 1/2 dozen frozen mini-fillo shells, thawed

Per Serving
Calories: 48
% Calories from fat: 30
Fat (gm): 1.6
Sat. fat (gm): 0.2
Cholesterol (mg): 23.7
Sodium (mg): 61
Protein (gm): 3.9
Carbohydrate (gm): 4.3
Exchanges
Milk: 0.0
Vegetable: 0.0
Fruit: 0.0
Bread: 0.5
Meat: 0.0
Fat: 0.5

1. Mix cottage cheese, Parmesan cheese, fat-free milk, flour, spinach, oregano, and thyme; season to taste with salt and pepper. Stir in eggs.

2. Arrange fillo shells on cookie sheet or in mini-muffin tins; fill with cheese mixture. Bake at 325 degrees until puffed and beginning to brown on the tops, about 20 minutes.

RED TOMATO SALSA

16 servings (about 2 tablespoons each)

2 large tomatoes, cut into wedges
1 small onion, finely chopped
1 small poblano chili, veins and seeds discarded, chopped
1/4 jalapeno chili, seeds and veins discarded, chopped
1 clove garlic, minced
1/4 cup loosely packed cilantro, finely chopped
Salt, to taste
Baked tortilla chips

Per Serving
Calories: 9
% Calories from fat: 10
Fat (gm): 0.1
Sat. fat (gm): 0
Cholesterol (mg): 0
Sodium (mg): 4
Protein (gm): 0.4
Carbohydrate (gm): 1.9
Exchanges
Milk: 0.0
Vegetable: 0.5
Fruit: 0.0
Bread: 0.0
Meat: 0.0
Fat: 0.0

1. Process tomatoes, onion, chilies, and garlic in food processor or blender until finely chopped. Mix in cilantro; season to taste with salt.

2. Spoon salsa into bowl; serve with baked tortilla chips (not included in nutritional data).

PINTO PARTY DIP

8 servings

- 1 can (15 1/2 ounces) kidney, *or* pinto, beans, rinsed, drained
- 2 cloves garlic, minced
- 1/4 cup chopped shallots
- 1 medium rib celery, chopped
- 3 tablespoons mild salsa
- 1/4 cup (1 ounce) shredded mozzarella cheese
- Chopped parsley, as garnish
- Dippers—assorted vegetables, baked pita chips

Per Serving
Calories: 63
% Calories from fat: 13
Fat (gm): 1
Sat. fat (gm): 0.5
Cholesterol (mg): 1.9
Sodium (mg): 255
Protein (gm): 4.1
Carbohydrate (gm): 10.2
Exchanges
Milk: 0.0
Vegetable: 0.0
Fruit: 0.0
Bread: 0.5
Meat: 0.5
Fat: 0.0

1. Process all ingredients, except cheese, parsley, and dippers in food processor or blender until almost smooth.

2. Transfer to microwave-safe bowl and microwave at High until hot, 1 to 2 minutes, stirring after 1 minute. Sprinkle with cheese; microwave at High until cheese is melted, about 30 seconds. Sprinkle with parsley. Serve with vegetables and baked tortilla chips (not included in nutritional data).

MEXICAN BEAN DIP

12 servings (about 2 tablespoons each)

- Vegetable cooking spray
- 1/2 cup thinly sliced green onions and tops
- 1-2 cloves garlic, minced
- 1 can (15 ounces) black beans, rinsed, drained
- 3/4 cup (3 ounces) shredded reduced-fat Cheddar cheese
- 1/4 teaspoon salt
- 1/3 cup vegetable broth, *or* water
- 1-2 tablespoons finely chopped cilantro
- Baked tortilla chips

Per Serving
Calories: 48
% Calories from fat: 21
Fat (gm): 1.3
Sat. fat (gm): 0.5
Cholesterol (mg): 3.8
Sodium (mg): 254
Protein (gm): 4.5
Carbohydrate (gm): 7
Exchanges
Milk: 0.0
Vegetable: 0.0
Fruit: 0.0
Bread: 0.5
Meat: 0.0
Fat: 0.0

1. Spray small skillet with cooking spray, heat over medium heat until hot. Saute onions and garlic until tender, about 3 minutes.

2. Process black beans, cheese, and salt in food processor or blender until almost smooth, adding enough broth to make desired dipping consistency. Mix in onion mixture and cilantro.

3. Spoon dip into bowl; serve with baked tortilla chips (not included in nutritional data).

QUESADILLAS

6 servings

Vegetable cooking spray
1 poblano chili, *or* green bell pepper, sliced
1 medium onion, finely chopped
1 teaspoon ground cumin
2 tablespoons finely chopped cilantro
1 cup (4 ounces) shredded reduced-fat Cheddar cheese
6 flour tortillas
3/4 cup mild, *or* medium, salsa
6 tablespoons fat-free sour cream

Per Serving
Calories: 165
% Calories from fat: 26
Fat (gm): 4.8
Sat. fat (gm): 1.7
Cholesterol (mg): 10.1
Sodium (mg): 393
Protein (gm): 8.3
Carbohydrate (gm): 22.9
Exchanges
Milk: 0.0
Vegetable: 1.5
Fruit: 0.0
Bread: 1.0
Meat: 0.5
Fat: 0.5

1. Spray large skillet with cooking spray; heat over medium heat until hot. Saute poblano chili, onion, and cumin until vegetables are tender, 3 to 5 minutes; stir in cilantro.

2. Sprinkle cheese on half of each tortilla; spoon vegetable mixture over. Fold tortillas in half.

3. Spray large skillet with cooking spray; heat over medium heat until hot. Cook quesadillas over medium to medium-high heat until browned on the bottoms, 2 to 3 minutes. Spray tops of quesadillas with cooking spray; turn and cook until browned on the other side. Cut into wedges and serve warm with salsa and sour cream.

NACHOS

6 servings

- Baked tortilla chips (purchased)
- 1 can (15 1/2 ounces) pinto beans, rinsed, drained, coarsely mashed
- 1 cup Red Tomato Salsa (see p. 513), divided
- 1/2-1 teaspoon chili powder
- 3/4 teaspoon dried oregano leaves
- 2-3 cloves garlic, minced
- Salt, to taste
- 1/2 cup (2 ounces) shredded reduced-fat Cheddar, *or* Monterey Jack, cheese
- 1 medium tomato, chopped
- 1/2 small avocado, chopped
- 2 green onions and tops, sliced
- 6 pitted ripe olives, sliced, optional
- 1/4 cup fat-free sour cream

Per Serving
Calories: 200
% Calories from fat: 22
Fat (gm): 5.4
Sat. fat (gm): 1.2
Cholesterol (mg): 5.1
Sodium (mg): 455
Protein (gm): 10.5
Carbohydrate (gm): 32.5

Exchanges
Milk: 0.0
Vegetable: 1.0
Fruit: 0.0
Bread: 2.0
Meat: 0.0
Fat: 1.0

1. Spread baked tortilla chips in a single layer in jelly roll pan. Mix beans, 1/4 cup salsa, chili powder, oregano, and garlic; season to taste with salt. Spoon bean mixture over tortilla chips; sprinkle with cheese. Bake at 350 degrees until beans are hot and cheese melted, 5 to 10 minutes.

2. Sprinkle with tomato, avocado, onions, and olives; garnish with dollops of sour cream. Serve with remaining salsa.

EASY MICROWAVE NACHOS

4 servings

16 baked tortilla chips (purchased)
1/4 cup (1 ounce) shredded reduced-fat mozzarella cheese
1/4 cup mild, *or* medium, salsa

Per Serving
Calories: 75
% Calories from fat: 22
Fat (gm): 1.8
Sat. fat (gm): 0.7
Cholesterol (mg): 4
Sodium (mg): 156
Protein (gm): 3.3
Carbohydrate (gm): 11.3

Exchanges
Milk: 0.0
Vegetable: 0.0
Fruit: 0.0
Bread: 1.0
Meat: 0.0
Fat: 0.0

1. Line platter with wax paper and arrange tortilla chips over it. Sprinkle cheese over each chip; microwave on High just until cheese melts, 30 to 60 seconds. Serve while warm with salsa.

BAKED ASPARAGUS WITH HAM

4 servings

Vegetable cooking spray
1 1/2 pounds asparagus
Salt
8 thin slices smoked ham
1/4 cup (1 ounce) freshly grated Parmesan cheese
2 tablespoons white wine

Per Serving
Calories: 114
% Calories from fat: 29
Fat (gm): 3.9
Sat. fat (gm): 1.8
Cholesterol (mg): 19.9
Sodium (mg): 464
Protein (gm): 12.6
Carbohydrate (gm): 7.7

Exchanges
Milk: 0.0
Vegetable: 1.5
Fruit: 0.0
Bread: 0.0
Meat: 1.5
Fat: 0.0

1. Spray an 11 x 7 baking dish with vegetable cooking spray. Tie asparagus together in 1 or 2 bunches with string. Pour cold salted water 2 to 3 inches deep in an asparagus cooker or tall steamer. Place asparagus upright in cooker and heat to boiling. Reduce heat and simmer, covered, until tender, about 6 minutes, depending on size. Drain on paper towels; remove string.

2. Divide asparagus into 4 bundles. Wrap 2 ham slices around each bundle. Arrange wrapped asparagus bundles in a single layer in baking dish. Sprinkle with Parmesan cheese and pour white wine around asparagus. Bake at 350 degrees 8 to 10 minutes or until cheese is melted.

ASPARAGUS PROVENÇAL

4 servings

- 2 1/4 pounds asparagus
- 1 cup diced tomatoes
- Vegetable cooking spray
- 1 yellow bell pepper, chopped
- 1 onion, chopped
- 1 clove garlic, minced
- 1 teaspoon herbes de Provence
- 1/2 cup fat-free Italian dressing
- 2 tablespoons chopped fresh parsley

Per Serving
Calories: 113
% Calories from fat: 8
Fat (gm): 1.2
Sat. fat (gm): 0.2
Cholesterol (mg): 0
Sodium (mg): 18
Protein (gm): 7.6
Carbohydrate (gm): 21.1
Exchanges
Milk: 0.0
Vegetable: 4.0
Fruit: 0.0
Bread: 0.0
Meat: 0.0
Fat: 0.0

1. Place asparagus in a steamer basket over simmering water. Steam until tender, 6 to 10 minutes. Drain well, and divide among 4 hot individual gratin dishes. Top with tomatoes and set aside.

2. Spray a small skillet with vegetable cooking spray; saute yellow pepper, onion, garlic, and herbes de Provence 5 minutes. Add to Italian dressing and pour over asparagus. Sprinkle with parsley.

ENDIVE LEAVES WITH RATATOUILLE

20 servings (2 appetizers each)

- Vegetable cooking spray
- 1 small eggplant, cut into 1/2-inch cubes
- 1 small zucchini, diced
- 2 small tomatoes, diced
- 1 small onion, diced
- 1/4 cup chopped fresh thyme
- 3 cloves garlic, minced
- Pepper, to taste
- 40 large leaves Belgian endive

Per Serving
Calories: 14
% Calories from fat: 8
Fat (gm): 0.1
Sat. fat (gm): 0
Cholesterol (mg): 0
Sodium (mg): 3.4
Protein (gm): 0.5
Carbohydrate (gm): 3.2
Exchanges
Milk: 0.0
Vegetable: 0.5
Fruit: 0.0
Bread: 0.0
Meat: 0.0
Fat: 0.0

1. Spray a large saucepan with vegetable cooking spray; add eggplant, zucchini, tomatoes, and onion and saute 5 minutes. Add thyme and garlic. Cover and cook over low heat until tender, about 10 minutes, stirring occasionally. Season to taste with pepper; cool.

2. Spoon vegetable mixture into endive leaves. Arrange filled leaves in a fan pattern on a large platter.

TABOULEH

10 servings

- 1 cup bulgur wheat
- 2 cups boiling water
- 1/2 cup chopped scallions
- 5 tablespoons chopped fresh mint
- 2 medium tomatoes, peeled, seeded, and chopped
- 1 cup chopped parsley
- 1 tablespoon olive oil
- 6 tablespoons fresh lemon juice
- 10 large lettuce leaves

Per Serving
Calories: 73
% Calories from fat: 19
Fat (gm): 1.7
Sat. fat (gm): 0.2
Cholesterol (mg): 0
Sodium (mg): 10
Protein (gm): 2.4
Carbohydrate (gm): 13.6
Exchanges
Milk: 0.0
Vegetable: 0.0
Fruit: 0.0
Bread: 1.0
Meat: 0.0
Fat: 0.0

1. Put bulgur in medium bowl and add boiling water. Stir; cover bowl, and let stand 35 minutes. Drain any remaining water. Mix in scallions, mint, tomatoes, parsley, olive oil, and lemon juice. Serve on lettuce-lined plates.

CAPONATA

10 servings

Vegetable cooking spray
1 medium eggplant (about 1 pound), peeled and cut into 1/2-inch cubes
3/4 cup chopped onion
1/3 cup chopped celery
1 can (14 1/2 ounces) diced tomatoes, undrained
3 tablespoons wine vinegar
2 tablespoons tomato paste
1 teaspoon sugar
1 tablespoon dried basil leaves
1 teaspoon dried oregano leaves
Dash cayenne pepper
1 tablespoon chopped parsley
1 teaspoon lemon juice

Per Serving
Calories: 30
% Calories from fat: 7
Fat (gm): 0.3
Sat. fat (gm): 0.04
Cholesterol (mg): 0
Sodium (mg): 74
Protein (gm): 1.1
Carbohydrate (gm): 7.1

Exchanges
Milk: 0.0
Vegetable: 1.5
Fruit: 0.0
Bread: 0.0
Meat: 0.0
Fat: 0.0

1. Spray large skillet with cooking spray; add eggplant, onion, and celery and cook, covered, over medium heat until just tender, 5 to 8 minutes. Stir in remaining ingredients, except parsley and lemon juice. Cook, uncovered, over low heat until thickened, about 5 minutes, stirring occasionally. Remove from heat.

2. Stir in parsley and lemon juice. Cool; cover and refrigerate. Let stand at room temperature for 30 minutes before serving.

POTATO PANCAKES WITH GINGER YOGURT

8 servings

- 4 large baking potatoes (about 2 pounds), peeled
- 3/4 cup grated onion
- 2 egg whites, slightly beaten
- 1/4 teaspoon baking soda
- 1/2 teaspoon dried basil leaves, crumbled
- Canola oil, *or* vegetable cooking spray
- Ginger Yogurt (recipe follows)

Per Serving
Calories: 116
% Calories from fat: 2
Fat (gm): 0.2
Sat. fat (gm): 0.1
Cholesterol (mg): 1
Sodium (mg): 101
Protein (gm): 5.9
Carbohydrate (gm): 23.1
Exchanges
Milk: 0.0
Vegetable: 0.0
Fruit: 0.0
Bread: 1.5
Meat: 0.0
Fat: 0.0

1. Grate potatoes into deep mixing bowl, working quickly as potatoes brown fast. Mix in remaining ingredients except oil and Ginger Yogurt. Cover bowl with plastic wrap and let stand in refrigerator 20 minutes. Stir before using.

2. Spray large nonstick skillet with canola oil or cooking spray. Spoon tablespoons of mixture into hot skillet, making pancakes, about 1 1/2 inches in diameter. Fry pancakes until cooked and golden brown on both sides.

3. Place bowl of Ginger Yogurt on serving platter and surround with hot pancakes.

Ginger Yogurt

makes about 2 cups

- 2 cups plain nonfat yogurt
- 2 teaspoons minced candied ginger
- 1/2 cup minced fresh chives

1. Combine all ingredients in small bowl. Cover and refrigerate; stir before serving.

POTATO SEAFOOD CAKES

8 servings

- 2 cups mashed potatoes
- 1 cup chopped crabmeat, shrimp, *or* surimi
- 2 egg whites, slightly beaten
- 1/2 teaspoon Worcestershire sauce
- 1/4 teaspoon red pepper flakes
- 1/4 cup minced parsley
- 2-3 teaspoons margarine

Per Serving
Calories: 72
% Calories from fat: 19
Fat (gm): 1.6
Sat. fat (gm): 0.4
Cholesterol (mg): 17.9
Sodium (mg): 235
Protein (gm): 5.4
Carbohydrate (gm): 9.5
Exchanges
Milk: 0.0
Vegetable: 0.0
Fruit: 0.0
Bread: 0.5
Meat: 0.5
Fat: 0.0

1. Combine potatoes, crabmeat, egg whites, Worcestershire sauce, red pepper flakes, and parsley in medium bowl. Shape batter into patties; cook in margarine in nonstick skillet over medium heat until browned, 3 to 4 minutes on each side.

SWEET-AND-SOUR CHICKEN CHUNKS

20 servings

- Vegetable cooking spray
- 2 medium onions, thinly sliced
- 2 medium green bell peppers, seeded and cut into thin strips
- 1 clove garlic, finely chopped
- 2 1/2 pounds cooked boneless, skinless chicken breast, cut into 3/4-inch pieces
- Sweet-and-Sour Sauce (see p. 508)

Per Serving
Calories: 99
% Calories from fat: 16
Fat (gm): 1.8
Sat. fat (gm): 0.5
Cholesterol (mg): 43.6
Sodium (mg): 100
Protein (gm): 16.8
Carbohydrate (gm): 3
Exchanges
Milk: 0.0
Vegetable: 0.0
Fruit: 0.0
Bread: 0.0
Meat: 2.0
Fat: 0.0

1. Spray large skillet with cooking spray; heat over medium heat until hot. Saute onions, green peppers, and garlic until tender, about 5 minutes. Add chicken and Sweet-and-Sour Sauce; cook 2 minutes or until bubbly.

Tip: For easy convenience, 1 cup jarred sweet-and-sour sauce can be substituted for the home-made sauce.

BAKED CLAMS

6 servings

12 clams in shells
3/4 cup dry unseasoned bread crumbs
6 tablespoons white wine
1/4 cup chopped parsley
3 cloves garlic, finely chopped
1 teaspoon Italian seasoning
1/2 teaspoon pepper

Per Serving
Calories: 145
% Calories from fat: 11
Fat (gm): 1.7
Sat. fat (gm): 0.2
Cholesterol (mg): 37.2
Sodium (mg): 157
Protein (gm): 16.1
Carbohydrate (gm): 12.9
Exchanges
Milk: 0.0
Vegetable: 0.0
Fruit: 0.0
Bread: 0.5
Meat: 2.0
Fat: 0.0

1. Open clams above bowl; remove clam muscle. Reserve clam liquor and shells. Scrub shells under cold running water and place in a single layer in a shallow baking dish.

2. Mix bread crumbs, wine, parsley, garlic, Italian seasoning, and pepper in medium bowl. Place 1 clam in each shell in baking dish. Spoon bread crumb mixture over clams and drizzle with reserved liquor. Bake uncovered at 375 degrees for 15 to 20 minutes or until brown.

MUSSELS IN SPICY SAUCE

6 servings

3 cups canned mussels, drained
3 jars (2 1/2 ounces each) chopped pimiento, drained
6 tablespoons fat-free mayonnaise
2 tablespoons Dijon mustard
1 tablespoon dry sherry
1 1/2 teaspoons lemon juice

Per Serving
Calories: 161
% Calories from fat: 22
Fat (gm): 3.9
Sat. fat (gm): 0.7
Cholesterol (mg): 42.9
Sodium (mg): 548
Protein (gm): 18.7
Carbohydrate (gm): 11.3
Exchanges
Milk: 0.0
Vegetable: 0.0
Fruit: 0.0
Bread: 0.0
Meat: 3.0
Fat: 0.0

1. Place mussels on platter. Combine remaining ingredients; serve with mussels.

SALMON FISH MOLD

6 servings

- 1 package (3 ounces) fat-free cream cheese
- 1 can (10 1/2 ounces) reduced-fat cream of mushroom soup
- 2 envelopes unflavored gelatin
- 1/4 cup cold water
- 1 can (7 1/2 ounces) salmon, bones and skin removed
- 1/2 cup chopped celery
- 1/2 cup chopped green onions and tops
- 1 cup fat-free mayonnaise
- 1/2 cup plain nonfat yogurt
- 1 green olive, cut in half
- Chopped parsley, cucumber slices, pimiento strips, cherry tomatoes, as garnish

Per Serving
Calories: 155
% Calories from fat: 34
Fat (gm): 5.8
Sat. fat (gm): 1.6
Cholesterol (mg): 16.2
Sodium (mg): 968
Protein (gm): 14.2
Carbohydrate (gm): 10.9
Exchanges
Milk: 0.0
Vegetable: 0.0
Fruit: 0.0
Bread: 0.0
Meat: 1.5
Fat: 5.0

1. Heat cream cheese and soup in medium saucepan over medium heat until cheese is melted and mixture is smooth. Sprinkle gelatin over water in small saucepan; let stand 5 minutes. Heat over low heat until gelatin is dissolved, 2 to 3 minutes; stir into cream cheese mixture. Stir in remaining ingredients, except garnishes.

2. Spoon mixture into a greased 5-cup fish-shaped mold. Chill till firm, 4 to 6 hours.

3. To unmold, dip mold briefly in hot water; loosen edge of mold with tip of sharp knife. Unmold onto platter. Place olive half on the eye of the fish. Sprinkle parsley along the outer rim of cucumber slices; overlap cucumber slices to resemble scales along the side of the fish. Decorate the mouth and tail with pimiento strips. Decorate platter with cherry tomatoes.

SHRIMP COCKTAIL

8 servings

2 quarts water
1/4 cup sliced onion
1 clove garlic, quartered
1 bay leaf
2 ribs celery with leaves
1/2 lemon, sliced
2 pounds medium shrimp in shells
Zesty Cocktail Sauce (see p. 514)

Per Serving
Calories: 124
% Calories from fat: 8
Fat (gm): 1.1
Sat. fat (gm): 0.3
Cholesterol (mg): 174
Sodium (mg): 264
Protein (gm): 19.4
Carbohydrate (gm): 9.7
Exchanges
Milk: 0.0
Vegetable: 1.0
Fruit: 0.0
Bread: 0.0
Meat: 2.0
Fat: 0.0

1. Heat water, onion, garlic, bay leaf, celery, and lemon to boiling in large saucepan; add shrimp. Reduce heat and simmer until shrimp turn pink, 3 to 4 minutes. Drain immediately and chill.
2. Shell and devein shrimp, leaving tails intact. Serve with Zesty Cocktail Sauce.

SHRIMP REMOULADE

12 servings

1/2 cup fat-free mayonnaise
2 teaspoons chopped fresh tarragon, *or* 1/2 teaspoon dried tarragon leaves
3 cloves garlic, minced
2 teaspoons dry mustard
1 tablespoon drained capers
6 gherkins, *or* small dill pickles, minced
1 1/2 pounds shrimp, shelled, deveined, cooked
Parsley sprigs and lemon wedges, as garnish

Per Serving
Calories: 67
% Calories from fat: 11
Fat (gm): 0.8
Sat. fat (gm): 0.2
Cholesterol (mg): 110.5
Sodium (mg): 290
Protein (gm): 12.1
Carbohydrate (gm): 1.9
Exchanges
Milk: 0.0
Vegetable: 0.0
Fruit: 0.0
Bread: 0.0
Meat: 2.0
Fat: 0.0

1. Combine all ingredients except shrimp and garnishes in bowl; refrigerate several hours for flavors to blend. Arrange shrimp in bowl and garnish with parsley and lemon; serve with sauce for dipping. Or, arrange shrimp on serving plates and garnish; spoon sauce over shrimp.

ORIENTAL SKEWERED SHRIMP

6 servings

- 36 medium shrimp, peeled and deveined (about 1 1/4 pounds)
- 6 cherry tomatoes
- 6 yellow pickled peppers
- 3/4 cup dry sherry
- 1/4 cup soy sauce
- 1/2 teaspoon ground ginger
- 1 teaspoon sugar

Per Serving
Calories: 131
% Calories from fat: 7
Fat (gm): 0.9
Sat. fat (gm): 0.2
Cholesterol (mg): 145.1
Sodium (mg): 523
Protein (gm): 17
Carbohydrate (gm): 5.6
Exchanges
Milk: 0.0
Vegetable: 1.0
Fruit: 0.0
Bread: 0.0
Meat: 2.0
Fat: 0.0

1. Thread shrimp lengthwise on six 9-inch skewers. Thread a cherry tomato and a yellow pickled pepper at the end of each skewer. Place skewers on a platter and drizzle with combined sherry, soy sauce, and ginger; refrigerate for 1 hour, turning skewers occasionally. Drain and reserve marinade.

2. Grill over medium coals or broil 6 inches from heat source until shrimp are cooked, 6 to 10 minutes, turning once. Add sugar to reserved marinade and heat to boiling; drizzle over shrimp just before serving.

CITRUS SCALLOPS

12 servings

- 2 pounds scallops
- 1 tablespoon olive oil, *or* canola oil
- 1 cup thinly sliced onion, separated into rings
- 2 cloves garlic, minced
- 1/4 cup fresh orange juice
- 1/2 cup fresh lime juice
- 1/4 teaspoon hot pepper sauce, *or* to taste
- 1 orange, thinly sliced, seeds removed
- 1 lime, thinly sliced, seeds removed

Per Serving
Calories: 100
% Calories from fat: 18
Fat (gm): 2.1
Sat. fat (gm): 0.2
Cholesterol (mg): 32.2
Sodium (mg): 151
Protein (gm): 14.5
Carbohydrate (gm). 6.8
Exchanges
Milk: 0.0
Vegetable: 0.0
Fruit: 0.0
Bread: 0.0
Meat: 2.0
Fat: 0.0

1. Saute scallops in oil in large skillet until opaque and tender. Place scallops in deep glass bowl, layering them with onion rings and garlic.

2. Combine remaining ingredients and pour over scallops. Cover and chill up to 24 hours, stirring occasionally.

TWO

Soups AND Chowders

BEEF STOCK

20 servings (about $3^1/_2$ quarts)

- 2 pounds short ribs of beef
- 2 pounds beef marrow bones, cut into pieces
- 1 pound ground beef chuck
- 1 large onion, coarsely chopped
- 4 medium carrots, cut into quarters
- 3 ribs celery with leaves
- 1/2 cup dried mushrooms
- 1 clove garlic
- 10 peppercorns
- 1 bay leaf
- 1 teaspoon dried basil leaves
- 1 teaspoon dried thyme leaves
- 3 sprigs parsley
- 1 cup dry red wine
- 1 tablespoon soy sauce
- Cold water

Per Serving
Calories: 24
% Calories from fat: 19
Fat (gm): 0.5
Sat. fat (gm): 0.2
Cholesterol (mg): 3.2
Sodium (mg): 64
Protein (gm): 2.3
Carbohydrate (gm): 0.5

Exchanges
Milk: 0.0
Vegetable: 0.0
Fruit: 0.0
Bread: 0.0
Meat: 0.0
Fat: 0.0

1. Combine all ingredients into 6- or 8-quart stockpot; add cold water to cover by 2 inches. Cover with a loose-fitting lid and heat to boiling; reduce heat and simmer, covered, 4 hours; cool.

2. Strain stock into container and refrigerate. When cold, remove and discard all fat congealed on surface. Refrigerate stock, or freeze.

CHICKEN STOCK

16 servings (about 4 quarts)

Per Serving
Calories: 35
% Calories from fat: 25
Fat (gm): 0.9
Sat. fat (gm): 0.3
Cholesterol (mg): 10
Sodium (mg): 11
Protein (gm): 3.3
Carbohydrate (gm): 0.8

Exchanges
Milk: 0.0
Vegetable: 0.0
Fruit: 0.0
Bread: 0.0
Meat: 0.5
Fat: 0.0

- 1 chicken stewing hen (4-5 pounds)
- 2 1/2 pounds chicken necks and wings
- 1 veal knuckle, cracked, optional
- 2 medium onions, stuck with several cloves
- 6 medium carrots, cut into quarters
- 2 medium leeks, cut into 1-inch pieces
- 3 ribs celery, including leaves
- 1/2 teaspoon dried basil leaves
- 1/2 teaspoon dried thyme leaves
- 1/2 teaspoon dried tarragon leaves
- 1 clove garlic
- 10 peppercorns
- 6 sprigs parsley
- 1 cup dry white wine
- Cold water

1. Combine all ingredients into large 10-quart stockpot; add cold water to cover by 2 inches. Place loose-fitting lid on top and heat to boiling; reduce heat and simmer, covered 3 to 4 hours; cool.

2. Strain stock into container and refrigerate. When cold, remove and discard all fat congealed on surface. Refrigerate, or freeze.

FISH STOCK

4 servings (about 4 cups)

$1^1/_2$ pounds fresh, *or* frozen, fish
1 medium onion, finely chopped
3 ribs celery with leaves, cut in half
1 medium carrot, finely diced
3 sprigs parsley
3 slices lemon
8 peppercorns
$^3/_4$ cup white wine
3 cups cold water

Per Serving
Calories: 47
% Calories from fat: 2
Fat (gm): 0.1
Sat. fat (gm): 0
Cholesterol (mg): 6.7
Sodium (mg): 15
Protein (gm): 2.9
Carbohydrate (gm): 1.3
Exchanges
Milk: 0.0
Vegetable: 0.0
Fruit: 0.0
Bread: 0.0
Meat: 0.5
Fat: 0.0

1. Combine all ingredients in large saucepan. Heat to boiling; reduce heat and simmer, covered, 30 minutes; cool.
2. Strain into container. Refrigerate, or freeze.

VEGETABLE STOCK

12 servings (about 9 cups)

Vegetable cooking spray
4 cloves garlic, crushed
2 cups chopped onions
3 ribs celery, sliced
3 cups sliced carrots
1 cup sliced turnips
1 cup cubed, peeled potato
$^1/_2$ cup chopped parsley
2 bay leaves
$^1/_2$ teaspoon dried thyme leaves
$^1/_2$ teaspoon pepper
3 quarts water

Per Serving
Calories: 4
% Calories from fat: 3
Fat (gm): 0
Sat. fat (gm): 0
Cholesterol (mg): 0
Sodium (mg): 3
Protein (gm): 0.1
Carbohydrate (gm): 1.1
Exchanges
Milk: 0.0
Vegetable: 0.0
Fruit: 0.0
Bread: 0.0
Meat: 0.0
Fat: 0.0

1. Spray large saucepan with cooking spray. Add garlic, onions, and celery and saute 5 minutes, covered, over medium heat, stirring occasionally. Add remaining ingredients, except water, and continue cooking 5 minutes. Add water and heat to boiling; reduce heat and simmer, covered, 2 hours, stirring occasionally. Cool.

2. Strain through double layer of cheesecloth. Refrigerate, or freeze.

APPLE SQUASH SOUP

8 servings

Per Serving
Calories: 155
% Calories from fat: 15
Fat (gm): 2.8
Sat. fat (gm): 0.5
Cholesterol (mg): 1.3
Sodium (mg): 48
Protein (gm): 3.3
Carbohydrate (gm): 32.6
Exchanges
Milk: 0.0
Vegetable: 0.0
Fruit: 0.0
Bread: 2.0
Meat: 0.0
Fat: 0.5

1 1/2 cups chopped onions
2 teaspoons ground cinnamon
1/4 teaspoon ground ginger
1/4 teaspoon ground cloves
1/8 teaspoon ground nutmeg
1 1/2 tablespoons margarine
1 large butternut squash, peeled, seeded, cubed (about 2 1/2 pounds)
2 tart cooking apples, peeled, cored, chopped
1 1/3 cups apple cider
3 cups Chicken Stock (see p. 47)
Salt and pepper, to taste
Spiced Sour Cream (recipe follows)

1. Saute onions and spices in margarine in large saucepan over very low heat until onions are very tender, about 20 minutes, stirring frequently; add squash, apples, cider, and Chicken Stock. Heat to boiling; reduce heat and simmer, covered, until squash and apples are tender, about 25 minutes.

2. Process mixture in food processor or blender until smooth; return mixture to saucepan and heat to simmering. Season to taste with salt and pepper. Ladle soup into bowls and serve with Spiced Sour Cream.

Spiced Sour Cream

makes about 1 cup

1/2 cup fat-free sour cream
1 teaspoon sugar
1/2 teaspoon ground cinnamon
1/8 teaspoon ground ginger
Lemon juice, to taste

1. Combine sour cream, sugar, and spices; season to taste with lemon juice.

SMOKY THREE BEAN SOUP

8 servings (about 1 1/2 cups each)

- 8 ounces turkey smoked sausage, cut into scant 1/2-inch slices
- 1 cup chopped onion
- 1 cup sliced celery
- 2 teaspoons minced garlic
- 1 tablespoon vegetable oil
- 1 1/2 quarts chicken broth
- 2 cups cubed, peeled sweet potatoes
- 2 cups cubed, peeled Idaho potato
- 1 can (15 ounces) navy beans, rinsed, drained
- 1 can (15 ounces) pinto beans, rinsed, drained
- 1 can (15 ounces) black beans, rinsed, drained
- 3/4 teaspoon dried thyme leaves
- 1 bay leaf
- 1 1/2-2 teaspoons salt
- 1/2 teaspoon pepper

Per Serving
Calories: 305
% Calories from fat: 19
Fat (gm): 8.6
Sat. fat (gm): 1.5
Cholesterol (mg): 17.5
Sodium (mg): 1850
Protein (gm): 16.7
Carbohydrate (gm): 46.8

Exchanges
Milk: 0.0
Vegetable: 0.0
Fruit: 0.0
Bread: 3.0
Meat: 1.0
Fat: 1.0

1. Saute smoked sausage, onion, celery, and garlic in oil in Dutch oven until sausage is browned, 5 to 8 minutes. Add remaining ingredients and heat to boiling; reduce heat and simmer, covered, until potatoes are tender, 10 to 15 minutes.

SOUTHWEST SUCCOTASH SOUP

4 servings

Per Serving
Calories: 233
% Calories from fat: 14
Fat (gm): 3.7
Sat. fat (gm): 2.1
Cholesterol (mg): 10.7
Sodium (mg): 50.5
Protein (gm): 11.3
Carbohydrate (gm): 39.2
Exchanges
Milk: 0.5
Vegetable: 0.0
Fruit: 0.0
Bread: 2.0
Meat: 0.0
Fat: 1.0

1/2 cup chopped onion
1/2 cup chopped red bell pepper
1 large jalapeno chili, chopped
1 teaspoon chopped garlic
1/2 teaspoon chili powder
1/2 teaspoon ground cumin
1/2 teaspoon dried thyme leaves
1 tablespoon butter
2 tablespoons flour
2 cups fat-free milk
1 can (13 1/4 ounces) baby lima beans, rinsed, drained
1 cup frozen whole-kernel corn
1/2 teaspoon salt

1. Saute onion, bell pepper, jalapeno, garlic, chili powder, cumin, and thyme in butter in medium saucepan until tender, about 5 minutes. Stir in flour; cook 1 minute. Stir in milk and heat to boiling; stir until thickened, about 2 minutes. Stir in remaining ingredients; heat to boiling. Reduce heat and simmer 5 minutes.

HEARTY SPLIT PEA, BEAN, AND BARLEY SOUP

9 servings

Per Serving
Calories: 180
% Calories from fat: 8
Fat (gm): 1.7
Sat. fat (gm): 2.3
Cholesterol (mg): 8
Sodium (mg): 523
Protein (gm): 12
Carbohydrate (gm): 31
Exchanges
Milk: 0.0
Vegetable: 5.0
Fruit: 0.0
Bread: 0.5
Meat: 0.5
Fat: 0.0

2 cups dried Great Northern beans, sorted, rinsed
2 1/4 quarts water
1 meaty ham bone, *or* 2 pork hocks
1/4 cup pearl barley
2 cups chopped onions
2 large carrots, peeled, sliced
2 large ribs celery, including leaves, sliced
3-5 beef bouillon cubes

2 garlic cloves, minced
3 bay leaves
$1^1/_2$ teaspoons dried thyme leaves
$^1/_4$ teaspoon ground celery seeds
$^1/_4$ teaspoon pepper
3 cups thinly sliced cabbage
1 can (8 ounces) reduced-sodium tomato sauce
Salt, to taste

1. Cover beans with 2 inches of water in Dutch oven and heat to boiling; boil 2 minutes. Remove from heat and let stand, covered, 1 hour. Drain.

2. Return beans to Dutch oven with remaining ingredients except cabbage, tomato sauce, and salt; heat to boiling. Reduce heat and simmer, covered, 30 minutes. Add cabbage and simmer 30 to 40 minutes or until beans are very tender.

3. Remove ham bone and cut meat into small pieces; return to soup. Discard bone and bay leaves; skim fat from surface of soup. Add tomato sauce and simmer 10 minutes. Season to taste with salt.

WHITE BEAN SOUP PROVENÇAL

8 servings

1 pound dried cannellini, *or* navy, beans
Olive oil cooking spray
1 cup chopped onion
1 cup chopped celery
3 cloves garlic, minced
2 teaspoons dried sage leaves
$1^1/_2$ quarts Chicken Stock (see p. 47), *or* reduced-sodium fat-free chicken broth
2 cups water
3 large plum tomatoes, chopped
2 teaspoons lemon juice
Salt and pepper, to taste
Mixed Herb Pesto (see p. 515)

Per Serving
Calories: 283
% Calories from fat: 21
Fat (gm): 6.9
Sat. fat (gm): 1.2
Cholesterol (mg): 3.6
Sodium (mg): 199
Protein (gm): 16.2
Carbohydrate (gm): 41.9

Exchanges
Milk: 0.0
Vegetable: 2.0
Fruit: 0.0
Bread: 2.0
Meat: 1.0
Fat: 1.0

1. Cover beans with 2 inches water in large saucepan and heat to boiling; boil, uncovered, 2 minutes. Remove from heat and let stand, covered, 1 hour; drain.

2. Spray large saucepan with cooking spray; heat over medium heat until hot. Saute onion, celery, and garlic 3 to 4 minutes. Stir in beans, sage, Chicken Stock, and water; heat to boiling. Reduce heat and simmer, covered, until beans are tender, 45 to 60 minutes.

3. Process in food processor or blender until smooth; return to saucepan. Stir in tomatoes and lemon juice; season to taste with salt and pepper.

4. Serve soup in bowls; stir 1 tablespoon Mixed Herb Pesto into each bowl.

ITALIAN BEAN SOUP

14 servings

- 1 cup dried navy beans
- 2 quarts water
- 1 cup chopped onion
- 1 cup chopped green bell pepper
- 1 cup chopped carrots
- 1/2 cup chopped celery
- 1 teaspoon dried basil leaves
- 1 teaspoon oregano leaves
- 1 teaspoon vegetable-flavored bouillon granules
- 1/4 teaspoon dry mustard
- 2 cloves garlic, minced
- 3 cans (8 ounces each) tomato sauce
- 1/2 cup whole wheat elbow macaroni, uncooked
- 1 can (15 ounces) garbanzo beans, drained

Per Serving
Calories: 125
% Calories from fat: 7
Fat (gm): 1
Sat. fat (gm): 0.2
Cholesterol (mg): 0
Sodium (mg): 489
Protein (gm): 6.3
Carbohydrate (gm): 24.4

Exchanges
Milk: 0.0
Vegetable: 0.5
Fruit: 0.0
Bread: 1.5
Meat: 0.0
Fat: 0.0

1. Sort and wash beans; place in Dutch oven. Cover with water 2 inches above beans; heat to boiling and cook over high heat 3 minutes. Remove from heat; cover and let stand 1 hour.

2. Drain beans and return to pan; add water and remaining ingredients, except macaroni and garbanzo beans. Heat to boiling; reduce heat and simmer until beans are tender, about 1 hour, stirring occasionally. Add macaroni and garbanzo beans and cook about 15 minutes or until macaroni is tender.

NEAPOLITAN BEAN BISQUE

6 servings (about 1 cup each)

1/2 cup chopped onion
6 large cloves garlic, cut in halves
1 tablespoon olive oil
1 teaspoon dried rosemary leaves
1/2 teaspoon dried thyme leaves
2 cans (15 ounces each) Great Northern, *or* navy, beans, rinsed, drained
1 quart reduced-sodium vegetable broth
1 tablespoon balsamic vinegar
1/2 teaspoon salt
1/2 teaspoon pepper
1/2 cup frozen spinach
3-4 tablespoons basil pesto
1/4 cup roasted red bell pepper
Parmesan cheese curls, as garnish

Per Serving
Calories: 221
% Calories from fat: 29
Fat (gm): 7.4
Sat. fat (gm): 1
Cholesterol (mg): 1.3
Sodium (mg): 823
Protein (gm): 9.7
Carbohydrate (gm): 29.8
Exchanges
Milk: 0.0
Vegetable: 0.0
Fruit: 0.0
Bread: 2.0
Meat: 0.0
Fat: 1.5

1. Saute onion and garlic in oil in large saucepan until tender, about 5 minutes; stir in herbs and cook 1 to 2 minutes. Stir in beans, broth, vinegar, salt, and pepper. Heat to boiling; reduce heat and simmer 5 minutes.

2. Puree half the soup (about 2 1/2 cups) in blender with spinach and pesto until smooth; place in small saucepan. Puree remaining soup in blender with roasted pepper until smooth; return to saucepan.

3. Heat both soups over medium heat until hot. Ladle both soups into bowls simultaneously; swirl lightly with knife. Garnish with Parmesan cheese.

BORSCHT

14 servings

- 4 pounds beef shank
- 1 large beef marrow bone
- 1 tablespoon plus 1 1/2 teaspoons salt, divided
- 2 quarts water
- 1 can (15 ounces) tomatoes, undrained
- 1 medium onion, quartered
- 1 rib celery, cut into 2-inch pieces
- 3 parsley sprigs
- 10 whole black peppercorns
- 2 bay leaves
- 3 cups coarsely shredded cabbage
- 1 1/2 cups thickly sliced carrots
- 1 cup chopped onion
- 2 tablespoons fresh, *or* 1 tablespoon dried, dill weed
- 1/3 cup apple cider vinegar
- 1 can (15 ounces) julienne beets, undrained
- 1 teaspoon sugar
- Fat-free sour cream, as garnish
- Snipped fresh dill weed *or* dried basil leaves, as garnish

Per Serving
Calories: 215
% Calories from fat: 25
Fat (gm): 5.9
Sat. fat (gm): 2.1
Cholesterol (mg): 69.3
Sodium (mg): 891
Protein (gm): 31.3
Carbohydrate (gm): 8.3

Exchanges
Milk: 0.0
Vegetable: 1.0
Fruit: 0.0
Bread: 0.0
Meat: 3.5
Fat: 0.0

1. Combine beef shank, marrow bone, 1 tablespoon salt, and water in large Dutch oven. Heat to boiling; reduce heat and simmer, covered, 1 hour. Add tomatoes and juice, onion, celery, parsley, peppercorns, and bay leaves; simmer, covered, 2 hours.

2. Remove beef from soup with slotted spoon. Strain soup through colander into large bowl. Discard bones and vegetables. Return soup and beef to Dutch oven. Add cabbage, carrots, chopped onion, dill, vinegar, beets, sugar, and remaining 1 1/2 teaspoons salt. Heat to boiling; reduce heat and simmer, covered, 30 minutes, or until beef and vegetables are tender.

3. Serve in bowls; garnish with dollops of sour cream; sprinkle with snipped dill weed.

BROCCOLI BISQUE

5-6 servings

2 medium broccoli stalks
1/2 small head cauliflower
1 cup chopped green onions and tops
2 teaspoons margarine
1 tablespoon flour
3 cups Chicken Stock (see p. 47)
1 1/3 cups coarsely chopped peeled potatoes
3 tablespoons finely chopped fresh chives, *or* 1 1/2 tablespoons dried chives
2 1/2 teaspoons dried basil leaves
1 1/2 cups 2% reduced-fat milk
Salt and pepper, to taste

Per Serving
Calories: 169
% Calories from fat: 26
Fat (gm): 5.2
Sat. fat (gm): 1.1
Cholesterol (mg): 2.5
Sodium (mg): 594
Protein (gm): 11.9
Carbohydrate (gm): 21.5
Exchanges
Milk: 0.5
Vegetable: 3.0
Fruit: 0.0
Bread: 0.0
Meat: 0.0
Fat: 1.0

1. Cut broccoli and cauliflower into florets. Reserve 3/4 cup small broccoli florets and 3/4 cup small cauliflower florets; coarsely chop remaining broccoli and cauliflower.

2. Saute green onions in margarine in large saucepan until tender, about 4 minutes. Stir in flour; cook 1 minute. Stir in Chicken Stock, chopped broccoli and cauliflower, potatoes, chives, and basil; heat to boiling. Reduce heat and simmer, uncovered, until potatoes are tender, about 12 minutes.

3. Process in food processor or blender until smooth. Return puree to saucepan; add milk and reserved broccoli and cauliflower florets. Heat to boiling; reduce heat and simmer until florets are crisp-tender, about 5 minutes. Season to taste with salt and pepper.

CARROT SOUP WITH DILL

4 servings (about 1 cup each)

1/4 cup sliced green onions and tops
3 tablespoons chopped parsley
2 teaspoons margarine
1 tablespoon arrowroot
1 1/2 cups Chicken Stock (see p. 47)
2 cups sliced carrots, steamed
1/2 cup evaporated fat-free milk
Salt and pepper, to taste
2 tablespoons chopped fresh dill weed

Per Serving
Calories: 156
% Calories from fat: 3
Fat (gm): 0.5
Sat. fat (gm): 0.1
Cholesterol (mg): 0.3
Sodium (mg): 245
Protein (gm): 10
Carbohydrate (gm): 28.7
Exchanges
Milk: 0.0
Vegetable: 4.0
Fruit: 0.0
Bread: 0.5
Meat: 0.0
Fat: 0.0

1. Saute green onions and parsley in margarine in medium saucepan until softened. Sprinkle with arrowroot and cook 2 minutes. Stir in Chicken Stock, heat to boiling, stirring until smooth and slightly thickened.

2. Process carrots in blender or food processor with 1 cup stock mixture until smooth. Place carrot mixture in saucepan with remaining stock mixture; add evaporated milk. Heat until hot; do not boil. Season to taste with salt and pepper. Ladle into soup cups and sprinkle with dill.

CREAM OF CAULIFLOWER SOUP WITH CHEESE

6 servings

Vegetable cooking spray
1/2 cup chopped onion
2 cloves garlic, minced
2 tablespoons flour
3 1/2 cups reduced-sodium fat-free chicken broth
12 ounces cauliflower, cut into florets
1 large Idaho potato, peeled, cubed
1/4-1/2 cup fat-free half-and-half, *or* fat-free milk

Per Serving
Calories: 108
% Calories from fat: 20
Fat (gm): 2.3
Sat. fat (gm): 1.1
Cholesterol (mg): 7.6
Sodium (mg): 312
Protein (gm): 8.8
Carbohydrate (gm): 12.2
Exchanges
Milk: 0.0
Vegetable: 2.0
Fruit: 0.0
Bread: 0.0
Meat: 0.5
Fat: 0.5

- 3/4 cup (3 ounces) shredded reduced-fat Cheddar cheese
- Salt and white pepper, to taste
- Ground mace, *or* nutmeg, as garnish

1. Spray large saucepan with cooking spray; heat over medium heat until hot. Saute onion and garlic until tender, about 10 minutes. Stir in flour; cook 1 to 2 minutes longer. Add broth, cauliflower, and potato; heat to boiling. Reduce heat and simmer, covered, until vegetables are tender, 10 to 15 minutes.

2. Remove about half the vegetables from the soup with a slotted spoon and reserve. Process remaining soup in food processor or blender until smooth. Return soup to saucepan; stir in reserved vegetables, half-and-half, and cheese; cook over low heat until cheese is melted, 3 to 4 minutes, stirring frequently. Season to taste with salt and white pepper.

3. Pour soup into bowls; sprinkle lightly with mace or nutmeg.

Variations: **Fennel Bisque with Walnuts**—Make soup as above, substituting 1 large leek, sliced, for the onion, and 2 large fennel bulbs, sliced, for the cauliflower. Complete soup as above, omitting Cheddar cheese. Ladle soup into bowls; sprinkle with 3 ounces crumbled blue cheese and 1/4 cup toasted walnuts.

Cream of Turnip Soup—Make soup as above, substituting chopped turnips for the cauliflower and reduced-fat Swiss, Gouda, or Havarti cheese for the Cheddar; add 1/2 teaspoon dried thyme leaves.

CONFETTI SOUP

8 servings

- Vegetable cooking spray
- 2 carrots, sliced
- 1 cup sliced leeks, white parts only, *or* green onions and tops
- 1 package (10 ounces) frozen chopped broccoli
- 1 package (10 ounces) frozen cauliflower
- 1 1/2 cups reduced-sodium fat-free chicken broth

Per Serving
Calories: 75
% Calories from fat: 4
Fat (gm): 0.4
Sat. fat (gm): 0.1
Cholesterol (mg): 1.7
Sodium (mg): 104
Protein (gm): 6.3
Carbohydrate (gm): 12.6

Exchanges
Milk: 0.0
Vegetable: 3.0
Fruit: 0.0
Bread: 0.0
Meat: 0.0
Fat: 0.0

3 cups fat-free milk, divided
1 tablespoon cornstarch
Pepper, to taste

1. Spray large saucepan with cooking spray; heat over medium heat until hot. Saute carrots and leeks until lightly browned, about 8 minutes. Add broccoli, cauliflower, and chicken broth; heat to boiling. Reduce heat and simmer, covered, until vegetables are tender, about 5 minutes.

2. Process half the vegetable mixture in blender or food processor until smooth; return to saucepan and heat to boiling. Stir in combined 1/2 cup milk and cornstarch; boil, stirring, until thickened, about 1 minute. Stir in remaining 2 1/2 cups milk; simmer, covered, 5 minutes longer. Season to taste with pepper.

IOWA CORN SOUP

8 servings

1 cup sliced onion
1 tablespoon canola oil
2 tablespoons flour
3 cups frozen whole kernel corn
5 cups 2% reduced-fat milk
1/4 cup parsley, minced
Salt and pepper, to taste

Per Serving
Calories: 170
% Calories from fat: 11
Fat (gm): 2.1
Sat. fat (gm): 0.3
Cholesterol (mg): 3.5
Sodium (mg): 258
Protein (gm): 10.3
Carbohydrate (gm): 29.5
Exchanges
Milk: 1.0
Vegetable: 0.5
Fruit: 0.0
Bread: 1.0
Meat: 0.0
Fat: 0.0

1. Saute onion in oil in large saucepan until tender, about 5 minutes. Sprinkle with flour and cook 1 minute. Stir in corn and milk. Heat to boiling; reduce heat and simmer 5 minutes. Stir in parsley; season to taste with salt and pepper.

CUCUMBER AND SORREL SOUP

6 servings (about $1^1/_4$ cups each)

Vegetable cooking spray
$^1/_4$ cup plus 2 tablespoons sliced green onions and tops, divided
1 clove garlic, minced
3 cups peeled, seeded, chopped cucumbers (about $1^1/_2$ pounds)
1 cup coarsely chopped sorrel, *or* spinach
2 cups fat-free milk
2 cups reduced-sodium fat-free chicken broth
1 tablespoon cornstarch
2 tablespoons water
Salt and white pepper, to taste
$1^1/_2$ cups herb croutons (purchased)

Per Serving
Calories: 77
% Calories from fat: 8
Fat (gm): 0.6
Sat. fat (gm): 0.2
Cholesterol (mg): 1.5
Sodium (mg): 247
Protein (gm): 6.2
Carbohydrate (gm): 11.5

Exchanges
Milk: 0.0
Vegetable: 3.0
Fruit: 0.0
Bread: 0.0
Meat: 0.0
Fat: 0.0

1. Spray large saucepan with cooking spray, heat over medium heat until hot. Saute $^1/_4$ cup green onions and garlic until tender, 3 to 4 minutes. Add cucumbers and sorrel and cook over medium heat 5 minutes.

2. Add milk and broth to saucepan; heat to boiling. Reduce heat and simmer, covered, until cucumbers are tender, 5 to 10 minutes. Process soup in food processor or blender until smooth; return to saucepan.

3. Heat soup to boiling. Mix cornstarch and water; whisk into boiling soup. Boil, whisking constantly, until thickened, about 1 minute. Season to taste with salt and white pepper. Cool; refrigerate until chilled, 3 to 4 hours.

4. Pour soup into bowls; top with herb croutons and remaining 2 tablespoons green onions.

CUCUMBER-YOGURT SOUP

4 servings

3 cups low-fat plain yogurt
1 1/2 cups grated, peeled, seeded cucumber
3/4 cup cold water
3 tablespoons minced chives
1 tablespoon minced dill weed
1 tablespoon minced garlic
1 teaspoon white pepper
4 thin slices cucumber

Per Serving
Calories: 119
% Calories from fat: 20
Fat (gm): 2.7
Sat. fat (gm): 0
Cholesterol (mg): 1.7
Sodium (mg): 121
Protein (gm): 9.5
Carbohydrate (gm): 14.4
Exchanges
Milk: 1.0
Vegetable: 1.0
Fruit: 0.0
Bread: 0.0
Meat: 0.0
Fat: 0.5

1. Combine all ingredients, except cucumber slices, in mixing bowl; chill. Top each serving with cucumber slice.

PEASANT GARLIC SOUP

6 servings

1 1/2 cups peeled, cubed potatoes
1 cup sliced carrots
1 cup sliced celery
1/2 cup chopped onion
2 heads garlic, peeled
3 cups Chicken Stock (see p. 47), *or* reduced-sodium, fat-free chicken broth
1 teaspoon dried thyme leaves
1 slice French, *or* Italian, bread, cubed
Salt and pepper, to taste
Chopped parsley, *or* chives, as garnish

Per Serving
Calories: 105
% Calories from fat: 6
Fat (gm): 0.7
Sat. fat (gm): 0.1
Cholesterol (mg): 1.7
Sodium (mg): 58
Protein (gm): 3.4
Carbohydrate (gm): 22.3
Exchanges
Milk: 0.0
Vegetable: 1.0
Fruit: 0.0
Bread: 1.0
Meat: 0.0
Fat: 0.0

1. Combine potatoes, carrots, celery, onion, garlic, Chicken Stock, and thyme in large saucepan. Heat to boiling; reduce heat and simmer, covered, until vegetables are very tender, about 2 minutes.

2. Process soup with bread cubes in food processor or blender until smooth. Return to saucepan; heat until hot. Season to taste with salt and pepper. Garnish with parsley.

GARDEN GREEN SOUP

4 servings

4 shallots, sliced
3 cloves garlic, minced
1 teaspoon canola oil
4 cups mixed greens, rinsed, shredded (romaine, red leaf, *or* Boston lettuce; spinach, escarole, *or* sorrel)
2 cups fat-free milk
1 cup reduced-sodium fat-free chicken broth
1 tablespoon oat bran
1/4 cup chopped fresh, *or* 1 tablespoon dried, basil leaves
Grated rind of 1 lemon
Salt and pepper, to taste

Per Serving
Calories: 81
% Calories from fat: 17
Fat (gm): 1.7
Sat. fat (gm): 0.3
Cholesterol (mg): 2.2
Sodium (mg): 123
Protein (gm): 7.3
Carbohydrate (gm): 10.4
Exchanges
Milk: 0.5
Vegetable: 1.0
Fruit: 0.0
Bread: 0.0
Meat: 0.0
Fat: 0.5

1. Saute shallots and garlic in oil in large saucepan until tender, about 3 minutes. Add greens and stir until wilted. Add remaining ingredients, except lemon rind, salt, and pepper, and heat to boiling; reduce heat and simmer 5 minutes. Process in blender or food processor until smooth. Stir in lemon rind; season to taste with salt and pepper.

LEEK AND CARROT YOGURT SOUP

8 servings

1 tablespoon canola oil
Canola oil, *or* vegetable cooking spray
2 large leeks, washed and thinly sliced
2 cups carrots, sliced, cooked, and drained
1/2 teaspoon ground cinnamon
1/2 teaspoon freshly ground nutmeg
1/2 teaspoon salt
1/4 teaspoon white pepper

Per Serving
Calories: 85
% Calories from fat: 25
Fat (gm): 2.5
Sat. fat (gm): 0.2
Cholesterol (mg): 0.8
Sodium (mg): 222
Protein (gm): 4.6
Carbohydrate (gm): 11.7
Exchanges
Milk: 0.0
Vegetable: 2.5
Fruit: 0.0
Bread: 0.0
Meat: 0.0
Fat: 0.5

1¹/4 quarts reduced-sodium fat-free chicken broth
1¹/2 cups plain nonfat yogurt

1. Heat oil in heavy pot coated with canola oil or cooking spray. Add leeks and saute until soft, stirring occasionally. Mix in carrots. Add remaining ingredients, except yogurt. Simmer, covered, until carrots are tender.
2. Remove carrots and leeks and puree in blender or food processor fitted with steel blade. Return vegetables to soup in pot. Slowly add yogurt, stirring constantly. Heat through but do not boil.

LEEK AND PUMPKIN SOUP

8 servings

Butter-flavored vegetable cooking spray
1 tablespoon canola oil
3 leeks, washed and sliced thin
1 large potato, peeled and cubed
1 can (16 ounces) pumpkin
3 cups reduced-sodium fat-free chicken broth
¹/2 teaspoon ground cinnamon
¹/4 teaspoon ground allspice
¹/4 teaspoon ground nutmeg
1 can (12 ounces) evaporated fat-free milk

Per Serving
Calories: 120
% Calories from fat: 17
Fat (gm): 2.4
Sat. fat (gm): 0.3
Cholesterol (mg): 1.3
Sodium (mg): 87
Protein (gm): 5.7
Carbohydrate (gm): 20.1
Exchanges
Milk: 0.5
Vegetable: 1.0
Fruit: 0.0
Bread: 0.5
Meat: 0.0
Fat: 0.5

1. Coat nonstick saucepan with cooking spray. Heat oil and saute leeks and potatoes until soft, stirring constantly, about 5 minutes. Mix in pumpkin and chicken broth. Simmer 15 minutes, covered, stirring occasionally. Blend in cinnamon, allspice, nutmeg, and milk. Simmer until soup is warm and vegetables are tender. Serve hot.

SUMMER MINESTRONE

6 main-dish servings (about 1 1/3 cups each)

Vegetable cooking spray
2 medium potatoes, cubed
2 medium carrots, thinly sliced
1 small zucchini, cubed
1 cup halved green beans
1 cup thinly sliced, *or* shredded, cabbage
1/2 cup thinly sliced celery
1 medium onion, coarsely chopped
3-4 cloves garlic, minced
2 teaspoons Italian seasoning
1-2 teaspoons dried oregano leaves
1 quart reduced-sodium, fat-free chicken broth
1 can (15 ounces) no-salt-added stewed tomatoes
1 can (15 ounces) kidney beans, rinsed, drained
2 cups water
1 1/2 cups (4 ounces) mostaccioli (penne), uncooked
1/2 teaspoon pepper
2 tablespoons grated Parmesan, *or* Romano, cheese

Per Serving
Calories: 264
% Calories from fat: 9
Fat (gm): 2.7
Sat. fat (gm): 0.6
Cholesterol (mg): 1.6
Sodium (mg): 216
Protein (gm): 12.3
Carbohydrate (gm): 50.5
Exchanges
Milk: 0.0
Vegetable: 3.0
Fruit: 0.0
Bread: 2.0
Meat: 1.0
Fat: 0.0

1. Spray bottom of large saucepan with cooking spray; heat over medium heat until hot. Saute fresh vegetables (next 8 ingredients) until crisp-tender, 10 to 12 minutes. Stir in Italian seasoning and oregano; cook 1 to 2 minutes more.

2. Add broth, tomatoes, beans, and water; heat to boiling. Reduce heat and simmer, covered, 10 minutes.

3. Heat soup to boiling; add pasta to saucepan. Reduce heat and simmer, uncovered, until pasta is al dente, 10 to 12 minutes. Stir in pepper and Parmesan.

ITALIAN MUSHROOM SOUP

4 servings

Vegetable cooking spray
2 medium onions, chopped
1 pound mushrooms (white, cremini, *or* chanterelles), thinly sliced
1 quart Chicken Stock (see p. 47), *or* fat-free chicken broth
6 tablespoons tomato puree
6 tablespoons sweet vermouth
1 tablespoon minced fresh, *or* 1 teaspoon dried, basil leaves
1/4 cup minced chives
Parmesan cheese, grated, as garnish

Per Serving
Calories: 139
% Calories from fat: 19
Fat (gm): 3
Sat. fat (gm): 0.5
Cholesterol (mg): 1
Sodium (mg): 138
Protein (gm): 9.8
Carbohydrate (gm): 13.3
Exchanges
Milk: 0.0
Vegetable: 3.0
Fruit: 0.0
Bread: 0.0
Meat: 0.0
Fat: 1.0

1. Spray large saucepan with cooking spray; heat over medium heat until hot. Saute onions and mushrooms until tender, about 10 minutes. Add Chicken Stock, tomato puree, and vermouth; heat to boiling. Reduce heat and simmer, covered, 5 minutes. Stir in basil and chives; sprinkle with Parmesan.

MUSHROOM BARLEY SOUP WITH HERBS

8 servings (about 1 1/2 cups each)

2 cups finely chopped onions
1 cup diced carrots
1/2 cup finely chopped celery
1 tablespoon vegetable oil
16 ounces mushrooms, sliced
1 teaspoon minced garlic
1 teaspoon dried thyme leaves
1 teaspoon dried basil leaves
1 teaspoon dried tarragon leaves
1/2 teaspoon celery seeds
2 cups Beef Stock (see p. 46)
2 cups Chicken Stock (see p. 47)

Per Serving
Calories: 105
% Calories from fat: 20
Fat (gm): 2.5
Sat. fat (gm): 0.3
Cholesterol (mg): 0.9
Sodium (mg): 20
Protein (gm): 3.7
Carbohydrate (gm): 18.7
Exchanges
Milk: 0.0
Vegetable: 2.0
Fruit: 0.0
Bread: 0.5
Meat: 0.0
Fat: 0.5

2 cups water
1/2 cup pearl barley
Salt and pepper, to taste
3 tablespoons chopped parsley

1. Saute onions, carrots, and celery in oil in large saucepan until lightly browned, about 8 minutes. Stir in mushrooms, garlic, and herbs; saute 3 minutes. Stir in Beef Stock, Chicken Stock, water, and barley. Heat to boiling; reduce heat and simmer, covered, until barley is tender, 45 to 60 minutes. Season to taste with salt and pepper; stir in parsley.

JELLIED MUSHROOM SOUP

8 servings

Per Serving
Calories: 41
% Calories from fat: 6
Fat (gm): 0.2
Sat. fat (gm): 0
Cholesterol (mg): 0
Sodium (mg): 605
Protein (gm): 3.4
Carbohydrate (gm): 4
Exchanges
Milk: 0.0
Vegetable: 1.5
Fruit: 0.0
Bread: 0.0
Meat: 0.0
Fat: 0.0

Butter-flavored cooking spray
1 pound mushrooms, trimmed and minced
1 quart chicken consomme
2 envelopes unflavored gelatin
1/2 cup water
1/2 teaspoon salt
1/4 teaspoon pepper
1 teaspoon fresh crushed tarragon, *or* 1/2 teaspoon dried tarragon
1/4 cup sherry
Watercress leaves

1. Heat pot coated with cooking spray. Saute mushrooms until tender, stirring often. Cover if necessary to cook mushrooms. Add consomme and simmer 5 minutes. Place gelatin in 1/2 cup water and allow to stand 5 minutes to dissolve; stir it into hot soup. Stir in salt, pepper, tarragon, and sherry. Pour soup into individual small bowls and refrigerate until set. Garnish with watercress leaves before serving.

JAPANESE MUSHROOM SOUP WITH NOODLES

6 servings

- 1 ounce dried mushrooms
- 1/2 small onion
- 1 clove garlic
- 1 1/2 pounds fresh mushrooms, minced, divided
- 2 tablespoons margarine
- 1/4 teaspoon thyme
- 1 quart reduced-sodium fat-free chicken broth
- 1 cup dry white wine
- 1/4 pound no-yolk noodles
- 1/2 pound snow peas
- 1/2 cup radishes, sliced
- 1 tablespoon red wine vinegar
- Pepper, freshly ground, to taste
- 2 teaspoons parsley, chopped

Per Serving
Calories: 214
% Calories from fat: 24
Fat (gm): 5.9
Sat. fat (gm): 1.2
Cholesterol (mg): 0.7
Sodium (mg): 575
Protein (gm): 10.3
Carbohydrate (gm): 24.9

Exchanges
Milk: 0.0
Vegetable: 3.0
Fruit: 0.0
Bread: 1.0
Meat: 0.0
Fat: 1.0

1. Pour 3 cups boiling water over dried mushrooms and let stand 30 minutes. Drain, reserving mushrooms and liquid. Process softened mushrooms, onion, garlic, and 1 pound fresh mushrooms in food processor until minced.

2. Saute minced mushroom mixture in margarine in large saucepan 2 minutes. Add thyme, chicken broth, wine, and mushroom liquid; heat to boiling. Reduce heat and simmer, covered, 30 minutes. Strain broth and discard vegetables.

3. Return broth to saucepan and heat to boiling; add noodles and cook until tender, about 10 minutes. Add remaining 1/2 pound mushrooms, snow peas, and radishes and simmer until snow peas are crisp-tender, 2 to 3 minutes. Stir in vinegar and parsley; season to state with pepper.

RED ONION AND APPLE SOUP WITH CURRY

5-6 servings (about 1¼ cups each)

1¼ pounds red onions (about 4 medium), thinly sliced
1 tablespoon margarine
1½ quarts Chicken Stock (see p. 47)
2 cups peeled, coarsely grated tart cooking apples, divided
½ cup shredded carrots
1 large bay leaf
1 teaspoon mild curry powder
¼ teaspoon chili powder
⅛ teaspoon dried thyme leaves
⅛ teaspoon ground allspice
Salt and pepper, to taste
Mango chutney, as garnish

Per Serving
Calories: 106
% Calories from fat: 18
Fat (gm): 2.3
Sat. fat (gm): 0.4
Cholesterol (mg): 0
Sodium (mg): 393
Protein (gm): 6.4
Carbohydrate (gm): 16.4
Exchanges
Milk: 0.0
Vegetable: 2.0
Fruit: 0.5
Bread: 0.0
Meat: 0.0
Fat: 0.5

1. Saute onions in margarine in large saucepan until tender and lightly browned, about 15 minutes. Stir in Chicken Stock, 1 cup apples, carrots, and herbs; heat to boiling. Reduce heat and simmer, covered, until vegetables are tender, about 20 minutes.

2. Stir in remaining 1 cup apples and simmer 5 minutes. Discard bay leaf. Season to taste with salt and pepper. Serve with chutney.

FRENCH ONION SOUP

8 servings (about 1¼ cups each)

Vegetable cooking spray
6 cups thinly sliced Spanish onions (1½ pounds)
2 cloves garlic, minced
1 teaspoon sugar
6 cups reduced-sodium fat-free beef broth
2 bay leaves
Salt and white pepper, to taste

Per Serving
Calories: 144
% Calories from fat: 6
Fat (gm): 1
Sat. fat (gm): 0.2
Cholesterol (mg): 0
Sodium (mg): 390
Protein (gm): 9
Carbohydrate (gm): 24.3
Exchanges
Milk: 0.0
Vegetable: 3.0
Fruit: 0.0
Bread: 1.0
Meat: 0.0
Fat: 0.0

8 slices, French bread, toasted
8 tablespoons (2 ounces) shredded fat-free Swiss, or mozzarella, cheese

1. Spray Dutch oven with cooking spray; heat over medium heat until hot. Add onions and garlic and cook covered, over medium-low heat until wilted, 8 to 10 minutes. Stir in sugar and cook, uncovered, over medium-low to low heat until onions are lightly browned, about 15 minutes.

2. Stir in broth and bay leaves; heat to boiling. Reduce heat and simmer, covered, 30 minutes. Discard bay leaves; season to taste with salt and white pepper.

3. Top each toast slice with 1 tablespoon cheese; broil 6 inches from heat source until melted. Pour soup into bowls; top each with a toast slice.

PARSLEY SOUP

4 servings

2 Idaho potatoes, peeled, diced
2 medium onions, chopped
1 tablespoon margarine
3/4 cup water
1 can (10 3/4 ounces) reduced-sodium fat-free chicken broth
1 cup packed parsley sprigs
Dash Worcestershire sauce
2 cans (12 ounces each) evaporated fat-free milk
Salt and white pepper, to taste

Per Serving
Calories: 271
% Calories from fat: 11
Fat (gm): 3.5
Sat. fat (gm): 0.8
Cholesterol (mg): 6.9
Sodium (mg): 321
Protein (gm): 18.7
Carbohydrate (gm): 41.4

Exchanges
Milk: 1.0
Vegetable: 0.0
Fruit: 0.0
Bread: 2.0
Meat: 0.0
Fat: 1.0

1. Combine potatoes, onions, margarine, and 3/4 cup water in large saucepan and heat to boiling; reduce heat and simmer, covered, until potatoes are tender, about 15 minutes. Add chicken broth, parsley, and Worcestershire sauce and heat to boiling; reduce heat and simmer, uncovered, until parsley is wilted, 2 to 3 minutes.

2. Process soup in blender or food processor until smooth. Return to saucepan, add milk, and cook over medium heat until hot, about 5 minutes. Season to taste with salt and white pepper.

SOUTHWEST-STYLE POTATO CORN CHOWDER

5-6 servings

Per Serving
Calories: 324
% Calories from fat: 18
Fat (gm): 6.8
Sat. fat (gm): 3
Cholesterol (mg): 18.1
Sodium (mg): 648
Protein (gm): 12.8
Carbohydrate (gm): 55.3

Exchanges
Milk: 0.5
Vegetable: 0.0
Fruit: 0.0
Bread: 3.0
Meat: 0.0
Fat: 1.0

- 1 large onion, chopped
- 1 garlic clove, minced
- 2 teaspoons olive oil
- 3 1/2 cups fat-free chicken broth, divided
- 3 1/2 cups cubed, peeled red potatoes (1/2-inch)
- 1 large bay leaf
- 3/4 teaspoon dried thyme leaves
- 1/4 teaspoon dry mustard
- 2 1/2 cups 1% low-fat milk
- 2 1/2 cups frozen whole-kernel corn
- 6 ounces Canadian bacon, julienned
- Salt and white pepper, to taste

1. Saute onion and garlic in oil in large saucepan until tender, about 5 minutes. Add broth, potatoes, bay leaf, thyme, and mustard; heat to boiling. Reduce heat and simmer, covered, until potatoes are tender, about 10 minutes.

2. Add milk and corn; heat to boiling. Reduce heat and simmer, covered, 5 minutes or until corn is cooked. Discard bay leaf.

3. Process half the vegetables and liquid in food processor or blender until smooth; return to saucepan. Stir in Canadian bacon and simmer, covered, 5 minutes. Season to taste with salt and white pepper.

Variation: **Colcannon Chowder**—Make recipe as above, sauteing 2 cups thinly sliced cabbage with the onion and garlic, reducing milk to 2 cups, and omitting corn. Do not puree the mixture. Combine ½ cup reduced-fat sour cream and 1 tablespoon flour; stir into the chowder with the Canadian bacon.

POTATO BARLEY SOUP

8 servings

Olive oil, *or* vegetable cooking spray
1 cup chopped onions
3 cloves garlic, minced
3 cups Idaho potatoes, peeled, diced
2 large carrots, sliced
3 ribs celery, sliced
1 parsnip, sliced
2 bay leaves
1 cup tomato juice
3/4 cup barley
4 cups Vegetable Stock (see p. 48)
1/2 teaspoon each ingredient: salt, pepper, thyme, marjoram

Per Serving
Calories: 169
% Calories from fat: 3
Fat (gm): 0.6
Sat. fat (gm): 0.1
Cholesterol (mg): 0
Sodium (mg): 271
Protein (gm): 4.6
Carbohydrate (gm): 37.8
Exchanges
Milk: 0.0
Vegetable: 2.0
Fruit: 0.0
Bread: 2.0
Meat: 0.0
Fat: 0.0

1. Coat Dutch oven lightly with olive oil; heat over medium heat until hot. Saute onions, garlic, and potatoes 5 minutes, over medium heat. Add remaining ingredients. Simmer, partially covered, 25 minutes or until vegetables and barley are tender, stirring occasionally. Discard bay leaves. For smoother taste, puree soup, reheat, and serve.

POTATO PISTOU

6 servings

2 quarts water
2 cups chopped onions
4 Idaho potatoes, peeled, diced
5 tomatoes, peeled, seeded, chopped
3/4 cup green beans, trimmed, cut into 1 1/2-inch pieces
2 medium zucchini, sliced
1/4 teaspoon pepper
1/4 teaspoon marjoram

Per Serving
Calories: 159
% Calories from fat: 11
Fat (gm): 2
Sat. fat (gm): 0.9
Cholesterol (mg): 3.3
Sodium (mg): 97
Protein (gm): 6.1
Carbohydrate (gm): 32.1
Exchanges
Milk: 0.0
Vegetable: 3.0
Fruit: 0.0
Bread: 1.0
Meat: 0.0
Fat: 0.5

- 1 1/2 cups firmly packed fresh basil leaves
- 6 cloves garlic
- 1/4 cup (1 ounce) freshly grated Parmesan cheese
- Salt and pepper, to taste

1. Heat water to boiling in large stock pot; add onions and potatoes; reduce heat and simmer 15 minutes. Add remaining vegetables, pepper, and marjoram; simmer 20 minutes longer.

2. Process soup in food processor or blender until smooth; return to stock pot. Simmer over medium heat until hot.

3. Process basil, garlic, and cheese in food processor until smooth. Stir mixture into soup; season to taste with salt and pepper, and serve.

VICHYSSOISE

8 servings (about 1 1/2 cups each)

- Vegetable cooking spray
- 1 quart sliced leeks, white parts only
- 1 cup sliced onion
- 4 large boiling potatoes, peeled, sliced thin
- 1 1/4 quarts Chicken Stock (see p. 47)
- 1 can (13 ounces) fat-free evaporated milk
- 1/2 teaspoon white pepper
- 1/4 teaspoon salt
- 1/2 cup non-fat plain yogurt
- 2 tablespoons fresh mint, chopped

Per Serving
Calories: 160
% Calories from fat: 3
Fat (gm): 0.5
Sat. fat (gm): 0.2
Cholesterol (mg): 4.3
Sodium (mg): 161
Protein (gm): 7.9
Carbohydrate (gm): 31.8
Exchanges
Milk: 0.0
Vegetable: 0.0
Fruit: 0.0
Bread: 2.0
Meat: 0.0
Fat: 0.0

1. Spray large saucepan with cooking spray; heat over medium heat until hot. Saute leeks, onion, and potatoes 10 minutes. Stir in Chicken Stock; heat to boiling. Reduce heat and simmer, covered, 15 minutes. Stir in milk; simmer 10 minutes, stirring occasionally.

2. Process soup in food processor or blender until smooth. Return soup to pan and stir in pepper, salt, and yogurt. Heat until hot, 2 to 3 minutes; do not boil. Serve hot, or refrigerate and serve chilled. Serve in bowls; sprinkle with mint.

Variation: **Celery Vichyssoise**—Make soup as above, adding 3 large ribs sliced celery to the vegetables. Omit mint; garnish each bowl with a dollop of dill sour cream and celery leaves.

SPINACH SOUP

10 servings (about 1 cup each)

1 large leek white part only, thinly sliced
1 carrot, sliced
1 rib celery, sliced
1 tablespoon olive oil
2 quarts Chicken Stock (see p. 47)
2 pounds fresh spinach
Salt and pepper, to taste
1/2 cup grated Parmesan cheese
Plain flavor croutons, as garnish

Per Serving
Calories: 113
% Calories from fat: 31
Fat (gm): 3.8
Sat. fat (gm): 1.2
Cholesterol (mg): 4
Sodium (mg): 229
Protein (gm): 9.1
Carbohydrate (gm): 9.9
Exchanges
Milk: 0.0
Vegetable: 2.0
Fruit: 0.0
Bread: 0.0
Meat: 0.5
Fat: 0.5

1. Saute leek, carrot, and celery in oil in large saucepan until tender. Add Chicken Stock and heat to boiling. Add spinach and cook uncovered, for 2 minutes, until spinach wilts.

2. Process in food processor or blender until smooth. Return soup to saucepan and heat until hot; season to taste with salt and pepper. Ladle soup into bowls; sprinkle with cheese and croutons.

GAZPACHO

4-6 servings

2 cans (14 1/2 ounces) plum tomatoes, undrained
1 small garlic clove, minced
1-2 tablespoons chopped scallions, *or* chives
1 medium cucumber, peeled, seeded, diced
1 rib celery, diced
1/2 large green bell pepper, diced
2-3 drops red pepper sauce

Per Serving
Calories: 38
% Calories from fat: 9
Fat (gm): 0.4
Sat. fat (gm): 0.1
Cholesterol (mg): 0
Sodium (mg): 230
Protein (gm): 1.8
Carbohydrate (gm): 8.2
Exchanges
Milk: 0.0
Vegetable: 2.0
Fruit: 0.0
Bread: 0.0
Meat: 0.0
Fat: 0.0

- $1/4$ teaspoon black pepper salt, to taste
- 4-6 sprigs parsley, as garnish

1. Process tomatoes and liquid with garlic in blender or food processor until smooth. Transfer to mixing bowl and add remaining ingredients except salt and parsley. Chill, covered, several hours. Season to taste with salt; garnish with fresh parsley sprigs.

ANDALUSIAN GAZPACHO

6 servings (about $1\frac{1}{2}$ cups each)

- 5 large tomatoes, seeded, chopped, divided
- 2 cups reduced-sodium tomato juice
- 2 cloves garlic
- 2 tablespoons lime juice
- 1 teaspoon dried oregano leaves
- 1 small seedless cucumber, coarsely chopped
- 1 cup chopped yellow bell pepper
- 1 cup chopped celery
- 6 green onions and tops, thinly sliced, divided
- 2 tablespoons finely chopped cilantro
- Salt and pepper, to taste
- Avocado Sour Cream (recipe follows)
- Red pepper sauce, optional

Per Serving
Calories: 76
% Calories from fat: 17
Fat (gm): 1.6
Sat. fat (gm): 0.3
Cholesterol (mg): 0.1
Sodium (mg): 46
Protein (gm): 17
Carbohydrate (gm): 3.3

Exchanges
Milk: 0.0
Vegetable: 2.0
Fruit: 0.0
Bread: 0.0
Meat: 0.0
Fat: 0.5

1. Reserve 1 cup tomatoes; process remaining tomatoes, tomato juice, garlic, lime juice, and oregano in food processor or blender until smooth.

2. Mix tomato mixture, reserved 1 cup tomatoes, cucumber, bell pepper, celery, 5 green onions, and cilantro in large bowl; season to taste with salt and pepper. Refrigerate until chilled, 3 to 4 hours.

3. Serve soup in chilled bowls; top each with a dollop of Avocado Sour Cream and sprinkle with remaining green onion. Serve with red pepper sauce.

Avocado Sour Cream

makes about 2/3 cup

- 1/2 medium avocado, peeled, chopped
- 1/4 cup fat-free sour cream
- 2 tablespoons fat-free milk
- Salt and white pepper, to taste

1. Process avocado, sour cream, and milk in food processor until smooth; season to taste with salt and white pepper.

TOMATO-VEGETABLE SOUP

5-6 servings

- 1 medium onion, coarsely chopped
- 1 large rib celery, coarsely chopped
- 1 medium carrot, coarsely chopped
- 3/4 cup chopped red bell pepper
- 1 1/2 teaspoons olive oil
- 1 cup Beef Stock (see p. 46)
- 1 can (32 ounces) imported Italian (plum) tomatoes, undrained
- 1/4 cup dry white wine, *or* Beef Stock
- 1 teaspoon lemon juice
- 3/4 teaspoon celery salt
- Pinch crushed red pepper
- Salt and pepper, to taste
- Finely chopped chives, as garnish

Per Serving
Calories: 123
% Calories from fat: 13
Fat (gm): 1.8
Sat. fat (gm): 0.6
Cholesterol (mg): 4.1
Sodium (mg): 500
Protein (gm): 6.5
Carbohydrate (gm): 20.1

Exchanges
Milk: 0.0
Vegetable: 0.0
Fruit: 0.5
Bread: 1.5
Meat: 0.0
Fat: 0.5

1. Saute onion, celery, carrot, and bell pepper in oil in large saucepan until vegetables are tender, about 10 minutes. Stir in remaining ingredients, except salt, pepper, and chives, and heat to boiling. Reduce heat and simmer, covered, 10 minutes.

2. Process soup in blender or food processor until smooth. Transfer to serving bowl; season to taste with salt and pepper. Refrigerate until chilled. Garnish with chopped chives.

TOMATO-ORANGE SOUP

6 servings

Per Serving
Calories: 78
% Calories from fat: 3
Fat (gm): 0.3
Sat. fat (gm): 0
Cholesterol (mg): 0
Sodium (mg): 157
Protein (gm): 3.2
Carbohydrate (gm): 13.7
Exchanges
Milk: 0.0
Vegetable: 3.0
Fruit: 0.0
Bread: 0.0
Meat: 0.0
Fat: 0.0

- 2 small oranges
- 3 medium tomatoes, peeled, seeded, cubed
- 3/4 cup chopped onion
- 1 can (14 1/2 ounces) reduced-sodium fat-free chicken broth
- 1 cup reduced-sodium tomato juice
- 1/2 cup dry white wine
- 1 tablespoon red wine vinegar
- 1 tablespoon sugar
- 1/4 teaspoon salt
- 3/4 teaspoon pepper

1. Remove the zest of 1 orange, cut into julienne strips, and set aside. Remove and discard peel from both oranges. Coarsely chop oranges and place in bowl; stir in tomatoes and remaining ingredients. Cover and chill for at least 1 hour to allow flavors to develop.

2. Serve soup in bowls; garnish with orange zest.

FRESH TOMATO SOUP

6 servings (about 1 1/4 cups each)

Per Serving
Calories: 87
% Calories from fat: 17
Fat (gm): 1.8
Sat. fat (gm): 0.3
Cholesterol (mg): 0.4
Sodium (mg): 36
Protein (gm): 4
Carbohydrate (gm): 11.6
Exchanges
Milk: 0.0
Vegetable: 2.0
Fruit: 0.0
Bread: 0.0
Meat: 0.0
Fat: 0.5

- 4 green onions and tops, sliced
- 4 cloves garlic, minced
- 1 teaspoon vegetable oil
- 2 1/2 pounds tomatoes, peeled, seeded, chopped, divided
- 2 1/2 cups Chicken Stock (see p. 47)
- 1/4 cup chopped fresh, *or* 1 1/2 teaspoons dried, basil leaves
- 1 bay leaf
- 2 teaspoons sugar
- 1/2 cup dry white wine
- 1/4 cup chopped parsley
- Salt and pepper, to taste

1. Saute green onions and garlic in oil in large saucepan until transparent, about 2 minutes. Reserve 2 cups chopped tomatoes. Process remaining tomatoes in food processor or blender until smooth; stir into saucepan and cook 5 minutes. Stir in Chicken Stock, basil, bay leaf, and sugar. Heat to boiling; reduce heat and simmer, uncovered, 30 minutes.

2. Stir in wine and reserved 2 cups tomatoes; heat to boiling. Reduce heat and simmer, uncovered, 15 minutes. Stir in parsley; discard bay leaf and season to taste with salt and pepper.

CRUNCHY VEGETABLE SOUP

4 servings

- 1½ cups cut asparagus (1-inch pieces)
- 1 medium carrot, finely chopped
- 1 rib celery; finely chopped
- 2 tablespoons chopped onion
- 2 medium mushrooms, sliced
- 1 cup reduced-sodium fat-free chicken broth
- 1 cup fat-free plain yogurt
- Pinch dried tarragon leaves
- Dash cayenne pepper
- Black pepper, to taste
- Diced pimientos, as garnish

Per Serving
Calories: 63
% Calories from fat: 4
Fat (gm): 0.3
Sat. fat (gm): 0.1
Cholesterol (mg): 1
Sodium (mg): 102
Protein (gm): 6.3
Carbohydrate (gm): 9.3

Exchanges
Milk: 0.0
Vegetable: 2.0
Fruit: 0.0
Bread: 0.0
Meat: 0.0
Fat: 0.0

1. Process vegetables and chicken broth in blender or food processor until finely chopped. Pour into medium saucepan. Heat to boiling; reduce heat and simmer 6 to 8 minutes or until vegetables are crisp-tender. Stir in yogurt, tarragon, cayenne pepper, and black pepper; garnish each serving with pimientos.

TANGY ZUCCHINI SOUP

4-5 servings

1 medium onion, finely chopped
1 small garlic clove, minced
2 cups diced zucchini
1/2 cup peeled, diced potato
3 cups Chicken Stock (see p. 47), *or* reduced-fat chicken broth
2 tablespoons chopped parsley
1/4 teaspoon dry mustard
Dash cayenne pepper
1/2 cup buttermilk
1/2 cup whole milk
Salt and white pepper, to taste
Thinly sliced zucchini, as garnish

Per Serving
Calories: 77
% Calories from fat: 14
Fat (gm): 1.2
Sat. fat (gm): 0.7
Cholesterol (mg): 4.2
Sodium (mg): 243
Protein (gm): 5.8
Carbohydrate (gm): 11.6
Exchanges
Milk: 0.0
Vegetable: 2.0
Fruit: 0.0
Bread: 0.0
Meat: 0.0
Fat: 0.5

1. Combine onion, garlic, diced zucchini, potato, Chicken Stock, parsley, mustard, and cayenne pepper in large saucepan; heat to boiling. Reduce heat and simmer, covered, until potato is very tender, about 15 minutes.

2. Process in blender or food processor until smooth; transfer to serving bowl. Stir in buttermilk and milk; season to taste with salt and white pepper. Refrigerate until chilled. Garnish with sliced zucchini.

EASY SPINACH-PASTA SOUP WITH BASIL

4-5 servings

1 small onion, finely chopped
1 small garlic clove, minced
2 teaspoons olive oil
1 1/2 quarts Chicken Stock (see p. 47), *or* fat-free chicken broth
1 cup water
3/4 cup uncooked broken vermicelli (2-inch pieces)

Per Serving
Calories: 193
% Calories from fat: 18
Fat (gm): 3.9
Sat. fat (gm): 0.9
Cholesterol (mg): 2
Sodium (mg): 563
Protein (gm): 13.3
Carbohydrate (gm): 27.6
Exchanges
Milk: 0.0
Vegetable: 0.0
Fruit: 0.0
Bread: 2.0
Meat: 1.0
Fat: 0.0

- 1 package (10 ounces) frozen chopped spinach, thawed
- 1/4 cup chopped fresh, *or* 1 1/2 tablespoons dried, basil leaves
- 1/4 teaspoon pepper
- 1 cup chopped plum tomatoes
- 1 cup cooked, *or* canned, drained and rinsed, garbanzo beans
- Salt, to taste
- 2 tablespoons grated Parmesan cheese, as garnish

1. Saute onion and garlic in oil in large saucepan until tender, about 5 minutes. Add Chicken Stock and water; heat to boiling. Add vermicelli; reduce heat, and simmer, uncovered, until tender, 7 to 10 minutes.

2. Add remaining ingredients, except salt and Parmesan cheese; simmer 5 minutes. Season to taste with salt. Sprinkle each serving with Parmesan cheese.

SEAFOOD PASTA SOUP

6 servings

- 1/2 cup chopped onion
- 1/2 cup diced green bell pepper
- 1/2 cup diced red, *or* yellow, bell pepper
- 1/2 teaspoon minced garlic
- 8 ounces mushrooms, sliced
- 2 tablespoons olive oil
- 1 can (14 ounces) Italian plum tomatoes, undrained, chopped
- 2 cups reduced-sodium fat-free chicken broth
- 1/2 cup dry white wine, *or* fat-free chicken broth
- 1 pound sea scallops, halved
- 1/4 cup finely chopped parsley
- 1/2 pound uncooked small pasta, cooked

Per Serving
Calories: 323
% Calories from fat: 20
Fat (gm): 7.4
Sat. fat (gm): 1.3
Cholesterol (mg): 34.8
Sodium (mg): 382
Protein (gm): 24.1
Carbohydrate (gm): 37.4

Exchanges
Milk: 0.0
Vegetable: 1.0
Fruit: 0.0
Bread: 2.0
Meat: 2.5
Fat: 0.0

$^1/_4$-$^1/_2$ cup (1-2 ounces) grated Parmesan cheese
Salt and pepper, to taste

1. Saute onion, bell peppers, garlic, and mushrooms in oil in large saucepan until mushrooms are tender, about 10 minutes. Add remaining ingredients, except Parmesan cheese, salt, and pepper; heat to boiling. Remove from heat and let stand, covered, 5 minutes. Stir in Parmesan cheese; season to taste with salt and pepper.

PASTA E FAGIOLI

12 servings

1 cup chopped onion
$^1/_2$ cup diced celery
$^1/_2$ cup diced carrot
$1^1/_2$ tablespoons minced garlic
2 tablespoons olive oil
2 cups dried Great Northern, *or* cannellini, beans, soaked overnight, drained
$2^1/_4$ quarts water
$4^1/_2$ cups peeled, seeded, diced tomatoes
5 ounces elbow macaroni, *or* other pasta, cooked
Pepper, to taste
Grated Parmesan cheese, as garnish

Per Serving
Calories: 124
% Calories from fat: 21
Fat (gm): 3.1
Sat. fat (gm): 1.1
Cholesterol (mg): 10.2
Sodium (mg): 18
Protein (gm): 5
Carbohydrate (gm): 20.4

Exchanges
Milk: 0.0
Vegetable: 1.0
Fruit: 0.0
Bread: 1.0
Meat: 0.0
Fat: 0.5

1. Saute onion, celery, carrot, and garlic in oil in Dutch oven until soft, about 5 minutes. Add beans and water; heat to boiling. Reduce heat and simmer, covered, until beans are tender, 45 to 60 minutes.

2. Add tomatoes and simmer, covered, 10 minutes; add pasta and simmer, covered, 5 minutes. Season to taste with pepper. Sprinkle each serving with Parmesan cheese.

CALDO DE PESCADO

10 servings

- 2 cups chopped onions
- 3 cloves garlic, minced
- 1 large red bell pepper, chopped
- 1 tablespoon olive oil
- 2 cups peeled, sliced potatoes
- 3 cups Fish Stock (see p. 48)
- 1 can (28 ounce) crushed red tomatoes, undrained
- 2 large ears corn, husked, cut into 1-inch pieces
- 1/4 teaspoon grated orange rind
- 1/4 teaspoon cayenne pepper
- 1/4 teaspoon turmeric
- 16 ounces Pacific rockfish fillets, cut into 1-inch strips
- 12 ounces red snapper fillets, cut into 1-inch strips
- 12 ounces large shrimp, peeled, deveined, cut into 1-inch pieces
- Salt, to taste

Per Serving
Calories: 223
% Calories from fat: 13
Fat (gm): 3.1
Sat. fat (gm): 0.6
Cholesterol (mg): 82
Sodium (mg): 305
Protein (gm): 24.9
Carbohydrate (gm): 22.1
Exchanges
Milk: 0.0
Vegetable: 2.0
Fruit: 0.0
Bread: 1.0
Meat: 2.0
Fat: 0.0

1. Saute onions, garlic, and bell pepper in oil in large saucepan until onion is soft. Add remaining ingredients, except fish, shrimp, and salt, and heat to boiling. Reduce heat and simmer, covered, 15 to 20 minutes. Add fish and shrimp and cook until fish is tender and flakes with a fork, 5 to 10 minutes; season to taste with salt.

Note: To make clam chowder, substitute six, 10-ounce cans minced clams, *or* 4 pounds fresh clams, for the fish. Add clams just before serving.

CIOPPINO MEDITERRANEAN

6 servings

Per Serving
Calories: 224
% Calories from fat: 18
Fat (gm): 4.5
Sat. fat (gm): 0.8
Cholesterol (mg): 156.7
Sodium (mg): 312
Protein (gm): 29.4
Carbohydrate (gm): 14.4

Exchanges
Milk: 0.0
Vegetable: 2.0
Fruit: 0.0
Bread: 0.0
Meat: 3.0
Fat: 0.0

1/4 cup chopped green bell pepper
2 tablespoons finely chopped onion
1 clove garlic, minced
1 tablespoon olive oil
2 cans (16 ounces each) whole tomatoes, undrained, chopped
1 can (6 ounces) low-sodium tomato paste
1 cup water
1/2 cup dry red wine
3 tablespoons chopped parsley
1 teaspoon dried oregano leaves
1 teaspoon dried basil leaves
16 ounces fillet of sole, cut into bite-size pieces
16 ounces shrimp, peeled, deveined
1 can (7 1/2 ounce) minced clams, undrained
Salt and pepper, to taste

1. Saute bell pepper, onion, and garlic in oil in large saucepan until tender, about 5 minutes. Add remaining ingredients, except seafood, salt, and pepper, and heat to boiling. Reduce heat and simmer, covered, 20 minutes.

2. Add sole, shrimp, and clams and liquor; simmer until sole is tender and flakes with a fork, about 5 minutes. Season to taste with salt and pepper.

GUMBO

6 servings

Per Serving
Calories: 239
% Calories from fat: 8
Fat (gm): 2
Sat. fat (gm): 0.4
Cholesterol (mg): 111.8
Sodium (mg): 146
Protein (gm): 25.9
Carbohydrate (gm): 26

Exchanges
Milk: 0.0
Vegetable: 2.0
Fruit: 0.0
Bread: 1.0
Meat: 2.0
Fat: 0.0

Vegetable cooking spray
1 cup sliced onion
2 cups sliced okra
3 cups peeled, seeded, chopped tomatoes
1 quart Fish Stock, *or* Chicken Stock (see pp. 48, 47)
1 green bell pepper, sliced
1 bay leaf
1/4 teaspoon crushed red pepper
12 ounces red snapper fillets
12 ounces extra-large shrimp, peeled, deveined
1 teaspoon gumbo file powder
Salt and pepper, to taste
2 cups cooked rice, warm

1. Spray large saucepan with cooking spray; saute onions and okra until onions are tender, about 5 minutes. Add tomatoes and Fish Stock and heat to boiling; reduce heat and simmer, covered, 5 minutes.

2. Add remaining ingredients, except file powder, salt, pepper, and rice; simmer, uncovered, until fish is tender and flakes with a fork, about 10 minutes. Discard bay leaf; stir in gumbo file and season to taste with salt and pepper. Serve over rice.

KAKAVIA

12 servings

Per Serving
Calories: 241
% Calories from fat: 15
Fat (gm): 3.9
Sat. fat (gm): 0.9
Cholesterol (mg): 81.7
Sodium (mg): 249
Protein (gm): 34.2
Carbohydrate (gm): 13.4

Exchanges
Milk: 0.0
Vegetable: 2.0
Fruit: 0.0
Bread: 0.0
Meat: 4.0
Fat: 0.0

Vegetable cooking spray
4 cups chopped onions
2 ribs celery, chopped
1 tablespoon minced garlic
2 leeks, white parts only, sliced
3 large carrots, peeled, chopped
1 can (16 ounces) plum tomatoes, undrained, coarsely chopped
1 quart water
1 cup dry white wine
1 teaspoon pepper
3 tablespoons lemon juice
4-6 pounds fish fillets (striped bass, sea bass, *or* red snapper), cut into bite-size pieces
12 clams, scrubbed
12 shrimp, peeled, deveined
12 mussels, scrubbed
3 bay leaves
1/2 teaspoon dried thyme leaves
1/4 cup minced parsley
Salt, to taste

1. Spray large saucepan with cooking spray, heat over medium heat until hot. Saute onions, celery, garlic, leeks, and carrots until onions are tender, about 10 minutes.

2. Add tomatoes and liquid, water, wine, pepper, and lemon juice; heat to boiling. Add remaining ingredients, except parsley and salt; reduce heat and simmer, covered, until fish is tender and clams and mussels open, about 10 minutes. Discard any unopened clams and mussels; discard bay leaves. Stir in parsley; season to taste with salt.

FIFTEEN-MINUTE CLAM SOUP

6 servings

Vegetable cooking spray
1/2 medium onion, finely chopped
2 cloves garlic, chopped
4 thin slices day-old bread, cubed
2 medium tomatoes, peeled, seeded, finely chopped
3 cups clam juice, *or* Fish Stock (see p. 48)
3 cups water
1/2 cup dry sherry
1 teaspoon paprika
24 clams, *or* mussels, scrubbed
Salt and pepper, to taste
2 tablespoons chopped parsley, as garnish

Per Serving
Calories: 101
% Calories from fat: 8
Fat (gm): 0.9
Sat. fat (gm): 0.1
Cholesterol (mg): 12.1
Sodium (mg): 374
Protein (gm): 6.6
Carbohydrate (gm): 12.8
Exchanges
Milk: 0.0
Vegetable: 1.0
Fruit: 0.0
Bread: 0.5
Meat: 0.0
Fat: 0.5

1. Spray large saucepan with cooking spray, heat over medium heat until hot. Saute onion, garlic, and bread until onion is soft, about 5 minutes. Add remaining ingredients, except salt, pepper, and parsley; simmer, covered, until clams or mussels open, about 10 minutes. Discard shellfish that do not open. Season broth to taste with salt and pepper. Sprinkle servings with parsley.

WHITE CLAM CHOWDER WITH CORN

4-5 servings

1 medium onion, chopped
1 large rib celery, chopped
1 tablespoon margarine, *or* butter
1 tablespoon flour
1 cup clam juice, *or* fat-free chicken broth
1 can (10 1/2 ounces) minced clams, undrained
1 large bay leaf

Per Serving
Calories: 224
% Calories from fat: 15
Fat (gm): 4.1
Sat. fat (gm): 1.2
Cholesterol (mg): 40.7
Sodium (mg): 157
Protein (gm): 11.1
Carbohydrate (gm): 39.6
Exchanges
Milk: 0.0
Vegetable: 0.0
Fruit: 0.0
Bread: 2.5
Meat: 1.0
Fat: 0.0

- 1/2 teaspoon dried marjoram leaves
- 1/8 teaspoon black pepper
- 2 cups peeled, cubed red potatoes (1/4-inch)
- 2 cups whole-kernel corn
- 1 cup 2% reduced-fat milk
- Salt, to taste

1. Saute onion and celery in margarine in large saucepan until onion is tender, about 5 minutes. Stir in flour, cook 1 minute longer. Stir in clam juice; stir in liquor from minced clams. Reserve minced clams.

2. Stir in herbs, pepper, potatoes, and corn; heat to boiling. Reduce heat and simmer, covered, stirring occasionally, until potatoes are tender, 8 to 10 minutes. Discard bay leaf.

3. Process half the chowder in blender or food processor until smooth; return to saucepan. Stir in milk and minced clams; simmer 5 minutes. Season to taste with salt.

NEW YORK CITY CLAM CHOWDER

6 servings

Per Serving
Calories: 228
% Calories from fat: 5
Fat (gm): 1.3
Sat. fat (gm): 0.2
Cholesterol (mg): 38.2
Sodium (mg): 332
Protein (gm): 19
Carbohydrate (gm): 34.8

Exchanges
Milk: 0.0
Vegetable: 1.0
Fruit: 0.0
Bread: 2.0
Meat: 1.0
Fat: 0.0

- 36 littleneck clams, *or* other fresh small clams
- 3 cups water
- Olive oil cooking spray
- 4 potatoes, peeled, cubed
- 1 cup sliced onion
- 2 carrots, chopped
- 1 can (28 ounces) crushed tomatoes, undrained
- 1/2 cup clam juice
- 1/3 cup chopped parsley
- 1/2 teaspoon dried thyme leaves
- 1/4 teaspoon pepper
- 2 bay leaves
- 1/4 teaspoon red pepper sauce, optional
- Salt and pepper, to taste

1. Wash clams and discard any that are open. Place clams in large saucepan; add 3 cups water and heat to boiling. Reduce heat and simmer, covered, 5 to 8 minutes or until clams open. Discard any clams that do not open. Strain liquid through double layer of cheesecloth and reserve.

2. Spray Dutch oven with cooking spray; heat over medium heat until hot. Saute potatoes, onion, and carrots 5 minutes. Mix in reserved clam liquid and remaining ingredients, except salt and pepper.

3. Heat chowder to boiling; reduce heat and simmer, covered, 20 minutes or until vegetables are tender. Add clams in shells and cook 3 minutes longer. Discard bay leaves; season to taste with salt and pepper.

MAINE CLAM CHOWDER

6 servings

- 36 littleneck clams, *or* other fresh small clams
- 6 cups water
- Vegetable cooking spray
- 1 cup chopped onion
- 1/2 cup chopped celery
- 1 carrot, thinly sliced
- 4 red potatoes, peeled, cubed
- 2 cups fat-free milk, divided
- 1/2 cup clam juice
- 1/4 cup all-purpose flour
- 1/4 teaspoon white pepper
- Salt, to taste

Per Serving
Calories: 158
% Calories from fat: 4
Fat (gm): 0.8
Sat. fat (gm): 0.2
Cholesterol (mg): 19.6
Sodium (mg): 164
Protein (gm): 11.6
Carbohydrate (gm): 27.5

Exchanges
Milk: 0.0
Vegetable: 0.0
Fruit: 0.0
Bread: 1.5
Meat: 1.0
Fat: 0.0

1. Wash clams and discard any that are open. Place clams in saucepan with 6 cups water; heat to boiling. Reduce heat and simmer, covered, 5 to 8 minutes or until clams open. Discard any clams that do not open. Remove clams from shells, chop, and reserve. Strain liquid through double layer of cheesecloth and reserve.

2. Spray large saucepan with cooking spray; heat over medium heat until hot. Saute onion, celery, carrot, and potatoes for 5 minutes over medium heat. Add 1 1/2 cups milk, reserved clam liquid, and clam juice. Cover and simmer 20 to 30 minutes or until vegetables are tender.

3. Heat chowder to boiling; whisk in combined flour and remaining 1/2 cup milk. Boil, whisking, until thickened, 1 to 2 minutes. Stir in white pepper; season to taste with salt. Add reserved clams and cook 2 to 3 minutes longer.

SHERRIED CRAB AND MUSHROOM CHOWDER

5-6 servings

- 1 1/4 pounds fresh mushrooms, sliced
- 2/3 cup chopped onion
- 2 tablespoons chopped celery with leaves
- 2 tablespoons chopped carrot
- 1 tablespoon margarine
- 1 1/2 tablespoons flour
- 2 1/2 cups Chicken Stock (see p. 47), divided
- 3/4 cup peeled, diced red potatoes
- 1/8 teaspoon dried thyme leaves
- 1 tablespoon tomato paste
- 1 1/2 teaspoons reduced-sodium soy sauce
- 1 1/3 cups whole milk
- 6 ounces fresh lump crabmeat, shells removed
- 1 tablespoon chopped chives
- 2 tablespoons dry sherry
- Salt and white pepper, to taste

Per Serving
Calories: 159
% Calories from fat: 27
Fat (gm): 5
Sat. fat (gm): 1.7
Cholesterol (mg): 33.8
Sodium (mg): 371
Protein (gm): 10.8
Carbohydrate (gm): 18.1

Exchanges
Milk: 0.0
Vegetable: 0.0
Fruit: 0.0
Bread: 1.0
Meat: 1.0
Fat: 0.5

1. Saute mushrooms, onion, celery, and carrot in margarine in large skillet until tender, about 8 minutes. Reserve about 1/3 mushroom mixture; transfer remaining mixture to large saucepan and stir in flour. Cook 1 to 2 minutes over medium heat.

2. Stir in 1 1/2 cups Chicken Stock, potatoes, and thyme; heat to boiling. Reduce heat and simmer, covered, until potatoes are tender, about 10 minutes.

3. Process chowder in food processor or blender until smooth; return to saucepan. Add remaining 1 cup Chicken Stock, tomato paste, soy sauce, milk, reserved mushroom mixture, crabmeat, chives, and sherry; simmer 5 minutes. Season to taste with salt and white pepper.

HEARTY FISH CHOWDER

6 servings

Vegetable cooking spray
1/4 cup finely chopped onion
2 ribs celery, sliced
2 carrots, sliced
1 green bell pepper, chopped
3 cans (16 ounces each) low-sodium whole tomatoes, undrained, chopped
1 bottle (6 ounces) clam juice
3 medium potatoes, peeled, diced
1 teaspoon dried oregano leaves
1/2 teaspoon pepper
8 ounces fillet of sole, cut into bite-size pieces
8 ounces flounder, cut into bite-size pieces
8 ounces orange roughy, cut into bite-size pieces
1 cup dry white wine, *or* water
Salt and pepper, to taste
6 tablespoons chopped parsley
2 tablespoons finely chopped basil

Per Serving
Calories: 242
% Calories from fat: 6
Fat (gm): 1.7
Sat. fat (gm): 0.3
Cholesterol (mg): 46.7
Sodium (mg): 204
Protein (gm): 23.3
Carbohydrate (gm): 28.6

Exchanges
Milk: 0.0
Vegetable: 2.0
Fruit: 0.0
Bread: 1.0
Meat: 2.0
Fat: 0.0

1. Spray large saucepan with cooking spray; heat over medium heat until hot. Saute onion, celery, carrots, and bell pepper until tender, about 5 minutes. Add tomatoes and liquid, clam juice, potatoes, oregano, and pepper and heat to boiling; reduce heat and simmer, covered, 20 minutes.

2. Add fish and wine; simmer, uncovered, until fish is tender and flakes with a fork, about 10 minutes. Season to taste with salt; stir in parsley and basil.

WHITE FISH CHOWDER

6 servings

2 teaspoons margarine
1 large onion, finely chopped
1 large clove garlic, chopped
1 large rib celery, diced
2 cups Fish Stock (see p. 48), *or* vegetable, *or* chicken broth, divided
2 cups 2% reduced-fat milk, divided
2 1/2 cups potatoes, peeled, cut into 3/4-inch cubes
1 cup frozen baby lima beans
1 large carrot, diced
1 1/2 teaspoons dried basil leaves
1/2 teaspoon dried marjoram leaves
1/4 teaspoon dried thyme leaves
1/4 teaspoon dry mustard
1/4 teaspoon ground celery seeds
1/4 teaspoon white pepper
1 tablespoon plus 1 teaspoon cornstarch
1 pound skinless founder fillets, *or* halibut, *or* orange roughy, cut into 1-inch pieces
1 cup frozen whole kernel corn
Salt, to taste

Per Serving
Calories: 291
% Calories from fat: 13
Fat (gm): 4.3
Sat. fat (gm): 1.6
Cholesterol (mg): 43.7
Sodium (mg): 152
Protein (gm): 21.2
Carbohydrate (gm): 40.9

Exchanges
Milk: 0.3
Vegetable: 2.0
Fruit: 0.0
Bread: 2.0
Meat: 2.0
Fat: 0.0

1. Saute onion, garlic, and celery in margarine in large saucepan until onion is tender, about 5 minutes. Add Fish Stock, 1 cup milk, potatoes, lima beans, carrot, basil, marjoram, thyme, dry mustard, celery seeds, and pepper. Heat to boiling; reduce heat and simmer, covered, about 15 minutes or until potatoes are tender.

2. Heat soup to boiling. Mix cornstarch and remaining 1 cup of milk and stir into soup; cook, stirring, until soup is thickened, about 1 minute. Add flounder and corn; reduce heat to simmering and cook an additional 5 or 6 minutes, or until flounder flakes with a fork. Season to taste with salt.

SLOW COOKER CHICKEN GUMBO

6 servings

- 1 package (10 ounces) frozen blackeyed peas, thawed
- 2 large onions, finely chopped
- 1 medium pork hock (about 3/4 pound)
- 1 pound boneless, skinless chicken breasts
- 2 large ribs celery, chopped
- 1/2 cup diced red, *or* green, bell pepper
- 3 tablespoons long-grain white rice
- 1 large bay leaf
- 1 package (10 ounces) frozen succotash, thawed
- 1 cup sliced fresh, *or* frozen, thawed, okra
- 4 cups reduced-fat chicken broth
- 1 can (15 ounces) diced tomatoes, undrained
- 2 tablespoons chopped parsley
- 1/4 teaspoon dried thyme leaves
- 1/4 teaspoon black pepper

Per Serving
Calories: 263
% Calories from fat: 12
Fat (gm): 3.6
Sat. fat (gm): 0.8
Cholesterol (mg): 36.2
Sodium (mg): 789
Protein (gm): 21.6
Carbohydrate (gm): 39.5
Exchanges
Milk: 0.0
Vegetable: 2.0
Fruit: 0.0
Bread: 2.0
Meat: 1.5
Fat: 0.0

1. Combine all ingredients, except tomatoes, parsley, thyme, and pepper in slow cooker. Cover; cook on High 30 minutes. Continue cooking on High 3 hours longer, or reduce heat to Low and continue cooking 7 hours longer.

2. Remove chicken pieces from slow cooker with slotted spoon. Discard pork hock and bay leaf. Stir in remaining ingredients; cook on Low 15 minutes longer, or until soup is thoroughly heated.

3. Cut chicken into bite-size pieces; stir into gumbo and cook 5 minutes longer. If gumbo is too thick, thin with a little hot water before serving.

CHINESE HOT POT

8 servings

Per Serving
Calories: 200
% Calories from fat: 6
Fat (gm): 1.4
Sat. fat (gm): 0.3
Cholesterol (mg): 22.9
Sodium (mg): 574
Protein (gm): 11.6
Carbohydrate (gm): 30.3
Exchanges
Milk: 0.0
Vegetable: 0.0
Fruit: 0.0
Bread: 2.0
Meat: 1.0
Fat: 0.0

- 4 cans (13 3/4-ounces each) low-sodium chicken broth
- 1 cup dry white wine *or* low-sodium chicken broth
- 1/4 cup tamari soy sauce
- 2 packages (3 1/2-ounces each) ramen noodles (flavor packets discarded), broken in half
- 1 package (8 ounces) frozen Oriental-style vegetables
- 1 can (4 ounces) baby corn, drained
- 1 cup fresh snow peas
- 1 pound boneless, skinless chicken breasts, cut into bite-size pieces
- 1 bunch watercress, trimmed
- 4 green onions and tops, cut into 1-inch lengths

1. Combine broth, wine, and soy sauce in large saucepan. Heat to boiling. Add noodles, Oriental-style vegetables, baby corn, snow peas, and chicken. Heat to boiling; reduce heat and simmer until vegetables are tender and chicken is cooked, 5 to 8 minutes. Remove pan from heat. Stir in watercress and onions. Serve immediately.

EGG DROP SOUP

8 servings

6 cups Chicken Stock (see p. 47), *or* reduced-fat chicken broth
2 tablespoons cornstarch
2 tablespoons water
2 scallions, cut into 1-inch pieces
2 egg whites, lightly beaten
White pepper, to taste

Per Serving
Calories: 39
% Calories from fat: 17
Fat (gm): 0.7
Sat. fat (gm): 0.2
Cholesterol (mg): 7.6
Sodium (mg): 22
Protein (gm): 3.4
Carbohydrate (gm): 2.6
Exchanges
Milk: 0.0
Vegetable: 0.5
Fruit: 0.0
Bread: 0.0
Meat: 0.5
Fat: 0.0

1. Heat Chicken Stock to boiling in medium saucepan. Add combined cornstarch and water slowly, stirring until thickened; boil, stirring until thickened, about 1 minute. Stir in scallions; remove from heat. Stir in egg whites with a fork. Season to taste with white pepper.

GREEK LEMON-RICE SOUP

4 servings (about 1 cup each)

3 1/2 cups reduced-fat chicken broth
1/4 cup converted long-grain rice
2 large cloves garlic, minced
1/4-1/3 cup lemon juice
1 egg, lightly beaten
2 tablespoons finely chopped parsley
Salt and white pepper, to taste

Per Serving
Calories: 107
% Calories from fat: 23
Fat (gm): 2.7
Sat. fat (gm): 0.4
Cholesterol (mg): 75
Sodium (mg): 237
Protein (gm): 8.7
Carbohydrate (gm): 11.3
Exchanges
Milk: 0.0
Vegetable: 0.0
Fruit: 0.0
Bread: 0.0
Meat: 0.0
Fat: 0.0

1. Heat broth to boiling in medium saucepan; stir in rice and garlic. Reduce heat and simmer, covered, until rice is tender, about 25 minutes. Reduce heat to low.

2. Mix lemon juice and egg; slowly stir mixture into soup. Stir in parsley; season to taste with salt and white pepper. Pour soup into bowls.

CHICKEN-IN-THE-POT

8 servings

- 5 pounds chicken pieces
- 1 large onion, studded with 1 whole clove
- 8 medium carrots, cut into 2-inch pieces, divided
- 6 leeks (white parts only) cut into 2-inch pieces, divided
- 8 ribs celery, cut into 2-inch pieces, divided
- 8 sprigs parsley, divided
- 1/2 cup sliced mushrooms
- 1/2 pound small white onions
- Salt and pepper, to taste
- 4 cups cooked rice, warm

Per Serving
Calories: 362
% Calories from fat: 18
Fat (gm): 7.1
Sat. fat (gm): 1.9
Cholesterol (mg): 80.4
Sodium (mg): 133
Protein (gm): 30.7
Carbohydrate (gm): 42.8
Exchanges
Milk: 0.0
Vegetable: 3.0
Fruit: 0.0
Bread: 2.0
Meat: 2.5
Fat: 0.0

1. Combine chicken, onion, 1 carrot, 2 leeks, 2 ribs celery, and 4 sprigs parsley in large saucepan; add water to cover. Heat to boiling; reduce heat and simmer, covered, 1 hour.

2. Strain soup; discard vegetables and reserve chicken pieces, keeping chicken warm; return broth to saucepan. Add remaining carrots, leeks, celery, and parsley to broth and simmer until vegetables are almost tender. Add mushrooms and white onions and simmer another 20 minutes or until vegetables are tender. Season to taste with salt and pepper.

3. Remove chicken from bones and cut into large pieces. Spoon 1/2 cup rice into each soup bowl; spoon chicken and vegetables over rice; ladle hot broth over all.

MATZO BALL AND VEGETABLE SOUP

6 servings

- 6-8 cups Chicken Stock (see p. 47), *or* reduced-fat chicken broth
- 1 rib celery, sliced
- 1 large carrot, diced
- 1 cup frozen baby lima beans
- $1^1/_2$ cups small cauliflower florets
- $^1/_8$ teaspoon black pepper
- Matzo Balls (recipe follows)

Per Serving
Calories: 164
% Calories from fat: 24
Fat (gm): 4.4
Sat. fat (gm): 0.8
Cholesterol (mg): 45.9
Sodium (mg): 180
Protein (gm): 9.3
Carbohydrate (gm): 19.4

Exchanges
Milk: 0.0
Vegetable: 1.0
Fruit: 0.0
Bread: 1.0
Meat: 0.5
Fat: 1.0

1. Combine all ingredients except Matzo Balls in Dutch oven. Heat to boiling; reduce heat and simmer, covered, 20 to 25 minutes or until vegetables are tender. Gently add Matzo Balls to soup; simmer 4 to 5 minutes.

Matzo Balls

makes 12 balls

- 1 egg
- 2 egg whites
- 1 tablespoon canola, safflower, *or* corn oil
- $^1/_2$ cup plus 1 tablespoon matzo meal
- $^1/_4$ teaspoon salt
- $2^1/_2$ tablespoons Chicken Stock (see p. 47), *or* reduced-fat chicken broth
- 3 quarts water

1. Lightly beat egg, egg whites, and oil in bowl, using a fork. Add remaining ingredients and blend well, making sure matzo meal is completely moistened. Cover mixture and refrigerate at least 1 hour or up to 6 hours.

2. When matzo ball mixture is thoroughly chilled, heat 3 quarts of water to boiling in large saucepan. To form matzo balls, scoop up about 2 teaspoons of mixture and shape into a $1^1/_4$-inch ball with moistened fingers. Make sure ball is fairly round and smooth, but do not press it together too tightly. Drop matzo ball into boiling water. Repeat with remaining mixture, making 12 balls. Gently simmer, covered, 30 to 35 minutes, until matzo balls are cooked through.

MALAYSIAN-STYLE CHICKEN AND SCALLION SOUP

6 servings

5 cups Chicken Stock (see p. 47), *or* reduced-fat chicken broth, divided
2 tablespoons chopped gingerroot
1 large clove garlic, minced
1 lemon slice, 1/4-inch thick
1/2 teaspoon anise seeds
1/2 teaspoon coriander seeds
1/4 teaspoon cumin seeds
1/4 teaspoon black peppercorns
2 medium skinless, boneless chicken breast halves, cut into 1-inch by 1/8-inch-thick strips
1 cup green onions and tops, sliced
Chopped fresh cilantro, as garnish

Per Serving
Calories: 87
% Calories from fat: 21
Fat (gm): 2
Sat. fat (gm): 0.5
Cholesterol (mg): 33.6
Sodium (mg): 32.6
Protein (gm): 12.4
Carbohydrate (gm): 2.4

Exchanges
Milk: 0.0
Vegetable: 0.5
Fruit: 0.0
Bread: 0.0
Meat: 1.5
Fat: 0.0

1. Combine Chicken Stock, gingerroot, garlic, lemon, anise, coriander, cumin, and peppercorns in large saucepan. Heat to boiling; reduce heat and simmer, covered, 30 minutes. Strain and discard seasoning ingredients; return stock to saucepan.

2. Heat chicken with water to cover in medium saucepan to boiling; reduce heat and simmer until chicken is cooked, about 5 minutes. Drain; rinse chicken and drain. Add chicken and green onions to stock and simmer 1 to 2 minutes. Garnish each serving with chopped cilantro.

MULLIGATAWNY

6 servings

- 2 large onions, coarsely chopped
- 2 large ribs celery, coarsely chopped
- 1 large clove garlic, minced
- 2 teaspoons canola, safflower, *or* corn oil
- 2 large Winesap, *or* other tart cooking apples, peeled, coarsely chopped
- 2 medium carrots, coarsely chopped
- 1/4 cup chopped parsley
- 2 tablespoons chopped red, *or* green, bell pepper
- 4 cups Chicken Stock (see p. 47), *or* reduced-fat chicken broth
- 1 cup water
- 1 1/2 pounds bony chicken pieces (wings, backs, necks, etc.)
- 1 pound boneless, skinless chicken breasts
- 1/2 cup peeled, diced potato
- 2 1/2 teaspoons curry powder
- 1 teaspoon chili powder
- 1/2 teaspoon ground allspice
- 1/4 teaspoon dried thyme leaves
- 1/4 teaspoon pepper
- 1 can (15 1/2 ounces) diced tomatoes, undrained
- Salt, to taste
- Finely chopped parsley, as garnish

Per Serving
Calories: 200
% Calories from fat: 22
Fat (gm): 5
Sat. fat (gm): 1
Cholesterol (mg): 40.8
Sodium (mg): 148
Protein (gm): 16.7
Carbohydrate (gm): 22

Exchanges
Milk: 0.0
Vegetable: 3.0
Fruit: 0.0
Bread: 0.5
Meat: 1.5
Fat: 0.0

1. Saute onions, celery, and garlic in oil in large saucepan 4 to 5 minutes, or until onions are softened. Add apples, carrots, parsley, and bell pepper and cook, stirring, 3 to 4 minutes longer. Add Chicken Stock and remaining ingredients, except tomatoes, salt, and parsley. Heat to boiling; reduce heat and simmer, covered, 1 hour and 10 minutes.

2. Remove chicken from pan; discard bony pieces and reserve breasts. Skim off and discard fat on soup surface, using large, shallow spoon. Stir in tomatoes and juice. Process about 2 cups vegetables and liquid in blender or food processor until smooth; return to pan.

3. Cut chicken breasts into bite-size pieces; add to soup. Heat soup until hot; season to taste with salt. Garnish with parsley.

SPICY NORTH AFRICAN-STYLE CHICKEN SOUP

7 servings

- 3 cups chopped red, *or* yellow, onions
- 2 large cloves garlic, minced
- 2 teaspoons olive oil
- 5 cups Chicken Stock (see p. 47), *or* reduced-sodium fat-free chicken broth, divided
- 1 cup water
- 2 skinless chicken breast halves (about 1 pound)
- 2 large ribs celery, thinly sliced
- 1/2 cup chopped parsley
- 1 can (15 1/2 ounces) diced tomatoes, undrained
- 1 cinnamon stick, 3 inches long
- 2 large bay leaves
- 1 teaspoon dried thyme leaves
- 3/4 teaspoon dried marjoram leaves
- 1/8 teaspoon ground cloves
- Dash cayenne pepper
- 1/4 teaspoon black pepper
- 1/2 cup bulgur wheat, *or* brown rice

Per Serving
Calories: 166
% Calories from fat: 19
Fat (gm): 3.6
Sat. fat (gm): 0.7
Cholesterol (mg): 33.4
Sodium (mg): 143
Protein (gm): 14.8
Carbohydrate (gm): 17.9

Exchanges
Milk: 0.0
Vegetable: 2.0
Fruit: 0.0
Bread: 0.5
Meat: 1.5
Fat: 0.0

1. Saute onion and garlic in oil in large saucepan, about 5 minutes or until onion is tender. Add remaining ingredients, except bulgur wheat. Heat to boiling; reduce heat and simmer, covered, about 30 minutes or until chicken is tender. With a slotted spoon, remove chicken and reserve. Remove cinnamon stick and bay leaves and discard.

2. Heat soup to boiling. Stir in bulgur wheat. Reduce heat and simmer an additional 40 to 45 minutes until bulgur is tender. Meanwhile, remove chicken meat from bones, and cut into bite-size pieces. When bulgur is tender, return chicken to pan and simmer an additional 2 to 3 minutes.

MOROCCAN CHICKEN-GARBANZO SOUP

6 servings (about 1 3/4 cups each)

Per Serving
Calories: 304
% Calories from fat: 14
Fat (gm): 4.7
Sat. fat (gm): 1.7
Cholesterol (mg): 38
Sodium (mg): 786
Protein (gm): 20
Carbohydrate (gm): 46.4

Exchanges
Milk: 0.0
Vegetable: 2.0
Fruit: 0.0
Bread: 3.0
Meat: 1.0
Fat: 0.0

- 1 cup chopped onion
- 3/4 cup chopped celery
- 1 teaspoon grated gingerroot
- 1 teaspoon ground turmeric
- 1/2 teaspoon ground cinnamon
- 1/4 teaspoon crushed red pepper
- 1 tablespoon butter, *or* margarine
- 2 cans (15 ounces each) garbanzo beans, rinsed, drained
- 1 can (28 ounces) whole tomatoes in juice, undrained, chopped
- 1 quart reduced-sodium fat-free chicken broth
- 8 ounces boneless, skinless chicken breast, cooked, cubed
- 2 ounces angel hair pasta, broken into pieces
- 1/4 cup chopped parsley
- 1/2-1 teaspoon salt

1. Saute onion, celery, gingerroot, turmeric, cinnamon, and crushed red pepper in butter in large saucepan until tender, about 8 minutes. Stir in beans, tomatoes and liquid, broth, and chicken. Heat to boiling; reduce heat and simmer 5 minutes.

2. Stir in pasta; simmer until pasta is tender, about 3 minutes. Stir in parsley and salt.

HAMBURGER SOUP

8 servings (about 1 cup each)

- 1 pound lean ground beef
- 1 small onion, chopped
- 1 can (16 ounces) diced tomatoes, undrained
- 2 cups sliced carrots
- 2 cups broccoli florets
- 3 cups reduced-sodium beef broth
- 1 can (15 ounces) black beans, rinsed, drained
- 1 can (15 ounces) Great Northern beans, rinsed, drained
- 1/2 teaspoon dried thyme leaves
- Salt and pepper, to taste

Per Serving
Calories: 252
% Calories from fat: 31
Fat (gm): 8.7
Sat. fat (gm): 3.2
Cholesterol (mg): 37.6
Sodium (mg): 510
Protein (gm): 19.3
Carbohydrate (gm): 23.5
Exchanges
Milk: 0.0
Vegetable: 2.0
Fruit: 0.0
Bread: 1.0
Meat: 2.0
Fat: 0.5

1. Cook beef and onions in large saucepan until beef is browned, about 10 minutes. Stir in remaining ingredients and heat to boiling. Reduce heat and simmer, covered, until vegetables are tender, about 10 minutes. Season to taste with salt and pepper.

RICH BEEF AND LENTIL SOUP

10 servings

- 16 ounces lean beef stew cubes, fat trimmed
- 1 1/2 cups finely chopped onions
- 1-2 tablespoons vegetable oil
- 2 tablespoons flour
- 3 quarts reduced-sodium fat-free beef broth
- 3 cups dried lentils, sorted, rinsed
- 1 medium leek white part only, finely chopped

Per Serving
Calories: 313
% Calories from fat: 12
Fat (gm): 4.2
Sat. fat (gm): 1.1
Cholesterol (mg): 28.4
Sodium (mg): 234
Protein (gm): 31.7
Carbohydrate (gm): 37.3
Exchanges
Milk: 0.0
Vegetable: 1.0
Fruit: 0.0
Bread: 2.0
Meat: 2.5
Fat: 0.0

3 large carrots, finely chopped
1/2 cup chopped celery
1/4 cup dry white wine, *or* beef broth
Salt and pepper, to taste

1. Cook beef and onions in oil in large saucepan over medium to medium-high heat until beef is browned and crusty and onions are well browned, about 10 minutes; stir in flour.

2. Add beef broth, lentils, leek, carrots, and celery; heat to boiling. Reduce heat and simmer, covered, until beef is tender, 1 to 1 1/2 hours, stirring in wine during last 15 minutes. Season to taste with salt and pepper.

SPICY BEEF AND CABBAGE SOUP

8 servings

Per Serving
Calories: 172
% Calories from fat: 30
Fat (gm): 5.8
Sat. fat (gm): 2.1
Cholesterol (mg): 26
Sodium (mg): 523
Protein (gm): 10.8
Carbohydrate (gm): 20.1

Exchanges
Milk: 0.0
Vegetable: 2.0
Fruit: 0.0
Bread: 0.5
Meat: 1.0
Fat: 0.5

3/4 pound ground beef round
1 large onion, finely chopped
1 large clove garlic, minced
4 cups beef bouillon, reconstituted from cubes
3 cups water
2 ribs celery, including leaves, thinly sliced
2 large carrots, thinly sliced
3 bay leaves
1 can (15 ounces) reduced-sodium tomato sauce
3 cups grated, *or* very finely shredded, cabbage
1/2 teaspoon dry mustard
2 tablespoons apple cider vinegar
2 tablespoons sugar
1/2 teaspoon dried thyme leaves
1/2 teaspoon dried marjoram leaves
1/4 teaspoon ground cinnamon

- 1/8 teaspoon ground cloves
- 1/2 teaspoon black pepper
- 1/3 cup uncooked white rice
- Salt, to taste

1. Combine ground round, onion, and garlic in large saucepan. Cook over medium heat, stirring frequently, until meat is browned. Remove from heat; drain off any fat.

2. Add remaining ingredients, except rice and salt. Heat to boiling; reduce heat and simmer, covered, 15 minutes. Add rice; simmer about 25 minutes or until cabbage and rice are cooked and flavors are well blended. Season to taste with salt.

EASY BEEF SAUSAGE AND BLACK BEAN SOUP

6 servings

- 1 cup thinly sliced carrots
- 1 cup thinly sliced celery
- 3/4 cup water
- 1/2 pound reduced-fat smoked beef sausage links, thinly sliced
- 2 cans (19 ounces each) low-sodium black bean soup
- Fat-free plain yogurt, as garnish
- Chopped parsley, as garnish

Per Serving
Calories: 195
% Calories from fat: 24
Fat (gm): 5.3
Sat. fat (gm): 1
Cholesterol (mg): 24
Sodium (mg): 359
Protein (gm): 12.9
Carbohydrate (gm): 24.2
Exchanges
Milk: 0.0
Vegetable: 0.5
Fruit: 0.0
Bread: 1.5
Meat: 1.0
Fat: 0.5

1. Combine carrots, celery, and water in medium saucepan. Heat to boiling; reduce heat and simmer, covered, 5 minutes or until vegetables are crisp-tender. Add sausage and bean soup to vegetables, stirring to blend. Heat to boiling; reduce heat and simmer, uncovered, 10 minutes, stirring occasionally. Ladle soup into bowls; garnish with dollops of yogurt and sprinkle with parsley.

SLOW COOKER GOULASH SOUP

8 servings

- 1 large onion, finely chopped
- 1 large carrot, thinly sliced
- 1 large rib celery, diced
- 2 large cloves garlic, minced
- 2 cups peeled, diced potatoes
- 1 cup cut fresh, *or* frozen, green beans
- 2 tablespoons pearl barley
- 1 pound beef round, fat trimmed, cut into 3/4-inch cubes
- 5 cups water
- 4 beef bouillon cubes
- 1 bay leaf
- 2 teaspoons sugar
- 1 1/2 teaspoons paprika
- 1/2 teaspoon dry mustard
- 1/2 teaspoon dried thyme leaves
- 1/4 teaspoon black pepper
- 1 can (15 ounces) reduced-sodium tomato sauce
- 2 tablespoons tomato paste
- Salt, to taste

Per Serving
Calories: 181
% Calories from fat: 14
Fat (gm): 2.9
Sat. fat (gm): 0.8
Cholesterol (mg): 30.3
Sodium (mg): 551
Protein (gm): 14.9
Carbohydrate (gm): 25.3

Exchanges
Milk: 0.0
Vegetable: 2.0
Fruit: 0.0
Bread: 1.0
Meat: 1.0
Fat: 0.0

1. Combine all ingredients, except tomato sauce, tomato paste, and salt, in slow cooker. Cook on High 1 hour. Reduce heat to Low; cook 5 to 6 hours longer.

2. Stir tomato sauce and tomato paste to slow cooker. Cook an additional 1 to 1 1/2 hours on High. Season to taste with salt.

LAMB AND WHITE BEAN SOUP

8 servings

- $1^1/_2$ cups dry Great Northern, *or* navy, beans, sorted, washed
- 2 lamb shanks (about $1^3/_4$ pounds), cracked
- 6 cups beef broth
- 2 cups water
- 2 large carrots, sliced
- 2 large ribs celery, sliced
- 1 large onion, finely chopped
- 2 large cloves garlic, minced
- 3 bay leaves
- $1^1/_2$ teaspoons dried thyme leaves
- $1^1/_4$ teaspoons dried marjoram leaves
- $^1/_2$ teaspoon ground celery seed
- $^1/_2$ teaspoon dry mustard
- $^1/_4$ teaspoon pepper
- 3 cups cabbage, thinly sliced
- Salt, to taste

Per Serving
Calories: 193
% Calories from fat: 20
Fat (gm): 4.4
Sat. fat (gm): 1.3
Cholesterol (mg): 59.4
Sodium (mg): 763
Protein (gm): 22.9
Carbohydrate (gm): 16.6

Exchanges
Milk: 0.0
Vegetable: 2.0
Fruit: 0.0
Bread: 0.5
Meat: 2.0
Fat: 0.0

1. Put beans in large saucepan and cover with 2 inches cold water. Bring to a boil over high heat. Cover, lower heat, and simmer 2 minutes. Remove pot from heat and let stand at room temperature for 1 hour. Drain. Return beans to pan; add remaining ingredients except cabbage and salt. Heat to boiling; reduce heat, and simmer, covered, until beans are tender, about 1 hour. Add cabbage and simmer until tender, about 10 minutes.

2. Remove and discard bay leaves. Remove lamb shanks with slotted spoon; remove meat and cut into bite-size pieces. Discard bones and return meat to pan. Season to taste with salt.

CHINESE PORK AND WATERCRESS SOUP

6 servings

Per Serving
Calories: 72
% Calories from fat: 21
Fat (gm): 1.6
Sat. fat (gm): 0.5
Cholesterol (mg): 13.7
Sodium (mg): 46.7
Protein (gm): 5.3
Carbohydrate (gm): 6.1

Exchanges
Milk: 0.0
Vegetable: 0.0
Fruit: 0.0
Bread: 0.5
Meat: 0.5
Fat: 0.0

Vegetable cooking spray
2 1/2 ounces fresh pork loin, fat trimmed, cut into very thin 1-inch-long strips
1 small clove garlic, halved
1 1/4-inch-thick slice fresh gingerroot
5 cups Chicken Stock (see p. 47), *or* reduced-fat chicken broth, divided
4-5 scallions, including 1 inch of green top, quartered lengthwise and cut into 1-inch lengths
1 tablespoon dry sherry
1 teaspoon reduced-sodium soy sauce
2/3 cup cooked rice
1 1/2 cups (lightly packed) watercress sprigs

1. Spray large saucepan with cooking spray; add pork strips, garlic, and gingerroot and cook over medium heat until pork is cooked. Add Chicken Stock, scallions, sherry, soy sauce, and rice. Heat to boiling; reduce heat and simmer, covered, 2 minutes. Stir in watercress; remove pan from heat and let stand 30 seconds or until watercress is wilted. Discard gingerroot. Serve immediately.

THREE

Salads and Salad Dressings

TROPICAL FRUIT BOATS WITH BANANA DRESSING

4 servings

2 small pineapples, cut in half
1 cup sliced strawberries
1 medium banana, sliced
1 cup blueberries
1 cup watermelon balls
1 cup cantaloupe balls
2 kiwi fruit, peeled and sliced
Banana Dressing (recipe follows)
2 tablespoons grated orange rind

Per Serving
Calories: 254
% Calories from fat: 6
Fat (gm): 2
Sat. fat (gm): 0.4
Cholesterol (mg): 1.3
Sodium (mg): 126
Protein (gm): 6.2
Carbohydrate (gm): 59
Exchanges
Milk: 0.0
Vegetable: 0.0
Fruit: 4.0
Bread: 0.0
Meat: 0.5
Fat: 0.0

1. Run a serrated knife around perimeter of each pineapple half and remove pineapple flesh, leaving 1/4-inch shell. Cut pineapple into cubes, removing and discarding core. Combine pineapple, strawberries, banana, blueberries, watermelon, cantaloupe, and kiwi fruit in large bowl; toss well to mix. Spoon fruit into pineapple halves; spoon Banana Dressing over fruit. Sprinkle with orange rind.

Banana Dressing

makes about 3/4 cup

1/2 cup reduced-fat cottage cheese
1 medium banana, cut up
2-3 tablespoons pineapple juice
1 tablespoon honey

1. Place all ingredients in food processor or blender and process until smooth.

CRANBERRY CREAM SALAD

6 servings

1 cup boiling water
1 package (3 ounces) cherry-flavored gelatin
1 can (16 ounces) whole berry cranberry sauce
1/2 cup diced celery
1/4 cup golden raisins
1 cup Mock Sour Cream (see p. 501)

Per Serving
Calories: 200
% Calories from fat: 2
Fat (gm): 0.4
Sat. fat (gm): 0.2
Cholesterol (mg): 1
Sodium (mg): 150
Protein (gm): 4.2
Carbohydrate (gm): 47.3

Exchanges
Milk: 0.0
Vegetable: 0.0
Fruit: 3.0
Bread: 0.0
Meat: 0.5
Fat: 0.0

1. Pour boiling water over gelatin in medium bowl; stir until dissolved. Cool; refrigerate until syrupy, about 20 minutes. Stir in cranberry sauce, celery, and raisins. Fold in Mock Sour Cream. Pour mixture into 1-quart mold. Refrigerate until firm, 2-3 hours or overnight.

2. To unmold, dip mold briefly in warm water; loosen edge of gelatin with tip of sharp knife. Unmold onto serving plate.

COTTAGE CHEESE LIME MOLD

6 servings

1 package (3 ounces) sugar-free lime flavored gelatin
1/2 cup plain fat-free yogurt
1/2 cup fat-free mayonnaise
1 teaspoon lemon juice
1-2 tablespoons sugar
2 cups 1% reduced-fat cottage cheese
1/2 small cantaloupe, finely diced

Per Serving
Calories: 135
% Calories from fat: 11
Fat (gm): 1.6
Sat. fat (gm): 0.9
Cholesterol (mg): 6.7
Sodium (mg): 597
Protein (gm): 13.7
Carbohydrate (gm): 16.9

Exchanges
Milk: 0.0
Vegetable: 0.0
Fruit: 1.0
Bread: 0.0
Meat: 1.5
Fat: 0.0

1. Prepare gelatin according to package directions, but do not add cold water. With electric mixer, mix in yogurt, mayonnaise, and lemon juice; refrigerate until syrupy, about 20 minutes. Combine sugar, cottage cheese, and cantaloupe in small bowl. Fold cottage cheese mixture into gelatin mixture. Pour into 1-quart mold. Refrigerate until set, 3 to 4 hours or overnight.

2. To unmold, dip mold briefly in warm water; loosen edge of gelatin with tip of sharp knife. Unmold onto serving plate.

THREE-BEAN AND CORN SALAD

8 servings

1 can (16 ounces) whole green beans, rinsed, drained
1 can (15 ounces) garbanzo beans, rinsed, drained
1 can (15 ounces) kidney beans, rinsed, drained
1 can (12 ounces) whole kernel corn with sweet peppers, drained
1 medium onion, thinly sliced and separated into rings
1/2 cup fat-free French dressing
1/2 cup (2 ounces) shredded reduced-fat Mexican blend cheese
8 lettuce leaves

Per Serving
Calories: 175
% Calories from fat: 12
Fat (gm): 2.4
Sat. fat (gm): 0.2
Cholesterol (mg): 3.7
Sodium (mg): 721
Protein (gm): 8.6
Carbohydrate (gm): 30.3
Exchanges
Milk: 0.0
Vegetable: 0.0
Fruit: 0.0
Bread: 2.0
Meat: 0.5
Fat: 0.0

1. Toss beans, corn, and onion with dressing. Refrigerate at least 1 hour. Toss with cheese and spoon into lettuce leaves.

GARBANZO BEAN AND PARSLEY SALAD

12 servings

4 cups chopped parsley
2 cans (15½ ounces each) garbanzo beans, rinsed, drained
1 large green bell pepper, chopped
½ cup sliced green onions and tops
1 large tomato, seeded and diced
¼ cup lemon juice
1 clove garlic, minced
2 tablespoons olive oil
Salt and pepper, to taste

Per Serving
Calories: 105
% Calories from fat: 31
Fat (gm): 3.8
Sat. fat (gm): 0.5
Cholesterol (mg): 0
Sodium (mg): 304
Protein (gm): 4.2
Carbohydrate (gm): 14.9
Exchanges
Milk: 0.0
Vegetable: 0.5
Fruit: 0.0
Bread: 1.0
Meat: 0.0
Fat: 0.5

1. Combine parsley, beans, green pepper, green onions, and tomatoes in bowl. Combine lemon juice and garlic in small bowl, and whisk in olive oil in a thin stream. Toss dressing with salad; season to taste with salt and pepper.

6-BEAN SALAD WITH GINGER DRESSING

16 servings (about ⅔ cup each)

12 ounces cut green beans, cooked
1 can (15 ounces) dark red kidney beans
1 can (15 ounces) garbanzo beans
1 can (15 ounces) Great Northern beans
1 can (15 ounces) pinto beans
1 can (15 ounces) black beans
¼ cup sliced green onions and tops
Ginger Dressing (recipe follows)

Per Serving
Calories: 240
% Calories from fat: 28
Fat (gm): 7.6
Sat. fat (gm): 0.6
Cholesterol (mg): 0
Sodium (mg): 691
Protein (gm): 7
Carbohydrate (gm): 37
Exchanges
Milk: 0.0
Vegetable: 1.0
Fruit: 0.0
Bread: 2.0
Meat: 0.0
Fat: 1.5

1. Rinse and drain all beans. Combine all ingredients, tossing to mix well.

Ginger Dressing

makes about 1 2/3 cups

- 1/2 cup canola oil
- 3/4 cup pineapple, *or* apricot, preserves
- 1/3 cup cider, *or* rice wine, vinegar
- 1/4 cup sugar
- 2 teaspoons minced gingerroot, *or* 1-2 teaspoons ground ginger
- 2-3 teaspoons salt
- 1/2 teaspoon pepper

1. Mix all ingredients.

MANDARIN BEETS WITH CITRUS DRESSING

6 servings

- 6 medium beets, cooked, cooled, thinly sliced
- 1 small red onion, thinly sliced
- Citrus Dressing (recipe follows)
- 1 can (11 ounces) mandarin orange segments, drained

Per Serving
Calories: 104
% Calories from fat: 20
Fat (gm): 2.4
Sat. fat (gm): 0.3
Cholesterol (mg): 0
Sodium (mg): 312
Protein (gm): 1.9
Carbohydrate (gm): 20.2
Exchanges
Milk: 0.0
Vegetable: 2.0
Fruit: 0.5
Bread: 0.0
Meat: 0.0
Fat: 0.5

1. Combine beets and onion in medium bowl; pour dressing over and toss. Add oranges and toss just before serving.

Citrus Dressing

makes about 1/3 cup

- 1 tablespoon vegetable oil
- 2 tablespoons orange marmalade
- 2 tablespoons lemon juice
- 3/4 teaspoon salt
- Dash pepper

1. Combine all ingredients.

PICKLED BEET SALAD

4 servings

- 1 can (15 ounces) sliced beets, undrained
- 1 tablespoon red wine vinegar
- 1 bay leaf
- 1 whole clove
- 1-2 teaspoons sugar
- Shredded lettuce
- 1/2 small onion, sliced and separated into rings

Per Serving
Calories: 41
% Calories from fat: 2
Fat (gm): 0.1
Sat. fat (gm): 0
Cholesterol (mg): 0
Sodium (mg): 324
Protein (gm): 1.2
Carbohydrate (gm): 9.7

Exchanges
Milk: 0.0
Vegetable: 2.0
Fruit: 0.0
Bread: 0.0
Meat: 0.0
Fat: 0.0

1. Drain beet juice into small skillet. Add vinegar, bay leaf, clove, and sugar. Heat to boiling; reduce heat and simmer 1 minute. Cool.

2. Pour cooled juice over beets and allow to marinate overnight in refrigerator. Lift beets with slotted spoon from juice and serve on bed of shredded lettuce. Garnish with onion rings.

CRUNCHY BROCCOLI SALAD

4 servings

- 2 pounds fresh broccoli florets, cooked crisp-tender, cooled
- 1/2 pound sliced mushrooms
- 1 can (8 ounces) sliced water chestnuts, drained
- 1/4 cup fat-free yogurt
- 1/2 cup fat-free mayonnaise
- 1 teaspoon sugar
- 1/8 teaspoon pepper
- 1 teaspoon grated onion
- 1 clove garlic, crushed
- Salt and pepper, to taste

Per Serving
Calories: 142
% Calories from fat: 7
Fat (gm): 1.2
Sat. fat (gm): 0.2
Cholesterol (mg): 0.4
Sodium (mg): 477
Protein (gm): 9.4
Carbohydrate (gm): 28.9

Exchanges
Milk: 0.0
Vegetable: 5.0
Fruit: 0.0
Bread: 0.0
Meat: 0.0
Fat: 0.0

1. Combine broccoli, mushrooms, and water chestnuts in bowl; add combined yogurt, mayonnaise, sugar, pepper, onion, and garlic and mix well. Season to taste with salt and pepper. Cover and refrigerate 2 hours or more to blend flavors.

SLAW POLONAISE

5 servings

- 1/2 cup low-fat yogurt
- 1/4 cup buttermilk
- 1 teaspoon sugar
- 2 tablespoons minced dill pickle
- 1 teaspoon poppy seeds
- 1 teaspoon garlic powder
- 1 pound cabbage, shredded
- Salt and pepper, to taste
- Paprika

Per Serving
Calories: 44
% Calories from fat: 11
Fat (gm): 0.6
Sat. fat (gm): 0.1
Cholesterol (mg): 0.9
Sodium (mg): 96
Protein (gm): 2.9
Carbohydrate (gm): 7.7
Exchanges
Milk: 0.0
Vegetable: 1.5
Fruit: 0.0
Bread: 0.0
Meat: 0.0
Fat: 0.0

1. Process yogurt, buttermilk, sugar, pickle, poppy seeds, and garlic powder in blender until smooth. Toss dressing with cabbage; season to taste with salt and pepper. Spoon slaw into serving bowl and sprinkle with paprika.

CHINESE COLESLAW

4 servings

- 1 tablespoon olive oil
- 1/2 cup white vinegar
- 1/3 cup sugar
- 1 teaspoon salt
- 1/4 teaspoon pepper
- 2 teaspoons dried shallots
- 1 small head cabbage, shredded
- 1/2 cup sliced radishes

Per Serving
Calories: 158
% Calories from fat: 20
Fat (gm): 3.9
Sat. fat (gm): 0.5
Cholesterol (mg): 0
Sodium (mg): 588
Protein (gm): 4.6
Carbohydrate (gm): 30.8
Exchanges
Milk: 0.0
Vegetable: 2.0
Fruit: 0.0
Bread: 1.0
Meat: 0.0
Fat: 1.0

1. Combine oil, vinegar, sugar, salt, pepper, and shallots; pour over cabbage and radishes and mix well. Refrigerate.

FAMILY FAVORITE COLESLAW

6 servings

- 1/4 cup Dijon mustard
- 1/4 cup fat-free mayonnaise
- 2 teaspoons sugar
- 1 teaspoon fresh lemon juice
- 1/2 teaspoon salt
- 1 medium cabbage, shredded

Per Serving
Calories: 34
% Calories from fat: 18
Fat (gm): 0.7
Sat. fat (gm): 0.1
Cholesterol (mg): 0
Sodium (mg): 624
Protein (gm): 1.2
Carbohydrate (gm): 6.4
Exchanges
Milk: 0.0
Vegetable: 1.5
Fruit: 0.0
Bread: 0.0
Meat: 0.0
Fat: 0.0

1. Mix all ingredients except cabbage in large bowl. Add cabbage and toss well.

CRISP CUCUMBER SALAD

6 servings

- 3 medium cucumbers, peeled, thinly sliced
- 1 medium red onion, thinly sliced, separated into rings
- 1/2 cup white distilled vinegar
- 3 tablespoons sugar
- 1/4 teaspoon ground ginger
- 1 tablespoon chopped chives
- 1/8 teaspoon dried oregano leaves
- 1 teaspoon salt
- 1/4 teaspoon pepper

Per Serving
Calories: 75
% Calories from fat: 5
Fat (gm): 0.4
Sat. fat (gm): 0.1
Cholesterol (mg): 0
Sodium (mg): 363
Protein (gm): 2.4
Carbohydrate (gm): 18
Exchanges
Milk: 0.0
Vegetable: 0.0
Fruit: 0.0
Bread: 1.0
Meat: 0.0
Fat: 0.0

1. Layer cucumbers and onions in bowl. Combine remaining ingredients; pour over cucumbers and refrigerate several hours. Toss before serving.

BIBB LETTUCE SALAD WITH RASPBERRY VINAIGRETTE

8 servings

Per Serving
Calories: 222
% Calories from fat: 31
Fat (gm): 8
Sat. fat (gm): 1.2
Cholesterol (mg): 0
Sodium (mg): 398
Protein (gm): 7.6
Carbohydrate (gm): 32.3
Exchanges
Milk: 0.0
Vegetable: 2.0
Fruit: 0.0
Bread: 1.5
Meat: 0.0
Fat: 1.5

2 heads Bibb lettuce, torn into bite-size pieces
1 bunch watercress, torn into bite-size pieces
1 pound mushrooms, sliced
1 can (16 ounces) quartered artichoke hearts, drained
1 bunch white radishes, sliced
Raspberry Vinaigrette (recipe follows)
1 cup raspberries
10 small French rolls, halved, toasted

1. Combine greens, mushrooms, artichoke hearts, and radishes in large bowl. Toss with Raspberry Vinaigrette. Spoon salad onto salad plates and top with berries; serve with French rolls.

Raspberry Vinaigrette

makes about 1/3 cup

1/4 cup olive oil
1 tablespoon raspberry vinegar
1-2 tablespoons water
1/4 teaspoon Dijon mustard
1/8 teaspoon salt
1/4 teaspoon pepper

1. Combine all ingredients.

GREEK ISLANDS SALAD

6 servings

- 4 tomatoes, cored and quartered
- 1 cucumber, peeled, cut into 1/4-inch slices
- 1 green bell pepper, cut into thin, round slices
- 1 yellow bell pepper, cut into thin, round slices
- 1 red bell pepper, cut into thin, round slices
- 2-3 anchovies, optional
- 12 black olives, optional
- 1 medium red onion, thinly sliced
- 2-4 tablespoons crumbled feta cheese
- 3/4 cup fat-free Italian dressing

Per Serving
Calories: 70
% Calories from fat: 20
Fat (gm): 1.6
Sat. fat (gm): 0.9
Cholesterol (mg): 4.7
Sodium (mg): 489
Protein (gm): 2.4
Carbohydrate (gm): 12.1

Exchanges
Milk: 0.0
Vegetable: 2.5
Fruit: 0.0
Bread: 0.0
Meat: 0.0
Fat: 0.0

1. Combine tomatoes, cucumber, peppers, anchovies, olives, onions, and feta cheese in large bowl. Pour dressing over and toss.

HARLEQUIN SALAD

6 servings

- 3 medium tomatoes, sliced
- 4 ounces part-skim mozzarella cheese, sliced
- 1 small cucumber, peeled and sliced
- 1/2 cup Dijonnaise Sauce (see p. 500)
- 1/4 cup dry white wine
- 2 tablespoons lemon juice
- 1/4 teaspoon dry mustard
- 2 tablespoons capers
- 6 fresh basil leaves, chopped
- Fresh oregano sprigs

Per Serving
Calories: 92
% Calories from fat: 32
Fat (gm): 3.6
Sat. fat (gm): 2
Cholesterol (mg): 10.7
Sodium (mg): 315
Protein (gm): 5.7
Carbohydrate (gm): 10

Exchanges
Milk: 0.0
Vegetable: 2.5
Fruit: 0.0
Bread: 0.0
Meat: 0.0
Fat: 0.5

1. Arrange tomato, cheese, and cucumber slices attractively on serving platter; top tomato slices with dollops of Dijonnaise Sauce. Combine remaining ingredients, except oregano, in small bowl. Drizzle over salad; garnish with oregano.

COUNTRY POTATO SALAD WITH MUSTARD DRESSING

8 servings

- 24 unpeeled new potatoes (about 1 1/4 pounds), cooked, cubed
- 4 hard-cooked egg whites, chopped
- 1 cup diced celery
- 1 cup roasted red peppers, chopped, drained
- 1/4 cup plain fat-free yogurt
- 3 tablespoons reduced-fat mayonnaise
- 2 teaspoons stone-ground mustard
- 1/2 teaspoon white pepper
- 1/2 teaspoon garlic powder

Per Serving
Calories: 92
% Calories from fat: 16
Fat (gm): 1.7
Sat. fat (gm): 0.4
Cholesterol (mg): 0.1
Sodium (mg): 108
Protein (gm): 3.6
Carbohydrate (gm): 16
Exchanges
Milk: 0.0
Vegetable: 0.0
Fruit: 0.0
Bread: 1.0
Meat: 0.0
Fat: 0.5

1. Combine potatoes, egg whites, celery, and red peppers. Mix yogurt, mayonnaise, mustard, pepper, and garlic powder; spoon over salad and mix well.

BASQUE TOMATOES

8 servings

- 8 ripe medium tomatoes
- 1/2 cup chopped parsley
- 2-3 teaspoons olive oil
- 2-3 tablespoons tarragon vinegar
- 1 teaspoon Dijon-style mustard
- 1 clove garlic, minced
- 1/2-1 teaspoon sugar
- 1 teaspoon salt
- 1/4 teaspoon pepper
- Sliced black olives, as garnish

Per Serving
Calories: 41
% Calories from fat: 31
Fat (gm): 1.6
Sat. fat (gm): 0.2
Cholesterol (mg): 0
Sodium (mg): 288
Protein (gm): 1.2
Carbohydrate (gm): 6.9
Exchanges
Milk: 0.0
Vegetable: 1.5
Fruit: 0.0
Bread: 0.0
Meat: 0.0
Fat: 0.0

1. Slice tomatoes and arrange in shallow dish. Sprinkle with parsley. Combine remaining ingredients, except olives; drizzle over tomatoes. Garnish with black olives.

TOMATO-BASIL ASPIC

6 servings

- 1 envelope unflavored gelatin
- 1/4 cup cold water
- 1 1/4 cups boiling water
- 3 tablespoons sweet basil vinegar
- 1/8 teaspoon black pepper
- Dash salt
- 2 tablespoons onion juice
- 1 can (4 ounces) tomato paste
- 1 teaspoon sugar
- Lettuce leaves
- Parsley sprigs, as garnish

Per Serving
Calories: 22
% Calories from fat: 6
Fat (gm): 0.2
Sat. fat (gm): 0
Cholesterol (mg): 0
Sodium (mg): 151
Protein (gm): 1.7
Carbohydrate (gm): 4.1

Exchanges
Milk: 0.0
Vegetable: 1.0
Fruit: 0.0
Bread: 0.0
Meat: 0.0
Fat: 0.0

1. Sprinkle gelatin over cold water in small bowl; let stand 5 minutes. Add boiling water and stir until gelatin is dissolved. Stir in vinegar, pepper, salt, onion juice, tomato paste, and sugar. Pour into 6 individual molds and chill until set, about 3 hours.

2. To unmold, dip molds briefly into warm water; loosen edges of gelatin with sharp knife. Unmold on lettuce-lined plates and garnish with parsley.

ITALIAN TOMATO AND VEGETABLE SALAD

4 servings

- 6 Italian plum tomatoes, sliced
- 1/2 cup chopped scallions
- 1 pound green beans, cooked crisp-tender
- 1/2 cup chopped mushrooms
- 1/3 cup fat-free Italian dressing
- Parsley sprigs, as garnish

Per Serving
Calories: 99
% Calories from fat: 7
Fat (gm): 0.8
Sat. fat (gm): 0.1
Cholesterol (mg): 0
Sodium (mg): 192
Protein (gm): 3.4
Carbohydrate (gm): 21.7
Exchanges
Milk: 0.0
Vegetable: 1.5
Fruit: 0.0
Bread: 1.0
Meat: 0.0
Fat: 0.0

1. Arrange vegetables on plates. Drizzle with dressing and garnish with parsley.

ORIENTAL-STYLE WILTED SPINACH SALAD

4 servings

- 3 quarts baby spinach leaves
- 2-3 teaspoons vegetable oil
- 1 tablespoon plus 1 teaspoon lemon juice
- 1 tablespoon plus 1 teaspoon hoisin sauce
- 1-2 teaspoons sesame oil
- 1 teaspoon sugar
- 1 cup sliced mushrooms
- 1 teaspoon sesame seeds
- 8 small breadsticks

Per Serving
Calories: 95
% Calories from fat: 26
Fat (gm): 2.6
Sat. fat (gm): 0.8
Cholesterol (mg): 38.2
Sodium (mg): 418
Protein (gm): 3.4
Carbohydrate (gm): 12.6
Exchanges
Milk: 0.0
Vegetable: 1.0
Fruit: 0.0
Bread: 0.5
Meat: 0.0
Fat: 0.5

1. Place spinach in large salad bowl. Heat vegetable oil, lemon juice, hoisin sauce, and sesame oil in small skillet over medium heat, stirring constantly, until bubbly; stir in sugar. Pour warm dressing over spinach and toss until greens are slightly wilted and well coated. Add mushrooms and toss; sprinkle with sesame seeds. Serve with breadsticks.

BEANY MACARONI SALAD

8 servings (about 1 cup each)

- 1 1/2 cups cooked macaroni, cold
- 1 pound cooked chicken breast, cut into scant 1/2-inch cubes
- 2 cans (15 ounces each) light red kidney beans, rinsed, drained
- 1/2 cup sliced celery
- 1/2 cup sliced carrots
- Honey Dressing (recipe follows)
- Salt and pepper, to taste

Per Serving
Calories: 241
% Calories from fat: 9
Fat (gm): 2.3
Sat. fat (gm): 0.6
Cholesterol (mg): 43.6
Sodium (mg): 397
Protein (gm): 23.5
Carbohydrate (gm): 30.9
Exchanges
Milk: 0.0
Vegetable: 0.0
Fruit: 0.0
Bread: 2.0
Meat: 2.0
Fat: 0.0

1. Combine all ingredients, except salt and pepper, in large bowl, mixing well. Season to taste with salt and pepper.

Honey Dressing

makes about 3/4 cup

- 1/3 cup fat-free mayonnaise
- 2-3 tablespoons honey
- 2 teaspoons prepared yellow mustard

1. Whisk all ingredients in medium bowl.

CHEESY MACARONI SALAD

6 servings

- 8 ounces uncooked small elbow macaroni, cooked
- 1/2 cup frozen peas, thawed
- 1/2 cup diced celery
- 1/4 cup chopped green onions and tops
- 1 cup small curd low-fat cottage cheese
- 1/4 cup low-fat plain yogurt
- 2 tablespoons cider vinegar
- 2 tablespoons prepared mustard
- 1 teaspoon sugar

Per Serving
Calories: 219
% Calories from fat: 6
Fat (gm): 1.3
Sat. fat (gm): 0.5
Cholesterol (mg): 2.3
Sodium (mg): 234
Protein (gm): 12.6
Carbohydrate (gm): 38.5
Exchanges
Milk: 0.0
Vegetable: 0.0
Fruit: 0.0
Bread: 2.5
Meat: 0.5
Fat: 0.0

1 tablespoon lemon juice
1/4 teaspoon celery seeds
1/4 teaspoon dried oregano leaves
1/8 teaspoon pepper

1. Combine macaroni, peas, celery, and green onions in bowl. Combine remaining ingredients; spoon over macaroni and toss.

EASY PASTA SALAD

8 servings

2 green bell peppers, chopped
1 cup chopped sweet onion
1 cup quartered artichoke hearts
1 cup chopped tomatoes
1 pound rotini, *or* other small pasta, cooked al dente
1 cup plain fat-free yogurt
3 tablespoons red wine vinegar
1/2 teaspoon salt
1/4 teaspoon white pepper
1/2 teaspoon garlic powder
1 teaspoon Worcestershire sauce

Per Serving
Calories: 241
% Calories from fat: 7
Fat (gm): 1.8
Sat. fat (gm): 0.3
Cholesterol (mg): 0.5
Sodium (mg): 193
Protein (gm): 10.7
Carbohydrate (gm): 46.1
Exchanges
Milk: 0.0
Vegetable: 2.0
Fruit: 0.0
Bread: 2.5
Meat: 0.0
Fat: 0.0

1. Toss vegetables with pasta in large bowl. Combine remaining ingredients; spoon over salad and toss.

ROTINI SALAD WITH TUNA

6 servings

8 ounces rotini, cooked, cooled
2 cans (6 1/2-ounces each) water pack white tuna, drained
2 medium tomatoes, chopped
1 cup sliced mushrooms
1 jar (4 ounces) marinated artichoke hearts, drained
1/4 cup diced green bell pepper
1/4 cup sliced radishes
1/4 cup (1 ounce) shredded fat-free mozzarella cheese
1/4 cup sliced pitted black olives
1/2 cup prepared fat-free Italian salad dressing

Per Serving
Calories: 267
% Calories from fat: 16
Fat (gm): 4.6
Sat. fat (gm): 0.7
Cholesterol (mg): 25.8
Sodium (mg): 521
Protein (gm): 21.3
Carbohydrate (gm): 34.6
Exchanges
Milk: 0.0
Vegetable: 1.0
Fruit: 0.0
Bread: 2.0
Meat: 2.0
Fat: 0.0

1. Combine all ingredients in large bowl; toss well. Chill.

ITALIAN-STYLE RICE SALAD

6 servings

1 1/2 cups long-grain rice, cooked, warm
1/2 cup fat-free Italian salad dressing
3 scallions, chopped
1 tablespoon chopped parsley
1 tablespoon chopped fresh basil leaves
1/3 cup diced red, *or* green, bell pepper
1/3 cup diced celery
1/3 cup peeled, diced cucumber
2 large firm tomatoes, peeled, seeded, diced
1/4 cup chopped Italian hot marinated peppers
2 tablespoons capers
1/4 cup pitted Italian black olives, chopped

Per Serving
Calories: 273
% Calories from fat: 28
Fat (gm): 8.7
Sat. fat (gm): 1.9
Cholesterol (mg): 3.5
Sodium (mg): 335
Protein (gm): 5.2
Carbohydrate (gm): 41.8
Exchanges
Milk: 0.0
Vegetable: 1.0
Fruit: 0.0
Bread: 2.5
Meat: 0.0
Fat: 1.5

Salt and pepper, to taste
Tomato wedges, black *or* green olives, parsley, as garnish

1. Toss rice with Italian dressing and scallions. Set aside to cool.
2. Add remaining ingredients, except salt and pepper, and garnishes, mixing well. Season to taste with salt and pepper. Mound salad on serving platter and garnish with tomato wedges, olives, and parsley.

WEST COAST SALAD

4 servings

- 2 1/2 cups water
- 1/4 cup raspberry vinegar
- 1 pound boneless, skinless chicken breast
- 1 cup fresh raspberries
- 1/2 cup sliced mushrooms
- 1/2 pound fresh spinach
- Honey-Raspberry Dressing (recipe follows)
- 1 cup alfalfa sprouts

Per Serving
Calories: 171
% Calories from fat: 30
Fat (gm): 5.8
Sat. fat (gm): 1
Cholesterol (mg): 45.7
Sodium (mg): 86
Protein (gm): 19.1
Carbohydrate (gm): 11.8
Exchanges
Milk: 0.0
Vegetable: 2.0
Fruit: 0.0
Bread: 0.0
Meat: 2.0
Fat: 0.0

1. Heat 2 1/2 cups water and 1/4 cup vinegar to boiling in large, non-aluminum skillet. Add chicken; cover, reduce heat, and simmer 10 minutes or until chicken is done. Drain. Cut chicken into cubes.
2. Divide chicken, raspberries, and mushrooms evenly among 4 spinach-lined plates. Drizzle with Honey-Raspberry Dressing. Top with alfalfa sprouts.

Honey-Raspberry Dressing

makes about 1/3 cup

- 3 tablespoons raspberry flavored vinegar
- 1 tablespoon vegetable oil
- 1 1/2 teaspoons water
- 1 tablespoon honey

1. Whisk all ingredients in small bowl. Refrigerate, covered.

CONFETTI CHICKEN SALAD

4 servings

3 medium bell peppers (assorted colors), sliced
2 cups cubed cooked chicken breast
$1^1/_2$ cups whole kernel corn
1 green onion and top, sliced
2 tablespoons apple cider vinegar
2 tablespoons olive oil
1 tablespoon chopped parsley
1 clove garlic, minced
$^1/_2$ teaspoon dried oregano leaves
Salt and pepper, to taste

Per Serving
Calories: 253
% Calories from fat: 34
Fat (gm): 9.7
Sat. fat (gm): 1.9
Cholesterol (mg): 59.5
Sodium (mg): 58
Protein (gm): 24.4
Carbohydrate (gm): 18.9
Exchanges
Milk: 0.0
Vegetable: 1.0
Fruit: 0.0
Bread: 1.0
Meat: 3.0
Fat: 0.0

1. Combine peppers, chicken, corn, and green onion in large bowl. Combine remaining ingredients, except salt and pepper. Pour over chicken mixture and toss; season to taste with salt and pepper.

CREOLE CHICKEN SALAD

4 servings

2 small heads Boston lettuce, torn into pieces
6 plum tomatoes, sliced
2 small onions, sliced
4 teaspoons cayenne pepper
1 tablespoon paprika
2 teaspoons ground black pepper
1 teaspoon chili powder
1 teaspoon garlic powder
1 pound boneless, skinless chicken breast
Louisiana Dressing (recipe follows)
Salt, to taste

Per Serving
Calories: 242
% Calories from fat: 27
Fat (gm): 7.8
Sat. fat (gm): 1.4
Cholesterol (mg): 45.7
Sodium (mg): 271
Protein (gm): 21.5
Carbohydrate (gm): 24
Exchanges
Milk: 0.0
Vegetable: 2.0
Fruit: 0.0
Bread: 1.0
Meat: 2.0
Fat: 0.0

1. Toss lettuce, tomatoes, and onions in large bowl and set aside. Combine spices in small bowl, mixing well. Season both sides of chicken breasts well with spice mixture.

2. Broil or grill chicken 5 to 6 minutes per side until cooked through; cool. Cut into 1-inch pieces and add to vegetables. Pour Louisiana Dressing over all and toss well; season to taste with salt.

Louisiana Dressing

makes about 1/2 cup

- 1/4 cup fat-free mayonnaise
- 2-4 tablespoons Dijon-style mustard
- 2 tablespoons dry white wine
- 1-2 tablespoons honey
- 1 1/2 teaspoons sugar

1. Mix all ingredients in small bowl. Refrigerate, covered.

GREEK SMOKED CHICKEN SALAD

4 servings

- 2 slices turkey bacon, cut into 1/2-inch pieces
- 6 tablespoons Dijon mustard
- 2 tablespoons red wine vinegar
- 2 tablespoons water
- 1-2 ounces fat-free feta cheese, crumbled
- 10 ounces fresh spinach leaves
- 1 bunch bok choy, stems trimmed, leaves sliced
- 6 ounces smoked boneless, skinless chicken breast, cut into thin strips

Per Serving
Calories: 102
% Calories from fat: 24
Fat (gm): 2.3
Sat. fat (gm): 0.3
Cholesterol (mg): 23.7
Sodium (mg): 1270
Protein (gm): 13
Carbohydrate (gm): 3.3
Exchanges
Milk: 0.0
Vegetable: 0.0
Fruit: 0.0
Bread: 0.0
Meat: 2.0
Fat: 0.0

1. Cook bacon in large skillet until crisp; add mustard and vinegar to skillet, and whisk over very low heat until smooth. Whisk in water. Add feta, stirring until heated through, but do not boil.

2. Combine spinach, bok choy, and chicken in large bowl. Pour dressing over greens and chicken, tossing until well mixed.

ORIENTAL CHICKEN SALAD

6 servings

- 3 cups torn lettuce leaves
- 1 1/2 cups chopped cooked chicken breast
- 1 can (8 ounces) sliced water chestnuts, drained
- 1/4 cup diagonally sliced green onions and tops
- 1 package (10 ounces) snow peas, thawed
- 1 cup thinly sliced red cabbage
- Oriental Dressing (recipe follows)
- Chow mein noodles, as garnish

Per Serving
Calories: 146
% Calories from fat: 30
Fat (gm): 4.9
Sat. fat (gm): 1
Cholesterol (mg): 29
Sodium (mg): 620
Protein (gm): 12.7
Carbohydrate (gm): 13.5

Exchanges
Milk: 0.0
Vegetable: 3.0
Fruit: 0.0
Bread: 0.0
Meat: 1.5
Fat: 0.0

1. Combine all ingredients except chow mein noodles in bowl; toss with Oriental Dressing and sprinkle with chow mein noodles.

Oriental Dressing

makes about 1/3 cup

- 3 1/2 tablespoons tamari soy sauce
- 1 tablespoon vegetable oil
- 2 tablespoons balsamic vinegar
- 1 tablespoon sugar
- 1 clove garlic, minced
- 2 tablespoons chopped fresh chives

1. Whisk all ingredients in small bowl. Refrigerate, covered.

CHICKEN WITH SPINACH AND BEAN SALAD

4 servings

- Vegetable cooking spray
- 2 cloves garlic, minced
- 2 tablespoons pine nuts
- 10 ounces fresh baby spinach
- 2 tablespoons water
- Pepper, to taste
- 4 boneless, skinless chicken breast halves (5 ounces each), pounded to flatten
- Bean Salad (recipe follows)

Per Serving
Calories: 298
% Calories from fat: 17
Fat (gm): 5.8
Sat. fat (gm): 0.8
Cholesterol (mg): 57.2
Sodium (mg): 127
Protein (gm): 32.6
Carbohydrate (gm): 29.3

Exchanges
Milk: 0.0
Vegetable: 1.0
Fruit: 0.0
Bread: 1.5
Meat: 2.8
Fat: 0.0

1. Spray large skillet with cooking spray; heat over medium heat until hot. Saute garlic and pine nuts 1-2 minutes. Add spinach and water; cook, covered, until wilted, about 4 minutes. Drain excess water. Season with pepper.

2. Broil chicken breasts 6 inches from heat source, turning once, until they are cooked through, 3 to 4 minutes on each side.

3. Spoon spinach mixture on serving plates and top with chicken; spoon Bean Salad to the side.

Bean Salad

makes about 2 cups

- 3 tablespoons white wine
- 1 teaspoon balsamic vinegar
- 1/2 teaspoon dried oregano leaves
- 1/2 teaspoon dried tarragon leaves
- 1 can (15 ounces) Great Northern beans, rinsed, drained
- 1/2 cup chopped celery
- 1/2 cup chopped tomato
- 1/4 cup chopped red onion
- Salt and pepper, to taste

1. Whisk wine, vinegar, oregano, and tarragon until blended; pour over combined beans, celery, tomato, and red onion. Season to taste with salt and pepper.

CHICKEN AND RASPBERRY SALAD

8 servings

- 2 large pears, peeled, cored, julienned
- 2 tablespoons lime juice
- 3 cups radicchio, *or* other lettuce, washed, dried, and torn into bite-size pieces
- 1 small red onion, sliced paper-thin and separated into rings
- $2^1/_2$ cups julienned cooked chicken breast
- Raspberry Dressing (recipe follows)
- 1 cup fresh raspberries

Per Serving
Calories: 134
% Calories from fat: 27
Fat (gm): 4.1
Sat. fat (gm): 0.8
Cholesterol (mg): 36.9
Sodium (mg): 130
Protein (gm): 14.4
Carbohydrate (gm): 10.4

Exchanges
Milk: 0.0
Vegetable: 0.0
Fruit: 0.5
Bread: 0.0
Meat: 2.0
Fat: 0.0

1. Toss pears with lime juice in large serving bowl. Add radicchio, onion rings, chicken and Raspberry Dressing; toss well to combine. Sprinkle with fresh raspberries.

Raspberry Dressing

makes about $^1/_3$ cup

- $^1/_4$ cup raspberry vinegar
- 1 tablespoon olive oil
- 1 tablespoon honey mustard
- $^1/_4$ teaspoon salt
- $^1/_4$ teaspoon black pepper

1. Whisk all ingredients in small bowl.

CHICKEN AND WILD RICE SALAD

6 servings

$1^1/_4$ cups wild rice, cooked
$^1/_2$ tablespoon white wine vinegar
1 tablespoon olive oil
2 whole smoked boneless, skinless chicken breasts, cut into 1-inch cubes
$^1/_2$ cup sliced green onions and tops
$^1/_4$ cup golden raisins
Curried Chutney Dressing (recipe follows)
Salt and pepper, to taste
Lettuce leaves

Per Serving
Calories: 290
% Calories from fat: 26
Fat (gm): 8.5
Sat. fat (gm): 1.3
Cholesterol (mg): 30
Sodium (mg): 751
Protein (gm): 17.9
Carbohydrate (gm): 36.2
Exchanges
Milk: 0.0
Vegetable: 0.0
Fruit: 1.0
Bread: 1.5
Meat: 2.0
Fat: 0.5

1. Toss rice with vinegar and oil; add chicken, green onions, raisins, and Curried Chutney Dressing and toss well. Season to taste with salt and pepper. Serve on lettuce leaves.

Curried Chutney Dressing

makes about 1 cup

1 clove garlic, minced
1 tablespoon white wine vinegar
2 tablespoons lemon juice
2 teaspoons curry powder
$1^1/_2$ tablespoons mango chutney
2 tablespoons olive oil
$^1/_4$ cup fat-free sour cream
1-2 tablespoons water
$^1/_4$ cup chopped cilantro

1. Process all ingredients, except cilanto, in food processor or blender until smooth. Stir in cilanto.

CURRIED RICE, CHICKEN, AND FRUIT SALAD

7 servings

- 1 pound boneless, skinless chicken breasts, cooked; shredded *or* cubed
- 1 can (15 1/4-ounce) pineapple tidbits in juice, drained
- 2 1/4 cups cooked rice
- 1 large red, *or* green, bell pepper, cubed
- 1 1/2 cups green seedless grapes
- 2 tablespoons sliced green onions and tops
- Curry Dressing (recipe follows)

Per Serving
Calories: 210
% Calories from fat: 17
Fat (gm): 3.9
Sat. fat (gm): 0.7
Cholesterol (mg): 30
Sodium (mg): 62
Protein (gm): 12.9
Carbohydrate (gm): 31.3

Exchanges
Milk: 0.0
Vegetable: 0.0
Fruit: 1.0
Bread: 1.0
Meat: 1.5
Fat: 0.0

1. Combine all ingredients in large bowl. Toss to coat well. Cover and refrigerate several hours, stirring occasionally.

Curry Dressing

makes about 3/4 cup

- 1/2 cup reduced-fat mayonnaise
- 1/4 cup fat-free buttermilk
- 2 teaspoons mild curry powder, or to taste
- 1/2 teaspoon salt
- 1/4 teaspoon white pepper

1. Place mayonnaise in medium bowl; gradually whisk in buttermilk. Whisk in remaining ingredients.

BROWN RICE AND CHICKEN SALAD WITH TARRAGON DRESSING

8 servings

2 cups brown rice, cooked
4 cups diced cooked chicken breast
12 scallions, thinly sliced
2 ribs celery, chopped
2 medium green bell peppers, chopped
1/4 cup chopped pimiento
1/2 pint cherry tomatoes, halved
1/2 cup chopped parsley
1/2 cup sliced radishes
Tarragon Dressing (recipe follows)
Salt and pepper, to taste

Per Serving
Calories: 252
% Calories from fat: 30
Fat (gm): 8.3
Sat. fat (gm): 1.5
Cholesterol (mg): 59.5
Sodium (mg): 132
Protein (gm): 24.6
Carbohydrate (gm): 18.9

Exchanges
Milk: 0.0
Vegetable: 1.0
Fruit: 0.0
Bread: 1.0
Meat: 3.0
Fat: 0.0

1. Toss rice and remaining ingredients, except Tarragon Dressing and salt and pepper in large bowl; toss with Tarragon Dressing and season to taste with salt and pepper.

Tarragon Dressing

makes about 1/2 cup

3 tablespoons olive oil
1/4 cup white wine vinegar
1 tablespoon fresh, *or* 1 1/2 teaspoons dried, tarragon leaves

1. Mix all ingredients.

SMOKED TURKEY POTATO SALAD

8 servings

- 2 1/2 cups unpeeled red, *or* new, potatoes, cooked, sliced
- 1 tablespoon margarine
- 1 1/2 cups smoked skinless white turkey meat, cubed *or* shredded
- 1 cup chopped celery
- 1/4 cup chopped onion
- 1/2 cup chopped parsley
- 3 hard-cooked egg whites, chopped
- 1/2 teaspoon dried basil leaves
- 1/2 teaspoon paprika
- 1/4 teaspoon salt
- 1/4 teaspoon pepper
- 1/4 cup fat-free mayonnaise
- 1/4 cup plain fat-free yogurt

Per Serving
Calories: 144
% Calories from fat: 16
Fat (gm): 2.6
Sat. fat (gm): 0.6
Cholesterol (mg): 17.8
Sodium (mg): 193
Protein (gm): 10.2
Carbohydrate (gm): 20.6

Exchanges
Milk: 0.0
Vegetable: 1.0
Fruit: 0.0
Bread: 1.0
Meat: 1.0
Fat: 0.0

1. Fry potatoes in margarine in large skillet, stirring as they brown, 3 to 5 minutes. Potatoes will break up into pieces. Toss potatoes with remaining ingredients, except mayonnaise and yogurt in bowl. Spoon combined mayonnaise and yogurt over salad and toss.

THAI PORK SALAD

6 servings

- 12 ounces pork tenderloin, fat trimmed, cut into thin strips
- 1 1/2 tablespoons reduced-sodium soy sauce
- 2 teaspoons apple cider vinegar
- 1/4 teaspoon pepper
- Vegetable cooking spray
- Thai Dressing (recipe follows)
- 3 cups sliced lettuce, *or* Asian lettuce blend

Per Serving
Calories: 263
% Calories from fat: 30
Fat (gm): 8.8
Sat. fat (gm): 2
Cholesterol (mg): 25.5
Sodium (mg): 300
Protein (gm): 13.8
Carbohydrate (gm): 31.2

Exchanges
Milk: 0.0
Vegetable: 0.5
Fruit: 0.0
Bread: 1.5
Meat: 2.0
Fat: 0.5

- 1 can (15 ounces) black beans, rinsed, drained
- 1 large tomato, diced
- 1 large cucumber, peeled, seeded, sliced
- 1 large red bell pepper, diced
- 3/4 cup chopped cilantro
- 2 tablespoons sliced green onion tops
- 3 1/2 ounces rice sticks, *or* angel hair pasta, cooked

1. Toss pork in small bowl with soy sauce, vinegar, and black pepper; let stand 15 minutes. Spray large skillet with cooking spray; heat over medium-high heat until hot. Stir-fry pork until cooked through, about 5 minutes. Transfer pork and pan juices to large bowl; stir in Thai Dressing.

2. Add remaining ingredients and toss to mix well. Refrigerate 1 or 2 hours, stirring occasionally, or up to 6 hours before serving.

Thai Dressing

makes about 1/2 cup

- 1 1/2 tablespoons reduced-sodium soy sauce
- 3 tablespoons dry sherry
- 2 tablespoons chicken broth
- 1 teaspoon apple cider vinegar
- 2 tablespoons sesame oil
- 2 teaspoons granulated sugar
- 3/4 teaspoon ground ginger
- 2-3 drops hot chili oil, *or* hot pepper sauce

1. Whisk all ingredients in small bowl.

SALADE NIÇOISE

10 servings

Per Serving
Calories: 423
% Calories from fat: 34
Fat (gm): 17.2
Sat. fat (gm): 2.3
Cholesterol (mg): 17.9
Sodium (mg): 184
Protein (gm): 30.6
Carbohydrate (gm): 43.7

Exchanges
Milk: 0.0
Vegetable: 2.0
Fruit: 0.0
Bread: 2.0
Meat: 4.0
Fat: 1.0

2 pounds green beans, cut in 1 1/2-inch lengths, cooked crisp-tender
2 green bell peppers, cut into thin rounds
2 cups sliced celery
1 pint cherry tomatoes
5 medium red potatoes, unpeeled, cooked, sliced
3 cans (6 1/2 ounces each) water pack tuna, drained
10 large pitted black olives
1 small red onion, thinly sliced
1/4 cup chopped scallions
2 tablespoons chopped fresh basil, *or* 1 tablespoon dried basil leaves
1/3 cup chopped parsley
Niçoise Dressing (recipe follows)

1. Arrange beans, green peppers, celery, tomatoes, potatoes, tuna, olives, and onion on serving platter in attractive pattern. Sprinkle with basil, parsley, and scallions. Drizzle with Nicoise Dressing.

Niçoise Dressing

makes about 1/2 cup

2 teaspoons Dijon-style mustard
2 tablespoons wine vinegar
6 tablespoons olive oil
2 cloves garlic, minced
1 teaspoon chopped fresh , *or* 1/2 teaspoon dried, thyme leaves
1/2 teaspoon pepper

1. Shake all dressing ingredients in tightly covered jar, or whisk in small bowl.

CALIFORNIA CRAB SALAD

4 servings

Per Serving
Calories: 147
% Calories from fat: 14
Fat (gm): 2.7
Sat. fat (gm): 0.5
Cholesterol (mg): 59.2
Sodium (mg): 412
Protein (gm): 18.6
Carbohydrate (gm): 13.6

Exchanges
Milk: 0.0
Vegetable: 1.5
Fruit: 0.0
Bread: 0.0
Meat: 2.0
Fat: 0.0

- 8 ounces crabmeat, flaked
- 4 stalks cooked asparagus, sliced
- 1/2 cup sliced water chestnuts
- 1/2 cup thinly sliced celery
- 1/4 cup sliced green onions and tops
- California Dressing (recipe follows)
- 4 large Boston lettuce leaves
- 4 artichoke bottoms, canned *or* fresh, cooked
- 2 tablespoons chopped pimiento
- 2 tablespoons chopped parsley
- 1 cup fresh bean sprouts

1. Combine crabmeat, asparagus, water chestnuts, celery, and green onions in medium bowl; pour California Dressing over and toss. Place lettuce leaves on salad plates; top with artichoke bottoms and fill with scoops of crab salad. Sprinkle with pimiento and parsley. Top with bean sprouts.

California Dressing

makes about 2/3 cup

- 1/2 cup cottage cheese
- 2 tablespoons prepared horseradish
- 1 tablespoon reduced-fat mayonnaise
- 1 tablespoon lemon juice
- 1 teaspoon Worcestershire sauce
- 1/2 teaspoon dry mustard
- 1 tablespoon sugar
- 2 tablespoons minced parsley

1. Process all ingredients, except parsley, in blender or food processor until smooth. Mix in parsley.

CRAB SALAD LOUIS

4 servings

- 1/4 cup chopped green bell pepper
- 1/4 cup chopped green onions
- 2 tablespoons chopped green olives
- Juice of 1/2 lemon
- 2 cups imitation crabmeat chunks
- 1/3 cup fat-free mayonnaise
- 2/3 cup low-fat plain yogurt
- 2 tablespoons fat-free milk
- 1/4 cup low-sodium chili sauce
- Lettuce leaves
- 1/4 cup minced chives

Per Serving
Calories: 124
% Calories from fat: 14
Fat (gm): 2
Sat. fat (gm): 0.6
Cholesterol (mg): 13.9
Sodium (mg): 887
Protein (gm): 9.8
Carbohydrate (gm): 17.4
Exchanges
Milk: 0.0
Vegetable: 0.0
Fruit: 0.0
Bread: 1.0
Meat: 1.0
Fat: 0.0

1. Combine bell pepper, green onions, olives, lemon juice, and crabmeat. Whisk mayonnaise, yogurt, milk, and chili sauce in medium bowl until smooth; spoon over crabmeat mixture and toss. Spoon salad into lettuce-lined salad bowls and sprinkle with chives.

ISLAND FISH SALAD WITH AVOCADO DRESSING

6 servings

- 1 1/4 pounds mahi mahi, *or* monkfish, fillets
- 1 tablespoon grated orange rind
- Vegetable cooking spray
- Avocado Dressing (recipe follows)
- 4 cups assorted lettuce (Boston, head, romaine, *or* oak leaf), torn into bite-size pieces
- 1 large tomato, sliced thin
- 1 orange, sliced thin
- 1/2 cup thinly sliced red onions

Per Serving
Calories: 143
% Calories from fat: 14
Fat (gm): 2.2
Sat. fat (gm): 0.4
Cholesterol (mg): 69.2
Sodium (mg): 314
Protein (gm): 19.5
Carbohydrate (gm): 11.4
Exchanges
Milk: 0.0
Vegetable: 2.0
Fruit: 0.0
Bread: 0.0
Meat: 2.0
Fat: 0.0

1. Sprinkle fish with orange rind. Spray large skillet with cooking spray; heat over medium heat until hot. Cook fish until it flakes with a fork, 6 to 8 minutes, turning once; cool. Refrigerate, covered, until well chilled.

2. Cut fish into thin slices or chunks and toss with Avocado Dressing.

3. Spoon fish onto lettuce-lined plates. Arrange tomato and orange slices around salad and sprinkle with onion.

Avocado Dressing

makes about 3/4 cup

- 1/4 medium avocado, peeled, pitted
- 1/4 cup fat-free plain yogurt
- 2 teaspoons red wine vinegar
- 1/4 teaspoon hot pepper sauce
- 1/4 teaspoon salt
- 1/4 teaspoon dried tarragon leaves
- 1/4 cup fat-free mayonnaise

1. Mash avocado; mix in yogurt, vinegar, hot pepper sauce, salt, and tarragon. Add mayonnaise and blend well.

FOUR

Fish

AND

Seafood

POACHED COD WITH ASPARAGUS

4 servings

- 1 pound fresh asparagus, ends trimmed
- 2 cloves garlic, chopped
- 1 tablespoon chopped parsley
- 2 tablespoons olive oil
- Salt and pepper, to taste
- 1½ pounds cod, cut into 4 pieces
- 1 tablespoon lemon juice
- 1 tablespoon chopped fresh, *or* 1 teaspoon dried, basil leaves

Per Serving
Calories: 216
% Calories from fat: 34
Fat (gm): 8
Sat. fat (gm): 1.2
Cholesterol (mg): 72.9
Sodium (mg): 75
Protein (gm): 31.8
Carbohydrate (gm): 3.6
Exchanges
Milk: 0.0
Vegetable: 1.0
Fruit: 0.0
Bread: 0.0
Meat: 3.0
Fat: 0.0

1. Simmer asparagus in water in large skillet, uncovered, 5 to 8 minutes until almost tender. Drain asparagus, reserving 1 cup cooking water; keep warm.

2. Saute garlic and parsley in oil in large skillet 2 minutes. Sprinkle fish lightly with salt and pepper and add to skillet. Add reserved asparagus cooking water, lemon juice and basil. Heat to boiling; reduce heat and simmer, covered, until cod is tender and flakes with a fork, 8 to 10 minutes. Arrange fish and asparagus on platter.

BAKED COD PROVENÇAL

4 servings

- Vegetable cooking spray
- 1 medium onion, chopped
- 2 cloves garlic, chopped
- 1½ pounds tomatoes, seeded, chopped
- 1 tablespoon drained capers
- ¼ cup chopped fresh, *or* 1 tablespoon dried, basil leaves
- 4 pitted black olives, sliced
- 1 tablespoon lemon juice
- 1 teaspoon dried oregano leaves
- Salt and pepper, to taste
- 4 cod fillets (about 1¼ pounds)

Per Serving
Calories: 169
% Calories from fat: 12
Fat (gm): 2.2
Sat. fat (gm): 0.3
Cholesterol (mg): 56.2
Sodium (mg): 157
Protein (gm): 25.5
Carbohydrate (gm): 13.2
Exchanges
Milk: 0.0
Vegetable: 1.0
Fruit: 0.0
Bread: 0.0
Meat: 3.0
Fat: 0.0

1. Spray large skillet with cooking spray; heat over medium heat until hot. Saute onion and garlic 3 to 5 minutes or until onions are translucent. Add tomatoes, capers, basil, olives, lemon juice, and oregano; heat to boiling. Reduce heat and simmer until thickened, 8 to 10 minutes, stirring occasionally. Season to taste with salt and pepper.

2. Sprinkle fish lightly with salt and pepper; arrange in lightly greased baking dish. Bake at 450 degrees until fish is tender and flakes with a fork, about 10 minutes. Spoon tomato sauce over fish.

FLOUNDER WITH MIXED HERB PESTO

4 servings

- 4 sole, *or* flounder, fillets (about 5 ounces each)
- 1/4 cup Mixed Herb Pesto (see p. 515)
- 2 tablespoons lemon juice
- 2 tablespoons chopped shallots
- 1 clove garlic, minced
- 1/2 teaspoon pepper
- 3 cups cooked rice

Per Serving
Calories: 354
% Calories from fat: 21
Fat (gm): 8.1
Sat. fat (gm): 1.4
Cholesterol (mg): 68.8
Sodium (mg): 288
Protein (gm): 31.5
Carbohydrate (gm): 36.9

Exchanges
Milk: 0.0
Vegetable: 0.0
Fruit: 0.0
Bread: 2.0
Meat: 4.0
Fat: 0.0

1. Place each fillet on a 9 x 9-inch piece of heavy foil or parchment paper. Fold each fillet in half; spread Mixed Herb Pesto evenly on each fillet. Combine lemon juice, shallots, garlic, and pepper in small bowl; spoon evenly over fish.

2. Seal each square of foil or paper by folding edges together. Place on baking pan sheet. Bake at 400 degrees until packets puff slightly, about 15 minutes. Serve fish with rice.

CAJUN-STYLE FISH

4 servings

1 cup chopped onion
1 clove garlic, minced
2 teaspoons margarine
1 can (15 1/2 ounces) diced tomatoes, undrained
1 large green bell pepper, chopped
2 cups cubed zucchini *and/or* yellow squash
1/2 teaspoon dried basil leaves
1/2 teaspoon dried thyme leaves
1/4 teaspoon dried marjoram leaves
2-3 drops hot pepper sauce
Salt and pepper, to taste
Vegetable cooking spray
1 pound skinless fish fillets (flounder, sole, halibut, turbot, *or* other lean white fish)
3 cups cooked rice, warm

Per Serving
Calories: 221
% Calories from fat: 10
Fat (gm): 2.6
Sat. fat (gm): 0.4
Cholesterol (mg): 35.5
Sodium (mg): 193
Protein (gm): 16.5
Carbohydrate (gm): 32.7

Exchanges
Milk: 0.0
Vegetable: 2.0
Fruit: 0.0
Bread: 1.0
Meat: 2.0
Fat: 0.0

1. Saute onion and garlic in margarine in large skillet until almost tender, about 5 minutes. Add tomatoes, green pepper, squash, and herbs. Heat to boiling; reduce heat and cook, covered, about 10 minutes or until vegetables are tender. Season to taste with hot pepper sauce, salt, and pepper.

2. While vegetables are cooking, cook fish. Spray large skillet with cooking spray; heat over medium heat until hot. Add fish and cook over medium heat until fish is tender and flakes with a fork, about 4 minutes on each side. Season to taste with salt and pepper.

3. Spoon rice onto large serving platter; top with vegetables and fish.

BAKED FLOUNDER WITH ORANGE SAUCE

6 servings

Butter-flavored vegetable cooking spray
1 medium onion, minced
1 clove garlic, minced
1 large orange, peeled, seeded, chopped
1/2 cup seasoned dry bread crumbs
6 flounder fillets (5 ounces each)
Orange Sauce (recipe follows)

Per Serving
Calories: 208
% Calories from fat: 9
Fat (gm): 2
Sat. fat (gm): 0.5
Cholesterol (mg): 66.5
Sodium (mg): 369
Protein (gm): 26
Carbohydrate (gm): 20.3
Exchanges
Milk: 0.0
Vegetable: 0.0
Fruit: 1.0
Bread: 0.0
Meat: 3.0
Fat: 0.0

1. Spray large skillet with cooking spray; heat over medium heat until hot. Saute onion and garlic until tender, about 5 minutes. Remove from heat; stir in orange and bread crumbs. Spoon crumb mixture on to thick end of each fillet. Roll up fillets; place rolls, seam sides down, in greased baking dish. Bake at 400 degrees until fish is tender and flakes with a fork, 10 to 12 minutes. Serve with Orange Sauce.

Orange Sauce

makes about 1 1/2 cups

1 1/2 cups fresh orange juice
1 1/2 tablespoons grated orange rind
1 teaspoon sugar
1/4 teaspoon ground ginger
1/4 teaspoon dry mustard
1 1/2 tablespoons cornstarch

1. Whisk all ingredients in small saucepan; heat to boiling over medium heat, whisking constantly until sauce thickens, about 2 minutes.

FINNAN HADDIE

6 servings

- 1½ pounds finnan haddie (smoked haddock)
- 2 cups fat-free milk
- 1 medium onion, thinly sliced
- 2 cups sliced mushrooms
- 1 teaspoon margarine
- 1 teaspoon stone-ground mustard
- 3 hard-boiled egg whites, chopped
- 2 tablespoons chopped chives

Per Serving
Calories: 192
% Calories from fat: 10
Fat (gm): 2.1
Sat. fat (gm): 0.4
Cholesterol (mg): 88.1
Sodium (mg): 956
Protein (gm): 34
Carbohydrate (gm): 7.7

Exchanges
Milk: 0.0
Vegetable: 1.0
Fruit: 0.0
Bread: 0.0
Meat: 4.0
Fat: 0.0

1. Cover fish with water in bowl and let stand 1 hour; drain and cut into quarters. Heat finnan haddie and milk to boiling in medium saucepan; reduce heat and simmer 15 to 20 minutes, covered. Drain and flake fish with fork. Discard milk.

2. Saute onion and mushrooms in medium skillet until tender, about 5 minutes; stir in mustard and flaked fish. Spoon fish onto individual dishes; sprinkle with egg whites and chives.

SWEET-SOUR GROUPER

4 servings

- Olive oil cooking spray
- 4 large grouper filets (about 6 ounces each)
- 1 cup sliced onions
- ⅓ cup red wine vinegar
- 1½ teaspoons sugar
- 1 tablespoon chopped parsley
- 1 teaspoon dried basil leaves
- ½ teaspoon dried mint leaves
- ¼ teaspoon white pepper

Per Serving
Calories: 156
% Calories from fat: 9
Fat (gm): 1.5
Sat. fat (gm): 0.3
Cholesterol (mg): 52
Sodium (mg): 60
Protein (gm): 28
Carbohydrate (gm): 6.4

Exchanges
Milk: 0.0
Vegetable: 1.0
Fruit: 0.0
Bread: 0.0
Meat: 2.5
Fat: 0.0

1. Spray large skillet with cooking spray; heat over medium heat until hot. Add grouper and saute until fish is tender and flakes with a fork, about 10 minutes, turning once.

2. While fish is cooking, saute onions in skillet coated with cooking spray until tender, 4 to 5 minutes. Stir in vinegar, sugar, parsley, basil, mint, and pepper. Simmer, covered, 4 to 5 minutes. Serve onion mixture over fish.

MICROWAVE LEMON HALIBUT

4 servings

- $1\frac{1}{4}$ pounds halibut, *or* haddock, fillets, cut into 4 pieces
- Juice of 2 lemons
- Dill weed, to taste
- Paprika, to taste
- Pepper, to taste
- Parsley sprigs, as garnish

Per Serving
Calories: 160
% Calories from fat: 19
Fat (gm): 3.2
Sat. fat (gm): 0.5
Cholesterol (mg): 45.5
Sodium (mg): 77
Protein (gm): 29.6
Carbohydrate (gm): 2
Exchanges
Milk: 0.0
Vegetable: 0.0
Fruit: 0.0
Bread: 0.0
Meat: 3.0
Fat: 0.0

1. Place fish in lightly greased glass baking dish. Drizzle lemon juice over fish; sprinkle lightly with dill weed, paprika, and pepper. Cover with vented plastic wrap, and microwave on High for 4 minutes, or until fish flakes easily with fork. Garnish with parsley sprigs.

CURRIED PINEAPPLE FLOUNDER

4 servings

- 1 pound flounder, *or* other white fish, fillets *or* steaks
- 2 tablespoons margarine
- $1\frac{1}{4}$ cups pineapple juice, divided
- 2 tablespoons minced onion
- 1 tablespoon diced pimiento
- 1 teaspoon salt
- 1 teaspoon parsley flakes
- $\frac{1}{2}$ teaspoon curry powder
- 2 tablespoons fresh lemon juice
- 1 tablespoon cornstarch

Per Serving
Calories: 376
% Calories from fat: 18
Fat (gm): 7.5
Sat. fat (gm): 1.5
Cholesterol (mg): 54.4
Sodium (mg): 749
Protein (gm): 25
Carbohydrate (gm): 50.4
Exchanges
Milk: 0.0
Vegetable: 0.0
Fruit: 0.0
Bread: 3.0
Meat: 3.0
Fat: 0.0

1-2 tablespoons sugar
3 cups cooked rice

1. Place fish in baking pan; dot with margarine. Bake at 400 degrees until fish is tender and flakes with a fork, about 10 minutes.

2. While fish is baking, combine 1 cup pineapple juice and remaining ingredients, except cornstarch, sugar and rice in small saucepan; heat to boiling. Stir in combined cornstarch and remaining 1/4 cup pineapple juice; boil, stirring, until thickened, 1 to 2 minutes. Season to taste with sugar.

3. Arrange fish over rice on serving platter; spoon pineapple sauce over.

BOUILLABAISSE

10 servings

1 cup chopped onion
1/2 cup chopped celery
1 clove garlic, minced
2 tablespoons olive oil
1 1/2 cups clam juice, *or* reduced-fat chicken broth
1/2 cup dry white wine, clam juice, *or* reduced-fat chicken broth
2 cans (15 ounces each) small diced tomatoes, undrained
3 leeks (white parts only), julienned
1 bay leaf
1 teaspoon dried thyme leaves
1 teaspoon grated orange rind
2 pounds halibut, *or* other white fish steaks, boned, skinned, cubed
1/2 pound crabmeat, flaked into large pieces
1/2 pound bay scallops
12 mussels, scrubbed
1/4 cup chopped parsley

Per Serving
Calories: 244
% Calories from fat: 25
Fat (gm): 6.7
Sat. fat (gm): 0.9
Cholesterol (mg): 68.2
Sodium (mg): 704
Protein (gm): 33.9
Carbohydrate (gm): 11.7

Exchanges
Milk: 0.0
Vegetable: 2.0
Fruit: 0.0
Bread: 0.0
Meat: 5.0
Fat: 0.0

1. Saute onion, celery, and garlic in olive oil in Dutch oven until tender, about 7 minutes. Add clam juice and wine. Stir in tomatoes, leeks, herbs, and orange rind; heat to boiling. Reduce heat to low and simmer, covered, 10 minutes. Stir in halibut, crab, scallops, and mussels; simmer, covered, until fish is tender and flakes with a fork, 5 to 8 minutes. Discard any mussels that did not open. Discard bay leaf; stir in parsley.

SAVORY FISH AND VEGETABLE STEW

6 servings

- 1 large red onion, sliced
- 4-6 cloves garlic, chopped
- 2 tablespoons olive oil
- 1 pound small red potatoes, cut into 1/2-inch slices
- 2 large carrots, cut into 1-inch pieces
- 1-2 ribs celery, cut into 1/2-inch pieces
- 1 teaspoon dried basil leaves
- Pepper, to taste
- 1 tablespoon flour
- 2 pounds fresh fish fillets, cut into 2-inch pieces
- 3-4 tablespoons lemon juice
- Salt, to taste

Per Serving
Calories: 348
% Calories from fat: 18
Fat (gm): 6.8
Sat. fat (gm): 1.1
Cholesterol (mg): 88.7
Sodium (mg): 160
Protein (gm): 34.8
Carbohydrate (gm): 36.6
Exchanges
Milk: 0.0
Vegetable: 1.0
Fruit: 0.0
Bread: 1.5
Meat: 4.0
Fat: 0.0

1. Saute onion and garlic in oil in large saucepan 3 to 4 minutes. Add potatoes, carrots, celery, basil, and pepper; saute 5 minutes. Stir in flour and cook 1 minute longer. Add water to almost cover vegetables; heat to boiling. Reduce heat and simmer, covered, until vegetables are crisp-tender, about 8 minutes.

2. Add fish and simmer, covered, until fish is tender and flakes with a fork, about 5 minutes. Season to taste with lemon juice and salt.

MONKFISH WITH SPINACH AND MUSHROOMS

4 servings

- 1 1/2 pounds monkfish, cut into large chunks
- Flour
- 1 tablespoon minced shallots
- 1 large yellow bell pepper, cut into thin strips
- 1 large red bell pepper, cut into thin strips
- 1/2 cup sliced mushrooms
- 1 tablespoon margarine
- 1/2 pound fresh spinach, torn into pieces
- Juice of 2 lemons
- Salt and pepper, to taste

Per Serving
Calories: 188
% Calories from fat: 27
Fat (gm): 5.8
Sat. fat (gm): 0.6
Cholesterol (mg): 43.1
Sodium (mg): 111
Protein (gm): 27.5
Carbohydrate (gm): 7.2

Exchanges
Milk: 0.0
Vegetable: 1.0
Fruit: 0.0
Bread: 0.0
Meat: 3.5
Fat: 0.0

1. Coat monkfish lightly with flour. Saute shallots, bell peppers, and mushrooms in margarine in large skillet until tender, about 5 minutes. Move vegetables to sides of skillet; add monkfish and cook over medium heat until fish is tender and flakes with a fork, turning pieces occasionally, about 8 minutes. Add spinach and lemon juice; cook, covered, just until spinach wilts, about 2 minutes. Season to taste with salt and pepper.

ORANGE ROUGHY IN PARCHMENT

6 servings

- Cooking parchment, *or* aluminum foil
- 1 1/2 pounds orange roughy fillets, cut into 6 serving pieces
- 6 red bell pepper rings
- 6 large mushrooms, thinly sliced
- 3 tablespoons chopped parsley
- 1/4 teaspoon ground nutmeg
- 1 teaspoon dried tarragon leaves
- 1/2 teaspoon salt

Per Serving
Calories: 85
% Calories from fat: 10
Fat (gm): 0.9
Sat. fat (gm): 0.1
Cholesterol (mg): 22.6
Sodium (mg): 263
Protein (gm): 17
Carbohydrate (gm): 1.4

Exchanges
Milk: 0.0
Vegetable: 0.0
Fruit: 0.0
Bread: 0.0
Meat: 2.0
Fat: 0.0

1. Cut 6 pieces of cooking parchment about 18 x 12-inches. Fold each sheet in half and round off unfolded edges to form half circles. Unfold each sheet. Place fillets in center of each sheet and top with red pepper rings and mushrooms; sprinkle with parsley, nutmeg, tarragon, and salt.

2. Fold paper over fish and roll edges tightly to seal. Place packets on baking sheet. Bake at 425 degrees until packets puff, about 10 minutes.

SALMON SALAD FARFALLE

4 servings

12 ounces cooked salmon, cubed *or* flaked
2 medium tomatoes, chopped
1 small onion, thinly sliced, separated into rings
1/4 cup sliced pitted black olives, optional
1/4 cup shredded carrot
2 cloves garlic, crushed
2 tablespoons olive oil
2 tablespoons minced parsley
1 teaspoon dried oregano leaves
1/2 teaspoon dried basil leaves
1/4 teaspoon pepper
8 ounces farfalle (bow ties), cooked, room temperature

Per Serving
Calories: 477
% Calories from fat: 35
Fat (gm): 18.5
Sat. fat (gm): 3.2
Cholesterol (mg): 53.5
Sodium (mg): 64
Protein (gm): 27.2
Carbohydrate (gm): 49.4

Exchanges
Milk: 0.0
Vegetable: 0.0
Fruit: 0.0
Bread: 3.0
Meat: 3.0
Fat: 2.0

1. Mix all ingredients, except lettuce, in large bowl. Refrigerate covered until ready to serve.

SALMON STEAKS BAKED WITH HERBED YOGURT

4 servings

- 4 salmon steaks (3-4 ounces each)
- 1 cup plain yogurt
- 1/2 teaspoon dry mustard
- 1/2 teaspoon dried dill weed
- 1/2 teaspoon dried thyme leaves
- 1 tablespoon lemon juice
- 1/2 teaspoon pepper
- Paprika, as garnish
- 2 tablespoons minced parsley
- 3 cups cooked rice

Per Serving
Calories: 399
% Calories from fat: 30
Fat (gm): 12.8
Sat. fat (gm): 2.8
Cholesterol (mg): 67.5
Sodium (mg): 117
Protein (gm): 29.5
Carbohydrate (gm): 38.9
Exchanges
Milk: 0.5
Vegetable: 0.0
Fruit: 0.0
Bread: 2.0
Meat: 3.0
Fat: 1.0

1. Arrange salmon in greased baking pan. Combine remaining ingredients, except paprika, parsley, and rice, and spread over fish; sprinkle with paprika. Bake, uncovered, at 375 degrees 20 minutes, or until fish is tender and flakes easily with fork; sprinkle with parsley. Serve with rice.

FISH TERIYAKI

6 servings

- 1 1/2 pounds fish fillets (salmon, orange roughy, red snapper, whitefish), cut into 1-inch pieces
- 1/4 cup light soy sauce
- 1 teaspoon sugar
- 2 tablespoons sake, *or* dry white wine
- 2 cloves garlic, minced
- 1/2 teaspoon minced fresh ginger
- 1/4 teaspoon red pepper flakes

Per Serving
Calories: 115
% Calories from fat: 19
Fat (gm): 2.3
Sat. fat (gm): 0.6
Cholesterol (mg): 47
Sodium (mg): 195
Protein (gm): 21.4
Carbohydrate (gm): 0.6
Exchanges
Milk: 0.0
Vegetable: 0.0
Fruit: 0.0
Bread: 0.0
Meat: 2.5
Fat: 0.0

1. Place fish in glass baking dish. Combine remaining ingredients; drizzle over fish and toss to coat. Let stand at room temperature 20 minutes.

2. Arrange fish pieces on greased broiling pan. Broil fish 5 inches from heat source 7 to 8 minutes, or until fish flakes easily when tested with fork.

MICROWAVE SALMON TARRAGON

4 servings

1 pound salmon fillet, cut into 4 pieces
Salt and pepper, to taste
1/4 cup lemon juice
1/2 teaspoon dried tarragon leaves
1 tablespoon chopped pimiento

Per Serving
Calories: 109
% Calories from fat: 30
Fat (gm): 3.8
Sat. fat (gm): 0.8
Cholesterol (mg): 20.3
Sodium (mg): 69
Protein (gm): 16.3
Carbohydrate (gm): 1.6
Exchanges
Milk: 0.0
Vegetable: 0.0
Fruit: 0.0
Bread: 0.0
Meat: 2.0
Fat: 0.0

1. Arrange fish in glass baking dish with thick sides toward the outside of the dish; sprinkle lightly with salt and pepper. Combine lemon juice and tarragon; spoon over fish. Let stand at room temperature several minutes.

2. Microwave, loosely covered, on Medium-High 5 to 6 minutes, or until fish flakes easily with fork. Sprinkle with pimiento.

BALSAMIC-GLAZED SALMON FILLETS

6 servings

6 salmon fillets (about 5 ounces each)
Balsamic Glaze (recipe follows)
1 tablespoon chopped fresh, *or* 1 teaspoon dried, oregano leaves
Salt and pepper, to taste
12 fresh basil leaves, julienned

Per Serving
Calories: 163
% Calories from fat: 29
Fat (gm): 5
Sat. fat (gm): 1
Cholesterol (mg): 25.4
Sodium (mg): 914
Protein (gm): 20.6
Carbohydrate (gm): 7.2
Exchanges
Milk: 0.0
Vegetable: 0.0
Fruit: 0.0
Bread: 0.0
Meat: 3.0
Fat: 0.0

1. Arrange fish in greased baking pan. Brush with warm Balsamic Glaze and sprinkle with oregano. Bake, uncovered, at 475 degrees until fish flakes with a fork, 10 to 14 minutes. Brush with any remaining glaze. Sprinkle lightly with salt and pepper; sprinkle with basil.

Balsamic Glaze

makes about 1/3 cup

- Vegetable cooking spray
- 4 cloves garlic, minced
- 1 tablespoon dry white wine, *or* water
- 1 tablespoon honey
- 1/3 cup balsamic vinegar
- 4 teaspoons Dijon-style mustard

1. Spray small skillet with cooking spray; heat over medium heat until hot. Saute garlic until tender, about 2 minutes. Do not brown. Add remaining ingredients; heat to boiling. Reduce heat and simmer, uncovered, until slightly thickened, 2-3 minutes.

SALMON CAKES WITH DILL SAUCE

6 servings

- 1 pound potatoes, peeled, cooked, mashed
- 1 can (15 1/2-ounces) salmon, bones and skin discarded
- 1/4 cup fat-free plain yogurt
- 1/4 cup sliced green onions and tops
- 3 tablespoons chopped parsley
- 2 tablespoons lemon juice
- 1/4 teaspoon pepper
- 1 cup fresh bread crumbs
- 2 tablespoons olive oil
- 1 teaspoon margarine
- Dill Sauce (see p. 502)

Per Serving
Calories: 316
% Calories from fat: 35
Fat (gm): 11.2
Sat. fat (gm): 2.1
Cholesterol (mg): 32.8
Sodium (mg): 567
Protein (gm): 21.5
Carbohydrate (gm): 32.1

Exchanges
Milk: 0.0
Vegetable: 0.0
Fruit: 0.0
Bread: 2.0
Meat: 2.0
Fat: 1.0

1. Combine all ingredients except olive oil, margarine, and Dill Sauce in large bowl; mix well. Shape into 6 large patties. Cook patties in oil and margarine over medium heat until browned, about 5 minutes per side. Serve with Dill Sauce.

DILLED SALMON BURGERS

4 servings

- 1 can ($12^1/_2$-ounces) salmon, undrained, *or* $1^1/_2$ cups flaked cooked salmon
- 1 egg white, lightly beaten
- $^1/_2$ cup seasoned dry bread crumbs
- $^1/_4$ cup chopped onion
- $^1/_2$ teaspoon dried thyme leaves
- $^1/_2$ teaspoon pepper
- 1 tablespoon corn oil
- 2 small pita bread rounds, halved
- Shredded lettuce, as garnish
- Chopped tomato, as garnish
- Dill Sauce (see p. 502)

Per Serving
Calories: 388
% Calories from fat: 32
Fat (gm): 13.4
Sat. fat (gm): 2.8
Cholesterol (mg): 24.2
Sodium (mg): 716
Protein (gm): 27.5
Carbohydrate (gm): 37.8

Exchanges
Milk: 0.5
Vegetable: 0.0
Fruit: 0.0
Bread: 2.0
Meat: 3.0
Fat: 1.0

1. Drain salmon, reserving 2 tablespoons of liquid; discard skin and bones. Combine reserved liquid, egg white, bread crumbs, onion, thyme, and pepper. Add salmon; mix well. Shape into 4 patties, $^1/_2$-inch thick.

2. Cook patties in oil in large skillet over medium heat until browned, 2 to 3 minutes on each side. Place patties in pita halves; top with lettuce, tomato, and Dill Sauce.

SNAPPER EN PAPILLOTE

6 servings

Cooking parchment, *or* aluminum foil
2 tablespoons margarine, softened
2 tablespoons chopped parsley
2 tablespoons dry white wine
3 tablespoons minced garlic
Dash white pepper
6 red snapper or pompano fillets (about 6 ounces each)
6 slices tomatoes
3/4 cup julienned zucchini
3/4 cup thinly sliced leek (white part only)
3/4 teaspoon dried thyme leaves
3/4 teaspoon dried oregano leaves

Per Serving
Calories: 285
% Calories from fat: 22
Fat (gm): 6.9
Sat. fat (gm): 1.4
Cholesterol (mg): 72.8
Sodium (mg): 149
Protein (gm): 42.7
Carbohydrate (gm): 11.2
Exchanges
Milk: 0.0
Vegetable: 2.0
Fruit: 0.0
Bread: 0.0
Meat: 4.0
Fat: 0.0

1. Cut 6 pieces of parchment about 18 x 12-inches. Fold each sheet in half and round off unfolded edges to form half circles. Unfold each sheet.

2. Mix margarine, parsley, wine, garlic and pepper in small bowl until smooth. Place fish fillets on parchment pieces; top with tomato slices. Place 2 tablespoons of zucchini and 2 tablespoons of leek on top of tomato; sprinkle with 1/8 teaspoon thyme and 1/8 teaspoon oregano. Spoon generous tablespoon margarine mixture on top.

3. Fold paper over fish and roll edges tightly to seal. Place packets on baking sheet. Bake fish at 425 degrees until packets puff, about 10 minutes.

GRILLED RED SNAPPER WITH JALAPEÑO MAYONNAISE

4 servings

1 lemon, sliced
3 pounds whole red snapper, dressed
2 tablespoons tarragon wine vinegar
1 tablespoon chopped fresh, *or* 1 teaspoon dried, tarragon leaves
Jalapeño Mayonnaise (recipe follows)

Per Serving
Calories: 395
% Calories from fat: 11
Fat (gm): 4.8
Sat. fat (gm): 1
Cholesterol (mg): 125.3
Sodium (mg): 762
Protein (gm): 72.3
Carbohydrate (gm): 12.6
Exchanges
Milk: 0.0
Vegetable: 0.0
Fruit: 0.0
Bread: 0.5
Meat: 7.0
Fat: 0.0

1. Place lemon slices in fish cavity; sprinkle inside of fish with vinegar and tarragon. Set fish in lightly greased fish-shaped grill rack. Place fish on grill and cook, covered, until fish is tender and flakes with a fork, about 20 minutes; turn fish once or twice during cooking. Remove fish to serving platter; serve with Jalapeño Mayonnaise.

Jalapeño Mayonnaise

makes about 1 cup

1/2 cup fat-free mayonnaise
1/2 cup plain fat-free yogurt
2 jalapeño chilies, seeded, chopped
1/4 cup chopped cilantro
1/4 teaspoon ground cumin

1. Combine all ingredients in small bowl; refrigerate covered until ready to serve. Stir before serving.

RED SNAPPER WITH CAYENNE TOMATO RELISH

4 servings

- 4 red snapper steaks, *or* fillets (about 4 ounces each)
- Juice of 1 lemon
- 1/2 cup dry white wine
- Cayenne Tomato Relish (recipe follows)
- 2 tablespoons chopped parsley

Per Serving
Calories: 178
% Calories from fat: 15
Fat (gm): 2.7
Sat. fat (gm): 0.6
Cholesterol (mg): 41.4
Sodium (mg): 444
Protein (gm): 25.5
Carbohydrate (gm): 8.5

Exchanges
Milk: 0.0
Vegetable: 1.0
Fruit: 0.0
Bread: 0.0
Meat: 3.0
Fat: 0.0

1. Place fish in greased baking pan; add lemon juice and wine. Bake, uncovered, at 400 degrees until fish flakes easily with fork, about 10 minutes. Remove fish to serving platter and spoon Cayenne Tomato Relish over. Sprinkle with parsley.

Cayenne Tomato Relish

makes about 2 cups

- Vegetable cooking spray
- 1/2 cup chopped green onions and tops
- 1 clove garlic, minced
- 1 can (15 ounces) small diced tomatoes, drained
- 1/2 cup finely chopped green bell pepper
- 1/2 cup sliced mushrooms
- 1 tablespoon dried basil leaves
- 1 teaspoon cayenne pepper
- 1 tablespoon lemon juice

1. Spray medium skillet with cooking spray; cook over medium heat until hot. Add onions and garlic; saute until tender, about 5 minutes. Add remaining ingredients, except lemon juice and heat to boiling. Reduce heat and simmer until mixture thickens slightly, about 12 to 15 minutes. Stir in lemon juice.

MICROWAVE SOLE DIJON

4 servings

- $1^1/_4$ pounds fillet of sole
- 6 stalks asparagus, cut diagonally into 2-inch pieces
- 1 tablespoon reduced-fat mayonnaise
- $1^1/_2$ tablespoons Dijon-style mustard
- Juice of 1 lemon
- 1 tablespoon chopped chives
- Salt and pepper, to taste
- Paprika, to taste
- Chopped parsley, as garnish

Per Serving
Calories: 137
% Calories from fat: 20
Fat (gm): 2.9
Sat. fat (gm): 0.5
Cholesterol (mg): 67.8
Sodium (mg): 183
Protein (gm): 24.7
Carbohydrate (gm): 2.2

Exchanges
Milk: 0.0
Vegetable: 0.0
Fruit: 0.0
Bread: 0.0
Meat: 2.5
Fat: 0.0

1. Place fillets in single layer in glass baking dish, tucking under thin edges, and arranging thick parts toward outside of dish. Arrange asparagus around outside edges of dish.

2. Mix mayonnaise, mustard, lemon juice, and chives in small bowl; spread over fish. Sprinkle lightly with salt, pepper, and paprika. Microwave, loosely covered, on High 3 to 4 minutes. Rotate dish; cover and microwave 1 minute, or until fish flakes easily with fork. Let stand covered 1 to 2 minutes. Sprinkle with parsley.

MICROWAVE SOLE ORIENTAL

4 servings

- $1^1/_4$ pounds fillet of sole, *or* flounder
- 2 teaspoons low-sodium soy sauce
- 1 tablespoon frozen orange juice concentrate
- 1 clove garlic, minced
- 1 tablespoon sesame oil
- 2 teaspoons chopped gingerroot
- Pepper, to taste
- 1 teaspoon toasted sesame seeds
- Chopped parsley, as garnish

Per Serving
Calories: 159
% Calories from fat: 31
Fat (gm): 5.3
Sat. fat (gm): 0.9
Cholesterol (mg): 66.5
Sodium (mg): 191
Protein (gm): 24.2
Carbohydrate (gm): 2.3

Exchanges
Milk: 0.0
Vegetable: 0.0
Fruit: 0.0
Bread: 0.0
Meat: 2.5
Fat: 0.5

1. Arrange fish in glass baking dish, tucking under any thin edges. Combine soy sauce, orange juice, garlic, sesame oil, and gingerroot in small bowl; drizzle over fish. Let stand 15 minutes. Microwave, loosely covered, on High 3 to 4 minutes, or until fish flakes with a fork. Let stand 1 minute. Sprinkle with pepper, sesame seeds, and parsley.

SOLE WITH ROSEMARY POTATOES

4 servings

- 4 small baking potatoes, cut into wedges
- Vegetable cooking spray
- 2 tablespoons dried rosemary leaves
- 1/2 teaspoon garlic powder
- 1/4 teaspoon pepper
- 4 shallots, minced
- 1 small red onion, chopped
- 1 large clove garlic, minced
- 1 1/4 pounds sole fillets

Per Serving
Calories: 279
% Calories from fat: 7
Fat (gm): 2.1
Sat. fat (gm): 0.6
Cholesterol (mg): 68
Sodium (mg): 127
Protein (gm): 30.1
Carbohydrate (gm): 34.4
Exchanges
Milk: 0.0
Vegetable: 0.0
Fruit: 0.0
Bread: 2.0
Meat: 3.0
Fat: 0.0

1. Place potatoes on baking sheet; spray lightly with cooking spray and sprinkle with rosemary, garlic powder, and pepper. Bake potatoes at 400 degrees until fork-tender, about 45 minutes.

2. About 15 minutes before potatoes are done, spray large skillet with cooking spray; heat over medium heat until hot. Saute shallots, onion, and garlic until tender, about 5 minutes. Fold each sole fillet in half and add to skillet. Cook fish over medium heat until fish is tender and flakes with a fork, about 6 minutes, turning once. Place fish on serving platter; spoon shallot mixture over fish. Surround with hot rosemary potatoes.

BASQUE-STYLE FISH

4 servings

Vegetable cooking spray
1 pound fish fillets *or* steaks (sole, grouper, orange roughy, cod, swordfish, salmon, *or* flounder)
1/4 cup bottled clam juice
1/2 cup dry white wine, *or* clam juice
1/2 cup canned crushed tomatoes
2 tablespoons chopped parsley
1-3 tablespoons chopped scallions
1 teaspoon dried thyme leaves
1 bay leaf
1/4 teaspoon pepper

Per Serving
Calories: 140
% Calories from fat: 9
Fat (gm): 1.3
Sat. fat (gm): 0.3
Cholesterol (mg): 41.8
Sodium (mg): 261
Protein (gm): 23.9
Carbohydrate (gm): 3.9
Exchanges
Milk: 0.0
Vegetable: 0.0
Fruit: 0.0
Bread: 0.0
Meat: 3.0
Fat: 0.0

1. Spray large skillet with cooking spray; heat over medium heat until hot. Add fish, and combined remaining ingredients; heat to boiling. Reduce heat and simmer, covered, until fish is tender and flakes with a fork, 10 to 15 minutes. Discard bay leaf.

2. Remove fish to heated platter and keep warm. Simmer tomato sauce, uncovered, until liquid is reduced to about 1/4 cup; spoon over fish.

GRILLED SWORDFISH WITH CHILI-LIME SAUCE

6 servings

1-2 teaspoons olive oil
2 tablespoons lime juice
1/4 teaspoon pepper
2 tablespoons minced parsley
6 swordfish steaks (about 4 ounces each)
Chili-Lime Sauce (recipe follows)

Per Serving
Calories: 153
% Calories from fat: 29
Fat (gm): 4.8
Sat. fat (gm): 1.2
Cholesterol (mg): 37.2
Sodium (mg): 365
Protein (gm): 19.7
Carbohydrate (gm): 7.3
Exchanges
Milk: 0.0
Vegetable: 1.0
Fruit: 0.0
Bread: 0.0
Meat: 2.5
Fat: 0.0

1. Mix olive oil, lime juice, pepper, and parsley in small bowl; brush on swordfish; refrigerate, covered 1 hour.

2. Grill fish over hot coals until fish is tender and flakes with a fork, about 8 minutes, turning once. Serve fish with Chili-Lime Sauce.

Chili-Lime Sauce

makes about 2 cups

- 1/4 cup chili sauce
- 2 cups chopped tomatoes
- 1/2-1 small jalapeño chili, seeded, chopped
- Juice of 1/2 lime

1. Mix all ingredients.

TROUT WITH VEGETABLE GARNI

4 servings

- 4 fresh, *or* frozen, thawed pan-dressed rainbow trout, *or* lake perch (about 8 ounces each)
- Pepper, to taste
- 1/2 cup dry white wine, *or* clam juice
- 1/4 cup clam juice, *or* reduced-sodium fat-free chicken broth
- 1 tablespoon lemon juice
- 1/2 teaspoon dried thyme leaves
- 1/2 teaspoon dried oregano leaves
- Vegetable cooking spray
- 1 cup sliced mushrooms
- 1 medium carrot, chopped
- 1 small onion, chopped
- 1 clove garlic, minced
- Vegetable cooking spray

Per Serving
Calories: 311
% Calories from fat: 24
Fat (gm): 7.9
Sat. fat (gm): 1.5
Cholesterol (mg): 129.8
Sodium (mg): 117
Protein (gm): 47.9
Carbohydrate (gm): 4.5

Exchanges
Milk: 0.0
Vegetable: 1.0
Fruit: 0.0
Bread: 0.0
Meat: 5.5
Fat: 0.0

1. Place fish in shallow baking dish and sprinkle with pepper. Pour combined wine, clam juice, lemon juice, thyme, and oregano over fish. Cover, and refrigerate 2 hours. Drain fish, reserving marinade.

2. Coat large skillet with cooking spray; heat over medium heat until hot. Saute mushrooms, carrot, onion, and garlic until tender but not brown, about 5 minutes. Push vegetables to edges of skillet. Add fish, and cook over medium heat until browned, 2 to 3 minutes on each side. Add reserved marinade; simmer, covered, until fish is tender and flakes with a fork, about 5 minutes.

3. Transfer fish and vegetables to platter; keep warm. Simmer marinade mixture until reduced to 1/4 cup; spoon over fish.

PAN-FRIED TROUT

4 servings

- 1 1/4 pounds trout fillets
- 1/3 cup white, *or* yellow, cornmeal
- 1/4 teaspoon anise seeds
- 1/4 teaspoon black pepper
- 1/2 cup minced cilantro, *or* parsley
- Vegetable cooking spray
- Lemon wedges

Per Serving
Calories: 207
% Calories from fat: 23
Fat (gm): 5.2
Sat. fat (gm): 1
Cholesterol (mg): 81.1
Sodium (mg): 42
Protein (gm): 30.2
Carbohydrate (gm): 8
Exchanges
Milk: 0.0
Vegetable: 0.0
Fruit: 0.0
Bread: 0.5
Meat: 3.0
Fat: 0.0

1. Coat fish with combined cornmeal, spices, and cilantro, pressing it gently into fish.

2. Spray large skillet with cooking spray; heat over medium heat until hot. Add fish and cook until fish is tender and flakes with a fork, about 5 minutes on each side. Serve with lemon wedges.

MICROWAVE WHITEFISH WITH CUMBERLAND SAUCE

4 servings

- 1 pound whitefish fillets (about 4 ounces each)
- 1/4 cup thinly sliced green onions and tops
- Paprika
- 1 cucumber, scored with fork, thinly sliced
- Fresh dill sprigs, as garnish
- Cumberland Sauce (recipe follows)

Per Serving
Calories: 149
% Calories from fat: 16
Fat (gm): 2.5
Sat. fat (gm): 0.4
Cholesterol (mg): 24
Sodium (mg): 87
Protein (gm): 13.4
Carbohydrate (gm): 17

Exchanges
Milk: 0.0
Vegetable: 0.0
Fruit: 0.0
Bread: 1.0
Meat: 2.0
Fat: 0.0

1. Arrange fish in glass baking dish, folding thin ends under; sprinkle with green onions and paprika. Cover with vented plastic wrap. Microwave 5 minutes on High, or until fish flakes with fork.

2. Place fish on serving platter; garnish with cucumbers and dill sprigs. Serve with Cumberland Sauce.

Cumberland Sauce

makes about 2 cups

- 1 cup chopped peeled, seeded cucumber
- 1 cup fat-free sour cream
- 1/4 cup fat-free plain yogurt
- 2 tablespoons chopped fresh, *or* 2 teaspoons dried, dill weed
- 2 cloves garlic, minced

1. Process all ingredients in food processor or blender until smooth; refrigerate covered until ready to serve.

SALMON LOAF WITH CUCUMBER SAUCE

6 servings

1 can (16 ounces) salmon, undrained
2 egg whites, lightly beaten
2 tablespoons minced onion
1/2 cup chopped celery
2 tablespoons minced green bell pepper
2 tablespoons minced chives
1 tablespoon chopped fresh, *or* 1 teaspoon dried, dill weed
1 cup dry unseasoned bread crumbs
1 tablespoon lemon juice
Cucumber Sauce (recipe follows)

Per Serving
Calories: 201
% Calories from fat: 24
Fat (gm): 5.2
Sat. fat (gm): 1.4
Cholesterol (mg): 29.9
Sodium (mg): 567
Protein (gm): 21.1
Carbohydrate (gm): 16.2
Exchanges
Milk: 0.0
Vegetable: 0.0
Fruit: 0.0
Bread: 1.0
Meat: 3.0
Fat: 0.0

1. Drain salmon, reserving juice; discard skin and bones. Add water to salmon juice to make 1/2 cup. Combine liquid, salmon, and remaining ingredients, except Cucumber Sauce, in large bowl. Spoon into greased 9 x 5-inch loaf pan. Bake at 350 degrees until golden, 30 to 40 minutes.

2. Unmold onto serving platter. Serve with Cucumber Sauce.

Cucumber Sauce

makes about 1 cup

1/2 cup fat-free plain yogurt
2/3 cup seeded, finely chopped cucumber
1 teaspoon dried dill weed

1. Mix all ingredients; refrigerate until ready to serve.

BAKED FISH WITH SUN-DRIED TOMATO STUFFING

8 servings

Sun-Dried Tomato Stuffing (recipe follows)
1-2 whole whitefish, red snapper, *or* trout, dressed (about 2 pounds)
2 tablespoons sliced almonds, toasted

Per Serving
Calories: 230
% Calories from fat: 33
Fat (gm): 8.5
Sat. fat (gm): 1.3
Cholesterol (mg): 69.6
Sodium (mg): 231
Protein (gm): 25.1
Carbohydrate (gm): 13.5
Exchanges
Milk: 0.0
Vegetable: 1.0
Fruit: 0.0
Bread: 0.5
Meat: 3.0
Fat: 0.0

1. Spoon stuffing into greased baking dish; arrange fish on top. Bake, uncovered, at 400 degrees until fish is tender and flakes with a fork. Sprinkle with almonds.

Sun-Dried Tomato Stuffing

makes about 2 1/2 cups

Olive oil cooking spray
1 cup chopped onion
1/2 cup minced shallots
1 cup sliced celery
3/4 cup sun-dried tomatoes, reconstituted in hot water, chopped
2 cups chopped tomatoes
1/2 cup dry unseasoned bread crumbs
1/4 teaspoon dried chervil leaves
1/4 teaspoon white pepper

1. Spray large skillet with cooking spray; heat over medium heat until hot. Saute onions, shallots, and celery over medium heat until tender, about 5 minutes. Add sun-dried, and chopped, tomatoes and continue cooking 5 minutes. Mix in bread crumbs, chervil, and white pepper.

EASY JAMBALAYA

4 servings

1 cup diced smoked ham
1/2 cup chopped green bell pepper
1/2 cup chopped onion
2 cloves garlic, minced
1-2 tablespoons olive oil
1 can (15 ounces) diced tomatoes with Italian herbs, undrained
1/2 cup water
1 medium bay leaf
1/2 teaspoon Italian seasoning
1/4 teaspoon red pepper sauce
1/4 teaspoon salt
Dash pepper
12-16 ounces peeled, deveined shrimp
3 cups cooked rice, warm
Red pepper sauce

Per Serving
Calories: 381
% Calories from fat: 20
Fat (gm): 7.7
Sat. fat (gm): 1.7
Cholesterol (mg): 145.7
Sodium (mg): 1176
Protein (gm): 28.2
Carbohydrate (gm): 42.4

Exchanges
Milk: 0.0
Vegetable: 2.0
Fruit: 0.0
Bread: 2.0
Meat: 3.0
Fat: 0.0

1. Saute ham, green pepper, onion, and garlic in oil in large saucepan until tender, about 5 minutes. Add tomatoes and liquid, water, bay leaf, Italian seasoning, 1/4 teaspoon red pepper sauce, salt, and pepper. Heat to boiling; reduce heat and simmer, covered, 15 minutes. Add shrimp; simmer until cooked, 2 to 3 minutes; discard bay leaf. Serve over rice with additional red pepper sauce.

MICROWAVE CREOLE SHRIMP

4 servings

1 can (16 ounces) Italian plum tomatoes, undrained, coarsely chopped
1 medium onion, chopped
1 medium green bell pepper, diced
1/2 teaspoon chili powder
1/8 teaspoon red pepper flakes
1 bay leaf
1 pound medium shrimp, peeled, deveined
Salt, to taste

Per Serving
Calories: 129
% Calories from fat: 10
Fat (gm): 1.4
Sat. fat (gm): 0.3
Cholesterol (mg): 174.2
Sodium (mg): 389
Protein (gm): 20.3
Carbohydrate (gm): 8.9

Exchanges
Milk: 0.0
Vegetable: 1.5
Fruit: 0.0
Bread: 0.0
Meat: 2.0
Fat: 0.0

1. Combine all ingredients, except shrimp and salt in 2-quart measure or casserole. Cover with vented plastic wrap, and microwave on High until onion is tender and mixture is bubbly, 5 to 8 minutes, stirring once. Add shrimp and microwave, covered, on High 2 to 3 minutes, or until shrimp are pink. Remove bay leaf and let stand for 3 minutes; season to taste with salt. Serve over rice if desired.

QUICK 'N EASY SPICED SHRIMP

4 servings

1 can (15 ounces) tomato puree
1/2 cup water
3 tablespoons white vinegar
3 tablespoons Worcestershire sauce
2 tablespoons frozen orange juice concentrate
1 tablespoon prepared mustard
1/4 teaspoon red pepper sauce
1/2 teaspoon garlic powder
1/4 teaspoon salt
12-16 ounces peeled, deveined shrimp, cooked

Per Serving
Calories: 172
% Calories from fat: 8
Fat (gm): 1.4
Sat. fat (gm): 0.3
Cholesterol (mg): 166.1
Sodium (mg): 509
Protein (gm): 20.6
Carbohydrate (gm): 18.3

Exchanges
Milk: 0.0
Vegetable: 2.0
Fruit: 0.5
Bread: 0.0
Meat: 2.0
Fat: 0.0

1. Heat all ingredients, except shrimp, in medium saucepan; heat to boiling. Reduce heat and simmer, covered, 5 minutes. Add shrimp and simmer until hot through, 2 to 3 minutes. Serve over rice, if desired.

SHRIMP WITH ARTICHOKES

4 servings

- 2 tablespoons shallots, finely minced
- 1/2 cup thinly sliced mushrooms
- 1 tablespoon margarine
- 1/4 cup dry white wine, *or* chicken broth
- 8 artichoke hearts, halved
- 1/4 cup chopped chives
- 1/4 cup chopped pimiento
- 1 pound medium shrimp, shelled, deveined, cooked
- Salt and pepper, to taste
- 1 lemon, sliced
- Parsley sprigs, as garnish

Per Serving
Calories: 158
% Calories from fat: 18
Fat (gm): 4.1
Sat. fat (gm): 0.9
Cholesterol (mg): 174.2
Sodium (mg): 277
Protein (gm): 21
Carbohydrate (gm): 9.7
Exchanges
Milk: 0.0
Vegetable: 2.0
Fruit: 0.0
Bread: 0.0
Meat: 2.0
Fat: 0.0

1. Saute shallots and mushrooms in margarine in medium skillet until tender, about 5 minutes. Add wine, artichoke hearts, chives, and pimiento; heat just to boiling. Add shrimp and reduce heat; simmer, covered, until hot, about 2 minutes. Season to taste with salt and pepper. Serve with lemon; garnish with parsley. Serve with rice or couscous, if desired.

SHRIMP WITH FETA CHEESE

4 servings

Vegetable cooking spray
4 scallions, finely chopped
2 green bell peppers, finely chopped
1 small red chili, finely chopped
1 teaspoon dried oregano leaves
4 medium tomatoes, peeled, chopped
1 small bunch parsley, finely chopped
1 teaspoon sugar
1 pound medium shrimp, peeled, deveined
1/4 cup (1 ounce) crumbled feta cheese
3 tablespoons fat-free milk
Salt and pepper, to taste

Per Serving
Calories: 196
% Calories from fat: 21
Fat (gm): 4.6
Sat. fat (gm): 1.9
Cholesterol (mg): 180.8
Sodium (mg): 300
Protein (gm): 26.8
Carbohydrate (gm): 12.4
Exchanges
Milk: 0.0
Vegetable: 2.0
Fruit: 0.0
Bread: 0.0
Meat: 3.0
Fat: 0.0

1. Spray large skillet with cooking spray; heat over medium heat until hot. Add scallions, green peppers, chili, and oregano; saute until vegetables are tender, 4 to 8 minutes. Add tomatoes, parsley, and sugar; simmer 5 minutes. Add shrimp, cheese, and milk and simmer, uncovered, until hot through, about 5 minutes. Season to taste with salt and pepper.

SESAME SHRIMP STIR-FRY

4 servings

Vegetable cooking spray
1 small red bell pepper, seeded, chopped
1/4 cup thinly sliced green onions and tops
2 large cloves garlic, minced
2-3 teaspoons sesame oil
2 drops hot chili oil
8 ounces snow peas, ends trimmed
1 pound medium shrimp, peeled, deveined
2 tablespoons dry sherry, *or* reduced-sodium fat-free chicken broth

Per Serving
Calories: 367
% Calories from fat: 13
Fat (gm): 5.1
Sat. fat (gm): 0.9
Cholesterol (mg): 173.2
Sodium (mg): 557
Protein (gm): 29.3
Carbohydrate (gm): 48.6
Exchanges
Milk: 0.0
Vegetable: 0.0
Fruit: 0.0
Bread: 3.0
Meat: 3.0
Fat: 0.0

2 tablespoons reduced-sodium fat-free chicken broth
2 tablespoons reduced-sodium soy sauce
2 tablespoons hoisin sauce
1/4 cup water
2 teaspoons cornstarch
Salt and pepper, to taste
3 cups cooked rice, warm

1. Spray wok or large skillet with cooking spray; heat over medium heat until hot. Stir-fry red pepper, green onions, and garlic 2 to 3 minutes. Add sesame oil, hot chili oil, and snow peas; cook over medium heat, covered, until snow peas are crisp-tender, about 5 minutes, stirring occasionally.

2. Add shrimp and cook until pink, 2 to 3 minutes. Stir in combined dry sherry, chicken broth, soy sauce, and hoisin sauce; heat to boiling. Stir in combined water and cornstarch; boil, stirring, until thickened, 1 to 2 minutes. Season to taste with salt and pepper. Serve over rice.

HOT GARLIC SHRIMP

4 servings

1 pound large shrimp, peeled, deveined
1 tablespoon olive oil
4 cloves garlic, minced
1/2-1 teaspoon red pepper flakes
1/2 teaspoon ground cumin
3 tablespoons lemon juice
Minced parsley, as garnish

Per Serving
Calories: 126
% Calories from fat: 32
Fat (gm): 4.4
Sat. fat (gm): 0.7
Cholesterol (mg): 174.2
Sodium (mg): 200
Protein (gm): 18.6
Carbohydrate (gm): 2.1
Exchanges
Milk: 0.0
Vegetable: 0.0
Fruit: 0.0
Bread: 0.0
Meat: 2.5
Fat: 0.0

1. Combine shrimp, olive oil and garlic in 1-quart glass casserole; sprinkle with red pepper flakes, cumin, and lemon juice. Cover with plastic wrap and vent edge; microwave on High until shrimp are pink and cooked, 3 to 4 minutes, turning shrimp once. Let stand, covered, 1 minute. Sprinkle with parsley.

PEKING SHRIMP

4 servings

- 6 dried black mushrooms
- Vegetable cooking spray
- 4 green onions and tops, diagonally sliced
- 16 snow peas, ends trimmed, halved
- 2 teaspoons finely chopped garlic
- 3/4 pound medium shrimp, peeled, deveined
- 1 teaspoon cornstrach
- 1/4 cup reduced-fat chicken broth

Per Serving
Calories: 98
% Calories from fat: 8
Fat (gm): 0.9
Sat. fat (gm): 0.2
Cholesterol (mg): 131.2
Sodium (mg): 151
Protein (gm): 15.4
Carbohydrate (gm): 6.9
Exchanges
Milk: 0.0
Vegetable: 1.0
Fruit: 0.0
Bread: 0.0
Meat: 1.5
Fat: 0.0

1. Soak mushrooms in hot water 20 minutes or until soft; drain. Remove and discard stems; cut caps into thin strips.

2. Spray large skillet or wok with cooking spray; heat over medium heat until hot. Add onions, snow peas, and garlic; stir-fry until crisp-tender, about 4 minutes. Add shrimp; stir-fry until shrimp are pink, 2 to 4 minutes. Stir in combined cornstarch and chicken broth; stir until thickened, about 1 minute.

THAI COCONUT SHRIMP

6 servings

- 1/2 cup chopped onion
- 1/2 cup chopped green bell pepper
- 1/2 cup chopped red bell pepper
- 2 cloves garlic, minced
- 1 jalapeño chili, minced
- 2-3 teaspoons chopped gingerroot
- 1 teaspoon dark sesame oil
- 1 can (14 ounces) light unsweetened coconut milk
- 3-4 tablespoons reduced-fat peanut butter
- 2 cans (15 ounces each) kidney, *or* pinto beans, rinsed, drained

Per Serving
Calories: 462
% Calories from fat: 19
Fat (gm): 9.6
Sat. fat (gm): 3.5
Cholesterol (mg): 114.9
Sodium (mg): 885
Protein (gm): 28.6
Carbohydrate (gm): 64.9
Exchanges
Milk: 0.0
Vegetable: 0.0
Fruit: 0.0
Bread: 4.0
Meat: 2.0
Fat: 1.0

2 cups cubed seeded tomatoes (1-inch)
1 pound peeled, deveined shrimp
1-2 tablespoons lime juice
1 tablespoon chopped cilantro
1/2-1 teaspoon salt
4 cups cooked rice, warm

1. Saute onion, bell peppers, garlic, chili, and gingerroot in sesame oil in large saucepan until tender, about 5 minutes. Stir in coconut milk and peanut butter; heat to boiling over medium heat, stirring until smooth. Reduce heat and simmer, uncovered, 5 minutes.

2. Stir in beans and tomatoes; heat to boiling. Stir in shrimp. Simmer, uncovered, until shrimp curl and turn pink, about 5 minutes. Stir in lime juice, cilantro, and salt. Serve over rice.

SCALLOPS IN TOMATO-GINGER SAUCE

4 servings

Per Serving
Calories: 187
% Calories from fat: 19
Fat (gm): 3.7
Sat. fat (gm): 0
Cholesterol (mg): 36
Sodium (mg): 720
Protein (gm): 19.1
Carbohydrate (gm): 16.8
Exchanges
Milk: 0.0
Vegetable: 0.0
Fruit: 0.0
Bread: 0.0
Meat: 2.0
Fat: 0.0

Vegetable cooking spray
1-inch piece gingerroot, minced
4 large cloves garlic, minced
2 green onions and tops, finely chopped
1/2 teaspoon crushed red pepper
3 tablespoons sugar
2 teaspoons reduced-sodium soy sauce
3 tablespoons catsup
1/4 cup dry white wine, *or* reduced-sodium fat-free chicken broth
1 teaspoon white vinegar
1 pound sea scallops

1. Spray large skillet with cooking spray; heat over medium heat until hot. Saute ginger, garlic, and green onion 2 minutes; stir in combined red pepper, sugar, soy sauce, catsup, wine, and vinegar. Heat to boiling; reduce heat and simmer 1 to 2 minutes.

2. Thread drained scallops onto skewers. Place scallops on greased broiler pan; broil 6 inches from heat source until scallops are tender and cooked, 6 to 8 minutes, turning scallops once. Serve with warm sauce.

SCALLOPS IN WHITE WINE

4 servings

- 1 tablespoon chopped shallots
- 1 teaspoon dried tarragon leaves
- 1 teaspoon dried thyme leaves
- 1/4 cup margarine
- 1/3 cup dry white wine, *or* reduced-sodium fat-free chicken broth
- 1 pound scallops
- 1/2 pound mushrooms, sliced
- 3 tablespoons minced parsley
- Salt and pepper, to taste

Per Serving
Calories: 188
% Calories from fat: 33
Fat (gm): 6.9
Sat. fat (gm): 1.1
Cholesterol (mg): 37.8
Sodium (mg): 317
Protein (gm): 20.5
Carbohydrate (gm): 7
Exchanges
Milk: 0.0
Vegetable: 1.0
Fruit: 0.0
Bread: 0.0
Meat: 2.5
Fat: 0.5

1. Saute shallots, tarragon, and thyme in margarine in large skillet 1 minute; add wine and heat to boiling. Reduce heat and simmer 1 to 2 minutes. Add scallops and mushrooms; cook over medium heat until scallops are tender and cooked, about 5 minutes. Stir in parsley. Season to taste with salt and pepper.

SCALLOPS WITH LINGUINE

6 servings

- 1 cup chopped onion
- 3/4 cup shredded carrots
- 1 cup chopped roasted, peeled mild green chilies
- 1-2 tablespoons olive oil
- 12 ounces bay scallops
- 1/4 cup minced basil, *or* cilantro
- 1/4 cup minced parsley
- 1-2 teaspoons white Worcestershire sauce

Per Serving
Calories: 265
% Calories from fat: 18
Fat (gm): 5.4
Sat. fat (gm): 0.3
Cholesterol (mg): 18
Sodium (mg): 374
Protein (gm): 16.4
Carbohydrate (gm): 37.4
Exchanges
Milk: 0.0
Vegetable: 1.0
Fruit: 0.0
Bread: 2.0
Meat: 2.0
Fat: 0.0

Salt and pepper, to taste
12 ounces linguine, cooked

1. Saute onion, carrots, and chilies in oil in large skillet until onion is tender, 5 to 8 minutes. Move vegetables to edges of skillet; add scallops and saute until cooked and tender, about 5 minutes. Stir in basil and parsley; season to taste with Worcestershie sauce, salt, and pepper. Serve over linguine.

SCALLOPS WITH CRISP SNOW PEAS AND APPLES

4 servings

1 medium onion, chopped
1 small red bell pepper, chopped
3 cloves garlic, minced
2 tablespoons peanut, *or* canola oil, divided
2 small apples, cored, diced
1 cup snow peas, ends trimmed
12-16 ounces sea scallops, halved
1/4 cup apple cider *or* juice
1 tablespoon tamari soy sauce
2 teaspoons cornstarch
Salt and pepper, to taste

Per Serving
Calories: 243
% Calories from fat: 29
Fat (gm): 8
Sat. fat (gm): 1
Cholesterol (mg): 28.4
Sodium (mg): 397
Protein (gm): 16.7
Carbohydrate (gm): 27.6
Exchanges
Milk: 0.0
Vegetable: 1.0
Fruit: 1.0
Bread: 0.0
Meat: 2.0
Fat: 1.0

1. Stir-fry onion, bell pepper, and garlic in 1 tablespoon oil in wok or large skillet 3 to 4 minutes; add apples and snow peas and stir-fry 3 to 4 minutes longer. Move vegetable mixture to sides of wok; add remaining 1 tablespoon oil and scallops. Stir-fry until scallops are cooked and tender, 5 to 8 minutes. Stir in combined apple cider, soy sauce, and cornstarch; cook over medium-high heat until thickened, 1 to 2 minutes. Season to taste with salt and pepper.

GRILLED SCALLOP KABOBS

4 servings

1 pound sea scallops, halved
1/4 cup dry white wine, *or* clam juice
2 tablespoons fresh lime, *or* lemon juice
1 tablespoon minced parsley
1 clove garlic, minced
1/2 teaspoon dried basil leaves
1/2 teaspoon dried oregano leaves
1 medium zucchini, cut into 1/2-inch pieces, steamed until crisp-tender
1 medium green or red bell pepper, cut into 1-inch squares, steamed until crisp-tender
8 fresh mushrooms
8 cherry tomatoes
Salt and pepper, to taste

Per Serving
Calories: 159
% Calories from fat: 23
Fat (gm): 3.9
Sat. fat (gm): 0.1
Cholesterol (mg): 36
Sodium (mg): 495
Protein (gm): 20.5
Carbohydrate (gm): 8.6
Exchanges
Milk: 0.0
Vegetable: 2.0
Fruit: 0.0
Bread: 0.0
Meat: 2.0
Fat: 0.0

1. Arrange scallops in glass baking dish; toss with combined wine, lime juice, parsley, garlic, basil, and oregano. Refrigerate, covered, 3 to 4 hours. Drain; reserve marinade.

2. Thread scallops and vegetables alternately on skewers. Grill over hot coals until scallops are cooked and tender, 8 to 10 minutes, basting with marinade and turning occasionally. Season to taste with salt and pepper.

MICROWAVE SEA SCALLOPS

4 servings

1 pound sea scallops, halved
1/2 cup dry white wine, *or* reduced-sodium fat-free chicken broth
1/2 small jalapeño chili, minced
1-2 teaspoons olive oil
2 cloves garlic, minced
1/4 cup finely chopped shallots
Juice of 1/2 lemon
1/2 cup frozen, thawed peas
1/4 cup chopped red bell pepper
1 cup sliced mushrooms
1/2 teaspoon dried dill weed
Salt and pepper, to taste
Minced parsley, as garnish

Per Serving
Calories: 185
% Calories from fat: 26
Fat (gm): 4.8
Sat. fat (gm): 0.2
Cholesterol (mg): 36
Sodium (mg): 509
Protein (gm): 20.4
Carbohydrate (gm): 10
Exchanges
Milk: 0.0
Vegetable: 2.0
Fruit: 0.0
Bread: 0.0
Meat: 2.0
Fat: 0.0

1. Combine scallops, wine, and jalapeño chili in glass bowl; toss well. Refrigerate 1 to 2 hours.

2. Microwave oil, garlic, and shallots in 8 x 12-inch glass baking dish on High 2 minutes. Add lemon juice, peas, bell pepper, mushrooms, and dill and mix well. Microwave on High 2 minutes. Stir in scallop mixture; microwave, loosely covered, until scallops are tender and cooked, about 3 minutes. Season to taste with salt and pepper; sprinkle with parsley.

MICROWAVE SCALLOPS TERIYAKI

4 servings

2 tablespoons dry sherry, *or* reduced-sodium fat-free chicken broth
1 tablespoon reduced-sodium soy sauce
2 tablespoons water
1 tablespoon sesame oil
2 teaspoons gingerroot, minced
1 teaspoon frozen orange juice concentrate
2 cloves garlic, minced
1 pound sea scallops
1 tablespoon lemon juice
Paprika
Minced parsley, as garnish

Per Serving
Calories: 147
% Calories from fat: 27
Fat (gm): 4.3
Sat. fat (gm): 0.6
Cholesterol (mg): 37.8
Sodium (mg): 314
Protein (gm): 19.6
Carbohydrate (gm): 5
Exchanges
Milk: 0.0
Vegetable: 0.0
Fruit: 0.0
Bread: 0.0
Meat: 2.5
Fat: 0.0

1. Combine sherry, soy sauce, water, oil, ginger root, orange juice, and garlic in 8 x 10-inch glass baking dish. Add scallops and refrigerate up to 4 hours.

2. Cover dish with vented plastic wrap and microwave on High until scallops are tender and cooked, 4 to 6 minutes, stirring once. Let stand, covered, 3 minutes. Spoon lemon juice over scallops; sprinkle with paprika and parsley.

STEAMED CLAMS AND PASTA

4 servings

Vegetable cooking spray
4 cloves garlic, minced
1 cup finely chopped onion
1/4 cup minced parsley
1/2 teaspoon dried oregano leaves
1/4 teaspoon white pepper
24 fresh clams, scrubbed
1 cup clam juice, *or* water
4 cups cooked spaghetti, warm
2 tablespoons grated Parmesan cheese

Per Serving
Calories: 292
% Calories from fat: 8
Fat (gm): 2.6
Sat. fat (gm): 0.7
Cholesterol (mg): 30.9
Sodium (mg): 499
Protein (gm): 23.3
Carbohydrate (gm): 46.4
Exchanges
Milk: 0.0
Vegetable: 0.0
Fruit: 0.0
Bread: 3.0
Meat: 2.0
Fat: 0.0

1. Spray skillet with cooking spray; heat over medium heat until hot. Saute garlic and onion 3 to 4 minutes; add parsley, oregano, and white pepper. Add clams and clam juice; heat to boiling. Reduce heat and simmer, covered, until clams open, about 5 minutes. Discard any unopened clams.

2. Spoon spaghetti into shallow bowls. Arrange clams on spaghetti; pour broth over. Sprinkle with Parmesan cheese.

FIVE

Chicken, Turkey, AND Cornish Hen

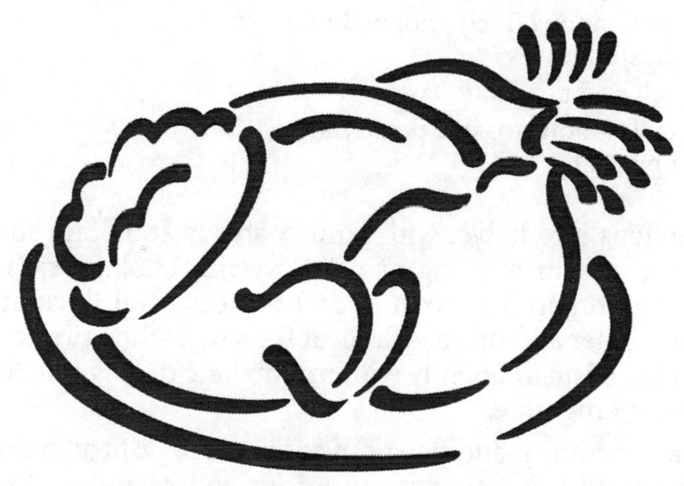

GLAZED CORNISH HENS WITH WILD RICE

4 servings

- 2 Rock Cornish game hens (1 to 1 1/4 pounds each)
- Vegetable cooking spray
- Paprika
- 1/3 cup orange marmalade
- 1/4 cup sliced green onion and tops
- 1/4 cup sliced celery
- 1 package (6 1/4 ounces) fast-cooking long-grain white-and-wild rice, spice packet discarded
- 1 can (14 1/2 ounces) reduced-sodium fat-free chicken broth
- 1 can (11 ounces) mandarin orange segments, drained
- 2 tablespoons raisins
- 2 tablespoons finely chopped mint, *or* parsley, leaves
- Salt and pepper, to taste
- 2 tablespoons toasted pecan halves, optional

Per Serving
Calories: 473
% Calories from fat: 21
Fat (gm): 11.1
Sat. fat (gm): 0.8
Cholesterol (mg): 40.1
Sodium (mg): 217
Protein (gm): 31.4
Carbohydrate (gm): 63.5
Exchanges
Milk: 0.0
Vegetable: 0.0
Fruit: 0.5
Bread: 3.5
Meat: 3.0
Fat: 0.5

1. Cut hens into halves with poultry shears and place cut sides down on rack in roasting pan. Spray with cooking spray and sprinkle with paprika. Roast at 350 degrees until thickest parts are fork-tender and drumstick meat feels soft when pressed, 1 to 1 1/4 hours. Baste frequently with marmalade during last 30 minutes of cooking time.

2. Spray medium saucepan with cooking spray; heat over medium heat until hot. Saute green onions and celery until tender, about 5 minutes. Add rice and chicken broth; heat to boiling. Reduce heat and simmer, covered, until rice is tender, about 5 minutes. Stir in orange segments, raisins, and mint; cook 2 to 3 minutes longer. Season to taste with salt and pepper.

3. Spoon rice onto serving platter and sprinkle with pecans; arrange hens on rice.

GRILLED CORNISH HENS WITH FRUIT SAUCE

6 servings

3 Cornish hens
1/4 cup whole cloves, soaked briefly in water, drained
1 large lemon, cut into 6 wedges, divided
Fruit Sauce (recipe follows)
Nonstick cooking spray

Per Serving
Calories: 353
% Calories from fat: 30
Fat (gm): 11.6
Sat. fat (gm): 3.2
Cholesterol (mg): 137.7
Sodium (mg): 233
Protein (gm): 44.9
Carbohydrate (gm): 12.2

Exchanges
Milk: 0.0
Vegetable: 0.0
Fruit: 1.0
Bread: 0.0
Meat: 5.5
Fat: 0.0

1. Prepare barbecue grill for indirect grilling method. When briquets become ashen, sprinkle drained cloves over them as an aromatic.

2. Place 1 lemon wedge in each hen cavity, and arrange hens on grill coated with cooking spray, breast side up, over drip pan. Grill, covered, over indirect heat 45 minutes or until joints move easily and juices run clear when hens are pierced in thigh with fork. Cut hens in half and transfer to serving platter. Discard cooked lemon wedges and garnish with remaining wedges. Serve with Fruit Sauce.

Fruit Sauce

makes about 1 1/2 cups

1/2 cup port wine, *or* cranberry juice
1/2 cup cranberry juice
1/4 cup cherry all-fruit preserves
2 tablespoons fresh lemon juice
1/4 teaspoon ground nutmeg
1/4 teaspoon salt
1/4 teaspoon black pepper

1. Combine all ingredients in small saucepan, and heat to boiling; reduce heat and simmer 5 minutes or until preserves are dissolved and sauce is hot. Serve warm.

CORNISH HENS WITH GRILLED PAPAYA

6 servings

- 3 Cornish hens (about 2 pounds)
  Papaya Basting Sauce (recipe follows)
- 3 tablespoons light brown sugar
- 2 teaspoons light rum
- 1 ripe papaya, seeds removed, cut into 6 slices

Per Serving
Calories: 359
% Calories from fat: 30
Fat (gm): 11.6
Sat. fat (gm): 3.2
Cholesterol (mg): 137.7
Sodium (mg): 137
Protein (gm): 45.2
Carbohydrate (gm): 15.7
Exchanges
Milk: 0.0
Vegetable: 0.0
Fruit: 1.0
Bread: 0.0
Meat: 5.5
Fat: 0.0

1. Butterfly hens by cutting down length of backbone with kitchen scissors or poultry shears. Open bird to flat position. Use heel of your hand to pound sharply on breastbone until it cracks and hens lie flat. Brush hens with Papaya Basting Sauce.

2. Prepare grill for indirect grilling method. When coals become ashen, place butterflied hens, skin side up, on grill. Grill, covered, about 20 minutes, turning every 4 minutes with long-handled tongs. Brush hens twice more with basting sauce as you turn them. Hens are done if juices run clear when pricked with fork. Pass extra Basting Sauce at table or pour over hens before serving.

3. Five minutes before hens are done, mix sugar and rum and brush cut sides of papaya slices with mixture. Place papaya slices on grill screen 1minute. Serve with hens.

Papaya Basting Sauce

makes about 1 1/2 cups

- 1 ripe papaya, peeled, seeded, and cut into 1/2-inch cubes
- 1/2 cup orange juice

1. Process papaya and orange juice in food processor or blender until smooth.

SAUTEED CHICKEN BREASTS WITH SAGE

4 servings

- 4 boneless, skinless chicken breast halves
- 1/4 cup fresh lemon juice
- 2-8 fresh sage leaves
- Vegetable cooking spray
- 1/2 teaspoon Italian seasoning
- Black pepper, to taste
- 4 slices lemon

Per Serving
Calories: 147
% Calories from fat: 21
Fat (gm): 3.4
Sat. fat (gm): 1
Cholesterol (mg): 68.6
Sodium (mg): 60
Protein (gm): 25.5
Carbohydrate (gm): 3.2
Exchanges
Milk: 0.0
Vegetable: 0.0
Fruit. 0.0
Bread: 0.0
Meat: 3.0
Fat: 0.0

1. Place chicken in 8-inch-square glass baking dish; add lemon juice, and sage leaves. Cover, and let stand 30 minutes. Remove chicken and pat dry; reserve. Strain and reserve lemon juice and sage leaves separately.

2. Coat medium skillet with vegetable cooking spray, place chicken breasts, smooth side down, and cook over medium heat until nicely browned on the bottom, about 5 minutes. Turn breasts and sprinkle with Italian seasoning and pepper. Tuck reserved sage leaves around chicken, and cook until chicken is browned on bottom and no longer pink in the center, about 5 minutes longer.

3. Transfer chicken to cutting board. Slice chicken breasts diagonally, 1/2-inch thick, and arrange on warm platter. Place sage leaves over chicken. Cover loosely with foil.

4. Discard grease from skillet; heat skillet over medium-high heat until hot. Pour in reserved lemon juice and stir with wooden spoon, scraping up brown bits from bottom of pan. Sauce will boil almost immediately. As soon as it becomes a brown glaze (in less than 1 minute), pour sauce over chicken, and garnish with lemon slices.

CHICKEN BREASTS BAKED WITH STUFFING

6 servings

- Vegetable-Bread Stuffing (recipe follows)
- 6 large skinless chicken breast halves (2 1/2-3 lbs.)
- 1 teaspoon margarine
- 1/4 teaspoon dried basil leaves
- 1/4 teaspoon dried thyme leaves
- 1/4 teaspoon salt
- 1/8 teaspoon black pepper
- Minced parsley, as garnish

Per Serving
Calories: 272
% Calories from fat: 22
Fat (gm): 6.7
Sat. fat (gm): 1.2
Cholesterol (mg): 76.2
Sodium (mg): 396
Protein (gm): 32
Carbohydrate (gm): 20.2

Exchanges
Milk: 0.0
Vegetable: 1.0
Fruit: 0.0
Bread: 1.0
Meat: 3.0
Fat: 0.0

1. Spoon Vegetable-Bread Stuffing into 13 x 9-inch baking pan; arrange chicken breasts, bone sides down, on top. Spread margarine over chicken and sprinkle evenly with basil, thyme, salt, if desired, and black pepper. Bake, covered, at 350 degrees 50 to 60 minutes, until chicken is cooked through. Sprinkle with parsley.

Vegetable-Bread Stuffing

makes about 4 cups

- 2 cups chopped onions
- 2 large ribs celery, diced
- 1 cup finely chopped cabbage
- 1 small carrot, diced
- 2 tablespoons chopped parsley leaves
- 1 tablespoon margarine
- 1 cup reduced-sodium fat-free chicken broth, divided
- 1/2 teaspoon dried basil leaves
- 1/8 teaspoon black pepper
- 3 1/2 cups seasoned cube-style stuffing

1. Saute onion, celery, cabbage, carrot, and parsley in margarine in large non-stick skillet 5 minutes; add 1/4 cup broth. Cook over medium heat, stirring frequently, until onion is tender, 3 to 4 minutes. Stir in basil and black pepper. Add stuffing and remaining 3/4 cup broth. Stir to mix well.

GRILLED CHICKEN BREASTS WITH SAUERKRAUT

6 servings

3 large boneless, skinless chicken breast halves
1/4 cup canola oil
1/3 cup dry red wine, *or* reduced-sodium fat-free chicken broth
1 clove garlic, minced
1/2 teaspoon paprika
1/4 cup minced parsley
1/4 teaspoon pepper
Butter-flavored vegetable cooking spray
3 cups prepared sauerkraut
1 teaspoon caraway seeds

Per Serving
Calories: 220
% Calories from fat: 27
Fat (gm): 6.5
Sat. fat (gm): 1.2
Cholesterol (mg): 73
Sodium (mg): 813
Protein (gm): 29.1
Carbohydrate (gm): 10.7
Exchanges
Milk: 0.0
Vegetable: 2.0
Fruit: 0.0
Bread: 0.0
Meat: 3.0
Fat: 0.0

1. Place chicken, oil, wine, garlic, paprika, and parsley in large plastic bag; seal bag and turn chicken a few times to coat. Place bag on cookie sheet. Let stand 1 hour at room temperature (or 2 hours in refrigerator), turning occasionally. Drain, discarding marinade.

2. Grill chicken breasts over medium-hot coals, or broil 6 inches from heat source until cooked through, 10 to 15 minutes on each side.

3. Spray large skillet with cooking spray and heat over medium heat. Add sauerkraut and caraway seeds. Simmer, uncovered, until all visible liquid has evaporated. Sauerkraut should be very dry.

4. Spoon sauerkraut onto serving platter; arrange chicken on top.

GRILLED CHICKEN BREASTS WITH FENNEL

6 servings

- 6 boneless, skinless chicken breast halves
- 1/4 cup fennel seeds, optional
- 1 tablespoon olive oil
- 2 large bulbs fennel, thickly sliced, steamed until crisp-tender
- 1/4 teaspoon black pepper, freshly ground
- 1 tangerine, peeled and divided into sections, as garnish

Per Serving
Calories: 173
% Calories from fat: 29
Fat (gm): 5.4
Sat. fat (gm): 1.2
Cholesterol (mg): 73
Sodium (mg): 71
Protein (gm): 27
Carbohydrate (gm): 2.7
Exchanges
Milk: 0.0
Vegetable: 0.0
Fruit: 0.0
Bread: 0.0
Meat: 3.0
Fat: 0.0

1. Grill chicken breasts over medium-hot coals until cooked through, 5 to 8 minutes on each side.

2. Sprinkle fennel seeds, if using, on hot coals. Brush oil over fennel bulb and sprinkle with pepper. Grill fennel until tender 2 to 3 minutes on each side. Serve chicken and grilled fennel with tangerine sections.

ROAST CHICKEN WITH CORNBREAD STUFFING

6 servings (with about 2/3 cup stuffing each)

- 1 roasting chicken (about 3 pounds)
- Vegetable cooking spray
- 1 1/2 teaspoons dried rosemary, divided
- 1 1/2 cups thinly sliced celery
- 3/4 cup chopped onion
- 1/4 cup coarsely chopped pecans, optional
- 3/4 teaspoon dried sage leaves
- 1/4 teaspoon dried thyme leaves
- 3 cups cornbread stuffing mix
- 1 1/2 cups reduced-sodium fat-free chicken broth
- Salt and pepper, to taste
- 2 egg whites, *or* 1/4 cup real egg product

Per Serving
Calories: 258
% Calories from fat: 22
Fat (gm): 6.1
Sat. fat (gm): 1.6
Cholesterol (mg): 57.9
Sodium (mg): 548
Protein (gm): 24.4
Carbohydrate (gm): 25.3
Exchanges
Milk: 0.0
Vegetable: 0.5
Fruit: 0.0
Bread: 1.5
Meat: 2.5
Fat: 0.0

1. Spray chicken with cooking spray; sprinkle with 1 teaspoon rosemary. Roast chicken on rack in roasting pan at 375 degrees until meat thermometer inserted in thickest part of thigh, away from bone, registers 170 degrees (chicken leg will move freely and juices will run clear), about 1 1/2 hours. Let chicken stand 10 minutes before carving.

2. Spray medium skillet with cooking spray; heat over medium heat until hot. Saute celery, onion, and pecans (if using) until vegetables are tender, 3 to 5 minutes. Stir in sage, thyme, and remaining 1/2 teaspoon rosemary; cook over medium heat 1 to 2 minutes.

3. Add vegetable mixture to stuffing mix in large bowl; add chicken broth and toss. Season to taste with salt and pepper. Mix in egg whites. Spoon stuffing into sprayed 2-quart casserole. Bake, covered, in oven with chicken during last 30 to 45 minutes roasting time.

CRISP OVEN-FRIED CHICKEN

6 servings

- 4 egg whites, *or* 1/2 cup real egg product
- 1/4 cup 2% reduced-fat milk
- 6 skinless chicken breast halves (about 6 ounces each)
- 1/4 cup all-purpose flour
- 1 1/2 cups finely crushed corn flakes
- 3/4 cup dry unseasoned breadcrumbs
- Butter-flavor vegetable cooking spray
- Salt and pepper, to taste

Per Serving
Calories: 387
% Calories from fat: 13
Fat (gm): 5.4
Sat. fat (gm): 1.5
Cholesterol (mg): 104.2
Sodium (mg): 557
Protein (gm): 44.8
Carbohydrate (gm): 36

Exchanges
Milk: 0.0
Vegetable: 0.0
Fruit: 0.0
Bread: 2.5
Meat: 4.0
Fat: 0.0

1. Beat egg whites and milk in shallow bowl until blended. Coat chicken breasts with flour; dip in egg mixture, then coat generously with combined corn flakes and breadcrumbs.

2. Spray baking pan with cooking spray. Place chicken, meat sides up, in baking pan; spray generously with cooking spray and sprinkle lightly with salt and pepper. Bake at 350 degrees until chicken is browned and juices run clear, 45 to 60 minutes.

Note: If desired, 1/2 teaspoon each dried rosemary leaves and sage leaves, and 1/4 teaspoon dried thyme leaves can be added to the corn flake mixture.

MICROWAVE CHICKEN CRUNCH

6 servings

- 2 1/2 pound chicken pieces
- 1 cup buttermilk
- 1/2 teaspoon garlic powder
- 1/2 teaspoon paprika
- 1/4 teaspoon dried thyme leaves
- 1/4 teaspoon salt
- 2 cups corn flakes cereal, finely crushed

Per Serving
Calories: 217
% Calories from fat: 31
Fat (gm): 7.2
Sat. fat (gm): 2
Cholesterol (mg): 85.7
Sodium (mg): 276
Protein (gm): 28.7
Carbohydrate (gm): 7.3
Exchanges
Milk: 0.0
Vegetable: 0.0
Fruit: 0.0
Bread: 0.5
Meat: 3.5
Fat: 0.0

1. Dip chicken pieces into buttermilk. Combine remaining ingredients in paper bag. Shake chicken pieces in bag until coated, and place in 12-inch glass baking dish with thicker pieces toward outside.

2. Cover dish with waxed paper. Microwave on High 7 to 8 minutes, then turn chicken pieces and rotate dish. Microwave on High until chicken is cooked through, another 6 to 8 minutes.

APPLE CIDER CHICKEN

4 servings

- Vegetable cooking spray
- 3 pounds chicken pieces
- 6 tart apples, peeled, cored, divided
- Pepper
- 3 tablespoons all-purpose flour
- 2 cups apple cider, divided
- Bouquet garni (sprig of parsley and 1/2 teaspoon each: dried thyme, rosemary, and tarragon leaves, tied in cheesecloth bag)
- 3/4 cup fat-free half-and-half, *or* evaporated skim milk
- 2 tablespoons parsley, chopped

Per Serving
Calories: 598
% Calories from fat: 24
Fat (gm): 15.6
Sat. fat (gm): 4.3
Cholesterol (mg): 180.7
Sodium (mg): 230
Protein (gm): 62.8
Carbohydrate (gm): 39.7
Exchanges
Milk: 0.5
Vegetable: 0.0
Fruit: 2.0
Bread: 0.0
Meat: 8.0
Fat: 0.0

1. Spray Dutch oven with cooking spray; heat over medium heat until hot. Add chicken and cook until browned on all sides, 5 to 8 minutes; remove chicken from pan.

2. Slice 2 of the apples, sprinkle with pepper, and add to Dutch oven; saute until beginning to brown, 2 to 3 minutes. Sprinkle in flour and cook gently, stirring occasionally, until flour is light brown. Add 1 1/4 cups cider and heat to boiling, stirring constantly. Replace chicken pieces and add bouquet garni. Cover with tight-fitting lid and bake at 375 degrees 1 hour.

3. Cut remaining 4 apples into quarters. Coat small oven-proof skillet with vegetable cooking spray; add apples and saute until browned lightly, 2 to 3 minutes. Cook, covered, just until tender, about 5 minutes. Remove from heat and reserve.

4. Arrange chicken pieces on platter. Discard bouquet garni. Add remaining 3/4 cup cider to Dutch oven and heat to boiling; boil rapidly 10 minutes. Strain mixture into small saucepan. Add reserved apple quarters and half-and-half. Reheat very gently without boiling. Pour sauce over chicken. Garnish with parsley.

MICROWAVE CHICKEN DIJON

4 servings

2 tablespoons Dijon mustard
2 tablespoons fat-free mayonnaise
1/2 teaspoon pepper
1/2 teaspoon paprika
4 boneless, skinless chicken breast halves (about 4 ounces each), pounded thin
Chives, chopped, for garnish

Per Serving
Calories: 102
% Calories from fat: 22
Fat (gm): 2.4
Sat. fat (gm): 0.6
Cholesterol (mg): 45.7
Sodium (mg): 235
Protein (gm): 17.2
Carbohydrate (gm): 1.9

Exchanges
Milk: 0.0
Vegetable: 0.0
Fruit: 0.0
Bread: 0.0
Meat: 2.0
Fat: 0.0

1. Mix mustard, mayonnaise, pepper and paprika; spread one side of chicken with half the mixture and place in 8-inch glass baking dish. Cover with microwave-safe paper towel. Microwave on High 3 minutes. Turn chicken and coat with remaining mustard sauce. Cover and microwave on High another 3 minutes, until chicken is cooked through. Garnish with dash of paprika and sprinkling of chopped chives.

MICROWAVE SESAME CHICKEN

4 servings

Per Serving
Calories: 133
% Calories from fat: 31
Fat (gm): 4.4
Sat. fat (gm): 0.9
Cholesterol (mg): 45.7
Sodium (mg): 620
Protein (gm): 19.1
Carbohydrate (gm): 3.4
Exchanges
Milk: 0.0
Vegetable: 0.0
Fruit: 0.0
Bread: 0.0
Meat: 2.5
Fat: 0.0

1/4 cup reduced-sodium soy sauce
1 scallion, sliced
1 tablespoon Dijon mustard
1 teaspoon sesame oil
1 tablespoon chopped gingerroot
1 tablespoon frozen orange juice concentrate
1 pound boneless, skinless chicken breasts, cut into 1-inch cubes
1 tablespoon toasted sesame seeds
1 tablespoon chopped parsley

1. Combine soy sauce, scallion, mustard, oil, gingerroot, and orange juice concentrate; pour over chicken in 9-inch glass baking dish and refrigerate, covered, stirring a few times.

2. Cover dish with waxed paper and microwave on High for 3 to 4 minutes. Turn chicken pieces, cover, and microwave on High until chicken is cooked through, 2 to 3 minutes. Sprinkle with sesame seeds and parsley.

CHICKEN LIMONE

4 servings

Per Serving
Calories: 318
% Calories from fat: 31
Fat (gm): 10.8
Sat. fat (gm): 2
Cholesterol (mg): 91.5
Sodium (mg): 81
Protein (gm): 35.2
Carbohydrate (gm): 13.2
Exchanges
Milk: 0.0
Vegetable: 0.0
Fruit: 0.0
Bread: 1.0
Meat: 4.5
Fat: 0.0

2 pounds boneless and skinless chicken breasts, pounded thin
1/2 cup all-purpose flour
Salt, to taste
White pepper, to taste
2 tablespoons olive oil
Juice of 1 lemon
1/2 cup dry white wine
1 tablespoon chopped Italian parsley
Sliced lemon for garnish

1. Coat chicken lightly with flour, salt, and pepper. Saute chicken in oil in large skillet until cooked through and browned, 2 to 3 minutes on each side; remove from skillet.

2. Add lemon juice and wine; heat to boiling. Boil until liquid is reduced by half, stirring and scraping up browned bits from skillet. Return chicken to skillet and cook 1 to 2 minutes, turning pieces to coat with juices.

3. Arrange chicken on serving platter; pour pan juices over chicken, sprinkle with parsley and garnish with lemon.

MICROWAVE LEMON CHICKEN

4 servings

- 4 boneless, skinless chicken breast halves (about 4 ounces each), pounded thin
- Salt, to taste
- 1/2 teaspoon black pepper
- 2 teaspoons margarine
- 1/4 cup Chicken Stock (see p. 47), or reduced-sodium fat-free chicken broth
- 2 cloves garlic, minced
- 2 tablespoons lemon juice
- 4 slices lemon
- Paprika
- 2 tablespoons chopped parsley, for garnish

Per Serving
Calories: 115
% Calories from fat: 30
Fat (gm): 3.8
Sat. fat (gm): 1
Cholesterol (mg): 48
Sodium (mg): 48
Protein (gm): 17.3
Carbohydrate (gm): 2.9

Exchanges
Milk: 0.0
Vegetable: 0.0
Fruit: 0.0
Bread: 0.0
Meat: 2.0
Fat: 0.0

1. Sprinkle both sides of chicken with salt and pepper, and set aside in glass baking dish. Microwave margarine in 1-cup glass measure at 50% for 1 minute, or until melted. Combine with Chicken Stock, garlic, and lemon juice and pour over chicken. Cover with waxed paper, and microwave at High until chicken is no longer pink in the center, 5 to 6 minutes.

2. Garnish each chicken breast with lemon slice; sprinkle lightly with paprika and parsley. Spoon sauce over.

MICROWAVE CHICKEN TARRAGON

4 servings

2 cloves garlic, minced
1-2 teaspoons sesame oil
1 pound chicken tenders
2 tablespoons low-sodium soy sauce
2 tablespoons water
Juice of 1 lemon
2 teaspoons dried tarragon leaves
Salt and pepper, to taste

Per Serving
Calories: 111
% Calories from fat: 26
Fat (gm): 3.1
Sat. fat (gm): 0.7
Cholesterol (mg): 45.7
Sodium (mg): 304
Protein (gm): 17.8
Carbohydrate (gm): 2.4

Exchanges
Milk: 0.0
Vegetable: 0.0
Fruit: 0.0
Bread: 0.0
Meat: 2.0
Fat: 0.0

1. Microwave garlic and sesame oil in 1-quart glass casserole at High 1 minute. Add chicken, soy sauce, water, lemon juice and tarragon, stirring to coat chicken. Let stand 15 minutes.

2. Cover casserole with vented plastic wrap. Microwave at Medium until chicken is cooked through, 4 to 6 minutes, stirring after 2 minutes.

PLOUGHMAN'S CHICKEN

6 servings

2 teaspoons olive oil
1 large onion, thinly sliced
2 ribs celery, cut into 1-inch pieces
3 pounds chicken pieces
1/2 cup dry vermouth, *or* reduced-sodium fat-free chicken broth
3/4 cup Chicken Stock (see p. 47), or reduced-sodium fat-free chicken broth
1 teaspoon minced garlic
1/2 teaspoon dried thyme leaves
4 new potatoes, cut into 1 1/2-inch cubes
Salt and pepper, to taste
Parsley sprigs

Per Serving
Calories: 306
% Calories from fat: 17
Fat (gm): 5.7
Sat. fat (gm): 1.3
Cholesterol (mg): 91.5
Sodium (mg): 138
Protein (gm): 36.2
Carbohydrate (gm): 21.6

Exchanges
Milk: 0.0
Vegetable: 0.0
Fruit: 0.0
Bread: 1.5
Meat: 4.0
Fat: 0.0

1. Heat oil in large skillet and saute onion and celery over medium heat 3 to 4 minutes. Add chicken and cook until browned on all sides, 5 to 7 minutes. Add vermouth and heat to boiling for 1 minute; boil 1 minute. Add remaining ingredients, except potatoes, salt and pepper, and parsley. Heat to boiling; reduce heat and simmer, covered, 20 minutes.

2. Add potatoes and simmer, covered, until tender, about 20 minutes. Season to taste with salt and pepper; garnish with parsley.

CHICKEN WITH SHERRIED MUSHROOM SAUCE

4 servings

- 4 skinless chicken breast halves
- 1/4-1/2 cup (1-2 ounces) grated Parmesan cheese
- 1-2 tablespoons olive oil
- 2 cloves garlic, minced
- 3 tablespoons all-purpose flour
- 1 1/2 cups Chicken Stock (see p. 47), or reduced-sodium fat-free chicken broth
- 1/2 cup dry sherry, *or* reduced-sodium fat-free chicken broth
- 1 cup mushroom caps
- 1 teaspoon dried thyme leaves
- 1 teaspoon dried tarragon leaves
- 2 tablespoons chopped parsley
- 8 ounces spaghetti, cooked

Per Serving
Calories: 385
% Calories from fat: 16
Fat (gm): 7.6
Sat. fat (gm): 2
Cholesterol (mg): 73.4
Sodium (mg): 162
Protein (gm): 38.3
Carbohydrate (gm): 51.8

Exchanges
Milk: 0.0
Vegetable: 0.0
Fruit: 0.0
Bread: 3.0
Meat: 3.0
Fat: 0.0

1. Coat chicken breasts generously with cheese. Cook in oil in large skillet over medium-low to medium heat until browned, 2 to 3 minutes on each side. Transfer chicken to 1 1/2-quart casserole.

2. Add garlic to skillet and saute 1 to 2 minutes; add flour, stirring until smooth. Add Chicken Stock, sherry, mushrooms, and herbs. Heat to boiling; reduce heat and simmer, stirring, until smooth and slightly thickened.

3. Pour broth mixture over chicken. Bake at 350 degrees until chicken is cooked through, 30 to 40 minutes. Sprinkle with parsley; serve with spaghetti.

SLOW COOKER COQ AU VIN

6 servings

Vegetable cooking spray
2/3 cup green onions and tops, chopped
2 1/2 pounds chicken pieces
8 small white onions, peeled
8 ounces small mushrooms
1 clove garlic, crushed
1/4 teaspoon pepper
1/2 teaspoon dried tarragon leaves
1/2 teaspoon dried thyme leaves
8 small new potatoes, scrubbed
1 cup Chicken Stock (see p. 47), or reduced-sodium fat-free chicken broth
Parsley, chopped
1 cup dry red wine

Per Serving
Calories: 379
% Calories from fat: 18
Fat (gm): 7.6
Sat. fat (gm): 2.1
Cholesterol (mg): 87
Sodium (mg): 119
Protein (gm): 32.6
Carbohydrate (gm): 38
Exchanges
Milk: 0.0
Vegetable: 1.0
Fruit: 0.0
Bread: 2.0
Meat: 4.0
Fat: 0.0

1. Spray large skillet with cooking spray; add green onions and chicken and cook over medium heat until chicken is browned on all sides, 8 to 10 minutes.

2. Combine all ingredients, except wine, and add to slow cooker. Cover and cook on Low 8 to 10 hours. During last hour, add wine. Excellent served with rice.

CHICKEN VERONIQUE

4 servings

1 cup sliced mushrooms
3 tablespoons sliced green onions and tops
2 tablespoons vegetable oil
4 boneless, skinless chicken breast halves, cut into 1-inch pieces
1 cup Chicken Stock (see p. 47), or reduced-sodium fat-free chicken broth
1 tablespoon all-purpose flour

Per Serving
Calories: 355
% Calories from fat: 27
Fat (gm): 10.5
Sat. fat (gm): 1.9
Cholesterol (mg): 75.5
Sodium (mg): 99
Protein (gm): 30.5
Carbohydrate (gm): 30.4
Exchanges
Milk: 0.0
Vegetable: 0.0
Fruit: 0.5
Bread: 1.5
Meat: 4.0
Fat: 0.0

1 cup halved seedless green grapes
1/4 cup dry white wine
1 tablespoon drained capers
2 cups cooked rice

1. Saute mushrooms and onions in oil in large skillet about 2 minutes or until soft. Add chicken and cook until chicken is cooked through, about 5 minutes. Stir combined Chicken Stock and flour into skillet; heat to boiling. Boil, stirring, until thickened, 1 to 2 minutes. Stir in grapes, wine, and capers; cook 1 minute longer. Serve with rice.

NAPA VALLEY BRAISED CHICKEN

4 servings

Per Serving
Calories: 325
% Calories from fat: 19
Fat (gm): 6.6
Sat. fat (gm): 1.2
Cholesterol (mg): 73
Sodium (mg): 70
Protein (gm): 27.7
Carbohydrate (gm): 12.9
Exchanges
Milk: 0.0
Vegetable: 0.0
Fruit: 1.0
Bread: 0.0
Meat: 3.5
Fat: 1.5

4 boneless, skinless chicken breast halves
1 tablespoon canola oil
1 clove garlic, minced
2 tablespoons chopped onion
2 tablespoons all-purpose flour
2 tablespoons chopped parsley
1 bay leaf
1 cup dry white wine, *or* reduced-sodium fat-free chicken broth
1 cup dry sherry, or reduced-fat chicken broth
1 cup halved green seedless grapes
Salt and pepper, to taste

1. Cook chicken in oil in large skillet over medium heat until browned, 3 to 4 minutes on each side; add garlic and onion and cook 2 minutes longer. Stir in flour, parsley, and bay leaf; cook 1 minute. Add wine and sherry and heat to boiling; reduce heat and simmer, covered, until chicken is tender, about 50 minutes, adding grapes during last 10 minutes of cooking. Season to taste with salt and pepper.

BRAISED CHICKEN WITH TOMATOES

6 servings

Vegetable cooking spray
6 boneless, skinless chicken breast halves (about 1 1/2 pounds)
Black pepper, to taste
3 cloves garlic, minced
1/2 cup dry white wine
1/4 cup balsamic vinegar
5 plum tomatoes, seeded and chopped
2 tablespoons sliced black olives, optional
1 tablespoon dried rosemary leaves
2 tablespoons fresh oregano, *or* 1 tablespoon dried, oregano leaves

Per Serving
Calories: 179
% Calories from fat: 10
Fat (gm): 1.9
Sat. fat (gm): 0.5
Cholesterol (mg): 65.8
Sodium (mg): 87
Protein (gm): 27.2
Carbohydrate (gm): 8.9

Exchanges
Milk: 0.0
Vegetable: 0.0
Fruit: 0.0
Bread: 0.0
Meat: 3.0
Fat: 0.0

1. Spray large skillet with cooking spray and heat over medium-high heat. Add chicken, and brown on all sides, turning occasionally, about 10 minutes. Transfer chicken to platter and sprinkle with pepper; cover with aluminum foil to keep warm.

2. Drain off all but about 3 tablespoons of pan drippings. Saute garlic in pan drippings for about 1 minute. Add wine and simmer rapidly until wine is reduced by half. Add vinegar, chopped tomatoes, olives, rosemary, and oregano.

3. Return chicken to pan and simmer, covered, 10 to 12 minutes or until juices run clear when chicken thigh is pierced with a fork.

MICROWAVE CHICKEN PAPRIKASH

4 servings

- 1 pound chicken tenders
- 1 teaspoon canola oil
- 2 medium onions, finely chopped
- 2 cloves garlic, minced
- 1 medium green bell pepper, chopped
- 1 cup sliced mushrooms
- 1 cup stewed tomatoes
- 2 1/2 teaspoons sweet Hungarian paprika
- 1 teaspoon poppy seeds
- 1/4 cup fat-free sour cream
- Salt and pepper, to taste

Per Serving
Calories: 173
% Calories from fat: 24
Fat (gm): 4.6
Sat. fat (gm): 1
Cholesterol (mg): 46.5
Sodium (mg): 220
Protein (gm): 20.7
Carbohydrate (gm): 12.5
Exchanges
Milk: 0.0
Vegetable: 2.5
Fruit: 0.0
Bread: 0.0
Meat: 2.0
Fat: 0.0

1. Microwave chicken in glass baking dish until cooked through, about 5 minutes; reserve.

2. Microwave oil, onions, garlic, and green pepper in 2-quart glass measure or casserole at High 3 minutes. Add mushrooms and microwave at High 2 minutes. Mix in tomatoes, paprika, reserved chicken, and poppy seeds. Cover with waxed paper and microwave at High until hot through, about 4 minutes. Let stand, covered, 5 minutes; stir in sour cream. Season to taste with salt and pepper.

ORANGE-SCENTED CHICKEN STEW

6 servings

- 2 cups thinly sliced onions
- 2 tablespoons chopped garlic
- 2 tablespoons olive oil
- 1 teaspoon ground cinnamon
- 1/2 teaspoon ground coriander
- 1/2 teaspoon ground ginger
- 1 pound boneless, skinless chicken breast, cut into strips
- 2 cans (15 ounces each) red, *or* pinto, beans, rinsed, drained

Per Serving
Calories: 279
% Calories from fat: 20
Fat (gm): 6
Sat. fat (gm): 0.9
Cholesterol (mg): 43.8
Sodium (mg): 781
Protein (gm): 26.3
Carbohydrate (gm): 30
Exchanges
Milk: 0.0
Vegetable: 0.0
Fruit: 0.0
Bread: 2.0
Meat: 3.0
Fat: 0.0

1 cup reduced sodium fat-free chicken broth
1/4 cup orange juice
Grated rind of 1/2 orange *or* lemon
1/2 cup chopped parsley
1 teaspoon salt
1/4 teaspoon cayenne pepper

1. Cook onions and garlic in oil in large skillet over low heat, covered, until very tender, about 15 minutes; stir in spices and cook 1 minute longer. Increase heat to medium; add chicken and cook until browned, about 10 minutes.

2. Stir in remaining ingredients and heat to boiling; reduce heat and simmer, covered, until chicken is tender, about 5 minutes.

CHICKEN STEW WITH PARSLEY DUMPLINGS

6 servings

Per Serving
Calories: 233
% Calories from fat: 20
Fat (gm): 5.1
Sat. fat (gm): 1.4
Cholesterol (mg): 35.5
Sodium (mg): 383
Protein (gm): 19.2
Carbohydrate (gm): 26.7
Exchanges
Milk: 0.0
Vegetable: 2.0
Fruit: 0.0
Bread: 1.0
Meat: 1.5
Fat: 0.5

Vegetable cooking spray
1 cup chopped onion
3 carrots, cut into 3/4-inch pieces
1/2 cup sliced celery
3 cups reduced-sodium fat-free chicken broth, divided
1 1/2 cups boneless, skinless chicken breast halves, cut into 1-inch pieces
1/2-3/4 teaspoon dried sage
1/2 cup frozen peas
2 tablespoons finely chopped parsley leaves
5 tablespoons all-purpose flour
Salt and pepper, to taste
Parsley Dumplings (recipe follows)

1. Spray large saucepan with cooking spray; heat over medium heat until hot. Saute onion, carrot, and celery 5 minutes. Add 2 1/2 cups chicken broth, chicken, and sage; heat to boiling. Reduce heat and simmer, covered, until chicken is cooked and vegetables are tender, 10 to 15 minutes.

2. Stir peas and parsley into stew; heat to boiling. Mix flour and remaining 1/2 cup chicken broth; stir into stew. Boil, stirring constantly, until thickened, 1 to 2 minutes. Season to taste with salt and pepper.

3. Spoon dumpling dough into 6 mounds on top of boiling chicken and vegetables (do not drop directly in liquid). Reduce heat and simmer, covered, 10 minutes. Simmer, uncovered, 10 minutes longer.

Parsley Dumplings

makes 6 dumplings

3/4 cup all-purpose flour
1 teaspoon baking powder
1/4 teaspoon salt
1 1/2 tablespoons vegetable shortening
1/3 cup 2% reduced-fat milk
1 tablespoon finely chopped fresh parsley

1. Combine flour, baking powder, and salt in small bowl. Cut in shortening with pastry blender until mixture resembles coarse crumbs. Stir in milk to make a soft dough; stir in parsley.

CHICKEN FRICASSEE

6 servings

Vegetable cooking spray
6 skinless chicken breast halves (about 6 ounces each)
1 medium onion, cut into wedges
4 medium carrots, cut into 1-inch pieces
4 ribs celery, cut into 1-inch pieces
2 cloves garlic, minced
3 tablespoons all-purpose flour
2 cans (14 1/2 ounces each) reduced-sodium fat-free chicken broth
16 whole cloves
2 bay leaves
1 teaspoon lemon juice

Per Serving
Calories: 349
% Calories from fat: 11
Fat (gm): 4.2
Sat. fat (gm): 0.8
Cholesterol (mg): 48.5
Sodium (mg): 28
Protein (gm): 28
Carbohydrate (gm): 48.4

Exchanges
Milk: 0.0
Vegetable: 1.0
Fruit: 0.0
Bread: 3.0
Meat: 2.0
Fat: 0.0

1/2 teaspoon sugar
1/2 teaspoon salt
1/4 teaspoon pepper
12 ounces cooked fettuccine, *or* no-yolk noodles, warm
Minced parsley leaves, as garnish

1. Spray large skillet or Dutch oven with cooking spray; heat over medium heat until hot. Cook chicken until browned, about 8 minutes. Remove from skillet. Add vegetables to skillet; saute 5 minutes. Stir in flour and cook 1 minute, stirring constantly.

2. Return chicken to skillet. Add chicken broth, cloves and bay leaves tied in cheesecloth, lemon juice, and sugar. Heat to boiling; reduce heat and simmer, covered, until chicken is tender, about 20 minutes. Simmer, uncovered, until sauce is thickened to medium consistency, about 10 minutes. Discard spice packet; stir in salt and pepper.

3. Serve chicken and vegetables over pasta; sprinkle with parsley.

SLOW COOKER CHICKEN CREOLE

5 servings

1 cup reduced-sodium fat-free chicken broth
1 can (6 ounces) tomato paste
1 large onion, chopped
2 cups chopped cabbage
1 large green bell pepper, diced
2 large cloves garlic, minced
1 bay leaf
1 tablespoon lemon juice
1 tablespoon Worcestershire sauce
1 tablespoon granulated sugar
2 teaspoons dried basil leaves
2 teaspoons Dijon mustard
1/4 teaspoon black pepper
3-4 drops hot pepper sauce

Per Serving
Calories: 423
% Calories from fat: 11
Fat (gm): 5
Sat. fat (gm): 1.3
Cholesterol (mg): 91.5
Sodium (mg): 482
Protein (gm): 40.3
Carbohydrate (gm): 53.6

Exchanges
Milk: 0.0
Vegetable: 2.5
Fruit: 0.0
Bread: 2.5
Meat: 3.5
Fat: 0.0

5 large skinless chicken breast halves (about $2^1/_2$ pounds)
4 cups cooked rice

1. Mix all ingredients, except chicken and rice in large slow cooker. Add chicken; cover and cook on High 1 hour. Reduce heat to low, and cook an additional 5 to 6 hours. Remove and discard bay leaf. Arrange chicken breasts on rice on serving platter; spoon sauce over.

CAROLINA CHICKEN AND BEAN PILAU

6 servings

Per Serving
Calories: 386
% Calories from fat: 9
Fat (gm): 4
Sat. fat (gm): 1.1
Cholesterol (mg): 47.4
Sodium (mg): 69.6
Protein (gm): 30.5
Carbohydrate (gm): 55.5
Exchanges
Milk: 0.0
Vegetable: 0.0
Fruit: 0.0
Bread: 4.0
Meat: 2.0
Fat: 0.0

4-6 slices bacon
1 pound boneless skinless chicken breast, cubed
1 cup chopped onion
1 cup chopped green bell pepper
1 cup chopped celery
1 teaspoon chopped garlic
1 teaspoon dried thyme leaves
1/2 teaspoon dried tarragon leaves
2 bay leaves
3/4-1 teaspoon salt
1/2 teaspoon black pepper
1/2 teaspoon cayenne pepper
3 tablespoons all-purpose flour
1 quart reduced-sodium fat-free chicken broth
2 cans (15 ounces each) Great Northern, *or* pinto, beans, rinsed, drained
1 cup rice
1 cup sliced carrots

1. Cook bacon in Dutch oven until crisp; remove, crumble, and reserve. Pour all but 2 tablespoons bacon fat from pan; add chicken and cook over medium heat until browned on all sides, about 10 minutes. Remove chicken from pan and reserve. Saute onion, green pepper, celery, and garlic in fat remaining in pan until very tender, about 10 minutes.

2. Stir in thyme, tarragon, bay leaves, salt, black pepper, cayenne pepper, and flour; cook over medium heat until flour is beginning to brown, about 5 minutes, stirring frequently.

3. Stir in broth; heat to boiling, stirring until smooth. Stir in reserved chicken and bacon, beans, rice, and carrots. Heat to boiling; reduce heat and simmer, covered, until rice is tender, about 20 minutes. Let stand, covered, 10 minutes and remove bay leaves before serving.

CHICKEN-VEGETABLE STIR-FRY

4 servings

- 2 teaspoons vegetable oil
- 8 ounces boneless chicken breast, cut into strips
- 1 bunch green onions and tops, sliced
- 1 red bell pepper, sliced
- 2-3 teaspoons minced fresh, *or* 1/2-3/4 teaspoon ground, gingerroot
- 1 teaspoon minced garlic
- 3 cups thinly sliced Chinese cabbage
- 2 cups fresh, *or* canned, drained bean sprouts
- 1 can (15 ounces) butter beans, rinsed, drained
- 3/4 cup vegetable broth, chicken broth, *or* water
- 1-2 tablespoons reduced-sodium tamari soy sauce
- 2 teaspoons cornstarch
- 3 cups cooked rice, warm

Per Serving
Calories: 373
% Calories from fat: 9
Fat (gm): 3.8
Sat. fat (gm): 0.6
Cholesterol (mg): 32.9
Sodium (mg): 650
Protein (gm): 25.5
Carbohydrate (gm): 59.4

Exchanges
Milk: 0.0
Vegetable: 3.0
Fruit: 0.0
Bread: 3.0
Meat: 2.0
Fat: 0.0

1. Heat oil in wok or large skillet over medium high heat until hot. Add chicken and stir-fry until browned, 2 to 3 minutes; add green onions, bell pepper, gingerroot, and garlic and stir-fry 1 minute. Stir in Chinese cabbage, bean sprouts, and beans and stir-fry until cabbage is slightly wilted, about 3 minutes. Stir in combined broth, soy sauce, and cornstarch and heat to boiling. Serve over rice.

SWEET-AND-SOUR CHICKEN

8 servings

	Vegetable cooking spray
1	pound chicken breast strips *or* tenders
2	cups sliced carrots
1	cup diced green bell peppers
1/2	cup sliced green onions and tops
1	can (20 ounces) pineapple chunks, undrained
2	cans (15 ounces each) dark red kidney beans, rinsed, drained
1-1 1/3	cups orange juice
2	tablespoons cornstarch
1/4	cup low-sodium soy sauce
1/4	cup packed light brown sugar
1/4	cup white vinegar
	Salt and pepper, to taste
4	cups cooked rice, warm

Per Serving
Calories: 350
% Calories from fat: 3
Fat (gm): 1.3
Sat. fat (gm): 0.3
Cholesterol (mg): 18.1
Sodium (mg): 555
Protein (gm): 16.9
Carbohydrate (gm): 68.5

Exchanges
Milk: 0.0
Vegetable: 0.0
Fruit: 1.0
Bread: 3.0
Meat: 2.0
Fat: 0.0

1. Spray large skillet or wok with cooking spray; heat over medium heat until hot. Stir-fry chicken, carrots, green peppers, and green onions until chicken is cooked, about 10 minutes.

2. Drain pineapple, reserving juice. Add pineapple and beans to pan. Combine reserved pineapple juice with enough orange juice to make 2 cups; whisk in cornstarch. Add juice mixture and remaining ingredients, except salt, pepper, and rice, to skillet; heat to boiling. Reduce heat and simmer uncovered until chicken and vegetables are tender, about 10 minutes. Season to taste with salt and pepper; serve over rice.

CHICKEN-FRIED RICE

6 servings

- 3 cups water
- 3 tablespoons reduced-sodium soy sauce
- 1 teaspoon five-spice powder
- 1/4 teaspoon salt
- 1/8 teaspoon red pepper flakes
- 1 1/2 cups long-grain white rice
- 3 tablespoons reduced-sodium fat-free chicken broth, *or* water
- 2 teaspoons sesame oil
- 4 cups thinly sliced bok choy leaves and stems
- 1 red bell pepper, seeded and diced
- 1/4 cup thinly sliced green onion
- 1 boneless, skinless chicken breast, cooked, cut into small cubes
- 1 can (8 ounces) sliced water chestnuts, well drained
- 2 teaspoons hoisin sauce
- 2 teaspoons rice vinegar

Per Serving
Calories: 275
% Calories from fat: 11
Fat (gm): 3.3
Sat. fat (gm): 0.7
Cholesterol (mg): 32.1
Sodium (mg): 310
Protein (gm): 16.6
Carbohydrate (gm): 43.5
Exchanges
Milk: 0.0
Vegetable: 1.0
Fruit: 0.0
Bread: 2.5
Meat: 1.5
Fat: 0.0

1. Combine water, soy sauce, five-spice powder, salt, and red pepper flakes in medium saucepan. Heat to boiling; add rice, reduce heat and simmer, covered, until rice is tender, about 20 minutes. Remove from heat.

2. Combine broth and sesame oil in large nonstick skillet. Add bok choy, red bell pepper, and green onion and cook over medium-high heat, stirring, 2 to 3 minutes. Add rice mixture, chicken, water chestnuts, hoisin sauce, and vinegar and cook additional 3 to 4 minutes or until flavors are well blended.

CANTONESE CHICKEN

6 servings

6 boneless, skinless chicken breast halves, (about 2 pounds)
6 dried Chinese, *or* Japanese, shiitake mushrooms soaked in hot water 20-30 minutes, squeezed dry, cut into strips
3 tablespoons low-sodium soy sauce
2 tablespoons oyster sauce
2 tablespoons dry sherry, optional
2 teaspoons minced garlic
2 teaspoons minced gingerroot, peeled
1 1/2 tablespoons cornstarch
1 teaspoon sesame oil
1/2 teaspoon sugar
Salt, to taste
Vegetable cooking spray
4 scallions, green part only, cut into 2-inch lengths

Per Serving
Calories: 163
% Calories from fat: 19
Fat (gm): 3.4
Sat. fat (gm): 0.9
Cholesterol (mg): 62.6
Sodium (mg): 503
Protein (gm): 23.7
Carbohydrate (gm): 7.1
Exchanges
Milk: 0.0
Vegetable: 1.5
Fruit: 0.0
Bread: 0.0
Meat: 2.5
Fat: 0.0

1. Place chicken and mushrooms in large mixing bowl. Combine remaining ingredients, except scallions, and pour over chicken and mushrooms; toss well. Cover, and marinate at room temperature 30 to 40 minutes.

2. Spray large skillet with cooking spray; add scallions and cook over medium-high heat 1 minute. Add chicken and marinade. Heat to boiling; reduce heat and simmer, covered, until chicken is cooked through, about 20 minutes, stirring occasionally. Serve with rice or oriental noodles.

CHICKEN CHINA MOON

4 servings

- 1 tablespoon sesame seeds, toasted
- 2 teaspoons finely chopped gingerroot
- 2 tablespoons sugar
- 2 tablespoons low-sodium soy sauce
- 4 boneless, skinless chicken breast halves, pounded thin
- 2 tablespoons chopped green onion

Per Serving
Calories: 166
% Calories from fat: 24
Fat (gm): 4.2
Sat. fat (gm): 1
Cholesterol (mg): 73
Sodium (mg): 328
Protein (gm): 28
Carbohydrate (gm): 2.5
Exchanges
Milk: 0.0
Vegetable: 0.0
Fruit: 0.0
Bread: 0.0
Meat: 3.0
Fat: 0.0

1. Combine sesame seeds, ginger, sugar, and soy sauce and stir well. Grill chicken over medium hot coals, or broil 6 inches from heat source, until cooked through, about 4 minutes on each side; baste with soy mixture frequently. Garnish with green onion. Serve over rice.

STIR-FRY CHICKEN WITH BROCCOLI AND RICE

6 servings

- 1/4 cup light soy sauce
- 1 1/2 tablespoons dry sherry
- 3/4 teaspoon ground ginger
- 1 1/2 pounds boneless, skinless chicken breast, cut into 1-inch pieces
- Vegetable cooking spray
- 1/2 cup sliced mushrooms
- 1/4 cup chopped pimiento
- 1/2 cup sliced celery
- 1/2 cup sliced scallions
- 1 large clove garlic, crushed
- 1 pound broccoli florettes, steamed until crisp-tender
- 3 cups cooked rice

Per Serving
Calories: 232
% Calories from fat: 9
Fat (gm): 2.5
Sat. fat (gm): 0.7
Cholesterol (mg): 45.7
Sodium (mg): 423
Protein (gm): 22.5
Carbohydrate (gm): 28.9
Exchanges
Milk: 0.0
Vegetable: 1.0
Fruit: 0.0
Bread: 1.5
Meat: 2.0
Fat: 0.0

1. Combine soy sauce, sherry, ginger, and chicken in small bowl. Let stand 10 minutes.

2. Spray wok or large skillet with cooking spray; heat over medium heat until hot. Add mushrooms, pimiento, celery, scallions, and garlic. Cook 4 minutes, stirring constantly. Transfer mixture to bowl. Add chicken mixture to wok and cook until chicken is cooked through. Add mushroom mixture and broccoli; cook 1 to 2 minutes. Serve with rice.

CANTON CHICKEN AND RICE

4 servings

Vegetable cooking spray
3/4 pound chicken tenders
2 scallions, minced
1 large clove garlic, minced
1 teaspoon finely chopped gingerroot
1/4 cup low-sodium soy sauce
3 tablespoons dry sherry
1 teaspoon cider vinegar
2 tablespoons honey
1/4 teaspoon cayenne pepper
1 tablespoon sugar
4 cups cooked rice

Per Serving
Calories: 344
% Calories from fat: 5
Fat (gm): 1.9
Sat. fat (gm): 0.5
Cholesterol (mg): 34.3
Sodium (mg): 560
Protein (gm): 18.4
Carbohydrate (gm): 58.6
Exchanges
Milk: 0.0
Vegetable: 0.0
Fruit: 0.0
Bread: 3.5
Meat: 1.5
Fat: 0.0

1. Spray wok or skillet with cooking spray; heat over medium heat until hot. Add chicken, scallions, garlic, and gingerroot and stir-fry until chicken is nicely browned, 4 to 5 minutes. Stir in combined remaining ingredients, except rice, and cook 3 to 4 minutes. Serve over rice.

MICROWAVE CHICKEN CHOW MEIN

4 servings

- 1 cup diagonally sliced celery
- 1 medium green bell pepper, cut into thin strips
- 1 medium onion, cut into thin wedges
- 1 teaspoon canola oil
- 1 cup sliced mushrooms
- 12 ounces fresh bean sprouts, rinsed and drained
- 1 can (8 ounes) water chestnuts, rinsed and drained
- 1 jar (ounces) pimientos, drained and chopped
- 2 tablespoons reduced-sodium soy sauce
- 1/2 cup Chicken Stock (see p. 47), or reduced-sodium fat-free chicken broth
- 12 ounces cooked chicken breasts, sliced thinly against grain

Per Serving
Calories: 311
% Calories from fat: 12
Fat (gm): 5.2
Sat. fat (gm): 1.1
Cholesterol (mg): 73.5
Sodium (mg): 372
Protein (gm): 37.2
Carbohydrate (gm): 33.9

Exchanges
Milk: 0.0
Vegetable: 5.0
Fruit: 0.0
Bread: 0.0
Meat: 3.5
Fat: 0.0

1. Combine celery, green pepper, onions, and oil in microwave-safe 2-quart casserole. Microwave on High until tender, about 3 to 4 minutes, stirring once.

2. Microwave mushrooms for 2 minutes in separate dish and drain when tender. Combine cooked vegetables, bean sprouts, water chestnuts, and pimientos; stir in soy sauce and Chicken Stock. Cover with waxed paper and microwave on High 5 to 6 minutes, stirring twice. Add chicken, mix, and let stand, covered, for 6 or 7 minutes until warmed through. Microwave on High for another minute to heat if necessary. Serve with rice, if desired.

CHICKEN WITH PICANTE SALSA

6 servings

6 chicken thighs
1 teaspoon garlic powder
Picante Salsa (recipe follows)
2 cups cooked brown, *or* white, rice

Per Serving
Calories: 160
% Calories from fat: 23
Fat (gm): 3.9
Sat. fat (gm): 1.1
Cholesterol (mg): 30.9
Sodium (mg): 210
Protein (gm): 10.8
Carbohydrate (gm): 19.6
Exchanges
Milk: 0.0
Vegetable: 1.0
Fruit: 0.0
Bread: 1.0
Meat: 1.0
Fat: 0.0

1. Sprinkle chicken thighs with garlic powder and arrange in baking pan. Spoon about 1/2 cup Picante Salsa over chicken. Bake, loosely covered, at 375 degrees until chicken is cooked through, 50 to 60 minutes. Arrange thighs over hot rice on serving platter. Serve with remaining Picante Sauce.

Picante Salsa

makes about 2 cups

1 1/2 cups peeled, finely chopped tomatoes
1/2 cup chopped onion
1/4 cup finely chopped cilantro
2 jalapeño chilies, minced
1/4 cup tomato juice

1. Combine all ingredients. Serve at room temperature.

SANTA FE CHICKEN

6 servings

6 boneless, skinless chicken breast halves (about 4 ounces each)
2 teaspoons ground cumin, divided
1 teaspoon garlic salt
1 tablespoon canola oil
1 cup canned black beans, rinsed and drained
1 cup frozen whole kernel corn
2/3 cup picante sauce
1/2 cup diced red bell pepper
2-4 tablespoons chopped cilantro

Per Serving
Calories: 239
% Calories from fat: 23
Fat (gm): 6.2
Sat. fat (gm): 1.1
Cholesterol (mg): 73
Sodium (mg): 602
Protein (gm): 30.6
Carbohydrate (gm): 15.8
Exchanges
Milk: 0.0
Vegetable: 0.0
Fruit: 0.0
Bread: 1.0
Meat: 3.0
Fat: 0.0

1. Season chicken with 1 teaspoon cumin and the garlic salt. Heat oil in skillet; add chicken, and cook over medium heat until browned, 3 to 4 minutes on each side.

2. Combine beans, corn, picante sauce, bell pepper, and remaining 1 teaspoon cumin; add to skillet, spooning some of the mixture over the chicken. Heat to boiling; reduce heat and simmer, covered, until chicken is cooked through, 10 to 15 minutes.

3. Arrange chicken on platter, spooning bean mixture over; sprinkle with cilantro.

QUICK CHICKEN CHILI

8 servings

Vegetable cooking spray
1 cup chopped onion
3 cloves garlic, minced
3 tablespoons chili powder
1 teaspoon ground cumin
1 can (14 1/2 ounces) crushed tomatoes, undrained
3 cups cooked cubed chicken breast

Per Serving
Calories: 172
% Calories from fat: 17
Fat (gm): 3.3
Sat. fat (gm): 0.7
Cholesterol (mg): 44.3
Sodium (mg): 377
Protein (gm): 20.8
Carbohydrate (gm): 15.5
Exchanges
Milk: 0.0
Vegetable: 1.0
Fruit: 0.0
Bread: 0.5
Meat: 2.0
Fat: 0.0

1 can (16 ounces) red kidney beans, drained
Coarsely crumbled tortilla chips, as garnish

1. Spray large skillet with cooking spray; add onion and garlic and saute until tender, about 5 minutes. Add chili powder, cumin, and tomatoes. Simmer 5 minutes. Stir in chicken and beans, and cook until hot through, about 5 minutes. Serve in bowls; sprinkle with tortilla chips.

MICROWAVE SOUTHWEST CHICKEN

2 servings

12 ounces chicken tenders
3 tablespoons lemon juice
1 teaspoon olive oil
2 cloves garlic, minced
2 medium onions, sliced
1 small red, *or* green, bell pepper, julienned
1 teaspoon ground cumin
1½ teaspoons dried oregano leaves
2 teaspoons finely chopped jalapeño chili, *or* 1 teaspoon crushed red pepper flakes
Salt and black pepper, to taste
2 tablespoons finely chopped cilantro, *or* parsley

Per Serving
Calories: 289
% Calories from fat: 17
Fat (gm): 5.5
Sat. fat (gm): 1.1
Cholesterol (mg): 98.5
Sodium (mg): 100
Protein (gm): 41.9
Carbohydrate (gm): 17.7
Exchanges
Milk: 0.0
Vegetable: 1.0
Fruit: 0.0
Bread: 0.0
Meat: 5.0
Fat: 0.0

1. Sprinkle chicken with lemon juice. Microwave oil, garlic, and onions in 2-quart casserole, uncovered, at High, for 2 minutes. Stir in pepper strips, cumin, oregano, and jalapeño chili. Microwave, covered with waxed paper, on High until crisp-tender, 2 to 4 minutes, stirring once.

2. Microwave chicken in small glass baking dish, covered with waxed paper, on High until cooked through, 4 to 6 minutes, stirring halfway through cooking time. Stir chicken into vegetables; microwave at High until hot, about 1 minute. Season to taste with salt and pepper; garnish with cilantro.

CANCUN CHICKEN LOAF

4 servings

- 1 pound extra-lean ground chicken
- 1/4 cup uncooked rolled oats
- 1/2 cup onion, minced
- Dash garlic powder
- 1/8 teaspoon ground coriander
- 1/8 teaspoon dried thyme leaves, crushed
- 1/4 cup tomato sauce
- 1 egg, beaten
- 1 tablespoon toasted sunflower seeds
- 3 tablespoons canned chopped green chilies
- 1/2-1 teaspoon salt
- 1/4 teaspoon pepper

Per Serving
Calories: 247
% Calories from fat: 27
Fat (gm): 7.2
Sat. fat (gm): 1.8
Cholesterol (mg): 140
Sodium (mg): 169
Protein (gm): 36.2
Carbohydrate (gm): 7.2
Exchanges
Milk: 0.0
Vegetable: 1.0
Fruit: 0.0
Bread: 0.0
Meat: 4.0
Fat: 0.0

1. Mix all ingredients and shape into loaf in greased baking pan; bake at 350 degrees until cooked through, about 1 hour.

ARROZ CON POLLO

7 servings

- 1 pound boneless, skinless chicken breasts, cut into bite-size pieces
- Vegetable cooking spray
- 2 teaspoons olive oil
- 1 large onion, chopped
- 2 cloves garlic, minced
- 2 1/2 cups reduced-sodium fat-free chicken broth, divided
- 1/2 cup dry sherry, *or* reduced-sodium fat-free chicken broth
- 1 large green bell pepper, seeded and diced
- 1 large red bell pepper, seeded and diced
- 1/4 teaspoon saffron threads, optional

Per Serving
Calories: 246
% Calories from fat: 12
Fat (gm): 3.2
Sat. fat (gm): 0.6
Cholesterol (mg): 26.1
Sodium (mg): 147
Protein (gm): 15.8
Carbohydrate (gm): 34.5
Exchanges
Milk: 0.0
Vegetable: 1.0
Fruit: 0.0
Bread: 2.0
Meat: 1.5
Fat: 0.0

- 1/4 teaspoon black pepper
- Dash cayenne pepper
- 1 cup long-grain white rice
- 1 1/2 cups fresh, *or* frozen, peas
- Vegetable cooking spray

1. Spray Dutch oven with cooking spray and heat over medium heat until hot. Add chicken and cook over medium heat, turning frequently, 6 or 8 minutes, until they begin to brown and are cooked through. Remove and set aside in medium bowl.

2. Add oil to Dutch oven; add onion, garlic, and 1/4 cup broth, stirring up any brown bits from pan bottom. Cook over medium heat, stirring frequently, 6 or 7 minutes, or until onion is tender. If liquid begins to evaporate, add a bit more broth.

3. Add remaining 1 1/4 cups broth, sherry, green and red peppers, and reserved chicken. Stir in saffron (if using), black pepper, cayenne pepper, rice, and peas. Heat to boiling; reduce heat and simmer, covered, 20 minutes or until rice is tender. Stir before serving.

CHICKEN TOSTADAS WITH HOT GREEN SALSA

6 servings

- Vegetable cooking spray
- 6 corn tortillas
- 1 cup shredded lettuce
- 1 cup chopped tomatoes
- 2 cups cooked shredded chicken breast, warm
- Hot Green Salsa (recipe follows)
- Fat-free sour cream, optional

Per Serving
Calories: 174
% Calories from fat: 18
Fat (gm): 3.5
Sat. fat (gm): 0.7
Cholesterol (mg): 39.3
Sodium (mg): 309
Protein (gm): 17.1
Carbohydrate (gm): 18.8

Exchanges
Milk: 0.0
Vegetable: 0.5
Fruit: 0.0
Bread: 1.0
Meat: 2.0
Fat: 0.0

1. Spray medium skillet generously cooking spray; heat over medium heat until hot. Cook each tortilla, turning with tongs until both sides are golden brown. Arrange tortillas on serving plates; top each with shredded lettuce, tomatoes, and chicken; serve with Hot Green Salsa and sour cream.

Hot Green Salsa

makes about 1 1/2 cups

1 can (12 ounces) tomatillos, drained
1/2 cup chopped onion
2 jalapeño chilies, seeded
3 cloves garlic, halved
1/4 teaspoon salt
1/4 cup packed cilantro sprigs

1. Process tomatillos, onion, chilies, garlic, salt, and cilantro in food processor until finely chopped.

FAJITA PITAS

4 servings

1 pound chicken tenders
1 medium red, *or* green, bell pepper, cut into strips
1 small onion, thinly sliced
1 tablespoon canola oil
1 1/2 teaspoons ground cumin
3/4 teaspoon dried oregano leaves
1/8-1/4 teaspoon crushed red pepper
2 whole pitas, cut into halves, warm
1/2 cup mild, *or* medium, salsa
4 tablespoons fat-free sour cream

Per Serving
Calories: 288
% Calories from fat: 19
Fat (gm): 5.8
Sat. fat (gm): 0.8
Cholesterol (mg): 65.6
Sodium (mg): 444
Protein (gm): 31.2
Carbohydrate (gm): 25.9

Exchanges
Milk: 0.0
Vegetable: 0.0
Fruit: 0.0
Bread: 2.0
Meat: 3.0
Fat: 0.0

1. Saute chicken, red pepper, and onion in oil in large skillet until chicken is cooked through and vegetables are crisp-tender, 5 to 8 minutes; sprinkle with cumin, oregano, and crushed red pepper and cook 1 minute longer.

2. Serve chicken mixture in pitas with salsa and sour cream.

CHICKEN BURRITOS WITH A BITE

8 servings

1 pound ground chicken
1 tablespoon canola oil
1/2 teaspoon ground cumin
1/2 teaspoon garlic powder
1/2 teaspoon dried basil leaves
1 cup chopped onion
1 can (16 ounces) pinto beans, drained and rinsed
1 can (4 ounces) chopped hot, *or* mild, green chilies
8 flour tortillas, warm
1/2 cup shredded reduced-fat Cheddar cheese
Taco sauce

Per Serving
Calories: 290
% Calories from fat: 24
Fat (gm): 7.7
Sat. fat (gm): 1.7
Cholesterol (mg): 47.1
Sodium (mg): 586
Protein (gm): 23.8
Carbohydrate (gm): 30.3
Exchanges
Milk: 0.0
Vegetable: 0.0
Fruit: 0.0
Bread: 2.0
Meat: 2.5
Fat: 0.0

1. Cook chicken in oil in large skillet until browned, crumbling with a fork; stir in cumin, garlic powder, basil, and onion and cook 3 to 4 minutes longer. Stir in beans and chilies; simmer until hot through, about 5 minutes. Spoon chicken mixture on each tortilla and sprinkle with cheese; roll up, and tuck in edges. Serve with taco sauce.

CHICKEN CACCIATORE

4 servings

8 ounces boneless, skinless chicken breast
8 ounces boneless, skinless chicken thighs
2 teaspoons dried basil, divided
1/2 teaspoon dried oregano
1/4 teaspoon garlic powder
Olive oil cooking spray
Salt and pepper, to taste
1 cup chopped onion

Per Serving
Calories: 411
% Calories from fat: 15
Fat (gm): 7.2
Sat. fat (gm): 1.7
Cholesterol (mg): 65.5
Sodium (mg): 199
Protein (gm): 30.9
Carbohydrate (gm): 53.7
Exchanges
Milk: 0.0
Vegetable: 4.0
Fruit: 0.0
Bread: 2.0
Meat: 3.0
Fat: 0.0

1 cup chopped green bell pepper
6 cloves garlic, minced
3 cups medium mushrooms, cut into quarters
2 cans ($14^1/_2$ ounces each) reduced-sodium whole tomatoes, undrained, coarsely chopped
$^1/_2$ cup dry red, *or* white, wine
1 bay leaf
4 teaspoons cornstarch
2 tablespoons water
Salt and pepper, to taste
3 cups cooked no-yolk broad noodles
Finely chopped basil, *or* parsley leaves, as garnish

1. Cut chicken into serving-size pieces; sprinkle with combined 1 teaspoon basil, oregano, and garlic powder. Spray large skillet with cooking spray; heat over medium heat until hot. Cook chicken on medium heat until browned, 5 to 8 minutes; remove from skillet and sprinkle with salt and pepper.

2. Add onion, green pepper, and garlic to skillet; saute 3 to 4 minutes. Add mushrooms, tomatoes with liquid, wine, and bay leaf; heat to boiling. Add reserved chicken; reduce heat and simmer, covered, until chicken is tender, 20 to 30 minutes.

3. Heat to boiling; stir in combined cornstarch and water. Boil, stirring constantly, until thickened. Discard bay leaf; season to taste with salt and pepper. Serve chicken and sauce over noodles; sprinkle with basil.

Note: 4 skinless chicken breast halves (6 ounces each) can be substituted for the boneless breasts and thighs, if desired.

CHICKEN RISOTTO

8 servings

Per Serving
Calories: 349
% Calories from fat: 21
Fat (gm): 8
Sat. fat (gm): 2.4
Cholesterol (mg): 55.5
Sodium (mg): 188
Protein (gm): 23.4
Carbohydrate (gm): 43.8

Exchanges
Milk: 0.0
Vegetable: 1.0
Fruit: 0.0
Bread: 2.5
Meat: 3.0
Fat: 0.0

- 1 pound boneless, skinless chicken breasts, cubed
- 2 tablespoons olive oil, divided
- 2 cloves garlic, minced
- 1 large onion, thinly sliced
- 1 large red bell pepper, seeded and chopped
- 1 1/2 cups uncooked arborio rice
- 2 1/2-3 cups reduced-sodium fat-free chicken broth
- 1/4 teaspoon salt
- 1/4 teaspoon black pepper
- 1 tablespoon grated Parmesan cheese

1. Saute chicken in 1 tablespoon oil in large saucepan until cooked through, about 5 minutes; remove chicken. Add garlic, onion, and bell pepper and saute until tender, about 5 minutes.

2. Add rice to saucepan and cook, stirring frequently, 3 to 4 minutes. Heat chicken broth to boiling; add 1 cup broth to rice; cook, stirring constantly, until liquid is absorbed. Continue adding broth, 1/2 cup at a time, cooking until absorbed before adding more. Stir in chicken; cook 2 to 3 minutes, until hot. Stir in salt and black pepper; spoon into serving bowl and sprinkle with cheese.

CHICKEN AND VEGETABLE TETRAZZINI

8 servings

3 cups cooked rotini, *or* other shaped pasta
1 cup (8 ounces) cooked cubed chicken breast
1/2 cup frozen peas
1 can (15 ounces) pinto, *or* red kidney, beans, rinsed, drained
2 tablespoons sliced green onions and tops
1/4 teaspoon salt
1/8 teaspoon pepper
White Sauce (recipe follows)
1/2 cup (2 ounces) shredded Cheddar cheese

Per Serving
Calories: 304
% Calories from fat: 30
Fat (gm): 10
Sat. fat (gm): 5.7
Cholesterol (mg): 38.5
Sodium (mg): 339
Protein (gm): 16.1
Carbohydrate (gm): 36.9
Exchanges
Milk: 0.0
Vegetable: 0.0
Fruit: 0.0
Bread: 2.5
Meat: 1.0
Fat: 1.5

1. Combine pasta, chicken, peas, beans, green onions, salt and pepper; spoon into lightly greased 13 x 9-inch baking dish. Pour White Sauce over; sprinkle with cheese.

2. Bake at 350 degrees until cheese is browned and sauce is bubbly, about 30 minutes.

White Sauce

makes 2 cups

4 tablespoons butter or margarine
1/4 cup flour
2 cups fat-free milk

1. Melt butter in medium saucepan; whisk in flour. Cook over medium heat 1 minute; whisk in milk. Heat to boiling, whisking until smooth.

BREAST OF CHICKEN IN PORCINI SAUCE

4 servings

Per Serving
Calories: 181
% Calories from fat: 18
Fat (gm): 3.6
Sat. fat (gm): 1.3
Cholesterol (mg): 70.9
Sodium (mg): 191
Protein (gm): 26.9
Carbohydrate (gm): 6.7
Exchanges
Milk: 0.0
Vegetable: 1.0
Fruit: 0.0
Bread: 0.0
Meat: 3.0
Fat: 0.0

1/4 ounce dried porcini, *or* shiitake, mushrooms
Vegetable cooking spray
1/4 cup chopped onion
4 ounces mushrooms, sliced
1/3 cup dry white wine
1/2 pound plum tomatoes (4-5), peeled, seeded, chopped
Black pepper, to taste
1 tablespoon chopped fresh, *or* 1/2 teaspoon dried, rosemary leaves
1 tablespoon fresh chopped, *or* 1 teaspoon dried, basil leaves
1 tablespoon fresh chopped, *or* 1 teaspoon dried, oregano leaves
4 boneless skinless chicken breast halves (about 1 1/2 pounds)
1/2 cup reduced-sodium fat-free chicken broth

1. Soak dried porcini in about 1/2 cup hot water until soft, about 10 minutes; strain, reserving mushrooms and liquid.

2. Spray small skillet with cooking spray; heat over medium heat until hot. Add onion and mushrooms, and saute for about 2 minutes, until onions are soft and mushrooms give off their moisture. Add wine, and simmer 1 minute. Add tomatoes, and crush with back of spoon. Add reserved porcini and liquid. Simmer sauce over medium-high heat to reduce slightly, about 3 minutes. Season with pepper, rosemary, basil, and oregano.

3. Spray large skillet with vegetable cooking spray; heat over medium-high heat until hot. Cook chicken breasts for 5 minutes, turning once, until nicely browned, about 5 minutes on each side. Drain off excess pan drippings. Add chicken broth, and cook, covered, until chicken is cooked through, about 5 minutes. Add mushroom sauce to chicken. Stir well, and cook for 1 minute.

CHICKEN CATALAN-STYLE

4 servings

Per Serving
Calories: 427
% Calories from fat: 28
Fat (gm): 13.4
Sat. fat (gm): 3.6
Cholesterol (mg): 153.6
Sodium (mg): 348
Protein (gm): 53.1
Carbohydrate (gm): 18.3
Exchanges
Milk: 0.0
Vegetable: 3.0
Fruit: 0.0
Bread: 0.0
Meat: 6.5
Fat: 0.0

Vegetable cooking spray
3 pounds chicken pieces
1 tablespoon chopped fresh, *or* 1 teaspoon dried, oregano leaves
Black pepper
2 onions, finely chopped
1 clove garlic, minced
2 tomatoes, peeled, seeded, and chopped
1 bay leaf
1/2 cup dry white wine
1 small eggplant, unpeeled, cubed
2 zucchini, sliced
1/2 cup water
2 green, *or* red, bell peppers, chopped
1/2 cup tomato sauce
1 teaspoon chopped cilantro
1 tablespoon chopped fresh, *or* 1 teaspoon dried, basil leaves
2 tablespoons chopped fresh parsley

1. Spray large skillet with vegetable cooking spray; add chicken and cook over medium heat until browned on all sides, 8 to 10 minutes. Remove chicken and sprinkle oregano and pepper. Place chicken in casserole.

2. Saute onions and garlic in same skillet 3 minutes. Add tomatoes, bay leaf, and white wine. Simmer, covered, 5 minutes. Transfer to casserole. Cover and bake at 350 degrees 30 minutes.

3. Add eggplant, zucchini, and water to skillet. Saute over medium heat 5 minutes until lightly browned. Add peppers to skillet and saute 5 minutes; stir in tomato sauce, cilantro, and basil. Add vegetable mixture to casserole. Continue baking, covered, 30 minutes, or until chicken is cooked through. Sauce should be thick. Remove bay leaf. Sprinkle chicken with parsley.

4. Arrange chicken pieces and sauce on hot serving dish. Top with parsley.

CHICKEN MARENGO

4 servings

Per Serving
Calories: 246
% Calories from fat: 22
Fat (gm): 6.1
Sat. fat (gm): 1.1
Cholesterol (mg): 48.3
Sodium (mg): 57.9
Protein (gm): 20
Carbohydrate (gm): 17.7

Exchanges
Milk: 0.0
Vegetable: 1.0
Fruit: 0.0
Bread: 1.0
Meat: 2.5
Fat: 0.0

4 boneless, skinless chicken breast halves
1/4 cup all-purpose flour
Dash salt and pepper
1 tablespoon olive oil
1 clove garlic, crushed
3 tablespoons chopped onion
4 tomatoes, quartered
1 cup dry white wine
Bouquet garni (sprig of parsley and 1/2 teaspoon each: dried thyme, rosemary, and tarragon leaves, tied in cheesecloth bag)
1 cup sliced mushrooms
1/2 cup sliced pitted black olives, optional
1/2 cup reduced-sodium fat-free chicken broth
2 tablespoons cornstarch

1. Shake chicken in bag containing flour, salt, and pepper. Brown chicken in oil in medium skillet over medium heat; add garlic and onions and cook 3 to 4 minutes longer. Add tomatoes, wine, herb bouquet, mushrooms, and olives, if using. Heat to boiling; reduce heat and simmer, covered, over low heat about 1/2 hour.

2. Remove chicken from skillet and discard bouquet garni. Heat tomato mixture to boiling; gradually stir in combined chicken broth and cornstarch. Boil, stirring, until mixture thickens, 1 to 2 minutes. Arrange chicken on hot platter. Spoon tomato sauce over. Excellent served with rice.

EASY CHICKEN SALTIMBOCCA

6 servings

- 3 boneless skinless chicken breast halves, cut in half lengthwise, pounded thin
- 6 thin slices boiled ham
- 1 medium tomato, seeded and chopped
- 1 teaspoon dried oregano leaves
- 1/3 cup dry unseasoned bread crumbs
- 3 tablespoons shredded part-skim mozzarella cheese
- 2 tablespoons minced parsley

Per Serving
Calories: 199
% Calories from fat: 23
Fat (gm): 4.8
Sat. fat (gm): 1.6
Cholesterol (mg): 82.5
Sodium (mg): 293
Protein (gm): 31.5
Carbohydrate (gm): 5.6

Exchanges
Milk: 0.0
Vegetable: 0.5
Fruit: 0.0
Bread: 0.0
Meat: 3.5
Fat: 0.0

1. Place a ham slice on each chicken breast; top with combined tomato and oregano. Bake at 350 degrees, loosely covered, until chicken is cooked through, 40 to 45 minutes. Sprinkle combined bread crumbs, cheese and parsley over chicken; bake until cheese is melted, about 10 minutes.

QUICK AND EASY PAELLA

5 servings

- 1/2 pound boneless, skinless chicken breast, cut into bite-size pieces
- 2 teaspoons olive oil
- 1 large onion, chopped
- 2 cloves garlic, minced
- 2 3/4 cups reduced-sodium fat-free chicken broth, divided
- 1/4 teaspoon crushed saffron threads, optional
- 1 can (14 3/4 ounces) Italian-style tomatoes, undrained
- 1 can (14 3/4 ounces) artichoke hearts, drained
- 1 large red bell pepper, diced
- 1 large green bell pepper, diced
- 1 teaspoon dried thyme leaves

Per Serving
Calories: 376
% Calories from fat: 13
Fat (gm): 5.7
Sat. fat (gm): 1.1
Cholesterol (mg): 96.2
Sodium (mg): 719
Protein (gm): 27.9
Carbohydrate (gm): 56.1

Exchanges
Milk: 0.0
Vegetable: 2.0
Fruit: 0.0
Bread: 3.0
Meat: 2.0
Fat: 0.0

- 1/2 teaspoon dried basil leaves
- 1/8 teaspoon cayenne pepper
- 1/8 teaspoon black pepper
- 1/4 pound Canadian bacon, cut into thin strips
- 1 1/4 cups uncooked long-grain white rice
- 1/2 pound peeled, deveined medium shrimp
- 1/4 teaspoon salt

1. Cook chicken pieces in oil in large saucepan over medium heat until browned, 2 to 3 minutes; add onion and garlic and cook until onion is tender, about 5 minutes. Add chicken broth and saffron (if using); add remaining ingredients, except rice, shrimp, and salt. Heat to boiling; add rice, reduce heat, and simmer, covered, 15 minutes or until rice is almost tender. Add shrimp and cook an additional 5 to 6 minutes until shrimp is cooked and rice is tender. Stir in salt.

CHICKEN VESUVIO

8 servings

- 8 skinless chicken breast halves (about 3 lbs.)
- 4 large red potatoes, unpeeled, cut into quarters
- 1/4 cup chopped green onions and tops
- 1 tablespoon olive oil
- 1/4 cup fresh lemon juice
- 1 tablespoon chopped fresh, *or* 1 teaspoon dried, rosemary leaves
- 1 tablespoon chopped fresh, *or* 1 teaspoon dried, oregano leaves
- 1 tablespoon minced garlic
- 1/4 cup sliced pitted black olives
- 1 cup sliced mushrooms

Per Serving
Calories: 183
% Calories from fat: 19
Fat (gm): 3.8
Sat. fat (gm): 0.8
Cholesterol (mg): 45.7
Sodium (mg): 44.2
Protein (gm): 18.6
Carbohydrate (gm): 18.4
Exchanges
Milk: 0.0
Vegetable: 0.0
Fruit: 0.0
Bread: 1.0
Meat: 2.0
Fat: 0.0

1. Place chicken, potatoes, and onions in 2-quart casserole. Drizzle olive oil and lemon juice over chicken and potatoes; sprinkle with rosemary, oregano, and garlic. Refrigerate at least 30 minutes, turning occasionally.

2. Bake chicken, covered, at 425 degrees 30 minutes. Lower oven temperature to 400 degrees and add olives and mushrooms. Bake, covered, until chicken is cooked through, about 30 minutes. Place chicken on platter and pour pan juices over all.

MIDDLE-EASTERN CHICKEN

6 servings

Vegetable cooking spray
1 pound boneless, skinless chicken breasts, cut into 6 pieces
1 large onion, chopped
2 cloves garlic, minced
2 teaspoons olive oil
1 3/4 cups reduced-sodium fat-free chicken broth
1 green bell pepper, seeded and diced
2 cups chopped tomato
1 can (15 ounces) garbanzo beans, rinsed, drained
1/2 cup raisins
1 large bay leaf
1 1/2 teaspoons dried thyme leaves
1 teaspoon ground cumin
1/4 teaspoon ground allspice
1/8 teaspoon ground cloves
1/8 teaspoon black pepper
1 cup uncooked couscous, cooked
Salt, to taste
Chopped parsley for garnish

Per Serving
Calories: 334
% Calories from fat: 13
Fat (gm): 5.1
Sat. fat (gm): 0.9
Cholesterol (mg): 30.5
Sodium (mg): 419
Protein (gm): 21.3
Carbohydrate (gm): 52.6
Exchanges
Milk: 0.0
Vegetable: 1.0
Fruit: 0.5
Bread: 2.5
Meat: 1.5
Fat: 0.0

1. Spray small Dutch oven with cooking spray; add chicken pieces and cook over medium heat until browned, 3 to 4 minutes. Add onion, garlic, and oil; cook until onion is tender, 3 to 4 minutes. Add broth, green pepper, tomato, garbanzos, raisins, bay leaf, thyme, cumin, allspice, cloves, and black pepper. Heat to boiling; reduce heat, and simmer, covered, 20 to 25 minutes or until chicken is tender. Remove bay leaf and discard. Add salt to taste.

2. Arrange couscous on serving platter and top with chicken and sauce. Garnish with chopped parsley.

GRECIAN CHICKEN

4 servings

- 2 pounds chicken pieces
- 3 tablespoons dried oregano leaves
- 1 1/4 teaspoons garlic powder
- 1/4 teaspoon salt
- 1/4 teaspoon pepper
- 1 tablespoon margarine, melted
- 1 cup fresh lemon juice
- 1 cup dry white wine, *or* reduced-sodium fat-free chicken broth
- 1 teaspoon Worcestershire sauce
- 2 tablespoons cornstarch
- 1/4 cup water

Per Serving
Calories: 346
% Calories from fat: 31
Fat (gm): 12.4
Sat. fat (gm): 3.7
Cholesterol (mg): 145.1
Sodium (mg): 370
Protein (gm): 37.9
Carbohydrate (gm): 13.3

Exchanges
Milk: 0.0
Vegetable: 0.0
Fruit: 1.0
Bread: 0.0
Meat: 0.5
Fat: 0.0

1. Sprinkle chicken pieces with combined oregano, garlic powder, salt, and pepper. Place chicken skin side up in nonstick shallow casserole. Brush chicken pieces with margarine. Bake, covered, at 375 degrees 40 minutes.

2. Combine lemon juice, wine, and Worcestershire sauce; pour over chicken. Cover and bake until tender, about 20 minutes. Remove chicken to serving platter.

3. Heat pan juices to boiling; stir in combined cornstarch and water. Boil, stirring until thickened, 1 to 2 minutes. Serve sauce over chicken.

MOROCCAN-STYLE CORNISH HENS STUFFED WITH COUSCOUS

8 servings

Per Serving
Calories: 555
% Calories from fat: 27
Fat (gm): 16.4
Sat. fat (gm): 4
Cholesterol (mg): 153.6
Sodium (mg): 509
Protein (gm): 53.6
Carbohydrate (gm): 43.5
Exchanges
Milk: 0.0
Vegetable: 0.0
Fruit: 1.0
Bread: 2.0
Meat: 6.5
Fat: 0.0

3 tablespoons dry white wine, *or* water
3/4 cup raisins
1/2 teaspoon saffron threads, chopped, optional
2 medium onions, chopped
2 tablespoons olive oil
2 teaspoons ground cinnamon
3/4 teaspoon dried rosemary leaves
1 tablespoon honey
1 cup couscous, cooked
Pepper, to taste
4 Rock Cornish game hens, about 1 1/2 pounds each, skinned
Honey Baste (recipe follows)

1. Pour wine over raisins and saffron (if using) in small bowl; let stand 30 minutes.

2. Saute onions in oil in medium skillet until tender, about 5 minutes; stir in cinnamon, rosemary, and honey. Stir onion mixture into couscous; stir in raisin mixture. Season to taste with pepper. Stuff hens with couscous mixture and place in roasting pan. Bake at 450 degrees until juices run clear when thighs are pierced, about 45 minutes.

Honey Baste

makes about 1/4 cup

1/4 cup dark honey
3/4 teaspoon ground cinnamon
1/4 teaspoon ground turmeric, *or* ground cumin
Pepper, freshly ground

1. Combine all ingredients.

UNITED NATIONS CHICKEN

4 servings

1 tablespoon olive oil
4 boneless, skinless chicken breast halves
Pepper
1/2 cup chopped onion
1/4 cup chopped green bell pepper
Sauce/topping of your choice (recipes follow)

Per Serving
Calories: 164
% Calories from fat: 27
Fat (gm): 4.8
Sat. fat (gm): 0.8
Cholesterol (mg): 65.7
Sodium (mg): 60
Protein (gm): 26.5
Carbohydrate (gm): 2.3
Exchanges
Milk: 0.0
Vegetable: 0.0
Fruit: 0.0
Bread: 0.0
Meat: 3.0
Fat: 0.0

1. Heat olive oil in medium skillet over medium-high heat. Add chicken and sprinkle with pepper. Cook until golden, about 4 to 5 minutes on each side. Add chopped onion and green pepper and cook until tender, about 3 to 4 minutes.

2. Serve chicken with desired sauce/topping.

Sauces for United Nations Chicken (all serve 4)

Greek-Style Sauce

makes about 3/4 cup

3/4 cup Chicken Stock (see p. 47), or reduced-sodium fat-free chicken broth
2 tablespoons fresh lemon juice
1 tablespoon grated lemon peel
1 teaspoon dried oregano leaves
8 sliced black olives, as garnish

Per Serving
Calories: 10
% Calories from fat: 19
Fat (gm): 0.2
Sat. fat (gm): 0.1
Cholesterol (mg): 1.9
Sodium (mg): 2
Protein (gm): 0.7
Carbohydrate (gm): 1.3
Exchanges
Milk: 0.0
Vegetable: 0.0
Fruit: 0.0
Bread: 0.5
Meat: 0.0
Fat: 0.0

1. Heat all ingredients, except olives, in small saucepan until hot; do not boil. Spoon over chicken; garnish with olives.

French-Style Sauce

makes about 2 cups

- 1/3 cup Chicken Stock (see p. 47), or reduced-sodium fat-free chicken broth
- 1/3 cup dry red wine
- 1/2 pound mushrooms, sliced
- 1/2 cup jarred pearl onions, drained
- 1 teaspoon dried thyme leaves
- Minced parsley, as garnish

Per Serving
Calories: 42
% Calories from fat: 8
Fat (gm): 0.3
Sat. fat (gm): 0.1
Cholesterol (mg): 0.8
Sodium (mg): 107
Protein (gm): 1.9
Carbohydrate (gm): 4.9

Exchanges
Milk: 0.0
Vegetable: 0.0
Fruit: 0.0
Bread: 0.5
Meat: 0.0
Fat: 0.0

1. Heat Chicken Stock and wine to boiling in large skillet; add mushrooms, reduce heat and simmer, covered, until mushrooms are wilted, about 5 minutes. Stir in onions and thyme; cook, uncovered, over medium heat until liquid is almost evaporated, about 5 minutes. Spoon over chicken; garnish with parsley.

Italian-Style Sauce

makes about 1/2 cup

- 1/2 cup low-fat yogurt
- 1 tablespoon fresh, *or* 1 teaspoon dried, basil leaves
- 1 small tomato, chopped
- 1 tablespoon fresh, *or* 1 teaspoon dried, oregano leaves
- Dash pepper
- 4 anchovies, *or* fresh parsley, as garnish

Per Serving
Calories: 27
% Calories from fat: 19
Fat (gm): 0.6
Sat. fat (gm): 0.3
Cholesterol (mg): 1.8
Sodium (mg): 24
Protein (gm): 1.9
Carbohydrate (gm): 3.7

Exchanges
Milk: 0.0
Vegetable: 0.0
Fruit: 0.0
Bread: 0.0
Meat: 0.0
Fat: 0.0

1. Heat all ingredients, except anchovies, over low heat in small saucepan until warm. Spoon over chicken; garnish with anchovies.

Mexican-Style Sauce

makes about 1 cup

Vegetable cooking spray
1/4 cup finely chopped onion
1 small jalapeño chili, minced
1 teaspoon chili powder
1 small tomato, diced
3/4 cup Chicken Stock (see p. 47), or reduced-sodium fat-free chicken broth
1/3 cup low-fat yogurt or sour cream
2 teaspoons finely chopped cilantro

Per Serving
Calories: 33
% Calories from fat: 20
Fat (gm): 0.7
Sat. fat (gm): 0.3
Cholesterol (mg): 3.1
Sodium (mg): 26
Protein (gm): 2.2
Carbohydrate (gm): 4.5
Exchanges
Milk: 0.0
Vegetable: 0.0
Fruit: 0.0
Bread: 0.5
Meat: 0.0
Fat: 0.0

1. Spray small skillet with cooking spray; add onion and jalapeño chili and cook over medium heat until onion is tender, 2 to 3 minutes. Stir in chili powder and tomato; cook 1 to 2 minutes. Stir in Chicken Stock and heat to boiling; reduce heat and simmer until stock is reduced to about 1/2 cup. Reduce heat to low; stir in yogurt and cilantro. Spoon over chicken.

Chinese-Style Sauce

makes about 2 cups

1/3 cup Chicken Stock (see p. 47), or reduced-sodium fat-free chicken broth
1/2 pound mushrooms, sliced
1/2 cup sliced water chestnuts
4 scallions, sliced
3 tablespoons sesame seeds, toasted, as garnish

Per Serving
Calories: 32
% Calories from fat: 9
Fat (gm): 0.4
Sat. fat (gm): 0.1
Cholesterol (mg): 0.8
Sodium (mg): 8
Protein (gm): 2.3
Carbohydrate (gm): 6.1
Exchanges
Milk: 0.0
Vegetable: 0.0
Fruit: 0.0
Bread: 0.5
Meat: 0.0
Fat: 0.0

1. Heat Chicken Stock to boiling in large skillet; add mushrooms, water chestnuts, and scallions. Reduce heat and simmer, covered, until mushrooms are wilted, about 5 minutes. Cook, uncovered, over medium heat until liquid is almost evaporated, about 5 minutes. Spoon over chicken; sprinkle with sesame seeds.

APRICOT TURKEY BREAST

4 servings

1 pound boneless turkey breast cutlets, pounded to 1/4 inch thickness
1 teaspoon paprika
1/4 teaspoon cayenne pepper
Vegetable cooking spray
Salt and pepper, to taste
1 1/2 tablespoons apricot preserves
2 teaspoons Dijon mustard
2 tablespoons chopped parsley

Per Serving
Calories: 137
% Calories from fat: 17
Fat (gm): 2.6
Sat. fat (gm): 0.8
Cholesterol (mg): 49.6
Sodium (mg): 81.1
Protein (gm): 21.7
Carbohydrate (gm): 5.8

Exchanges
Milk: 0.0
Vegetable: 0.0
Fruit: 0.5
Bread: 0.0
Meat: 2.5
Fat: 0.0

1. Sprinkle turkey with combined paprika and cayenne pepper. Spray large skillet with cooking spray; add turkey and saute until cooked through, 2 to 3 minutes on each side. Sprinkle lightly with salt and pepper. Brush combined preserves and mustard on turkey; sprinkle with parsley.

TURKEY MARSALA

4 servings

12 ounces turkey breast cutlets, pounded to 1/4 inch thickness
All-purpose flour
Vegetable cooking spray
1 teaspoon dried rosemary leaves
2 tablespoons Marsala wine, *or* dry sherry
1/4 cup dry white wine, *or* reduced-sodium fat-free chicken broth
Salt and pepper, to taste
Parsley sprigs, as garnish

Per Serving
Calories: 100
% Calories from fat: 17
Fat (gm): 1.8
Sat. fat (gm): 0.6
Cholesterol (mg): 37.2
Sodium (mg): 39.7
Protein (gm): 16.1
Carbohydrate (gm): 0.4

Exchanges
Milk: 0.0
Vegetable: 0.0
Fruit: 0.0
Bread: 0.0
Meat: 2.0
Fat: 0.0

1. Coat cutlets lightly with flour. Spray large skillet with cooking spray; saute turkey cutlets until cooked through, 2 to 3 minutes on each side. Move cutlets to side of skillet. Add rosemary, Marsala and wine; simmer until reduced to a thin glaze, stirring brown bits from bottom of skillet. Coat turkey with wine mixture; season to taste with salt and pepper. Garnish with parsley.

TURKEY PEPPERCORN

4 servings

1 pound turkey breast cutlets, pounded to 1/4-inch thickness
1 tablespoon black, *or* green, peppercorns, crushed in blender
Vegetable cooking spray
1/2 cup dry white wine, *or* reduced-sodium fat-free chicken broth
1 tablespoon brandy, optional
Salt and pepper, to taste
1 tablespoon chopped parsley, as garnish

Per Serving
Calories: 145
% Calories from fat: 15
Fat (gm): 2.4
Sat. fat (gm): 0.8
Cholesterol (mg): 49.6
Sodium (mg): 48
Protein (gm): 21.6
Carbohydrate (gm): 1.3
Exchanges
Milk: 0.0
Vegetable: 0.0
Fruit: 0.0
Bread: 0.0
Meat: 2.5
Fat: 0.0

1. Sprinkle both sides of turkey with peppercorns and press firmly onto surface of meat. Spray large skillet with cooking spray; saute turkey cutlets until cooked through, 2 to 3 minutes on each side. Move cutlets to side of skillet. Stir in wine and brandy (if using); simmer until reduced to a thin glaze, stirring brown bits from bottom of skillet. Coat turkey with glaze; season to taste with salt and pepper. Sprinkle with parsley.

POACHED TURKEY AND VEGETABLES GREMOLATA

4 servings

1/2 cup reduced-sodium fat-free chicken broth
1/4 cup dry white wine, *or* reduced-sodium fat-free chicken broth
1 pound turkey breast cutlets
4 medium red-skinned potatoes, quartered
4 large carrots, cut into 2-inch pieces
1 cup halved green beans
1 cup cubed zucchini
Salt and pepper, to taste
Finely chopped parsley

Per Serving
Calories: 302
% Calories from fat: 6
Fat (gm): 1.9
Sat. fat (gm): 0.6
Cholesterol (mg): 67.9
Sodium (mg): 145
Protein (gm): 30.5
Carbohydrate (gm): 39.7
Exchanges
Milk: 0.0
Vegetable: 1.0
Fruit: 0.0
Bread: 2.0
Meat: 3.0
Fat: 0.0

1. Heat chicken broth and wine to boiling in large skillet; add turkey cutlets and vegetables. Reduce heat and simmer, covered, until turkey is cooked through and vegetables are tender, 10 to 15 minutes. Arrange turkey and vegetables on platter; cover to keep warm. Heat pan juices to boiling; boil until reduced to 1/4 cup; drizzle over turkey and vegetables. Season to taste with salt and pepper; sprinkle with parsley. Serve with Gremolata.

Gremolata

makes about 1/4 cup

1 cup chopped parsley
1 tablespoon minced garlic
2 tablespoons lemon juice
1 tablespoon olive oil

1. Process all ingredients in food processor or blender until smooth.

TURKEY TERIYAKI

4 servings

1/4 cup dry sherry, *or* reduced-sodium fat-free chicken broth
2 tablespoons low-sodium soy sauce
2 tablespoons water
1 tablespoon Dijon-style mustard
2 tablespoons finely chopped gingerroot
2 cloves garlic, minced
1 tablespoon minced orange rind
1 pound turkey breast, cut into strips
Vegetable cooking spray
1-2 teaspoons sesame oil
2 cups sliced mushrooms
1 cup frozen peas, thawed

Per Serving
Calories: 198
% Calories from fat: 18
Fat (gm): 3.9
Sat. fat (gm): 1
Cholesterol (mg): 49.6
Sodium (mg): 364
Protein (gm): 25.4
Carbohydrate (gm): 11
Exchanges
Milk: 0.0
Vegetable: 0.5
Fruit: 0.0
Bread: 0.5
Meat: 2.5
Fat: 0.0

1. Combine sherry, soy sauce, water, mustard, gingerroot, garlic, and orange rind; pour over turkey in bowl, tossing to coat turkey; refrigerate 1 hour. Drain.

2. Spray wok or large skillet with cooking spray; add sesame oil and heat over medium heat until hot. Add turkey mixture and stir-fry 2 to 3 minutes. Add mushrooms and peas; stir-fry until turkey and mushrooms are cooked, about 5 minutes. Serve with rice, if desired.

TURKEY MEATBALLS WITH TOMATO-BASIL SAUCE

4 servings

Per Serving
Calories: 318
% Calories from fat: 31
Fat (gm): 11.2
Sat. fat (gm): 2.7
Cholesterol (mg): 42.2
Sodium (mg): 543
Protein (gm): 21.9
Carbohydrate (gm): 28.5

Exchanges
Milk: 0.0
Vegetable: 2.5
Fruit: 0.0
Bread: 1.0
Meat: 2.0
Fat: 1.5

1 pound ground turkey
3/4 cup Italian-seasoned dry bread crumbs
1 medium onion, chopped
2 egg whites
1/2 teaspoon dried marjoram leaves
1 teaspoon dried oregano leaves
1 teaspoon dried basil leaves
1/4 teaspoon black pepper
1/2 cup white wine, *or* reduced-sodium fat-free chicken broth
2 cups Basic Tomato-Basil Sauce (half recipe) (see p. 510), *or* purchased spaghetti sauce

1. Combine turkey, bread crumbs, onion, egg whites, marjoram, oregano, basil, and pepper. This is best mixed with your hands. Slowly add wine to turkey mixture, mixing with hands until mixture forms large ball. Shape mixture into 16 meatballs and arrange in greased baking pan.

2. Bake at 350 degrees until meatballs are firm, about 15 minutes. Spoon Basic Tomato-Basil Sauce over meatball and bake, loosely covered, until meatballs are firm and no longer pink in center and sauce is bubbly, about 20 minutes. Spoon meatballs and sauce over cooked pasta, rice, or polenta.

ITALIAN TURKEY BURGERS

4 servings

- 8 ounces ground turkey
- 1 egg
- 1/2 teaspoon salt, optional
- 1/4 teaspoon pepper
- 3/4 cup Italian-flavored dry bread crumbs, divided
- Vegetable cooking spray
- 1 cup thinly sliced mushrooms
- 1/2 cup red wine, *or* reduced-sodium fat-free chicken broth
- 1/2 cup plain fat-free yogurt

Per Serving
Calories: 200
% Calories from fat: 22
Fat (gm): 4.9
Sat. fat (gm): 1.4
Cholesterol (mg): 21.6
Sodium (mg): 648
Protein (gm): 14.1
Carbohydrate (gm): 19.6

Exchanges
Milk: 0.0
Vegetable: 0.0
Fruit: 0.0
Bread: 1.0
Meat: 1.5
Fat: 1.0

1. Combine turkey, egg, salt, pepper, and 1/4 cup bread crumbs; shape into 4 burgers. Coat burgers with remaining bread crumbs. Spray medium skillet with cooking spray; cook burgers over medium-low to medium heat until browned and no longer pink in the center, 5 to 8 minutes on each side.

2. While burgers are cooking, spray medium skillet with cooking spray; add mushrooms and saute mushrooms 5 minutes or until softened. Stir in wine and heat to boiling; reduce heat and simmer, uncovered, until wine is almost gone. Reduce heat to low and stir in yogurt.

3. Place burgers on serving plates; spoon mushroom mixture over.

TEX-MEX PITAS WITH HOMEMADE SALSA

8 servings

Per Serving
Calories: 230
% Calories from fat: 26
Fat (gm): 8.5
Sat. fat (gm): 2
Cholesterol (mg): 47.3
Sodium (mg): 280
Protein (gm): 16.7
Carbohydrate (gm): 25.6

Exchanges
Milk: 0.0
Vegetable: 2.0
Fruit: 0.0
Bread: 1.0
Meat: 2.0
Fat: 0.0

Vegetable cooking spray
1 pound ground turkey
1 cup chopped onion
1 tablespoon minced garlic
1 teaspoon pepper
1 tablespoon chili powder
1 teaspoon ground cumin
1 teaspoon dried oregano leaves
1/2-3/4 cup (2-3 ounces) reduced-fat mozzarella cheese
Salsa (recipe follows)
4 pita breads, cut in half
Shredded lettuce
1/2 cup fat-free sour cream

1. Spray large skillet with cooking spray; cook turkey, onion, and garlic until turkey is browned. Crumble turkey with a fork. Stir in pepper and spices and cook 2 minutes longer; remove from heat and stir in cheese.

2. Spoon mixture into pita halves; top with lettuce, salsa, and dollops of sour cream.

Salsa

makes about 2 cups

2 cups seeded, chopped tomato
1/2 cup thinly sliced green onions and tops
1 jalapeño chili, seeds discarded, minced
1/4 cup minced cilantro
1/2 teaspoon celery seed
1 tablespoon red wine vinegar
Black pepper, freshly ground

1. Mix all ingredients.

SIX

Beef, Veal, Pork, AND Lamb

MICROWAVE MEAT LOAF

4 servings

- 1 pound ground beef top round
- 1/4 cup chopped green bell pepper
- 1/4 cup chopped red bell pepper
- 3/4 cup chopped onion
- 3 cloves garlic, minced
- 1/2 cup whole wheat bread crumbs
- 1 tablespoon reduced-sodium soy sauce
- 1 tablespoon mustard
- 1 teaspoon salt, optional
- 1/4 teaspoon pepper
- 1 large dill pickle, chopped

Per Serving
Calories: 242
% Calories from fat: 24
Fat (gm): 6.3
Sat. fat (gm): 2
Cholesterol (mg): 72
Sodium (mg): 560
Protein (gm): 30
Carbohydrate (gm): 15
Exchanges
Milk: 0.0
Vegetable: 0.0
Fruit: 0.0
Bread: 0.5
Meat: 4.0
Fat: 0.0

1. Mix all ingredients and mold into long, round loaf, about 2 inches high in 9-inch pie plate. Microwave on High 3 to 4 minutes. Rotate pie plate and microwave on High until meat loaf is no longer pink in the center, 3 to 4 minutes.

ALL-AMERICAN MEAT LOAF

8 servings

- 1 pound ground lean beef
- 1 pound ground turkey
- 1 tablespoon garlic powder
- 1/4 teaspoon pepper
- 1/4 teaspoon ground allspice
- 2 tablespoons Worcestershire sauce
- 1 1/2 cups quick cooking oats
- 1 can zesty tomato soup
- 1/2 cup chili sauce
- 1/2 cup plain fat-free yogurt
- 2 tablespoons dried onions
- 2 egg whites
- 1/2 cup chopped parsley

Per Serving
Calories: 330
% Calories from fat: 35
Fat (gm): 12.9
Sat. fat (gm): 4.2
Cholesterol (mg): 57.4
Sodium (mg): 882
Protein (gm): 24
Carbohydrate (gm): 29.2
Exchanges
Milk: 0.0
Vegetable: 3.0
Fruit: 0.0
Bread: 1.0
Meat: 3.0
Fat: 0.5

- 1/2 cup tomato sauce
- 1/2 cup barbecue sauce
- Parsley sprigs

1. Combine meat with remaining ingredients, except tomato and barbecue sauce, and parsley sprigs. Form into loaf in greased 13 x 9-inch baking pan; refrigerate, covered, 1 hour.

2. Bake at 350 degrees, loosely covered, until loaf is no longer pink in the center, about 1 hour.

3. While meat loaf is cooking, heat tomato and barbecue sauces to boiling in small saucepan; reduce heat and simmer until thickened, about 15 minutes. Spread on top of meat 20 minutes before end of baking time. Remove from pan and drain; garnish with parsley.

BEEF STROGANOFF

4 servings

Per Serving
Calories: 423
% Calories from fat: 21
Fat (gm): 39
Sat. fat (gm): 45.1
Cholesterol (mg): 10
Sodium (mg): 2.2
Protein (gm): 64
Carbohydrate (gm): 167
Exchanges
Milk: 0.0
Vegetable: 1.0
Fruit: 0.0
Bread: 2.5
Meat: 4.0
Fat: 0.0

- 1 pound beef eye of round, *or* sirloin steak, fat trimmed, cut into 1 1/2 x 1/2-inch strips
- 1 tablespoon margarine
- 3 cups sliced mushrooms
- 1/2 cup sliced onion
- 2 cloves garlic, minced
- 2 tablespoons flour
- 1 1/2 cups reduced-sodium beef broth
- 1 teaspoon Dijon-style mustard
- 1/4 teaspoon dried thyme leaves
- 1/2 cup fat-free sour cream
- Salt and pepper, to taste
- 3 cups cooked no-yolk noodles, warm
- Finely chopped parsley leaves, as garnish

1. Saute beef in margarine in large skillet until browned on all sides, about 5 minutes; remove from pan. Add mushrooms, onion, and garlic; saute until tender, 5 to 8 minutes. Stir in flour and cook, stirring, 1 to 2 minutes longer.

2. Add beef, beef broth, mustard, and thyme. Heat to boiling; reduce heat and simmer, covered, until beef is tender, 45 to 60 minutes. Reduce heat to low; stir in sour cream and cook 2 to 3 minutes. Season to taste with salt and pepper. Serve over warm noodles; sprinkle with parsley.

BEEF PAPRIKASH

4 servings

- 1 pound boneless beef top sirloin steak, cut 1-inch thick, fat trimmed
- 1 tablespoon vegetable oil
- 2 medium onions, sliced
- 1 package (16 ounces) sauerkraut, rinsed and drained
- 1 tablespoon paprika
- 1 can (13 3/4 ounces) reduced-sodium beef broth
- 2-4 tablespoons tomato paste
- 1/2 teaspoon caraway seeds
- 1/8 teaspoon cayenne pepper
- 1/4 cup fat-free sour cream
- Salt and black pepper, to taste
- 4 cups cooked noodles
- Parsley, chopped

Per Serving
Calories: 540
% Calories from fat: 35
Fat (gm): 20.6
Sat. fat (gm): 6.6
Cholesterol (mg): 122.7
Sodium (mg): 999
Protein (gm): 32.7
Carbohydrate (gm): 53.9

Exchanges
Milk: 0.0
Vegetable: 2.0
Fruit: 0.0
Bread: 3.0
Meat: 3.0
Fat: 2.0

1. Cut beef into 1/2-inch pieces; cook in oil in large saucepan over medium heat until browned, 8 to 10 minutes; remove from skillet. Add onions and saute until tender, 8 to 10 minutes; stir in sauerkraut, paprika, broth, tomato paste, caraway seeds, and cayenne pepper; heat to boiling. Return beef to saucepan; reduce heat and simmer, covered, until beef is tender, about 10 minutes. Stir in sour cream; season to taste with salt and pepper.

2. Serve mixture over noodles; sprinkle with parsley.

SLOW COOKER BEEF STEW

6 servings

- 1 large onion, finely chopped
- 2 garlic cloves, minced
- 1 pound boiling potatoes, cut into 3/4-inch cubes
- 1 1/2 cups coarsely shredded cabbage
- 1 large carrot, sliced
- 1/4 cup long-grain rice
- 16 ounces beef round, fat trimmed, cut into bite-sized pieces
- 1 1/2 cups fat-free beef broth
- 3/4 cup dry red wine, *or* beef broth
- 1/4 cup catsup
- 2 teaspoons brown sugar
- 1 1/2 teaspoons cider vinegar
- 1 1/2 teaspoons dried thyme leaves
- 1 teaspoon chili powder
- 1/2 teaspoon dry mustard
- 1/4 teaspoon pepper
- Salt, to taste

Per Serving
Calories: 289
% Calories from fat: 18
Fat (gm): 6.0
Sat. fat (gm): 1.9
Cholesterol (mg): 51
Sodium (mg): 287
Protein (gm): 21
Carbohydrate (gm): 34

Exchanges
Milk: 0.0
Vegetable: 1.5
Fruit: 0.0
Bread: 1.5
Meat: 2.5
Fat: 0.0

1. Combine all ingredients, except salt, in slow cooker and stir well. Cover and cook on High 1 hour. Stir and cook on Low until beef is tender, 6 1/2 to 8 hours. Season to taste with salt.

SLOW COOKER BEEF BOURGUIGNON

8 servings

Per Serving
Calories: 177
% Calories from fat: 25
Fat (gm): 4.8
Sat. fat (gm): 1.5
Cholesterol (mg): 37.5
Sodium (mg): 116
Protein (gm): 21.4
Carbohydrate (gm): 10

Exchanges
Milk: 0.0
Vegetable: 1.0
Fruit: 0.0
Bread: 0.0
Meat: 3.0
Fat: 0.0

Vegetable cooking spray
2 pounds boneless beef chuck, fat trimmed, cut into 1 1/2-inch cubes
1 large carrot, sliced
1 medium onion, sliced
3 tablespoons flour
2 cups Beef Stock (see p. 46), *or* reduced-fat beef broth
1 tablespoon tomato paste
2 cloves garlic, minced
1 teaspoon dried thyme leaves
1 teaspoon dried tarragon leaves
1 bay leaf
1/2 pound pearl onions, peeled
1 pound mushrooms, sliced
1/2 cup dry red, *or* burgundy, wine

1. Spray large skillet with cooking spray; heat over medium heat until hot. Add beef, carrot, and sliced onion; cook until beef is browned. Add flour and cook 1 to 2 minutes; stir in Beef Stock and heat to boiling. Boil, stirring, until thickened, 1 to 2 minutes. Transfer to slow cooker.

2. Add remaining ingredients, except mushrooms and wine. Cover and cook on Low until beef is tender, 8 to 10 hours. Add mushrooms and wine during last hour of cooking. Discard bay leaf.

BEEF AND MUSHROOMS WITH PASTA

4 servings

- 1 pound thinly sliced beef round tip steaks (1/8 to 1/4-inch thick)
- 2 cloves garlic, minced
- 1 tablespoon olive oil
- 1/4 teaspoon salt
- 1/8 teaspoon pepper
- 3 cups sliced mushrooms
- 1 cup halved cherry tomatoes
- 1/4 cup fat-free Italian dressing
- 1 1/2 cups uncooked medium shell, *or* farfalle (bow tie), pasta, cooked
- 1 tablespoon grated Parmesan cheese
- 1 tablespoon chopped parsley

Per Serving
Calories: 353
% Calories from fat: 24
Fat (gm): 9.5
Sat. fat (gm): 2.5
Cholesterol (mg): 64.7
Sodium (mg): 434
Protein (gm): 29.8
Carbohydrate (gm): 36.1

Exchanges
Milk: 0.0
Vegetable: 1.0
Fruit: 0.0
Bread: 2.0
Meat: 3.5
Fat: 0.0

1. Cut steaks into scant 1/2-inch strips; cut crosswise into 1-inch-wide pieces. Saute beef and garlic in oil in large skillet until browned, 3 to 4 minutes; stir in salt and pepper. Remove beef mixture from skillet.

2. Add mushrooms to skillet and saute until tender, 5 to 8 minutes. Return beef mixture to skillet; add tomatoes and Italian dressing and heat through.

3. Spoon beef mixture over hot pasta; sprinkle with cheese and parsley.

WEST AFRICAN BEEF JOLLOF

8 servings

- 8 ounces beef stew meat, cut into 1/2-inch cubes
- 1 tablespoon vegetable oil
- 1 medium onion, chopped, divided
- 3 tablespoons tomato paste
- 1 teaspoon ground coriander
- 1 teaspoon ground cumin
- 1 teaspoon garlic powder
- 4 medium tomatoes, quartered
- 1 tablespoon crushed red pepper
- 2 1/2 cups reduced-sodium beef broth
- 1 cup rice
- 2 cans (15 ounces each) black beans, rinsed, drained
- 1/2-1 teaspoon salt

Per Serving
Calories: 255
% Calories from fat: 14
Fat (gm): 4
Sat. fat (gm): 1
Cholesterol (mg): 13.3
Sodium (mg): 496
Protein (gm): 14.6
Carbohydrate (gm): 39.5

Exchanges
Milk: 0.0
Vegetable: 2.0
Fruit: 0.0
Bread: 2.0
Meat: 1.0
Fat: 0.0

1. Cook meat in oil in Dutch oven over medium-high heat until brown on all sides, about 8 minutes. Stir in half the onion, the tomato paste, coriander, cumin, and garlic powder; cook over low heat until onion is tender, about 5 minutes, stirring frequently.

2. Process remaining onion, the tomatoes, and red pepper in food processor until smooth. Stir into beef mixture; stir in broth and heat to boiling. Reduce heat and simmer, covered, 40 minutes.

3. Stir in rice, beans, and salt; simmer until rice and meat are tender, about 20 minutes longer.

STUFFED FLANK STEAK BRAZIL

8 servings

- 1 beef flank steak (2 pounds), butterflied
- 1/4 cup red wine vinegar
- 2 teaspoons minced garlic
- 2 teaspoons dried thyme leaves
- 1 teaspoon salt
- Black Bean Filling (recipe follows)
- 2 cups loosely packed spinach leaves
- 4 whole thin carrots, cooked
- 3 hard-cooked eggs, quartered
- 4 cups reduced-sodium fat-free beef broth

Per Serving
Calories: 314
% Calories from fat: 28
Fat (gm): 9.6
Sat. fat (gm): 3.7
Cholesterol (mg): 122.8
Sodium (mg): 730
Protein (gm): 34.5
Carbohydrate (gm): 20.6

Exchanges
Milk: 0.0
Vegetable: 1.0
Fruit: 0.0
Bread: 1.0
Meat: 4.0
Fat: 0.0

1. Lay meat flat on counter; cover with waxed paper and pound to an even thickness, using flat side of meat mallet. Sprinkle all surfaces of meat with vinegar, garlic, thyme, and salt. Let stand while preparing filling, or transfer to jelly roll pan and refrigerate, covered, up to 12 hours.

2. Spread Black Bean Filling over meat; cover with spinach leaves. Place carrots about 3 inches apart on spinach, parallel to grain of meat; place egg quarters between carrots. Roll meat, starting from short end, to form a thick roll; tie with kitchen string at 2-inch intervals.

3. Place meat in roasting pan; pour broth around meat, adding water if necessary to come 1/3 of the way up the side of meat. Cover tightly with lid or foil. Bake at 375 degrees 1 hour, or until meat reaches internal temperature of 130 degrees. Place meat on platter and let stand 5 minutes before slicing. Or chill, slice, and serve cold.

Black Bean Filling

makes about 3 cups

1 cup boiling water
1 ancho chili
2 cans (15 ounces each) black beans, rinsed, drained
1/4 cup chopped onion
1/4 cup chopped parsley
1 teaspoon ground cumin

1. Pour water over ancho chili in small bowl, and let stand until softened, about 10 minutes; drain and remove stem from chili. Puree chili in blender with a small amount of soaking water until smooth.

2. Coarsely mash beans in medium bowl; stir in chili puree, onion, parsley, and cumin.

TIP: Ask your butcher to butterfly the flank steak. Or, to butterfly flank steak, place on cutting board; with sharp knife, cut in half horizontally to within 1/2-inch of one long side.

GRILLED STUFFED PEPPERS

4 servings

1 pound lean ground beef, ground
1/2 cup dry unseasoned bread crumbs
1 teaspoon ground ginger
3 cloves garlic, minced
1/2-1 teaspoon salt
1/4 teaspoon pepper
2/3 cup finely chopped onion
1/2 cup minced water chestnuts
1/4 cup dry white wine, *or* fat-free milk
1-2 tablespoons reduced-sodium soy sauce
4 large red bell peppers, seeded and halved lengthwise

Per Serving
Calories: 264
% Calories from fat: 21
Fat (gm): 6.1
Sat. fat (gm): 1.9
Cholesterol (mg): 56.5
Sodium (mg): 606
Protein (gm): 24.8
Carbohydrate (gm): 24.9

Exchanges
Milk: 0.0
Vegetable: 2.0
Fruit: 0.0
Bread: 1.0
Meat: 3.0
Fat: 0.0

1. Combine all ingredients, except bell peppers. Spoon mixture into pepper halves. Place on grill, meat sides down, and grill 3 to 4 minutes. Turn peppers and grill until meat is no longer pink in the center, 5 to 8 minutes (peppers will be charred). Or, broil 6 inches from heat source, meat sides down, until peppers are charred; turn and broil until meat is no longer pink in the center, about 5 minutes.

STEAK ON A STICK

---

6 servings

- 1 1/2 pounds beef eye of round, *or* sirloin, fat trimmed, cut into 3/4-inch cubes
- 1 large tomato, cut into 6 wedges
- 2 tablespoons reduced-fat beef broth
- 2 tablespoons dry red wine, *or* reduced-fat beef broth
- 1 clove garlic, minced
- 1/4 teaspoon pepper
- 1/4 teaspoon sugar
- 1 teaspoon dried rosemary leaves
- 4 cups cooked rice, warm

Per Serving
Calories: 328
% Calories from fat: 26
Fat (gm): 9.1
Sat. fat (gm): 3.4
Cholesterol (mg): 64.6
Sodium (mg): 66
Protein (gm): 26.9
Carbohydrate (gm): 31.2
Exchanges
Milk: 0.0
Vegetable: 0.0
Fruit: 0.0
Bread: 2.0
Meat: 3.0
Fat: 0.0

1. Thread beef on skewers, with a tomato wedge on the end of each; place on broiler pan. Combine remaining ingredients except rice. Broil 6 inches from heat source to desired degree of doneness, about 5 minutes on each side for medium, brushing with beef broth mixture.

2. Serve with rice.

GRILLED STEAK WITH TOMATO-TARRAGON SAUCE

4 servings

1 pound beef eye of round steak, fat trimmed
1 teaspoon canola oil
2 tablespoons red wine vinegar
1 tablespoon chopped fresh, *or* 1 teaspoon dried, tarragon leaves
Tomato-Tarragon Sauce (recipe follows)

Per Serving
Calories: 232
% Calories from fat: 31
Fat (gm): 7.7
Sat. fat (gm): 2
Cholesterol (mg): 72
Sodium (mg): 374
Protein (gm): 28.3
Carbohydrate (gm): 9.5
Exchanges
Milk: 0.0
Vegetable: 1.0
Fruit: 0.0
Bread: 0.0
Meat: 4.0
Fat: 0.0

1. Brush both sides of steak with combined oil, vinegar, and tarragon; refrigerate 1 hour.

2. Grill steak over medium-hot coals to desired degree of doneness, about 5 minutes on each side, depending upon thickness of meat. Slice steak into thin strips, across grain, and serve with Tomato-Tarragon Sauce.

Tomato-Tarragon Sauce

makes about 3/4 cup

3 medium shallots, minced
2 cloves garlic, minced
1 teaspoon canola oil
2 teaspoons sugar
2 tablespoons tarragon vinegar
3/4 cup tomato puree
1/4 teaspoon salt
1/2 teaspoon dried tarragon
1/8 teaspoon pepper

1. Saute shallots and garlic in oil in small saucepan until tender, 2 to 3 minutes; add remaining ingredients and heat to boiling; reduce heat and simmer, uncovered, 5 minutes. Serve hot.

STEAK DA VINCI

4 servings

Vegetable cooking spray
1 1/4 pounds lean, boneless beef round steak, cut into 1-inch cubes
1 cup chopped onion
1 cup chopped green bell peppers
1 clove garlic, minced
1/4 cup diced shallots
1 can (14 1/2 ounces) whole tomatoes, undrained, chopped
1 teaspoon beef bouillon crystals
1 teaspoon dried oregano leaves
1/2 teaspoon dried basil leaves
1 teaspoon garlic powder
1/2 cup sliced mushrooms
Salt and pepper, to taste
8 ounces linguine, cooked, warm
1/4 cup chopped Italian parsley
1/4 cup (1 ounce) grated Parmesan cheese

Per Serving
Calories: 443
% Calories from fat: 21
Fat (gm): 10.5
Sat. fat (gm): 3.4
Cholesterol (mg): 87
Sodium (mg): 434
Protein (gm): 42.1
Carbohydrate (gm): 44.3
Exchanges
Milk: 0.0
Vegetable: 3.0
Fruit: 0.0
Bread: 2.0
Meat: 4.0
Fat: 0.0

1. Spray large skillet with cooking spray; heat over medium heat until hot. Saute beef, onion, bell peppers, garlic, and shallots until meat is browned and onion tender, about 10 minutes.

2. Add remaining ingredients, except salt and pepper, linguine, parsley, and Parmesan cheese, and simmer, covered, until meat is tender, 45 to 60 minutes. Simmer, uncovered until thickened to desired consistency, about 15 minutes. Season to taste with salt and pepper. Serve over linguine; sprinkle with parsley and Parmesan cheese.

STEAK AND MESCLUN SALAD

4 servings

12 ounces boneless beef eye of round, *or* sirloin steaks, fat trimmed
2-3 teaspoons olive oil
1 cup snow peas, ends trimmed
Salt and coarse ground pepper, to taste
6 cups mesclun, *or* assorted salad greens
1/2 cup shredded carrots
1/2 cup halved grape tomatoes
1/2 cup fat-free ranch, *or* blue cheese, dressing

Per Serving
Calories: 237
% Calories from fat: 35
Fat (gm): 8.9
Sat. fat (gm): 2.8
Cholesterol (mg): 48.5
Sodium (mg): 417
Protein (gm): 19.6
Carbohydrate (gm): 17.6
Exchanges
Milk: 0.0
Vegetable: 3.0
Fruit: 0.0
Bread: 0.0
Meat: 2.0
Fat: 1.0

1. Cook steak in oil in medium skillet over medium heat to desired degree of doneness, about 5 minutes on each side for medium; remove from skillet. Add snow peas to skillet; cook, covered, until crisp-tender, 3 to 4 minutes, stirring occasionally.
2. Slice steak across grain into thin slices; season with salt and pepper. Toss beef, snow peas, mesclun, carrots, and tomatoes with dressing; serve immediately.

GRILLED STEAK AND VEGETABLES WITH CREAMY HORSERADISH SAUCE

6 servings

6 boneless beef eye of round, *or* sirloin steaks (about 4 ounces each), trimmed of all fat
2 large cloves garlic, halved
Salt and coarsely ground pepper, to taste
3 medium tomatoes, halved
1 large red onion, cut into 1/2-inch thick slices
Creamy Horseradish Sauce (recipe follows)

Per Serving
Calories: 233
% Calories from fat: 36
Fat (gm): 8.9
Sat. fat (gm): 3.4
Cholesterol (mg): 64.6
Sodium (mg): 170
Protein (gm): 25.9
Carbohydrate (gm): 10.4
Exchanges
Milk: 0.0
Vegetable: 2.0
Fruit: 0.0
Bread: 0.0
Meat: 3.0
Fat: 0.0

1. Rub both sides of steaks with cut sides of garlic; sprinkle with salt and pepper. Grill steaks, tomato halves, and onion slices over hot coals until steaks are desired degree of doneness, 5 to 8 minutes per side for medium. Turn onion slices when browned on the bottom. Remove onion slices and tomatoes when tender. Serve with Creamy Horseradish Sauce.

Creamy Horseradish Sauce

makes about 3/4 cup

1/2 cup fat-free sour cream
1/4 cup fat-free mayonnaise
1-2 tablespoons prepared horseradish

1. Mix all ingredients; cover and refrigerate until serving time.

SLOW COOKER POT ROAST

6 servings

6 small potatoes, peeled and sliced
6 carrots, peeled and sliced
2 onions, peeled and sliced
2 ribs celery with tops, sliced
1/2 teaspoon dried thyme leaves
1/2 teaspoon dried marjoram leaves
1 beef chuck arm roast (3 pounds)
Salt and pepper, to taste
1/2 cup Beef Stock (see p. 46), *or* reduced-fat beef broth

Per Serving
Calories: 425
% Calories from fat: 25
Fat (gm): 11.7
Sat. fat (gm): 4.2
Cholesterol (mg): 161
Sodium (mg): 134
Protein (gm): 54.9
Carbohydrate (gm): 22.3
Exchanges
Milk: 0.0
Vegetable: 1.5
Fruit: 0.0
Bread: 1.0
Meat: 7.0
Fat: 0.0

1. Put vegetables in slow cooker and sprinkle with herbs. Season meat with salt and pepper and place in crock pot. Add Beef Stock; cover and cook on Low 10 to 12 hours or on High 4 to 5 hours.

Variations: **German-Style Pot Roast**—Add 3 or 4 medium dill pickles, 1 teaspoon dried dill weed, and 1 tablespoon wine vinegar to slow cooker with vegetables.

Italian-Style—Add 1 cup of tomato sauce to crockpot with vegetables; substitute Italian seasoning for the thyme and marjoram.

Mexican-Syle—Add 1/2 cup chopped green onions and tops, 1 tablespoon minced garlic, 1 cup beef broth, 2 tablespoons tomato paste, and 2 to 4 tablespoons chili powder to slow cooker with vegetables.

BEEF AND BEAN BURRITOS

8 servings

- 1 pound lean ground beef
- 1 medium onion, chopped
- 1 tablespoon chili powder
- 1 teaspoon ground cumin
- 1 teaspoon garlic powder
- 3/4 teaspoon dried oregano leaves
- 1/4-1/2 teaspoon ground red pepper
- 1/2 teaspoon salt
- 1 can (8 ounces) tomato sauce
- 1 can (15 ounces) pinto beans, drained and mashed
- 8 flour tortillas (each about 8 inches), warmed
- Thinly sliced lettuce, chopped tomatoes, and sliced green onions, optional

Per Serving
Calories: 279
% Calories from fat: 31
Fat (gm): 9.7
Sat. fat (gm): 3.1
Cholesterol (mg): 35.2
Sodium (mg): 728
Protein (gm): 16.8
Carbohydrate (gm): 31
Exchanges
Milk: 0.0
Vegetable: 0.0
Fruit: 0.0
Bread: 2.0
Meat: 2.0
Fat: 0.5

1. Cook ground beef and onion in large skillet over medium heat until beef is browned, about 10 minutes, crumbling with a fork. Drain. Mix in herbs, salt, and tomato sauce; heat to boiling. Reduce heat and simmer 10 minutes, stirring occasionally. Stir in beans and simmer 2 to 3 minutes.

2. Serve on tortillas with lettuce, tomato, and onion, if desired.

SPEEDY CHILI

8 servings

Vegetable cooking spray
$1^1/_2$ pounds lean ground beef
2 pounds ground turkey breast
2 large onions, chopped
3 cloves garlic, minced
$^1/_2$ teaspoon pepper
1 can (6 ounces) reduced-sodium tomato paste
2 cans ($10^1/_2$ ounces each) zesty tomato sauce
2 cans ($15^1/_2$ ounces each) kidney beans, rinsed, drained
2 tablespoons chili powder
1 teaspoon dried oregano leaves
Salt and pepper, to taste
Finely chopped parsley, as garnish

Per Serving
Calories: 415
% Calories from fat: 29
Fat (gm): 13.2
Sat. fat (gm): 4.9
Cholesterol (mg): 97.5
Sodium (mg): 911
Protein (gm): 43.7
Carbohydrate (gm): 28.7
Exchanges
Milk: 0.0
Vegetable: 0.0
Fruit: 0.0
Bread: 2.0
Meat: 4.0
Fat: 0.0

1. Spray large Dutch oven with cooking spray; heat over medium heat until hot. Add ground beef, turkey, onions, garlic, and $^1/_2$ teaspoon pepper, and cook until meat is browned, 10 to 12 minutes; drain fat and crumble meat with a fork. Stir in remaining ingredients, except salt, pepper, and parsley, and heat to boiling; reduce heat and simmer, covered, 15 minutes. Season to taste with salt and pepper; sprinkle each serving with parsley.

MICROWAVE ORIENTAL BEEF

4 servings

2 tablespoons reduced-sodium soy sauce
2 tablespoons water
1 teaspoon sesame oil
1 clove garlic, minced
1 teaspoon Dijon-style mustard
1 teaspoon minced gingerroot
1 pound beef eye of round steak, sliced thinly across the grain
1 red bell pepper, julienned
4 scallions, chopped
1 teaspoon toasted sesame seeds
Chopped parsley, as garnish

Per Serving
Calories: 145
% Calories from fat: 26
Fat (gm): 4
Sat. fat (gm): 1.2
Cholesterol (mg): 54.2
Sodium (mg): 330
Protein (gm): 23.7
Carbohydrate (gm): 2.4
Exchanges
Milk: 0.0
Vegetable: 0.0
Fruit: 0.0
Bread: 0.0
Meat: 3.0
Fat: 0.0

1. Combine soy sauce, water, sesame oil, garlic, mustard and gingerroot; pour over beef in 2-quart glass casserole, tossing to coat. Mix in peppers and scallions. Microwave on High 3 to 4 minutes, stirring once. Check doneness of beef; continue microwaving, 1 minutes at a time, to desired doneness. Garnish with parsley and serve.

SUKIYAKI

6 servings

1-2 tablespoons peanut oil
1 pound boneless beef sirloin steak, fat trimmed, diagonally sliced into very thin strips
1/4 cup water
1/4 cup sugar
2 tablespoons soy sauce
1/4 cup sake (rice wine)
1/4 teaspoon beef-flavored bouillon granules
1 cup diagonally sliced carrots

Per Serving
Calories: 300
% Calories from fat: 21
Fat (gm): 7
Sat. fat (gm): 2.8
Cholesterol (mg): 50.4
Sodium (mg): 435
Protein (gm): 19.8
Carbohydrate (gm): 37.7
Exchanges
Milk: 0.0
Vegetable: 1.5
Fruit: 0.0
Bread: 2.0
Meat: 2.0
Fat: 0.0

2 medium onions, cut into thin strips
6 green onions, cut into 1 1/2-inch pieces
2 cups sliced mushrooms
4 cups sliced Chinese cabbage
1 cup bamboo shoots
1 package (5 ounces) transparent noodles (bean threads), cooked, cut into 3-inch lengths

1. Heat oil in wok or large skillet until hot; add beef and stir-fry until browned, 2 to 3 minutes. Combine water, sugar, soy sauce, sake and bouillon; add half the soy mixture, carrots, and onions to wok and stir-fry 2 minutes. Add remaining soy mixture and remaining vegetables; stir-fry until cabbage is crisp-tender, about 5 minutes. Stir in noodles; cook 1 to 2 minutes longer.

THAI-STYLE BEEF AND PASTA

4 servings

1 pound boneless beef eye of round, *or* sirloin steaks, 1-inch thick
2 tablespoons teriyaki sauce
Vegetable cooking spray
Satay Sauce (recipe follows)
6 ounces vermicelli, *or* thin spaghetti, cooked
1/2 cup seeded, chopped cucumber

Per Serving
Calories: 410
% Calories from fat: 28
Fat (gm): 11.7
Sat. fat (gm): 4
Cholesterol (mg): 64.6
Sodium (mg): 1399
Protein (gm): 30.3
Carbohydrate (gm): 39.2
Exchanges
Milk: 0.0
Vegetable: 0.0
Fruit: 0.0
Bread: 2.5
Meat: 4.0
Fat: 0.0

1. Cut steak lengthwise into 1/8-inch-thick strips; toss with teriyaki sauce.

2. Spray wok or large skillet with cooking spray; heat over high heat until hot. Add beef and stir-fry until browned, about 5 minutes. Add beef and Satay Sauce to vermicelli and toss; sprinkle with cucumber.

Satay Sauce

makes about 1/3 cup

3 tablespoons teriyaki sauce
2 tablespoons reduced-fat peanut butter
1 tablespoon water
1/8-1/4 teaspoon ground ginger
1/8-1/4 teaspoon crushed red pepper

1. Combine all ingredients.

WOK STEAK SWEET-AND-SOUR

4 servings

Per Serving
Calories: 490
% Calories from fat: 23
Fat (gm): 12.4
Sat. fat (gm): 3.2
Cholesterol (mg): 46.9
Sodium (mg): 220
Protein (gm): 27.8
Carbohydrate (gm): 64.7

Exchanges
Milk: 0.0
Vegetable: 0.0
Fruit: 0.0
Bread: 4.0
Meat: 3.0
Fat: 0.5

1 tablespoon vegetable oil
1 pound beef tenderloin, *or* flank steak, fat trimmed, thinly sliced across grain
1 medium onion, sliced
1 large zucchini, sliced
1/2 pound snow peas, ends trimmed
1/2 pound mushrooms, sliced
1/2 can (8 ounce-size) sliced water chestnuts, drained
1 tablespoon sesame seeds
2/3 cup sweet-sour sauce
Salt and pepper, to taste
3 cups cooked rice

1. Heat oil in wok or large skillet; add beef and stir-fry until browned, 3 to 4 minutes. Move beef to side of wok; add vegetables and stir-fry until crisp-tender, about 5 minutes. Add sesame seeds and sweet-sour sauce, stirring to combine; season to taste with salt and pepper. Serve over rice.

5-SPICE BEEF STIR-FRY

4 servings

- 1 pound beef flank steak, diagonally cut into strips ($1^1/_2$ x $^1/_2$-inch)
- 5-spice Marinade (recipe follows)
- 1 tablespoon sesame oil
- 1 medium yellow, *or* white, onion, sliced into rings
- $^3/_4$ cup reduced-fat reduced-sodium beef broth
- 1 tablespoon hoisin sauce
- 2 medium tomatoes, peeled, seeded, chopped
- 1 can (8 ounces) sliced water chestnuts, drained
- 2 tablespoons chopped green onions and tops
- Salt and pepper, to taste
- 4 cups cooked rice

Per Serving
Calories: 488
% Calories from fat: 23
Fat (gm): 11.7
Sat. fat (gm): 3.8
Cholesterol (mg): 43.4
Sodium (mg): 453
Protein (gm): 30.6
Carbohydrate (gm): 58.7

Exchanges
Milk: 0.0
Vegetable: 0.0
Fruit: 0.0
Bread: 4.0
Meat: 4.0
Fat: 0.0

1. Arrange flank steak in glass baking dish; pour 5-spice Marinade over. Let stand 15 to 20 minutes, stirring occasionally. Drain; reserving marinade.

2. Heat sesame oil in wok or large skillet until hot; add onion and stir-fry until almost tender, 4 to 5 minutes. Add beef to wok; stir-fry until browned, 2 to 3 minutes. Add reserved marinade and beef broth; heat to boiling. Reduce heat and cook, stirring, until mixture has thickened slightly.

3. Stir in hoisin sauce, tomatoes, water chestnuts, and green onions; stir-fry 2 minutes longer. Season to taste with salt and pepper. Serve over rice.

5-Spice Marinade

makes about 1/3 cup

- 3 tablespoons dry sherry
- 2 tablespoons reduced-sodium soy sauce
- 1 teaspoon 5-spice powder
- 1 tablespoon rice wine vinegar
- 1/4 teaspoon ground ginger
- Pepper, to taste
- 2-3 drops hot chili oil
- 1 tablespoon cornstarch

1. Mix all ingredients.

VEAL AND MUSHROOM MARSALA

4 servings

- Vegetable cooking spray
- 1 pound veal scaloppini, pounded thin
- 1/2 teaspoon dried rosemary leaves
- Salt and pepper, to taste
- 1 teaspoon olive oil
- 2 cloves garlic, minced
- 2 cups sliced mushrooms
- 1 teaspoon cornstarch
- 1/3 cup reduced-sodium fat-free chicken broth
- 1/2 cup dry Marsala wine

Per Serving
Calories: 159
% Calories from fat: 23
Fat (gm): 4.1
Sat. fat (gm): 1.2
Cholesterol (mg): 80.5
Sodium (mg): 132
Protein (gm): 23.2
Carbohydrate (gm): 3.4

Exchanges
Milk: 0.0
Vegetable: 0.5
Fruit: 0.0
Bread: 0.0
Meat: 3.0
Fat: 0.0

1. Spray large skillet with cooking spray; heat over medium heat until hot. Sprinkle veal with rosemary, salt, and pepper. Add oil and garlic to skillet; add veal and saute until browned, 2 to 3 minutes on each side. Remove from skillet.

2. Add mushrooms to skillet; saute until lightly browned, about 5 minutes. Stir in combined cornstarch, chicken broth, and wine; heat to boiling. Reduce heat and simmer, stirring, until thickened, 1 to 2 minutes. Return veal to skillet; cook until hot through, 1 to 2 minutes.

VEAL PEPERONATA

4 servings

Per Serving
Calories: 254
% Calories from fat: 15
Fat (gm): 4.5
Sat. fat (gm): 1.1
Cholesterol (mg): 80.4
Sodium (mg): 224
Protein (gm): 25.8
Carbohydrate (gm): 17.6

Exchanges
Milk: 0.0
Vegetable: 2.0
Fruit: 0.0
Bread: 0.5
Meat: 3.0
Fat: 0.0

1 pound veal scaloppini, pounded until thin
Flour
Olive oil cooking spray
1 small yellow bell pepper, sliced
1 small red bell pepper, sliced
1 small green bell pepper, sliced
3 cloves garlic, minced
2 teaspoons minced fresh, *or* 3/4 teaspoon dried basil leaves
1 teaspoon fresh, *or* 1/2 teaspoon dried rosemary leaves
1 teaspoon fresh, *or* 1/4 teaspoon dried thyme leaves
1 1/2 cups peeled, chopped, and seeded ripe tomatoes
1 cup reduced-sodium beef broth
1 cup dry red wine
6 pitted black olives, sliced
Juice of 1/2 lemon
Salt and pepper, to taste
Chopped basil, as garnish
Chopped parsley, as garnish

1. Coat veal lightly with flour. Spray large skillet with cooking spray; heat over medium heat until hot. Add veal, spray lightly with cooking spray, and saute until browned, 2 to 3 minutes on each side; remove from skillet. Add bell peppers, garlic, and herbs; saute until tender, 5 to 8 minutes. Remove from skillet.

2. Add tomatoes, broth, wine, and olives to skillet; heat to boiling; reduce heat and simmer until thickened to a sauce consistency, about 10 minutes. Return veal and peppers to skillet; stir in lemon juice and season to taste with salt and pepper. Sprinkle with chopped basil and parsley.

VEAL WITH HONEY-DIJON MUSHROOMS

4 servings

1 pound veal scaloppini, pounded until thin
Flour
Salt and pepper, to taste
1-2 tablespoons olive oil
Juice of 1 lemon
1/2 cup dry white wine, *or* reduced-sodium fat-free chicken broth
Honey-Dijon Mushrooms (recipe follows)

Per Serving
Calories: 228
% Calories from fat: 24
Fat (gm): 5.7
Sat. fat (gm): 1.1
Cholesterol (mg): 61.2
Sodium (mg): 141
Protein (gm): 18.9
Carbohydrate (gm): 15.8
Exchanges
Milk: 0.0
Vegetable: 1.0
Fruit: 0.5
Bread: 0.0
Meat: 3.0
Fat: 0.0

1. Lightly coat veal with flour; sprinkle lightly with salt and pepper. Saute veal in oil in large skillet until browned, 2 to 3 minutes on each side. Add lemon juice and wine; simmer until thickened to a sauce consistency, 3 to 4 minutes. Arrange veal on platter; spoon Honey-Dijon Mushrooms over.

Honey-Dijon Mushrooms

makes about 1 1/2 cups

3/4 cup reduced-fat chicken broth
3/4 cup dry white wine, *or* reduced-sodium fat-free chicken broth
1 small onion, chopped
3 tablespoons lemon juice
10 whole peppercorns
1/4 cup minced chives
2 tablespoons honey
2 teaspoons Dijon-style mustard
1 1/2 cups sliced mushrooms
2 tablespoons water
2 teaspoons flour
Salt and pepper, to taste
1/4 cup chopped parsley
Lemon slices

1. Heat chicken broth, wine, onion, lemon juice, peppercorns, and chives to boiling in large saucepan; reduce heat and simmer, uncovered, 10 minutes; strain, discarding onion and spices. Return broth to saucepan; add honey, mustard, and mushrooms and heat to boiling; reduce heat and simmer, covered, 10 minutes.

2. Heat mushroom mixture to boiling. Stir in combined water and flour; boil, stirring, until slightly thickened, 1 to 2 minutes. Remove from heat; season to taste with salt and pepper. Add parsley and lemon slices.

VEAL PICCATA

4 servings

1 pound veal scaloppini, pounded until thin
3 tablespoons flour
Olive oil cooking spray
$1\frac{1}{2}$ cups sliced mushrooms
Juice of $\frac{1}{2}$ lemon
$\frac{1}{2}$ cup dry white wine, *or* reduced-sodium fat-free chicken broth
3 tablespoons chopped fresh parsley
Lemon slices, as garnish

Per Serving
Calories: 171
% Calories from fat: 15
Fat (gm): 2.9
Sat. fat (gm): 1
Cholesterol (mg): 80.4
Sodium (mg): 58
Protein (gm): 23.4
Carbohydrate (gm): 9

Exchanges
Milk: 0.0
Vegetable: 0.0
Fruit: 0.0
Bread: 0.5
Meat: 3.0
Fat: 0.0

1. Coat veal lightly with flour. Spray large skillet with cooking spray; heat over medium heat until hot. Add veal, spray lightly with cooking spray, and cooked until browned, about 2 minutes on each side.

2. Add mushrooms and saute 3 to 4 minutes. Squeeze lemon juice over veal; add wine and heat to boiling. Reduce heat and simmer until thickened to a thin sauce consistency, 2 to 3 minutes. Sprinkle with parsley; garnish with lemon slices.

HERBED VEAL CHOPS

6 servings

Vegetable cooking spray
6 veal chops (about 4 ounces each), fat trimmed
1/3 cup white wine, *or* reduced-sodium fat-free chicken broth
2 tablespoons minced parsley
1/2 teaspoon dried basil leaves
1/2 teaspoon dried sage leaves
Salt and pepper, to taste

Per Serving
Calories: 176
% Calories from fat: 30
Fat (gm): 5.6
Sat. fat (gm): 1.6
Cholesterol (mg): 100.1
Sodium (mg): 77
Protein (gm): 27.2
Carbohydrate (gm): 0.4
Exchanges
Milk: 0.0
Vegetable: 0.0
Fruit: 0.0
Bread: 0.0
Meat: 3.0
Fat: 0.0

1. Spray large skillet with cooking spray; heat over medium heat until hot. Saute veal chops until browned, 2 to 3 minutes on each side; continue to cook over low heat 10 minutes, turning several times. Add wine and herbs and heat to boiling; reduce heat and simmer, covered, until chops are tender, about 10 minutes. Season to taste with salt and pepper. Arrange chops on platter; spoon remaining wine over.

VEAL AND MUSHROOM ROULADE

8 servings

Butter-flavored cooking spray
2 cloves garlic, minced
1 cup sliced onion
1 pound mushrooms, sliced
8 veal scallops (about 2 pounds), pounded thin
1/4 teaspoon salt
1/4 teaspoon pepper
1 cup dry white wine, *or* reduced-sodium fat-free chicken broth
1 cup reduced-sodium fat-free chicken broth

Per Serving
Calories: 137
% Calories from fat: 27
Fat (gm): 4.1
Sat. fat (gm): 1.5
Cholesterol (mg): 70.8
Sodium (mg): 143
Protein (gm): 18.6
Carbohydrate (gm): 4.8
Exchanges
Milk: 0.0
Vegetable: 1.0
Fruit: 0.0
Bread: 0.0
Meat: 2.0
Fat: 0.0

1. Coat large nonstick skillet with cooking spray; heat over medium heat until hot. Saute garlic, onion, and mushrooms until tender, 6 to 8 minutes, stirring occasionally.

2. Sprinkle veal with salt and pepper. Divide mushroom mixture on scallops, and roll up, tying with kitchen string. Return veal rolls to skillet; spray lightly with cooking spray. Saute until browned on all sides, 3 to 4 minutes. Pour wine and broth into skillet and heat to boiling; reduce heat and simmer 10 to 15 minutes, or until veal is tender.

VEAL STEW WITH WINE

6 servings

Vegetable cooking spray
1 large onion, chopped
1 large garlic clove, minced
1 1/4 pounds lean veal, fat trimmed, cut into 1/2-inch cubes
1/4 cup water
1/2 cup tomato sauce
1 cup dry white wine, *or* reduced-sodium fat-free chicken broth
Salt and pepper, to taste

Per Serving
Calories: 256
% Calories from fat: 31
Fat (gm): 8.5
Sat. fat (gm): 3.1
Cholesterol (mg): 128.1
Sodium (mg): 243
Protein (gm): 32.5
Carbohydrate (gm): 4.3

Exchanges
Milk: 0.0
Vegetable: 1.0
Fruit: 0.0
Bread: 0.0
Meat: 4.0
Fat: 0.0

1. Spray large skillet with cooking spray; heat over medium heat until hot. Saute onion, garlic, and veal until browned, about 10 minutes. Add remaining ingredients and heat to boiling; reduce heat and simmer, covered, until veal is tender, about 30 minutes.

BAYOU PORK CHOPS

4 servings

- Vegetable cooking spray
- 4 loin pork chops (5-6 ounces each), fat trimmed
- 1 medium onion, chopped
- 1 small green bell pepper, sliced
- 1/2 cup sliced celery
- 2 large cloves garlic, minced
- 1 can (14-ounces) stewed tomatoes, drained
- 1 can (4 ounces) chopped green chilies
- 2 tablespoons chopped fresh parsley
- Salt and pepper, to taste
- 4 cups cooked rice

Per Serving
Calories: 438
% Calories from fat: 15
Fat (gm): 7.3
Sat. fat (gm): 2.1
Cholesterol (mg): 57.5
Sodium (mg): 628
Protein (gm): 27.3
Carbohydrate (gm): 63.9

Exchanges
Milk: 0.0
Vegetable: 3.0
Fruit: 0.0
Bread: 3.0
Meat: 3.0
Fat: 0.0

1. Spray large skillet with cooking spray; heat over medium heat until hot. Cook pork chops until browned, 3 to 4 minutes on each side. Remove from skillet.

2. Add onion, bell pepper, celery, and garlic to skillet; saute until tender, 3 to 4 minutes. Stir in tomatoes and chilies; heat to boiling. Reduce heat and simmer, uncovered, 5 minutes. Add pork chops; simmer, covered, until pork chops are tender, about 20 minutes. Stir in parsley; season to taste with salt and pepper. Serve over rice.

SLOW COOKER PORK CHOPS AND SWEET POTATOES

6 servings

Vegetable cooking spray
6 loin pork chops (5-6 ounces each), fat trimmed
Salt and pepper, to taste
2 medium sweet potatoes, peeled, cut into 1-inch cubes
1 large onion, sliced
2 small apples, peeled, cored, cubed
3 tablespoons packed light brown sugar
1 large green bell pepper, sliced
1 teaspoon dried oregano leaves
1 teaspoon dried thyme leaves
2 cups apple cider

Per Serving
Calories: 472
% Calories from fat: 29
Fat (gm): 15.7
Sat. fat (gm): 5.3
Cholesterol (mg): 94.5
Sodium (mg): 89
Protein (gm): 29.5
Carbohydrate (gm): 55.6
Exchanges
Milk: 0.0
Vegetable: 0.0
Fruit: 2.0
Bread: 2.0
Meat: 4.0
Fat: 0.0

1. Spray large skillet with cooking spray; heat over medium heat until hot. Add pork chops and cook until browned, 3 to 4 minutes on each side; season to taste with salt and pepper.

2. Place pork chops in slow cooker; add remaining ingredients. Cover and cook on Low until pork chops are tender, 8 to 10 hours or on High 3 to 4 hours.

PORK CHOPS PARMESAN

4 servings

3 tablespoons yellow cornmeal
1 tablespoon grated Parmesan cheese
1/2 teaspoon pepper
1/2 teaspoon dried basil leaves
4 pork loin chops (5-6 ounces each), fat trimmed
1-2 tablespoons olive oil
3 green onions and tops, chopped

Per Serving
Calories: 312
% Calories from fat: 25
Fat (gm): 8.6
Sat. fat (gm): 2.2
Cholesterol (mg): 58.5
Sodium (mg): 82
Protein (gm): 25.7
Carbohydrate (gm): 30.5
Exchanges
Milk: 0.0
Vegetable: 0.0
Fruit: 0.0
Bread: 2.0
Meat: 3.0
Fat: 0.0

1 clove garlic, minced
1/4 teaspoon fennel seeds, crushed
3 tablespoons chopped fresh parsley
4 cups cooked no-yolk noodles, warm

1. Combine cornmeal, Parmesan cheese, pepper, and basil; coat pork chops with mixture. Cook pork chops in oil over medium heat in large skillet until browned, 3 to 4 minutes on each side. Add green onions, garlic, and fennel seeds; reduce heat to low and cook, covered, until pork chops are cooked in the center, 5 to 8 minutes, turning occasionally. Garnish with parsley and serve with noodles.

ROSEMARY-SAGE PORK MEDALLIONS

4 servings

Vegetable cooking spray
1 pound pork tenderloin, cut into scant 1/2-inch slices
1 clove garlic, minced
1/2 teaspoon dried rosemary leaves
1/2 teaspoon dried sage leaves
2 teaspoons lemon juice
Salt and pepper, to taste

Per Serving
Calories: 126
% Calories from fat: 25
Fat (gm): 3.4
Sat. fat (gm): 1.2
Cholesterol (mg): 67.6
Sodium (mg): 52
Protein (gm): 22
Carbohydrate (gm): 0.6
Exchanges
Milk: 0.0
Vegetable: 0.0
Fruit: 0.0
Bread: 0.0
Meat: 3.0
Fat: 0.0

1. Spray large skillet with cooking spray; heat over medium heat until hot. Add pork and garlic and sprinkle with herbs; cook until pork is browned and no longer pink in the center, 2 to 3 minutes on each side. Sprinkle with lemon juice; sprinkle lightly with salt and pepper.

SLOW COOKER PORK ROAST

8 servings

1 boneless pork loin roast (about 4 pounds)
1 tablespoon chopped fresh, *or* 2 teaspoons dried rosemary leaves
1 teaspoon coarse ground pepper
Salt, to taste
2 cloves garlic, cut into slivers
Vegetable cooking spray
2 medium onions, sliced, divided
2 bay leaves
1 whole clove
1 cup hot water
2 tablespoons white wine, optional

Per Serving
Calories: 422
% Calories from fat: 34
Fat (gm): 15.5
Sat. fat (gm): 5.3
Cholesterol (mg): 140.5
Sodium (mg): 161
Protein (gm): 62
Carbohydrate (gm): 4.4
Exchanges
Milk: 0.0
Vegetable: 1.0
Fruit: 0.0
Bread: 0.0
Meat: 7.5
Fat: 0.0

1. Rub pork roast with rosemary and pepper; sprinkle lightly with salt. Make tiny slits in meat and insert slivers of garlic. Spray large skillet with cooking spray; heat over medium heat until hot. Cook pork until browned on all sides, 8 to 10 minutes.

2. Arrange 1 sliced onion in bottom of slow cooker. Add pork, remaining onion, bay leaves, clove, water and wine. Cover and cook on Low until pork is tender and no longer pink in center, about 10 hours. Dicard bay leaves.

Tip: To make gravy, blend 2 tablespoons cornstarch and 1/4 cup water to form smooth paste; stir into juices in slow cooker. Cook, covered on High until mixture boils and thickens, about 15 minutes.

PORK AND VEGETABLE STIR-FRY

4 servings

- 6 teaspoons cornstarch, divided
- 1/2 cup dry sherry, *or* reduced-sodium fat-free chicken broth, divided
- 1 pound boneless pork loin, fat trimmed, cut into thin strips
- 2 tablespoons vegetable oil
- 2 cloves garlic
- 1 tablespoon peeled, minced gingerroot
- 4 cups broccoli florets
- 2 zucchini, sliced 1/2 inch thick
- 1/4 cup shredded carrots
- 2-3 teaspoons light soy sauce
- 3 cups cooked rice, warm

Per Serving
Calories: 435
% Calories from fat: 26
Fat (gm): 11.8
Sat. fat (gm): 2.5
Cholesterol (mg): 46.6
Sodium (mg): 189
Protein (gm): 24.4
Carbohydrate (gm): 49.7
Exchanges
Milk: 0.0
Vegetable: 1.0
Fruit: 0.0
Bread: 3.0
Meat: 3.0
Fat: 0.0

1. Combine 4 teaspoons cornstarch and 1/4 cup dry sherry; pour over pork in glass baking dish and toss to coat. Let stand 10 minutes.

2. Heat oil in wok or large skillet until hot; stir-fry pork mixture, garlic, and gingerroot 2 to 3 minutes. Add broccoli, zucchini, and carrots; stir-fry until crisp-tender, 4 to 5 minutes. Stir in combined remaining 1/4 cup dry sherry and 2 teaspoons cornstarch; heat to boiling. Cook, stirring until thickened, 1 to 2 minutes. Add soy sauce; serve over rice.

PORK ORIENTAL IN ORANGE SAUCE

4 servings

Per Serving
Calories: 425
% Calories from fat: 33
Fat (gm): 15.5
Sat. fat (gm): 3.2
Cholesterol (mg): 46.6
Sodium (mg): 587
Protein (gm): 22.7
Carbohydrate (gm): 47.6

Exchanges
Milk: 0.0
Vegetable: 0.0
Fruit: 0.0
Bread: 3.0
Meat: 3.0
Fat: 1.0

2 tablespoons vegetable oil
1 pound boneless lean pork loin, cut into 1/2-inch pieces
2 large carrots, thinly sliced
2 ribs celery, chopped
1 tablespoon shredded orange rind
1/2 cup orange juice
2 tablespoons soy sauce
2 teaspoons cornstarch
1/8 teaspoon ground ginger
1/4 cup cashews, optional
2 teaspoons sugar
3 cups cooked rice, warm

1. Heat oil in wok or large skillet until hot; stir-fry pork until browned, 3 to 4 minutes. Add carrots and celery; stir-fry until crisp tender, about 5 minutes. Stir in combined remaining ingredients, except rice; heat to boiling. Cook, stirring, until thickened, 1 to 2 minutes. Serve over rice.

SWEET-AND-SOUR PORK

4 servings

Per Serving
Calories: 312
% Calories from fat: 14
Fat (gm): 4.8
Sat. fat (gm): 1.6
Cholesterol (mg): 47.8
Sodium (mg): 220
Protein (gm): 21.3
Carbohydrate (gm): 43.8

Exchanges
Milk: 0.0
Vegetable: 0.0
Fruit: 0.0
Bread: 3.0
Meat: 2.0
Fat: 0.0

Vegetable cooking spray
1/2 cup red bell pepper, cut in strips
1/4 cup sliced scallions
1/4 cup shredded carrots
2 cloves garlic, minced
1 pound boneless pork loin, fat trimmed, cut into cubes
1/2 cup Chicken Stock (see p. 47), *or* reduced-sodium fat-free chicken broth
2 teaspoons red wine vinegar
2 teaspoons soy sauce

1 teaspoon brown sugar
1 tablespoon water
2 teaspoons cornstarch
1/2 cup pineapple chunks
3 cups cooked rice, warm

1. Spray wok or large skillet with cooking spray and heat over medium heat until hot; stir-fry vegetables until crisp-tender, 3 to 4 minutes. Move vegetables to side of wok; add pork and stir fry until browned, about 5 minutes. Stir in combined remaining ingredients, except rice; heat to boiling. Cook, stirring, until thickened, 1 to 2 minutes. Serve over rice.

SAVORY LAMB SHANKS

6 servings

2 pounds lamb shanks, fat trimmed
Flour
2 teaspoons olive oil
2 cups chopped onions
2 garlic cloves, minced
2 cups reduced-sodium fat-free chicken broth
1 can (14 1/2 ounces) tomatoes, undrained, coarsely chopped
2 large carrots, sliced
1/2 cup brown lentils
1 medium green bell pepper, seeded, diced
1/4 cup chopped fresh parsley
2 bay leaves
2 teaspoons dried thyme leaves
1/4 teaspoon ground cinnamon
1/4 teaspoon ground cloves
1/4 teaspoon pepper
Salt and pepper, to taste
1 1/4 cups uncooked brown rice, cooked, warm
Parsley sprigs, as garnish

Per Serving
Calories: 325
% Calories from fat: 26
Fat (gm): 7.8
Sat. fat (gm): 2.2
Cholesterol (mg): 56
Sodium (mg): 246
Protein (gm): 25
Carbohydrate (gm): 40

Exchanges
Milk: 0.0
Vegetable: 1.5
Fruit: 0.0
Bread: 2.0
Meat: 2.0
Fat: 0.0

1. Coat lamb shanks lightly with flour; brown in oil in Dutch oven. Stir in onions and garlic and cook until lightly browned, about 5 minutes. Stir in remaining ingredients, except salt, pepper, rice, and parsley sprigs and heat to boiling. Reduce heat and simmer, covered, 1 1/2 hours or until lamb shanks are tender. Discard bay leaves.

2. Remove lamb shanks; remove lean meat and cut into bite-sized pieces. Discard bones. Return meat to stew; season to taste with salt and pepper.

3. Arrange rice on serving platter and spoon lamb stew over. Garnish with parsley sprigs.

GINGERED INDIAN LAMB

4 servings

1 pound lean lamb, fat trimmed, cut into 1-inch pieces
Flour
Olive oil cooking spray
1/4 cup peeled, finely chopped gingerroot
1 medium onion, chopped
4 cloves garlic, minced
1 can (15 ounces) Italian plum tomatoes, undrained
Juice of 1/2 lemon
1/4 teaspoon ground turmeric
1/4 teaspoon celery seeds
1/2 teaspoon ground cumin
1 tablespoon curry powder, mild *or* hot
1/4 cup fat-free plain yogurt
1 cup frozen peas
1/2 cup sliced mushrooms
Salt and pepper, to taste

Per Serving
Calories: 204
% Calories from fat: 25
Fat (gm): 5.8
Sat. fat (gm): 1.9
Cholesterol (mg): 57.6
Sodium (mg): 204
Protein (gm): 22.6
Carbohydrate (gm): 15.7

Exchanges
Milk: 0.0
Vegetable: 1.0
Fruit: 0.0
Bread: 0.5
Meat: 2.5
Fat: 0.0

1. Coat veal cubes light with flour. Spray large saucepan with cooking spray; heat over medium heat until hot. Add veal and cook over medium heat until browned, about 5 minutes. Add gingerroot, onion and garlic; cook until tender, about 5 minutes.

Add tomatoes and liquid, lemon juice and spices; heat to boiling. Reduce heat and simmer, covered, until lamb is tender, 30 to 45 minutes.

2. Reduce to heat low; stir in yogurt, peas, and mushrooms. Simmer 5 minutes. Season to taste with salt and pepper.

SLOW COOKER IRISH STEW

6 servings

- 1 1/2 pounds boneless lamb shoulder, fat trimmed, cut into 1-inch cubes
- 6 small potatoes, thinly sliced
- 6 small white onions, quartered
- 6 carrots, sliced
- 2 teaspoons dried rosemary leaves
- 1/2 teaspoon dried thyme leaves
- 1 bay leaf
- 2 cups water
- Salt and pepper, to taste

Per Serving
Calories: 320
% Calories from fat: 17
Fat (gm): 6.5
Sat. fat (gm): 2.3
Cholesterol (mg): 47.2
Sodium (mg): 74
Protein (gm): 18.5
Carbohydrate (gm): 48.5

Exchanges
Milk: 0.0
Vegetable: 3.0
Fruit: 0.0
Bread: 2.0
Meat: 2.0
Fat: 0.0

1. Combine all ingredients, except salt and pepper, in slow cooker. Cover and cook on High 1 hour. Reduce heat to Low and cook until lamb and vegetables are very tender, 10 to 12 hours. Season to taste with salt and pepper. Discard bay leaf.

SHEPHERD'S PIE

6 servings

- 1 1/2 pounds boneless lamb leg steaks, fat trimmed, cut into 1/2-inch cubes
- 1 tablespoon margarine
- 3/4 cup chopped onion
- 3/4 cup chopped green bell pepper
- 1/2 cup chopped celery
- 3 cloves garlic, minced
- 3 tablespoons flour
- 2 1/2 cups reduced-sodium beef broth

Per Serving
Calories: 274
% Calories from fat: 27
Fat (gm): 8.4
Sat. fat (gm): 2.3
Cholesterol (mg): 48.5
Sodium (mg): 179
Protein (gm): 21.7
Carbohydrate (gm): 28.5

Exchanges
Milk: 0.0
Vegetable: 2.0
Fruit: 0.0
Bread: 1.0
Meat: 2.5
Fat: 0.5

- 1 1/2 cups sliced carrots
- 1 tablespoon tomato paste
- 1/2 teaspoon dried rosemary leaves
- 1/4-1/2 teaspoon dried thyme leaves
- 1 bay leaf
- 3/4 cup frozen peas
- Salt and pepper, to taste
- 2 cups Real Mashed Potatoes (see p. 664)

1. Saute lamb in margarine in large saucepan until browned on all sides, 5 to 8 minutes; remove from pan. Add onion, bell pepper, celery, and garlic; saute until tender, 8 to 10 minutes. Stir in flour; cook over medium heat 1 to 2 minutes, stirring constantly.

2. Return lamb to saucepan; add broth, carrots, tomato paste, and herbs. Heat to boiling; reduce heat and simmer, covered, until lamb is tender, about 25 minutes, adding peas during last 5 minutes cooking time. Discard bay leaf; season to taste with salt and pepper.

3. Pour stew into 1 1/2-quart casserole. Spoon Real Mashed Potatoes around edge of casserole. Bake at 400 degrees until potatoes are browned, about 10 minutes.

GRILLED MINTED LAMB PATTIES

4 servings

- 1 pound ground lean lamb
- 1/2 cup chopped onion
- 3 tablespoons minced parsley
- 1/4 tablespoon salt
- 1/4 teaspoon pepper
- 2 tablespoons lemon juice
- 1/4 cup cooked rice
- 1/4 teaspoon ground cinnamon
- 1/4 teaspoon ground allspice
- 3 teaspoons chopped fresh, *or* dried, mint
- Olive-oil cooking spray
- Sliced cucumbers, as garnish
- Halved cherry tomatoes, as garnish

Per Serving
Calories: 111
% Calories from fat: 27
Fat (gm): 3.3
Sat. fat (gm): 1.1
Cholesterol (mg): 42.5
Sodium (mg): 192
Protein (gm): 14.1
Carbohydrate (gm): 5.7

Exchanges
Milk: 0.0
Vegetable: 0.0
Fruit: 0.0
Bread: 0.0
Meat: 2.0
Fat: 0.0

1. Combine ground lamb with all ingredients, except cooking spray, cucumbers, and tomatoes. Make lamb patties; spray both sides of patties with cooking spray. Grill over hot coals, until no longer pink in the center, 4 to 5 minutes on each side, or broil 6 inches from heat source until cooked through, 4 to 5 minutes on each side. Garnish with cucumber and tomatoes.

EL PASO LAMB KABOBS

8 servings

- 2 pounds boneless lamb shoulder *or* leg, cut into $1^1/_2$-inch cubes
- Salt and pepper, to taste
- 1 tablespoon minced fresh, *or* 1 teaspoon dried, thyme leaves
- Vegetable cooking spray
- 3 small plum tomatoes, halved
- El Paso Sauce (recipe follows)

Per Serving
Calories: 120
% Calories from fat: 16
Fat (gm): 4.7
Sat. fat (gm): 1.6
Cholesterol (mg): 45.3
Sodium (mg): 43
Protein (gm): 14.4
Carbohydrate (gm): 4.9

Exchanges
Milk: 0.0
Vegetable: 0.0
Fruit: 0.0
Bread: 0.0
Meat: 2.0
Fat: 0.0

1. Sprinkle meat lightly with salt, pepper, and thyme. Thread meat onto skewers with tomatoes and grill over hot coals to desired degree of doneness, 3 to 4 minutes on each side for medium; brush lamb with El Paso Sauce occasionally. Serve meat with remaining El Paso Sauce.

El Paso Sauce

makes about $^1/_2$ cup

- $^1/_2$ cup boiling water
- 3 small, dried, hot red chilies, such as cayenne, tepin, or hontaka
- 2 teaspoons cumin
- 2 teaspoons paprika
- 5 cloves garlic, minced
- $^1/_4$ cup lemon juice
- 2 tablespoons white wine, *or* water
- 3 tablespoons chopped fresh cilantro
- $^1/_2$ lemon *or* lime, with rind, coarsely chopped

1. Pour boiling water over chilies; let stand 10 minutes. Drain. Process chilies, and remaining ingredients, except lemon, in food processor or blender until smooth. Add lemon and process until finely chopped.

MOUSSAKA

12 servings

Olive oil cooking spray
1 large eggplant, unpeeled, sliced
1 pound potatoes, unpeeled, sliced
3 cups chopped onions
8 ounces carrots, sliced
3 cloves garlic, minced
1 teaspoon ground cinnamon
1 teaspoon dried oregano leaves
1/2 teaspoon dried thyme leaves
3/4 cup fat-free beef broth
2 cups chopped tomatoes
2 cups sliced mushrooms
1 pound ground lean lamb, *or* beef, cooked, drained
2 cups cooked barley
1 small zucchini, sliced
Salt and pepper, to taste
Custard Topping (recipe follows)
Ground nutmeg, to taste

Per Serving
Calories: 265
% Calories from fat: 29
Fat (gm): 8.9
Sat. fat (gm): 2.3
Cholesterol (mg): 44.7
Sodium (mg): 152
Protein (gm): 15
Carbohydrate (gm): 32.7
Exchanges
Milk: 0.0
Vegetable: 3.0
Fruit: 0.0
Bread: 1.0
Meat: 1.0
Fat: 1.0

1. Spray aluminum foil-lined jelly roll pan with cooking spray; arrange eggplant on pan and spray with cooking spray. Bake at 350 degrees until eggplant is tender but still firm to touch, about 20 minutes. Arrange eggplant on bottom of 13 x 9-inch baking pan.

2. Heat potatoes, onions, carrots, garlic, cinnamon, oregano, thyme, and broth to boiling in large skillet; reduce heat and simmer, uncovered, 5 minutes. Add tomatoes and mushrooms; simmer, uncovered, until tomatoes are soft. Add lamb, barley, and zucchini; cook, uncovered, until mixture is thick, about 5 minutes. Season to taste with salt and pepper.

3. Spoon vegetable mixture over eggplant. Pour Custard Topping over and sprinkle with nutmeg. Bake at 350 degrees until lightly browned on the top, about 45 minutes. Cool 5 to 10 minutes before cutting.

Custard Topping

- 1/3 cup margarine
- 1/2 cup all-purpose flour
- 3 cups fat-free milk
- 1 egg
- 2 egg whites
- Salt and white pepper, to taste

1. Melt margarine in medium saucepan; stir in flour. Cook over medium heat until bubbly, about 2 minutes, stirring constantly. Stir in milk; heat to boiling. Boil, stirring constantly, until thickened, about 1 minute.
2. Beat egg and egg whites in small bowl. Stir about 1 cup milk mixture into eggs; stir egg mixture into saucepan. Cook over low heat until thickened, 2 to 3 minutes. Season to taste with salt and white pepper.

SEVEN

Vegetable Entrées

VEGETABLE FRITTATA WITH PARMESAN TOAST

4 servings

Vegetable cooking spray
1 medium poblano chili, sliced
1 medium onion, sliced
2 cups sliced mushrooms
2 cloves garlic, minced
2 tablespoons chopped parsley
1/4 cup vegetable broth
6 eggs
1/4 cup fat-free milk
1/2 cup cooked brown rice
1/2 cup (2 ounces) shredded reduced-fat Cheddar cheese
1/4 teaspoon salt
1/8 teaspoon pepper
4 slices Italian, *or* French, bread
4 teaspoons grated Parmesan cheese

Per Serving
Calories: 294
% Calories from fat: 33
Fat (gm): 10.7
Sat. fat (gm): 3.7
Cholesterol (mg): 322.5
Sodium (mg): 632
Protein (gm): 20
Carbohydrate (gm): 29.7
Exchanges
Milk: 0.0
Vegetable: 0.0
Fruit: 0.0
Bread: 2.0
Meat: 2.0
Fat: 1.0

1. Spray medium ovenproof skillet with cooking spray; heat over medium heat until hot. Saute vegetables 5 minutes; add parsley and broth. Cook, covered, over medium heat until vegetables are tender and liquid is absorbed, about 5 minutes.

2. Beat together eggs and milk; mix in cooked rice, Cheddar cheese, salt, and pepper. Pour mixture over vegetables in skillet. Cook without stirring, uncovered, over medium-low heat until egg is set and lightly browned on bottom, about 10 minutes.

3. Broil frittata 6 inches from heat source until frittata is cooked on top, 3 to 4 minutes; invert frittata onto plate, slide back into skillet, and cook until lightly browned, 3 to 5 minutes.

4. Sprinkle bread with Parmesan cheese; broil 6 inches from heat source until browned, 2 to 3 minutes. Slide frittata onto serving plate; cut into wedges. Serve with Parmesan toast.

VEGETABLE PUFF

6 servings

- Vegetable cooking spray
- 4 ounces sliced mushrooms
- 1/2 cup chopped red bell pepper
- 1/2 cup finely chopped shallots
- 2 cloves garlic, minced
- 1 pound broccoli, cooked, coarsely chopped
- 1 cup finely shredded carrots, cooked
- 2/3 cup frozen whole kernel corn, thawed
- 2 teaspoons lemon juice
- 3/4 teaspoon dried thyme leaves
- 1/2 teaspoon salt
- 1/2 teaspoon pepper
- 1 cup fat-free half-and-half, *or* 2% reduced-fat milk
- 2 tablespoons flour
- 1 cup no-cholesterol real egg product
- 5 large egg whites
- 1/2 teaspoon cream of tartar

Per Serving
Calories: 133
% Calories from fat: 3
Fat (gm): 0.5
Sat. fat (gm): 0.1
Cholesterol (mg): 0
Sodium (mg): 359
Protein (gm): 11.8
Carbohydrate (gm): 21.2
Exchanges
Milk: 0.0
Vegetable: 2.0
Fruit: 0.0
Bread: 0.5
Meat: 1.0
Fat: 0.0

1. Spray large skillet with cooking spray; heat over medium heat until hot. Saute mushrooms, bell pepper, shallots, and garlic until tender, about 4 minutes. Stir in broccoli, carrots, corn, lemon juice, and thyme; saute 5 minutes. Transfer mixture to large bowl and season with salt and pepper.

2. Whisk half-and-half and flour until smooth in small saucepan. Heat to boiling; boil, whisking constantly, until thickened, about 1 minute. Whisk about half the mixture into egg product; whisk egg mixture back into half-and-half. Stir into vegetable mixture.

3. Beat egg whites in large mixing bowl until foamy. Add cream of tartar and continue beating until stiff peaks form; fold into vegetable mixture. Transfer mixture to a lightly greased 1 1/2-quart casserole. Place casserole in a large roasting pan on center rack of oven; add 2 inches hot water to pan.

4. Bake, uncovered, at 375 degrees 35 minutes or until casserole is puffed and lightly browned on top. Serve immediately.

SWEET POTATO HASH WITH POACHED EGGS

4 servings (scant 1 cup each)

Butter-flavored cooking spray
2 cups cubed (1/2 inch) peeled sweet potatoes
2 cups cubed (1/2 inch) unpeeled Idaho potatoes
1/2 cup chopped onion
1/2 cup chopped red bell pepper
1 teaspoon dried rosemary leaves
1/2 teaspoon dried thyme leaves
Salt and pepper, to taste
4 poached, *or* fried, eggs

Per Serving
Calories: 393
% Calories from fat: 13
Fat (gm): 5.8
Sat. fat (gm): 1.7
Cholesterol (mg): 212
Sodium (mg): 171
Protein (gm): 12.3
Carbohydrate (gm): 74.4
Exchanges
Milk: 0.0
Vegetable: 0.5
Fruit: 0.0
Bread: 4.5
Meat: 1.0
Fat: 0.0

1. Spray large skillet with cooking spray; heat over medium heat until hot. Add vegetables and herbs and cook, covered, over medium heat 5 minutes.

2. Spray vegetables lightly with cooking spray and stir. Cook uncovered, until vegetables are browned and tender, about 10 minutes. Season to taste with salt and black pepper.

3. Spoon hash onto plates; top each serving with an egg.

VEGETABLE CREPES

4 servings (2 crepes each)

Vegetable cooking spray
2 cups thinly sliced cabbage
1 cup thinly sliced celery
1/2 medium green bell pepper, thinly sliced
1/2 cup sliced mushrooms
1/3 cup chopped green onions and tops
2-3 teaspoons sugar

Per Serving
Calories: 215
% Calories from fat: 25
Fat (gm): 5.8
Sat. fat (gm): 1.4
Cholesterol (mg): 107.2
Sodium (mg): 530
Protein (gm): 14.7
Carbohydrate (gm): 25.1
Exchanges
Milk: 0.5
Vegetable: 1.0
Fruit: 0.0
Bread: 1.0
Meat: 1.0
Fat: 0.5

2 tablespoons water
2-3 teaspoons lemon juice
Salt and pepper, to taste
8 Crepes (see p. 497), warm
Mock Hollandaise Sauce (see p. 502)

1. Spray large skillet with cooking spray; heat over medium heat until hot. Add cabbage, celery, bell pepper, mushrooms, green onions, sugar, and water. Cook, covered, over medium heat until cabbage and mushrooms are wilted, about 5 minutes. Cook, uncovered, until vegetables are tender, about 5 minutes longer. Season to taste with lemon juice, salt, and pepper.

2. Spoon vegetable mixture along centers of crepes; roll up and arrange, seam sides down, on serving plates. Serve with Mock Hollandaise Sauce.

VEGETABLE STRUDEL WITH WILD MUSHROOM SAUCE

4 servings

Butter-flavored vegetable cooking spray
1/2 cup chopped red bell pepper
1/2 cup chopped yellow bell pepper
1/4 cup chopped shallots
2 cloves garlic, minced
1 1/2 cups cubed butternut, *or* acorn, squash, cooked
1 1/2 cups broccoli florets, cooked
Wild Mushroom Sauce (see p. 505), divided
3/4 cup (3 ounces) shredded reduced-fat brick, *or* Swiss, cheese
Salt and pepper, to taste
5 sheets frozen fillo pastry, thawed

Per Serving
Calories: 207
% Calories from fat: 19
Fat (gm): 4.6
Sat. fat (gm): 2.4
Cholesterol (mg): 15.2
Sodium (mg): 85
Protein (gm): 11.8
Carbohydrate (gm): 27.9

Exchanges
Milk: 0.0
Vegetable: 3.0
Fruit: 0.0
Bread: 1.0
Meat: 1.0
Fat: 0.0

1. Spray large skillet with cooking spray; heat over medium heat until hot. Saute bell peppers, shallot, and garlic until tender, 5 to 8 minutes. Stir in squash, broccoli, and half of the Wild Mushroom Sauce; cook until hot through, 2 to 3 minutes. Remove from heat and stir in cheese; season to taste with salt and pepper.

2. Lay 1 sheet of fillo on clean towel on table; spray generously with cooking spray. Cover with second sheet of fillo and spray generously with cooking spray; repeat with remaining fillo.

3. Spoon vegetable mixture along long edge of fillo, 3 to 4 inches from the edge. Fold edge of fillo over filling and roll up, using towel to help lift and roll; place seam side down on greased cookie sheet. Spray top of fillo generously with cooking spray.

4. Bake at 375 degrees until golden, about 30 minutes. Let stand 5 minutes before cutting.

5. Cut strudel into 4 pieces and arrange on plates. Spoon remaining Wild Mushroom Sauce over or alongside each serving.

BLACK-EYED PEAS AND GREENS WITH MILLET

4 servings (about 1 1/2 cups each)

Vegetable cooking spray
1 medium onion, sliced
2 cloves garlic, minced
1 can (14 1/2 ounces) reduced-sodium vegetable broth
3 tablespoons red wine vinegar
6 cups coarsely chopped turnip greens
2 large tomatoes, cut in wedges
1 can (15 ounces) black-eyed peas, rinsed, drained
1 cup millet
2 tablespoons finely chopped cilantro leaves
Salt and pepper, to taste
Red pepper sauce, to taste

Per Serving
Calories: 322
% Calories from fat: 6
Fat (gm): 2.3
Sat. fat (gm): 1.1
Cholesterol (mg): 0
Sodium (mg): 385
Protein (gm): 12.4
Carbohydrate (gm): 63.9
Exchanges
Milk: 0.0
Vegetable: 2.0
Fruit: 0.0
Bread: 3.5
Meat: 0.5
Fat: 0.0

1. Spray large saucepan with cooking spray; heat over medium heat until hot. Saute onion and garlic until tender, about 5 minutes. Add broth and vinegar; heat to boiling. Add greens and tomatoes to saucepan; reduce heat and simmer, covered, until greens are wilted, about 5 minutes.

2. Stir black-eyed peas and millet into saucepan; simmer, covered, until all liquid is absorbed, about 20 minutes. Remove from heat and let stand 5 to 10 minutes. Stir in cilantro; season to taste with salt, pepper, and red pepper sauce.

EGGPLANT PROVENÇAL

4 servings (1 1/2 cups each)

Per Serving
Calories: 226
% Calories from fat: 28
Fat (gm): 7.6
Sat. fat (gm): 1.2
Cholesterol (mg): 0
Sodium (mg): 549
Protein (gm): 6.6
Carbohydrate (gm): 37.3

Exchanges
Milk: 0.0
Vegetable: 4.0
Fruit: 0.0
Bread: 1.0
Meat: 0.0
Fat: 1.0

Olive oil cooking spray
1 cup chopped onion
1 clove garlic, minced
2 small eggplants (about 1 pound each), peeled, cut into 3/4-inch cubes
2 medium green bell peppers, cut into inch strips
2 cups chopped tomatoes
1/4 cup finely chopped parsley
1/4 cup sliced, pitted ripe, *or* pimiento stuffed, olives
1 tablespoon drained capers
3/4 teaspoon dried basil leaves
3/4 teaspoon dried oregano leaves
Salt and pepper, to taste
1/2 cup dry unseasoned bread crumbs
2 tablespoons grated, fat-free Parmesan cheese
1 tablespoon margarine, melted

1. Spray large skillet with cooking spray; heat over medium heat until hot. Saute onion and garlic 3 to 4 minutes; add eggplant, bell pepper, and tomatoes. Cook, covered, over medium heat until vegetables are tender, 8 to 10 minutes, stirring occasionally.

2. Stir parsley, olives, capers, and herbs into mixture; season to taste with salt and pepper. Spoon mixture into 11 x 7-inch baking dish. Combine breadcrumbs, Parmesan cheese, and margarine; sprinkle over casserole. Bake at 350 degrees, uncovered, until mixture is bubbly and top browned, about 30 minutes.

SWEET POTATO CAKES

2 servings

- 2 cups shredded sweet potatoes
- 1/2 cup shredded carrot
- 1/2 cup shredded zucchini
- 1/2 cup shredded potato
- 1/4 cup finely chopped onion
- 1/4 teaspoon dried sage leaves
- Salt and pepper, to taste
- 1 egg
- 2 egg whites
- 1/4 cup all-purpose flour
- Butter-flavored vegetable cooking spray
- 4 tablespoons fat-free sour cream, optional

Per Serving
Calories: 303
% Calories from fat: 9
Fat (gm): 3.2
Sat. fat (gm): 0.9
Cholesterol (mg): 106.5
Sodium (mg): 116
Protein (gm): 12.1
Carbohydrate (gm): 56.8

Exchanges
Milk: 0.0
Vegetable: 2.0
Fruit: 0.0
Bread: 2.5
Meat: 1.0
Fat: 0.0

1. Combine vegetables and sage in medium bowl; season to taste with salt and pepper. Mix in egg, egg whites, and flour.

2. Spray medium skillet with cooking spray; heat over medium heat until hot. Add half the vegetable mixture to skillet, pressing down firmly to make a 7- to 8-inch cake. Cook over medium heat until browned on the bottom, 8 to 10 minutes. Loosen cake with spatula and invert onto plate.

3. Spray skillet generously with cooking spray and slide cake back into skillet. Cook until browned on the bottom, 8 to 10 minutes. Repeat with remaining potato mixture. Cut each cake in half and top with 1 tablespoon sour cream if desired.

ROASTED STUFFED PORTOBELLO MUSHROOMS WITH MIXED HERB PESTO

4 servings (2 stuffed mushrooms each)

8 large portobello mushrooms (5-6 inches diameter)
Vegetable cooking spray
1 cup finely chopped zucchini
1 cup shredded carrots
3 green onions and tops, thinly sliced
4 tablespoons dry unseasoned bread crumbs
Mixed Herb Pesto (see p. 515)
Salt and pepper, to taste
1/2 cup (2 ounces) shredded reduced-fat mozzarella cheese

Per Serving
Calories: 185
% Calories from fat: 20
Fat (gm): 3.9
Sat. fat (gm): 1.8
Cholesterol (mg): 7.6
Sodium (mg): 206
Protein (gm): 16
Carbohydrate (gm): 19.1
Exchanges
Milk: 0.0
Vegetable: 4.0
Fruit: 0.0
Bread: 0.5
Meat: 1.0
Fat: 0.0

1. Remove and chop mushroom stems. Spray large skillet with cooking spray; heat over medium heat until hot. Saute mushroom stems, zucchini, carrots, and green onions until crisp-tender, 8 to 10 minutes. Stir in breadcrumbs and pesto. Season to taste with salt and pepper. Spoon vegetable mixture onto mushrooms.

2. Spray aluminum-foil-lined jelly roll pan with cooking spray; arrange mushrooms on pan. Roast mushrooms at 425 degrees until mushrooms are tender, about 20 minutes, sprinkling with cheese the last 5 minutes of roasting time.

GRILLED VEGETABLE KABOBS

6 servings

- 1 package (9 ounces) frozen artichoke hearts, thawed
- 3 medium zucchini, cut into 1/2-inch slices
- 24 cherry tomatoes
- 3 frozen, Mexican-style all-vegetable "burgers," thawed, cut into quarters
- 1/2 cup fat-free French, *or* Italian, salad dressing
- 1/2-1 teaspoon ground cumin
- 3-4 teaspoons lime juice
- 2 teaspoons grated lime rind
- Salt and pepper, to taste
- Black Beans and Rice (see p. 377)

Per Serving
Calories: 375
% Calories from fat: 17
Fat (gm): 7.4
Sat. fat (gm): 0.1
Cholesterol (mg): 0
Sodium (mg): 678
Protein (gm): 20
Carbohydrate (gm): 62.2
Exchanges
Milk: 0.0
Vegetable: 3.0
Fruit: 0.0
Bread: 2.5
Meat: 0.5
Fat: 1.0

1. Alternate vegetables and "burgers" on metal skewers. Mix salad dressing, cumin, lime juice and rind in small bowl.

2. Grill kabobs over medium-hot coals until vegetables are tender, 8 to 10 minutes, turning occasionally and basting generously with dressing mixture. Sprinkle lightly with salt and pepper.

3. Spoon Black Beans and Rice onto plates and top with kabobs.

TOMATOES STUFFED WITH PEPPER-ROASTED MUSHROOMS

6 servings

Per Serving
Calories: 136
% Calories from fat: 16
Fat (gm): 2.9
Sat. fat (gm): 0.2
Cholesterol (mg): 0
Sodium (mg): 143
Protein (gm): 6.4
Carbohydrate (gm): 26.6
Exchanges
Milk: 0.0
Vegetable: 4.0
Fruit: 0.0
Bread: 0.5
Meat: 0.0
Fat: 0.0

Olive oil cooking spray
1 pound mushrooms
1/2 teaspoon coarse-grind pepper
1 cup cooked rice
1/4 cup dry unseasoned bread crumbs
2 tablespoons fat-free red wine vinaigrette
3 tablespoons finely chopped fresh, *or* 1 1/2 teaspoons dried, dill weed
3 tablespoons finely chopped chives
6 large tomatoes (10-12 ounces each), cored
Salt, to taste

1. Spray aluminum-foil-lined jelly roll pan with cooking spray. Arrange mushrooms on pan in single layer; spray with cooking spray and sprinkle with pepper.

2. Roast mushrooms at 425 degrees until tender, about 20 minutes; cool slightly. Chop mushrooms; combine with rice, bread crumbs, vinaigrette, and herbs.

3. Slice tops from tomatoes and scoop out pulp with grapefruit spoon. Chop pulp and stir into mushroom mixture; season to taste with salt. Spoon mushroom mixture into tomatoes. Bake in baking pan at 425 degrees until hot through, 10 to 15 minutes.

ORIENTAL VEGETABLE SATAY

4 servings

- 1/2 medium acorn squash, peeled, seeded, cut into 1-inch pieces
- 1 pound broccoli florets
- 1/2 pound fresh, *or* frozen, thawed, whole okra
- 2 medium yellow summer squash, cut into 1-inch slices
- 8 ounces pearl onions, peeled
- 3/4 cup teriyaki sauce, divided
- 3 cups cooked rice, warm
- Peanut Satay Sauce (recipe follows)

Per Serving
Calories: 452
% Calories from fat: 20
Fat (gm): 10.3
Sat. fat (gm): 1.8
Cholesterol (mg): 0
Sodium (mg): 775
Protein (gm): 13.4
Carbohydrate (gm): 78.9

Exchanges
Milk: 0.0
Vegetable: 3.0
Fruit: 0.0
Bread: 4.0
Meat: 0.0
Fat: 2.0

1. Cook acorn squash in 2 inches simmering water in medium saucepan until beginning to soften, about 2 minutes; drain.

2. Arrange vegetables on skewers and place on lightly greased aluminum-foil-lined jelly roll pan. Roast at 425 degrees until lightly browned, about 10 minutes. Baste with half the teriyaki sauce, and roast 2 to 3 minutes longer. Turn vegetables and repeat for other side, using remainder of sauce.

3. Arrange skewers on plates; serve with rice and Peanut Satay Sauce.

Peanut Satay Sauce

makes about 1/3 cup

- 3 tablespoons reduced-sodium soy sauce
- 3 tablespoons chunky peanut butter
- 2 1/2 tablespoons sugar
- 1/4 cup thinly sliced green onion, green and white parts
- 1 tablespoon grated gingerroot

1. Combine all ingredients.

SZECHUAN VEGETABLE STIR-FRY

4 servings (about 1 1/4 cups each)

- 1 cup vegetable broth, divided
- 1/3 cup orange juice
- 1/4 cup reduced-sodium tamari soy sauce
- 1/8-1/4 teaspoon crushed red pepper
- 1 package (8 ounces) tempeh, *or* light firm tofu, cut into 3/4-inch cubes
- Vegetable cooking spray
- 8 ounces asparagus, cut into 1 1/2-inch pieces
- 4 ounces snow peas, strings removed
- 1 cup sliced carrots
- 1 cup sliced green onions and tops
- 1 medium red bell pepper, sliced
- 2-3 teaspoons minced gingerroot
- 4 cloves garlic, minced
- 1/2 cup sliced shiitake, *or* cremini, mushrooms
- 2 tablespoons cornstarch
- Salt and pepper, to taste
- 4 cups cooked brown rice, warm
- 1/4 cup peanuts, optional

Per Serving
Calories: 455
% Calories from fat: 15
Fat (gm): 8.0
Sat. fat (gm): 1.3
Cholesterol (mg): 0
Sodium (mg): 663
Protein (gm): 23.3
Carbohydrate (gm): 75.8

Exchanges
Milk: 0.0
Vegetable: 3.0
Fruit: 0.0
Bread: 4.0
Meat: 1.0
Fat: 1.0

1. Combine 1/2 cup vegetable broth, orange juice, soy sauce, and red pepper; pour over tempeh in shallow glass dish and let stand 30 minutes. Drain, reserving marinade.

2. Spray wok or large skillet with cooking spray; heat over medium heat until hot. Add tempeh; stir-fry 2 to 3 minutes. Add asparagus, snow peas, carrots, green onions, bell pepper, gingerroot, and garlic; spray with cooking spray. Stir-fry until vegetables are crisp-tender, 8 to 10 minutes. Add mushrooms; stir-fry 3 to 4 minutes longer.

3. Add reserved marinade to wok; heat to boiling. Mix cornstarch and remaining 1/2 cup stock; stir into boiling mixture. Boil, stirring constantly, until thickened, about 1 minute. Season to taste with salt and pepper.

4. Spoon vegetable mixture over rice on serving plates; sprinkle with peanuts, if using.

THAI STIR-FRY

4 servings

Vegetable cooking spray
8 green onions and tops, sliced
8 ounces broccoli florets
8 ounces carrots, thinly sliced
1 cup Thai peanut sauce
1/2 cup canned reduced-sodium vegetable broth
2 teaspoons cornstarch
1 package (6 1/4 ounces) Thai coconut ginger rice, cooked according to package directions, warm
1/4 cup finely chopped cilantro
1/4 cup dry roasted peanuts, optional

Per Serving
Calories: 361
% Calories from fat: 14
Fat (gm): 5.3
Sat. fat (gm): 1
Cholesterol (mg): 0
Sodium (mg): 1726
Protein (gm): 13.1
Carbohydrate (gm): 63
Exchanges
Milk: 0.0
Vegetable: 3.0
Fruit: 0.0
Bread: 3.0
Meat: 0.0
Fat: 1.0

1. Spray large skillet with cooking spray; heat over medium heat until hot. Saute onions, broccoli, and carrots until crisp-tender; 4 to 5 minutes. Stir in peanut sauce. Stir in combined vegetable broth and cornstarch; heat to boiling. Boil until thickened, about 1 minute. Serve vegetable mixture over rice; sprinkle with cilantro and peanuts (if using).

CURRIED COUSCOUS

4 servings (about 1 1/2 cups each)

Vegetable cooking spray
8 ounces fresh, *or* frozen, thawed, whole okra
1 medium onion, chopped
2 cloves garlic, chopped
2 tablespoons finely chopped parsley
1 cup frozen whole-kernel corn, thawed
1 cup sliced mushrooms
2 medium carrots, sliced
1 1/2 teaspoons curry powder

Per Serving
Calories: 304
% Calories from fat: 11
Fat (gm): 3.9
Sat. fat (gm): 0.6
Cholesterol (mg): 0.5
Sodium (mg): 55
Protein (gm): 9.5
Carbohydrate (gm): 60.1
Exchanges
Milk: 0.0
Vegetable: 3.0
Fruit: 1.0
Bread: 2.0
Meat: 0.0
Fat: 0.5

1 cup reduced-sodium vegetable broth
2/3 cup couscous
1 medium tomato, chopped
Salt and pepper, to taste
Cucumber Sauce (see p. 163)
Onion-Chutney Relish (recipe follows)
1/4 cup chopped unsalted peanuts
1/4 cup dark raisins

1. Spray large saucepan with cooking spray; heat over medium heat until hot. Saute okra, onion, garlic, and parsley until onion is tender, about 5 minutes. Stir in corn, mushrooms, carrots, and curry powder; cook 2 minutes.

2. Add stock to saucepan and heat to boiling; reduce heat and simmer, covered, until vegetables are tender, 8 to 10 minutes. Stir in couscous and tomato. Remove from heat and let stand, covered, until couscous is tender and broth absorbed, about 5 minutes. Season to taste with salt and pepper.

3. Spoon couscous mixture into serving bowl; serve with Cucumber Sauce, Onion-Chutney Relish, peanuts, and raisins.

Onion-Chutney Relish

makes about 1 cup

Vegetable cooking spray
4 medium onions, chopped
1/2 cup chopped mango chutney
1-1 1/2 teaspoons dried mint leaves

1. Spray large skillet with cooking spray; heat over medium heat until hot. Saute onions 3 to 5 minutes; reduce heat to low and cook until they are very soft and golden, about 15 minutes.

2. Mix onions, chutney, and mint; refrigerate until ready to serve.

VEGETABLE CURRY

4 servings

Vegetable cooking spray
1/2 cup chopped onion
2 cloves garlic, minced
1 large head cauliflower, cut into florets
2 medium potatoes, peeled, cut into 1/2-inch cubes
2 large carrots, cut into 1/2-inch slices
1 1/2 cups Vegetable Stock (see p. 48), *or* vegetable broth
3/4 teaspoon ground turmeric
1/4 teaspoon dry mustard
1/4 teaspoon ground cumin
1/4 teaspoon ground coriander
1 tablespoon flour
2 tablespoons cold water
1 large tomato, chopped
2 tablespoons finely chopped parsley
1-2 tablespoons lemon juice
Salt, cayenne, and black pepper, to taste

Per Serving
Calories: 81
% Calories from fat: 6
Fat (gm): 0.6
Sat. fat (gm): 0
Cholesterol (mg): 0
Sodium (mg): 57.2
Protein (gm): 3.7
Carbohydrate (gm): 15.8

Exchanges
Milk: 0.0
Vegetable: 2.0
Fruit: 0.0
Bread: 0.5
Meat: 0.0
Fat: 0.0

1. Spray large saucepan with cooking spray; heat over medium heat until hot. Saute onion and garlic 3 to 4 minutes. Add cauliflower, potatoes, carrots, Vegetable Stock, and herbs to saucepan; heat to boiling. Reduce heat and simmer, covered, until vegetables are tender, 10 to 15 minutes.

2. Heat vegetable mixture to boiling. Mix flour and water; stir into boiling mixture. Cook, stirring constantly, until thickened. Stir in tomato, parsley, and lemon juice; simmer 2 to 3 minutes longer. Season to taste with salt, cayenne, and black pepper.

LENTIL RAVIOLI WITH GINGERED TOMATO RELISH

4 servings (6 ravioli each)

Olive oil cooking spray
1/4 cup finely chopped fennel bulb, *or* celery
2 teaspoons grated gingerroot
1 teaspoon curry powder
1/2 teaspoon ground cumin
1/4 teaspoon ground turmeric
1/4 teaspoon ground cinnamon
1/4 teaspoon cayenne pepper
2 2/3 cups water
2/3 cup dried lentils, cleaned, rinsed
2 tablespoons finely chopped cilantro
Salt, to taste
48 wonton wrappers
Gingered Tomato Relish (see p. 512)
Cilantro, *or* parsley sprigs, as garnish

Per Serving
Calories: 324
% Calories from fat: 5
Fat (gm): 1.8
Sat. fat (gm): 0.3
Cholesterol (mg): 12
Sodium (mg): 569
Protein (gm): 12.1
Carbohydrate (gm): 65.4
Exchanges
Milk: 0.0
Vegetable: 2.0
Fruit: 0.0
Bread: 4.0
Meat: 0.0
Fat: 0.0

1. Coat large skillet with cooking spray; heat over medium heat until hot. Saute fennel and gingerroot 2 to 3 minutes; add spices and cook 1 minute longer.

2. Add water and lentils to skillet; heat to boiling. Reduce heat and simmer, covered, until lentils are just tender, about 15 minutes. Simmer uncovered, until excess liquid is gone, about 5 minutes. Stir in chopped cilantro; season to taste with salt.

3. Place 1 tablespoon lentil mixture in center of 1 wonton wrapper; brush edges of wrapper with water. Place second wonton wrapper on top and press edges to seal. Repeat with remaining wonton wrappers and filling.

4. Heat about 3 quarts water to boiling in large saucepan; add 4 to 6 ravioli. Reduce heat and simmer, uncovered, until ravioli float to surface and are cooked al dente, 3 to 4 minutes. Remove ravioli with slotted spoon; repeat cooking procedure with remaining ravioli.

5. Arrange ravioli on plates and top with Gingered Tomato Relish; garnish with cilantro.

ROASTED VEGETABLES WITH MUSHROOM TORTELLINI

4 servings

Vegetable cooking spray
3 medium Italian plum tomatoes
8 ounces small okra, ends trimmed
4 ounces small mushrooms, halved
1 medium zucchini, cut into 1/4-inch slices
1 medium yellow summer squash, cut into 1/4-inch slices
4 ounces broccoli rabe, rinsed, dried, cut into 3-inch pieces, *or* broccoli, cut into small florets
1 1/2 teaspoons Italian seasoning
Salt and pepper, to taste
1 package (9 ounces) mushroom, *or* herb, tortellini, cooked, warm
1-2 tablespoons olive oil

Per Serving
Calories: 256
% Calories from fat: 19
Fat (gm): 5.6
Sat. fat (gm): 1.3
Cholesterol (mg): 3.8
Sodium (mg): 337
Protein (gm): 14.6
Carbohydrate (gm): 40.5

Exchanges
Milk: 0.0
Vegetable: 2.0
Fruit: 0.0
Bread: 2.0
Meat: 1.0
Fat: 0.0

1. Line large jelly roll pan with aluminum foil; spray with cooking spray.

2. Cut each tomato into 6 wedges; cut wedges in halves. Arrange tomatoes and remaining vegetables on jelly roll pan; spray generously with cooking spray. Sprinkle vegetables with Italian seasoning; sprinkle lightly with salt and pepper.

3. Roast vegetables at 425 degrees until tender and browned, about 40 minutes, removing broccoli rabe after about 20 minutes. Combine vegetables and tortellini in serving bowl; drizzle with olive oil and toss.

ROASTED EGGPLANT WITH PASTA

6 servings

Per Serving
Calories: 140
% Calories from fat: 19
Fat (gm): 3
Sat. fat (gm): 0.5
Cholesterol (mg): 0
Sodium (mg): 7
Protein (gm): 4.5
Carbohydrate (gm): 24
Exchanges
Milk: 0.0
Vegetable: 1.5
Fruit: 0.0
Bread: 1.0
Meat: 0.0
Fat: 0.5

- 1 medium eggplant (3/4 pound)
- 1 large tomato, seeded, coarsely chopped
- 4 green onions and tops, sliced
- 2 tablespoons balsamic vinegar, *or* red wine vinegar
- 1 tablespoon olive oil
- 1-2 teaspoons lemon juice
- 1 tablespoon finely chopped parsley
- 1 1/2 cups (6 ounces) fusilli, *or* rotini (spirals or corkscrews), cooked, room temperature

1. Pierce eggplant 6 to 8 times with fork; place in baking pan. Bake, uncovered, at 425 degrees until tender, about 20 minutes. Cool until warm enough to handle easily. Cut eggplant in half; scoop out pulp with large spoon, and cut pulp into 3/4-inch pieces.

2. Combine eggplant pulp, tomato, and onions in bowl; stir in vinegar, oil, lemon juice, and parsley. Spoon over pasta and toss.

SESAME PASTA WITH SUMMER VEGETABLES

6 side-dish servings

Per Serving
Calories: 192
% Calories from fat: 30
Fat (gm): 6.6
Sat. fat (gm): 0.7
Cholesterol (mg): 0
Sodium (mg): 428
Protein (gm): 7.2
Carbohydrate (gm): 28.3
Exchanges
Milk: 0.0
Vegetable: 1.5
Fruit: 0.0
Bread: 1.5
Meat: 0.0
Fat: 1.0

- 1 small eggplant
- 1 cup sliced carrots, steamed until crisp-tender
- 1 cup sliced yellow summer squash, steamed until crisp-tender
- 1 cup broccoli florets, steamed until crisp-tender
- 1 medium red bell pepper, sliced
- 1/4 cup sliced green onions and tops
- Sesame Dressing (recipe follows)
- 8 ounces thin spaghetti, cooked, room temperature
- 2 teaspoons toasted sesame seeds

1. Heat oven to 400 degrees. Pierce eggplant 6 to 8 times with fork; place in baking pan. Bake, uncovered, until tender, about 30 minutes. Cool until able to handle easily. Cut eggplant in half; scoop out pulp with a large spoon and cut pulp into 3/4-inch pieces.
2. Combine eggplant and remaining vegetables in bowl; pour Sesame Dressing over and toss. Add pasta and toss; sprinkle with sesame seeds.

Sesame Dressing

makes about 1 1/3 cups

2 tablespoons reduced-sodium soy sauce
2 tablespoons sesame oil
1 teaspoon hot chili oil, optional
1 tablespoon balsamic, *or* red wine vinegar
1 1/2 tablespoons sugar
1 clove garlic, minced
1 tablespoon finely chopped cilantro, *or* parsley

1. Mix all ingredients; refrigerate until serving time. Mix again before using.

CURRIED PASTA AND VEGETABLES

4 servings

Vegetable cooking spray
1/2 cup chopped red bell pepper
1/2 cup chopped yellow bell pepper
1 cup small cauliflower florets
1 cup peas, *or* cut green beans
1/2 teaspoon crushed red pepper
1/4 cup water
Salt and pepper, to taste
2 cups (double recipe) Curry Sauce (see p. 407)
8 ounces angel hair pasta, cooked, warm
2-4 tablespoons chopped dry-roasted peanuts

Per Serving
Calories: 390
% Calories from fat: 13
Fat (gm): 5.6
Sat. fat (gm): 1.1
Cholesterol (mg): 63.8
Sodium (mg): 84.7
Protein (gm): 13.6
Carbohydrate (gm): 68.7
Exchanges
Milk: 0.0
Vegetable: 2.0
Fruit: 0.5
Bread: 3.5
Meat: 0.0
Fat: 1.0

2 tablespoons finely chopped cilantro
1/4 cup chopped mango chutney

1. Spray medium skillet with cooking spray; heat over medium heat until hot. Saute bell peppers until tender, 3 to 4 minutes. Add cauliflower, peas, crushed red pepper, and water; heat to boiling. Reduce heat and simmer, covered, until vegetables are tender, 5 to 8 minutes; cook uncovered, until water has evaporated. Season to taste with salt and pepper.

2. Toss Curry Sauce and pasta in serving bowl; spoon vegetables over and toss. Spoon pasta onto serving plates and sprinkle with peanuts and cilantro; serve a spoonful of chutney on the side of each plate.

POTATO GNOCCHI WITH SAGE CREAM

6 servings

2 cups fat-free half-and-half, *or* 2% reduced-fat milk
16-20 medium sage leaves, thinly sliced, *or* 3/4 teaspoon dried sage leaves
1 cup chopped onion
2 teaspoons margarine
4 cups small broccoflower, *or* broccoli, florets
1/2 cup water, divided
2 tablespoons flour
1/2 teaspoon ground nutmeg
1 package (16 ounces) potato gnocchi, cooked, warm
Salt and pepper, to taste
Fat-free Parmesan cheese, grated, as garnish

Per Serving
Calories: 263
% Calories from fat: 2
Fat (gm): 0.6
Sat. fat (gm): 0.2
Cholesterol (mg): 0.9
Sodium (mg): 150
Protein (gm): 13.4
Carbohydrate (gm): 52.4
Exchanges
Milk: 0.0
Vegetable: 2.0
Fruit: 0.0
Bread: 2.5
Meat: 0.0
Fat: 0.0

1. Heat half-and-half and sage leaves (if using dried sage, tie leaves in small cheesecloth bag) to boiling in medium saucepan; reduce heat and simmer 10 minutes. Strain, discarding sage.

2. Saute onion in margarine in large skillet 2 to 3 minutes; add broccoflower and 1/4 cup water and heat to boiling. Reduce heat and simmer, covered, until broccoflower is tender and water gone, 5 to 8 minutes.

3. Heat half-and-half mixture to boiling. Mix flour, nutmeg, and remaining 1/4 cup water; whisk into half-and-half. Boil, whisking constantly, until thickened, about 1 minute.

4. Pour sauce over vegetables in skillet; mix in gnocchi and season to taste with salt and pepper. Spoon into serving bowl; sprinkle very lightly with Parmesan cheese.

ROASTED RED PEPPER AND SPINACH LASAGNE

8 servings

Olive oil cooking spray
1 cup chopped onion
2 teaspoons minced garlic
1 teaspoon dried marjoram leaves
1/2-3/4 teaspoon dried oregano leaves
3 cups fat-free milk, divided
1/4 cup plus 2 tablespoons all-purpose flour
1 cup (4 ounces) grated fat-free Parmesan cheese, divided
1/2 package (8-ounce size) fat-free cream cheese, cubed
2/3 cup finely chopped parsley
Salt and pepper, to taste
2 packages (10 ounces each) frozen, thawed, chopped spinach, very well drained
2/3 cup fat-free ricotta cheese
12 lasagne noodles (10 ounces), cooked
1 jar (15 ounces) roasted red peppers, drained, cut into 1-inch slices
1 cup (4 ounces) shredded reduced-fat mozzarella cheese

Per Serving
Calories: 261
% Calories from fat: 13
Fat (gm): 3.8
Sat. fat (gm): 1.7
Cholesterol (mg): 9.1
Sodium (mg): 386
Protein (gm): 21.4
Carbohydrate (gm): 36.8

Exchanges
Milk: 0.5
Vegetable: 2.0
Fruit: 0.0
Bread: 1.5
Meat: 1.0
Fat: 0.0

1. Spray large saucepan with cooking spray; heat over medium heat until hot. Saute onion and garlic until tender, 5 to 8 minutes; stir in marjoram and oregano and cook 1 to 2 minutes longer.

2. Add 2 cups milk to saucepan; heat to boiling. Mix remaining 1 cup milk and flour; whisk into boiling milk mixture. Boil, whisking constantly, until thickened, about 1 minute. Remove from heat; mix in Parmesan and cream cheese, stirring until cream cheese is melted. Stir in parsley; season with salt and pepper.

3. Mix spinach and ricotta cheese; season to taste with salt and pepper.

4. Spread 1/2 cup sauce in bottom of 13 x 9-inch baking pan. Arrange 4 noodles in pan, overlapping edges. Top with 1/2 of spinach mixture and 1/2 of red pepper slices; spread with generous 1 cup sauce. Repeat layers. Place remaining 4 noodles on top of lasagne and spread with remaining 1 1/4 cups sauce. Sprinkle with mozzarella cheese.

5. Bake lasagne at 350 degrees, loosely covered, until hot through, about 45 minutes. Let stand 10 minutes before serving.

MEXICAN-STYLE GRAIN AND VEGETABLE CASSEROLE

---

6 servings

Vegetable cooking spray
1 large red bell pepper, chopped
1 medium onion, chopped
3 cloves garlic, minced
1 jalapeño chili, finely chopped
2 medium chayote squash, peeled, seeded, cubed, *or* 2 medium zucchini, cubed
2 cups halved small mushrooms
1 cup frozen, thawed, whole-kernel corn
3/4 teaspoon dried oregano leaves
1/2 teaspoon ground cumin
1/2 teaspoon chili powder
Salt and pepper, to taste
2 cups cooked rice
2 cups cooked millet
1 cup fat-free sour cream

Per Serving
Calories: 293
% Calories from fat: 12
Fat (gm): 4.1
Sat. fat (gm): 1.7
Cholesterol (mg): 10.1
Sodium (mg): 156
Protein (gm): 14
Carbohydrate (gm): 52.6

Exchanges
Milk: 0.0
Vegetable: 2.0
Fruit: 0.0
Bread: 3.0
Meat: 0.5
Fat: 0.0

$^{3}/_{4}$ cup (3 ounces) shredded reduced-fat Monterey Jack cheese
2 green onions and tops, sliced

1. Spray large skillet with cooking spray; heat over medium heat until hot. Saute bell pepper, onion, garlic, and jalapeño chili 5 minutes; add squash, mushrooms, corn, oregano, cumin, and chili powder. Cook, covered, over medium heat until squash and mushrooms are tender, 8 to 10 minutes, stirring occasionally. Season to taste with salt and pepper.

2. Combine rice and millet; season to taste with salt and pepper. Spoon half the mixture into lightly greased 2-quart casserole; top with vegetable mixture and sour cream. Spoon remaining grain mixture on top.

3. Bake casserole, loosely covered, at 300 degrees until hot through, 30 to 40 minutes. Uncover, sprinkle with cheese, and bake until cheese is melted, 5 to 10 minutes longer. Sprinkle with green onions.

SWEET POTATO CHIPOTLE CHILI

4 servings

2 cups frozen stir-fry pepper blend
1 teaspoon minced garlic
1-2 teaspoons minced gingerroot
1 teaspoon cumin seeds
1-2 tablespoons peanut, *or* vegetable, oil
3 cups cubed ($^{1}/_{2}$-inch), peeled sweet potatoes
1 can (14$^{1}/_{2}$ ounces) chili-style chunky tomatoes, undrained
2 cans (15 ounces each) black beans, rinsed, drained
1-2 chipotle chilies in adobo sauce, chopped
1 cup water, *or* vegetable broth
Salt, to taste

Per Serving
Calories: 349
% Calories from fat: 10
Fat (gm): 3.9
Sat. fat (gm): 0.6
Cholesterol (mg): 0
Sodium (mg): 1228
Protein (gm): 13.5
Carbohydrate (gm): 64.8

Exchanges
Milk: 0.0
Vegetable: 0.0
Fruit: 0.0
Bread: 4.0
Meat: 0.0
Fat: 1.0

1. Saute pepper blend, garlic, gingerroot, and cumin seeds in oil in large saucepan until tender, about 5 minutes. Add remaining ingredients, except salt, to saucepan; heat to boiling. Reduce heat and simmer, covered, until potatoes are tender, about 15 minutes. Season to taste with salt.

GRILLED VEGETABLE FAJITAS

4 servings (2 fajitas each)

- 4 medium poblano chilies, *or* green bell peppers, cut into1-inch slices
- 3 large tomatoes, cut into wedges
- 2 medium onions, cut into wedges
- 4 large cactus paddles (nopales), cut into 1-inch slices
- Vegetable cooking spray
- 2 tablespoons olive oil, *or* vegetable oil
- 2 tablespoons white distilled vinegar
- 1 tablespoon lime juice
- 2 cloves garlic, minced
- 3-4 dashes cayenne pepper
- 8 flour, *or* corn, tortillas, warm
- 1/4 cup finely chopped cilantro
- 8 tablespoons fat-free sour cream
- 4 avocado slices

Per Serving
Calories: 414
% Calories from fat: 29
Fat (gm): 14.1
Sat. fat (gm): 2.3
Cholesterol (mg): 0
Sodium (mg): 47
Protein (gm): 12.6
Carbohydrate (gm): 64
Exchanges
Milk: 0.0
Vegetable: 3.0
Fruit: 0.0
Bread: 3.5
Meat: 0.0
Fat: 2.0

1. Spray vegetables with cooking spray; place on grill over medium-hot coals. Grill, turning occasionally, until vegetables are browned and tender, about 30 minutes (or bake on greased aluminum-foil-lined jelly roll pan at 400 degrees until brown and tender, 30 to 40 minutes). Combine vegetables in bowl.

2. Mix oil, vinegar, lime juice, garlic, and cayenne pepper; drizzle over vegetables and toss. Spoon about 1/2 cup of vegetables on each tortilla. Sprinkle with cilantro, top with 1 tablespoon sour cream, and roll up.

3. Place fajitas and avocado slices on serving plates.

Tip: Nopales can be found in Mexican grocery stores or produce section of large supermarkets.

GRILLED VEGETABLE BURRITOS

6 servings

2 medium red bell peppers
2 medium yellow bell peppers
2 medium poblano chilies, *or* green bell peppers
Vegetable cooking spray
1 medium onion, sliced
2 cloves garlic, minced
1/2 cup fat-free half-and-half, *or* fat-free sour cream
1/4 teaspoon dried oregano leaves
1/4 teaspoon dried thyme leaves
1 bay leaf
Salt and pepper, to taste
2 cups (2/3 recipe), Refried Beans (see p. 378), warm, *or* 1 can (15 ounces) refried beans
6 large flour tortillas (10-inch)
1 cup (1/2 recipe), Red Tomato Salsa (see p. 513), *or* prepared medium, *or* hot, salsa

Per Serving
Calories: 301
% Calories from fat: 10
Fat (gm): 3.5
Sat. fat (gm): 0.5
Cholesterol (mg): 0
Sodium (mg): 195
Protein (gm): 12.6
Carbohydrate (gm): 57.5
Exchanges
Milk: 0.0
Vegetable: 3.0
Fruit: 0.0
Bread: 3.0
Meat: 0.0
Fat: 0.0

1. Grill bell peppers and poblano chilies over medium-hot coals, turning frequently, until peppers are blistered and blackened, 5 to 8 minutes. Wrap peppers in towel or place in plastic bag; let stand 10 minutes. Peel peppers, discarding skins. Cut peppers into 1/4-inch slices.

2. Spray medium skillet with cooking spray; heat over medium heat until hot. Saute onion and garlic until tender, about 5 minutes. Add half-and-half, grilled vegetables, and herbs; heat to boiling. Reduce heat and simmer, uncovered, until slightly thickened; discard bay leaf. Season to taste with salt and pepper.

3. Spoon Refried Beans along center of tortillas; top with vegetable mixture. Fold ends of tortillas in and roll up. Serve salsa on the side.

VEGETARIAN BURRITOS WITH POBLANO CHILI SAUCE

4 servings

Olive oil cooking spray
3/4 cup chopped zucchini
3/4 cup chopped yellow summer squash
1 small onion, finely chopped
3 cloves garlic, minced
2 tablespoons finely chopped cilantro
1 teaspoon dried oregano leaves
1 can (15 ounces) pinto beans, rinsed, drained
1/4 cup water
1 cup chopped tomato
Salt and cayenne pepper, to taste
4 large (10-inch) flour tortillas
Poblano Chili Sauce (see p. 512), *or* 2 cups hot prepared salsa
1/2 cup fat-free sour cream

Per Serving
Calories: 319
% Calories from fat: 10
Fat (gm): 3.7
Sat. fat (gm): 0.5
Cholesterol (mg): 0
Sodium (mg): 620
Protein (gm): 18.3
Carbohydrate (gm): 58.9
Exchanges
Milk: 0.5
Vegetable: 2.0
Fruit: 0.0
Bread: 3.0
Meat: 0.5
Fat: 0.5

1. Spray medium skillet with cooking spray; heat over medium heat until hot. Saute zucchini, squash, onion, garlic, and herbs until onion is tender, 8 to 10 minutes. Add beans and water to skillet; mash coarsely with fork. Stir in tomato; cook over medium heat until hot. Season to taste with salt and cayenne pepper.

2. Spoon vegetable mixture along center of tortillas; top each with 1/4 cup Poblano Chili Sauce. Fold sides of tortillas in, overlapping filling; fold ends in, overlapping to make a square "package". Secure with toothpicks.

3. Spray large skillet with cooking spray; heat over medium heat until hot. Cook burritos until browned on all sides, brushing with Poblano Chili Sauce. Serve hot with sour cream and remaining Poblano Chili Sauce.

THREE-CHILI TAMALES

4 servings (3 tamales each)

Per Serving
Calories: 187
% Calories from fat: 26
Fat (gm): 5.6
Sat. fat (gm): 1
Cholesterol (mg): 0
Sodium (mg): 396
Protein (gm): 3.7
Carbohydrate (gm): 29.9

Exchanges
Milk: 0.0
Vegetable: 1.0
Fruit: 0.0
Bread: 1.5
Meat: 0.0
Fat: 1.0

12 corn husks
Hot water
2 ancho chilies, stems, seeds, and veins discarded
1/3 cup boiling water
1 large poblano chili, *or* green bell pepper, seeds and veins discarded, chopped
1 can (4 ounces) chopped green chilies, drained
3/4 teaspoon dried oregano leaves
1/2 teaspoon dried thyme leaves
Salt and pepper, to taste
Tamale Dough (recipe follows)

1. Soak corn husks in hot water until softened, about 1 hour. Drain well on paper toweling.

2. Crumble ancho chilies into bowl; pour 1/3 cup boiling water over and let stand until softened, 15 to 20 minutes. Cook ancho chilies and liquid, poblano chili, green chilies, and herbs over medium heat in medium skillet until chilies are tender, 5 to 8 minutes, stirring frequently. Season to taste with salt and pepper. Mix in Tamale Dough.

3. Spoon about 1/4 cup of tamale mixture onto center of each corn husk; fold sides of husks over filling. Tie ends of tamales with stips of cornhusk, making "bundles."

4. Place tamales on steamer rack in saucepan with 2 inches of water. Steam, covered, 2 hours, adding more water to saucepan if necessary. Serve warm.

Tamale Dough

1 cup masa harina
3/4 teaspoon baking powder
1 1/2 tablespoons margarine, softened
1/4-1/2 teaspoon salt
1 cup vegetable broth

1. Combine masa harina, baking powder, margarine, and salt; gradually stir in broth (mixture will be soft).

Tip: Masa harina is available in Mexican grocery stores and large supermarkets.

CHILIQUILES

8 servings

8 corn, *or* flour, tortillas
Vegetable cooking spray
1 medium green bell pepper, thinly sliced
1/2 teaspoon minced jalapeño chili
1/4 teaspoon cayenne pepper
2 cups enchilada, *or* taco, sauce
1 1/2 cups cooked black beans, *or* 1 can (15 ounces) black beans, rinsed, drained
1 cup frozen whole-kernel corn, thawed
2/3 package (12-ounce size) frozen pre-browned all-vegetable protein crumbles, thawed
1 large tomato, thinly sliced
Jalapeño con Queso Sauce (see p. 504), *or* 2 cups purchased Mexican-style cheese sauce
Medium, *or* hot, salsa, to taste

Per Serving
Calories: 272
% Calories from fat: 13
Fat (gm): 4.1
Sat. fat (gm): 2.2
Cholesterol (mg): 10.3
Sodium (mg): 737
Protein (gm): 24.3
Carbohydrate (gm): 36.8
Exchanges
Milk: 0.0
Vegetable: 0.8
Fruit: 0.0
Bread: 2.5
Meat: 2.0
Fat: 0.0

1. Spray both sides of tortillas lightly with cooking spray; cook in small skillet over medium-high heat to brown lightly, 30 to 60 seconds per side. Cool slightly; cut into 1/2-inch strips.

2. Spray small skillet with cooking spray; heat over medium heat until hot. Saute peppers until tender, 2 to 3 minutes; sprinkle with cayenne pepper. Stir in enchilada sauce; heat until hot.

3. Arrange 1/3 of the tortilla strips in bottom of 2-quart casserole. Top with 1/3 of peppers mixture. Layer on 1/2 cup black beans, 1/3 cup corn, 1/3 of the vegetable protein crumbles, 1/3 of the tomato slices, and 2/3 cup Jalapeño con Queso Sauce. Repeat layers 2 times.

4. Bake casserole, uncovered, at 350 degrees until hot through, 25 to 30 minutes. Serve hot with salsa.

MEXICAN ANCHO CHILI STEW

4 servings

Per Serving
Calories: 275
% Calories from fat: 13
Fat (gm): 4.3
Sat. fat (gm): 0.1
Cholesterol (mg): 0
Sodium (mg): 735
Protein (gm): 11.9
Carbohydrate (gm): 50.9
Exchanges
Milk: 0.0
Vegetable: 2.0
Fruit: 0.0
Bread: 2.5
Meat: 0.5
Fat: 0.5

4-6 ancho chilies, stems, seeds, and veins discarded
2 cups boiling water
4 medium tomatoes, cut into wedges
Vegetable cooking spray
6-8 Mexican-style all-vegetable "burgers," crumbled (18-24 ounces)
1 large onion, chopped
2 cloves garlic, minced
1 teaspoon minced serrano, *or* jalapeño, chili
1 teaspoon dried oregano leaves
1 teaspoon cumin seeds, crushed
2 tablespoons flour
Salt and pepper, to taste

1. Place ancho chilies in bowl; pour boiling water over. Let stand until chilies are softened, about 10 minutes. Process chilies, with water, and tomatoes in food processor or blender until smooth.

2. Spray large saucepan with cooking spray; heat over medium heat until hot. Cook crumbled "burgers," onion, garlic, serrano chili, and herbs until onion is tender, about 5 minutes. Stir in flour; cook over medium heat 1 to 2 minutes more.

3. Add chili and tomato mixture to saucepan; heat to boiling. Reduce heat and simmer, covered, 15 to 20 minutes. Season to taste with salt and pepper. Serve in shallow bowls.

HOT 'N SPICY BEAN AND VEGETABLE STEW

6 servings

Per Serving
Calories: 284
% Calories from fat: 5
Fat (gm): 2
Sat. fat (gm): 0.1
Cholesterol (mg): 0
Sodium (mg): 527
Protein (gm): 15.4
Carbohydrate (gm): 60.8
Exchanges
Milk: 0.0
Vegetable: 3.0
Fruit: 0.0
Bread: 3.0
Meat: 0.0
Fat: 0.0

Olive oil cooking spray
1 1/2 cups chopped onions
2-4 teaspoons minced jalapeño chilies
2-3 teaspoons minced garlic
1 tablespoon flour
1 1/2 teaspoons dried oregano leaves
3/4 teaspoon ground cinnamon
1 bay leaf
2 cans (16 ounces each) reduced-sodium diced tomatoes, undrained
1 1/2 cups Vegetable Stock (see p. 48), *or* water
1 tablespoon red wine vinegar
4 medium carrots, sliced
4 medium red potatoes, unpeeled, cubed
1 can (15 ounces) black beans, rinsed, drained
1 can (15 ounces) pinto beans, rinsed, drained
Salt and pepper, to taste

1. Spray Dutch oven or large saucepan with cooking spray; heat over medium heat until hot. Saute onions, chilies, and garlic 5 minutes; stir in flour and seasonings and cook 1 to 2 minutes longer.

2. Add remaining ingredients, except salt and pepper; heat to boiling. Reduce heat and simmer, covered, until vegetables are tender and stew thickened, 15 to 20 minutes. Discard bay leaf; season to taste with salt and pepper.

SPICED BEAN STEW WITH FUSILLI

8 servings

2 cups chopped onions
1/2 cup sliced celery
1 cup sliced mushrooms
1-2 tablespoons vegetable oil
2 cans (14 1/2 ounces each) diced tomatoes with roasted garlic
1 can (15 1/2 ounces) garbanzo beans, rinsed, drained
1 can (15 ounces) dark red kidney beans, rinsed, drained
1-2 tablespoons chili powder
1-2 teaspoons ground cumin
3/4 teaspoon dried oregano leaves
8 ounces fusilli, cooked, warm
Salt and pepper, to taste
3-4 tablespoons sliced green, *or* ripe, olives

Per Serving
Calories: 279
% Calories from fat: 12
Fat (gm): 3.8
Sat. fat (gm): 0.5
Cholesterol (mg): 0
Sodium (mg): 711
Protein (gm): 11.3
Carbohydrate (gm): 51.2
Exchanges
Milk: 0.0
Vegetable: 1.0
Fruit: 0.0
Bread: 3.0
Meat: 0.0
Fat: 0.5

1. Saute onions, celery, and mushrooms in oil in large saucepan 5 minutes. Add tomatoes, beans, and herbs. Heat to boiling. Reduce heat and simmer, covered, until vegetables are tender, about 10 minutes. Stir in pasta. Season to taste with salt and pepper. Serve stew in bowls; sprinkle with olives.

CARIBBEAN SWEET-AND-SOUR STEW

6 servings

Vegetable cooking spray
2 packages (10 1/2 ounces each) light tofu, cut into 1-inch cubes
2 medium onions, cut into 1-inch pieces
1 large red bell pepper, cut into strips
1 large green bell pepper, cut into strips
4 cloves garlic, minced
2 teaspoons minced gingerroot
1-2 jalapeño chilies, finely chopped

Per Serving
Calories: 388
% Calories from fat: 6
Fat (gm): 2.9
Sat. fat (gm): 0.2
Cholesterol (mg): 0
Sodium (mg): 361
Protein (gm): 17.8
Carbohydrate (gm): 76.8
Exchanges
Milk: 0.0
Vegetable: 2.0
Fruit: 1.0
Bread: 3.0
Meat: 1.0
Fat: 0.0

3 cups Vegetable Stock (see p. 48)
1 can (20 ounces) pineapple chunks in juice, undrained
2 tablespoons light brown sugar
2-3 teaspoons curry powder
2-3 tablespoons apple cider vinegar
2 tablespoons cornstarch
1/4 cup cold water
1 can (15 ounces) black beans, rinsed, drained
4 cups cooked rice, warm
3 small green onions and tops, sliced

1. Spray large skillet with cooking spray; heat over medium heat until hot. Add tofu and cook over medium heat until browned on all sides, 8 to 10 minutes. Remove from skillet and reserve.

2. Add onions, bell peppers, garlic, gingerroot, and jalapeño chilies to skillet; saute until onions are tender, about 5 minutes. Stir in stock, pineapple with juice, sugar, curry powder, vinegar, and reserved tofu; heat to boiling. Reduce heat and simmer, uncovered, 5 minutes.

3. Heat mixture to boiling. Mix cornstarch and water; stir into boiling mixture. Boil, stirring frequently, until mixture is thickened, about 1 minute. Stir in beans; cook over medium heat 2 to 3 minutes longer.

4. Serve mixture over rice; sprinkle each serving with green onions.

BLACK BEAN AND OKRA GUMBO

8 servings

Vegetable cooking spray
3 cups halved, small mushrooms
2 cups coarsely chopped onions
2 cups sliced carrots
1 cup chopped green bell pepper
1 cup chopped red bell pepper
4 teaspoons chili powder
1 teaspoon gumbo file powder
3 cups Vegetable Stock (see p. 48), *or* vegetable broth
3 cups cooked dried black beans
2 cups fresh, *or* frozen, cut, okra
Salt and pepper, to taste
8 pieces Green Chili Corn Bread (see p. 676)

Per Serving
Calories: 454
% Calories from fat: 15
Fat (gm): 8
Sat. fat (gm): 1.7
Cholesterol (mg): 28
Sodium (mg): 754
Protein (gm): 14.8
Carbohydrate (gm): 85.5
Exchanges
Milk: 0.0
Vegetable: 3.0
Fruit: 0.0
Bread: 4.5
Meat: 0.0
Fat: 1.5

1. Spray large skillet with cooking spray; heat over medium heat until hot. Add mushrooms, onions, carrots, and bell peppers and cook, covered, over medium heat until mushrooms are wilted, 5 to 8 minutes. Stir in chili powder and file powder; cook 2 to 3 minutes.

2. Add stock, beans, and okra; heat to boiling. Reduce heat and simmer, uncovered, until vegetables are tender and broth thickens, 8 to 10 minutes. Season to taste with salt and pepper.

3. Serve stew over corn bread in shallow bowls.

VEGGIE SHEPHERD'S PIE

4 servings

Vegetable cooking spray
1 1/2 cups frozen onion seasoning blend
1/2 cup sliced celery
1 teaspoon minced garlic
3/4 teaspoon dried savory leaves
2 cups vegetable broth
1 cup thinly sliced cabbage
1 cup sliced carrots
2 medium Idaho potatoes, unpeeled, cubed
3/4 cup sliced mushrooms
3 tablespoons flour
1/3 cup cold water
Salt and pepper, to taste
3/4 package (22-ounce size) frozen mashed potatoes, prepared according to package directions

Per Serving
Calories: 416
% Calories from fat: 16
Fat (gm): 6.2
Sat. fat (gm): 1.6
Cholesterol (mg): 7.6
Sodium (mg): 743
Protein (gm): 6.9
Carbohydrate (gm): 65.7
Exchanges
Milk: 0.0
Vegetable: 1.0
Fruit: 0.0
Bread: 4.0
Meat: 0.0
Fat: 1.0

1. Spray large saucepan with cooking spray; heat over medium heat until hot. Saute onion seasoning blend, celery, garlic, and savory 5 minutes. Stir in broth and remaining vegetables (except frozen mashed potatoes) and heat to boiling; reduce heat and simmer, covered, until vegetables are tender, about 10 minutes.

2. Heat vegetable mixture to boiling. Mix flour and cold water; stir into boiling mixture. Boil, stirring constantly, until thickened. Season to taste with salt and pepper. Pour mixture into 1 1/2-quart soufflé dish or casserole.

3. Spoon or pipe mashed potatoes around edge of casserole. Bake at 375 degrees until potatoes are lightly browned, about 20 minutes.

WILD RICE, CHEESE, AND VEGETABLE CASSEROLE

4 servings

- 1 package (6 1/4 ounces) wild and white rice mix, cooked without spice packet
- $1^1/_2$ cups cut asparagus spears, cooked
- $1^1/_2$ cups halved small Brussels sprouts, cooked
- 3 ounces fat-free cream cheese, cubed
- $^3/_4$ cup (3 ounces) shredded fat-free mozzarella cheese
- 3-4 ounces goat cheese, crumbled
- Salt and pepper, to taste

Per Serving
Calories: 307
% Calories from fat: 21
Fat (gm): 7.2
Sat. fat (gm): 4.3
Cholesterol (mg): 9.7
Sodium (mg): 200
Protein (gm): 21.7
Carbohydrate (gm): 39
Exchanges
Milk: 0.0
Vegetable: 2.0
Fruit: 0.0
Bread: 2.0
Meat: 1.5
Fat: 0.5

1. Mix rice, vegetables, and cheeses; season to taste with salt and pepper. Spoon into $1^1/_2$-quart casserole.

2. Bake, covered, at 350 degrees until casserole is hot and cheese is melted, about 30 minutes.

VEGETABLE AND MIXED RICE CASSEROLE

6 servings

- Vegetable cooking spray
- $1^1/_2$ cups sliced shiitake, *or* white, mushrooms
- 1 cup sliced zucchini
- $^1/_2$ cup chopped onion
- $^1/_2$ cup chopped green bell pepper
- $^1/_2$ cup chopped red bell pepper
- 1 teaspoon dried thyme leaves
- 1 package (6 ounces) brown and wild rice mix, cooked with spice packet
- 1 can (15 ounces) pinto beans, rinsed, drained
- 1 cup fresh, *or* frozen, whole-kernel corn
- 1 cup fat-free sour cream

Per Serving
Calories: 307
% Calories from fat: 12
Fat (gm): 4.2
Sat. fat (gm): 1.4
Cholesterol (mg): 10.1
Sodium (mg): 708
Protein (gm): 16.9
Carbohydrate (gm): 54.7
Exchanges
Milk: 0.0
Vegetable: 2.0
Fruit: 0.0
Bread: 3.0
Meat: 0.5
Fat: 0.5

1 cup (4 ounces) shredded reduced-fat Cheddar cheese, divided
Salt and pepper, to taste

1. Spray medium skillet with cooking spray; heat over medium heat until hot. Add mushrooms, zucchini, onion, bell peppers, and thyme; cook, covered, over medium heat until vegetables are tender, 8 to 10 minutes.

2. Combine rice, cooked vegetable mixture, beans, corn, sour cream, and 1/2 cup cheese; season to taste with salt and pepper. Spoon mixture into 2-quart casserole; sprinkle with remaining 1/2 cup cheese.

3. Bake, uncovered, at 350 degrees until hot through, 30 to 40 minutes.

GRILLED PORTOBELLO MUSHROOM SANDWICHES

4 servings

Per Serving
Calories: 239
% Calories from fat: 10
Fat (gm): 2.6
Sat. fat (gm): 0.5
Cholesterol (mg): 0
Sodium (mg): 546
Protein (gm): 10.3
Carbohydrate (gm): 43.8

Exchanges
Milk: 0.0
Vegetable: 3.0
Fruit: 0.0
Bread: 2.0
Meat: 0.0
Fat: 0.5

1 medium red bell pepper
1 medium yellow bell pepper
Salt and pepper, to taste
Olive oil cooking spray
4 large portobello, *or* porcini, mushrooms (4-5 inches diameter)
8 slices Italian bread
1 clove garlic, halved
4 tablespoons fat-free mayonnaise
3-4 tablespoons finely chopped basil

1. Grill bell peppers over medium-hot coals, turning frequently, until peppers are blistered and blackened, 5 to 8 minutes. Wrap peppers in towel or place in plastic bag; let stand 10 minutes. Peel peppers, discarding skins. Cut peppers into 1/2-inch slices; sprinkle lightly with salt and pepper.

2. Spray both sides of mushrooms with cooking spray. Grill, turning occasionally, until tender, about 8 minutes. Season to taste with salt and pepper.

3. Grill bread until toasted, 2 to 3 minutes; rub tops of bread slices with garlic. Mix mayonnaise and basil; spread on 4 bread slices. Top bread with mushrooms, peppers, and remaining bread slices.

VEGGIE PITAS

4 servings

Vegetable cooking spray
1 medium eggplant, unpeeled, cut into 1-inch cubes
1 large sweet potato, unpeeled, cut into 1/2-inch slices
1 medium green bell pepper, cut into 3/4-inch slices
1 large onion, sliced
1 large tomato, cut into 8 wedges
2 tablespoons balsamic, *or* red wine, vinegar
1 tablespoon olive oil, *or* vegetable oil
1 teaspoon lemon juice
2 cloves garlic, minced
1 teaspoon dried oregano leaves
1 teaspoon dried basil leaves
Salt and pepper, to taste
4 pita pockets, cut into halves

Per Serving
Calories: 292
% Calories from fat: 14
Fat (gm): 4.6
Sat. fat (gm): 0.6
Cholesterol (mg): 0
Sodium (mg): 334
Protein (gm): 7.9
Carbohydrate (gm): 56.3
Exchanges
Milk: 0.0
Vegetable: 3.0
Fruit: 0.0
Bread: 2.5
Meat: 0.0
Fat: 1.0

1. Spray aluminum-foil-lined jelly roll pan with cooking spray. Arrange vegetables on pan in single layer and spray generously with cooking spray. Bake at 400 degrees until vegetables are browned and tender, about 30 minutes. Combine vegetables in bowl.

2. Combine vinegar, oil, lemon juice, garlic, oregano, and basil; drizzle over vegetables and toss. Season to taste with salt and pepper. Spoon vegetables into pita pockets.

FALAFEL "BURGERS" WITH TAHINI DRESSING

4 servings

Per Serving
Calories: 291
% Calories from fat: 23
Fat (gm): 7.6
Sat. fat (gm): 0.3
Cholesterol (mg): 0.3
Sodium (mg): 194
Protein (gm): 13.2
Carbohydrate (gm): 45.0

Exchanges
Milk: 0.0
Vegetable: 2.0
Fruit: 0.0
Bread: 2.5
Meat: 0.5
Fat: 1.0

1½ cups cooked garbanzo beans, *or* 1 can (15 ounces) rinsed, drained garbanzo beans, coarsely pureed
¼ cup chopped parsley leaves
2 tablespoons chopped green onions and tops
2 cloves garlic, minced
1-2 tablespoons lemon juice
¼ cup all-purpose flour
1¼ teaspoons ground cumin
Salt and pepper, to taste
Olive oil cooking spray
2 pita breads, cut into halves
Tahini Dressing (recipe follows)
¼ cup chopped tomato
¼ cup chopped cucumber
¼ cup thinly sliced green onions and tops

1. Mix garbanzo beans, parsley, chopped green onions, garlic, lemon juice, flour, and cumin in bowl; season to taste with salt and pepper. Shape mixture into 4 "burgers."

2. Spray large skillet with cooking spray; heat over medium heat until hot. Cook "burgers" until browned on the bottoms, 3 to 4 minutes. Spray tops of "burgers" with cooking spray; turn and cook until browned on other side, 3 to 4 minutes.

3. Arrange "burgers" in pita breads; drizzle scant 2 tablespoons Tahini Dressing over each "burger." Spoon combined tomato, cucumber, and sliced green onions into pitas.

Tahini Dressing

⅓ cup fat-free yogurt
2-3 tablespoons tahini (sesame seed paste)
1 small clove garlic, minced
½-1 teaspoon lemon juice

1. Combine all ingredients; refrigerate until ready to use.

HERBED VEGGIE "BURGERS"

4 servings

Vegetable cooking spray
3/4 cup finely chopped broccoli florets
3/4 cup finely chopped mushrooms
1/4 cup finely chopped onion
2 cloves garlic
1 1/2 teaspoons dried basil leaves, divided
1/2 teaspoon dried marjoram leaves
1/4 teaspoon dried thyme leaves
2/3 cup cooked wild, *or* brown, rice
1/3 cup quick-cooking oats
1/3 cup coarsely chopped toasted walnuts
1/2 cup 1% low-fat cottage cheese
1/2 cup (2 ounces) shredded fat-free Cheddar cheese
Salt and pepper, to taste
2 egg whites
1/3 cup fat-free mayonnaise
4 multigrain, *or* whole wheat, buns, toasted
Lettuce leaves, as garnish

Per Serving
Calories: 313
% Calories from fat: 26
Fat (gm): 9.5
Sat. fat (gm): 1.3
Cholesterol (mg): 1.3
Sodium (mg): 700
Protein (gm): 19.6
Carbohydrate (gm): 40

Exchanges
Milk: 0.0
Vegetable: 0.0
Fruit: 0.0
Bread: 2.5
Meat: 2.0
Fat: 0.5

1. Spray medium skillet with cooking spray; heat over medium heat until hot. Saute broccoli, mushrooms, onion, and garlic until tender, 8 to 10 minutes. Add 1/2 teaspoon basil, marjoram, and thyme and cook 1 to 2 minutes longer. Remove from heat and cool slightly.

2. Stir rice, oats, walnuts, and cheeses into vegetable mixture; season to taste with salt and pepper. Stir in egg whites. Form mixture into 4 "burgers."

3. Spray large skillet with cooking spray; heat over medium heat until hot. Add "burgers" and cook over medium to medium-low heat until browned on the bottoms, 3 to 4 minutes. Spray tops of "burgers" with cooking spray and turn; cook until browned on other side, 3 to 4 minutes.

4. Mix mayonnaise and remaining 1 teaspoon basil. Spread on bottoms of buns and top with lettuce, "burgers," and bun tops.

CUCUMBER CHEESE MELT

4 servings

- 1/4 package (8-ounce size) fat-free cream cheese, softened
- 2 tablespoons crumbled blue cheese
- 8 slices multigrain bread, divided
- 1/4 cup apricot spreadable fruit
- 16 cucumber slices
- 4 slices (3 ounces) fat-free Swiss cheese
- Butter-flavored cooking spray

Per Serving
Calories: 249
% Calories from fat: 11
Fat (gm): 3.1
Sat. fat (gm): 1.1
Cholesterol (mg): 2.6
Sodium (mg): 673
Protein (gm): 13.6
Carbohydrate (gm): 42.9
Exchanges
Milk: 0.0
Vegetable: 2.0
Fruit: 0.0
Bread: 2.0
Meat: 1.0
Fat: 0.0

1. Mix cream cheese and blue cheese; spread on 4 slices of bread. Spread 1 tablespoon spreadable fruit over cheese mixture on each slice, top each with 4 cucumber slices, a slice of Swiss cheese, and remaining bread slices.

2. Spray large skillet with cooking spray; heat over medium heat until hot. Cook sandwiches over medium heat until browned on the bottoms, about 5 minutes. Spray tops of sandwiches with cooking spray and turn; cook until browned on the other side, about 5 minutes.

EGGPLANT PARMESAN SANDWICHES

4 servings

- 4 thick slices eggplant (scant 3/4-inch thick)
- 1 egg, lightly beaten
- 1/3 cup seasoned dry bread crumbs
- 2 tablespoons grated fat-free Parmesan cheese
- Vegetable cooking spray
- 4 ounces sliced fat-free mozzarella cheese
- 2 roasted red peppers, cut into halves
- 4 French rolls, *or* Hoagie buns, toasted
- Pizza Sauce (see p. 511)

Per Serving
Calories: 262
% Calories from fat: 8
Fat (gm): 2.2
Sat. fat (gm): 0.5
Cholesterol (mg): 0
Sodium (mg): 765
Protein (gm): 19.4
Carbohydrate (gm): 42.1
Exchanges
Milk: 0.0
Vegetable: 3.0
Fruit: 0.0
Bread: 2.0
Meat: 1.0
Fat: 0.0

1. Dip eggplant slices in egg; coat generously with combined bread crumbs and Parmesan cheese.

2. Spray large skillet with cooking spray; heat over medium heat until hot. Cook eggplant slices until browned on the bottoms, about 5 minutes. Spray eggplant slices generously with cooking spray and turn. Cook until eggplant slices are tender and browned on other side, about 5 minutes. Top each eggplant slice with 1 ounce cheese. Cook, covered, until cheese is melted, 2 to 3 minutes.

3. Place red peppers on bottoms of rolls; top with eggplant, Pizza Sauce, and roll tops.

EIGHT

Vegetable Side Dishes

ARTICHOKE DELIGHT

4 servings

Vegetable cooking spray
1 package (10 ounces) frozen artichokes
2 tablespoons finely chopped shallots
2 tablespoons finely chopped onion
1 clove garlic, minced
2 tablespoons white wine vinegar
1/4 cup white wine
Salt and pepper, to taste

Per Serving
Calories: 51
% Calories from fat: 2
Fat (gm): 0.1
Sat. fat (gm): 0
Cholesterol (mg): 0
Sodium (mg): 65
Protein (gm): 2.6
Carbohydrate (gm): 9.6
Exchanges
Milk: 0.0
Vegetable: 2.0
Fruit: 0.0
Bread: 0.0
Meat: 0.0
Fat: 0.0

1. Spray large skillet with cooking spray; heat over medium heat until hot. Saute artichokes, shallots, onion, and garlic until artichokes are separated and onion is softened but not browned. Stir in vinegar and wine. Heat to boiling; reduce heat and simmer, covered, until artichokes are tender, about 10 minutes. Season to taste with salt and pepper.

ARTICHOKES WITH HOLLANDAISE SAUCE

4-6 servings

4-6 whole artichokes, stems trimmed
Mock Hollandaise Sauce (see p. 502)

Per Serving
Calories: 114
% Calories from fat: 2
Fat (gm): 0.3
Sat. fat (gm): 0.1
Cholesterol (mg): 0.2
Sodium (mg): 396
Protein (gm): 11.9
Carbohydrate (gm): 17.5
Exchanges
Milk: 0.0
Vegetable: 4.0
Fruit: 0.0
Bread: 0.0
Meat: 0.0
Fat: 0.5

1. Slice 1 inch off tops of artichokes and discard. Trim tips of remaining leaves with scissors. Place artichokes in medium saucepan with 2 inches of water; heat to boiling. Reduce heat and simmer, covered, until artichoke leaves pull off easily and bottom is tender when pierced with a fork, about 30 minutes.

2. Place artichokes on serving plates with Mock Hollandaise Sauce on the side for dipping.

ASPARAGUS WITH PEANUT SAUCE

6 servings

2 tablespoons reduced-fat peanut butter
1/4 cup sugar
2-3 tablespoons reduced-sodium tamari soy sauce
3-4 teaspoons rice wine (sake), dry sherry, *or* water
1 teaspoon grated gingerroot
1 1/2 pounds asparagus spears, cooked until crisp-tender, chilled

Per Serving
Calories: 95
% Calories from fat: 21
Fat (gm): 2.3
Sat. fat (gm): 0.5
Cholesterol (mg): 0
Sodium (mg): 246
Protein (gm): 4.8
Carbohydrate (gm): 15
Exchanges
Milk: 0.0
Vegetable: 3.0
Fruit: 0.0
Bread: 0.0
Meat: 0.0
Fat: 0.5

1. Mix peanut butter, sugar, soy sauce, rice wine, and gingerroot until smooth.

2. Arrange asparagus on serving platter; spoon peanut sauce over.

MICROWAVE ASPARAGUS WITH PIMIENTO

4 servings

1 1/4 pounds asparagus
2 tablespoons lemon juice
2 tablespoons chopped pimiento
1 tablespoon toasted pine nuts

Per Serving
Calories: 48
% Calories from fat: 21
Fat (gm): 1.8
Sat. fat (gm): 0.1
Cholesterol (mg): 0
Sodium (mg): 5.9
Protein (gm): 4
Carbohydrate (gm): 6.8
Exchanges
Milk: 0.0
Vegetable: 1.0
Fruit: 0.0
Bread: 0.0
Meat: 0.0
Fat: 0.5

1. Arrange asparagus in single layer on microwave-safe platter. Drizzle with lemon juice, and sprinkle with pimiento. Cover with wax paper.

2. Microwave on High 5 to 6 minutes, or until tender, turning dish once. Sprinkle with pine nuts.

SANTA FE SUCCOTASH

8 servings (about 1/2 cup each)

- 1/2 cup chopped onion
- 1/2 cup chopped poblano chili, *or* sweet bell pepper
- 1/2 teaspoon minced jalapeño chili
- 1/2 teaspoon minced garlic
- 2 tablespoons margarine, *or* butter
- 1 tablespoon flour
- 2 teaspoons chili powder
- 1 teaspoon ground cumin
- 1 cup fat-free milk
- 1 can (15 ounces) lima beans, rinsed, drained
- 1 can (15 ounces) black-eyed peas, rinsed, drained
- 1 cup frozen or canned whole kernel corn
- 1 medium tomato, chopped
- 1/2 teaspoon salt

Per Serving
Calories: 145
% Calories from fat: 21
Fat (gm): 3.4
Sat. fat (gm): 0.7
Cholesterol (mg): 0.6
Sodium (mg): 366
Protein (gm): 6
Carbohydrate (gm): 22.8

Exchanges
Milk: 0.0
Vegetable: 0.0
Fruit: 0.0
Bread: 2.0
Meat: 0.0
Fat: 0.0

1. Saute onion, poblano chili, jalapeño chili, and garlic in margarine in medium saucepan until tender, about 5 minutes. Stir in flour, chili powder, and cumin; cook 1minute longer. Stir in milk; heat to boiling, stirring until thickened.

2. Stir in lima beans, blackeyes, and corn; heat to simmering. Stir in tomatoes and salt and serve.

MICROWAVE GREEN BEANS WITH PINE NUTS

4 servings

- 1 pound green beans, trimmed and washed
- 1/2 cup drained, crushed Italian plum tomatoes
- 2 tablespoons toasted pine nuts
- Pepper, to taste

Per Serving
Calories: 60
% Calories from fat: 35
Fat (gm): 2.8
Sat. fat (gm): 0
Cholesterol (mg): 0
Sodium (mg): 17
Protein (gm): 2.9
Carbohydrate (gm): 8.8
Exchanges
Milk: 0.0
Vegetable: 1.5
Fruit: 0.0
Bread: 0.0
Meat: 0.0
Fat: 0.5

1. Combine green beans and tomatoes in 8-inch microwave-safe dish. Cover with lid or wax paper. Microwave on High 7 to 9 minutes, or until tender, stirring twice. Drain excess liquid; toss with pine nuts, and season to taste with pepper.

GREEN BEANS IN SWEDISH MUSTARD SAUCE

6 servings

- 2 tablespoons margarine
- 2 tablespoons flour
- 1 teaspoon dry mustard
- 3/4 cup fat-free milk
- 3 tablespoons spicy brown, *or* Dijon-style, mustard
- 2 teaspoons apple cider vinegar
- 2 teaspoons sugar
- 1 tablespoon chopped fresh, *or* 1 teaspoon dried, dill weed
- Salt and pepper, to taste
- 1 1/2 pounds fresh green beans, trimmed, cooked crisp-tender, hot

Per Serving
Calories: 81
% Calories from fat: 29
Fat (gm): 2.8
Sat. fat (gm): 0.5
Cholesterol (mg): 0.5
Sodium (mg): 352
Protein (gm): 3.4
Carbohydrate (gm): 12.3
Exchanges
Milk: 0.0
Vegetable: 2.0
Fruit: 0.0
Bread: 0.0
Meat: 0.0
Fat: 0.5

1. Melt margarine in small saucepan over medium heat. Whisk in flour and dry mustard; cook 1 minute. Whisk in milk; heat to boiling, whisking until thickened and smooth, 2 or 3 minutes. Stir in mustard, vinegar, sugar, and dill. Season to taste with salt and pepper.

2. Place beans in serving bowl; pour sauce over.

ITALIAN GREEN BEANS

6 servings

- 1 pound green beans, cut into 2-inch pieces, cooked crisp-tender
- 2 teaspoons olive oil
- 1/4 cup seasoned dry bread crumbs
- 1/4 cup (1 ounce) grated Parmesan, *or* Romano, cheese
- 6 fresh basil leaves, chopped
- 1/2 cup sun-dried tomatoes (not oil-packed), softened, sliced
- Salt and pepper, to taste

Per Serving
Calories: 83
% Calories from fat: 32
Fat (gm): 3.1
Sat. fat (gm): 1.1
Cholesterol (mg): 3.3
Sodium (mg): 314
Protein (gm): 4.1
Carbohydrate (gm): 10.8
Exchanges
Milk: 0.0
Vegetable: 2.0
Fruit: 0.0
Bread: 0.0
Meat: 0.0
Fat: 0.5

1. Saute beans in oil in large skillet 3 minutes. Stir in bread crumbs, cheese, basil, and sun-dried tomatoes. Season to taste with salt and pepper.

BEETS DIJON

4 servings

- Butter-flavored vegetable cooking spray
- 1/3 cup finely chopped onion
- 2 cloves garlic, minced
- 1/3 cup fat-free sour cream
- 2 tablespoons Dijon-style mustard
- 2-3 teaspoons lemon juice
- Salt and pepper, to taste
- 1 1/2 pounds beets, cooked, cubed, *or* sliced, warm
- Parsley, minced, as garnish

Per Serving
Calories: 71
% Calories from fat: 7
Fat (gm): 0.6
Sat. fat (gm): 0.1
Cholesterol (mg): 0
Sodium (mg): 185
Protein (gm): 3.5
Carbohydrate (gm): 13.8
Exchanges
Milk: 0.0
Vegetable: 3.0
Fruit: 0.0
Bread: 0.0
Meat: 0.0
Fat: 0.0

1. Spray small saucepan with cooking spray; heat over medium heat until hot. Saute onion and garlic until tender, 3 to 4 minutes. Stir in sour cream, mustard, and lemon juice; heat over low heat until hot. Season to taste with salt and pepper.

2. Spoon sauce over beets; stir gently. Sprinkle with parsley.

MICROWAVE BOK CHOY

4 servings

- 1 pound bok choy (Chinese celery), thinly sliced (about 6 cups)
- 1 teaspoon reduced-sodium soy sauce
- 1 clove garlic, minced
- 1 tablespoon frozen apple juice concentrate
- 1/2 teaspoon dark sesame oil
- Dash ground ginger
- 1 tablespoon roasted pumpkin seeds

Per Serving
Calories: 37
% Calories from fat: 24
Fat (gm): 1
Sat. fat (gm): 0.1
Cholesterol (mg): 0
Sodium (mg): 65
Protein (gm): 2.5
Carbohydrate (gm): 4.5
Exchanges
Milk: 0.0
Vegetable: 1.0
Fruit: 0.0
Bread: 0.0
Meat: 0.0
Fat: 0.0

1. Combine all ingredients, except pumpkin seeds, in 2-quart glass measure or baking dish. Cover with vented plastic wrap, and microwave on High 3 to 4 minutes, or until wilted, stirring once. Toss with pumpkin seeds.

BROCCOLI PARMESAN

4 servings

- Butter-flavored vegetable cooking spray
- 3 tablespoons chopped shallots, *or* green onions
- 1 clove garlic, chopped
- 1 pound broccoli florets and cut stems, cooked crisp-tender
- 2 teaspoons balsamic vinegar, *or* lemon juice
- 1/3 cup (1 1/3 ounces) shredded Parmesan cheese
- 2 tablespoons chopped toasted pine nuts

Per Serving
Calories: 76
% Calories from fat: 29
Fat (gm): 2.4
Sat. fat (gm): 1.1
Cholesterol (mg): 4.7
Sodium (mg): 85
Protein (gm): 5.2
Carbohydrate (gm): 7.9
Exchanges
Milk: 0.0
Vegetable: 2.0
Fruit: 0.0
Bread: 0.0
Meat: 0.0
Fat: 0.5

1. Spray large skillet with cooking spray; heat over medium heat until hot. Saute shallots and garlic until tender, about 2 minutes. Stir in broccoli and saute until warm, about 3 minutes. Stir in vinegar and cheese; spoon into serving bowl and sprinkle with pine nuts.

MICROWAVE BRUSSELS SPROUTS ALMONDINE

4 servings

1 pound Brussels sprouts, cut in half
1/4 cup Chicken Stock (see p. 47), *or* reduced-fat chicken broth
1 tablespoon lemon juice
1 teaspoon Dijon-style mustard
1 clove garlic, minced
Salt and pepper, to taste
3 tablespoons toasted slivered almonds

Per Serving
Calories: 85
% Calories from fat: 32
Fat (gm): 3.6
Sat. fat (gm): 0.4
Cholesterol (mg): 0.6
Sodium (mg): 44.2
Protein (gm): 4.6
Carbohydrate (gm): 12.5
Exchanges
Milk: 0.0
Vegetable: 2.0
Fruit: 0.0
Bread: 0.0
Meat: 0.0
Fat: 1.0

1. Place Brussels sprouts and Chicken Stock in 1-quart casserole or microwave-safe serving dish. Cover with wax paper and microwave on High until tender, about 6 minutes, stirring once. Combine lemon juice, mustard, and garlic in small bowl; stir into Brussels sprouts. Season to taste with salt and pepper. Sprinkle with almonds.

CABBAGE BRAISED IN WINE

8 servings

Vegetable cooking spray
1 large onion, thinly sliced
1 large clove garlic, chopped
1 medium head cabbage, coarsely shredded
1 cup dry white wine, *or* reduced-sodium fat-free chicken broth
1 tablespoon tomato sauce

Per Serving
Calories: 46
% Calories from fat: 4
Fat (gm): 0.2
Sat. fat (gm): 0
Cholesterol (mg): 0.3
Sodium (mg): 21
Protein (gm): 1.2
Carbohydrate (gm): 5.9
Exchanges
Milk: 0.0
Vegetable: 1.5
Fruit: 0.0
Bread: 0.0
Meat: 0.0
Fat: 0.0

1 tablespoon fresh rosemary leaves, *or* 1 teaspoon dried rosemary leaves
1 teaspoon dried oregano leaves
Salt and pepper, to taste

1. Spray large saucepan with cooking spray; heat over medium heat until hot. Saute onion and garlic until tender, about 5 minutes. Add cabbage, and cook, stirring, over medium heat until cabbage begins to wilt, about 5 minutes. Stir in wine, tomato sauce, rosemary, and oregano; heat to boiling. Reduce heat and simmer, covered, until cabbage is tender, about 10 minutes. Uncover and cook until liquid is almost evaporated, about 5 minutes. Season to taste with salt and pepper.

MICROWAVE RUBY RED CABBAGE

6 servings

1 medium onion, chopped
4 cloves garlic, minced
2 teaspoons vegetable oil
3/4 pound red cabbage, shredded (about 3 cups)
1/4 cup balsamic vinegar
2 tablespoons frozen orange juice concentrate
1 cup Chicken Stock (see p. 47), *or* reduced-sodium fat-free chicken broth
3 tablespoons raisins
1 tablespoon chopped gingerroot
1/2 teaspoon ground cloves
1 bay leaf
Juice of 1 lemon

Per Serving
Calories: 79
% Calories from fat: 20
Fat (gm): 1.9
Sat. fat (gm): 0.2
Cholesterol (mg): 1.7
Sodium (mg): 11
Protein (gm): 1.9
Carbohydrate (gm): 14.5
Exchanges
Milk: 0.0
Vegetable: 2.0
Fruit: 0.5
Bread: 0.0
Meat: 0.0
Fat: 0.0

1. Place onion, garlic, and oil in 2-quart casserole and microwave on High 3 minutes. Stir in remaining ingredients; cover with wax paper, and microwave on High until cabbage is tender, about 8 minutes, stirring once. Discard bay leaf.

BABY CARROTS À L'ORANGE

4 servings

$1^1/_2$ cups reduced-sodium fat-free chicken broth
20 baby carrots, *or* 2 large carrots, peeled and sliced
1 medium onion, chopped
2 teaspoons sugar
1 small orange, peeled and diced

Per Serving
Calories: 48
% Calories from fat: 5
Fat (gm): 0.3
Sat. fat (gm): 0
Cholesterol (mg): 0
Sodium (mg): 26
Protein (gm): 1.5
Carbohydrate (gm): 10.8
Exchanges
Milk: 0.0
Vegetable: 2.0
Fruit: 0.0
Bread: 0.0
Meat: 0.0
Fat: 0.0

1. Combine chicken broth, carrots, onion, and sugar in medium saucepan. Heat to boiling; reduce heat and cook, covered 5 minutes. Uncover and boil until carrots are tender and liquid almost absorbed, about 5 minutes. Stir in orange.

CARROTS VICHY

4 servings

Vegetable cooking spray
2 large onions, chopped
1 pound carrots, sliced $^1/_2$-inch thick
1 cup water
1 teaspoon sugar
2 teaspoons butter
Salt and pepper, to taste
2 tablespoons chopped parsley

Per Serving
Calories: 96
% Calories from fat: 3
Fat (gm): 0.4
Sat. fat (gm): 0.1
Cholesterol (mg): 0
Sodium (mg): 398
Protein (gm): 2.2
Carbohydrate (gm): 20.6
Exchanges
Milk: 0.0
Vegetable: 3.5
Fruit: 0.0
Bread: 0.0
Meat: 0.0
Fat: 0.0

1. Spray large saucepan with cooking spray; heat over medium heat until hot. Saute onions until tender and lightly browned, about 8 minutes, stirring frequently. Stir in carrots, water, sugar, and butter. Heat to boiling; reduce heat and simmer, covered, 10 minutes or until tender. Season to taste with salt and pepper; sprinkle with parsley.

MICROWAVE CAULIFLOWER MEDLEY

4 servings

1 small head cauliflower, cut into florets
$1^1/_4$ cups chopped green bell pepper
1 medium carrot, diced
1 teaspoon caraway seeds
$^1/_4$ cup water
Salt and pepper, to taste

Per Serving
Calories: 54
% Calories from fat: 6
Fat (gm): 0.4
Sat. fat (gm): 0.1
Cholesterol (mg): 0
Sodium (mg): 14
Protein (gm): 2.9
Carbohydrate (gm): 11.5
Exchanges
Milk: 0.0
Vegetable: 2.0
Fruit: 0.0
Bread: 0.0
Meat: 0.0
Fat: 0.0

1. Place cauliflower in l-quart microwave-safe casserole; sprinkle with green peppers, carrots, and caraway seeds. Add water; cover and microwave on High until tender, 5 to 7 minutes, stirring once. Season to taste with salt and pepper.

CAULIFLOWER SICILIAN STYLE

6 servings

Vegetable cooking spray
$^1/_2$ cup thinly sliced leeks (white parts only), *or* onion
3 cloves garlic, minced
1 medium cauliflower, cut into small florets
1 medium tomato, thinly sliced
1 green bell pepper, thinly sliced
$^1/_2$ cup dry white wine, *or* reduced-sodium fat-free chicken broth
$^1/_2$ teaspoon dried oregano leaves
2 tablespoons chopped parsley
2 tablespoons chopped fresh basil leaves
2 tablespoons drained capers
2 tablespoons chopped pitted Italian black olives
Salt and pepper, to taste
1 lemon, cut into 6 wedges

Per Serving
Calories: 68
% Calories from fat: 17
Fat (gm): 1.6
Sat. fat (gm): 0.1
Cholesterol (mg): 0
Sodium (mg): 146
Protein (gm): 4.3
Carbohydrate (gm): 9.7
Exchanges
Milk: 0.0
Vegetable: 2.5
Fruit: 0.0
Bread: 0.0
Meat: 0.0
Fat: 0.0

1. Spray large skillet with cooking spray; heat over medium heat until hot. Saute leeks until lightly browned, about 5 minutes. Add garlic, and saute 1 minute. Stir in cauliflower, and cook over medium heat, stirring constantly, 3 minutes. Reduce heat, and cook, covered, 5 minutes.

2. Stir in tomato, bell pepper, white wine, and herbs. Simmer, covered, until cauliflower is tender, about 5 minutes. Stir in capers and olives. Season to taste with salt and pepper. Spoon into serving bowl and surround with lemon wedges.

MICROWAVE CORN AND PEPPERS

4 servings

- 1/2 cup diced green bell pepper
- 1/2 cup diced red bell pepper
- 1 teaspoon vegetable oil
- 2 cups whole kernel corn
- 1/4 teaspoon ground cumin
- 1/4 teaspoon chili powder
- Dash powdered ginger
- 1/8 teaspoon pepper

Per Serving
Calories: 93
% Calories from fat: 11
Fat (gm): 1.4
Sat. fat (gm): 0.1
Cholesterol (mg): 0
Sodium (mg): 7
Protein (gm): 3
Carbohydrate (gm): 20.7

Exchanges
Milk: 0.0
Vegetable: 1.0
Fruit: 0.0
Bread: 1.0
Meat: 0.0
Fat: 0.0

1. Place green and red peppers in 1-quart casserole with oil. Microwave on High 3 minutes. Add remaining ingredients and cover with wax paper. Microwave on High 4 minutes, stirring once.

BRAISED FENNEL

6 servings

- Vegetable cooking spray
- 1 leek, white and tender green parts, thinly sliced
- 3 cloves garlic, minced
- 4 fennel bulbs, cut into wedges 1-inch thick
- 1 cup reduced-sodium vegetable, *or* reduced-sodium fat-free chicken broth

Per Serving
Calories: 25
% Calories from fat: 13
Fat (gm): 0.4
Sat. fat (gm): 0.1
Cholesterol (mg): 1.1
Sodium (mg): 227
Protein (gm): 1.2
Carbohydrate (gm): 4.7

Exchanges
Milk: 0.0
Vegetable: 1.0
Fruit: 0.0
Bread: 0.0
Meat: 0.0
Fat: 0.0

1 teaspoon dried oregano leaves
1/2 teaspoon fennel seeds
Salt and pepper, to taste
1 tablespoon finely chopped fresh parsley

1. Spray large saucepan with cooking spray; heat over medium heat until hot. Saute leek, stirring frequently, until lightly browned, about 3 minutes. Stir in garlic and fennel bulbs, and saute 2 minutes.

2. Stir in broth, oregano, and fennel seeds. Heat to boiling; reduce heat and simmer, covered, stirring occasionally, 10 to 12 minutes, until fennel is cooked through but still firm. Season to taste with salt and pepper. Spoon into serving dish; sprinkle with parsley.

MICROWAVE KALE

4 servings

Per Serving
Calories: 73
% Calories from fat: 22
Fat (gm): 2.1
Sat. fat (gm): 0.3
Cholesterol (mg): 2.5
Sodium (mg): 22
Protein (gm): 4.9
Carbohydrate (gm): 11
Exchanges
Milk: 0.0
Vegetable: 2.0
Fruit: 0.0
Bread: 0.0
Meat: 0.0
Fat: 0.5

1/2 teaspoon olive oil
3/4 cup chopped onion
3 cloves garlic, minced
1 tablespoon grated gingerroot
3-4 leaves fresh basil, chopped, *or* 1/2 teaspoon dried basil leaves
1/2 teaspoon crushed red pepper
1 pound kale, *or* turnip greens, sliced
1 cup Chicken Stock (see p. 47), *or* reduced-sodium fat-free chicken broth
4 dashes dark sesame oil
Juice of 1 lemon
1 teaspoon toasted pine nuts

1. Combine oil, onion, garlic, ginger, basil, and crushed red pepper in 2-quart microwave-safe dish; microwave on High 2 minutes. Stir in kale and Chicken Stock; cover with vented plastic wrap, and microwave on High until tender, about 7 minutes, stirring once. Stir in sesame oil and lemon juice. Sprinkle with pine nuts.

MICROWAVE OKRA PROVENÇAL

6 servings

1 pound small okra, trimmed
1 can (15 ounces) stewed tomatoes, drained and crushed
4 scallions, chopped
2 cloves garlic, minced
1/2 cup chopped green bell pepper
8 small pimiento-stuffed olives
1/4 cup chopped parsley
Pinch dried thyme leaves
Pinch dried marjoram leaves
2 teaspoons dried basil leaves
Salt and pepper, to taste

Per Serving
Calories: 54
% Calories from fat: 13
Fat (gm): 1
Sat. fat (gm): 0.1
Cholesterol (mg): 0
Sodium (mg): 258
Protein (gm): 2.5
Carbohydrate (gm): 11.4
Exchanges
Milk: 0.0
Vegetable: 2.0
Fruit: 0.0
Bread: 0.0
Meat: 0.0
Fat: 0.0

1. Place okra on paper towels on microwave-safe plate or baking dish. Microwave on High 2 to 3 minutes, until tender, turning once.

2. Place remaining ingredients, except salt and pepper, in l-quart measure and cover with wax paper. Microwave on High 5 to 6 minutes. Stir, and add okra. Microwave 1 minute on High. Season to taste with salt and pepper.

ONIONS STUFFED WITH MUSHROOMS

6 servings

6 small red onions
1 1/2 cups finely chopped mushrooms
2 cloves garlic
1/4 cup seasoned dry bread crumbs
3 tablespoons grated Parmesan cheese
2 tablespoons chopped fresh parsley
2 tablespoons chopped fresh, *or* 2 teaspoons dried, oregano leaves
1/2 teaspoon pepper

Per Serving
Calories: 84
% Calories from fat: 15
Fat (gm): 1.5
Sat. fat (gm): 0.7
Cholesterol (mg): 2.5
Sodium (mg): 94
Protein (gm): 3.8
Carbohydrate (gm): 15.2
Exchanges
Milk: 0.0
Vegetable: 3.0
Fruit: 0.0
Bread: 0.0
Meat: 0.0
Fat: 0.0

1. Remove skin and 1 or 2 outer layers of onions. Place onions in large saucepan with 1 inch of water; heat to boiling. Cover and steam onions until half cooked, about 15 minutes. Drain onions; let stand until cool enough to handle. Cut onions in half crosswise. Scoop out pulp in center, leaving solid shell of 3 or 4 layers of onion with bottoms intact.

2. Chop 1/2 cup of onion pulp finely; combine chopped onion and remaining ingredients in small bowl. Fill onion halves with stuffing. Place snugly side by side in lightly greased baking dish. Bake at 350 degrees until tender and browned, about 30 minutes. Serve warm or at room temperature.

GREEN PEAS VALENCIA STYLE

4 servings

Vegetable cooking spray
1 medium onion, finely chopped
2 cloves garlic, minced
1 small yellow bell pepper, minced
8 ounces fresh, *or* frozen, thawed, green peas
1/4 cup dry white wine, *or* reduced-sodium fat-free chicken broth
1/4 cup water
2 tablespoons chopped fresh parsley
1 tablespoon chopped fresh thyme leaves
1 bay leaf, crushed
1/8 teaspoon saffron threads, optional
Salt and pepper, to taste
Pimiento strips, as garnish

Per Serving
Calories: 77
% Calories from fat: 4
Fat (gm): 0.4
Sat. fat (gm): 0.1
Cholesterol (mg): 0
Sodium (mg): 6
Protein (gm): 3.8
Carbohydrate (gm): 13.1
Exchanges
Milk: 0.0
Vegetable: 1.0
Fruit: 0.0
Bread: 0.5
Meat: 0.0
Fat: 0.0

1. Spray large skillet with cooking spray; heat over medium heat until hot. Saute onion and garlic until softened, about 3 minutes. Stir in bell pepper, peas, wine, water, and herbs; heat to boiling. Reduce heat and simmer, covered, until peas are tender, about 10 minutes. Stir in saffron (if using) and cook 1 minute longer; season to taste with salt and pepper. Garnish with pimiento.

TRICOLORED BELL PEPPER STIR-FRY

4 servings

Vegetable cooking spray
1 green bell pepper, julienned
1 red bell pepper, julienned
1 yellow bell pepper, julienned
1 medium onion, sliced
1/4 cup sliced green onions and tops
1 tablespoon minced fresh, *or* 1 teaspoon dried, basil leaves
1/2 teaspoon fresh, *or* 1/4 teaspoon dried thyme leaves
1 teaspoon garlic powder
3 tablespoons dry white wine
2 tablespoons chopped fresh parsley

Per Serving
Calories: 39
% Calories from fat: 4
Fat (gm): 0.2
Sat. fat (gm): 0
Cholesterol (mg): 0
Sodium (mg): 4
Protein (gm): 1.1
Carbohydrate (gm): 7.2
Exchanges
Milk: 0.0
Vegetable: 1.5
Fruit: 0.0
Bread: 0.0
Meat: 0.0
Fat: 0.0

1. Spray wok or large skillet with cooking spray; heat over high heat until hot. Stir in peppers, onion, green onions, basil, thyme, and garlic powder. Stir-fry 3 to 3 1/2 minutes or until vegetables are crisp-tender. Stir in wine; cook 1 minute. Sprinkle with parsley.

ROASTED GARLIC GRILLED POTATOES

8 servings

2 tablespoons olive oil, divided
1 tablespoon dried rosemary leaves, crumbled
2 teaspoons coarsely ground black pepper
4 large baking potatoes
1 head garlic
1/2 cup fat-free sour cream
1/2 cup chopped fresh chives

Per Serving
Calories: 168
% Calories from fat: 19
Fat (gm): 3.6
Sat. fat (gm): 0.5
Cholesterol (mg): 0
Sodium (mg): 22
Protein (gm): 3.8
Carbohydrate (gm): 30.7
Exchanges
Milk: 0.0
Vegetable: 0.0
Fruit: 0.0
Bread: 2.0
Meat: 0.0
Fat: 0.5

1. Combine 1 1/2 tablespoons oil, rosemary, and pepper in small bowl; rub each potato with mixture, pierce a few times with fork, and wrap in heavy-duty aluminum foil. Cut top off head of garlic, exposing cloves; place on square of aluminum foil and drizzle with remaining 1/2 tablespoon oil. Wrap tightly.

2. Remove grill rack and set potatoes and garlic directly on hot coals, around perimeter of barbecue grill. If you are grilling other food, replace grill rack and cook as directed. Potatoes should be turned every 10 minutes until done. Potatoes are cooked when easily pierced with tip of knife, 35 to 40 minutes. Garlic is done when tender when squeezed.

3. Unwrap potatoes and garlic. Cut potatoes in half horizontally. Squeeze a garlic clove over each potato half and mash. Combine sour cream and chives in small bowl, spoon over potatoes.

SPANAKOPITA BAKED POTATOES

8 servings

4 large baking potatoes
Vegetable cooking spray
4 cloves garlic, minced
1 cup chopped onion
3 cups chopped fresh spinach leaves
1/2 cup fat-free ricotta cheese
1/4 teaspoon dried basil leaves
1/4 teaspoon dried oregano leaves
1/4 teaspoon ground nutmeg
1/4 teaspoon pepper

Per Serving
Calories: 103
% Calories from fat: 2
Fat (gm): 0.2
Sat. fat (gm): 0.1
Cholesterol (mg): 1.5
Sodium (mg): 31
Protein (gm): 4.6
Carbohydrate (gm): 22

Exchanges
Milk: 0.0
Vegetable: 1.0
Fruit: 0.0
Bread: 1.0
Meat: 0.0
Fat: 0.0

1. Pierce potatoes several times with tip of sharp knife or fork. Set potatoes on baking sheet. Bake at 425 degrees 45 minutes to 1 hour or until tender.

2. Spray large skillet with cooking spray; heat over medium heat until hot. Saute garlic and onion until onions are soft, about 5 minutes. Stir in spinach and cook, stirring occasionally, until spinach is limp. Stir in remaining ingredients.

3. Cut hot baked potatoes in half horizontally and gently squeeze open. Place potatoes on serving plates and spoon spinach topping over.

MICROWAVE POTATOES WITH AVOCADO TOPPING

8 servings

- 4 large baking potatoes
- Vegetable oil
- 1 container (8 ounces) plain low-fat yogurt
- 1 ripe avocado, mashed
- 2 tablespoons fat-free milk
- 1 tablespoon fresh lemon juice
- 1 tablespoon grated onion
- 1/4 cup imitation bacon bits
- 2 tomatoes, cut into wedges

Per Serving
Calories: 156
% Calories from fat: 28
Fat (gm): 5.1
Sat. fat (gm): 1
Cholesterol (mg): 1.8
Sodium (mg): 115
Protein (gm): 4.9
Carbohydrate (gm): 24.1
Exchanges
Milk: 0.0
Vegetable: 0.0
Fruit: 0.0
Bread: 1.5
Meat: 0.0
Fat: 1.0

1. Rub potatoes with oil. Pierce in several places with fork. Microwave on High 9 minutes or until tender.

2. Mix remaining ingredients, except bacon bits and tomatoes, in medium bowl. Split potatoes lengthwise, and fluff pulp with fork. Spoon avocado topping over potatoes. Sprinkle with bacon bits and garnish with tomato wedges.

GARDEN-TOPPED POTATOES

8 servings

- 1 large green bell pepper, chopped
- 1 cup chopped green onions and tops
- 1 clove garlic, crushed
- 2 tablespoons margarine
- 1/2 cup sliced mushrooms
- 1 cup sliced zucchini
- 2 tomatoes, chopped
- 3/4 cup fat-free half-and-half *or* sour cream
- 1/4 cup (1 ounce) grated Parmesan cheese
- Dash pepper
- 2 tablespoons chopped parsley
- 4 large baking potatoes, cooked, hot

Per Serving
Calories: 145
% Calories from fat: 20
Fat (gm): 3.4
Sat. fat (gm): 1
Cholesterol (mg): 3.2
Sodium (mg): 145
Protein (gm): 5.6
Carbohydrate (gm): 24.2
Exchanges
Milk: 0.0
Vegetable: 0.5
Fruit: 0.0
Bread: 1.5
Meat: 0.0
Fat: 0.5

1. Saute bell pepper, onions, and garlic in margarine in large skillet until softened, about 3 minutes. Stir in mushrooms and zucchini and saute until lightly browned, about 5 minutes. Add tomatoes and cook 2 minutes. Stir in remaining ingredients, except potatoes, and cook until hot.

2. Split potatoes lengthwise, and fluff pulp with fork. Spoon topping over potatoes.

MICROWAVE MEXICAN-TOPPED POTATOES

12 servings

- 6 large baking potatoes, cooked, hot
- Vegetable oil
- 1/2 pound turkey sausage
- 1 pound fat-free mozzarella cheese, cubed
- 1/4 cup fat-free milk
- 1 can (10 ounces) tomatoes and green chilies, undrained, chopped
- Shredded lettuce
- Chopped tomato

Per Serving
Calories: 177
% Calories from fat: 14
Fat (gm): 2.8
Sat. fat (gm): 0.6
Cholesterol (mg): 23.5
Sodium (mg): 519
Protein (gm): 18.1
Carbohydrate (gm): 21

Exchanges
Milk: 0.0
Vegetable: 0.0
Fruit: 0.0
Bread: 1.0
Meat: 2.0
Fat: 0.0

1. Rub potatoes with oil; pierce several times with fork. Microwave on High until tender, about 10 minutes.

2. Place sausage in microwave-safe dish and cook on High until browned, about 8 minutes, stirring twice to crumble as it cooks; drain.

3. Place cheese and milk in microwave-safe dish and cook on High about 2 minutes or until cheese melts. Add to meat mixture with tomatoes and chilies, and mix well.

4. Split potatoes lengthwise, and fluff pulp with fork. Spoon topping over potatoes. Sprinkle with lettuce and tomato.

MICROWAVE POTATOES LYONNAISE

4 servings

- 1 pound baking potatoes, sliced 1/8-inch thick
- 2 medium onions, thinly sliced
- 1 tablespoon olive oil
- 3 cloves garlic, minced
- 1/4 teaspoon salt
- 1/8 teaspoon pepper
- 1/8 teaspoon paprika
- 1 tablespoon chopped parsley

Per Serving
Calories: 180
% Calories from fat: 18
Fat (gm): 3.6
Sat. fat (gm): 0.5
Cholesterol (mg): 0
Sodium (mg): 145
Protein (gm): 3.5
Carbohydrate (gm): 34.7
Exchanges
Milk: 0.0
Vegetable: 0.5
Fruit: 0.0
Bread: 2.0
Meat: 0.0
Fat: 0.5

1. Place all ingredients, except parsley, in microwave-safe 3-quart casserole. Cover loosely with plastic wrap and microwave on High 12 to 14 minutes, until tender, stirring gently a few times. Sprinkle with parsley; let stand a few minutes before serving.

ROSEMARY-SCENTED POTATOES GRATIN

12 servings

- 4 cloves garlic, minced
- 4 shallots, minced
- 1/4 cup chopped parsley
- 1 tablespoon chopped fresh, *or* 1 teaspoon dried, rosemary leaves
- 1/4 cup (1 ounce) grated Parmesan cheese
- 6 baking potatoes, peeled, sliced
- Pepper, to taste
- 2 cups Chicken Stock (see p. 47), or reduced-sodium fat-free chicken broth

Per Serving
Calories: 130
% Calories from fat: 6
Fat (gm): 0.9
Sat. fat (gm): 0.5
Cholesterol (mg): 3.3
Sodium (mg): 48
Protein (gm): 3.9
Carbohydrate (gm): 26.7
Exchanges
Milk: 0.0
Vegetable: 0.5
Fruit: 0.0
Bread: 1.5
Meat: 0.0
Fat: 0.0

1. Combine garlic, shallots, parsley, rosemary, and Parmesan cheese in small mixing bowl. Slightly overlap 1/3 of the potato slices to cover bottom of lightly greased 12-inch ovenproof gratin dish. Sprinkle about 1/3 of herb mixture over potatoes; sprinkle lightly with pepper. Repeat layers twice using remaining potatoes and herb mixture. Pour Chicken Stock over potatoes. Bake at 350 degrees 45 minutes or until potatoes are tender. Cool 5 minutes before serving.

QUICK POTATOES AND VEGETABLES AU GRATIN

6 servings

Vegetable cooking spray
1/2 red, *or* green, bell pepper, chopped
1/2 cup chopped onion
2 cups water
1 1/2 cups frozen, *or* fresh, broccoli florets
1/2 cup frozen tiny peas
1 1/2 ounces dried shiitake mushrooms, broken into small pieces (about 6 mushrooms)
1 package (4 1/2 ounces) dried julienned potatoes
3/4 cup fat-free milk
1-1 1/2 cups (4-6 ounces) shredded reduced fat Swiss, *or* Cheddar, cheese

Per Serving
Calories: 169
% Calories from fat: 7
Fat (gm): 1.4
Sat. fat (gm): 0.7
Cholesterol (mg): 7.2
Sodium (mg): 98
Protein (gm): 10.4
Carbohydrate (gm): 30.5
Exchanges
Milk: 0.0
Vegetable: 0.0
Fruit: 0.0
Bread: 2.0
Meat: 0.0
Fat: 0.5

1. Spray medium saucepan with cooking spray; heat over medium heat until hot. Saute bell pepper and onion until tender, about 5 minutes. Add water, broccoli, peas, and dried mushrooms; heat to boiling.

2. Pour potato and sauce packet into 2-quart casserole; pour boiling vegetable mixture over and mix well. Stir in milk and cheese. Bake, uncovered, at 400 degrees until golden, 20 to 30 minutes.

STIR-FRY POTATOES AND ASIAN VEGETABLES

8 servings

Per Serving
Calories: 108
% Calories from fat: 3
Fat (gm): 0.3
Sat. fat (gm): 0.1
Cholesterol (mg): 0.6
Sodium (mg): 141
Protein (gm): 4.4
Carbohydrate (gm): 23.8

Exchanges
Milk: 0.0
Vegetable: 1.0
Fruit: 0.0
Bread: 1.0
Meat: 0.0
Fat: 0.0

Vegetable cooking spray
4 cloves garlic, minced
1/2 teaspoon grated gingerroot
1 cup chopped green onions and tops
4 medium red potatoes, cooked, peeled, cut into 1/2-inch cubes
3 cups sliced bok choy
8 shittake mushrooms, softened in hot water for 20 minutes, drained, sliced
2 cups bean sprouts
1/2 cup Chicken Stock (see p. 47), *or* reduced-sodium fat-free chicken broth
1 tablespoon cornstarch
2 tablespoons light soy sauce
1/2 teaspoon curry powder
1/2 teaspoon pepper

1. Spray wok or large skillet with cooking spray; heat over medium heat until hot. Stir-fry garlic, ginger, and green onions about 2 minutes or until tender. Add potatoes and stir-fry over high heat until beginning to brown. Stir in remaining vegetables, stir-frying over high heat until vegetables are cooked crisp-tender, about 5 minutes. Stir in combined remaining ingredients. Heat to boiling.

SPINACH-STUFFED MUSHROOMS

8 servings (2 mushrooms each)

- 16 large mushrooms
- 1 clove garlic, crushed
- 1 tablespoon margarine
- 1 package (10-ounces) frozen chopped spinach, *or* 1 bunch fresh spinach, cooked, well-drained
- 1 teaspoon Worcestershire sauce
- 1/2 cup seasoned dry bread crumbs
- 1 teaspoon Dijon-style mustard
- 1/8 teaspoon pepper
- 2 tablespoons fat-free mayonnaise
- 2 tablespoons grated Parmesan cheese

Per Serving
Calories: 67
% Calories from fat: 34
Fat (gm): 2.7
Sat. fat (gm): 0.8
Cholesterol (mg): 1.4
Sodium (mg): 200
Protein (gm): 2.9
Carbohydrate (gm): 8.6

Exchanges
Milk: 0.0
Vegetable: 1.5
Fruit: 0.0
Bread: 0.0
Meat: 0.0
Fat: 0.5

1. Remove stems from mushrooms and chop. Saute mushroom stems and garlic in margarine in medium skillet until tender, about 5 minutes. Stir in remaining ingredients, except mushroom caps. Spoon spinach mixture into mushroom caps. Place mushrooms, stuffed side up, in lightly greased 11 x 7-inch baking pan. Bake at 350 degrees 20 minutes or until mushrooms are tender.

MICROWAVE SESAME SPINACH

4 servings

- 1 teaspoon sesame oil
- 2 cloves garlic, minced
- 1/2 small onion, chopped
- 1 1/2 pounds fresh spinach, stems removed
- 1 teaspoon reduced-sodium soy sauce
- 1/4 teaspoon minced gingerroot
- 2 tablespoons sliced water chestnuts
- 2 teaspoons toasted sesame seeds

Per Serving
Calories: 68
% Calories from fat: 28
Fat (gm): 2.5
Sat. fat (gm): 0.4
Cholesterol (mg): 0
Sodium (mg): 180
Protein (gm): 5.7
Carbohydrate (gm): 9

Exchanges
Milk: 0.0
Vegetable: 1.5
Fruit: 0.0
Bread: 0.0
Meat: 0.0
Fat: 0.5

1. Place oil, garlic, and onion in microwave-safe 4-quart casserole; microwave on High 1 minute. Stir in spinach; cover with vented plastic wrap, and microwave on High 4 to 6 minutes, stirring once, until wilted. Drain excess liquid. Stir in soy sauce, gingerroot, and water chestnuts, and microwave on High 1 minute longer. Toss with sesame seeds and serve.

BAKED ACORN SQUASH

4 servings

2 small acorn, *or* Hubbard, squash, halved, seeded
1 cup orange juice
2 tablespoons honey
1 teaspoon ground cinnamon
1 teaspoon ground nutmeg

Per Serving
Calories: 120
% Calories from fat: 4
Fat (gm): 0.6
Sat. fat (gm): 0.2
Cholesterol (mg): 0
Sodium (mg): 6
Protein (gm): 2.1
Carbohydrate (gm): 29.1

Exchanges
Milk: 0.0
Vegetable: 0.0
Fruit: 1.0
Bread: 1.0
Meat: 0.0
Fat: 0.0

1. Place squash in baking dish; fill centers with combined remaining ingredients. Bake, uncovered, at 350 degrees until tender, about 1 hour.

MICROWAVE ACORN SQUASH WITH CRANBERRY TOPPING

4 servings

1 large acorn squash, halved, seeded
1 tablespoon water
1/2 cup cranberries
3 tablespoons frozen orange juice concentrate
1 tablespoon dark raisins
2 tablespoons sugar

Per Serving
Calories: 178
% Calories from fat: 2
Fat (gm): 0.4
Sat. fat (gm): 0.1
Cholesterol (mg): 0
Sodium (mg): 11
Protein (gm): 3
Carbohydrate (gm): 45.9

Exchanges
Milk: 0.0
Vegetable: 0.0
Fruit: 0.5
Bread: 2.0
Meat: 0.0
Fat: 0.0

1. Place squash, cut side down, in glass pie plate; add 1 tablespoon water. Cover loosely with wax paper. Microwave on High 8 to 10 minutes, until tender, rotating plate halfway through cooking time. Drain; cut each half into halves. Return to pie plate, cut side up; reserve.

2. Combine remaining ingredients in 4-cup glass measure. Microwave 4 to 5 minutes, or until slightly thickened, stirring once. Spoon cranberry mixture over squash. Microwave 30 seconds to 1 minute.

FRUIT-FILLED SQUASH

4 servings

1 small cooking apple, cored, thinly sliced
1 medium Bartlett pear, cored, thinly sliced
1/4 cup raisins
1/3 cup packed dark brown sugar
1 teaspoon ground cinnamon, *or* ground allspice
1 tablespoon lemon juice
1 large acorn squash, quartered, seeded

Per Serving
Calories: 190
% Calories from fat: 2
Fat (gm): 0.5
Sat. fat (gm): 0.1
Cholesterol (mg): 0
Sodium (mg): 12
Protein (gm): 1.5
Carbohydrate (gm): 49.5
Exchanges
Milk: 0.0
Vegetable: 0.0
Fruit: 2.0
Bread: 1.0
Meat: 0.0
Fat: 0.0

1. Combine apple, pear, raisins, brown sugar, cinnamon, and lemon juice in medium bowl. Place squash in lightly greased baking pan. Fill centers with fruit mixture. Cover pan tightly with aluminum foil; bake at 350 degrees until squash is tender, about 1 hour, removing cover for last 10 minutes cooking time.

Note: Other fruits such as oranges, peaches, nectarines, or pineapple may be substituted for apples and pears.

GOLDEN SPAGHETTI SQUASH

6 servings

- 2 tablespoons margarine, softened
- 2 tablespoons honey
- 1/4 teaspoon ground cinnamon
- Dash salt
- 1 spaghetti squash (2 1/2 to 3 pounds), halved, seeded
- 1 orange, peeled, chopped

Per Serving
Calories: 59
% Calories from fat: 33
Fat (gm): 2.4
Sat. fat (gm): 0.4
Cholesterol (mg): 0
Sodium (mg): 45
Protein (gm): 1.6
Carbohydrate (gm): 9.6
Exchanges
Milk: 0.0
Vegetable: 1.5
Fruit: 0.0
Bread: 0.0
Meat: 0.0
Fat: 0.5

1. Combine margarine, honey, cinnamon, and salt in small bowl.

2. Place squash halves, cut side down, on shallow baking pan. Bake at 375 degrees 35 to 45 minutes, or until tender. Using fork, scrape squash into bowl, forming spaghetti-like strands. Toss with margarine mixture and orange.

MICROWAVE GREEN & YELLOW SQUASH

4 servings

- 1 medium yellow summer squash, sliced
- 1 medium zucchini, sliced
- 2 ounces chopped pimientos
- 1/2 teaspoon dried oregano leaves
- 1 bay leaf
- 2 cloves garlic, crushed
- 2 tablespoons lemon juice
- 1 teaspoon olive oil
- 1 tablespoon water
- Pepper, to taste
- Chopped chives, as garnish

Per Serving
Calories: 44
% Calories from fat: 14
Fat (gm): 1.5
Sat. fat (gm): 0.2
Cholesterol (mg): 0
Sodium (mg): 5.5
Protein (gm): 1.4
Carbohydrate (gm): 7.8
Exchanges
Milk: 0.0
Vegetable: 1.5
Fruit: 0.0
Bread: 0.0
Meat: 0.0
Fat: 0.0

1. Combine all ingredients, except pepper and chives, in 2-quart microwave-safe casserole. Stir to mix. Cover with vented plastic wrap and microwave on High 2 to 3 minutes. Stir, and microwave on High another 2 to 3 minutes, until crisp-tender. Let stand covered 2 minutes. Remove bay leaf; sprinkle with pepper, and chives.

SWEET POTATOES WITH PEPPERS AND TOMATOES

8 servings

- 2 sweet potatoes, peeled, cut into 1 1/2-inch cubes
- 8 banana peppers, cut in half horizontally, seeded, *or* 2 bell peppers, cubed
- 16 cherry tomatoes
- 2 teaspoons margarine, melted
- 1/4 teaspoon ground cumin
- 1/4 teaspoon ground cinnamon
- 1/4 cup chopped cilantro, *or* chives

Per Serving
Calories: 54
% Calories from fat: 19
Fat (gm): 1.2
Sat. fat (gm): 0.2
Cholesterol (mg): 0
Sodium (mg): 20
Protein (gm): 1.2
Carbohydrate (gm): 10.6

Exchanges
Milk: 0.0
Vegetable: 0.5
Fruit: 0.0
Bread: 0.5
Meat: 0.0
Fat: 0.0

1. Cook potatoes in water in medium saucepan until just fork-tender; drain. Thread 8 skewers with sweet potatoes, peppers, and cherry tomatoes.

2. Mix margarine with ground cumin, cinnamon, and cilantro. Brush kabobs with margarine mixture.

3. Place kabobs on lightly greased grill rack 6 inches over hot coals. Cook until well browned, about 10 minutes, turning frequently.

MICROWAVE STUFFED TOMATOES

4 servings

- 4 large tomatoes
- 3 tablespoons vegetable oil
- 2 medium onions, chopped
- 1 cup long-grain rice
- 1/2 cup sliced green onions and tops
- 1/3 cup chopped mushrooms
- 2 tablespoons seasoned dry bread crumbs
- 1/2 cup tomato juice

Per Serving
Calories: 329
% Calories from fat: 30
Fat (gm): 11.2
Sat. fat (gm): 1.5
Cholesterol (mg): 0
Sodium (mg): 149
Protein (gm): 6
Carbohydrate (gm): 52.3

Exchanges
Milk: 0.0
Vegetable: 2.0
Fruit: 0.0
Bread: 2.5
Meat: 0.0
Fat: 2.0

1. Slice off top of each tomato, 3/4 to 1 inch from top. Scoop out pulp; reserve pulp and tomato tops.

2. Combine oil and onions in microwave-safe casserole; microwave on High 3 1/2 to 4 minutes or until soft. Combine reserved tomato pulp with enough water to make 2 cups. Stir into onion mixture. Stir in rice, green onions, and mushrooms. Microwave, covered with wax paper, on High 5 minutes; reduce to 50% power, or Medium, and microwave 15 minutes. Let stand 5 minutes.

3. Stuff rice mixture into tomato shells, sprinkle with bread crumbs and replace tops. Place in small microwave-safe dish and pour tomato juice into dish. Microwave, uncovered, on High 4 to 5 minutes or until tomatoes are soft.

TOMATOES STUFFED WITH MUSHROOMS AND CHEESE

4 servings

4 large tomatoes
Vegetable cooking spray
1 pound mushrooms, chopped
1/2 cup chopped onion
1/2 small green bell pepper, chopped
3 cloves garlic, crushed
1/4 cup chopped parsley
1/2 teaspoon dried oregano leaves
1/4 teaspoon cayenne pepper
1/4 cup (1 ounce) grated Parmesan cheese

Per Serving
Calories: 106
% Calories from fat: 22
Fat (gm): 3
Sat. fat (gm): 1.3
Cholesterol (mg): 4.9
Sodium (mg): 138
Protein (gm): 6.9
Carbohydrate (gm): 16.4

Exchanges
Milk: 0.0
Vegetable: 3.0
Fruit: 0.0
Bread: 0.0
Meat: 0.0
Fat: 0.5

1. Slice off top of each tomato, 3/4 to 1 inch from top. Scoop out pulp; reserve.

2. Spray large skillet with cooking spray; heat over medium heat until hot. Saute mushrooms, onions, bell pepper, and garlic until tender, about 10 minutes. Stir in reserved tomato pulp, parsley, oregano, and cayenne pepper; cook 5 minutes longer.

3. Place tomatoes in lightly greased baking dish; fill with vegetable mixture. Sprinkle with Parmesan cheese and bake at 350 degrees 10 minutes, or until hot.

ZUCCHINI WITH GARLIC AND TOMATO

6 servings

Vegetable cooking spray
1 1/2 pounds zucchini, sliced into 1/2-inch rounds
4 cloves garlic, minced
2 large tomatoes, peeled, seeded, chopped, *or* 1 cup canned chopped Italian plum tomatoes
1 tablespoon chopped fresh basil leaves
1 tablespoon chopped fresh oregano leaves
2 tablespoons chopped parsley
Salt and pepper, to taste

Per Serving
Calories: 28
% Calories from fat: 6
Fat (gm): 0.2
Sat. fat (gm): 0
Cholesterol (mg): 0
Sodium (mg): 7
Protein (gm): 1.2
Carbohydrate (gm): 6.6
Exchanges
Milk: 0.0
Vegetable: 1.0
Fruit: 0.0
Bread: 0.0
Meat: 0.0
Fat: 0.0

1. Spray large skillet with cooking spray; heat over medium heat until hot. Saute zucchini and garlic until lightly browned, about 5 minutes. Stir in tomatoes, basil, and oregano; cook 5 more minutes. Stir in parsley; season to taste with salt and pepper.

ZUCCHINI GRATIN WITH TOMATOES

4 servings

1 can (14 1/2-ounces) diced tomatoes
1/2 cup chopped fresh, or 1 tablespoon dried, basil leaves
1/4 cup chopped parsley
2 tablespoons chopped cilantro
2 large zucchini, sliced
1/2 cup seasoned dry bread crumbs
1/4 cup (1 ounce) grated Parmesan cheese
1 tablespoon margarine

Per Serving
Calories: 129
% Calories from fat: 27
Fat (gm): 4.1
Sat. fat (gm): 1.6
Cholesterol (mg): 4.9
Sodium (mg): 718
Protein (gm): 6.7
Carbohydrate (gm): 17.6
Exchanges
Milk: 0.0
Vegetable: 2.0
Fruit: 0.0
Bread: 0.5
Meat: 0.0
Fat: 1.0

1. Combine tomatoes, basil, parsley, and cilantro in medium saucepan; heat to boiling. Reduce heat and simmer 3 minutes. Pour half of tomato mixture into shallow 8 x 12-inch baking dish. Arrange zucchini on top, and cover with remaining tomato mixture. Combine bread crumbs and Parmesan cheese and sprinkle over casserole. Dot with margarine.

2. Bake at 375 degrees 30 to 40 minutes until zucchini is tender and crust golden.

NINE

Rice, Grains, and Beans

BRAISED RICE

6 servings

Vegetable cooking spray
1/3 cup finely minced onion
1 cup long-grain white rice
1/4 cup dry vermouth
2 cups Chicken Stock (see p. 47), *or* reduced-sodium fat-free chicken broth, warm
1 medium bay leaf
Bouquet garni
Salt and pepper, to taste

Per Serving
Calories: 138
% Calories from fat: 4
Fat (gm): 0.5
Sat. fat (gm): 0.1
Cholesterol (mg): 3.4
Sodium (mg): 6
Protein (gm): 3.5
Carbohydrate (gm): 25.9
Exchanges
Milk: 0.0
Vegetable: 0.0
Fruit: 0.0
Bread: 2.0
Meat: 0.0
Fat: 0.0

1. Spray skillet with cooking spray; heat over medium heat until hot. Saute onion until soft, 3 to 4 minutes. Stir in rice, and saute, stirring, 3 to 4 minutes. Stir in vermouth and simmer, stirring occasionally, until absorbed. Stir in Chicken Stock, bay leaf, and bouquet garni; heat to boiling. Reduce heat and simmer, covered, until rice is tender and liquid absorbed, about 20 minutes. Discard bay leaf; season to taste with salt and pepper.

Note: To make a bouquet garni, tie a few sprigs of parsley, thyme, and basil or tarragon, and bay leaf, in a cheesecloth bag.

GOAT CHEESE AND VEGETABLE CASSEROLE

4 servings

1 package (6 1/4 ounces) fast-cooking long-grain and wild rice
1 1/2 cups cut asparagus (1 1/2-inch), cooked crisp-tender
1 package (9 ounces) frozen artichoke hearts, cooked according to package directions
3 ounces fat-free cream cheese, cubed
3/4 cup (3 ounces) shredded reduced-fat mozzarella cheese

Per Serving
Calories: 336
% Calories from fat: 26
Fat (gm): 10
Sat. fat (gm): 6.4
Cholesterol (mg): 27
Sodium (mg): 1014
Protein (gm): 19.9
Carbohydrate (gm): 45.1
Exchanges
Milk: 0.0
Vegetable: 3.0
Fruit: 0.0
Bread: 2.0
Meat: 2.0
Fat: 1.0

3-4 ounces goat cheese, crumbled
Salt and pepper, to taste

1. Cook rice with spice packet according to package directions. Mix rice, vegetables, and cheeses; season to taste with salt and pepper. Spoon into 1 1/2-quart casserole.

2. Bake, covered, at 375 degrees until casserole is hot and cheese is melted, 20 to 30 minutes.

WILD RICE AND CHICKEN SALAD

4 servings (about 3/4 cup each)

1 pound boneless, skinless chicken breast, cooked; diced *or* shredded
1 cup cooked wild rice
1/4 cup chopped celery
1/4 cup thinly sliced green onions and tops
2 tablespoons dried cranberries
2-4 tablespoons chopped toasted walnuts
2/3 cup fat-free mayonnaise
1 1/2 teaspoons curry powder
1 teaspoon lemon juice
Salt and pepper, to taste
Salad greens

Per Serving
Calories: 293
% Calories from fat: 12
Fat (gm): 3.9
Sat. fat (gm): 0.5
Cholesterol (mg): 42.7
Sodium (mg): 369
Protein (gm): 23.7
Carbohydrate (gm): 40.2
Exchanges
Milk: 0.0
Vegetable: 0.0
Fruit: 0.0
Bread: 2.0
Meat: 3.0
Fat: 0.0

1. In a large bowl, mix all ingredients, except salt, pepper, and salad greens; season to taste with salt and pepper. Refrigerate at least 1 hour for flavors to blend.

2. Spoon salad onto greens-lined plates.

MICROWAVE WILD RICE

4 servings

1 teaspoon canola oil
1/4 cup chopped shallots
1/2 cup chopped celery
3/4 cup wild rice
2 1/2 cups Chicken Stock (see p. 47), or reduced-sodium fat-free chicken broth
2 tablespoons pine nuts

Per Serving
Calories: 174
% Calories from fat: 23
Fat (gm): 4.6
Sat. fat (gm): 0.3
Cholesterol (mg): 6.3
Sodium (mg): 24
Protein (gm): 8.1
Carbohydrate (gm): 25.9

Exchanges
Milk: 0.0
Vegetable: 1.0
Fruit: 0.0
Bread: 1.5
Meat: 0.0
Fat: 1.0

1. Combine oil, shallots, and celery in 2-quart glass measure; microwave on High 2 minutes or until tender. Add rice and Chicken Stock; microwave on High 5 minutes, then stir. Microwave on Medium 30 minutes longer, or until rice is tender. Let stand, covered, 10 minutes, then drain any excess liquid. Stir in pine nuts.

SAFFRON RICE

8 servings

3 cups reduced-sodium fat-free chicken broth
1 cup dry white wine
1 cup minced onion
2 teaspoons minced fresh parsley
1/2 teaspoon saffron
1/2 teaspoon dried coriander
1/2 teaspoon fennel seeds, lightly crushed
1/4 teaspoon ground mace, *or* ground nutmeg
2 cups long-grain rice

Per Serving
Calories: 206
% Calories from fat: 4
Fat (gm): 0.8
Sat. fat (gm): 0.1
Cholesterol (mg): 0
Sodium (mg): 131
Protein (gm): 5.3
Carbohydrate (gm): 39.6

Exchanges
Milk: 0.0
Vegetable: 0.0
Fruit: 0.0
Bread: 3.0
Meat: 0.0
Fat: 0.0

1. Combine all ingredients, except rice, in medium saucepan; heat to boiling. Add rice, reduce heat, and simmer, covered, until rice is tender, about 20 minutes.

Note: Ground turmeric can be substituted for the saffron and will impart an attractive yellow color to the rice.

THAI FRIED RICE

4 servings

1 package (6 1/4 ounces) Thai coconut ginger rice, *or* 1 1/2 cups cooked rice, warm
1 package (16 ounces) frozen vegetable stir-fry blend with sugar snap peas
6 green onions and tops, sliced, divided
1/2-1 teaspoon hot chili sesame oil
2 eggs, lightly beaten
2-3 tablespoons Thai peanut sauce
1-2 tablespoons reduced-sodium tamari sauce

Per Serving
Calories: 280
% Calories from fat: 13
Fat (gm): 3.8
Sat. fat (gm): 1
Cholesterol (mg): 106.2
Sodium (mg): 752
Protein (gm): 10.6
Carbohydrate (gm): 48.2
Exchanges
Milk: 0.0
Vegetable: 1.0
Fruit: 0.0
Bread: 3.0
Meat: 0.0
Fat: 0.5

1. Cook rice according to package directions.

2. Stir-fry frozen vegetables and 4 green onions in sesame oil in large skillet until tender, 3 to 4 minutes. Move vegetables to side of skillet.

3. Add eggs to skillet; cook over medium heat until set, stirring occasionally, about 2 minutes. Break up eggs with spatula and mix with vegetables; stir in rice and peanut and tamari sauces. Spoon rice mixture into serving dish and sprinkle with remaining 2 sliced green onions.

Tip: Mix 1 to 2 tablespoons reduced-fat peanut butter, 2 to 3 teaspoons tamari soy sauce, and 1/2 to 1 teaspoon minced gingerroot as a substitute for the Thai peanut sauce.

ASIAN FRIED RICE

4 servings

1 package ($6^1/_4$ ounces) quick-cooking long-grain and wild rice
2 cups broccoli florets
2 ounces snow peas, cut into halves
2 medium carrots, sliced
$^3/_4$ cup bean sprouts
$^3/_4$ cup sliced shiitake, *or* white, mushrooms
$^1/_2$ cup chopped red, *or* green, bell pepper
1 teaspoon minced garlic
1 teaspoon finely chopped gingerroot
1-2 tablespoons vegetable oil
$^1/_2$ cup vegetable broth
2 tablespoons reduced-sodium soy sauce
1 egg, lightly scrambled, crumbled

Per Serving
Calories: 266
% Calories from fat: 18
Fat (gm): 5.5
Sat. fat (gm): 1
Cholesterol (mg): 53.1
Sodium (mg): 1039
Protein (gm): 9.6
Carbohydrate (gm): 48.2

Exchanges
Milk: 0.0
Vegetable: 3.0
Fruit: 0.0
Bread: 2.0
Meat: 0.0
Fat: 1.0

1. Cook rice according to package directions, discarding seasoning packet.

2. Stir-fry vegetables, garlic, and gingerroot in oil in wok over medium-high heat until crisp-tender, 5 to 8 minutes.

3. Add broth and soy sauce to wok; stir in rice and scrambled egg and cook 2 to 3 minutes more.

PORK FRIED RICE

8 servings

Vegetable cooking spray
2 eggs, lightly beaten
5 green onions and tops, chopped
4 cups cooked rice
1 cup shredded cooked lean pork
1 small carrot, shredded
1/2 cup sliced water chestnuts
1/2 cup cooked green peas
1-2 tablespoons reduced-sodium soy sauce
Salt and pepper, to taste

Per Serving
Calories: 147
% Calories from fat: 10
Fat (gm): 1.6
Sat. fat (gm): 0.5
Cholesterol (mg): 12.6
Sodium (mg): 371
Protein (gm): 10
Carbohydrate (gm): 22.6
Exchanges
Milk. 0.0
Vegetable: 0.0
Fruit: 0.0
Bread: 1.5
Meat: 1.0
Fat: 0.0

1. Spray skillet with cooking spray; heat over medium heat until hot. Add eggs and cook, scrambling lightly with a fork; remove from skillet.

2. Add green onions to skillet and saute until tender. Mix in remaining ingredients, except soy sauce, salt, and pepper; cook over medium heat until rice is browned, about 5 minutes. Return egg to skillet; cook 1 to 2 minutes. Season to taste with soy sauce, salt, and pepper.

RICE LOUISIANA

8 servings

Vegetable cooking spray
1/4 pound ground chicken breast
2 tablespoons margarine
1/2 cup finely chopped onion
1/2 cup finely chopped celery
1/2 cup finely chopped green bell pepper
2 teaspoons minced garlic
2 teaspoons cayenne pepper
1 1/2 teaspoons black pepper
1 1/4 teaspoons sweet paprika
1 teaspoon dry mustard

Per Serving
Calories: 130
% Calories from fat: 28
Fat (gm): 4
Sat. fat (gm): 0.8
Cholesterol (mg): 10
Sodium (mg): 52
Protein (gm): 5.5
Carbohydrate (gm): 17.5
Exchanges
Milk: 0.0
Vegetable: 0.0
Fruit: 0.0
Bread: 1.0
Meat: 0.5
Fat: 0.5

1 teaspoon ground cumin
1/2 teaspoon ground thyme
1/2 teaspoon dried oregano leaves
2 bay leaves
2 cups Chicken Stock (see p. 47), *or* reduced-sodium fat-free chicken broth
3/4 cup rice
Salt, to taste

1. Spray large skillet with cooking spray; heat over medium heat until hot. Add chicken and cook until browned, crumbling chicken with a fork. Add margarine to skillet; add vegetables and herbs and saute until vegetables are tender, about 5 minutes, stirring frequently and scraping bottom of skillet occasionally. Reduce heat to low; continue cooking 5 to 10 minutes, stirring occasionally.

2. Add Chicken Stock and heat to boiling; add rice. Reduce heat to low and simmer, covered, until rice is tender, about 20 minutes. Discard bay leaves. Season to taste with salt.

RICE ACAPULCO

6 servings

Vegetable cooking spray
1 1/2 cups long-grain rice
3 cloves garlic, minced
1 cup minced onion
1 large tomato, peeled and chopped
3 cups reduced-sodium fat-free chicken broth
1 teaspoon chili powder
1/2 teaspoon cumin seeds, lightly crushed
1/4 teaspoon salt
1/4 teaspoon pepper

Per Serving
Calories: 199
% Calories from fat: 5
Fat (gm): 1.1
Sat. fat (gm): 0.1
Cholesterol (mg): 0
Sodium (mg): 266
Protein (gm): 6.3
Carbohydrate (gm): 41.7

Exchanges
Milk: 0.0
Vegetable: 0.0
Fruit: 0.0
Bread: 3.0
Meat: 0.0
Fat: 0.0

1. Spray skillet with cooking spray; heat over medium heat until hot. Add rice and cook until rice begins to brown, 3 to 4 minutes, stirring occasionally. Mix in garlic, onion, and tomato; saute 2 to 3 minutes. Stir in broth and remaining ingredients; heat to boiling. Reduce heat and simmer, covered, 15 to 20 minutes or until rice is tender.

MICROWAVE MUSHROOM RISOTTO

6 servings

- 2 tablespoons margarine
- 2 tablespoons olive oil
- 1/2 cup minced onion
- 1 cup arborio rice
- 1/2 cup sliced mushrooms
- 3 cups Chicken Stock (see p. 47) or reduced-sodium fat-free chicken broth, hot
- 1/4 cup (1 ounce) grated Parmesan cheese
- Salt and pepper, to taste

Per Serving
Calories: 219
% Calories from fat: 35
Fat (gm): 8.4
Sat. fat (gm): 1.9
Cholesterol (mg): 8.3
Sodium (mg): 128
Protein (gm): 5.8
Carbohydrate (gm): 28.3
Exchanges
Milk: 0.0
Vegetable: 0.0
Fruit: 0.0
Bread: 2.0
Meat: 0.0
Fat: 1.5

1. Microwave margarine, olive oil, and onions in 2-quart glass measure on High 2 minutes. Stir in rice and mushrooms. Microwave, uncovered, on High 4 minutes, or until rice is opaque.

2. Pour in Chicken Stock; microwave on High about 15 minutes, or until liquid is almost absorbed and rice is al dente. Let stand, uncovered, 5 minutes to let rice absorb remaining liquid, stirring several times. Stir in Parmesan cheese; season to taste with salt and pepper.

Variation: **Microwave Risotto with Spring Peas**—Make risotto as above, adding 2 cloves minced garlic and 1/2 teaspoon dried thyme leaves with the onions. Stir in 1/2 cup frozen, thawed peas at the end of cooking time. Complete recipe as above.

SPINACH RISOTTO

6 servings

- 1 package (10 ounces) frozen chopped spinach, well drained
- 2 tablespoons olive oil
- 1 medium onion, chopped
- 1 clove garlic, minced
- 2 cups arborio rice
- 1 1/2-2 quarts Chicken Stock (see p. 47), or reduced-sodium, fat-free chicken broth
- 1/4 cup (1 ounce) grated Parmesan cheese
- Salt and pepper, to taste

Per Serving
Calories: 324
% Calories from fat: 19
Fat (gm): 6.9
Sat. fat (gm): 1.7
Cholesterol (mg): 10
Sodium (mg): 116
Protein (gm): 9.6
Carbohydrate (gm): 53.6

Exchanges
Milk: 0.0
Vegetable: 1.0
Fruit: 0.0
Bread: 3.0
Meat: 0.5
Fat: 1.0

1. Combine spinach, olive oil, onion, and garlic in large, heavy saucepan; cook over medium heat, stirring constantly, about 5 minutes. Process mixture in food processor until smooth; return to saucepan. Add rice and Chicken Stock.

2. Cook over low heat until liquid is absorbed and rice is tender, about 20 minutes. Stir occasionally. Stir in cheese; season to taste with salt and pepper.

LEMON RISOTTO

4 servings

- 1/4 cup minced onion
- Rind of 1 lemon, grated
- 2 tablespoons olive oil
- 1 1/2 cups arborio rice
- 1-1 1/2 quarts reduced-sodium fat-free chicken broth
- 2-4 tablespoons lemon juice
- 1/2 cup (2 ounces) grated Parmesan cheese
- Salt and pepper, to taste

Per Serving
Calories: 423
% Calories from fat: 27
Fat (gm): 12.5
Sat. fat (gm): 3.9
Cholesterol (mg): 11
Sodium (mg): 1109
Protein (gm): 15.9
Carbohydrate (gm): 59.7

Exchanges
Milk: 0.0
Vegetable: 0.0
Fruit: 0.0
Bread: 4.0
Meat: 1.5
Fat: 1.5

1. Saute onion and lemon rind in oil in large saucepan until onion is tender, 3 to 4 minutes. Add rice; cook over medium-high heat, stirring constantly, 1 to 2 minutes.

2. Heat chicken broth just to boiling in large saucepan; reduce heat to medium-low to keep broth hot. Add broth mixture to rice, 1/2 cup at a time, stirring constantly until broth is absorbed before adding next 1/2 cup. Continue process until rice is al dente and mixture is creamy in texture, 20 to 25 minutes. Stir in lemon juice and cheese; season to taste with salt and pepper.

SEAFOOD RISOTTO

6 servings

1 1/2 cups diced onion
2 tablespoons finely minced garlic
3 tablespoons olive oil
2 cups arborio rice
1 1/2-2 quarts Chicken Stock (see p. 47), or reduced-sodium fat-free chicken broth
1 3/4 pounds crabmeat, *or* scallops, *or* medium shrimp, shelled and deveined
2-3 cups chopped Italian plum tomatoes
6 canned artichoke hearts, quartered
3 tablespoons grated lemon rind
2 tablespoons lemon juice
8 basil leaves, chopped
1/4 cup chopped parsley
Salt and pepper, to taste

Per Serving
Calories: 425
% Calories from fat: 19
Fat (gm): 9
Sat. fat (gm): 1.3
Cholesterol (mg): 26.3
Sodium (mg): 467
Protein (gm): 16.6
Carbohydrate (gm): 66.9
Exchanges
Milk: 0.0
Vegetable: 2.0
Fruit: 0.0
Bread: 3.5
Meat: 1.0
Fat: 1.5

1. Saute onion and garlic in oil in large saucepan until onion is soft, 3 to 4 minutes. Stir in rice and cook, stirring, 2 to 3 minutes.

2. Heat Chicken Stock just to boiling in large saucepan; reduce heat to medium-low to keep stock hot. Add stock to rice, 1/2 cup at a time, stirring constantly until stock is absorbed before adding next 1/2 cup. Continue process until rice is al dente and mixture is creamy in texture, 20 to 25 minutes. Stir in remaining ingredients, except salt and pepper, cook, stirring, until seafood is cooked, about 5 minutes. Season to taste with salt and pepper.

CHEESE AND VEGETABLE RISOTTO PANCAKES

4 servings

Vegetable cooking spray
1/2 cup chopped onion
1 cup arborio rice
2 1/2 cups vegetable broth
1/2 cup dry white wine
1 cup (4 ounces) shredded Parmesan cheese
1/4-1/2 cup (1-2 ounces) crumbled blue cheese
4 egg whites, *or* 1/2 cup no-cholesterol egg product
6 canned artichoke hearts, coarsely chopped
1/4 cup coarsely chopped roasted red pepper
Salt and pepper, to taste
Finely chopped parsley, for garnish

Per Serving
Calories: 369
% Calories from fat: 25
Fat (gm): 9.7
Sat. fat (gm): 6.3
Cholesterol (mg): 30.3
Sodium (mg): 1221
Protein (gm): 19.6
Carbohydrate (gm): 44.4

Exchanges
Milk: 0.0
Vegetable: 3.0
Fruit: 0.0
Bread: 2.0
Meat: 2.0
Fat: 1.0

1. Spray large saucepan with cooking spray; heat over medium heat until hot. Add onion and saute 2 minutes. Add rice to saucepan; cook over medium heat until beginning to brown, 3 to 4 minutes.

2. Add vegetable broth and wine to saucepan; heat to boiling. Reduce heat and simmer, covered, until rice is tender and liquid absorbed, about 20 to 25 minutes, stirring occasionally. Remove from heat; stir in cheeses, egg whites, artichoke hearts, and red pepper. Season to taste with salt and pepper.

3. Spray two 10-inch skillets generously with cooking spray; heat over medium heat until hot. Spoon half the risotto mixture into each skillet, shaping into large pancakes. Cook over medium heat until lightly browned on the bottoms, 5 to 8 minutes. Invert pancakes onto plates; slide back into skillets and cook until lightly browned on other side, 5 to 8 minutes. Cut pancakes in half; invert onto serving plates and sprinkle with parsley.

MUSHROOM AND ASPARAGUS PILAF

8 servings

- 3 1/3 cups vegetable broth, divided
- 2 cups dried Chinese mushrooms
- Vegetable cooking spray
- 1 1/2 cups chopped onions
- 2 teaspoons minced garlic
- 2 teaspoons bouquet garni
- 1 1/2 pounds asparagus, cut into 1 1/2-inch pieces
- 1/4 cup dry sherry, *or* water
- 2 packages (6 ounces each) tabouleh wheat salad mix, spice packets discarded
- 1/4 teaspoon red pepper sauce
- Salt and pepper, to taste
- 4 green onions and tops, thinly sliced
- 1/4 cup toasted pecan halves

Per Serving
Calories: 214
% Calories from fat: 14
Fat (gm): 3.7
Sat. fat (gm): 0.4
Cholesterol (mg): 0
Sodium (mg): 818
Protein (gm): 8.8
Carbohydrate (gm): 43

Exchanges
Milk: 0.0
Vegetable: 2.0
Fruit: 0.0
Bread: 2.0
Meat: 0.0
Fat: 0.5

1. Heat 2 cups broth to boiling; pour over mushrooms in bowl and let stand until mushrooms are softened, about 10 minutes. Drain, reserving broth. Slice mushrooms, discarding tough stems.

2. Spray large skillet with cooking spray; heat over medium heat until hot. Saute mushrooms, onions, garlic, and bouquet garni (see p. 352) until onions are tender, about 5 minutes. Add asparagus; saute 5 minutes more.

3. Add sherry, reserved broth from mushrooms, and remaining 1 1/3 cups broth to skillet; heat to boiling. Stir in tabouleh. Reduce heat and simmer, covered, until broth is absorbed and tabouleh is tender, 3 to 5 minutes. Stir in red pepper sauce; season to taste with salt and pepper. Spoon into serving bowl; sprinkle with green onions and pecans.

SWEET BULGUR PILAF

4 servings

- 2/3 cup thinly sliced green onions and tops
- 1 teaspoon minced garlic
- 1 cup bulgur (cracked wheat)
- 1-2 tablespoons olive oil
- 2 1/4 cups vegetable broth
- 1/2-3/4 teaspoon ground cinnamon
- 2 cups cubed, peeled, seeded butternut, *or* acorn, squash
- 1/4 cup currants, *or* raisins
- 1/4 cup pine nuts, toasted
- 1/4 cup finely chopped parsley
- Salt and pepper, to taste

Per Serving
Calories: 276
% Calories from fat: 27
Fat (gm): 8.9
Sat. fat (gm): 1.2
Cholesterol (mg): 0
Sodium (mg): 577
Protein (gm): 9.1
Carbohydrate (gm): 46.5
Exchanges
Milk: 0.0
Vegetable: 0.0
Fruit: 0.0
Bread: 3.0
Meat: 0.0
Fat: 1.5

1. Saute green onions, garlic, and bulgur in oil in large saucepan over medium heat until onions are tender, about 3 minutes. Stir in broth and cinnamon and heat to boiling; reduce heat and simmer, covered, 10 minutes.

2. Stir squash and currants into bulgur mixture; simmer, covered, until squash is tender, about 15 minutes. Stir in pine nuts and parsley; season to taste with salt and pepper.

MICROWAVE BULGUR PILAF À L'ORANGE

6 servings

- 1/4 cup currants
- 2 tablespoons sunflower seeds, *or* slivered almonds
- Grated rind and juice of 1 orange
- 3/4 cup bulgur (cracked wheat)
- 1 teaspoon sesame oil
- 1 small onion, chopped
- 1 1/2 cups boiling water

Per Serving
Calories: 99
% Calories from fat: 22
Fat (gm): 2.5
Sat. fat (gm): 0.3
Cholesterol (mg): 0
Sodium (mg): 3
Protein (gm): 3.2
Carbohydrate (gm): 17.4
Exchanges
Milk: 0.0
Vegetable: 0.0
Fruit: 0.0
Bread: 1.0
Meat: 0.0
Fat: 0.5

1. Process currants, sunflower seeds, orange rind, and juice in food processor or blender until smooth; reserve.

2. Place bulgur, sesame oil, and onion in 2-quart microwave-safe dish; microwave on High 2 minutes. Stir in boiling water and microwave on High 5 minutes. Stir in orange mixture; reduce power to Medium (50 percent), and microwave 12 to 14 minutes, or until bulgur is tender. Let stand until liquid is absorbed.

SAVORY BULGUR WHEAT

6 servings

Butter-flavored vegetable cooking spray
1/2 cup chopped onion
1/2 cup chopped celery
1 cup bulgur (cracked wheat)
2 cups reduced-sodium fat-free chicken broth
1/2 cup raisins
1 teaspoon chopped fresh, *or* 1/2 teaspoon dried, tarragon leaves
3/4 teaspoon ground cinnamon
1/4 teaspoon pepper
1/2 teaspoon salt

Per Serving
Calories: 132
% Calories from fat: 5
Fat (gm): 0.8
Sat. fat (gm): 0.1
Cholesterol (mg): 0
Sodium (mg): 304
Protein (gm): 5.1
Carbohydrate (gm): 29.5
Exchanges
Milk: 0.0
Vegetable: 0.0
Fruit: 0.5
Bread: 1.5
Meat: 0.0
Fat: 0.0

1. Spray medium saucepan with cooking spray; heat over medium heat until hot. Saute onion and celery until tender, about 5 minutes. Stir in bulgur and continue cooking until grain is golden brown. Stir in remaining ingredients. Heat to boiling; reduce heat and simmer, covered, 15 minutes or until liquid has been absorbed.

COUSCOUS NIÇOISE

6 servings

- 1 1/4 cups Chicken Stock (see p. 47), *or* reduced-sodium fat-free chicken broth
- 2 cloves garlic, minced
- 1 1/2 teaspoons olive oil
- 1 1/2 cups instant couscous
- 8 cherry tomatoes, cut in half
- 1/4 cup sliced, pitted Greek olives
- 8 fresh basil leaves, julienned
- 1 tablespoon minced parsley
- 1 tablespoon red wine vinegar
- 1 tablespoon minced chives
- Black pepper, to taste

Per Serving
Calories: 217
% Calories from fat: 16
Fat (gm): 3.7
Sat. fat (gm): 0.5
Cholesterol (mg): 2.1
Sodium (mg): 194
Protein (gm): 7
Carbohydrate (gm): 37.7
Exchanges
Milk: 0.0
Vegetable: 1.0
Fruit: 0.0
Bread: 2.5
Meat: 0.0
Fat: 0.5

1. Combine Chicken Stock, garlic, and oil in medium saucepan. Heat to boiling. Stir in couscous and remove from heat. Cover and let stand 5 minutes. Uncover and fluff with fork until grains are separated.

2. Add tomatoes, olives, basil, parsley, vinegar, and chives. Season to taste with pepper.

MICROWAVE SESAME KASHA

4 servings

- 2 teaspoons sesame oil
- 1/2 cup kasha (buckwheat groats)
- 1 egg white
- 1 3/4 cups boiling water
- 2 cloves garlic, minced
- 1 teaspoon reduced-sodium soy sauce
- 2 teaspoons sesame seeds
- Salt and pepper, to taste

Per Serving
Calories: 106
% Calories from fat: 29
Fat (gm): 3.6
Sat. fat (gm): 0.5
Cholesterol (mg): 0
Sodium (mg): 61
Protein (gm): 3.9
Carbohydrate (gm): 16.2
Exchanges
Milk: 0.0
Vegetable: 0.0
Fruit: 0.0
Bread: 1.0
Meat: 0.0
Fat: 0.5

1. Combine sesame oil and kasha in 2-quart microwave-safe dish. Microwave on High 1 to 2 minutes until toasted. Stir in egg white and microwave on High 30 seconds.

2. Stir in boiling water and microwave on High 2 minutes. Add garlic and soy sauce and microwave on High another 30 seconds. Let stand 5 minutes. Add sesame seeds; season to taste with salt and pepper.

MICROWAVE MILLET WITH VEGETABLES

6 servings

- 3/4 cup millet
- 2 tablespoons olive oil
- 1 medium onion, chopped
- 2 ribs celery, diced
- 1 small green or red bell pepper, diced
- 1 small carrot, diced
- 1 small zucchini, diced
- 2 cloves garlic, minced
- 1 teaspoon chopped gingerroot
- 2 1/2 cups Chicken Stock (see p. 47) *or* reduced-sodium fat-free chicken broth
- 1-2 teaspoons curry powder
- 1/2 teaspoon dried dill weed
- Salt and pepper, to taste

Per Serving
Calories: 172
% Calories from fat: 32
Fat (gm): 6.1
Sat. fat (gm): 0.9
Cholesterol (mg): 4.2
Sodium (mg): 23
Protein (gm): 5
Carbohydrate (gm): 23.7

Exchanges
Milk: 0.0
Vegetable: 1.0
Fruit: 0.0
Bread: 1.5
Meat: 0.0
Fat: 1.0

1. Spread millet on 9-inch pie plate, and toast in microwave on High 1 minute.

2. Combine oil, onion, celery, bell pepper, carrot, zucchini, garlic, and gingerroot in 2-quart microwave-safe casserole; microwave on High until slightly softened, 3 to 4 minutes.

3. Add toasted millet, Chicken Stock, curry powder, and dill weed. Cover with vented plastic wrap and microwave on High until tender, about 20 minutes, stirring several times. Season to taste with salt and pepper.

MICROWAVE QUINOA PILAF

4 servings

- 1/4 cup diced red bell pepper
- 2 cloves garlic, minced
- 1 small onion, chopped
- 1 teaspoon sesame oil
- 3/4 cup quinoa
- 1 1/2 cups Chicken Stock (see p. 47) *or* reduced-sodium fat-free chicken broth
- 1/2 cup fresh, *or* frozen, thawed green peas

Per Serving
Calories: 173
% Calories from fat: 18
Fat (gm): 3.5
Sat. fat (gm): 0.5
Cholesterol (mg): 3.8
Sodium (mg): 13
Protein (gm): 7
Carbohydrate (gm): 28.5
Exchanges
Milk: 0.0
Vegetable: 1.0
Fruit: 0.0
Bread: 1.5
Meat: 0.0
Fat: 1.0

1. Place pepper, garlic, onion, and sesame oil in 4-cup glass measure. Microwave, uncovered, on High 2 minutes. Stir in quinoa and Chicken Stock and microwave on High 5 minutes, stirring once. Microwave on Medium (50 percent) until liquid is almost absorbed, about 12 minutes. Stir in peas. Microwave on High 2 minutes or until liquid is absorbed. Grains should be pearly, with white outline visible.

MICROWAVE GOLDEN BARLEY

4 servings

- 2 cups water
- 1/2 cup pearl barley
- 1 tablespoon golden raisins
- 1 tablespoon coarsely chopped almonds
- 1 tablespoon coarsely chopped peanuts
- 1/4 cup chopped celery
- Pinch ground cardamom
- Salt and pepper, to taste

Per Serving
Calories: 121
% Calories from fat: 17
Fat (gm): 2.4
Sat. fat (gm): 0.3
Cholesterol (mg): 0
Sodium (mg): 9
Protein (gm): 3.5
Carbohydrate (gm): 22.6
Exchanges
Milk: 0.0
Vegetable: 0.0
Fruit: 0.0
Bread: 1.5
Meat: 0.0
Fat: 0.5

1. Heat water to boiling in l-quart microwave-safe dish; stir in barley. Cook on High 30 minutes, or until tender, stirring several times. Drain and stir in remaining ingredients, except salt and pepper. Season to taste with salt and pepper.

Tip: This can also be chilled, tossed with any desired dressing, and served as a salad.

BARLEY AND VEGETABLE SALAD

6 to 8 servings

- 1 1/2 cups water
- 3/4 cup quick-cooking barley
- Vinaigrette Dressing (recipe follows)
- 1 cup sliced carrots
- 1/2 cup sliced radishes
- 1/2 cup chopped red onion
- 1 can (13 1/4 ounces) baby lima beans, rinsed, drained
- 1/4 cup chopped parsley

Per Serving
Calories: 188
% Calories from fat: 24
Fat (gm): 5
Sat. fat (gm): 0.7
Cholesterol (mg): 0
Sodium (mg): 284
Protein (gm): 5.9
Carbohydrate (gm): 30.4

Exchanges
Milk: 0.0
Vegetable: 0.0
Fruit: 0.0
Bread: 2.0
Meat: 0.0
Fat: 1.0

1. Heat water to boiling in medium saucepan; stir in barley. Reduce heat and simmer until tender, about 10 minutes. Transfer barley to large bowl; stir in Vinaigrette Dressing. Let cool to room temperature; stir in remaining ingredients. Serve immediately, or refrigerate and serve chilled.

Vinaigrette Dressing

makes about 1/3 cup

- 2 tablespoons olive oil
- 3 tablespoons red wine vinegar
- 1 teaspoon dried dill weed
- 1 teaspoon chopped garlic
- 1/2 teaspoon salt
- 1/4 teaspoon pepper

1. Whisk all ingredients in small bowl.

GREEK-STYLE 5-WAY CHILI

8 servings (about 1 cup each)

- 12 ounces lean ground beef
- 1/2 cup chopped onion
- 1 teaspoon minced garlic
- 2 tablespoons chili powder
- 2 teaspoons dried oregano leaves
- 1 teaspoon ground cinnamon
- 1/2 teaspoon dried mint leaves
- 1 tablespoon unsweetened cocoa
- 1 can (28 ounces) diced tomatoes, undrained
- 1 can (15 ounces) garbanzo beans, rinsed, drained
- 1 can (15 ounces) dark red kidney beans, rinsed, drained
- 2 teaspoons honey
- 8 ounces macaroni, cooked, warm
- Sliced green onions and tops, crumbled feta cheese, sliced Greek olives, as garnish

Per Serving
Calories: 345
% Calories from fat: 22
Fat (gm): 8.3
Sat. fat (gm): 2.8
Cholesterol (mg): 28.6
Sodium (mg): 655
Protein (gm): 18.4
Carbohydrate (gm): 49.2

Exchanges
Milk: 0.0
Vegetable: 0.0
Fruit: 0.0
Bread: 3.5
Meat: 1.0
Fat: 1.0

1. Saute ground beef, onion, and garlic in large saucepan until ground beef is browned, about 5 minutes; add spices, herbs, and cocoa and cook 1 to 2 minutes longer.

2. Stir in tomatoes, beans, and honey; heat to boiling. Reduce heat and simmer, covered, 15 minutes; uncover and simmer until thickened, about 15 minutes.

3. Spoon chili over macaroni in bowls; garnish with green onions, feta cheese, and olives.

ITALIAN-STYLE BEANS AND VEGETABLES

6 servings

- 1½ cups chopped onions
- 1½ cups chopped portobello mushrooms
- 3-4 tablespoons olive oil, divided
- 2 cups broccoli florets and sliced stems
- 1 cup sliced yellow summer squash
- 1 can (15 ounces) garbanzo beans, rinsed, drained
- 1 can (15 ounces) red kidney beans, rinsed, drained
- 1 can (14½ ounces) diced tomatoes with roasted garlic, undrained
- 1 teaspoon dried basil leaves
- ¼-½ teaspoon crushed red pepper
- Salt and pepper, to taste
- 1½ packages (16-ounce size) prepared polenta, cut into 12 slices

Per Serving
Calories: 673
% Calories from fat: 14
Fat (gm): 10.3
Sat. fat (gm): 1.1
Cholesterol (mg): 0
Sodium (mg): 582
Protein (gm): 18.8
Carbohydrate (gm): 129.7

Exchanges
Milk: 0.0
Vegetable: 3.0
Fruit: 0.0
Bread: 7.0
Meat: 0.0
Fat: 2.0

1. Saute onions and mushrooms in 2 tablespoons of oil in large saucepan for 5 minutes. Add broccoli and squash; cook, covered, over medium heat 2 to 3 minutes.

2. Stir in beans, tomatoes with liquid, basil, and crushed red pepper; heat to boiling. Reduce heat and simmer, covered, until broccoli is crisp-tender, 5 to 8 minutes. Season to taste with salt and pepper.

3. Saute slices of polenta in large skillet according to package directions, using remaining olive oil as needed. Serve bean mixture over polenta slices.

BASIC POLENTA

6 servings (about 1/2 cup each)

3 cups water
3/4 cup yellow cornmeal
Salt and pepper, to taste

Per Serving
Calories: 55
% Calories from fat: 9
Fat (gm): 0.5
Sat. fat (gm): 0.1
Cholesterol (mg): 0
Sodium (mg): 5
Protein (gm): 1.2
Carbohydrate (gm): 11.7

Exchanges
Milk: 0.0
Vegetable: 0.0
Fruit: 0.0
Bread: 1.0
Meat: 0.0
Fat: 0.0

1. In medium saucepan, heat water to boiling; gradually stir in cornmeal. Cook over medium to medium-low heat, stirring constantly, until polenta thickens enough to hold its shape but is still soft, 5 to 8 minutes. Season to taste with salt and pepper.

Variations: **Blue Cheese Polenta**—Stir 1/2 cup (2 ounces) crumbled blue cheese, *or* other blue veined cheese, into the cooked polenta.

Goat Cheese Polenta—Stir 1/4 to 1/2 cup (1 to 2 ounces) crumbled goat cheese into the cooked polenta.

Garlic Polenta—Saute 1/4 cup finely chopped onion and 4 to 6 cloves minced garlic in 1 tablespoon olive oil; add water, as above and complete recipe.

MICROWAVE DOUBLE-CORN POLENTA

4 servings

2 cups Chicken Stock (see p. 47) *or* reduced-sodium fat-free chicken broth
Pinch salt
1/4 teaspoon cayenne pepper
1/2 teaspoon dried thyme leaves
1/2 teaspoon dried oregano leaves
1/2 cup yellow cornmeal
1/2 cup whole kernel corn
1 tablespoon olive oil

Per Serving
Calories: 173
% Calories from fat: 28
Fat (gm): 5.8
Sat. fat (gm): 1.3
Cholesterol (mg): 7.5
Sodium (mg): 87
Protein (gm): 6.6
Carbohydrate (gm): 25.4

Exchanges
Milk: 0.0
Vegetable: 0.0
Fruit: 0.0
Bread: 2.0
Meat: 0.0
Fat: 1.0

2 tablespoons grated Parmesan cheese
Pepper, to taste
1/4 cup sliced pimientos, as garnish

1. Place Chicken Stock, salt, cayenne pepper, and herbs in 2-quart microwave-safe bowl; microwave on High 4 to 6 minutes, until boiling. Gradually stir in cornmeal, corn, and olive oil.

2. Microwave, uncovered, on High until liquid is absorbed, 12 to 15 minutes, stirring every 5 minutes. Stir in Parmesan cheese; season to taste with pepper. Spoon into serving dish and top with pimientos.

EGGPLANT POLENTA STACK

4 servings

8 slices (3/4-inch) eggplant (about 1 pound)
2 egg whites, lightly beaten, *or* 1/4 cup no-cholesterol egg product
1/2 cup Italian-seasoned dry bread crumbs
1/4 cup (1 ounce) grated Parmesan cheese
Olive oil cooking spray
1 package (16 ounces) prepared Italian-herb polenta, cut into 8 slices
8 slices (1/2-inch) tomato
Salt and pepper, to taste
2-4 ounces reduced-fat feta, *or* goat cheese, crumbled

Per Serving
Calories: 244
% Calories from fat: 21
Fat (gm): 5.8
Sat. fat (gm): 2.9
Cholesterol (mg): 34
Sodium (mg): 759
Protein (gm): 20.7
Carbohydrate (gm): 28.6
Exchanges
Milk: 0.0
Vegetable: 2.0
Fruit: 0.0
Bread: 1.0
Meat: 2.0
Fat: 0.0

1. Dip eggplant slices in egg whites and coat with combined bread crumbs and Parmesan cheese. Spray large skillet with cooking spray and heat over medium heat until hot. Cook eggplant until browned on the bottom, about 10 minutes; spray tops of slices with cooking spray and turn. Cook until eggplant is tender and browned on other side, about 10 minutes longer.

2. Arrange eggplant in baking pan; top each with a slice of polenta and tomato. Sprinkle tomatoes with salt and pepper; sprinkle with feta cheese.

3. Bake at 450 degrees until tomatoes are hot and cheese lightly browned, about 10 minutes.

CAJUN GRITS WITH BLACKEYE SALSA

4 servings (about 3/4 cup each)

- 2 cups water
- 1 tablespoon chopped jalapeño chili
- 1/2 teaspoon ground cumin
- 1/2 teaspoon salt
- 2/3 cup quick-cooking grits
- 1 cup (4 ounces) light shredded Mexican cheese blend
- 1/2 can (15-ounce size) black-eyed peas, rinsed, drained, coarsely chopped
- Blackeye Salsa (recipe follows)

Per Serving
Calories: 299
% Calories from fat: 29
Fat (gm): 9.8
Sat. fat (gm): 6.1
Cholesterol (mg): 25
Sodium (mg): 959
Protein (gm): 14.2
Carbohydrate (gm): 39.7

Exchanges
Milk: 0.0
Vegetable: 2.0
Fruit: 0.0
Bread: 2.0
Meat: 1.0
Fat: 1.0

1. Combine water, jalapeño chili, cumin, and salt in medium saucepan; heat to boiling. Gradually stir in grits; reduce heat and simmer, stirring occasionally, until thickened, about 5 minutes. Stir in cheese and blackeyes. Spoon grits onto plates; spoon Blackeye Salsa over grits.

Blackeye Salsa

makes about 2 1/2 cups

- 1/2 can (15-ounce size) blackeyes, rinsed, drained, coarsely chopped
- 2 cups chopped tomatoes
- 3 tablespoons chopped onion
- 1 tablespoon minced jalapeño chili
- 1 tablespoon lime juice
- 1/2 teaspoon ground cumin
- 1/2 teaspoon salt

1. Combine all ingredients; let stand 20-30 minutes before serving.

CURRIED MICROWAVE LENTILS

10 servings

Per Serving
Calories: 50
% Calories from fat: 31
Fat (gm): 1.8
Sat. fat (gm): 0.3
Cholesterol (mg): 3
Sodium (mg): 14
Protein (gm): 2.7
Carbohydrate (gm): 5.5

Exchanges
Milk: 0.0
Vegetable: 0.0
Fruit: 0.0
Bread: 0.5
Meat: 0.0
Fat: 0.5

1 tablespoon olive oil
3 shallots, minced
1 medium carrot, chopped
2 cloves garlic, minced
3/4 cup dried lentils
3 cups Chicken Stock (see p. 47), *or* reduced-sodium fat-free chicken broth
1/2 teaspoon chopped gingerroot
1 teaspoon curry powder
2 ribs celery, finely chopped
Few dashes reduced-sodium soy sauce
Few dashes sesame oil
2 tablespoons fat-free plain yogurt, optional

1. Combine olive oil, shallots, carrot, and garlic in 2-quart microwave-safe casserole. Microwave on High 3 minutes, or until tender, stirring once. Add lentils, Chicken Stock, and gingerroot; cover with vented plastic wrap.

2. Microwave on High until lentils are tender, but not mushy, about 30 minutes, stirring several times. Drain excess liquid. Stir in curry powder, celery, soy sauce, sesame oil and yogurt, if using.

LENTIL AND RICE PILAF

6 servings

- 1 onion, chopped
- 1 small jalapeño chili, minced
- 1 clove garlic, minced
- 2 tablespoons olive oil
- 1 cup dried lentils, washed
- 4 1/2 cups water
- 1 cup chopped, peeled tomatoes
- 1 bay leaf
- 3/4 cup long grain rice
- Salt and pepper, to taste

Per Serving
Calories: 188
% Calories from fat: 24
Fat (gm): 5
Sat. fat (gm): 0.7
Cholesterol (mg): 0
Sodium (mg): 6
Protein (gm): 5.8
Carbohydrate (gm): 30.5
Exchanges
Milk: 0.0
Vegetable: 0.0
Fruit: 0.0
Bread: 2.0
Meat: 0.0
Fat: 1.0

1. Saute onion, jalapeño, and garlic in oil in medium saucepan until tender, about 5 minutes. Stir in lentils, water, tomatoes, and bay leaf; heat to boiling. Reduce heat and simmer, covered, 20 minutes, stirring occasionally.

2. Stir in rice and simmer 20 minutes longer, until rice is cooked and lentils are tender. Add additional water if necessary, and stir occasionally to prevent mixture from sticking to pan. Discard bay leaf; season to taste with salt and pepper.

PESOLE

8 servings

- 1 can (20 ounces) pesole (white hominy), drained
- 1 medium onion, chopped
- 1 tablespoon chili powder
- 3 cloves garlic, minced
- 2 tablespoons ground cumin
- 1 tablespoon dried oregano leaves
- 2 cups chopped peeled tomatoes, *or* 1 can (16 ounces) diced tomatoes, drained
- 1/2 teaspoon salt
- 1/4 teaspoon pepper

Per Serving
Calories: 81
% Calories from fat: 15
Fat (gm): 1.4
Sat. fat (gm): 0.1
Cholesterol (mg): 0
Sodium (mg): 300
Protein (gm): 2.2
Carbohydrate (gm): 16
Exchanges
Milk: 0.0
Vegetable: 1.5
Fruit: 0.0
Bread: 0.5
Meat: 0.0
Fat: 0.0

1. Combine all ingredients in large saucepan; add water to cover. Heat to boiling; reduce heat and simmer, covered, until tender, about 15 minutes. Uncovered and simmer until thickened, about 5 minutes.

BLACK BEANS AND RICE

4 servings (about 1 1/2 cups each) or 8 servings of about 3/4 cup each as side dish

- 1 cup chopped onion
- 1 cup chopped green bell pepper
- 2 teaspoons chopped garlic
- 1 1/2 teaspoons ground cumin
- 1 teaspoon dried thyme leaves
- 1/2 teaspoon crushed red pepper
- 1 bay leaf
- 1 tablespoon olive oil
- 1 cup rice
- 1 can (14 1/2 ounces) diced tomatoes with green chilies
- 1 can (15 ounces) black beans, rinsed, drained
- 2 cups water
- 1 tablespoon apple cider vinegar
- 1/2-1 teaspoon salt
- 1/2 teaspoon pepper

Per Serving
Calories: 235
% Calories from fat: 11
Fat (gm): 4.1
Sat. fat (gm): 0.6
Cholesterol (mg): 0
Sodium (mg): 863
Protein (gm): 10.3
Carbohydrate (gm): 62.9
Exchanges
Milk: 0.0
Vegetable: 0.0
Fruit: 0.0
Bread: 4.0
Meat: 0.0
Fat: 1.0

1. Saute onion, bell pepper, garlic, cumin, thyme, crushed red pepper, and bay leaf in olive oil until onion is tender, about 5 minutes. Stir in remaining ingredients. Heat to boiling; reduce heat and simmer, covered, until rice is tender, about 20 minutes. Let stand 5 minutes before serving. Discard bay leaf.

REFRIED BEANS

6 servings (about 1/2 cup each)

- 1 1/4 cups dried pinto beans
- Water
- Vegetable cooking spray
- 1 medium onion, coarsely chopped
- Salt and pepper, to taste

Per Serving
Calories: 106
% Calories from fat: 3
Fat (gm): 0.4
Sat. fat (gm): 0.1
Cholesterol (mg): 0
Sodium (mg): 2
Protein (gm): 6.1
Carbohydrate (gm): 20
Exchanges
Milk: 0.0
Vegetable: 0.0
Fruit: 0.0
Bread: 1.5
Meat: 0.0
Fat: 0.0

1. Wash and sort beans, discarding any stones. Cover beans with 2 inches of water in a large saucepan; heat to boiling and boil, uncovered, 2 minutes. Remove from heat; let stand, covered, 1 hour. Drain beans; cover with 2 inches of water and heat to boiling. Reduce heat and simmer, covered, until beans are tender, 1 1/2 to 2 hours. Drain, reserving 2 cups liquid.

2. Spray large skillet with cooking spray; heat over medium heat until hot. Saute onion until tender, 3 to 5 minutes. Add 1 cup beans and 1 cup reserved liquid to skillet. Cook over high heat, mashing beans until almost smooth with end of meat mallet or potato masher. Add half the remaining beans and liquid; continue cooking and mashing beans. Repeat with remaining beans and liquid. Season to taste with salt and pepper.

CREOLE BUTTER BEANS WITH CORNBREAD

8 servings

Per Serving
Calories: 292
% Calories from fat: 21
Fat (gm): 6.8
Sat. fat (gm): 1.6
Cholesterol (mg): 27.9
Sodium (mg): 1153
Protein (gm): 10.7
Carbohydrate (gm): 46.3
Exchanges
Milk: 0.0
Vegetable: 1.0
Fruit: 0.0
Bread: 3.0
Meat: 0.0
Fat: 1.0

- 1 onion, thinly sliced
- 1 green bell pepper, thinly sliced
- 1 rib celery, thinly sliced
- 1 small jalapeño chili, chopped
- 1 teaspoon chopped garlic
- 1 teaspoon dried thyme leaves
- 1 tablespoon vegetable oil
- 1 tablespoon flour
- 1 can (28 ounces) diced tomatoes, undrained
- 2 cans (15 ounces each) butter beans, rinsed, drained, divided
- 1/2-1 teaspoon Worcestershire sauce
- 1/4-1/2 teaspoon red pepper sauce
- 1/2 teaspoon salt
- 1 package (10 ounces) cornbread mix, prepared according to package directions, warm

1. Saute onion, bell pepper, celery, jalapeño, garlic, and thyme in oil in large saucepan until tender, about 8 minutes. Sprinkle with flour and cook until lightly browned, about 3 minutes.

2. Stir in tomatoes, beans, Worcestershire sauce, red pepper sauce, and salt. Heat to boiling; reduce heat and simmer until thickened, about 5 minutes. Serve over squares of cornbread.

RED BEANS, GREENS, AND RICE

4 servings (about 1 cup each)

- 3 slices bacon, diced
- 4 ounces turkey smoked sausage
- 3/4 cup chopped onion
- 3/4 cup chopped green bell pepper
- 1 teaspoon minced jalapeño chili
- 1/2 teaspoon minced garlic
- 1/3 cup cider vinegar
- 3 tablespoons sugar
- 1 1/2 tablespoons vegetable oil
- 1/2 teaspoon salt
- 1/2 teaspoon pepper
- 1 can (15 ounces) red beans, rinsed, drained
- 2 cups sliced kale, turnip, *or* mustard, greens
- 2 cups cooked rice, room temperature

Per Serving
Calories: 374
% Calories from fat: 25
Fat (gm): 10.8
Sat. fat (gm): 2.4
Cholesterol (mg): 21.6
Sodium (mg): 881
Protein (gm): 15
Carbohydrate (gm): 56.8

Exchanges
Milk: 0.0
Vegetable: 2.0
Fruit: 0.0
Bread: 3.0
Meat: 1.0
Fat: 1.0

1. Cook bacon in large skillet until beginning to brown, about 5 minutes; add smoked sausage and cook until browned, about 3 minutes. Add onion, bell pepper, jalapeño chili, and garlic; saute 2 to 3 minutes, until vegetables are crisp-tender.

2. Stir in vinegar, sugar, oil, salt, and pepper; heat to simmering. Stir in beans and cook until warm, 2 to 3 minutes. Stir in kale and cook until wilted, 2 to 3 minutes.

3. Spoon rice onto serving plates; spoon bean mixture over rice.

GINGER VEGETABLE STIR-FRY

4 servings

Per Serving
Calories: 311
% Calories from fat: 9
Fat (gm): 3.1
Sat. fat (gm): 0.5
Cholesterol (mg): 0
Sodium (mg): 621
Protein (gm): 12.4
Carbohydrate (gm): 59.4
Exchanges
Milk: 0.0
Vegetable: 3.0
Fruit: 0.0
Bread: 3.0
Meat: 0.0
Fat: 0.5

2 teaspoons vegetable oil
1 bunch green onions and tops, sliced
1 red bell pepper, sliced
1-2 tablespoons minced gingerroot
1 teaspoon minced garlic
3 cups thinly sliced Chinese cabbage
2 cups fresh bean sprouts, *or* canned bean sprouts, drained
1 can (15 ounces) butter beans, rinsed, drained
3/4 cup vegetable broth, reduced-sodium fat-free chicken broth, *or* water
1-2 tablespoons reduced-sodium tamari soy sauce
2 teaspoons cornstarch
3 cups cooked rice, warm

1. Heat oil in wok or large skillet over medium high heat until hot. Add green onions, bell pepper, gingerroot, and garlic and stir-fry 1 minute. Stir in Chinese cabbage, bean sprouts, and beans and stir-fry until cabbage is slightly wilted, about 3 minutes. Stir in combined broth, soy sauce, and cornstarch and heat to boiling. Serve over rice.

BEAN FRITTERS WITH GINGER TOMATO SAUCE

6 servings (4 fritters each)

Per Serving
Calories: 121
% Calories from fat: 15
Fat (gm): 2
Sat. fat (gm): 0.4
Cholesterol (mg): 35.4
Sodium (mg): 633
Protein (gm): 6
Carbohydrate (gm): 19.4

Exchanges
Milk: 0.0
Vegetable: 1.0
Fruit: 0.0
Bread: 1.0
Meat: 0.0
Fat: 0.5

- 1 can (15 ounces) black-eyed peas, rinsed, drained
- 1 egg
- 2 tablespoons chopped onion
- 2-3 teaspoons chopped gingerroot
- 1 tablespoon chopped jalapeño chili
- 1/2 teaspoon salt
- 1/4 cup plain dry bread crumbs
- 1/4 cup cornmeal
- Vegetable oil, for frying
- Ginger Tomato Dipping Sauce (recipe follows)

1. Process blackeyes, egg, onion, gingerroot, jalapeño chili, and salt in food processor or blender until smooth; transfer mixture to medium bowl. Stir in bread crumbs.

2. To shape fritters: roll 1 tablespoon blackeye mixture into a ball or oval shape; coat lightly with cornmeal. Repeat with remaining mixture.

3. Heat oil in medium saucepan to 350 degrees; fry fritters, 4 or 5 at a time, until browned, about 2 minutes. Drain on paper towels; keep warm in 200 degree oven until ready to serve.

4. Spoon Ginger Dipping Sauce in center of small plates; arrange fritters on sauce.

Ginger Tomato Dipping Sauce

makes about 3/4 cup

- 1/2 can (14 1/2-ounce size) diced tomatoes, undrained
- 2 cloves garlic
- 2 tablespoons chopped onion
- 1 tablespoon chopped jalapeño chili
- 1 tablespoon chopped gingerroot, *or* 1-2 teaspoons ground ginger
- 1/2 teaspoon salt
- 1 teaspoon vegetable oil

1. Process all ingredients, except oil, in food processor or blender until smooth; saute sauce in oil in small skillet until thickened, about 5 minutes.

Tip: Fritters may be rolled and coated several hours before cooking; refrigerate, covered.

MASHED POTATOES 'N BEANS WITH CHICKEN

8 servings (about 1/2 cup each)

- 2 cans (15 ounces each) navy, *or* Great Northern beans, rinsed, drained
- 3 cups cubed, peeled, Idaho potatoes
- 2 teaspoons minced garlic
- 1/2 cup fat-free milk, warm
- 2 cups (8 ounces) shredded reduced-fat Cheddar cheese
- Salt and pepper, to taste
- 1 pound Italian-style chicken breast strips, *or* cooked grilled chicken, cut into strips, warm

Per Serving
Calories: 373
% Calories from fat: 29
Fat (gm): 12.2
Sat. fat (gm): 7
Cholesterol (mg): 84.5
Sodium (mg): 862
Protein (gm): 34.5
Carbohydrate (gm): 32.3
Exchanges
Milk: 0.0
Vegetable: 0.0
Fruit: 0.0
Bread: 2.0
Meat: 4.0
Fat: 0.0

1. Combine beans, potatoes, and garlic in large saucepan; add water to cover. Heat to boiling; reduce heat and simmer, uncovered, until potatoes are tender, about 15 minutes. Drain; mash beans and potatoes in large mixer until smooth, adding milk gradually. Beat in cheese, beating until cheese melts. Season to taste with salt and pepper.

2. Spoon bean mixture onto serving plates; top each with 2 ounces chicken breast strips.

NANTUCKET BAKED BEANS

6 servings (about 1 1/4 cups each)

- 8 ounces smoked reduced-fat sausage, *or* linguica, diced
- 4 ounces ground beef round
- 1 cup chopped onion
- 2 teaspoons chopped garlic
- 2 cans (15 ounces each) kidney, *or* navy, beans, rinsed, drained
- 1 cup tomato sauce
- 1 cup reduced-sodium fat-free chicken broth
- 1/2 cup dry white wine, *or* reduced-sodium fat-free chicken broth
- 1/4 cup packed light brown sugar
- 1 1/2 teaspoons ground cumin
- 1 1/2 teaspoons dried oregano leaves
- 1/2 teaspoon salt
- 1 teaspoon pepper
- 2/3 cup fresh white bread crumbs

1. Saute sausage, ground beef, onion, and garlic in large skillet until meat is browned and onion is tender, about 10 minutes. Drain well.

2. Combine meat mixture and remaining ingredients, except bread crumbs, in 2 1/2-quart casserole. Bake at 350 degrees, uncovered, 1 hour. Sprinkle top of casserole with bread crumbs and bake until crumbs are lightly browned, 20 to 25 minutes.

Note: Linguica is a Portugese smoked sausage traditionally used in many dishes along coastal New England. It is spiced with garlic, cumin, and red pepper; chorizo or other smoked sausage can be substituted.

Per Serving
Calories: 286
% Calories from fat: 11
Fat (gm): 3.3
Sat. fat (gm): 1
Cholesterol (mg): 25.8
Sodium (mg): 1146
Protein (gm): 17.4
Carbohydrate (gm): 43.8

Exchanges
Milk: 0.0
Vegetable: 0.0
Fruit: 0.0
Bread: 3.0
Meat: 1.0
Fat: 0.0

BOSTON BAKED BEANS

8 servings (about 1 cup each)

- 1 pound dried navy beans
- 8 ounces sliced bacon, cubed
- 2 cups chopped onions
- 2 teaspoons minced garlic
- 1/3 cup unsulphured molasses
- 1/3 cup packed light brown sugar
- 2 teaspoons prepared mustard
- 1/2 teaspoon dry mustard
- 1/4 teaspoon ground allspice
- 2 bay leaves
- 2 teaspoons salt
- 1 teaspoon pepper

Per Serving
Calories: 442
% Calories from fat: 30
Fat (gm): 14.9
Sat. fat (gm): 5.1
Cholesterol (mg): 24.1
Sodium (mg): 1065
Protein (gm): 21.9
Carbohydrate (gm): 56.8
Exchanges
Milk: 0.0
Vegetable: 0.0
Fruit: 0.0
Bread: 4.0
Meat: 2.0
Fat: 1.0

1. Place beans in large saucepan with water to cover by 2 inches; heat to boiling and boil 2 minutes. Let stand, covered, 1 hour; drain. Return beans to pan and enough water to come to the top of the beans; heat to boiling. Reduce heat and simmer, covered, until tender but not soft, 30 to 40 minutes. Transfer beans and liquid to bean pot or 3-quart casserole.

2. Stir remaining ingredients into beans. Bake, covered, at 250 degrees 1 hour; uncover and bake until desired thickness, 4-6 hours, stirring every hour. Discard bay leaves.

BRAZILIAN BLACK BEAN BAKE

8 servings (about 1 cup each)

- 2 cups chopped onions
- 2 tablespoons minced jalapeño chili
- 2-4 teaspoons minced gingerroot, *or* 1-2 teaspoons ground ginger
- 4 cans (15 ounces each) black beans, rinsed, drained
- 2 cans (14 1/2 ounces each) diced tomatoes, undrained
- 1/3 cup honey

Per Serving
Calories: 290
% Calories from fat: 1
Fat (gm): 0.2
Sat. fat (gm): 0
Cholesterol (mg): 0
Sodium (mg): 1097
Protein (gm): 11.6
Carbohydrate (gm): 60.4
Exchanges
Milk: 0.0
Vegetable: 0.0
Fruit: 0.0
Bread: 4.0
Meat: 0.0
Fat: 0.0

- 1/3 cup packed light brown sugar
- 3/4 teaspoon dried thyme leaves
- 1 teaspoon salt
- 1/3 cup cubed mango
- 1/3 cup sliced banana

1. Combine all ingredients, except mango and banana, in 3-quart casserole. Bake at 350 degrees, covered, 30 minutes; uncover and bake to desired thickness, about 1 hour. Spoon mango and banana on beans before serving.

TUSCAN BAKED BEANS WITH SAUSAGE

6 servings (about 1 cup each)

- 1 pound turkey Italian sausage links
- 1/4 cup water
- 1 small red bell pepper, sliced
- 1 small green bell pepper, sliced
- 1 medium red onion, sliced
- 1 teaspoon minced garlic
- 1-2 tablespoons olive oil
- 1 can (15 ounces) red beans, rinsed, drained
- 1 can (15 ounces) Great Northern beans, rinsed, drained
- 1 can (14 1/2 ounces) diced tomatoes, undrained
- 1/4 cup dry red wine, optional
- 1 teaspoon dried sage leaves
- 1/2 teaspoon salt
- 1/4 teaspoon pepper

Per Serving
Calories: 277
% Calories from fat: 31
Fat (gm): 9.7
Sat. fat (gm): 2.1
Cholesterol (mg): 37.6
Sodium (mg): 1354
Protein (gm): 19.9
Carbohydrate (gm): 29.3

Exchanges
Milk: 0.0
Vegetable: 0.0
Fruit: 0.0
Bread: 2.0
Meat: 1.0
Fat: 1.5

1. Cook sausage in covered skillet over medium heat with 1/4 cup water until sausage is cooked through, about 8 minutes; uncover and continue cooking until sausage is browned, 3 to 5 minutes. Cool slightly; cut into 1/2-inch slices.

2. Cook bell peppers, onion, and garlic in oil in covered large skillet over medium heat until vegetables are tender and soft, but not browned, about 10 minutes.

3. Combine sausage, peppers, and remaining ingredients in 2-quart casserole. Bake, covered, at 350 degrees 30 minutes; uncover and bake to desired thickness, about 1 hour.

SPICY SOUTHWEST BAKED BEANS

4 servings (about 1 cup each)

- 1 cup chopped onion
- 1/2 cup chopped poblano chili, *or* green bell pepper
- 1 jalapeño chili, chopped
- 2 cloves garlic, chopped
- 1 tablespoon olive oil
- 2 cans (15 ounces each) pinto, *or* black, beans, rinsed, drained
- 1/2 cup beer, *or* reduced-sodium fat-free chicken broth
- 1/4 cup softened, sliced sun-dried tomatoes
- 1/4 cup packed light brown sugar
- 1 teaspoon ground cumin
- 1/2 teaspoon dried thyme leaves
- 1 bay leaf
- 1/2 teaspoon salt

Per Serving
Calories: 318
% Calories from fat: 15
Fat (gm): 5.6
Sat. fat (gm): 0.9
Cholesterol (mg): 0
Sodium (mg): 810
Protein (gm): 12.2
Carbohydrate (gm): 55.7
Exchanges
Milk: 0.0
Vegetable: 2.0
Fruit: 0.0
Bread: 3.0
Meat: 0.0
Fat: 1.0

1. Saute onion, chilies, and garlic in oil in large skillet until tender, about 8 minutes. Combine onion mixture and remaining ingredients in 1 1/2-quart casserole. Bake at 350 degrees, covered, 30 minutes; uncover and bake 15 to 20 minutes, or until liquid is nearly absorbed. Discard bay leaf.

TEN

Pasta Entrées

HOMEMADE PASTA

4 servings (entrée servings)

- 1½ cups all-purpose flour
- 2 large eggs

Per Serving
Calories: 208
% Calories from fat: 13
Fat (gm): 3
Sat. fat (gm): 0.8
Cholesterol (mg): 106.5
Sodium (mg): 32
Protein (gm): 8
Carbohydrate (gm): 36.1

Exchanges
Milk: 0.0
Vegetable: 0.0
Fruit: 0.0
Bread: 2.5
Meat: 0.0
Fat: 0.5

1. Mound flour on cutting board, making well in center. Drop eggs into center of well.

2. Break egg yolks and mix with a fork. While mixing eggs, gradually start to incorporate flour into eggs. As flour is incorporated, it will be necessary to move mound of flour toward center, using your hands. Continue mixing until all or almost all flour has been incorporated, forming soft, but not sticky, ball of dough.

3. Make noodles using one of the following methods.

Machine Kneading and Cutting

To knead dough using pasta machine, set machine rollers on widest setting. Cut dough into 2 equal pieces. Lightly flour outside of 1 piece, and pass it through machine. Fold piece of dough into thirds; pass it through machine again, inserting open edges (not the fold) of dough first. Repeat folding and rolling 8 to 12 times or until dough feels smooth and satiny; lightly flour dough only if it begins to feel sticky.

Move machine rollers to next widest setting. Pass dough (do not fold dough any longer) through rollers, beginning to roll out and stretch dough. Move machine rollers to next widest setting; pass dough through rollers. Continue to process until pasta is as thin as desired. (Often narrowest setting on machine makes pasta too thin; 1 or 2 settings from end is usually best.) Lightly flour dough if it begins to feel even slightly sticky at any time.

To cut dough using a pasta machine, set cutting rollers for width of pasta desired; pass dough through cutters. Arrange cut pasta in single layer on lightly floured surface.

Repeat above procedures with second piece of dough.

Hand Kneading and Cutting

To knead dough by hand, knead on lightly floured surface until dough is smooth and satiny, about 10 minutes. Cover dough lightly with damp towel and let rest 10 minutes.

Place dough on lightly floured surface. Starting in center of dough, roll with rolling pin from center to edge. Continue rolling, always from center to edge (to keep dough as round as possible) until dough is about 1/16-inch thick. Lightly flour dough if it begins to feel even slightly sticky at any time.

To cut dough by hand, flour top of dough lightly and roll up. Cut into desired width with sharp knife. Immediately unroll cut pasta to keep noodles from sticking together, and arrange in single layer on lightly floured surface.

4. Pasta can be cooked fresh, or it can be frozen or dried to be cooked later. To freeze pasta, place in heavy plastic freezer bag and freeze. To dry pasta, let stand on floured surface (or hang over rack) until completely dried. (Be sure pasta is completely dried or it will turn moldy in storage.) Store at room temperature in airtight container.

5. To cook fresh, frozen, or dried pasta, heat 4 to 5 quarts lightly salted (optional) water to boiling. Add pasta and begin testing for doneness as soon as water returns to boil. Cooking time will vary from 1 to 2 minutes once water has returned to boil.

FETTUCCINE WITH CHICKEN PICCATA

6 servings

- 6 chicken breast halves, boneless and skinless (about 3 ounces each)
- Flour
- Vegetable cooking spray
- 1 tablespoon margarine
- 2 tablespoons flour
- 1 can (14 1/2 ounces) reduced-sodium fat-free chicken broth
- 1/2 cup dry white wine, *or* reduced-sodium fat-free chicken broth
- 2 tablespoons lemon juice
- 1 tablespoon finely chopped parsley
- 2 teaspoons drained capers, optional
- 12 ounces cooked, warm fettuccine

Per Serving
Calories: 301
% Calories from fat: 18
Fat (gm): 6
Sat. fat (gm): 0.9
Cholesterol (mg): 43.4
Sodium (mg): 175
Protein (gm): 24.3
Carbohydrate (gm): 35

Exchanges
Milk: 0.0
Vegetable: 0.0
Fruit: 0.0
Bread: 2.5
Meat: 2.0
Fat: 0.0

1. Pound chicken with flat side of meat mallet to scant 1/4-inch thickness; coat lightly with flour. Spray large skillet with cooking spray; heat over medium heat until hot. Cook chicken over medium to medium-high heat until browned and no longer pink in center, 3 to 5 minutes. Remove chicken from skillet.

2. Melt margarine in skillet; stir in 2 tablespoons flour and cook over medium heat 1 to 2 minutes. Stir in chicken broth, wine, and lemon juice; heat to boiling. Boil, stirring constantly until slightly thickened, 1 to 2 minutes. Reduce heat and simmer, uncovered, until thickened to medium sauce consistency, about 15 minutes more. Stir in parsley and capers, if using.

3. Return chicken to sauce; cook over medium-low heat until chicken is hot through, 2 to 3 minutes. Serve chicken and sauce over pasta.

MICROWAVE FETTUCCINE ALFREDO

6 servings

1 cup 2% reduced-fat milk
2 tablespoons all-purpose flour
2 tablespoons margarine
1/2 teaspoon salt
3 cloves garlic, minced
1/4 cup (1 ounce) grated Parmesan cheese
1 pound fettuccine, cooked

Per Serving
Calories: 344
% Calories from fat: 20
Fat (gm): 7.3
Sat. fat (gm): 2.3
Cholesterol (mg): 6.3
Sodium (mg): 326
Protein (gm): 13.8
Carbohydrate (gm): 54
Exchanges
Milk: 0.0
Vegetable: 0.0
Fruit: 0.0
Bread: 3.5
Meat: 0.5
Fat: 1.5

1. Whisk all ingredients, except fettuccine, in 2-quart glass measure. Microwave at High, uncovered, 2 minutes. Whisk and microwave on High until thick, 2 to 3 minutes, whisking after each minute. Stir in pasta and microwave, loosely covered, 1 to 2 minutes until hot.

FETTUCCINE WITH PORK, GREENS, AND CARAMELIZED ONIONS

4 servings

4 medium onions, sliced
1 tablespoon olive oil
1 teaspoon sugar
2 cans (14 1/2-ounces) reduced-sodium fat-free chicken broth
2 cups kale, *or* mustard greens, *or* Swiss chard, thinly sliced
2 cups curly endive, *or* spinach, thinly sliced
1/4 teaspoon salt
1/4 teaspoon pepper
Olive oil cooking spray
12 ounces lean pork tenderloin, fat trimmed, cut into 1/4 inch slices
8 ounces fettuccine, cooked, warm

Per Serving
Calories: 389
% Calories from fat: 22
Fat (gm): 9.6
Sat. fat (gm): 1.6
Cholesterol (mg): 60.5
Sodium (mg): 345
Protein (gm): 30.5
Carbohydrate (gm): 46.9
Exchanges
Milk: 0.0
Vegetable: 3.0
Fruit: 0.0
Bread: 2.5
Meat: 2.0
Fat: 0.5

1. Saute onions in oil over medium heat in large skillet 5 minutes; reduce heat to low and stir in sugar. Cook until onions are golden in color and very soft, about 20 minutes. Stir chicken broth into onions; heat to boiling. Reduce heat and simmer, uncovered, until broth is reduced by one-third, about 10 minutes. Add greens; simmer, covered, until greens are wilted, 5 to 7 minutes. Simmer, uncovered, until broth is almost absorbed by greens, about 5 minutes. Stir in salt and pepper.

2. Spray large skillet with cooking spray; heat over medium heat until hot. Cook pork slices over medium to medium-high heat until browned and no longer pink in center, about 5 minutes.

3. Spoon onion mixture over pasta and toss; add pork and toss.

FETTUCCINE WITH SHRIMP AND ASPARAGUS PARMESAN

6 servings

- 1 cup sliced mushrooms
- 2 cloves garlic, minced
- 1 tablespoon margarine
- 1 cup asparagus spears, diagonally sliced
- 18 large shrimp, peeled, deveined, cooked
- 1 egg white
- 1/4 cup low-fat yogurt
- 1/2-3/4 cup fat-free milk
- 1/2 cup (2 ounces) grated Parmesan cheese
- 1 pound fettuccine, cooked, warm
- Salt and pepper, to taste
- 2 tablespoons parsley, minced

Per Serving
Calories: 326
% Calories from fat: 19
Fat (gm): 7.2
Sat. fat (gm): 2
Cholesterol (mg): 39.9
Sodium (mg): 371
Protein (gm): 20.6
Carbohydrate (gm): 47

Exchanges
Milk: 0.0
Vegetable: 0.0
Fruit: 0.0
Bread: 3.0
Meat: 2.0
Fat: 0.0

1. Saute mushrooms and garlic in margarine in medium skillet 3 to 4 minutes; add asparagus and saute until crisp-tender, 3 to 4 minutes. Add shrimp and cook 2 to 3 minutes, until warm. Cover and remove from heat.

2. Mix egg white, yogurt, milk and Parmesan cheese until smooth in small saucepan; heat over medium-low heat until warm, 3 to 4 minutes. Spoon sauce over fettuccine and toss; add shrimp mixture and toss. Season to taste with salt and pepper; sprinkle with parsley.

FETTUCCINE AND SHRIMP À LA GRECQUE

4 servings

Vegetable cooking spray
1/4 cup chopped onion
2 teaspoons minced garlic
2 teaspoons dried oregano leaves
1 teaspoon dried basil leaves
1 1/2 cups low-sodium tomato sauce
3/4 pound medium shrimp, shelled and deveined, cooked
3 ounces feta cheese, cut into 1/2-inch pieces
Salt and pepper, to taste
12 ounces fettuccine, cooked
Parsley, as garnish

Per Serving
Calories: 415
% Calories from fat: 18
Fat (gm): 8.4
Sat. fat (gm): 3.4
Cholesterol (mg): 149.3
Sodium (mg): 553
Protein (gm): 29.9
Carbohydrate (gm): 56.5
Exchanges
Milk: 0.0
Vegetable: 2.0
Fruit: 0.0
Bread: 3.5
Meat: 2.0
Fat: 0.0

1. Spray medium saucepan with cooking spray; heat over medium heat until hot. Saute onion and garlic until tender, 2 to 3 minutes. Stir in herbs and cook 1 minute longer. Stir in tomato sauce and shrimp; cook, covered, until hot through, about 5 minutes. Stir in cheese; season to taste with salt and pepper. Serve sauce over fettucinne; sprinkle with parsley.

SPINACH-MUSHROOM LASAGNE

8 servings

1 cup diced green onions
3 cloves garlic, crushed
2 cups sliced mushrooms
2 tablespoons olive oil
2 pounds spinach leaves, stems removed
1 teaspoon dried oregano leaves
1/4 teaspoon cayenne pepper
1 cup low-fat cottage cheese
1/2 cup (2 ounces) grated Parmesan cheese
1 cup chopped pimientos

Per Serving
Calories: 331
% Calories from fat: 25
Fat (gm): 10
Sat. fat (gm): 2.6
Cholesterol (mg): 10.2
Sodium (mg): 404
Protein (gm): 19.4
Carbohydrate (gm): 47.2
Exchanges
Milk: 0.0
Vegetable: 1.0
Fruit: 0.0
Bread: 3.0
Meat: 1.0
Fat: 1.0

1 cup chopped Italian parsley
1 pound uncooked lasagne noodles, *or* spinach lasagne noodles, cooked, drained
1/2 cup (2 ounces) shredded mozzarella cheese

1. Saute green onions, garlic, and mushrooms in oil in large skillet, 3 minutes. Add spinach, oregano, and cayenne pepper; cook, covered, 5 minutes. Remove from heat. Combine cottage cheese, Parmesan cheese, pimientos and parsley in bowl.

2. Place a layer of noodles in bottom of 13 x 9-inch baking pan. Spoon 1/3 of spinach mixture over noodles; spoon 1/3 of cheese mixture over spinach mixture. Repeat layers 2 times, ending with cheese mixture.

3. Bake at 350 degrees, loosely covered with aluminum foil, until hot through, about 1 hour; remove foil and sprinkle with mozzarella cheese during last 15 minutes baking time.

ITALIAN SAUSAGE LASAGNE

8 servings

2 cups fat-free ricotta cheese
1/4 cup (1 ounce) grated Parmesan cheese
3 cups (12 ounces) shredded reduced-fat mozzarella cheese
Tomato Sauce with Italian Sausage (recipe follows)
12 lasagne noodles (10 ounces), cooked, room temperature

Per Serving
Calories: 375
% Calories from fat: 30
Fat (gm): 12.9
Sat. fat (gm): 6
Cholesterol (mg): 47.3
Sodium (mg): 679
Protein (gm): 31.3
Carbohydrate (gm): 33.9

Exchanges
Milk: 0.0
Vegetable: 2.5
Fruit: 0.0
Bread: 1.5
Meat: 3.5
Fat: 0.5

1. Combine cheeses in bowl. Spread 1 cup Tomato Sauce with Italian Sausage on bottom of 13 x 9-inch baking pan; top with 4 lasagne noodles, overlapping slightly. Spoon one-third of cheese mixture over noodles, spreading lightly with rubber spatula. Top with 1 cup Tomato Sauce with Italian Sausage. Repeat layers 2 times, ending with layer of noodles, cheese, and remaining Tomato Sauce with Italian Sausage.

2. Bake at 350 degrees, loosely covered with aluminum foil, until sauce is bubbly, about 1 hour.

Tomato Sauce with Italian Sausage

makes about 4 1/2 cups

- Olive oil cooking spray
- 2 cups chopped onions
- 3 cloves garlic, minced
- 1 teaspoon dried basil leaves
- 1 teaspoon dried tarragon leaves
- 1 teaspoon dried thyme leaves
- 2 cans (16 ounces) low-sodium whole tomatoes, undrained, coarsely chopped
- 2 cans (8 ounces) low-sodium tomato sauce
- 1 cup water
- 1 teaspoon sugar
- 8 ounces turkey Italian sausage, cooked, drained
- 1/4 teaspoon salt
- 1/4 teaspoon black pepper

1. Spray large saucepan with cooking spray; heat over medium heat until hot. Saute onions and garlic until tender, about 5 minutes; stir in herbs and cook 1 to 2 minutes more.

2. Add tomatoes and liquid, tomato sauce, and water; heat to boiling. Reduce heat and simmer, uncovered, until sauce is reduced to about 4 1/2 cups, 15 to 20 minutes. Stir in sugar, sausage, salt, and pepper.

MACARONI AND BEANS MARINARA

6 servings

2 cloves garlic, minced
2 tablespoons olive oil
2 cups Marinara Sauce (see p. 509)
1 teaspoon dried oregano leaves
1 teaspoon garlic powder
1 can (16 ounces) cannellini, *or* Great Northern, beans
1/2 pound elbow macaroni, cooked
Salt and pepper, to taste
Chopped parsley, as garnish
Grated Parmesan cheese, as garnish

Per Serving
Calories: 306
% Calories from fat: 27
Fat (gm): 9.9
Sat. fat (gm): 2
Cholesterol (mg): 3.8
Sodium (mg): 365
Protein (gm): 13.5
Carbohydrate (gm): 47.2
Exchanges
Milk: 0.0
Vegetable: 1.0
Fruit: 0.0
Bread: 3.0
Meat: 0.5
Fat: 1.0

1. Saute garlic in oil in medium saucepan until golden; add Marinara Sauce and heat to boiling. Reduce heat and simmer, 10 minutes. Stir in oregano, garlic powder, and beans; simmer 5 minutes longer. Stir in macaroni; season to taste with salt and pepper. Spoon into serving bowl; sprinkle with parsley and Parmesan cheese.

CREAMY MACARONI AND CHEESE

6 servings

1/4 cup finely chopped onion
2 tablespoons margarine
3 tablespoons flour
1 bay leaf
2 1/2 cups fat-free milk
3/4 cup (3 ounces) shredded reduced-fat American cheese
3/4 cup (3 ounces) shredded reduced-fat Cheddar cheese
1 teaspoon Dijon-style mustard
1/4 teaspoon pepper

Per Serving
Calories: 330
% Calories from fat: 28
Fat (gm): 10
Sat. fat (gm): 4
Cholesterol (mg): 18.5
Sodium (mg): 559
Protein (gm): 17.4
Carbohydrate (gm): 42
Exchanges
Milk: 0.5
Vegetable: 0.0
Fruit: 0.0
Bread: 2.5
Meat: 1.0
Fat: 1.0

10 ounces fusilli, *or* rotini (corkscrews), cooked
2 tablespoons grated Parmesan cheese

1. Saute onion in margarine in medium saucepan until tender, 2 to 3 minutes. Stir in flour and bay leaf and cook 1 to 2 minutes, stirring frequently. Stir in milk; heat to boiling. Boil until thickened, stirring constantly (sauce will be thin). Remove from heat; discard bay leaf. Stir in American and Cheddar cheeses, mustard, and pepper.

2. Mix sauce and pasta in 1-quart casserole; sprinkle with Parmesan cheese. Bake, uncovered, at 350 degrees until hot through and lightly browned on top, about 30 minutes.

MACARONI WITH OLIVE AND TOMATO SAUCE

6 servings

1 medium red onion, finely chopped
2 tablespoons olive oil
2 cups chopped, peeled tomato
4 thin curls of orange rind, grated
1 clove garlic, minced
1-2 cups water
1/2 cup dry red wine, *or* tomato juice
1/2 cup sliced pitted Kalamata olives
2 tablespoons drained capers
3 tablespoons chopped parsley
1 teaspoon dried thyme leaves
Pepper, to taste
1 pound macaroni, cooked, warm

Per Serving
Calories: 454
% Calories from fat: 28
Fat (gm): 14.3
Sat. fat (gm): 1.7
Cholesterol (mg): 0
Sodium (mg): 818
Protein (gm): 11.4
Carbohydrate (gm): 68.5
Exchanges
Milk: 0.0
Vegetable: 1.0
Fruit: 0.0
Bread: 4.0
Meat: 0.0
Fat: 3.0

1. Saute onion in oil in large saucepan until translucent, stirring with wooden spoon. Add tomatoes, orange rind, garlic, and 1 cup water; heat to boiling. Reduce heat simmer, covered, until sauce thickens, about 5 minutes, adding more water if necessary. Add wine and simmer, loosely covered, about 30 minutes. Add olives, capers, herbs and pepper; simmer 10 minutes more. Serve with macaroni.

CHICKEN-VEGETABLE MANICOTTI WITH SPINACH SAUCE

4 servings (3 manicotti each)

Per Serving
Calories: 459
% Calories from fat: 15
Fat (gm): 7.8
Sat. fat (gm): 2
Cholesterol (mg): 51.4
Sodium (mg): 596
Protein (gm): 36.3
Carbohydrate (gm): 60.7
Exchanges
Milk: 0.0
Vegetable: 3.0
Fruit: 0.0
Bread: 3.0
Meat: 3.0
Fat: 0.0

Olive oil cooking spray
1/2 cup chopped onion
3 cloves garlic, minced
2 cups chopped spinach leaves
1/2 cup chopped zucchini
1/2 cup chopped yellow summer squash
1 teaspoon dried basil leaves
1 teaspoon dried oregano leaves
8 ounces cooked boneless, skinless chicken, finely shredded
1/2 cup fat-free ricotta cheese
1/4 teaspoon salt
1/4 teaspoon pepper
1 package (8 ounces) manicotti, cooked
Spinach Sauce (recipe follows)

1. Spray large skillet with cooking spray; heat over medium heat until hot. Saute onion and garlic until tender, about 3 minutes. Add remaining vegetables; saute until tender, 5 to 8 minutes. Stir in herbs and cook 2 minutes more. Stir in chicken, cheese, salt, and pepper.

2. Spoon about 3 tablespoons chicken-vegetable mixture into each manicotti; arrange in baking pan. Spoon Spinach Sauce over manicotti. Bake at 350 degrees, loosely covered with aluminum foil, until manicotti are hot through and sauce is bubbly, 35 to 40 minutes.

Spinach Sauce

makes about 2 1/2 cups

2 cloves garlic, minced
1 tablespoon margarine
1/4 cup all-purpose flour
2 cups 1% reduced-fat milk
1 pound fresh spinach, chopped
2 teaspoons dried basil leaves

1/8 teaspoon ground nutmeg
4 dashes red pepper sauce
1/4 teaspoon salt

1. Saute garlic in margarine in large saucepan 1 to 2 minutes. Stir in flour and cook over medium heat 1 to 2 minutes more. Stir in milk; heat to boiling. Boil, stirring constantly, until thickened, 1 to 2 minutes.

2. Stir spinach and remaining ingredients into sauce. Cook, uncovered, over medium heat until spinach is cooked, 5 to 7 minutes.

SPINACH AND ZUCCHINI MOSTACCIOLI CASSEROLE

8 servings

1 package (10 ounces) frozen chopped spinach
1 cup chopped onion
2 cloves garlic, minced
2 teaspoons vegetable oil
1 pound zucchini, cut into 1-inch pieces
2 cans (14 1/2-ounces each) diced tomatoes, undrained
3 tablespoons tomato paste
1 1/2 teaspoons dried basil leaves
3/4 teaspoon dried oregano leaves
1/4 teaspoon crushed red pepper flakes
10 ounces mostaccioli, cooked
1/2 cup (2 ounces) grated Parmesan cheese, divided

Per Serving
Calories: 210
% Calories from fat: 18
Fat (gm): 4.4
Sat. fat (gm): 1.5
Cholesterol (mg): 4.9
Sodium (mg): 361
Protein (gm): 9.9
Carbohydrate (gm): 34.2
Exchanges
Milk: 0.0
Vegetable: 2.0
Fruit: 0.0
Bread: 2.0
Meat: 0.0
Fat: 0.5

1. Drain spinach on paper towels, squeezing until almost dry.

2. Saute onion and garlic in oil in large saucepan until tender, about 5 minutes. Add zucchini; cook until zucchini is just limp, about 4 minutes. Stir in tomatoes and liquid, tomato paste, and herbs. Heat to boiling; reduce heat and simmer, uncovered, 5 minutes, stirring occasionally.

3. Combine pasta, spinach, zucchini mixture, and 1/4 cup Parmesan cheese in bowl. Spoon into greased 13 x 9-inch baking pan; sprinkle with remaining 1/4 cup cheese. Bake at 350 degrees, uncovered, 20 minutes.

PASTA PRIMAVERA

6 servings

1 cup broccoli florets
1 cup cauliflower florets
1 cup quartered artichoke hearts
1 cup cut asparagus spears (1-inch pieces)
1 cup chopped green bell pepper
2 cloves garlic, chopped
1/2 teaspoon dried oregano leaves
1/2 teaspoon dried basil leaves
1/4 cup olive oil
1 cup halved cherry tomatoes
1 pound fettuccine, cooked, warm
1/2 cup (2 ounces) grated Parmesan cheese

Per Serving
Calories: 393
% Calories from fat: 32
Fat (gm): 14.7
Sat. fat (gm): 2.9
Cholesterol (mg): 6.6
Sodium (mg): 322
Protein (gm): 16.7
Carbohydrate (gm): 53.6

Exchanges
Milk: 0.0
Vegetable: 2.0
Fruit: 0.0
Bread: 3.0
Meat: 0.5
Fat: 2.0

1. Saute broccoli, cauliflower, artichoke hearts, asparagus, bell pepper, garlic, and herbs in oil in large skillet until crisp-tender, 8 to 10 minutes. Toss vegetables and tomatoes with pasta. Sprinkle with Parmesan cheese.

PASTA SANTA FE

4 servings

1 medium onion, sliced
3 cloves garlic, minced
2 tablespoons vegetable oil
2 medium zucchini, sliced
2 medium tomatoes, cut into wedges
2 poblano chilis, sliced
1 cup canned, *or* frozen, thawed, whole kernel corn
2 tablespoons chili powder
1 teaspoon dried oregano leaves
1/2 teaspoon ground cumin

Per Serving
Calories: 350
% Calories from fat: 24
Fat (gm): 9.6
Sat. fat (gm): 1.2
Cholesterol (mg): 0
Sodium (mg): 327
Protein (gm): 11.6
Carbohydrate (gm): 58

Exchanges
Milk: 0.0
Vegetable: 2.0
Fruit: 0.0
Bread: 3.0
Meat: 0.0
Fat: 2.0

- 2 tablespoons minced cilantro *or* parsley
- 1/2 teaspoon salt
- 1/4 teaspoon pepper
- 8 ounces trio maliano (combination of corkscrews, shells, and rigatoni), cooked, warm

1. Saute onion and garlic in oil in large skillet until tender, about 5 minutes. Add remaining vegetables, chili powder, oregano, and cumin. Cook, uncovered, over medium to medium-low heat until vegetables are crisp-tender, 12 to 15 minutes. Stir in cilantro, salt, and pepper. Spoon vegetable mixture over pasta and toss.

PASTA WITH TOMATO, EGGPLANT, AND BELL PEPPER SAUCE

6 servings

- 1 large eggplant, unpeeled, cut into bite-size cubes
- 4 large red bell peppers, cut into bite-size pieces
- 2 tablespoons olive oil
- 10 medium tomatoes (about 2 pounds), peeled, seeded, coarsely chopped
- 1/2 teaspoon crushed red pepper flakes
- 1 tablespoon herbes de Provence
- 1 pound rotini, cooked, warm

Per Serving
Calories: 370
% Calories from fat: 18
Fat (gm): 7.4
Sat. fat (gm): 1
Cholesterol (mg): 0
Sodium (mg): 29
Protein (gm): 12.7
Carbohydrate (gm): 65.7

Exchanges
Milk: 0.0
Vegetable: 2.0
Fruit: 0.0
Bread: 3.5
Meat: 0.0
Fat: 1.5

1. Saute eggplant and bell peppers in oil in large skillet 5 minutes; add tomatoes and herbs. Saute about 10 minutes, until tomatoes are soft. Simmer, covered, 30 minutes, stirring occasionally and adding water if sauce becomes too thick. Spoon sauce over pasta.

PASTA NIÇOISE

4 servings

3 cups cooked pasta, shells *or* twists
16 pitted black olives, sliced
2 cups green beans, cooked until crisp-tender
1/4 cup sliced scallions
1 tomato, diced
1/2 cup chopped parsley
1 can water-packed white albacore tuna, drained, flaked
Herb Dressing (recipe follows)

Per Serving
Calories: 251
% Calories from fat: 22
Fat (gm): 6.2
Sat. fat (gm): 0.9
Cholesterol (mg): 19
Sodium (mg): 351
Protein (gm): 18.1
Carbohydrate (gm): 31.9

Exchanges
Milk: 0.0
Vegetable: 1.0
Fruit: 0.0
Bread: 2.0
Meat: 1.5
Fat: 0.0

1. Toss all ingredients in large serving bowl.

Herb Dressing

makes about 1/3 cup

1/4 cup tarragon vinegar
2-4 tablespoons water
2 teaspoons canola, *or* safflower, oil
1 large clove garlic, crushed
1/2 teaspoon Dijon-style mustard
1 teaspoon dried oregano leaves
Pepper, to taste

1. Mix all ingredients.

PASTA PUTTANESCA

6 servings

- 1/2 cup minced onion
- 2 tablespoons minced garlic
- 2 tablespoons olive oil
- 2 1/2 cups chopped, peeled, seeded tomatoes
- 1 teaspoon crushed red pepper flakes
- 1 tablespoon drained capers
- 1 cup pitted Kalamata olives
- 1 pound spaghetti, cooked, warm
- 2 tablespoons minced parsley

Per Serving
Calories: 399
% Calories from fat: 21
Fat (gm): 9.4
Sat. fat (gm): 1.3
Cholesterol (mg): 0
Sodium (mg): 627
Protein (gm): 11.6
Carbohydrate (gm): 67.9
Exchanges
Milk: 0.0
Vegetable: 1.0
Fruit: 0.0
Bread: 4.0
Meat: 0.0
Fat: 2.0

1. Saute onion and garlic in oil until tender in medium saucepan, 3 to 4 minutes. Add tomatoes; simmer, covered, 10 minutes. Add pepper flakes, capers and olives; cook 1 minute. Toss mixture with pasta; sprinkle with parsley.

PASTA WITH SEAFOOD SAUCE

6 servings

- 1 medium onion, chopped
- 2 cloves garlic, minced
- 2 tablespoons olive oil
- 1/2 cup dry white wine
- 2 cups diced, peeled, seeded tomatoes
- 1 teaspoon dried oregano leaves
- 1 tablespoon dried basil leaves
- 1 teaspoon dried thyme leaves
- 1 cup chopped fresh Italian parsley
- 3 cups fresh seafood (mussels, clams, shrimp, crabmeat, lobster, cod, bass, *or* swordfish), chopped
- 1 pound linguine, cooked

Per Serving
Calories: 374
% Calories from fat: 22
Fat (gm): 9.3
Sat. fat (gm): 1
Cholesterol (mg): 21
Sodium (mg): 351
Protein (gm): 20.2
Carbohydrate (gm): 51.1
Exchanges
Milk: 0.0
Vegetable: 1.0
Fruit: 0.0
Bread: 3.0
Meat: 1.5
Fat: 1.0

1. Saute onion and garlic in olive oil in large saucepan 2 minutes; add white wine and simmer, covered, 5 minutes. Add tomatoes and herbs with parsley; simmer, covered, 5 minutes. Add seafood and cook, covered, until mussels and clams open, shrimp turns pink, and seafood flakes with a fork, 5 to 8 minutes. Discard any unopened clams and mussels. Serve over pasta.

PENNE WITH SAUSAGE, GOAT CHEESE, AND TOMATO RELISH

4 servings

Vegetable cooking spray
3/4 pound Italian turkey sausage
2 cups frozen, thawed petite peas
1 pound penne, cooked, warm
Tomato Relish (recipe follows)
1/4 cup crumbled goat cheese

Per Serving
Calories: 741
% Calories from fat: 29
Fat (gm): 23.9
Sat. fat (gm): 5.7
Cholesterol (mg): 82.3
Sodium (mg): 658
Protein (gm): 35.9
Carbohydrate (gm): 94.4
Exchanges
Milk: 0.0
Vegetable: 1.0
Fruit: 0.0
Bread: 6.0
Meat: 2.0
Fat: 4.0

1. Spray medium skillet with cooking spray; heat over medium heat until hot. Add sausage and cook until browned, about 5 minutes, crumbling with a fork. Add peas; cook over medium heat until hot. Toss with penne; add Tomato Relish and toss. Sprinkle with goat cheese.

Tomato Relish

4 ripe red tomatoes, peeled, seeded, chopped
1 tablespoon finely minced shallots *or* scallions
1/2 teaspoon red wine vinegar
1 tablespoon olive oil
8 basil leaves, chopped
Salt and pepper, to taste
2 tablespoons minced parsley

1. Combine tomatoes, shallots, vinegar, oil, and basil leaves in bowl. Let stand 10 minutes to blend flavors; drain well. Season to taste with salt and pepper; stir in parsley.

CHICKEN AND SWEET POTATO RAVIOLI WITH CURRY SAUCE

4 servings (4 ravioli each)

- 8 ounces baked chicken breast, boneless, skinless, and shredded
- 1 cup mashed sweet potatoes
- 2 small cloves garlic, minced
- 1/2 teaspoon ground ginger
- 1/4 teaspoon salt
- 1/4 teaspoon white pepper
- 32 wonton wrappers
- Water
- Curry Sauce (recipe follows)

Per Serving
Calories: 383
% Calories from fat: 13
Fat (gm): 5.5
Sat. fat (gm): 1.1
Cholesterol (mg): 37.2
Sodium (mg): 587
Protein (gm): 19.8
Carbohydrate (gm): 62.4
Exchanges
Milk: 0.0
Vegetable: 0.5
Fruit: 0.0
Bread: 4.0
Meat: 1.5
Fat: 0.0

1. Mix chicken, sweet potatoes, garlic, ginger, salt, and pepper. Spoon about 2 teaspoons chicken mixture onto wonton wrapper; brush edges of wrapper with water. Top with second wonton wrapper and press edges together to seal. Repeat with remaining wonton wrappers and chicken mixture.

2. Heat about 2 quarts water to boiling in large saucepan; add 4 to 6 ravioli. Reduce heat and simmer, uncovered, until ravioli float to surface and are al dente, 3 to 4 minutes. Remove ravioli with slotted spoon; repeat cooking procedure with remaining ravioli. Serve with Curry Sauce.

Curry Sauce

makes about 1 cup

- 2 tablespoons finely chopped onion
- 2 cloves garlic, minced
- 1 tablespoon margarine
- 1 tablespoon flour
- 2 teaspoons curry powder
- 1/8 teaspoon cayenne pepper
- 1 cup reduced-sodium fat-free chicken, *or* vegetable broth
- 2-4 tablespoons dry white wine, optional

1. Saute onion and garlic in margarine in small saucepan 2 to 3 minutes; stir in flour, curry powder, and pepper. Cook 1 minute more, stirring constantly. Stir chicken broth and wine if using, into saucepan; heat to boiling. Boil until sauce is thickened (sauce will be thin), stirring constantly.

SHRIMP AND ARTICHOKE RAVIOLI WITH TARRAGON SAUCE

4 servings (4 ravioli each)

Olive oil cooking spray
8 ounces shrimp, peeled, deveined, and finely chopped
1 can (14 ounces) artichoke hearts, drained, rinsed, and finely chopped
1 clove garlic, minced
1/4 teaspoon ground nutmeg
3 tablespoons dry white wine, *or* water
32 wonton wrappers
Water
Tarragon Sauce (recipe follows)

Per Serving
Calories: 331
% Calories from fat: 5
Fat (gm): 1.9
Sat. fat (gm): 0.4
Cholesterol (mg): 95.1
Sodium (mg): 719
Protein (gm): 20.4
Carbohydrate (gm): 53
Exchanges
Milk: 0.0
Vegetable: 2.0
Fruit: 0.0
Bread: 3.0
Meat: 1.0
Fat: 0.0

1. Spray large skillet with cooking spray; heat over medium heat until hot. Add shrimp, artichoke hearts, garlic, nutmeg, and wine. Cook over medium heat until shrimp are cooked and liquid is gone, about 5 minutes. Cool.

2. Place about 2 teaspoons shrimp mixture on wonton wrapper; brush edges of wrapper with water. Top with second wonton wrapper and press edges together to seal. Repeat with remaining wonton wrappers and shrimp mixture.

3. Heat about 2 quarts water to boiling in large saucepan; add 4 to 6 ravioli. Reduce heat and simmer, uncovered, until ravioli float to surface and are al dente, 3 to 4 minutes. Remove ravioli with slotted spoon; repeat cooking procedure with remaining ravioli. Serve with Tarragon Sauce.

Tarragon Sauce

makes about 1 cup

- 2 medium shallots, finely chopped
- 1 tablespoon finely chopped fresh, *or* 1/2 teaspoon dried, tarragon leaves
- 1/2 cup dry white wine, *or* reduced-sodium fat-free chicken broth
- 1 cup reduced-sodium fat-free chicken broth, divided
- 1 tablespoon flour
- 1/4 teaspoon salt
- 1/8 teaspoon ground white pepper

1. Heat shallots, tarragon, and wine to boiling in small saucepan; reduce heat and simmer, uncovered, until mixture is reduced to 1/4 cup.

2. Add 1/2 cup chicken broth; heat to boiling. Mix flour and remaining 1/2 cup chicken broth; stir into boiling mixture. Boil until thickened (sauce will be thin), stirring constantly. Stir in salt and pepper.

RIGATONI WITH VEGETABLES

8 servings

- 1 clove garlic, minced
- 1/2 cup chopped onion
- 3 carrots, minced
- 1 tablespoon chopped fresh parsley
- 2 tablespoons olive oil
- 1/4 head cabbage, shredded
- 1 zucchini, cubed
- 3 large tomatoes, peeled and cubed
- 1/2 cup Chicken Stock (see p. 47), *or* reduced-sodium fat-free chicken broth
- 1 tablespoon minced fresh basil
- 1/2 tablespoon minced fresh chervil
- 1 tablespoon minced fresh, *or* 1 teaspoon dried, oregano leaves

Per Serving
Calories: 349
% Calories from fat: 28
Fat (gm): 11.1
Sat. fat (gm): 4.3
Cholesterol (mg): 18.9
Sodium (mg): 333
Protein (gm): 16.9
Carbohydrate (gm): 46.3

Exchanges
Milk: 0.0
Vegetable: 1.5
Fruit: 0.0
Bread: 2.5
Meat: 1.0
Fat: 1.5

Salt and pepper, to taste
1 pound rigatoni, cooked, warm
1/2 cup (2 ounces) grated Romano cheese
1/2 cup (2 ounces) grated Parmesan cheese

1. Saute garlic, onion, carrots, and parsley in oil in large skillet until carrots are crisp-tender, about 8 minutes. Add cabbage, zucchini, tomatoes, Chicken Stock, and herbs. Heat to boiling; reduce heat and simmer, covered, stirring occasionally. Season to taste with salt and pepper. Pour sauce over pasta and toss; add cheeses and toss.

RIGATONI WITH ESCAROLE AND ITALIAN SAUSAGE

4 servings

Vegetable cooking spray
3/4 pound Italian turkey sausage, cut into scant 1/2-inch slices
1 head escarole, cut into1-inch long strips
2 cloves garlic, minced
1 pound rigatoni, cooked, warm
1/4 cup (1 ounce) grated Romano cheese
1/2-1 cup fresh bread crumbs

Per Serving
Calories: 628
% Calories from fat: 26
Fat (gm): 17.8
Sat. fat (gm): 3.7
Cholesterol (mg): 62.2
Sodium (mg): 669
Protein (gm): 30.5
Carbohydrate (gm): 85.8

Exchanges
Milk: 0.0
Vegetable: 1.0
Fruit: 0.0
Bread: 5.5
Meat: 2.0
Fat: 2.0

1. Spray large skillet with cooking spray; heat over medium heat until hot. Cook sausage over medium heat until brown and cooked through, about 10 minutes. Add escarole and garlic; saute 2 to 3 minutes. Cook, covered, until escarole is wilted, 2 to 3 minutes.

2. Toss sausage mixture, rigatoni, and cheese on oven-proof platter. Sprinkle with bread crumbs. Broil until bread crumbs are golden brown, about 1 minute.

MOSTACCIOLI WITH ITALIAN SAUSAGE AND FENNEL PESTO

6 servings

1 pound smoked Italian turkey sausage links, cut into 1/2-inch slices
1 1/2 cups thinly sliced fennel bulb, *or* celery
1 cup chopped onion
2 cloves garlic, minced
1 can (8 ounces) low-sodium whole tomatoes, drained and chopped
Fennel Pesto (recipe follows)
12 ounces mostaccioli, cooked,warm

Per Serving
Calories: 406
% Calories from fat: 29
Fat (gm): 13
Sat. fat (gm): 2.9
Cholesterol (mg): 48.2
Sodium (mg): 711
Protein (gm): 24.6
Carbohydrate (gm): 48.3
Exchanges
Milk: 0.0
Vegetable: 1.0
Fruit: 0.0
Bread: 2.5
Meat: 2.0
Fat: 2.0

1. Cook sausage in large skillet over medium heat until browned, 8 to 10 minutes. Remove sausage from skillet and drain on paper towels; drain excess fat from skillet.

2. Add fennel, onion, and garlic to skillet; saute until tender, 5 to 8 minutes. Stir in tomatoes and sausage; stir in Fennel Pesto. Heat to boiling; reduce heat and simmer, covered, about 15 minutes. Spoon sauce mixture over pasta and toss.

Fennel Pesto

makes about 1 1/3 cups

1 tablespoon fennel seeds
1 cup chopped fennel bulb, *or* celery
1/2 cup parsley, loosely packed
2 cloves garlic
14 walnut halves (about 1 ounce)
3 tablespoons water
1 tablespoon olive oil
1/4 cup (1 ounce) grated Parmesan cheese

1. Place fennel seeds in small bowl; pour hot water over to cover. Let stand 10 minutes; drain.

2. Process fennel, fennel seeds, parsley, and garlic in food processor or blender until finely chopped. Add walnuts, 3 tablespoons water, and oil; mix until walnuts are finely chopped. Stir in Parmesan cheese.

SPINACH-MUSHROOM ROTOLO WITH MARINARA SAUCE

6 servings

Olive oil cooking spray
2 cups sliced mushrooms
1 package (10 ounces) fresh spinach, washed and chopped
2 cloves garlic, minced
1 teaspoon dried basil leaves
1 teaspoon dried tarragon leaves
1/2 package (8-ounce size) reduced-fat cream cheese, room temperature
1/2 cup fat-free ricotta cheese
1/4 teaspoon salt
1/4 teaspoon pepper
12 lasagne noodles, cooked
Marinara Sauce (see p. 509)

Per Serving
Calories: 286
% Calories from fat: 30
Fat (gm): 10.3
Sat. fat (gm): 2.7
Cholesterol (mg): 8.7
Sodium (mg): 686
Protein (gm): 12.5
Carbohydrate (gm): 38
Exchanges
Milk: 0.0
Vegetable: 3.0
Fruit: 0.0
Bread: 1.5
Meat: 0.0
Fat: 2.0

1. Coat large skillet with cooking spray; heat over medium heat until hot. Cook mushrooms over medium heat, covered, until they release juices, 3 to 5 minutes. Add spinach, garlic, and herbs to skillet; cook, covered, until spinach is wilted, 2 to 3 minutes. Cook, uncovered, over medium to medium-high heat until liquid is gone, about 10 minutes; cool.

2. Combine cheeses, salt, and pepper in bowl; stir in mushroom mixture. Spread 3 to 4 tablespoons cheese mixture on each noodle; roll up and place in baking dish.

3. Spoon Marinara Sauce over rotolo. Bake at 350 degrees, loosely covered with aluminum foil, until rotoli are hot through and sauce is bubbly, 20 to 30 minutes.

RICOTTA-STUFFED SHELLS WITH SPINACH PESTO

4 servings (3 shells each)

Per Serving
Calories: 178
% Calories from fat: 24
Fat (gm): 4.7
Sat. fat (gm): 0.8
Cholesterol (mg): 7.2
Sodium (mg): 216
Protein (gm): 9.5
Carbohydrate (gm): 24.6
Exchanges
Milk: 0.0
Vegetable: 1.0
Fruit: 0.0
Bread: 1.5
Meat: 0.5
Fat: 0.5

Vegetable cooking spray
1/4 cup finely chopped onion
2 cloves garlic, minced
1/2 teaspoon dried basil leaves
1/2 cup chopped fresh spinach
3/4 cup low-fat ricotta cheese
1/4 teaspoon ground nutmeg
1/4 teaspoon salt
1/4 teaspoon black pepper
12 cooked conchiglie (jumbo pasta shells), about 4 ounces
Spinach Pesto (recipe follows)
2 tablespoons red, *or* green, bell peppers, roasted *or* raw, chopped
Basil sprigs, as garnish

1. Spray medium skillet with cooking spray; heat over medium heat until hot. Saute onion, garlic, and dried basil until onion is tender, 3 to 4 minutes. Add spinach; cook, covered, over medium heat until spinach is wilted, 3 to 5 minutes.

2. Blend spinach mixture into cheese; stir in nutmeg, salt, and pepper. Stuff mixture into shells; place in baking pan. Bake at 350 degrees, covered, until hot through, about 20 minutes.

3. Arrange shells on small serving plates; spoon Spinach Pesto over shells or serve on the side. Sprinkle with bell peppers; garnish with basil sprigs.

Spinach Pesto

makes about 1/2 cup

1 cup loosely packed spinach
3 tablespoons finely chopped fresh, *or* 1 tablespoon dried, basil leaves
1 clove garlic, minced
1 tablespoon grated Parmesan cheese
2 teaspoons olive oil
1 teaspoon fresh lemon juice

1. Process all ingredients in food processor or blender until smooth. Let stand 2 to 3 hours for flavors to blend, or refrigerate until serving time. Serve at room temperature.

SHELLS WITH FRESH TOMATO SAUCE

6 servings

1 medium onion, diced
3 cloves garlic, minced
2 teaspoons olive oil
5 tomatoes, chopped
3/4 cup dry white wine
Leaves from 1/2 bunch fresh basil, finely chopped
1 cup sliced mushrooms
1 tablespoon chopped fresh, *or* 1/2 teaspoon dried, marjoram leaves
Salt and pepper, to taste
12 ounces no-egg pasta shells, cooked, warm
1 tablespoon grated Parmesan cheese

Per Serving
Calories: 267
% Calories from fat: 13
Fat (gm): 3.8
Sat. fat (gm): 0.7
Cholesterol (mg): 0.8
Sodium (mg): 40
Protein (gm): 9.6
Carbohydrate (gm): 44.9

Exchanges
Milk: 0.0
Vegetable: 1.5
Fruit: 0.0
Bread: 3.0
Meat: 0.0
Fat: 0.5

1. Saute onion and garlic in oil in large skillet until soft. Add tomatoes, wine, and basil. Cook over medium heat 5 minutes, then add mushrooms, marjoram, salt, and pepper; cook 5 minutes more. Spoon sauce over pasta and sprinkle with Parmesan cheese.

CHEESE-STUFFED SHELLS MARINARA

6 servings

3 egg whites
1 pound low-fat cottage cheese
1 cup (4 ounces) shredded skim mozzarella cheese
$^1/_4$ cup chopped parsley
10 basil leaves, chopped
$^1/_8$ teaspoon pepper
24 uncooked giant pasta shells, cooked
Marinara Sauce (see p. 509)
Grated Parmesan cheese, as garnish

Per Serving
Calories: 412
% Calories from fat: 26
Fat (gm): 11.8
Sat. fat (gm): 4.6
Cholesterol (mg): 19.6
Sodium (mg): 752
Protein (gm): 28.2
Carbohydrate (gm): 48.3

Exchanges
Milk: 0.0
Vegetable: 2.0
Fruit: 0.0
Bread: 3.0
Meat: 2.5
Fat: 0.5

1. Combine egg whites, cottage cheese, mozzarella cheese, parsley, basil, and pepper in medium bowl. Stuff each shell with a few tablespoons of cheese mixture.

2. Cover bottom of large baking dish with about $^1/_2$ inch of Marinara Sauce. Arrange stuffed shells side by side in sauce. Spoon remaining sauce over top of shells and sprinkle with Parmesan cheese. Bake at 350 degrees, covered, until hot through and bubbly, 30 to 45 minutes.

SPAGHETTI AND ITALIAN MEATBALLS

8 servings

Italian Meatballs (recipe follows)
3 tablespoons olive oil
Marinara Sauce (see p. 509)
1 pound thin spaghetti, cooked, warm
Chopped parsley, as garnish

Per Serving
Calories: 502
% Calories from fat: 35
Fat (gm): 19.6
Sat. fat (gm): 5.1
Cholesterol (mg): 43.7
Sodium (mg): 345
Protein (gm): 25.1
Carbohydrate (gm): 56.1

Exchanges
Milk: 0.0
Vegetable: 1.5
Fruit: 0.0
Bread: 3.0
Meat: 3.0
Fat: 2.0

1. Saute Italian Meatballs in olive oil in large skillet over medium heat, turning often until golden on all sides, 10 to 15 minutes. Drain. Combine Italian Meatballs and Marinara Sauce in large saucepan; heat to boiling. Reduce heat and simmer until meatballs are cooked through, about 10 minutes

2. Serve Italian Meatballs and Marinara Sauce over spaghetti; sprinkle with parsley.

Italian Meatballs

makes 32 meatballs

- 1 pound ground turkey
- 1/2 pound ground lean beef
- 1 small onion, minced
- 1 clove garlic, minced
- 1/2 teaspoon dried oregano leaves
- 1/2 teaspoon dried basil leaves
- 1/2 teaspoon pepper
- 1/4 cup seasoned dry bread crumbs

1. Mix all ingredients; form into 32 meatballs.

TURKEY TETRAZZINI

8 servings

- 8 ounces mushrooms, sliced
- 2 tablespoons margarine
- 2 tablespoons flour
- 1 can (14 1/2 ounces) reduced-sodium fat-free chicken broth
- 1 cup fat-free milk
- 1/2 cup dry white wine, *or* fat-free milk
- 16 ounces cooked spaghettini (thin spaghetti)
- 12 ounces cooked turkey, *or* chicken, breast, cubed
- 1/4 cup (1 ounce) grated Parmesan cheese

Per Serving
Calories: 370
% Calories from fat: 16
Fat (gm): 6.5
Sat. fat (gm): 1.7
Cholesterol (mg): 35.7
Sodium (mg): 218
Protein (gm): 23.6
Carbohydrate (gm): 50.3

Exchanges
Milk: 0.0
Vegetable: 1.0
Fruit: 0.0
Bread: 3.0
Meat: 2.0
Fat: 0.5

1/4 teaspoon ground nutmeg
1/4 teaspoon salt
1/4 teaspoon pepper

1. Saute mushrooms in margarine in large saucepan until tender, about 5 minutes. Stir in flour; cook over medium heat 1 to 2 minutes more. Stir in chicken broth, milk, and wine and heat to boiling. Boil, stirring constantly, until thickened, 1 to 2 minutes (sauce will be very thin). Stir in pasta, turkey, Parmesan cheese, nutmeg, salt, and pepper.

2. Spoon pasta mixture into 2 quart casserole or baking dish. Bake, uncovered, until lightly browned on top and bubbly, about 45 minutes.

SPAGHETTI WITH ANCHOVIES

4 servings

4 large cloves garlic, minced
2 tablespoons olive oil
3/4 ounce canned anchovy fillets, drained and chopped
1 teaspoon lemon juice
8 ounces spaghetti, cooked, warm
Pepper, to taste
Chopped Italian parsley, as garnish
Grated Parmesan cheese, as garnish

Per Serving
Calories: 286
% Calories from fat: 26
Fat (gm): 8.2
Sat. fat (gm): 1.2
Cholesterol (mg): 4.5
Sodium (mg): 197
Protein (gm): 9
Carbohydrate (gm): 43.5
Exchanges
Milk: 0.0
Vegetable: 0.0
Fruit: 0.0
Bread: 3.0
Meat: 0.0
Fat: 1.5

1. Saute garlic in oil in small skillet 2 minutes. Add anchovies and cook until garlic just begins to color, about 3 minutes; stir in lemon juice. Toss anchovy mixture with spaghetti; season to taste with pepper. Sprinkle with parsley and cheese.

SPAGHETTI WITH GARLIC SHRIMP

6 servings

3 large cloves garlic, quartered
2 tablespoons olive oil
1 pound medium shrimp, peeled and deveined
1 teaspoon Italian seasoning
1/8 teaspoon pepper
3 tablespoons minced fresh parsley, divided
1/2 cup (2 ounces) grated Parmesan cheese
1 pound thin spaghetti, cooked, warm

Per Serving
Calories: 406
% Calories from fat: 20
Fat (gm): 8.9
Sat. fat (gm): 2.5
Cholesterol (mg): 42.6
Sodium (mg): 194
Protein (gm): 18.5
Carbohydrate (gm): 61.6
Exchanges
Milk: 0.0
Vegetable: 0.0
Fruit: 0.0
Bread: 4.0
Meat: 1.0
Fat: 1.0

1. Saute garlic in oil in large skillet until golden; discard garlic pieces. Add shrimp, Italian seasoning, pepper, and 2 tablespoons parsley to skillet. Saute until shrimp is cooked and tender, 2 to 3 minutes. Toss shrimp and cheese with spaghetti; sprinkle with remaining 1 tablespoon parsley.

CHICKEN TORTELLINI WITH TOMATO-MUSHROOM SAUCE

6 servings

Vegetable cooking spray
1/4 cup chopped onion
1 small leek (white part only), very thinly sliced
3 tablespoons chopped shallots
4 large mushrooms, chopped
1/4 cup dry sherry, *or* reduced-sodium fat-free chicken broth
1/4 teaspoon salt
1/4 teaspoon pepper
1 cup reduced-sodium fat-free chicken broth
1 medium tomato, chopped

Per Serving
Calories: 167
% Calories from fat: 16
Fat (gm): 3.1
Sat. fat (gm): 1.5
Cholesterol (mg): 20.2
Sodium (mg): 219
Protein (gm): 8.7
Carbohydrate (gm): 25.8
Exchanges
Milk: 0.0
Vegetable: 1.0
Fruit: 0.0
Bread: 1.5
Meat: 0.0
Fat: 0.5

$1^1/_2$ teaspoons dried thyme leaves
2 bay leaves
1 package (9 ounces) chicken tortellini, cooked, warm
2 tablespoons drained capers

1. Spray medium saucepan with cooking spray; heat over medium heat until hot. Saute onion, leek, shallots, and mushrooms until very soft, 7 to 10 minutes. Add sherry; cook over high heat until liquid is almost absorbed, 2 to 3 minutes. Stir in salt and pepper.

2. Add chicken broth, tomato, thyme, and bay leaves to saucepan; heat to boiling. Reduce heat and simmer, uncovered, until tomato is very soft, about 15 minutes; discard bay leaves. Process mixture in food processor or blender until smooth. Return to saucepan; cook over medium heat until hot, 2 to 3 minutes.

3. Spoon sauce over tortellini; sprinkle with capers.

TORTELLINI SALAD WITH ARTICHOKES AND TUNA

8 servings

12 ounces cheese tortellini, cooked, room temperature
$^1/_2$ cup fresh, *or* frozen, thawed, peas
$^1/_2$ chopped green bell pepper
$^1/_2$ cup chopped green onions and tops
1 can (14 ounces) artichoke hearts, drained and quartered
1 can ($6^1/_2$ ounces) water-packed tuna, drained, flaked
$^1/_4$ cup (1 ounce) grated Parmesan cheese
Tomato Dressing (recipe follows)
Salt and pepper, to taste

Per Serving
Calories: 209
% Calories from fat: 30
Fat (gm): 6.9
Sat. fat (gm): 1.8
Cholesterol (mg): 20.9
Sodium (mg): 408
Protein (gm): 14.1
Carbohydrate (gm): 22
Exchanges
Milk: 0.0
Vegetable: 1.0
Fruit: 0.0
Bread: 1.0
Meat: 1.5
Fat: 0.5

1. Combine tortellini, peas, bell pepper, green onions, artichoke hearts, tuna, and cheese in large salad bowl; pour Tomato Dressing over salad and toss. Season to taste with salt and pepper.

Tomato Dressing

makes about 1 cup

- 2 small tomatoes, cut into wedges
- 2-3 tablespoons olive oil
- 2 tablespoons white wine vinegar
- 2 teaspoons Dijon-style mustard
- 3 tablespoons sliced green onions and tops
- 1 clove garlic, minced
- 1/2 cup fresh parsley, chopped
- 1/4 cup chopped fresh, *or* 1 tablespoon dried, basil leaves
- 1 tablespoon chopped fresh, *or* 1 teaspoon dried, oregano leaves

1. Combine all ingredients in food processor or blender; process until finely chopped.

3-CAN LASAGNE

4-6 servings

- 6 no-boil lasagne noodles
- 1 can (15 ounces) cannellini, *or* Great Northern beans, rinsed, drained, slightly mashed
- 1 cup reduced-fat cottage cheese
- 1 can (16 ounces) Italian-style zucchini with mushrooms and tomato sauce, undrained
- 1-1 1/2 cups (4-6 ounces) shredded reduced-fat Italian 6-cheese blend, divided
- 1 can (14 1/2 ounces) diced tomatoes with roasted garlic

Per Serving
Calories: 372
% Calories from fat: 21
Fat (gm): 8.5
Sat. fat (gm): 4.7
Cholesterol (mg): 24.5
Sodium (mg): 1417
Protein (gm): 25
Carbohydrate (gm): 47.7

Exchanges
Milk: 0.0
Vegetable: 3.0
Fruit: 0.0
Bread: 2.0
Meat: 2.0
Fat: 1.0

1. Place 2 lasagne noodles in lightly greased 8-inch-square baking pan. Top with 1/2 the beans, 1/2 the cottage cheese, 1/2 the zucchini, and 1/3 cup shredded cheese. Repeat layers, ending with 2 lasagne noodles. Spoon diced tomatoes over top of lasagne.

2. Bake, covered with aluminum foil, at 375 degrees until noodles are fork-tender, about 30 minutes. Uncover and sprinkle with remaining 1/3 cup cheese; let stand 5 to 10 minutes before serving.

ROASTED EGGPLANT AND TOMATOES WITH ZITI

4 servings

Olive oil cooking spray
1 medium eggplant, unpeeled, cut into 1/2-inch slices
3 medium onions, cut into 1/2-inch wedges
1/2 teaspoon dried thyme leaves
1/2 teaspoon dried marjoram leaves
1/2 teaspoon dried savory leaves
Salt and pepper, to taste
1 can (14 1/2 ounces) diced tomatoes with roasted garlic
8 ounces ziti, cooked, warm

Per Serving
Calories: 301
% Calories from fat: 4
Fat (gm): 1.3
Sat. fat (gm): 0.2
Cholesterol (mg): 0
Sodium (mg): 382
Protein (gm): 10.9
Carbohydrate (gm): 62.6
Exchanges
Milk: 0.0
Vegetable: 3.0
Fruit: 0.0
Bread: 3.0
Meat: 0.0
Fat: 0.0

1. Line jelly roll pan with aluminum foil and spray with cooking spray. Cut eggplant slices into fourths; arrange on jelly roll pan with onions. Spray vegetables with cooking spray; sprinkle with herbs, salt, and pepper.

2. Roast vegetables at 450 degrees 20 minutes. Spoon tomatoes over vegetables, and roast until eggplant is tender; 5 to 10 minutes longer. Serve over ziti.

NOODLES WITH VEGETABLES PAPRIKASH

4 servings

Vegetable cooking spray
4 cups packaged coleslaw mix
1 cup chopped onion
1 medium zucchini, sliced
1 1/2 cups sliced mushrooms
1 medium tomato, chopped
3 tablespoons flour
1 tablespoon paprika
3/4 cup vegetable broth

Per Serving
Calories: 454
% Calories from fat: 13
Fat (gm): 6.9
Sat. fat (gm): 2.3
Cholesterol (mg): 90.9
Sodium (mg): 249
Protein (gm): 18.2
Carbohydrate (gm): 81.9
Exchanges
Milk: 0.0
Vegetable: 4.0
Fruit: 0.0
Bread: 4.0
Meat: 0.0
Fat: 1.0

- 1/2 cup reduced-fat sour cream
- Salt and pepper, to taste
- 12 ounces egg noodles, cooked, warm

1. Spray large skillet with cooking spray and heat over medium heat until hot. Cook coleslaw, onion, and zucchini, covered, 5 to 8 minutes. Add mushrooms and tomato. Cook over medium heat, covered, until mushrooms and tomato are wilted, about 2 minutes.

2. Stir in flour and paprika; cook 1 to 2 minutes, stirring constantly. Stir in broth; heat to boiling. Boil, stirring constantly, until sauce thickens, about 1 minute. Stir in sour cream; season to taste with salt and pepper. Serve over noodles.

FETTUCCINE WITH FRESH FENNEL AND SPROUTS

4 servings

- Olive oil cooking spray
- 1 fennel bulb, thinly sliced
- 1 medium onion, thinly sliced
- 8 ounces small Brussels sprouts, halved
- 1/4 cup water, *or* vegetable broth
- 1 tablespoon lemon juice
- Salt and pepper, to taste
- 8 ounces spinach fettuccine, cooked, warm
- 1/2 cup (2 ounces) shredded, *or* shaved, Parmesan cheese
- 4 tablespoons toasted pine nuts, *or* slivered almonds

Per Serving
Calories: 326
% Calories from fat: 28
Fat (gm): 10.6
Sat. fat (gm): 3.9
Cholesterol (mg): 70.6
Sodium (mg): 215
Protein (gm): 16.2
Carbohydrate (gm): 44

Exchanges
Milk: 0.0
Vegetable: 3.0
Fruit: 0.0
Bread: 2.0
Meat: 0.0
Fat: 2.0

1. Spray large skillet with cooking spray; heat over medium heat until hot. Saute fennel and onion 3 to 4 minutes. Add Brussels sprouts and water and heat to boiling; reduce heat and simmer, covered, until sprouts are crisp-tender, 5 to 8 minutes. Stir in lemon juice; season to taste with salt and pepper.

2. Spoon fennel and sprouts mixture over fettucini on serving platter; sprinkle with Parmesan cheese and pine nuts.

WINE-GLAZED RAVIOLI AND ASPARAGUS

4 servings

2 cups canned reduced-sodium vegetable broth
1 cup dry white wine
1 cup orange juice
1/4 teaspoon crushed red pepper flakes
1 pound asparagus, cut into 1-inch pieces
1 package (9 ounces) fresh mushroom ravioli, cooked, warm
2 tablespoons margarine
Salt and pepper, to taste

Per Serving
Calories: 259
% Calories from fat: 32
Fat (gm): 8.2
Sat. fat (gm): 3.4
Cholesterol (mg): 34.4
Sodium (mg): 462
Protein (gm): 8
Carbohydrate (gm): 29.8
Exchanges
Milk: 0.0
Vegetable: 0.0
Fruit: 0.0
Bread: 2.0
Meat: 1.0
Fat: 1.0

1. Heat vegetable broth, white wine, orange juice, and crushed red pepper to boiling in large skillet; boil, uncovered, 10 minutes or until liquid is reduced to about 1/2 cup.

2. Add asparagus to skillet; cook, covered, over medium heat until crisp-tender, 3 to 4 minutes. Add ravioli and margarine; season to taste with salt and pepper.

20-MINUTE RAVIOLI

4 servings

3/4 cup chopped onion
2 teaspoons minced garlic
1 tablespoon olive oil
3/4 cup canned kidney beans, rinsed, drained
1 large tomato, cubed
1/2 teaspoon dried thyme leaves
1 package (9 ounces) fresh sun-dried tomato ravioli, cooked, warm
Salt and pepper, to taste

Per Serving
Calories: 220
% Calories from fat: 34
Fat (gm): 8.3
Sat. fat (gm): 3.3
Cholesterol (mg): 34.4
Sodium (mg): 342
Protein (gm): 8.3
Carbohydrate (gm): 28.6
Exchanges
Milk: 0.0
Vegetable: 0.0
Fruit: 0.0
Bread: 2.0
Meat: 1.0
Fat: 1.0

1. Saute onion and garlic in oil in large skillet until tender, about 5 minutes. Stir in beans, tomato, and thyme; cook 2 to 3 minutes longer. Stir in ravioli and cook 2 to 3 minutes longer. Season to taste with salt and pepper.

PASTA AND PORTOBELLO MUSHROOMS VINAIGRETTE

4 servings

12 ounces sliced portobello mushrooms
1 tablespoon olive oil
2 medium tomatoes, cut into wedges
1 medium yellow squash, *or* zucchini, sliced
1 medium green bell pepper, sliced
1 large carrot, sliced
1 small red onion, sliced
8 ounces rotini, cooked, room temperature
1/2-3/4 cup reduced-fat Italian dressing
Lettuce leaves, for garnish

Per Serving
Calories: 339
% Calories from fat: 23
Fat (gm): 9.2
Sat. fat (gm): 1.2
Cholesterol (mg): 1.8
Sodium (mg): 255
Protein (gm): 11.7
Carbohydrate (gm): 56.2

Exchanges
Milk: 0.0
Vegetable: 2.0
Fruit: 0.0
Bread: 3.0
Meat: 0.0
Fat: 1.5

1. Saute mushrooms in oil in large skillet until tender, 5 to 8 minutes. Combine mushrooms, vegetables, and pasta in bowl; pour Italian dressing over and toss. Arrange lettuce leaves on salad plates; spoon salad over.

GREAT GARLIC PASTA

4 servings

1/3 cup slivered (1/4-inch pieces), *or* thinly sliced, garlic
2-3 teaspoons olive oil
2 tablespoons minced fresh parsley
1 tablespoon minced fresh, *or* 1 teaspoon crushed, dried, rosemary leaves
8 ounces (2 cups) orrechiette ("little ears"), or other small pasta
1 cup tiny peas
1/4-1/3 (1-1 1/3 ounces) cup freshly grated Parmesan cheese
Salt and pepper, to taste

Per Serving
Calories: 303
% Calories from fat: 15
Fat (gm): 4.9
Sat. fat (gm): 1.4
Cholesterol (mg): 3.9
Sodium (mg): 133
Protein (gm): 12.2
Carbohydrate (gm): 52.3

Exchanges
Milk: 0.0
Vegetable: 0.0
Fruit: 0.0
Bread: 3.5
Meat: 0.0
Fat: 1.0

1. Cook garlic over very low heat in oil in small skillet until very tender but not browned, about 10 minutes. Stir in herbs.

2. Cook pasta according to package directions, adding peas 1 minute before end of cooking time; drain. Toss pasta, garlic mixture, and cheese in serving bowl. Season to taste with salt and pepper.

ASPARAGUS AND WHITE BEANS WITH LINGUINE

4 servings

1 pound asparagus, cut into 2-inch pieces
2 teaspoons minced garlic
2-3 teaspoons olive oil
2 cups chopped Italian plum tomatoes
1 can (15 ounces) cannellini, *or* Great Northern, beans, rinsed, drained
1 teaspoon dried rosemary leaves, *or* Italian seasoning
1 cup canned reduced-sodium vegetable broth
Salt and pepper, to taste
8 ounces linguine, *or* thin spaghetti, cooked, warm
1/4-1/2 cup (1-2 ounces) shredded Parmesan cheese

Per Serving
Calories: 303
% Calories from fat: 12
Fat (gm): 4
Sat. fat (gm): 1.3
Cholesterol (mg): 6.2
Sodium (mg): 455
Protein (gm): 14.2
Carbohydrate (gm): 52.1

Exchanges
Milk: 0.0
Vegetable: 2.0
Fruit: 0.0
Bread: 3.0
Meat: 0.0
Fat: 1.0

1. Saute asparagus and garlic in oil in large skillet until crisp-tender, 3 to 4 minutes. Stir in remaining ingredients, except salt, pepper, linguine, and cheese. Heat to boiling; reduce heat and simmer rapidly until mixture has thickened, 3 to 5 minutes. Season to taste with salt and pepper.

2. Serve vegetable mixture over linguine; sprinkle with cheese.

PASTA WITH EGGPLANT AND VEGETABLE SAUTE

4 servings

1 large eggplant (about 1¼ pounds), unpeeled, cubed (½-inch)
3 cups frozen stir-fry pepper blend
4 teaspoons minced roasted garlic
¾ teaspoon dried rosemary leaves
½ teaspoon dried thyme leaves
2 teaspoons olive oil
1 can (15 ounces) cannellini, *or* Great Northern, beans, rinsed, drained
Salt and pepper, to taste
8 ounces whole wheat spaghetti, *or* any desired pasta, cooked, warm

Per Serving
Calories: 355
% Calories from fat: 9
Fat (gm): 3.7
Sat. fat (gm): 0.5
Cholesterol (mg): 0
Sodium (mg): 171
Protein (gm): 14.8
Carbohydrate (gm): 69.6
Exchanges
Milk: 0.0
Vegetable: 2.0
Fruit: 0.0
Bread: 4.0
Meat: 0.0
Fat: 0.5

1. Cook eggplant, pepper blend, garlic, and herbs in oil in large saucepan over medium heat, covered, until vegetables are tender, 8 to 10 minutes, stirring occasionally. Stir in beans; cook until hot through, 1 to 2 minutes. Season to taste with salt and pepper. Serve eggplant mixture over spaghetti.

SESAME VEGETABLE STIR-FRY WITH ORIENTAL NOODLES

4 servings

Vegetable cooking spray
8 ounces asparagus, cut into 1-inch pieces
¼ teaspoon crushed red pepper flakes
1 can (15 ounces) black beans, rinsed, drained
1 jar (14 ounces) sweet-and-sour sauce for noodles and rice
1 small tomato, coarsely chopped
1 package (18 ounces) Chinese egg noodles, cooked, warm

Per Serving
Calories: 362
% Calories from fat: 1
Fat (gm): 0.3
Sat. fat (gm): 0
Cholesterol (mg): 0
Sodium (mg): 506
Protein (gm): 7
Carbohydrate (gm): 82.9
Exchanges
Milk: 0.0
Vegetable: 1.0
Fruit: 2.0
Bread: 3.0
Meat: 0.0
Fat: 0.0

1. Spray wok or medium skillet with cooking spray; heat over medium heat until hot. Stir-fry asparagus 3 to 4 minutes or until browned. Add red pepper flakes; cook 1 minute longer.

2. Stir beans and sweet-and-sour sauce into skillet and cook 2 to 3 minutes; stir in tomato. Serve over noodles.

LINGUINE WITH FENNEL AND SUN-DRIED TOMATO PESTO

6 servings

- 1 cup thinly sliced onion
- 1 fennel bulb, thinly sliced
- 1-2 tablespoons olive oil
- 1/4 cup dry white wine, *or* water
- Sun-Dried Tomato Pesto (recipe follows)
- 12 ounces linguine, *or* angel hair pasta, cooked, warm
- Salt and pepper, to taste

Per Serving
Calories: 288
% Calories from fat: 33
Fat (gm): 10.5
Sat. fat (gm): 1.2
Cholesterol (mg): 0
Sodium (mg): 248
Protein (gm): 8.6
Carbohydrate (gm): 39.1

Exchanges
Milk: 0.0
Vegetable: 2.0
Fruit: 0.0
Bread: 2.0
Meat: 0.0
Fat: 2.0

1. Saute onion and fennel in oil in large skillet 2 to 3 minutes. Cook, covered, over medium-low heat until onions are very soft, 10 to 15 minutes. Stir in wine and simmer, covered, 15 to 20 minutes or until wine is almost gone and fennel is tender.

2. Spoon onion mixture and Sun-Dried Tomato Pesto over linguine in serving bowl and toss. Season to taste with salt and pepper.

Sun-Dried Tomato Pesto

makes 1 1/2 cups

- 1/2 cup sun-dried tomatoes (not in oil)
- 1/2 cup very hot water
- 1/2 cup packed basil leaves
- 1 teaspoon minced garlic
- 3-4 tablespoons olive oil
- 2 tablespoons grated fat-free Parmesan cheese
- Salt and pepper, to taste

1. Soak tomatoes in hot water in bowl until softened, 5 to 10 minutes. Drain, reserving liquid.

2. Process tomatoes, basil, garlic, oil, and cheese in food processor or blender, adding enough reserved liquid to make a smooth, spoonable paste. Season to taste with salt and pepper. Serve at room temperature.

PASTA PEPERONATA

4 servings

- 5 large bell peppers, assorted colors, sliced
- 4 medium onions, sliced
- 4 teaspoons minced garlic
- 3 tablespoons olive oil
- 3 tablespoons water
- 1 teaspoon sugar
- Salt and pepper, to taste
- 8 ounces spaghetti, cooked, warm
- 1/4 cup (1 ounce) shredded Parmesan cheese

Per Serving
Calories: 381
% Calories from fat: 31
Fat (gm): 13
Sat. fat (gm): 2.8
Cholesterol (mg): 6.2
Sodium (mg): 81
Protein (gm): 11.1
Carbohydrate (gm): 54.9

Exchanges
Milk: 0.0
Vegetable: 2.0
Fruit: 0.0
Bread: 3.0
Meat: 0.0
Fat: 2.0

1. Saute peppers, onions, and garlic in oil in large skillet 2 to 3 minutes. Add water; cook, covered, over medium to medium-high heat 2 to 3 minutes.

2. Stir sugar into peppers mixture; cook, uncovered, over medium-low heat until mixture is very soft and browned, about 20 minutes. Season to taste with salt and pepper. Toss with spaghetti and sprinkle with cheese.

ZITI WITH GREMOLATA

8 servings

- Olive oil cooking spray
- 1/2 cup chopped onion
- 8 ounces shiitake, *or* cremini, mushrooms, sliced
- 2 cans (14 1/2 ounces each) diced tomatoes with Italian seasoning, undrained
- Salt and pepper, to taste
- 1 pound ziti, *or* penne, cooked, warm
- Gremolata (recipe follows)

Per Serving
Calories: 257
% Calories from fat: 4
Fat (gm): 1.1
Sat. fat (gm): 0.2
Cholesterol (mg): 0
Sodium (mg): 483
Protein (gm): 9
Carbohydrate (gm): 52.9

Exchanges
Milk: 0.0
Vegetable: 2.0
Fruit: 0.0
Bread: 3.0
Meat: 0.0
Fat: 0.0

1. Spray large skillet with cooking spray; heat over medium heat until hot. Saute onion and mushrooms until tender, 5 to 8 minutes. Add tomatoes and liquid and heat to boiling; reduce heat and simmer, uncovered, until thickened, about 10 minutes. Season to taste with salt and pepper.

2. Toss pasta with tomato mixture and half the Gremolata; pass remaining Gremolata to be added as desired.

Gremolata

makes about 1/2 cup

- 1 cup packed fresh parsley leaves
- 1-2 teaspoons grated lemon rind
- 4 large cloves garlic

1. Process all ingredients in food processor until finely minced, using pulse technique. Refrigerate until serving time.

TAGLIATELLE WITH CHILI-MUSHROOM STROGANOFF SAUCE

6 servings

Per Serving
Calories: 376
% Calories from fat: 20
Fat (gm): 8
Sat. fat (gm): 2.8
Cholesterol (mg): 13.3
Sodium (mg): 428
Protein (gm): 10.5
Carbohydrate (gm): 61.3

Exchanges
Milk: 0.0
Vegetable: 0.0
Fruit: 0.0
Bread: 4.0
Meat: 0.0
Fat: 1.5

1 package (1 3/4 ounces) dried shiitake mushrooms
1-2 dried ancho chilies
3 cups boiling water, divided
2 cups vegetable broth, divided
1 cup chopped onion
8 ounces white mushrooms, halved or quartered
2 tablespoons margarine
1/4 cup all-purpose flour
1/2 teaspoon dried thyme leaves
1 cup reduced-fat sour cream
1 teaspoon Dijon-style mustard
Salt and pepper, to taste
12 ounces tagliatelle (flat pasta), *or* fettuccine, cooked, warm
Minced parsley, for garnish

1. Place shiitake mushrooms and chilies in separate bowls; pour 2 cups boiling water over the mushrooms and 1 cup over the chilies. Let stand until vegetables are softened, about 10 minutes.

2. Drain mushrooms, reserving liquid. Remove tough centers from mushrooms and slice. Drain chilies, discarding liquid. Process chilies and 1 cup broth in blender or food processor until smooth.

3. Saute onion, shiitake, and white mushrooms in margarine in large skillet until wilted, about 5 minutes. Stir in flour; cook 1 minute longer, stirring frequently. Stir in reserved mushroom liquid, chili mixture, remaining 1 cup broth, and thyme. Heat to boiling; reduce heat and simmer, covered, until shiitake mushrooms are tender, 10 to 15 minutes. Simmer, uncovered, if necessary, until thickened.

4. Stir in sour cream and mustard; cook until hot through, 2 to 3 minutes. Season to taste with salt and pepper. Toss pasta with sauce in serving; sprinkle generously with parsley.

CHINESE NOODLES WITH SWEET POTATOES AND SNOW PEAS

4 servings

Vegetable cooking spray
2 cups cubed ($^1/_2$ inch), peeled, sweet potatoes
$^3/_4$ cup diagonally sliced green onions and tops
3 teaspoons minced garlic
1-2 teaspoons minced gingerroot
2 cups halved snow peas
$^1/_2$ cup chopped red, *or* green, bell pepper
$^3/_4$ cup vegetable broth
1-2 teaspoons tamari soy sauce
$1^1/_2$ teaspoons cornstarch
Salt and pepper, to taste
1 package (8 ounces) fresh Chinese egg noodles, cooked, warm
1-2 teaspoons toasted sesame seeds

Per Serving
Calories: 299
% Calories from fat: 5
Fat (gm): 1.5
Sat. fat (gm): 0.1
Cholesterol (mg): 0
Sodium (mg): 634
Protein (gm): 9.5
Carbohydrate (gm): 63.3
Exchanges
Milk: 0.0
Vegetable: 0.0
Fruit: 0.0
Bread: 4.0
Meat: 0.0
Fat: 0.0

1. Spray wok or large skillet with cooking spray; heat over medium heat until hot. Stir-fry potatoes, green onions, garlic, and gingerroot 2 to 3 minutes; cook, covered, over low heat until potatoes are almost tender, 10 to 12 minutes, stirring occasionally.

2. Add snow peas and bell pepper to wok. Stir-fry over medium heat until peas are crisp-tender; about 5 minutes. Combine broth, soy sauce, and cornstarch; add to wok and heat to boiling. Boil, stirring constantly, until thickened, about 1 minute. Season to taste with salt and pepper.

3. Spoon vegetable mixture over noodles in serving bowl; sprinkle with sesame seeds.

STIR-FRIED RICE NOODLES WITH VEGETABLES

4 servings

1 package (8 ounces) rice noodles
Cold water
1 tablespoon vegetable oil
1 cup halved green beans
1 cup cubed yellow summer squash
1/2 cup sliced red, *or* green, bell pepper
4 green onions and tops, thinly sliced
1 tablespoon finely chopped fresh gingerroot
2 cups thinly sliced napa cabbage
1 cup vegetable broth
2-3 teaspoons soy sauce
1/2-1 teaspoon Szechwan chili sauce

1. Place noodles in large bowl; pour cold water over to cover. While you prepare vegetables, let noodles stand until separate and soft, about 15 minutes; drain.

2. Heat oil in wok or skillet over medium-high heat until hot. Add green beans, squash, bell pepper, green onions, and gingerroot. Stir-fry until vegetables are tender, 8 to 10 minutes.

3. Add cabbage to wok; stir-fry just until cabbage turns bright in color, about 1 minute. Stir in drained noodles, broth, soy sauce, and chili sauce. Heat to boiling; reduce heat and simmer, uncovered, until noodles have absorbed all liquid, about 5 minutes.

Per Serving
Calories: 271
% Calories from fat: 13
Fat (gm): 4.1
Sat. fat (gm): 0.5
Cholesterol (mg): 0
Sodium (mg): 483
Protein (gm): 2.7
Carbohydrate (gm): 57.3

Exchanges
Milk: 0.0
Vegetable: 2.0
Fruit: 0.0
Bread: 3.0
Meat: 0.0
Fat: 0.5

ARTICHOKE TORTELLINI BAKE

4 servings

Vegetable cooking spray
2 cups (4 ounces) sliced mushrooms
1 small onion, sliced
1 teaspoon minced garlic
2 tablespoons flour
1 cup fat-free milk
Salt and cayenne pepper, to taste
1 can (14 ounces) artichoke hearts, drained
1 package (9 ounces) mozzarella-garlic tortellini, cooked
1/2-1 cup (2-4 ounces) shredded reduced-fat Italian 6-cheese blend, divided
1-2 tablespoons seasoned dry bread crumbs

Per Serving
Calories: 296
% Calories from fat: 23
Fat (gm): 7.6
Sat. fat (gm): 3
Cholesterol (mg): 29.4
Sodium (mg): 608
Protein (gm): 17.4
Carbohydrate (gm): 39.2

Exchanges
Milk: 0.0
Vegetable: 2.0
Fruit: 0.0
Bread: 2.0
Meat: 1.0
Fat: 1.0

1. Spray large saucepan with cooking spray; heat over medium heat until hot. Saute mushrooms, onion, and garlic until tender, about 5 minutes. Stir in flour; cook 1 to 2 minutes. Add milk and heat to boiling; boil, stirring constantly, until thickened, 1 to 2 minutes. Season to taste with salt and cayenne pepper.

2. Stir in artichokes, tortellini, and all but 2 tablespoons of the cheese. Pour into greased 1 1/2-quart casserole; sprinkle with bread crumbs and remaining 2 tablespoons cheese.

3. Bake at 350 degrees until bubbly and browned on the top, about 20 minutes.

ELEVEN

Pizza

AND

Calzones

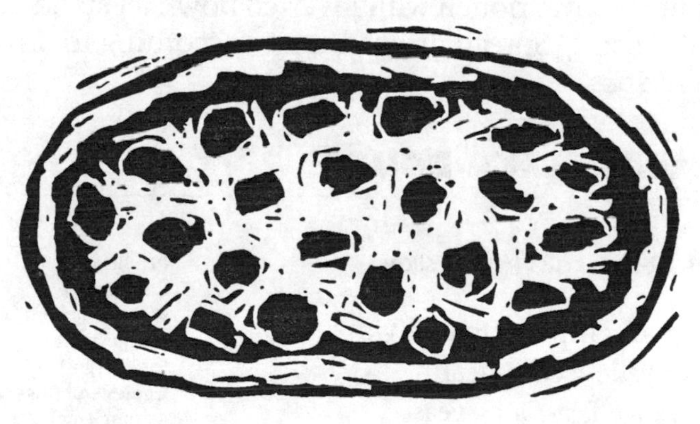

BASIC PIZZA DOUGH

Makes one 12-inch crust (6 large slices)

1¼ cups all-purpose flour, divided
1 package fast-rising yeast
½ teaspoon sugar
¼ teaspoon salt
½ cup very hot water (120 degrees)

Per Slice
Calories: 99.5
% Calories from fat: 2
Fat (gm): 0.3
Sat. fat (gm): 0
Cholesterol (mg): 0
Sodium (mg): 89
Protein (gm): 3.2
Carbohydrate (gm): 20.7
Exchanges
Milk: 0.0
Vegetable: 0.0
Fruit: 0.0
Bread: 1.5
Meat: 0.0
Fat: 0.0

1. Combine ¾ cup flour, yeast, sugar, and salt in medium bowl; add hot water, stirring until smooth. Mix in enough of remaining ½ cup flour to make a soft dough.

2. Knead dough on floured surface until smooth and elastic, 3 to 5 minutes. Cover dough with inverted bowl; let stand 15 minutes before using. Spread dough on pan according to directions in pizza recipes.

CORNMEAL PIZZA DOUGH

Makes one 12-inch crust (6 large slices)

1 cup all-purpose flour, divided
¼ cup yellow cornmeal
1 package fast-rising yeast
½ teaspoon sugar
½ cup very hot water (120 degrees)

Per Slice
Calories: 99
% Calories from fat: 4
Fat (gm): 0.4
Sat. fat (gm): 0.1
Cholesterol (mg): 0
Sodium (mg): 2.3
Protein (gm): 3.1
Carbohydrate (gm): 20.7
Exchanges
Milk: 0.0
Vegetable: 0.0
Fruit: 0.0
Bread: 1.5
Meat: 0.0
Fat: 0.0

1. Combine 1/2 cup flour, cornmeal, yeast, and sugar in medium bowl; add hot water, stirring until smooth. Mix in enough of remaining 1/2 cup flour to make a soft dough.

2. Knead dough on floured surface until smooth and elastic, 3 to 5 minutes. Cover dough with inverted bowl; let stand 15 minutes before using. Spread dough on pan according to directions in pizza recipes.

WHOLE WHEAT PIZZA DOUGH

Makes one 12-inch crust (6 large slices)

- 3/4 cup all-purpose flour, divided
- 1 package fast-rising yeast
- 1/4 teaspoon salt
- 1/2 cup very hot water (120 degrees)
- 2 teaspoons honey
- 1/2 cup whole wheat flour

Per Slice
Calories: 101
% Calories from fat: 0.3
Fat (gm): 0.3
Sat. fat (gm): 0.1
Cholesterol (mg): 0
Sodium (mg): 90
Protein (gm): 3.5
Carbohydrate (gm): 21.6
Exchanges
Milk: 0.0
Vegetable: 0.0
Fruit: 0.0
Bread: 1.5
Meat: 0.0
Fat: 0.0

1. Combine all-purpose flour, yeast, and salt in medium bowl; add hot water and honey, stirring until smooth. Mix in enough whole wheat flour to make a soft dough.

2. Knead dough on floured surface until smooth and elastic, 3 to 5 minutes. Cover dough with inverted bowl; let stand 15 minutes before using. Spread dough on pan according to directions in pizza recipes.

CHEESE PIZZA DOUGH

Makes one 12-inch crust (6 large slices)

- 1 1/4 cups all-purpose flour, divided
- 1 package fast-rising yeast
- 1/2 teaspoon sugar
- 2/3 cup very hot water (120 degrees)
- 2 tablespoons grated fat-free Parmesan cheese
- 1/4 cup (1 ounce) shredded fat-free Cheddar cheese

Per Slice
Calories: 112
% Calories from fat: 2
Fat (gm): 0.3
Sat. fat (gm): 0
Cholesterol (mg): 0
Sodium (mg): 49
Protein (gm): 5.4
Carbohydrate (gm): 21.7
Exchanges
Milk: 0.0
Vegetable: 0.0
Fruit: 0.0
Bread: 1.5
Meat: 0.0
Fat: 0.0

1. Combine 3/4 cup flour, yeast, and sugar in medium bowl; add hot water, stirring until smooth. Mix in Parmesan cheese and enough remaining 1/2 cup flour to make smooth dough.

2. Knead dough on floured surface until smooth, kneading in Cheddar cheese. Cover dough with inverted bowl; let stand 15 minutes before using. Spread dough on pan according to directions in pizza recipes.

BIG BATCH PIZZA CRUST

Makes four 12-inch crusts (32 slices)

- 1 envelope (2 teaspoons) active dry yeast
- 1 teaspoon granulated sugar
- 1 1/4 cups warm water (105-115 degrees)
- 5 cups all-purpose, *or* bread flour
- 2 large eggs
- 2 teaspoons salt
- Vegetable cooking spray

Per Slice
Calories: 77
% Calories from fat: 6
Fat (gm): 0.5
Sat. fat (gm): 0.1
Cholesterol (mg): 13.3
Sodium (mg): 137
Protein (gm): 2.5
Carbohydrate (gm): 15.2
Exchanges
Milk: 0.0
Vegetable: 0.0
Fruit: 0.0
Bread: 1.0
Meat: 0.0
Fat: 0.0

1. Stir yeast and sugar into water in small bowl. Let stand about 10 minutes until foamy.

2. Make dough according to one of the following methods:

To Make Dough in Food Processor

Place flour, eggs, and salt in food processor; turn on, and pour yeast mixture through feed tube in steady stream. Process until dough cleans sides of bowl, then process 45 seconds longer or until dough is smooth and elastic.

To Make Dough by Hand

To make dough by hand or with large electric mixer, mix yeast mixture and eggs in large bowl. Add flour and salt and stir or beat until dough pulls away from sides of bowl. Turn dough out on lightly floured surface, and knead 5 minutes or until smooth and elastic.

For Both Methods, Finish Crust as Follows

3. Put dough into large bowl coated with vegetable cooking spray. Turn dough to coat. Cover bowl with plastic wrap. Let dough rise in warm, draft-free place 1 hour or until doubled.

4. Punch down dough, and divide into 4 equal pieces. Shape pieces into smooth balls. (Dough can be made ahead up to this point and refrigerated or frozen.) Let rest 30 minutes so dough will be easier to handle. Dough will rise but not double in volume.

5. For each pizza, spray 12-inch-round pizza pan or large cookie sheet with cooking spray.

6. Place dough on lightly floured surface. With floured hands, pat into 6-inch round. Stretch or roll out dough with rolling pin into 11-inch circle. Lift onto prepared pan, and press dough with knuckles or fingers out to edges of pizza pan or into 12-inch circle.

7. Add sauce and toppings (not included in Nutritional Data) and bake at 500 degrees on lowest rack 10 to 12 minutes or until edges of crust are browned and crisp. Cut in wedges with pizza wheel or knife.

RAPID RISE PIZZA CRUST

Makes one 14-inch crust (8 large slices)

3 cups all-purpose flour, divided
1 package rapid-rising dry yeast
3/4 teaspoon salt
1 cup very warm water (125-130 degrees)
2 tablespoons olive oil
Cornmeal

Per Slice
Calories: 203
% Calories from fat: 17
Fat (gm): 3.8
Sat. fat (gm): 0.6
Cholesterol (mg): 0
Sodium (mg): 201
Protein (gm): 5.2
Carbohydrate (gm): 36.2
Exchanges
Milk: 0.0
Vegetable: 0.0
Fruit: 0.0
Bread: 2.5
Meat: 0.0
Fat: 0.5

1. In large bowl, combine 2 cups flour, yeast, and salt. Stir warm water and oil into dry ingredients. Stir in enough of remaining 1 cup flour to make soft dough.

2. Knead dough on lightly floured surface until smooth and elastic, about 4 to 6 minutes. Cover, let rest on floured surface 10 minutes.

3. Lightly oil pizza pan. Sprinkle with cornmeal. Form dough into smooth ball. Roll dough to fit pan. Top with sauce and toppings. Bake at 400 degrees 20 to 30 minutes or until browned.

Note: Sauce and toppings are not included in Nutritional Data above.

ZUCCHINI PIZZA CRUST

Makes one 12-inch crust (6 large slices)

4 medium zucchini, shredded (about 2 pounds)
Salt, to taste
2/3 cup finely chopped onion
1 clove garlic, minced
1/4 cup whole wheat flour
1/2 cup (2 ounces) shredded fat-free mozzarella cheese

Per Slice
Calories: 102
% Calories from fat: 17
Fat (gm): 2
Sat. fat (gm): 0.6
Cholesterol (mg): 71
Sodium (mg): 142
Protein (gm): 10.6
Carbohydrate (gm): 11.7
Exchanges
Milk: 0.0
Vegetable: 0.5
Fruit: 0.0
Bread: 0.5
Meat: 1.0
Fat: 0.0

$^{1}/_{4}$-$^{1}/_{2}$ cup (1-2 ounces) grated fat-free Parmesan cheese
1 teaspoon Italian seasoning
Pepper, to taste
2 eggs
2 egg whites
Vegetable cooking spray

1. Sprinkle zucchini lightly with salt; let stand in colander 10 minutes. Rinse and drain very well on paper toweling. Mix zucchini, onion, garlic, flour, cheeses, and Italian seasoning; season to taste with pepper. Mix in eggs and egg whites.

2. Spray 12-inch pizza pan with cooking spray, press zucchini mixture evenly on pan. Spray zucchini with cooking spray; bake at 375 degrees until browned, 30 to 40 minutes.

POTATO PIZZA CRUST

6 servings

1 package ($1^{1}/_{4}$ pounds) refrigerated shredded potatoes for hash browns
$^{1}/_{3}$ cup finely chopped onion
1 egg
1 egg white
$^{1}/_{4}$ teaspoon salt
$^{1}/_{4}$ teaspoon pepper
Butter-flavored vegetable cooking spray

Per Serving
Calories: 93
% Calories from fat: 9
Fat (gm): 0.9
Sat. fat (gm): 0.3
Cholesterol (mg): 35.5
Sodium (mg): 113
Protein (gm): 3.2
Carbohydrate (gm): 18.2
Exchanges
Milk: 0.0
Vegetable: 0.0
Fruit: 0.0
Bread: 1.5
Meat: 0.0
Fat: 0.0

1. Drain potatoes well on paper toweling. Mix potatoes, onion, egg, egg white, salt, and pepper.

2. Spray 12-inch skillet with cooking spray, press potato mixture evenly on bottom and 1 inch up side of skillet. Spray potato mixture with cooking spray. Bake at 400 degrees until browned, about 20 minutes.

PIZZA SUPREME

6 servings

Vegetable cooking spray
Basic Pizza Dough (see p. 436)
Pizza Sauce (see p. 511)
8 ounces Italian turkey sausage, cooked, crumbled
1/2 cup sliced mushrooms
1/2 cup sliced green bell peppers
1/2 cup sliced onion
1-2 tablespoons sliced ripe, *or* green, olives
1 teaspoon dried oregano leaves
1/2 teaspoon fennel seeds, crushed
3/4-1 cup (3-4 ounces) shredded reduced-fat mozzarella cheese

Per Serving
Calories: 222
% Calories from fat: 24
Fat (gm): 5.9
Sat. fat (gm): 2
Cholesterol (mg): 24.4
Sodium (mg): 484
Protein (gm): 13.9
Carbohydrate (gm): 29.3
Exchanges
Milk: 0.0
Vegetable: 1.0
Fruit: 0.0
Bread: 1.5
Meat: 1.5
Fat: 0.0

1. Spray 12-inch pizza pan with cooking spray, spread dough on pan, making rim around edge. Spread sauce over dough; sprinkle with sausage, mushrooms, bell peppers, onion, and olives. Sprinkle with oregano, fennel seeds, and cheese.

2. Bake pizza at 425 degrees until crust is browned, 15 to 20 minutes.

DELUXE SPINACH-CHEESE PIZZA

6 servings

2 ounces sun-dried tomatoes (not in oil)
Hot water
Olive oil cooking spray
2 cups sliced mushrooms
1 medium onion, sliced
3 cloves garlic, minced
Basic Pizza Dough (see p. 436)
1 cup fat-free ricotta cheese
1/2 cup (2 ounces) shredded fat-free mozzarella cheese
1/4 cup (1 ounce) grated fat-free Parmesan cheese

Per Serving
Calories: 224
% Calories from fat: 7
Fat (gm): 1.9
Sat. fat (gm): 1
Cholesterol (mg): 2.5
Sodium (mg): 317
Protein (gm): 17.7
Carbohydrate (gm): 37.5
Exchanges
Milk: 0.0
Vegetable: 1.0
Fruit: 0.0
Bread: 2.0
Meat: 1.0
Fat: 0.0

1 package (10 ounces) frozen spinach, thawed, well drained
3 tablespoons fat-free sour cream
1 tablespoon lemon juice
1/4 teaspoon ground nutmeg
Salt and pepper, to taste
1/4 cup (1 ounce) crumbled blue cheese

1. Place tomatoes in bowl and pour hot water over; let stand until softened, about 10 minutes. Drain; slice or coarsely chop.

2. Spray large skillet with cooking spray; heat over medium heat until hot. Cook mushrooms, onion, and garlic, covered, until mushrooms are wilted, about 5 minutes. Cook, uncovered, until vegetables are tender and excess liquid is gone, about 5 minutes.

3. Spray 12-inch pizza pan with cooking spray. Spread dough on pan, making rim around edge; bake at 425 degrees 10 minutes.

4. Mix ricotta, mozzarella, and Parmesan cheeses, spinach, sour cream, lemon juice, and nutmeg; season to taste with salt and pepper. Spread cheese mixture evenly on baked crust; top with vegetable mixture and sun-dried tomatoes. Sprinkle pizza with blue cheese.

5. Bake pizza until crust is browned and cheese is melted, about 15 minutes.

DEEP-DISH SPINACH PIZZA

6 servings

Vegetable cooking spray
1/4 cup finely chopped onion
1 clove garlic, minced
1 package (10 ounces) frozen chopped spinach, thawed, very well drained
Salt and pepper, to taste
Cornmeal Pizza Dough (see p. 436)
1/4 cup reduced-sodium tomato sauce
1 1/2 cups fat-free ricotta cheese
2 tablespoons fat-free sour cream

Per Serving
Calories: 195
% Calories from fat: 8
Fat (gm): 1.9
Sat. fat (gm): 1.1
Cholesterol (mg): 5.1
Sodium (mg): 151
Protein (gm): 16.3
Carbohydrate (gm): 30.5

Exchanges
Milk: 0.0
Vegetable: 1.0
Fruit: 0.0
Bread: 1.5
Meat: 1.0
Fat: 0.0

2 tablespoons grated fat-free Parmesan cheese
3/4 teaspoon dried oregano leaves
1 medium tomato, sliced
1/4 teaspoon Italian seasoning
1/2 cup (2 ounces) shredded reduced-fat mozzarella cheese

1. Spray medium skillet with cooking spray; heat over medium heat until hot. Saute onion and garlic until tender, 2 to 3 minutes; add spinach and cook until mixture is very dry. Season to taste with salt and pepper.

2. Roll dough on floured surface to circle 13 inches in diameter; ease dough into lightly greased 9-inch springform pan, covering bottom and 2 inches up side of pan. Spread tomato sauce on bottom of dough.

3. Mix ricotta cheese, sour cream, Parmesan cheese, and oregano; spoon onto dough and top with spinach mixture. Fold edge of dough over edge of filling; top center of pizza with tomato slices and sprinkle with Italian seasoning and mozzarella cheese.

4. Bake pizza at 400 degrees until dough is browned, about 20 to 30 minutes. Let stand 5 to 10 minutes before cutting.

BREAKFAST PIZZA

6 servings

Vegetable cooking spray
Cheese Pizza Dough, *or* Cornmeal Pizza Dough (see pp. 438, 436)
1 cup Pizza Sauce (see p. 511)
1/2 medium green bell pepper, sliced
1/2 small onion, sliced
1 cup (4 ounces) shredded fat-free mozzarella cheese
3 tablespoons real bacon bits
1 egg

Per Serving
Calories: 197
% Calories from fat: 9
Fat (gm): 1.9
Sat. fat (gm): 0.4
Cholesterol (mg): 35.5
Sodium (mg): 287
Protein (gm): 15.1
Carbohydrate (gm): 29.5
Exchanges
Milk: 0.0
Vegetable: 1.0
Fruit: 0.0
Bread: 1.5
Meat: 1.0
Fat: 0.0

1. Spray 12-inch pizza pan with cooking spray, spread dough on pan, making rim around edge. Spread sauce on dough and sprinkle with bell pepper, onion, cheese, and bacon bits.

2. Bake pizza at 425 degrees until crust is browned, 15 to 20 minutes. Remove from oven; break egg into center of pizza. Stir egg with fork and quickly spread over pizza. Return to oven and bake until egg is cooked, 1 to 2 minutes.

RANCH-STYLE PIZZA

6 servings

Vegetable cooking spray
Basic Pizza Dough (see p. 436)
1 cup (4 ounces) shredded fat-free mozzarella cheese
1/2 cup (2 ounces) shredded reduced-fat mozzarella cheese
1 cup thinly sliced spinach
1/2 cup sliced mushrooms
1/4 cup fat-free ranch salad dressing

Per Serving
Calories: 171
% Calories from fat: 9
Fat (gm): 1.7
Sat. fat (gm): 1.1
Cholesterol (mg): 5.1
Sodium (mg): 378
Protein (gm): 12.9
Carbohydrate (gm): 25

Exchanges
Milk: 0.0
Vegetable: 0.5
Fruit: 0.0
Bread: 1.5
Meat: 1.0
Fat: 0.0

1. Spray 12-inch pizza pan with cooking spray; spread dough on pan, making rim around edge. Sprinkle dough with cheeses. Toss spinach and mushrooms together; mound in center of pizza.

2. Bake pizza at 425 degrees until crust is browned, 15 to 20 minutes. Drizzle pizza with salad dressing before serving.

REUBEN PIZZA

6 servings

Vegetable cooking spray
12 ounces cabbage, thinly sliced
1/2 cup thinly sliced red onion
1 1/2 teaspoons caraway seeds, crushed, divided
2 tablespoons water
1/2 can (14.2-ounce size) Bavarian-style sweet mild sauerkraut with caraway, rinsed, very well drained
1/2-1 cup (2-4 ounces) shredded fat-free mozzarella cheese
2-3 teaspoons real bacon bits
Whole Wheat Pizza Dough (see p. 437)
1/2 cup rye flour
1/4 cup fat-free thousand island salad dressing

Per Serving
Calories: 185
% Calories from fat: 4
Fat (gm): 0.9
Sat. fat (gm): 0.1
Cholesterol (mg): 0
Sodium (mg): 402
Protein (gm): 8.8
Carbohydrate (gm): 36.9

Exchanges
Milk: 0.0
Vegetable: 1.0
Fruit: 0.0
Bread: 2.0
Meat: 0.5
Fat: 0.0

1. Spray large skillet with cooking spray; heat over medium heat until hot. Add cabbage, onion, and 1 teaspoon caraway seeds; saute 2 to 3 minutes. Add water to skillet; cook, covered, over medium to medium-low heat until cabbage is wilted, 5 to 8 minutes. Stir in sauerkraut; cook, uncovered, over medium-low heat until cabbage mixture is very tender, 15 to 20 minutes. Cool to room temperature; stir in cheese and bacon.

2. Make Whole Wheat Pizza Dough, substituting rye flour for the whole wheat flour, and adding the remaining 1/2 teaspoon caraway seeds.

3. Spray 12-inch pizza pan with cooking spray, spread dough on pan, making rim around edge. Spread salad dressing on dough. Spread cabbage mixture evenly over dough.

4. Bake pizza at 425 degrees until crust is browned, 15 to 20 minutes.

WEST COAST PIZZA

4 servings

Olive oil cooking spray
1 1/2 cups sliced mushrooms
1 cup small broccoli florets
3/4 cup thinly sliced red bell pepper
1/2 cup sliced carrot
1/4 cup thinly sliced green onions
4 cloves garlic, minced
1/2-3/4 cup cooked dried, *or* rinsed, drained, canned, Great Northern beans
Red Tomato Salsa (see p. 513), *or* 2 cups medium salsa, divided
1 thin-crust Italian bread shell (focaccia)
1/2-3/4 cup (2-3 ounces) shredded reduced-fat mozzarella cheese
1/2-3/4 cup (2-3 ounces) shredded fat-free mozzarella cheese
1/2-3/4 cup sprouted wheat berries, *or* alfalfa sprouts

Per Serving
Calories: 351
% Calories from fat: 18
Fat (gm): 7.1
Sat. fat (gm): 2.9
Cholesterol (mg): 13.8
Sodium (mg): 583
Protein (gm): 23.2
Carbohydrate (gm): 50.4
Exchanges
Milk: 0.0
Vegetable: 2.0
Fruit: 0.0
Bread: 2.5
Meat: 2.0
Fat: 0.0

1. Spray large skillet with cooking spray; heat over medium heat until hot. Saute mushrooms, broccoli, bell pepper, carrot, onions, and garlic until tender, 8 to 10 minutes.

2. Mash beans with 3 to 4 tablespoons salsa; spread mixture on bread shell. Spoon about 1/2 cup salsa over beans; top with sauteed vegetables and cheeses.

3. Bake pizza at 350 degrees until cheese is melted, about 15 minutes. Sprinkle with sprouts just before serving. Serve with remaining salsa.

CALYPSO PIZZA

6 servings

Vegetable cooking spray
Cheese Pizza Dough (see p. 438)
1 cup rinsed, drained, canned black beans
1 can (8 ounces) pineapple tidbits, drained
1/4 cup chopped red bell pepper
1 small jalapeño chili, finely chopped
1/2 teaspoon minced garlic
1/2 teaspoon ground cumin
1/4 cup hot, *or* mild, salsa
1 teaspoon lime juice
1 cup (4 ounces) shredded reduced-fat Monterey Jack cheese
1/2 cup (2 ounces) shredded fat-free Cheddar cheese

Per Serving
Calories: 219
% Calories from fat: 16
Fat (gm): 4
Sat. fat (gm): 2.1
Cholesterol (mg): 13.5
Sodium (mg): 373
Protein (gm): 14.1
Carbohydrate (gm): 33.9

Exchanges
Milk: 0.0
Vegetable: 1.0
Fruit: 0.5
Bread: 1.5
Meat: 1.0
Fat: 0.0

1. Spray 12-inch pizza pan with cooking spray, spread dough on pan, making rim around edge. Combine all ingredients, except cheeses, and arrange on crust; sprinkle with cheeses.

2. Bake pizza at 425 degrees until crust is browned, 15 to 20 minutes.

ORIENTAL PIZZA

6 servings

Oriental-flavored cooking spray
1 cup sliced shiitake, *or* cremini, mushrooms
1 cup thinly sliced bok choy
1/2 cup small broccoli florets
1 small onion, sliced
1/2 medium green bell pepper, sliced
1/2 cup (2 ounces) snow peas, trimmed
2 teaspoons minced gingerroot
1 clove garlic, minced
1-2 teaspoons reduced-sodium tamari soy sauce
Salt and pepper, to taste
Basic Pizza Dough (see p. 436)
1 can (5 1/2 ounces) crabmeat, flaked
3/4 cup (3 ounces) shredded fat-free mozzarella cheese

Per Serving
Calories: 152
% Calories from fat: 4
Fat (gm): 0.7
Sat. fat (gm): 0.1
Cholesterol (mg): 23.5
Sodium (mg): 345
Protein (gm): 9.2
Carbohydrate (gm): 27.7

Exchanges
Milk: 0.0
Vegetable: 2.0
Fruit: 0.0
Bread: 1.5
Meat: 0.0
Fat: 0.0

1. Spray large skillet with cooking spray; heat over medium heat until hot. Stir-fry mushrooms, bok choy, broccoli, onion, green pepper, snow peas, gingerroot, and garlic until tender, 8 to 10 minutes. Season to taste with soy sauce, salt, and pepper; cool to room temperature.

2. Spray 12-inch pizza pan with cooking spray. Spread dough on pan, making rim around edge. Spray dough with cooking spray. Arrange vegetables and crabmeat on dough; sprinkle with cheese.

3. Bake pizza at 425 degrees until crust is browned, 15 to 20 minutes.

FRENCH-STYLE ONION PIZZA

6 servings

Olive oil cooking spray
6 medium onions, thinly sliced (about 6 cups)
2 medium tomatoes, coarsely chopped
1/4 cup finely chopped parsley
1/2 teaspoon dried oregano leaves
1/4 teaspoon dried thyme leaves
Salt and pepper, to taste
Basic Pizza Dough (see p. 436)
2-4 tablespoons sliced ripe olives

Per Serving
Calories: 165
% Calories from fat: 9
Fat (gm): 1.6
Sat. fat (gm): 0.2
Cholesterol (mg): 0
Sodium (mg): 191
Protein (gm): 5.1
Carbohydrate (gm): 33.5

Exchanges
Milk: 0.0
Vegetable: 2.0
Fruit: 0.0
Bread: 1.5
Meat: 0.0
Fat: 0.0

1. Spray large skillet with cooking spray; heat over medium heat until hot. Cook onions over medium to medium-low heat until very tender, about 15 minutes. Add tomatoes, parsley, oregano, and thyme; cook over medium heat until mixture is thick, about 15 minutes. Season to taste with salt and pepper; cool to room temperature.

2. Spray 12-inch pizza pan with cooking spray, spread dough on pan, making rim around edge. Spread onion mixture over dough and sprinkle with olives.

3. Bake pizza at 425 degrees until crust is browned, 15 to 20 minutes.

FRESH TOMATO AND BASIL PIZZA

6 servings

Olive oil cooking spray
Basic Pizza Dough (see p. 436)
Pizza Sauce (see p. 511)
1-2 teaspoons minced garlic
1 cup (4 ounces) fat-free mozzarella cheese
1/2-3/4 cup (2-3 ounces) reduced-fat mozzarella cheese

Per Serving
Calories: 193
% Calories from fat: 9
Fat (gm): 1.8
Sat. fat (gm): 1.1
Cholesterol (mg): 5.1
Sodium (mg): 306
Protein (gm): 14.1
Carbohydrate (gm): 29.4

Exchanges
Milk: 0.0
Vegetable: 2.0
Fruit: 0.0
Bread: 1.5
Meat: 1.0
Fat: 0.0

2 medium tomatoes, thinly sliced
12 basil leaves, *or* 1 teaspoon dried basil leaves

1. Spray 12-inch pizza pan with cooking spray; spread dough on pan, making rim around edge. Mix Pizza Sauce and garlic; spread over dough. Sprinkle with cheeses; top with tomato slices and basil.

2. Bake pizza at 425 degrees until crust is browned, 15 to 20 minutes.

ARTICHOKE AND ROASTED PEPPER PIZZA

6 servings

Per Serving
Calories: 169
% Calories from fat: 18
Fat (gm): 3.6
Sat. fat (gm): 0.6
Cholesterol (mg): 2.5
Sodium (mg): 311
Protein (gm): 9
Carbohydrate (gm): 26.8

Exchanges
Milk: 0.0
Vegetable: 1.0
Fruit: 0.0
Bread: 1.5
Meat: 0.5
Fat: 0.0

Olive oil cooking spray
1 medium green bell pepper, cut into 1/2-inch slices
Basic Pizza Dough (see p. 436)
1/2 can (15 ounce size) reduced-sodium whole tomatoes, drained, coarsely chopped
1/2 can (15 ounce size) artichoke hearts, rinsed, drained, cut into fourths
1/2 teaspoon Italian seasoning
1/2 cup (2 ounces) shredded fat-free mozzarella cheese
1/4-1/2 cup (1-2 ounces) shredded reduced-fat mozzarella cheese
2 tablespoons grated fat-free Parmesan cheese

1. Spray aluminum-foil-lined small baking pan with cooking spray. Arrange bell pepper in pan; bake at 425 degrees until pepper is tender and browned, 20 to 30 minutes.

2. Spray 12-inch pizza pan with cooking spray, spread dough on pan, making rim around edge. Arrange bell pepper, tomatoes, and artichoke hearts on dough; sprinkle with Italian seasoning and cheeses.

3. Bake pizza until crust is browned, 15 to 20 minutes.

ROASTED PEPPERS AND CHEESE PIZZA

6 servings

Olive oil cooking spray
1 large red bell pepper, cut into 3/4-inch slices
Cornmeal Pizza Dough (see p. 436)
1 cup fat-free ricotta cheese
1/2 cup (2 ounces) shredded fat-free mozzarella cheese
1/4 cup (1 ounce) shredded fat-free Parmesan cheese
3 tablespoons fat-free sour cream
1 tablespoon lemon juice
1 clove garlic, minced
Salt and pepper, to taste
2 green onions, thinly sliced
12-18 fresh basil leaves

Per Serving
Calories: 172
% Calories from fat: 3
Fat (gm): 0.6
Sat. fat (gm): 0.1
Cholesterol (mg): 0
Sodium (mg): 124
Protein (gm): 14.4
Carbohydrate (gm): 29.4
Exchanges
Milk: 0.0
Vegetable: 1.0
Fruit: 0.0
Bread: 1.5
Meat: 1.0
Fat: 0.0

1. Spray aluminum-foil-lined baking pan with cooking spray. Arrange bell pepper slices in pan; spray with cooking spray. Roast at 425 degrees until peppers are soft, but not browned, 20 to 30 minutes.

2. Spray 12-inch pizza pan with cooking spray; spread dough on pan, making rim around edge. Bake dough at 425 degrees 15 to 20 minutes.

3. Mix cheeses, sour cream, lemon juice, and garlic; season to taste with salt and pepper. Spread cheese mixture evenly on crust; sprinkle with green onions. Arrange roasted pepper slices and basil leaves attractively on top.

4. Bake at 425 degrees until crust is browned, 15 to 20 minutes.

ROASTED CAPONATA PIZZA

6 servings

Olive oil cooking spray
2 cups diced, unpeeled eggplant
1 cup coarsely chopped onion
Whole Wheat Pizza Dough (see p. 437)
1 cup (1/2 recipe) Mediterranean Tomato-Caper Sauce (see p. 511)
1/2-1 cup (2-4 ounces) shredded fat-free mozzarella cheese
1/2 cup (2 ounces) crumbled reduced-fat feta cheese
1 tablespoon pine nuts, optional

Per Serving
Calories: 181
% Calories from fat: 9
Fat (gm): 1.9
Sat. fat (gm): 0.9
Cholesterol (mg): 3.4
Sodium (mg): 312
Protein (gm): 10
Carbohydrate (gm): 32.3
Exchanges
Milk: 0.0
Vegetable: 2.0
Fruit: 0.0
Bread: 1.5
Meat: 0.5
Fat: 0.0

1. Spray aluminum-foil-lined 13 x 9-inch baking pan with cooking spray. Arrange eggplant and onion in baking pan; bake at 425 degrees until eggplant is tender and browned, 20 to 30 minutes. Cool to room temperature.

2. Spray 12-inch pizza pan with cooking spray; spread dough on pan, making rim around edge. Spread sauce on dough; arrange eggplant mixture on sauce. Sprinkle with cheeses and pine nuts.

3. Bake pizza at 425 degrees until crust is browned, 15 to 20 minutes.

CHICKEN AND BLUE CHEESE PIZZA

12 appetizer servings

2 cups sliced mushrooms
2 cups coarsely chopped chicken breast
2 tablespoons margarine
1/2 teaspoon dried sage leaves
1/4 teaspoon salt
1/4 teaspoon pepper
Basic Pizza Dough (see p. 436)
1/3 cup (1 1/3 ounces) crumbled blue cheese
2 tablespoons chopped walnuts

Per Serving
Calories: 128
% Calories from fat: 32
Fat (gm): 4.4
Sat. fat (gm): 1.3
Cholesterol (mg): 20.7
Sodium (mg): 179
Protein (gm): 9.7
Carbohydrate (gm): 12
Exchanges
Milk: 0.0
Vegetable: 0.0
Fruit: 0.0
Bread: 1.0
Meat: 1.0
Fat: 0.0

1. Saute mushrooms and chicken in margarine in medium skillet until lightly browned. Stir in sage, salt, and pepper. Spread Basic Pizza Dough on lightly greased 12-inch pizza pan. Spread chicken mixture over dough. Top with blue cheese and walnuts.

2. Bake at 425 degrees 20 minutes or until pizzas are done. Crust will be brown and toppings hot.

GRILLED FAJITA PIZZA

12 appetizer servings

- 2 boneless skinless chicken breasts, cut into 1/2-inch strips
- Southwest Marinade (recipe follows)
- 1 cup sliced green bell pepper
- 1 cup sliced onion
- Basic Pizza Dough (see p. 436)
- 5 green onions and tops, sliced
- 1/2 cup chopped cilantro leaves

Per Serving
Calories: 150
% Calories from fat: 12
Fat (gm): 2
Sat. fat (gm): 0.4
Cholesterol (mg): 24.3
Sodium (mg): 104
Protein (gm): 11.2
Carbohydrate (gm): 20.2

Exchanges
Milk: 0.0
Vegetable: 1.0
Fruit: 0.0
Bread: 1.0
Meat: 1.0
Fat: 0.0

1. Combine chicken and Southwest Marinade in glass dish; refrigerate, covered, 45 minutes or several hours. Drain, reserving marinade.

2. Preheat barbecue grill. Spray rack with cooking spray. Brush peppers and onion with reserved marinade. Grill chicken, peppers, and onion over hot coals until done, about 5 minutes, turning once and brushing with marinade.

3. Stretch and shape dough into 12-inch round; place on paddle or cookie sheet that has been sprinkled with cornmeal. Arrange grilled foods on crust; sprinkle with green onions and cilantro.

4. Set pizza over hot coals on lightly greased rack. Cover grill and cook until crust is crisp and browned, about 5 to 6 minutes.

Southwest Marinade

makes about 2 cups

- 1½ cups beer
- 2 tablespoons mustard
- 5 tablespoons red wine vinegar
- 5 tablespoons dark brown sugar
- ½ teaspoon garlic powder

1. Combine all ingredients in small saucepan. Heat to boiling; reduce heat and simmer 5 minutes. Cool.

SEAFOOD AND ARTICHOKE PIZZA

6 servings

Per Serving
Calories: 271
% Calories from fat: 16
Fat (gm): 4.7
Sat. fat (gm): 1.8
Cholesterol (mg): 78.6
Sodium (mg): 566
Protein (gm): 23
Carbohydrate (gm): 30.9

Exchanges
Milk: 0.0
Vegetable: 2.0
Fruit: 0.0
Bread: 1.5
Meat: 2.0
Fat: 0.0

- 1 tablespoon plus 1 teaspoon cornstarch
- ¾ cup 2% reduced-fat milk
- ½ cup (2 ounces) shredded part-skim mozzarella cheese
- ¼ cup dry white wine
- ½ teaspoon garlic powder
- ½ teaspoon pepper
- Basic Pizza Dough (see p. 436)
- ½ pound small shrimp, peeled, deveined, cut into pieces
- ½ pound fresh bay scallops
- 6 green onions, sliced
- 1 can (14 ounces) artichoke hearts, drained, coarsely chopped
- 6 fresh basil leaves, sliced
- 2 tablespoons grated Parmesan cheese

1. Combine cornstarch and milk in medium saucepan; heat to boiling over medium heat. Cook 3 minutes or until thickened, stirring constantly. Remove from heat; stir in mozzarella cheese, wine, garlic powder, and pepper.

2. Spread Basic Pizza Dough on lightly greased 12-inch pizza pan. Spread sauce evenly over dough, leaving 1/2-inch border. Arrange shrimp, scallops, onions, artichokes, and basil leaves over sauce. Bake at 500 degrees 12 minutes. Sprinkle with Parmesan cheese and bake 5 minutes longer, or until cheese melts. Remove pizza to cutting board and let stand 5 minutes before cutting.

SHRIMP AND FETA PIZZA

8 servings

Whole Wheat Pizza Dough (see p. 437)
Olive oil cooking spray
1/2 teaspoon dried basil leaves
1/2 teaspoon dried oregano leaves
36 medium shrimp, shelled and deveined
2 cups thinly sliced snow peas
1 cup chopped scallions
2 cloves garlic, minced
4 1/2 ounces feta cheese, crumbled

Per Serving
Calories: 162
% Calories from fat: 28
Fat (gm): 5.1
Sat. fat (gm): 2.7
Cholesterol (mg): 62.6
Sodium (mg): 294
Protein (gm): 11.9
Carbohydrate (gm): 17.2

Exchanges
Milk: 0.0
Vegetable: 0.5
Fruit: 0.0
Bread: 1.0
Meat: 1.0
Fat: 0.5

1. Spread Whole Wheat Pizza Dough on lightly greased 12-inch pizza pan; pinch edges to form rim. Prick surface of dough with fork; spray with cooking spray. Sprinkle with basil and oregano. Bake at 475 degrees 10 to 12 minutes, until golden.

2. Spray large skillet with cooking spray; heat over medium heat until hot. Saute shrimp, snow peas, scallions, and garlic until shrimp are done, about 5 minutes. Spread shrimp mixture over crust. Sprinkle with cheese. Bake 5 to 8 minutes, or until cheese softens.

TUSCAN POTATO PIZZA

6 servings

Mesquite-flavored vegetable cooking spray
8 ounces small Russet potatoes, unpeeled, cut into scant 1/4-inch slices
1 medium red onion, thinly sliced
Salt and pepper, to taste
Whole Wheat Pizza Dough (see p. 137)
1-2 teaspoons minced garlic
1-2 teaspoons dried sage leaves
1/2 teaspoon dried thyme leaves
2 tablespoons sun-dried tomato bits
1 cup (4 ounces) shredded fat-free mozzarella cheese
1/2 cup (2 ounces) shredded smoked mozzarella cheese

Per Serving
Calories: 225
% Calories from fat: 8
Fat (gm): 2.1
Sat. fat (gm): 0.1
Cholesterol (mg): 5
Sodium (mg): 301
Protein (gm): 14.4
Carbohydrate (gm): 38.2

Exchanges
Milk: 0.0
Vegetable: 0.0
Fruit: 0.0
Bread: 2.5
Meat: 1.0
Fat: 0.0

1. Spray aluminum-foil-lined jelly roll pan with cooking spray. Arrange potatoes and onions on pan; spray with cooking spray. Bake at 425 degrees until potatoes are almost tender, about 10 minutes. Season to taste with salt and pepper, cool to room temperature.

2. Spray 12-inch pizza pan with cooking spray; spread dough on pan, making rim around edge. Spray dough lightly with cooking spray; spread garlic on crust. Arrange potatoes and onions on crust; sprinkle with herbs, tomato bits, and cheeses.

3. Bake pizza at 425 degrees until browned, 15 to 20 minutes.

PIZZA ON PASTA

6 servings

- Olive oil cooking spray
- 8 ounces Italian turkey sausage
- 1 cup sliced mushrooms
- 1 cup sliced zucchini
- 1/2 cup sliced red bell pepper
- 1/4 cup sliced green onions and tops
- 1 1/2 teaspoons minced garlic
- 1 1/2 teaspoons Italian seasoning
- 1/2 teaspoon dried oregano leaves
- Salt and pepper, to taste
- 8 ounces thin spaghetti, cooked
- 2 egg whites, lightly beaten
- 1 medium tomato, sliced
- 3/4-1 cup (3-4 ounces) shredded reduced-fat Muenster, *or* mozzarella, cheese
- Pizza Sauce (see p. 511), warm

Per Serving
Calories: 275
% Calories from fat: 22
Fat (gm): 6.7
Sat. fat (gm): 2.3
Cholesterol (mg): 27.8
Sodium (mg): 393
Protein (gm): 17.5
Carbohydrate (gm): 36.4

Exchanges
Milk: 0.0
Vegetable: 1.0
Fruit: 0.0
Bread: 2.0
Meat: 2.0
Fat: 0.0

1. Spray large skillet with cooking spray; heat over medium heat until hot. Add sausage, mushrooms, zucchini, bell pepper, green onions, and garlic; saute until sausage is cooked and vegetables are tender, about 8 minutes. Stir in Italian seasoning and oregano; cook 1 to 2 minutes longer. Season to taste with salt and pepper. Transfer to large bowl.

2. Spray clean large skillet with cooking spray; heat over medium heat until hot. Mix vegetable mixture, spaghetti, and egg whites. Add to skillet and pat into even layer with pancake turner. Cook, covered, over medium to medium-low heat until browned on the bottom, about 5 minutes. Loosen side and bottom of "pizza" with pancake turner; invert onto large plate. Slide "pizza" back into skillet.

3. Arrange tomato slices over top of "pizza" and sprinkle with cheese; cook, covered, over medium heat until cheese is melted, about 5 minutes. Slide "pizza" onto serving plate; cut into wedges and serve with Pizza Sauce.

ANTIPASTO PIZZA

6 servings

Per Serving
Calories: 209
% Calories from fat: 16
Fat (gm): 3.8
Sat. fat (gm): 1.5
Cholesterol (mg): 7.7
Sodium (mg): 517
Protein (gm): 11.8
Carbohydrate (gm): 33.1

Exchanges
Milk: 0.0
Vegetable: 2.0
Fruit: 0.0
Bread: 1.5
Meat: 1.0
Fat: 0.0

Olive oil cooking spray
Cornmeal Pizza Dough (see p. 436)
1 cup (1/2 recipe) Mediterranean Tomato-Caper Sauce (see p. 511)
1/2 small zucchini, thinly sliced
1/2 cup sliced mushrooms
1/2 cup sliced onion
1/2 medium red bell pepper, sliced
3 cloves garlic, minced
3-4 pepperoncini, sliced
3-4 cooked frozen, *or* canned, artichoke hearts, sliced
2-4 tablespoons sliced ripe olives
1 ounce thinly sliced hard salami, cut into slivers
3/4 cup (3 ounces) shredded fat-free mozzarella cheese
1/2 cup (2 ounces) crumbled reduced-fat feta cheese

1. Spray 12-inch pizza pan with cooking spray, spread dough on pan, making rim around edge. Spread sauce on dough; top with vegetables, salami, and cheeses.

2. Bake pizza at 425 degrees until crust is browned, 15 to 20 minutes.

LEEK AND FETA PIZZA WITH PESTO SAUCE

6 servings

Per Serving
Calories: 288
% Calories from fat: 27
Fat (gm): 8.9
Sat. fat (gm): 1.9
Cholesterol (mg): 3.4
Sodium (mg): 428
Protein (gm): 12.1
Carbohydrate (gm): 41.9

Exchanges
Milk: 0.0
Vegetable: 3.0
Fruit: 0.0
Bread: 1.5
Meat: 1.0
Fat: 1.0

Olive oil cooking spray
4 cups sliced leeks (white parts only)
1 teaspoon dried basil leaves
Salt and pepper, to taste
Basic Pizza Dough (see p. 436)
Sun-Dried Tomato Pesto (see p. 427)
1/2 cup (2 ounces) shredded fat-free mozzarella cheese
1/2 cup (2 ounces) crumbled reduced-fat feta cheese
2 tablespoons (1/2 ounce) grated fat-free Parmesan cheese

1. Spray large skillet with cooking spray; heat over medium heat until hot. Saute leeks until tender, 8 to 10 minutes. Sprinkle with basil and cook 1 to 2 minutes longer. Season to taste with salt and pepper; cool to room temperature.

2. Spray 12-inch pizza pan with cooking spray. Spread dough on pan, making rim around edge. Spread pesto on dough; top with leek mixture and sprinkle with cheeses.

3. Bake pizza at 425 degrees until crust is browned, 15 to 20 minutes.

WILD MUSHROOM PIZZA

6 servings

Per Serving
Calories: 194
% Calories from fat: 20
Fat (gm): 4.5
Sat. fat (gm): 0.7
Cholesterol (mg): 0.8
Sodium (mg): 336
Protein (gm): 12.5
Carbohydrate (gm): 26.7

Exchanges
Milk: 0.0
Vegetable: 2.0
Fruit: 0.0
Bread: 1.0
Meat: 1.0
Fat: 0.5

Olive oil cooking spray
5 cups sliced wild mushrooms (cremini, portobello, shiitake, etc.)
1/4 cup finely chopped shallots, *or* onions
1 teaspoon minced garlic
2 tablespoons water
1/4-1/2 teaspoon dried thyme leaves
Basic Pizza Dough (see p. 436)

- 1/4 cup (1/2 recipe) Mixed Herb Pesto (see p. 515)
- 1 cup (4 ounces) shredded fat-free mozzarella cheese, divided

1. Spray large skillet with cooking spray; heat over medium heat until hot. Add mushrooms, shallots, garlic, and water to skillet; cook, covered, over medium heat until mushrooms are wilted, about 5 minutes. Cook, uncovered, until mushrooms are tender and liquid is gone, 10 to 12 minutes. Stir in thyme.

2. Spray 12-inch pizza pan with cooking spray. Shape dough into a round; spread on 12-inch pizza pan, making rim around edge. Spread pesto on dough and sprinkle with 1/2 cup cheese. Spoon mushroom mixture on cheese; sprinkle with remaining 1/2 cup cheese

3. Bake pizza at 350 degrees until crust is browned, about 30 minutes.

GAZPACHO PIZZA

8 servings

- 1 1/4 packages (8-ounce size) fat-free cream cheese, softened
- 2 tablespoons fat-free mayonnaise
- 1/2 teaspoon dry mustard
- 2 teaspoons finely chopped parsley
- 2 teaspoons finely chopped chives
- 1 large whole wheat lavosh, *or* cracker bread (5 1/4 ounces)
- 1/2 cup chopped avocado
- 1 cup chopped seeded tomato
- 1 cup chopped seeded cucumber
- 1/2 cup chopped onion
- 1/2 cup chopped yellow bell pepper
- 1/2 cup chopped green bell pepper
- 1/4 cup fat-free Italian salad dressing
- 1 teaspoon minced garlic
- 1 teaspoon minced jalapeño chili
- Salt and pepper, to taste

Per Serving
Calories: 153
% Calories from fat: 29
Fat (gm): 5.1
Sat. fat (gm): 0.4
Cholesterol (mg): 0
Sodium (mg): 415
Protein (gm): 7.4
Carbohydrate (gm): 19.9
Exchanges
Milk: 0.0
Vegetable: 1.5
Fruit: 0.0
Bread: 1.0
Meat: 0.0
Fat: 1.0

1. Mix cream cheese, mayonnaise, dry mustard, parsley, and chives. Spread mixture on lavosh.

2. Combine vegetables in large bowl. Combine salad dressing, garlic, and jalapeño chili; pour over vegetables and toss. Season to taste with salt and pepper. Spoon mixture onto lavosh and serve immediately.

TOMATO FILLO PIZZA

8 servings

Olive oil cooking spray
8 sheets frozen fillo pastry, thawed
2 cups (8 ounces) shredded fat-free mozzarella cheese
1/2 cup thinly sliced onion
1 pound tomatoes, thinly sliced
Salt and pepper, to taste
1/4 cup (1 ounce) grated Parmesan cheese
3/4 teaspoon dried dill weed
1/2 teaspoon dried basil leaves

Per Serving
Calories: 79
% Calories from fat: 14
Fat (gm): 1.2
Sat. fat (gm): 0.6
Cholesterol (mg): 2.5
Sodium (mg): 270
Protein (gm): 12
Carbohydrate (gm): 5.4

Exchanges
Milk: 0.0
Vegetable: 0.0
Fruit: 0.0
Bread: 0.5
Meat: 1.0
Fat: 0.0

1. Spray jelly roll pan with cooking spray; place sheet of fillo on pan and spray generously with spray. Repeat with remaining sheets of fillo.

2. Sprinkle mozzarella cheese and onion over fillo; arrange tomato slices on top. Sprinkle lightly with salt and pepper. Sprinkle with Parmesan cheese and herbs.

3. Bake pizza at 375 degrees until fillo is browned and cheese melted, about 15 minutes.

PIZZA, SOUTHWEST-STYLE

6 servings

Mesquite-flavored vegetable cooking spray
1 medium poblano chili, sliced
3/4 cup sliced red bell pepper
1 medium onion, thinly sliced
1 small jalapeño chili, finely chopped
2 cloves garlic, minced
2/3 cup fresh, *or* frozen, thawed, whole-kernel corn
1 teaspoon dried marjoram leaves
Cornmeal Pizza Dough (see p. 436)
Pizza Sauce (see p. 511)
1/2 teaspoon ground cumin
1 cup (4 ounces) shredded fat-free pizza cheese

Per Serving
Calories: 192
% Calories from fat: 3
Fat (gm): 0.7
Sat. fat (gm): 0.1
Cholesterol (mg): 0
Sodium (mg): 161
Protein (gm): 11.9
Carbohydrate (gm): 35.9

Exchanges
Milk: 0.0
Vegetable: 2.0
Fruit: 0.0
Bread: 1.5
Meat: 0.5
Fat: 0.0

1. Spray large skillet with cooking spray; heat over medium heat until hot. Saute poblano chili, bell pepper, onion, jalapeño chili, and garlic until tender, about 8 minutes. Stir in corn and marjoram.

2. Spray 12-inch pizza pan with cooking spray, spread dough on pan, making rim around edge. Spray dough lightly with cooking spray. Mix Pizza Sauce and cumin; spread on dough. Top with vegetable mixture and sprinkle with cheese.

3. Bake pizza at 425 degrees until browned, 15 to 20 minutes.

TACO PIZZA

6 servings

12-16 ounces lean ground beef
1-2 tablespoons taco seasoning mix
2/3 cup water
Olive oil cooking spray
Cornmeal Pizza Dough (see p. 436)
1/2 cup (2 ounces) shredded fat-free Cheddar cheese
1/2 cup (2 ounces) shredded reduced-fat Monterey Jack cheese
1/2 large green bell pepper, sliced
1 cup chopped lettuce
1/2 cup chopped tomato
6 tablespoons fat-free sour cream
6 tablespoons reduced-sodium hot, *or* mild, salsa

Per Serving
Calories: 298
% Calories from fat: 35
Fat (gm): 11.3
Sat. fat (gm): 4.9
Cholesterol (mg): 44.8
Sodium (mg): 390
Protein (gm): 19.8
Carbohydrate (gm): 28.1

Exchanges
Milk: 0.0
Vegetable: 1.0
Fruit: 0.0
Bread: 1.5
Meat: 2.0
Fat: 1.0

1. Brown ground beef in small skillet; drain fat. Add taco seasoning mix, and water; heat to boiling. Reduce heat and simmer, uncovered, until mixture is dry, about 5 minutes. Cool to room temperature.

2. Spray 12-inch pizza pan with cooking spray, spread dough on pan, making rim around edge. Sprinkle dough with beef, cheeses, and bell pepper.

3. Bake pizza at 425 degrees until crust is browned, 15 to 20 minutes. Sprinkle with lettuce and tomato and serve immediately with sour cream and salsa.

BLACK BEAN AND JALAPEÑO PIZZA

6 servings

Olive oil cooking spray
Cornmeal Pizza Dough, *or* Cheese Pizza Dough (see pp. 436, 438)
1 cup (1/2 recipe) Red Tomato Salsa (see p. 513), *or* medium salsa, divided
1 cup cooked dried, *or* rinsed, drained, canned, black beans
1/4-1/3 cup drained, pickled sliced jalapeño chilies
1 cup (4 ounces) shredded reduced-fat Cheddar cheese

Per Serving
Calories: 191
% Calories from fat: 16
Fat (gm): 3.3
Sat. fat (gm): 1.5
Cholesterol (mg): 10.1
Sodium (mg): 334
Protein (gm): 9.9
Carbohydrate (gm): 30.3
Exchanges
Milk: 0.0
Vegetable: 1.0
Fruit: 0.0
Bread: 2.0
Meat: 0.5
Fat: 0.0

1. Spray 12-inch pizza pan with cooking spray; spread dough on pan, making rim around edge. Spread 3/4 cup salsa on dough.
2. Lightly mash black beans with remaining 1/4 cup salsa; spoon over pizza. Sprinkle jalapeño chilies and cheese over all.
3. Bake pizza at 425 degrees until crust is browned, 15 to 20 minutes.

CHILI POBLANO PIZZA

6 servings

Olive oil cooking spray
4 large poblano chilies, sliced
2 cups chopped onions
1 clove garlic, minced
Salt, to taste
Potato Pizza Crust (see p. 441)
1/2-1 cup (2-4 ounces) shredded reduced-fat Monterey Jack cheese

Per Serving
Calories: 154
% Calories from fat: 16
Fat (gm): 2.8
Sat. fat (gm): 1.3
Cholesterol (mg): 42.3
Sodium (mg): 190
Protein (gm): 7.3
Carbohydrate (gm): 26.1
Exchanges
Milk: 0.0
Vegetable: 1.0
Fruit: 0.0
Bread: 1.5
Meat: 0.5
Fat: 0.0

1. Spray large skillet with cooking spray; heat over medium heat until hot. Add poblano chilies, onions, and garlic, and cook over medium to medium-low heat until chilies are very soft, 20 to 30 minutes. Season to taste with salt.

2. Spread chili mixture in Potato Pizza Crust; sprinkle with cheese. Bake at 400 degrees until cheese is melted, 5 to 10 minutes.

HUEVOS RANCHEROS PIZZA

6 servings

Vegetable cooking spray
1 large poblano chili, sliced
1/2 large red bell pepper, sliced
1 small onion, sliced
2 cloves garlic, minced
Salt and pepper, to taste
Cornmeal Pizza Dough, *or* Cheese Pizza Dough (see pp. 436, 438)
1 cup (1/2 recipe) Red Tomato Salsa (see p. 513), *or* Pizza Sauce (see p. 511)
5 ounces chorizo, *or* spicy pork sausage, cooked, crumbled
1 cup (4 ounces) shredded fat-free Cheddar cheese
1 egg

Per Serving
Calories: 275
% Calories from fat: 35
Fat (gm): 10.5
Sat. fat (gm): 3.8
Cholesterol (mg): 56.2
Sodium (mg): 472
Protein (gm): 15.8
Carbohydrate (gm): 29.1
Exchanges
Milk: 0.0
Vegetable: 1.0
Fruit: 0.0
Bread: 1.5
Meat: 2.0
Fat: 0.0

1. Spray large skillet with cooking spray; heat over medium heat until hot. Saute poblano chili, bell pepper, onion, and garlic until tender, about 8 minutes. Season to taste with salt and pepper.

2. Spray 12-inch pizza pan with cooking spray, spread dough on pan, making rim around edge. Spread salsa on dough; top with sauteed vegetables, chorizo, and cheese.

3. Bake pizza at 425 degrees until crust is browned, 15 to 20 minutes. Remove from oven; break egg into center of pizza. Stir egg with fork and quickly spread over pizza. Return to oven and bake until egg is cooked, 1 to 2 minutes.

PIZZA WITH YELLOW AND GREEN SQUASH

6 servings

Vegetable cooking spray
1 medium zucchini, cut into scant 1/4-inch slices
1 medium yellow summer squash, cut into scant 1/4-inch slices
1 medium onion, thinly sliced
2 cloves garlic, minced
Salt and pepper, to taste
Cheese Pizza Dough (see p. 438)
1 medium tomato, thinly sliced
1/2 teaspoon dried basil leaves
1/2 teaspoon dried thyme leaves
1/4 teaspoon dried oregano leaves
1 cup (4 ounces) shredded reduced-fat mozzarella cheese

Per Serving
Calories: 189
% Calories from fat: 16
Fat (gm): 3.2
Sat. fat (gm): 2.1
Cholesterol (mg): 10.1
Sodium (mg): 188
Protein (gm): 11.8
Carbohydrate (gm): 27.5
Exchanges
Milk: 0.0
Vegetable: 1.0
Fruit: 0.0
Bread: 1.5
Meat: 1.0
Fat: 0.0

1. Spray large skillet with cooking spray; heat over medium heat until hot. Saute squash, onion, and garlic until crisp-tender, about 3 minutes; season to taste with salt and pepper.

2. Spray 12-inch pizza pan with cooking spray, spread Cheese Pizza Dough on pan, making rim around edge. Spray dough lightly with cooking spray. Arrange tomato slices on dough; top with squash mixture. Sprinkle with herbs and cheese.

3. Bake pizza at 425 degrees until browned, 15 to 20 minutes.

SMOKY BROCCOLI AND MUSHROOM PIZZA

6 servings

Mesquite-flavored vegetable cooking spray
1 cup broccoli florets
1 cup sliced cremini, *or* shiitake, mushrooms
1 medium onion, sliced
2 cloves garlic, finely chopped
1/8 teaspoon crushed red pepper flakes
Salt and pepper, to taste
Whole Wheat Pizza Dough (see p. 437)
1 cup fat-free ricotta cheese
3 tablespoons fat-free sour cream
1/2 teaspoon dried sage
1/2 cup (2 ounces) shredded smoked mozzarella cheese
1/2 cup (2 ounces) shredded fat-free mozzarella cheese

Per Serving
Calories: 201
% Calories from fat: 9
Fat (gm): 2.2
Sat. fat (gm): 1.1
Cholesterol (mg): 6.8
Sodium (mg): 256
Protein (gm): 16.5
Carbohydrate (gm): 32

Exchanges
Milk: 0.0
Vegetable: 1.0
Fruit: 0.0
Bread: 1.5
Meat: 1.5
Fat: 0.0

1. Spray large skillet with cooking spray; heat over medium heat until hot. Add broccoli, mushrooms, onion, and garlic and spray generously with cooking spray; saute until crisp-tender, 5 to 8 minutes. Stir in red pepper flakes; season to taste with salt and pepper. Cool to room temperature.

2. Spray 12-inch pizza pan with cooking spray; spread dough on pan, making rim around edge. Spray dough with cooking spray; bake at 425 degrees 10 minutes.

3. Mix ricotta cheese, sour cream, sage, and smoked mozzarella cheese; season to taste with salt and pepper. Spread cheese mixture evenly over dough; top with vegetable mixture. Sprinkle pizza with fat-free mozzarella cheese.

4. Bake pizza at 425 degrees until crust is browned, about 15 minutes.

SAGE-SCENTED SWEET POTATO PIZZA

6 servings

Vegetable cooking spray
2 cups sliced sweet potatoes
1 cup sliced onion
1 teaspoon dried sage leaves
Salt and pepper, to taste
Cornmeal Pizza Dough (see p. 436)
2 teaspoons minced roasted garlic
1 cup (4 ounces) shredded reduced-fat Colby-Jack cheese

Per Serving
Calories: 281
% Calories from fat: 13
Fat (gm): 4.2
Sat. fat (gm): 2.2
Cholesterol (mg): 13.5
Sodium (mg): 166
Protein (gm): 11.4
Carbohydrate (gm): 50.3
Exchanges
Milk: 0.0
Vegetable: 1.0
Fruit: 0.0
Bread: 3.0
Meat: 0.5
Fat: 0.5

1. Spray aluminum-foil-lined jelly roll pan with cooking spray. Arrange sweet potatoes and onion on pan; spray with cooking spray and sprinkle with sage. Roast potatoes at 425 degrees until almost tender, 10 to 15 minutes; cool to room temperature. Season to taste with salt and pepper.

2. Spray 12-inch pizza pan with cooking spray. Spread Cornmeal Pizza Dough on pan, making rim around edge. Sprinkle dough with garlic; arrange potato mixture on dough and sprinkle with cheese.

3. Bake pizza until crust is browned, 15 to 20 minutes.

ZUCCHINI AND MUSHROOM PIZZA WITH FILLO CRUST

8 servings

Olive oil cooking spray
1 cup sliced leeks (white part only), *or* 1/2 cup each: chopped green onions and onion
4 cups sliced wild mushrooms (cremini, shiitake, portobello, oyster, etc.)
1 teaspoon minced garlic
2 medium zucchini, thinly sliced
1/2 teaspoon dried thyme leaves
Salt and pepper, to taste

Per Serving
Calories: 69
% Calories from fat: 29
Fat (gm): 2.4
Sat. fat (gm): 1.3
Cholesterol (mg): 5.1
Sodium (mg): 223
Protein (gm): 5.1
Carbohydrate (gm): 8.1
Exchanges
Milk: 0.0
Vegetable: 0.5
Fruit: 0.0
Bread: 0.5
Meat: 0.5
Fat: 0.0

- 8 sheets frozen fillo pastry, thawed
- 1 cup (4 ounces) crumbled reduced-fat feta cheese
- 1/4 cup (1 ounce) grated fat-free Parmesan cheese

1. Spray large skillet with cooking spray; heat over medium heat until hot. Add leeks and cook, covered, over medium heat until wilted, 3 to 4 minutes. Add mushrooms and garlic; cook, covered, 5 minutes. Add zucchini and cook, uncovered, until vegetables are tender, 5 to 8 minutes. Stir in thyme; season to taste with salt and pepper.

2. Spray jelly roll pan with cooking spray, place sheet of fillo on pan and spray generously with spray. Repeat with remaining sheets of fillo. Spoon vegetable mixture evenly over fillo; sprinkle with cheeses.

3. Bake pizza at 375 degrees until fillo is browned and cheese melted, about 15 minutes.

GARDEN PATCH PIZZA

8 servings

- 1 1/4 packages (8-ounce size) fat-free cream cheese, softened
- 2 tablespoons fat-free sour cream
- 1 teaspoon Italian seasoning
- 1 large whole wheat lavosh, *or* cracker bread (5 1/4 ounces)
- 1 cup broccoli florets
- 1 cup chopped, seeded cucumber
- 2-3 marinated artichoke hearts, drained, sliced
- 1/4 cup sliced carrot
- 1/4 cup thinly sliced green onions and tops
- 1-2 tablespoons sliced ripe olives
- 1/2 cup (2 ounces) shredded reduced-fat Havarti cheese
- 1/4 cup French, Italian, or ranch fat-free salad dressing

Per Serving
Calories: 149
% Calories from fat: 28
Fat (gm): 4.6
Sat. fat (gm): 0.8
Cholesterol (mg): 5.1
Sodium (mg): 419
Protein (gm): 9.3
Carbohydrate (gm): 17.2
Exchanges
Milk: 0.0
Vegetable: 2.0
Fruit: 0.0
Bread: 0.5
Meat: 0.5
Fat: 0.5

1. Mix cream cheese, sour cream, and Italian seasoning; spread mixture on lavosh. Arrange vegetables and cheese attractively on top.

2. Serve immediately, or refrigerate no longer than 1 hour. Drizzle with salad dressing just before serving.

SPINACH SALAD PIZZA

8 servings

- 1 1/2 packages (8-ounce size) fat-free cream cheese, softened
- 5-6 tablespoons fat-free sweet-sour salad dressing, divided
- 1 large whole wheat lavosh, *or* cracker bread (5 1/4 ounces)
- 2 cups packed spinach leaves, torn into bite-sized pieces
- 1 cup sliced mushrooms
- 1/2 cup thinly sliced red onion
- 2 hard-cooked eggs, sliced
- 2 tablespoons bacon bits

Per Serving
Calories: 162
% Calories from fat: 25
Fat (gm): 4.6
Sat. fat (gm): 0.5
Cholesterol (mg): 53.3
Sodium (mg): 405
Protein (gm): 10.2
Carbohydrate (gm): 19.9
Exchanges
Milk: 0.0
Vegetable: 1.5
Fruit: 0.0
Bread: 1.0
Meat: 0.5
Fat: 0.5

1. Mix cream cheese and 2 tablespoons sweet-sour dressing. Spread mixture on lavosh; top with spinach, mushrooms, onion, hard-cooked eggs, and bacon bits.

2. Serve immediately, or refrigerate no longer than 1 hour. Drizzle with remaining sweet-sour dressing just before serving.

SALAD PIZZA

8 servings

Basic Pizza Dough (see p. 436)
1 cup thinly sliced radicchio
1 cup thinly sliced arugula
1½ cups thinly sliced red onion rings
2 large plum tomatoes, coarsely chopped
1 tablespoon balsamic vinegar
½ teaspoon salt
¼ teaspoon pepper
3 ounces part-skim mozzarella cheese, shredded

Per Serving
Calories: 92
% Calories from fat: 23
Fat (gm): 2.4
Sat. fat (gm): 1.2
Cholesterol (mg): 6
Sodium (mg): 89
Protein (gm): 4.5
Carbohydrate (gm): 13.5
Exchanges
Milk: 0.0
Vegetable: 1.0
Fruit: 0.0
Bread: 0.5
Meat: 0.0
Fat: 0.5

1. Press dough into lightly greased 12-inch pizza pan; pinch edges to form rim. Prick surface of dough with fork; bake at 475 degrees 10 to 15 minutes, until golden.

2. Combine radicchio, arugula, onion, and tomatoes in large bowl. Add vinegar, salt, and pepper; toss to mix well. Let stand 15 minutes. Place radicchio mixture onto baked dough to within 1 inch of edge. Sprinkle with cheese. Bake 5 to 10 minutes, or until cheese melts.

APPLE SALAD PIZZA

6 servings

Vegetable cooking spray
Basic Pizza Dough (see p. 436)
2 cups thinly sliced spinach
2 cups chopped, cored red apples
2 tablespoons lemon juice
¼ cup raisins
¼ cup coarsely chopped walnuts, *or* pecans
½ teaspoon curry powder, optional

Per Serving
Calories: 218
% Calories from fat: 19
Fat (gm): 4.9
Sat. fat (gm): 1.2
Cholesterol (mg): 3.5
Sodium (mg): 204
Protein (gm): 7.9
Carbohydrate (gm): 37.7
Exchanges
Milk: 0.0
Vegetable: 1.0
Fruit: 1.0
Bread: 1.5
Meat: 0.0
Fat: 0.5

- 1/4 cup (2 ounces) shredded fat-free Cheddar cheese
- 1/4 cup (1 ounce) crumbled blue cheese

1. Spray 12-inch pizza pan with cooking spray; spread dough on pan, making rim around edge.

2. Arrange spinach on dough. Sprinkle apples with lemon juice; toss apples with remaining ingredients and arrange on spinach.

3. Bake pizza at 425 degrees until dough is browned, 15 to 20 minutes.

FRUIT ORCHARD PIZZA

8 servings

- 1 1/2 packages (8-ounce size) fat-free cream cheese, softened
- 2 tablespoons maple syrup, *or* honey
- 1 teaspoon ground cinnamon
- 1 large whole wheat lavosh, *or* cracker bread (5 1/4 ounces)
- 5-6 cups assorted fresh fruit (strawberries, raspberries, blueberries, sliced peaches, pears, plums, kiwi, etc.)
- Raspberry Sauce (see p. 526)

Per Serving
Calories: 195
% Calories from fat: 14
Fat (gm): 3.2
Sat. fat (gm): 0
Cholesterol (mg): 0
Sodium (mg): 295
Protein (gm): 8.2
Carbohydrate (gm): 34.2

Exchanges
Milk: 0.0
Vegetable: 0.0
Fruit: 1.0
Bread: 1.5
Meat: 0.0
Fat: 0.5

1. Mix cream cheese, maple syrup, and cinnamon. Spread mixture on lavosh; arrange fruit attractively on top.

2. Serve immediately, or refrigerate no longer than 1 hour. Drizzle with Raspberry Sauce just before serving.

PEAR DESSERT PIZZA

6 servings

Basic Pizza Dough (see p. 436)
1/4 cup plus 2 tablespoons sugar, divided
Butter-flavored vegetable cooking spray
2 tablespoons honey
2 large ripe pears, cored, sliced
1/2 teaspoon ground cinnamon
1/4 cup (1 ounce) crumbled blue cheese
2 tablespoons raisins
2-4 tablespoons coarsely chopped walnuts

Per Serving
Calories: 244
% Calories from fat: 12
Fat (gm): 3.3
Sat. fat (gm): 1
Cholesterol (mg): 3.5
Sodium (mg): 156
Protein (gm): 5.2
Carbohydrate (gm): 50.2
Exchanges
Milk: 0.0
Vegetable: 0.0
Fruit: 1.5
Bread: 2.0
Meat: 0.0
Fat: 0.5

1. Make Basic Pizza Dough, adding 2 tablespoons sugar to flour.

2. Spray 12-inch pizza pan with cooking spray; spread dough on pan, making rim around edge. Drizzle dough with honey. Arrange pears on dough; spray with cooking spray and sprinkle with remaining 1/4 cup sugar and cinnamon. Sprinkle blue cheese, raisins, and walnuts over pears.

3. Bake pizza at 425 degrees until crust is browned, 15 to 20 minutes.

SAUSAGE CALZONES

8 servings

Olive oil cooking spray
8 ounces Italian-style turkey sausage
1 cup sliced carrots
1 cup cubed zucchini
1 cup sliced onions
1/2 cup chopped red bell pepper
1/2 cup sliced mushrooms
4 cloves garlic, minced
3/4 teaspoon Italian seasoning
1/2-3/4 teaspoon fennel seeds, crushed

Per Serving
Calories: 369
% Calories from fat: 22
Fat (gm): 8.7
Sat. fat (gm): 2
Cholesterol (mg): 19.3
Sodium (mg): 854
Protein (gm): 18.4
Carbohydrate (gm): 53.2
Exchanges
Milk: 0.0
Vegetable: 2.0
Fruit: 0.0
Bread: 3.0
Meat: 1.0
Fat: 1.0

- $1\frac{1}{2}$ cups chopped tomato
- 1 cup rinsed, drained, canned cannellini, *or* Great Northern, beans
- $\frac{1}{4}$ cup sliced ripe olives
- Salt and pepper, to taste
- 1 package (16 ounces) hot roll mix
- $1\frac{1}{4}$ cups very hot water (120 degrees)
- 1 tablespoon olive oil
- $\frac{3}{4}$ cup (3 ounces) shredded fat-free mozzarella cheese
- $\frac{3}{4}$ cup (3 ounces) shredded reduced-fat mozzarella cheese
- 2-3 tablespoons fat-free milk

1. Spray large skillet with cooking spray; heat over medium heat until hot. Cook sausage until browned, crumbling with fork while cooking. Drain excess fat. Add carrots, zucchini, onions, bell pepper, mushrooms, and garlic and cook, covered, 5 minutes. Add herbs and cook 1 to 2 minutes longer.

2. Add tomato, beans, and olives to skillet; cook, covered, until vegetables are just tender, 5 to 8 minutes, stirring occasionally. Season to taste with salt and pepper. Cool.

3. Make hot roll mix according to package directions for pizza crust, using $1\frac{1}{4}$ cups very hot water and 1 tablespoon oil. Divide dough into 8 equal pieces. Roll 1 piece dough on floured surface into circle 7 inches in diameter. Spoon about $\frac{3}{4}$ cup filling on dough and sprinkle with 3 tablespoons combined cheeses. Brush edge of dough with milk and fold in half. Flute edge of dough or press with tines of fork. Place on greased cookie sheet. Repeat with remaining dough, filling, and cheese.

4. Brush tops of calzones with milk. Bake calzones at 375 degrees until browned, about 15 minutes. Let cool on wire rack 5 minutes before serving.

CHEESE AND MUSHROOM CALZONES

8 servings

Vegetable cooking spray
6 cups sliced porcini, *or* portobello, mushrooms
1/2 cup chopped broccoli
1/2 cup chopped onion
2 teaspoons minced roasted garlic
1 teaspoon dried basil leaves
1 cup fat-free ricotta cheese
1 cup (4 ounces) shredded fat-free mozzarella cheese
2 tablespoons grated Parmesan cheese
1/4 cup fat-free sour cream
Salt and pepper, to taste
1 package (16 ounces) hot roll mix
1 1/4 cups water very hot (120 degrees)
1 tablespoon olive oil
Fat-free milk, to glaze

Per Serving
Calories: 312
% Calories from fat: 16
Fat (gm): 5.8
Sat. fat (gm): 1.1
Cholesterol (mg): 4.6
Sodium (mg): 387
Protein (gm): 18
Carbohydrate (gm): 48.4

Exchanges
Milk: 0.0
Vegetable: 1.0
Fruit: 0.0
Bread: 3.0
Meat: 1.0
Fat: 0.5

1. Spray large skillet with cooking spray; heat over medium heat until hot. Add mushrooms, broccoli, onion, garlic, and basil to skillet; spray generously with cooking spray. Cook, covered, over medium heat until mushrooms have wilted, about 5 minutes. Cook uncovered, until vegetables are tender, 5 to 8 minutes.

2. Mix sauteed vegetables, cheeses, and sour cream; season to taste with salt and pepper.

3. Make hot roll mix according to package directions for pizza, using 1 1/4 cups hot water and 1 tablespoon olive oil. Divide dough into 8 equal pieces. Roll 1 piece dough on floured surface into 6- to 7-inch circle; spoon about 2/3 cup mushroom mixture on dough. Brush edge of dough with milk and fold in half. Flute edges of dough or press together with tines of fork. Place on greased cookie sheet. Repeat with remaining dough and filling.

4. Brush tops of calzones with milk. Bake calzones at 375 degrees until browned, 15 to 20 minutes. Let cool on wire rack 5 minutes before serving.

SWEET FENNEL CALZONES

8 servings

Vegetable cooking spray
6 cups thinly sliced fennel bulb
1 1/2 cups chopped onion
2/3 cup chopped red bell pepper
2 cloves garlic, minced
1 cup (4 ounces) shredded fat free mozzarella cheese
1/2 cup fat-free sour cream
2 tablespoons finely chopped fennel leaves
Salt and pepper, to taste
1 package (16 ounces) hot roll mix
1 1/4 cups very hot water (120 degrees)
1 tablespoon olive oil
Fat-free milk, to glaze

Per Serving
Calories: 307
% Calories from fat: 15
Fat (gm): 5.3
Sat. fat (gm): 0.8
Cholesterol (mg): 3.4
Sodium (mg): 378
Protein (gm): 13.8
Carbohydrate (gm): 52

Exchanges
Milk: 0.0
Vegetable: 1.5
Fruit: 0.0
Bread: 3.0
Meat: 0.5
Fat: 0.5

1. Spray large skillet with cooking spray; heat over medium heat until hot. Add fennel, onion, bell pepper, and garlic; cook, covered, over medium to medium-low heat until tender, 15 to 20 minutes, stirring occasionally. Cool until warm; stir in cheese, sour cream, and fennel leaves. Season to taste with salt and pepper.

2. Make hot roll mix according to package directions for pizza, using 1 1/4 cups hot water and 1 tablespoon olive oil. Divide dough into 8 equal pieces. Roll 1 piece dough on floured surface into 6- to 7-inch circle; spoon about 2/3 cup fennel mixture on dough. Brush edge of dough with milk and fold in half. Flute edges of dough or press together with tines of fork. Place on greased cookie sheet. Repeat with remaining dough and filling.

3. Brush tops of calzones with milk. Bake calzones at 375 degrees until browned, 15 to 20 minutes. Let cool on wire rack 5 minutes before serving.

PIZZA RUSTICA

8 servings

- 1 clove garlic, minced
- 1 tablespoon olive oil
- 1 package (10 ounces) frozen chopped spinach, thawed, well drained
- 2 medium tomatoes, peeled, seeded, chopped
- 1/4 cup chopped fresh, *or* 1 tablespoon dried, basil leaves
- Whole Wheat Pizza Dough (see p. 437)
- 1 cup (4 ounces) shredded part-skim mozzarella cheese
- 1 egg white, lightly beaten
- 1 tablespoon water

Per Serving
Calories: 152
% Calories from fat: 30
Fat (gm): 5.2
Sat. fat (gm): 1.8
Cholesterol (mg): 8
Sodium (mg): 163
Protein (gm): 7.5
Carbohydrate (gm): 19.7

Exchanges
Milk: 0.0
Vegetable: 1.0
Fruit: 0.0
Bread: 1.0
Meat: 0.5
Fat: 0.5

1. Saute garlic in oil in medium skillet 30 seconds. Stir in spinach and cook 1 minute. Combine tomatoes and basil in small bowl.

2. Pat half of Whole Wheat Pizza Dough into bottom of lightly greased 12-inch pizza pan. Top with 1/2 the mozzarella cheese, spinach mixture, tomato-basil mixture, and remaining cheese, leaving 1-inch border.

3. On floured surface, roll remaining dough to 12-inch circle. Place over filling and seal to bottom crust, pressing filling down lightly and crimping crusts. Cover and let rise in warm place 1 hour.

4. Brush pizza with combined egg white and water. Bake at 375 degrees 40 minutes or until done, covering with foil last 10 minutes, if necessary, to prevent overbrowning.

VEGETARIAN TORTILLA PIZZA

2 servings

Vegetable cooking spray
3 tablespoons chopped onion
1 clove garlic, minced
1/2 cup sliced mushrooms
1/2 cup sun-dried tomatoes
1/3 cup coarsely shredded carrot
1/4 cup chopped red, green, *or* yellow, bell peppers
1 tablespoon minced fresh cilantro
2 (6-inch) flour tortillas
3/4 cup (3 ounces) shredded part-skim mozzarella cheese
1/2 cup canned kidney beans, drained

Per Serving
Calories: 337
% Calories from fat: 26
Fat (gm): 10.1
Sat. fat (gm): 4.8
Cholesterol (mg): 24
Sodium (mg): 878
Protein (gm): 19.7
Carbohydrate (gm): 44

Exchanges
Milk: 0.0
Vegetable: 2.0
Fruit: 0.0
Bread: 2.0
Meat: 1.5
Fat: 1.0

1. Spray large skillet with cooking spray; heat over medium heat until hot. Saute onion and garlic 1 minute. Stir in mushrooms, tomatoes, carrot, and peppers; cook until mushrooms are tender, about 5 minutes. Stir in cilantro; set aside.

2. Place tortillas on baking sheet and broil 6 inches from heat until lightly browned, about 2 minutes. Turn tortillas over; broil 1 minute or until crisp. Top each tortilla with 5 tablespoons cheese, 1/4 cup beans, half of vegetable mixture, and 1 tablespoon remaining cheese. Broil 6 inches from heat 1 minute or until cheese melts.

MICROWAVE FRENCH BREAD PIZZA

8 servings

- 4 ounces lean ground beef
- 4 ounces lean ground turkey
- 1/4 cup chopped green bell pepper
- 1/4 cup chopped onion
- 1 tablespoon garlic powder
- 1 cup Marinara Sauce (see p.509)
- 2 cups sliced mushrooms
- 1 teaspoon dried oregano leaves
- 1 loaf (1 pound) French bread
- 1/4 cup (2 ounces) shredded skim mozzarella cheese

Per Serving
Calories: 252
% Calories from fat: 24
Fat (gm): 6.9
Sat. fat (gm): 2.2
Cholesterol (mg): 18.1
Sodium (mg): 589
Protein (gm): 12.4
Carbohydrate (gm): 35.5

Exchanges
Milk: 0.0
Vegetable: 1.0
Fruit: 0.0
Bread: 2.0
Meat: 1.0
Fat: 0.5

1. Break up ground beef and turkey in very small chunks in 2-quart casserole. Add green pepper, onion, and garlic powder. Microwave on High 5 to 7 minutes, stirring every 2 minutes. Add Marinara Sauce, mushrooms, and oregano and microwave 4 minutes more.

2. Slice bread in half lengthwise; place cut sides up on microwave-safe plate. Spread meat mixture evenly over bread. Top with mozzarella cheese. Microwave 2 minutes or until cheese melts.

TWELVE

Breads, Muffins, and Breakfast

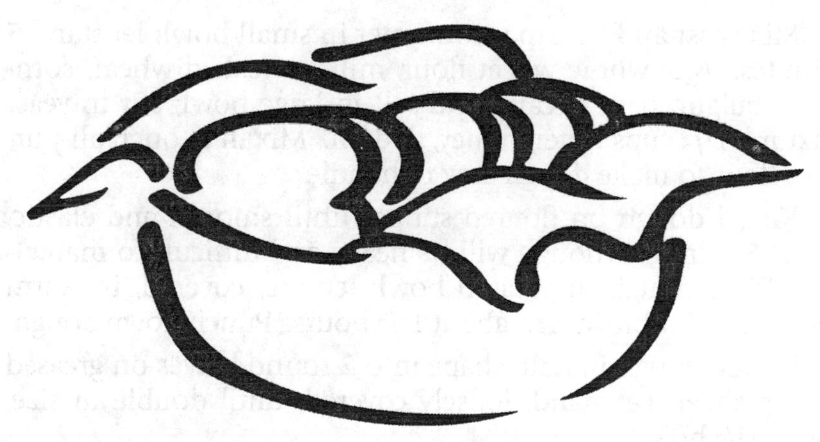

PEASANT BREAD

2 small loaves (8-10 servings each)

Per Slice
Calories: 197
% Calories from fat: 22
Fat (gm): 5
Sat. fat (gm): 0.6
Cholesterol (mg): 0
Sodium (mg): 137
Protein (gm): 5.4
Carbohydrate (gm): 34.2

Exchanges
Milk: 0.0
Vegetable: 0.0
Fruit: 0.0
Bread: 2.0
Meat: 0.0
Fat: 1.0

- 2 packages active dry yeast
- 1/2 cup warm water (110-115 degrees)
- 1 1/4 cups whole wheat flour
- 1/2 cup millet
- 1/2 cup cracked wheat
- 1/2 cup cornmeal
- 1/2 cup bulgur
- 1/2 cup quick cooking oats
- 1/2 cup ground pecans
- 1 teaspoon salt
- 1 1/4 cups lukewarm water
- 1/4 cup honey
- 2 tablespoons vegetable oil
- 1-2 cups unbleached all-purpose flour

1. Mix yeast and 1/2 cup warm water in small bowl; let stand 5 minutes. Mix whole wheat flour, millet, creaked wheat, cornmeal, bulgur, oats, pecans, and salt in large bowl; stir in yeast mixture, 1 1/4 cups water, honey, and oil. Mix in enough all-purpose flour to make dough easy to handle.

2. Knead dough on floured surface until smooth and elastic, about 5 minutes (dough will be heavy and difficult to maneuver). Place dough in greased bowl; let rise, covered, in warm place until double in size, about 1 1/2 hours. Punch down dough.

3. Divide dough in half; shape into 2 round loaves on greased baking sheet. Let stand, loosely covered, until double in size, about 1 1/2 hours.

4. Bake bread at 350 degrees until loaves are deep golden brown and sound hollow when tapped, about 40 minutes. Transfer to wire racks to cool.

MULTIGRAIN BATTER BREAD

2 loaves (16 servings each)

- 3 1/4 cups all-purpose flour
- 1 cup whole wheat flour
- 1/4 cup soy flour, *or* quick-cooking oats
- 3/4 cup quick-cooking oats
- 1/4 cup sugar
- 1/2 teaspoon salt
- 2 packages fast-rising yeast
- 1 cup cooked brown rice
- 2 1/4 cups fat-free milk, hot (125-130 degrees)
- 2 tablespoons vegetable oil

Per Slice
Calories: 97
% Calories from fat: 13
Fat (gm): 1.4
Sat. fat (gm): 0.2
Cholesterol (mg): 0.3
Sodium (mg): 43
Protein (gm): 3.5
Carbohydrate (gm): 17.9
Exchanges
Milk: 0.0
Vegetable: 0.0
Fruit: 0.0
Bread: 1.0
Meat: 0.0
Fat: 0.5

1. Combine flours, oats, sugar, salt, and yeast in large bowl; stir in rice. Add milk and oil, mixing until smooth. Spoon batter into 2 greased 8 1/2 x 4 1/2-inch bread pans; let stand, loosely covered, until double in size, about 30 minutes.

2. Bake bread at 375 degrees until loaves are browned and sound hollow when tapped, 35 to 40 minutes. Remove from pans and cool on wire racks.

POTATO BREAD

2 loaves (16 servings each)

- 1 package active dry yeast
- 1 1/2 cups warm water (110-115 degrees)
- 2 tablespoons sugar
- 3 tablespoons margarine, softened
- 2 eggs
- 1 cup mashed potatoes, lukewarm
- 6-6 1/2 cups all-purpose flour
- 1 cup whole wheat flour
- 1 teaspoon salt
- Fat-free milk

Per Slice
Calories: 121
% Calories from fat: 13
Fat (gm): 1.7
Sat. fat (gm): 0.4
Cholesterol (mg): 13.4
Sodium (mg): 103
Protein (gm): 3.6
Carbohydrate (gm): 22.7
Exchanges
Milk: 0.0
Vegetable: 0.0
Fruit: 0.0
Bread: 1.5
Meat: 0.0
Fat: 0.5

1. Mix yeast and warm water in large bowl; let stand 5 minutes. Mix in sugar, margarine, eggs, and mashed potatoes; mix in 5 1/2 cups all-purpose flour, whole wheat flour, and salt, to make soft dough. Mix in enough remaining 1 cup all-purpose flour to make smooth dough.

2. Knead dough on floured surface until smooth and elastic, about 5 minutes. Place dough in greased bowl; let rise, covered, in warm place until double in size, 1 to 1 1/2 hours. Punch down dough.

3. Divide dough into 2 equal pieces; shape into loaves and place in greased 9 x 5-inch loaf pans. Let stand, loosely covered, until double in size, about 45 minutes.

4. Brush tops of loaves with milk. Bake at 375 degrees until loaves are golden and sound hollow when tapped, about 45 minutes. Remove from pans and cool on wire racks.

QUICK SELF-RISING BISCUITS

18 servings (1 biscuit each)

2 cups self-rising flour
1 tablespoon vegetable shortening
3/4-1 cup fat-free milk
1 tablespoon margarine, melted

Per Serving
Calories: 65
% Calories from fat: 21
Fat (gm): 1.4
Sat. fat (gm): 0.3
Cholesterol (mg): 0.2
Sodium (mg): 189
Protein (gm): 1.7
Carbohydrate (gm): 10.8

Exchanges
Milk: 0.0
Vegetable: 0.0
Fruit: 0.0
Bread: 1.0
Meat: 0.0
Fat: 0.0

1. Measure flour into medium bowl; cut in shortening until mixture resembles coarse crumbs. Stir enough milk into flour mixture to make a soft dough. Roll dough on floured surface to 1/2 inch thickness; cut into 18 biscuits with 2 inch cutter.

2. Place biscuits in greased 13 x 9-inch baking pan; brush with melted margarine. Bake at 425 degrees until golden, about 15 minutes.

Variations: **Chive Biscuits**—Mix 3 tablespoons snipped fresh, *or* dried, chives into biscuit dough.

Parmesan Biscuits—Brush biscuits with melted margarine as above; sprinkle with 2 tablespoons grated fat-free Parmesan cheese.

STICKY BUNS

24 servings (1 bun each)

- 3 1/2 cups all-purpose flour, divided
- 1/3 cup plus 2 tablespoons sugar, divided
- 1 package active dry yeast
- 1 tablespoon plus 1 teaspoon ground cinnamon, divided
- 1 teaspoon salt
- 1 cup warm fat-free milk (110-115 degrees)
- 1/4 cup fat-free sour cream
- 1 egg, beaten
- Grated rind from 1 orange
- Vegetable cooking spray
- Sticky Bun Topping (recipe follows)
- 1/2 cup pecan pieces

Per Serving
Calories: 200
% Calories from fat: 17
Fat (gm): 3.8
Sat. fat (gm): 0.6
Cholesterol (mg). 9
Sodium (mg): 131
Protein (gm): 3.1
Carbohydrate (gm): 38.9
Exchanges
Milk: 0.0
Vegetable: 0.0
Fruit: 0.0
Bread: 2.5
Meat: 0.0
Fat: 0.5

1. Combine 2 cups flour, 1/3 cup sugar, yeast, 1 tablespoon cinnamon, and salt in large bowl. Stir in milk, sour cream, egg, and orange rind until smooth. Stir in enough remaining 1 1/2 cups flour to make soft dough.

2. Knead dough on floured surface until smooth and elastic, about 5 minutes. Place dough in greased bowl and let stand, covered, in warm place until double in size, 30 to 45 minutes. Punch dough down.

3. Spray three 9-inch-round cake pans with cooking spray; spoon about 1/2 cup hot Sticky Bun Topping into each and sprinkle with pecan pieces.

4. Combine remaining 2 tablespoons sugar and 1 teaspoon cinnamon in small bowl. Divide dough in half. Roll half the dough on floured surface into rectangle 12 x 7-inches; sprinkle with half the sugar mixture. Roll dough up, beginning with long side; cut into 12 equal slices. Repeat with remaining dough and sugar mixture. Place 8 rolls, cut sides up, in each pan, over the topping.

5. Let rolls rise, covered in warm place, until double in size, about 30 minutes. Bake at 375 degrees until golden, 15 to 20 minutes. Immediately invert rolls onto aluminum foil.

Sticky Bun Topping

- 4 tablespoons margarine
- 1 1/2 cups packed light brown sugar
- 1/2 cup light corn syrup
- 1/4 cup all-purpose flour

1. Melt margarine in small saucepan; stir in remaining ingredients and cook until bubbly.

Variation: **Cinnamon Rolls**—Do not make Sticky Bun Topping. Make dough as above, mixing in 1/2 cup raisins. Let dough rise, then roll and shape as above, sprinkling with double the amount of sugar and cinnamon. Place rolls, cut sides up, in sprayed muffin cups. Bake as above, and invert rolls onto wire racks. Mix 2 cups powdered sugar with enough skim milk to make a thick glaze; drizzle over slightly warm rolls.

FLORENTINE BREAD

24 servings

- 1 package active dry yeast
- 1 teaspoon salt
- 3 cups all-purpose flour
- 1 cup warm water (105 degrees)
- 3 tablespoons olive oil
- 1 tablespoon minced garlic
- Yellow cornmeal
- Coarse salt
- Olive oil
- 1/2 teaspoon dried rosemary leaves
- 1/2 teaspoon dried oregano leaves

Per Serving
Calories: 78
% Calories from fat: 23
Fat (gm): 2
Sat. fat (gm): 0.3
Cholesterol (mg): 0
Sodium (mg): 89
Protein (gm): 2.2
Carbohydrate (gm): 12.7

Exchanges
Milk: 0.0
Vegetable: 0.0
Fruit: 0.0
Bread: 1.0
Meat: 0.0
Fat: 0.0

1. Combine yeast, salt, and flour in large bowl; mix in combined water, oil, and garlic to form rough mass. Knead mixture in bowl until dough holds together, then knead on lightly floured surface until smooth and elastic, about 8 minutes. Form into ball, and let rest on lightly floured surface, covered, 1 hour.

2. Roll dough into 12 x 14-inch rectangle, and transfer to baking sheet sprinkled with cornmeal. Use fingertips to make indentations in dough at 2-inch intervals. Sprinkle dough lightly with coarse salt, and drizzle olive oil over top. Sprinkle with rosemary and oregano.

3. Bake at 375 degrees until golden, about 15 minutes. Remove from oven and brush lightly with olive oil. Cool slightly on rack; serve warm.

POLENTA SPOON BREAD

8 servings

Vegetable cooking spray
2 tablespoons minced garlic
1 medium red bell pepper, chopped
3 egg yolks
2 1/2 cups fat-free milk
1 cup polenta, *or* yellow cornmeal
1 1/2 teaspoons salt
1 teaspoon Italian seasoning
1/2 teaspoon red pepper flakes
2 tablespoons melted margarine
1/4 cup (1 ounce) grated Parmesan cheese
3 egg whites, beaten to stiff peaks

Per Serving
Calories: 141
% Calories from fat: 30
Fat (gm): 4.7
Sat. fat (gm): 1.3
Cholesterol (mg): 30.1
Sodium (mg): 578
Protein (gm): 6.8
Carbohydrate (gm): 18.2
Exchanges
Milk: 0.0
Vegetable: 0.0
Fruit: 0.0
Bread: 1.0
Meat: 0.0
Fat: 1.0

1. Spray small skillet with vegetable cooking spray; heat over medium heat until hot. Saute garlic and bell pepper until tender, 2 to 3 minutes. Cool.

2. Whisk egg yolks and milk until smooth in medium saucepan; heat to boiling, whisking constantly. Whisk in polenta and salt gradually; reduce heat to medium and whisk in bell pepper mixture, Italian seasoning, and pepper flakes. Simmer 2 minutes, stirring constantly with wooden spoon. Remove from heat; stir in margarine and cheese.

3. Fold egg whites into polenta mixture; pour into greased 2-quart souffle dish or casserole. Bake at 375 degrees until puffed and golden, about 30 minutes. Serve immediately.

BROWN SUGAR BANANA BREAD

16 servings

Per Serving
Calories: 151
% Calories from fat: 28
Fat (gm): 4.8
Sat. fat (gm): 0.9
Cholesterol (mg): 26.7
Sodium (mg): 160
Protein (gm): 2.9
Carbohydrate (gm): 24.9

Exchanges
Milk: 0.0
Vegetable: 0.0
Fruit: 0.5
Bread: 1.0
Meat: 0.0
Fat: 1.0

- 4 tablespoons margarine, softened
- 1/4 cup applesauce
- 2 eggs
- 2 tablespoons fat-free milk, *or* water
- 3/4 cup packed light brown sugar
- 1 cup mashed banana (2-3 medium bananas)
- 1 3/4 cups all-purpose flour
- 2 teaspoons baking powder
- 1/2 teaspoon baking soda
- 1/4 teaspoon salt
- 1/4 cup coarsely chopped walnuts, *or* pecans

1. Beat margarine, applesauce, eggs, milk, and brown sugar in large mixer bowl until smooth. Add banana and blend at low speed; beat at high speed 1 to 2 minutes.

2. Combine flour, baking powder, baking soda, and salt; mix into batter. Mix in walnuts. Pour batter into greased loaf pan, 8 x 4 x 2-inches.

3. Bake at 350 degrees until bread is golden and toothpick inserted in center comes out clean, 55 to 60 minutes. Cool in pan on wire rack 10 minutes; remove from pan and cool to room temperature.

COFFEE CAN GINGERBREAD

8 servings

Per Serving
Calories: 221
% Calories from fat: 13
Fat (gm): 3.3
Sat. fat (gm): 0.6
Cholesterol (mg): 0.6
Sodium (mg): 177
Protein (gm): 3.8
Carbohydrate (gm): 44.7

Exchanges
Milk: 0.0
Vegetable: 0.0
Fruit: 0.0
Bread: 3.0
Meat: 0.0
Fat: 0.5

1/4 cup margarine
1/2 cup sugar
2 egg whites
1/2 cup light molasses, warm
2 tablespoons hot water
1 1/2 cups all-purpose flour
1/2 teaspoon baking soda
1 teaspoon ground cinnamon
1 teaspoon ground ginger
1/2 teaspoon ground cloves
1/8 teaspoon ground nutmeg
1/2 teaspoon salt, optional
1/2 cup buttermilk

1. Beat margarine and sugar in large bowl until well blended; beat in egg whites. Mix in molasses and hot water, blending well. Mix in dry ingredients and buttermilk alternately, beginning and ending with dry ingredients.

2. Pour batter into greased and floured 2-pound coffee can. Cover with aluminum foil and place in slow cooker. Cook on High until wooden skewer inserted in center comes out clean, 2 to 3 hours.

BANANA BRAN MUFFINS

24 servings (1 muffin each)

Per Serving
Calories: 65
% Calories from fat: 5
Fat (gm): 0.4
Sat. fat (gm): 0.1
Cholesterol (mg): 0.2
Sodium (mg): 118
Protein (gm): 2.3
Carbohydrate (gm): 15.2

Exchanges
Milk: 0.0
Vegetable: 0.0
Fruit: 0.0
Bread: 1.0
Meat: 0.0
Fat: 0.0

1 1/2 cups whole wheat flour
1 1/2 cups unprocessed bran
2 teaspoons baking soda
2 teaspoons ground cinnamon
1 teaspoon ground nutmeg
1/2 teaspoon salt, optional
3 egg whites
1/2 cup honey

- 1/2 cup buttermilk
- 1/2 cup water
- 1 small ripe banana, mashed
- 1 teaspoon vanilla extract
- Grated rind of 1 orange

1. Combine flour, bran, baking soda, cinnamon, nutmeg, and salt in medium bowl; stir in combined remaining ingredients, mixing until just blended.

2. Pour batter into greased muffin tins, filling half full. Bake at 400 degrees until muffins are browned and toothpick inserted in center comes out clean, about 15 minutes. Cool in tins 5 minutes; invert and cool on wire racks.

OATMEAL BREAKFAST MUFFINS

12 servings (1 muffin each)

- 1 cup all-purpose flour
- 1 cup whole wheat flour
- 1 cup quick-cooking oatmeal
- 1/2 teaspoon ground cinnamon
- 1/4 teaspoon ground nutmeg
- 3 teaspoons baking powder
- 1/2 teaspoon salt, optional
- 1 cup apple juice
- 2 egg whites
- 1 egg yolk
- 1/4 cup corn oil

Per Serving
Calories: 156
% Calories from fat: 32
Fat (gm): 5.7
Sat. fat (gm): 0.8
Cholesterol (mg): 17.8
Sodium (mg): 93.5
Protein (gm): 4.4
Carbohydrate (gm): 22.4
Exchanges
Milk: 0.0
Vegetable: 0.0
Fruit: 0.0
Bread: 1.5
Meat: 0.0
Fat: 1.0

1. Mix flours, oatmeal, spices, baking powder, and salt. Stir in combined remaining ingredients, stirring just until blended.

2. Pour batter into greased muffin tins about three-quarters full. Bake at 400 degrees until muffins are browned and toothpick inserted in center comes out clean, 15 to 20 minutes. Cool in tins 5 minutes; invert and cool on wire racks.

ORANGE RAISIN MUFFINS

12 servings (1 muffin each)

- 2 cups whole wheat pastry flour
- $1^1/_2$ teaspoons baking powder
- $^1/_2$ teaspoon salt, optional
- 1 egg, beaten
- $^3/_4$ cup orange juice
- $^1/_4$ cup canola oil
- $^1/_3$ cup honey
- $^1/_2$ teaspoon vanilla extract
- $^1/_4$ cup golden raisins
- 1 tablespoon grated orange rind

Per Serving
Calories: 162
% Calories from fat: 29
Fat (gm): 5.4
Sat. fat (gm): 0.5
Cholesterol (mg): 17.8
Sodium (mg): 48
Protein (gm): 3.5
Carbohydrate (gm): 26.8
Exchanges
Milk: 0.0
Vegetable: 0.0
Fruit: 0.5
Bread: 1.0
Meat: 0.0
Fat: 1.0

1. Combine flour, baking powder, and salt in large bowl; stir in combined remaining ingredients, mixing just until blended.

2. Pour batter into greased muffin tins, filling about half full. Bake at 350 degrees until muffins are browned and toothpick inserted in center comes out clean, about 20 minutes.

CORN AND PIMIENTO MUFFINS

12 servings (1 muffin each)

- $^3/_4$ cup fat-free milk
- $^1/_4$ cup reduced-fat yogurt
- 3 tablespoons maple syrup
- 2 eggs
- 1 cup whole wheat pastry flour
- $^3/_4$ cup yellow cornmeal
- $^1/_2$ teaspoon baking soda
- $^1/_2$ teaspoon salt, optional
- $^1/_4$ cup well drained, chopped pimiento

Per Serving
Calories: 89
% Calories from fat: 14
Fat (gm): 1.4
Sat. fat (gm): 0.4
Cholesterol (mg): 36
Sodium (mg): 86
Protein (gm): 3.8
Carbohydrate (gm): 16.1
Exchanges
Milk: 0.0
Vegetable: 0.0
Fruit: 0.0
Bread: 1.0
Meat: 0.0
Fat: 0.0

1. Combine milk, yogurt, maple syrup, and eggs in large bowl, blending well. Stir in combined flour, cornmeal, baking soda, and salt, mixing just until blended; mix in pimiento.

2. Spoon batter into greased muffin tins. Bake at 375 degrees until muffins are golden and toothpick inserted in center comes out clean, 15 to 20 minutes. Cool in tins 5 minutes; invert and cool on wire rack.

PARMESAN-ROSEMARY MUFFINS

12 servings (1 muffin each)

- 1 cup all-purpose flour
- 1/4 cup whole wheat flour
- 1 teaspoon baking powder
- 1/2 teaspoon baking soda
- 1/4 teaspoon salt
- 1/3 cup (1 1/3 ounces) grated Parmesan cheese
- 1/2 teaspoon dried rosemary leaves
- 1 cup buttermilk
- 1 egg
- 1 1/2 tablespoons canola oil

Per Serving
Calories: 91
% Calories from fat: 34
Fat (gm): 3.4
Sat. fat (gm): 1
Cholesterol (mg): 21
Sodium (mg): 210
Protein (gm): 3.9
Carbohydrate (gm): 11

Exchanges
Milk: 0.0
Vegetable: 0.0
Fruit: 0.0
Bread: 1.0
Meat: 0.0
Fat: 0.5

1. Combine flours, baking powder, baking soda, salt, cheese, and rosemary in large bowl; stir in combined buttermilk, egg, and oil, mixing just until blended.

2. Pour batter into greased muffin tins; bake at 375 degrees until muffins are browned and toothpick inserted in center comes out clean, about 20 minutes. Cool in tins 5 minutes; invert and cool on wire rack.

FRUIT-FILLED MUFFINS

8 servings (1 muffin each)

- 2 cups all-purpose flour
- 1/4 cup sugar
- 1 tablespoon baking powder
- 1/4 teaspoon salt
- 1 large egg
- 1 cup plain yogurt
- 1/4 cup margarine, melted
- 1 teaspoon vanilla extract
- 1/4 cup any flavor spreadable fruit

Per Serving
Calories: 237
% Calories from fat: 25
Fat (gm): 6.9
Sat. fat (gm): 1.4
Cholesterol (mg): 27.2
Sodium (mg): 354
Protein (gm): 5.8
Carbohydrate (gm): 37.9
Exchanges
Milk: 0.0
Vegetable: 0.0
Fruit: 0.5
Bread: 2.0
Meat: 0.0
Fat: 1.0

1. Combine flour, sugar, baking powder, and salt in large bowl; stir in combined remaining ingredients, except spreadable fruit, mixing just until blended.

2. Pour half the batter into greased muffin tins; spoon about 1 teaspoon spreadable fruit in center of batter in each cup. Pour remaining batter over. Bake at 375 degrees until browned and toothpick inserted in center comes out clean, 25 to 30 minutes. Cool in tins 5 minutes; invert and cool on wire racks.

CHEESE-CARAWAY SCONES

8 servings (1 scone each)

- 1/2 cup all-purpose flour
- 1/4 cup whole wheat flour
- 1/4 cup yellow cornmeal
- 1 1/2 teaspoons baking powder
- 1/4 teaspoon salt
- 1 tablespoon margarine, softened
- 1 tablespoon canola, oil
- 1/4 cup (1 ounce) shredded mozzarella cheese
- 2 egg whites
- 1/3 cup fat-free milk
- 2 teaspoons caraway seeds
- Paprika

Per Serving
Calories: 104
% Calories from fat: 34
Fat (gm): 4
Sat. fat (gm): 0.8
Cholesterol (mg): 2.2
Sodium (mg): 217
Protein (gm): 3.9
Carbohydrate (gm): 13.3
Exchanges
Milk: 0.0
Vegetable: 0.0
Fruit: 0.0
Bread: 1.0
Meat: 0.0
Fat: 0.5

1. Combine flour, cornmeal, baking powder, and salt in large bowl; stir in, margarine, oil, and cheese, mixing until mixture is crumbly. Stir in combined egg whites, milk, and maple extract, mixing until blended; mix in caraway seeds.

2. Knead dough into ball on floured board. Roll into 7-inch circle and cut into 8 even wedges. Dust tops of each wedge with a little paprika. Arrange wedges in greased 9-inch pie pan. Bake at 375 degrees until scones are browned, 15 to 20 minutes.

POPPY SEED SCONES

12 servings (1 scone each)

- 2 2/3 cups all-purpose flour
- 3 tablespoons sugar
- 1 teaspoon baking powder
- 1/2 teaspoon salt, optional
- 6 tablespoons chilled margarine, cut into small pieces
- 3 egg whites, divided
- 1 egg yolk
- 1 cup fat-free plain yogurt
- 3 tablespoons poppy seeds
- 1 tablespoon water

Per Serving
Calories: 196
% Calories from fat: 34
Fat (gm): 7.3
Sat. fat (gm): 1.5
Cholesterol (mg): 18.9
Sodium (mg): 122
Protein (gm): 5.6
Carbohydrate (gm): 26.8

Exchanges
Milk: 0.0
Vegetable: 0.0
Fruit: 0.0
Bread: 1.5
Meat: 0.5
Fat: 1.5

1. Combine flour, sugar, baking powder, and salt in large bowl; cut in margarine with pastry blender until mixture resembles coarse meal. Mix 2 egg whites and egg yolk; stir into batter. Mix in yogurt and poppy seeds.

2. Knead dough briefly on floured board. Roll to 1-inch thickness. Cut into circles with 2-inch biscuit cutter; reroll and cut additional scones; place on greased cookie sheet. Mix remaining egg white and water and brush on tops of scones. Bake at 400 degrees until browned, about 20 minutes.

WHOLE WHEAT PANCAKES

4 servings (4 pancakes each)

- 1/2 cup all-purpose flour
- 1/2 cup whole wheat flour
- 1 teaspoon baking powder
- 1/4 teaspoon salt, optional
- 3/4 cup fat-free milk
- 2 tablespoons frozen apple juice concentrate, thawed
- 1 1/2 tablespoons vegetable oil
- 1 tablespoon brown sugar
- 2 egg whites, beaten
- Vegetable cooking spray
- 1/2-3/4 cup pancake or maple syrup, warm

Per Serving
Calories: 320
% Calories from fat: 15
Fat (gm): 5.7
Sat. fat (gm): 0.8
Cholesterol (mg): 0.9
Sodium (mg): 211
Protein (gm): 7
Carbohydrate (gm): 62.7
Exchanges
Milk: 0.0
Vegetable: 0.0
Fruit: 0.0
Bread: 2.0
Meat: 0.0
Fat: 1.0
Other carbohydrate: 2.0

1. Combine flours, baking powder, and salt in large bowl; stir in combined milk, apple juice concentrate, vegetable oil, brown sugar, and egg whites, mixing well.

2. Spray griddle or large skillet with cooking spray; heat over medium heat until hot. Pour batter onto griddle, using about 2 tablespoons batter per pancake. Turn pancakes when tops are covered with bubbles and bottoms are browned; cook until browned on second side. Serve with pancake syrup.

ORANGE-SCENTED FRENCH TOAST

4 servings (2 slices each)

- 2 eggs
- 1/4 cup fat-free milk
- 1/2 cup orange juice
- Grated rind of 1 orange
- 1/4 teaspoon ground cinnamon
- 8 slices whole wheat bread
- 2 tablespoons margarine
- 1/2 cup maple or pancake syrup

Per Serving
Calories: 341
% Calories from fat: 27
Fat (gm): 10.5
Sat. fat (gm): 2.4
Cholesterol (mg): 106.6
Sodium (mg): 374
Protein (gm): 8.9
Carbohydrate (gm): 55.9
Exchanges
Milk: 0.0
Vegetable: 0.0
Fruit: 0.0
Bread: 2.0
Meat: 0.0
Fat: 2.0
Other carbohydrate: 1.5

1. Whisk eggs, milk, orange juice, orange rind, and cinnamon in large pie plate. Dip bread slices in egg mixture to coat both sides generously. Cook in margarine in skillet over medium heat until browned, 2 to 3 minutes on each side. Serve with maple syrup.

SAVORY PARMESAN TOAST

6 servings (2 slices each)

- 4 eggs
- 1/4 cup fat-free milk
- 1/2 teaspoon pepper
- 1/4 teaspoon salt
- 2 cloves garlic, halved
- 12 slices Italian bread
- 1-2 tablespoons fennel seeds, lightly crushed
- Olive oil cooking spray
- 1/4 cup (1 ounce) grated Parmesan cheese

Per Serving
Calories: 236
% Calories from fat: 26
Fat (gm): 6.6
Sat. fat (gm): 2.2
Cholesterol (mg): 144.5
Sodium (mg): 558
Protein (gm): 11.4
Carbohydrate (gm): 32

Exchanges
Milk: 0.0
Vegetable: 0.0
Fruit: 0.0
Bread: 2.0
Meat: 1.0
Fat: 1.0

1. Whisk eggs, milk, pepper, and salt in large pie plate. Rub garlic cloves gently on both sides of bread slices. Dip bread in egg mixture to coat both sides generously; sprinkle both sides of bread slices with fennel seeds.

2. Spray griddle or large skillet with cooking spray; heat over medium heat until hot. Cook bread over medium heat until browned on the bottom, 2 to 3 minutes. Sprinkle top of each slice with about 1 teaspoon Parmesan cheese; turn and cook until browned, 2 to 3 minutes. Delicious served with pasta, grilled meats, or hearty soups.

CREPES

4 servings (2 each)

- 1/2 cup all-purpose flour
- 1/2 cup fat-free milk
- 1 egg
- 2 egg whites
- 1 tablespoon margarine, melted, *or* vegetable oil
- 1/4 teaspoon salt
- Vegetable cooking spray

Per Serving
Calories: 120
% Calories from fat: 33 (will decrease when filled)
Fat (gm): 4.3
Sat. fat (gm): 1
Cholesterol (mg): 53.8
Sodium (mg): 226
Protein (gm): 6
Carbohydrate (gm): 13.8

Exchanges
Milk: 0.0
Vegetable: 0.0
Fruit: 0.0
Bread: 1.0
Meat: 0.0
Fat: 1.0

1. Combine all ingredients, except cooking spray, in small bowl; beat until smooth (batter will be thin).

2. Spray 8-inch crepe pan or small skillet with cooking spray; heat over medium heat until hot. Pour scant 1/4 cup batter into pan, tilting pan to coat bottom evenly with batter.

3. Cook over medium heat until browned on the bottom, 2 to 3 minutes. Turn crepe and cook until browned on other side, 2 to 3 minutes.

Variation: **Dessert Crepes**—Add 1 to 2 tablespoons sugar to crepe batter; cook as above.

THIRTEEN

Dinner Sauces

AIOLI

8 servings (about 2 tablespoons each)

- 1 cup fat-free mayonnaise
- 5 cloves garlic, minced
- 2 tablespoons lemon juice
- 1/2 teaspoon dry mustard
- 1/2 teaspoon ground white pepper

Per Serving
Calories: 29
% Calories from fat: 2
Fat (gm): 0.1
Sat. fat (gm): 0
Cholesterol (mg): 0
Sodium (mg): 380
Protein (gm): 0.2
Carbohydrate (gm): 7
Exchanges
Milk: 0.0
Vegetable: 1.0
Fruit: 0.0
Bread: 0.0
Meat: 0.0
Fat: 0.0

1. Combine all ingredients.

DIJONNAISE SAUCE

8 servings (about 2 tablespoons each)

- 1 cup fat-free mayonnaise
- 3 tablespoons Dijon mustard
- 1 teaspoon fresh lemon juice

Per Serving
Calories: 29
% Calories from fat: 11
Fat (gm): 0.4
Sat. fat (gm): 0.1
Cholesterol (mg): 0
Sodium (mg): 455
Protein (gm): 0.3
Carbohydrate (gm): 6.4
Exchanges
Milk: 0.0
Vegetable: 0.0
Fruit: 0.0
Bread: 0.5
Meat: 0.0
Fat: 0.0

1. Combine all ingredients in small bowl. Refrigerate before serving.

HONEY DIJON SAUCE

10 servings (about 1/4 cup each)

- 1 1/2 cups Chicken Stock (see p. 47), *or* fat-free chicken broth
- 1/2 cup Dijon-style mustard
- 1/2 cup honey
- 2 tablespoons minced shallots
- 1 1/2 teaspoons paprika
- 1 1/2 teaspoons cornstarch
- 2 tablespoons white wine, *or* water

Per Serving
Calories: 74
% Calories from fat: 11
Fat (gm): 1
Sat. fat (gm): 0.2
Cholesterol (mg): 1.5
Sodium (mg): 164
Protein (gm): 1.3
Carbohydrate (gm): 15.3

Exchanges
Milk: 0.0
Vegetable: 0.0
Fruit: 0.0
Bread: 1.0
Meat: 0.0
Fat: 0.0

1. Combine Chicken Stock, mustard, honey, shallots, and paprika in small saucepan; heat to boiling. Reduce heat and simmer, uncovered, 10 minutes. Whisk in combined cornstarch and wine; simmer until thickened.

MOCK SOUR CREAM

8 servings (about 2 tablespoons each)

- 3/4 cup plain fat-free yogurt
- 1/4 cup cottage cheese
- 1 tablespoon fresh lemon juice

Per Serving
Calories: 18
% Calories from fat: 6
Fat (gm): 0.1
Sat. fat (gm): 0.1
Cholesterol (mg): 0.7
Sodium (mg): 45
Protein (gm): 2.1
Carbohydrate (gm): 2

Exchanges
Milk: 0.1
Vegetable: 0.0
Fruit: 0.0
Bread: 0.0
Meat: 0.1
Fat: 0.0

1. Place all ingredients in blender and process until smooth; refrigerate until chilled.

DILL SAUCE

16 servings (about 2 tablespoons each)

- 2 cups plain low-fat yogurt
- 3 tablespoons fresh, *or* 3 teaspoons dried, dill weed
- Salt and pepper, to taste

Per Serving
Calories: 19
% Calories from fat: 22
Fat (gm): 0.5
Sat. fat (gm): 0.3
Cholesterol (mg): 1.8
Sodium (mg): 20
Protein (gm): 1.5
Carbohydrate (gm): 2.1

Exchanges
Milk: 0.0
Vegetable: 0.0
Fruit: 0.0
Bread: 0.0
Meat: 0.0
Fat: 0.0

1. Combine all ingredients.

MOCK HOLLANDAISE SAUCE

6 servings (about 1/4 cup each)

- 6 ounces fat-free cream cheese
- 1/3 cup fat-free sour cream
- 3-4 tablespoons fat-free milk
- 1-2 teaspoons lemon juice
- 1/2-1 teaspoon Dijon-style mustard
- 1/8 teaspoon ground turmeric

Per Serving
Calories: 46
% Calories from fat: 8
Fat (gm): 0.4
Sat. fat (gm): 0.3
Cholesterol (mg): 2.4
Sodium (mg): 179
Protein (gm): 5.2
Carbohydrate (gm): 4.8

Exchanges
Milk: 0.0
Vegetable: 0.0
Fruit: 0.0
Bread: 0.0
Meat: 1.0
Fat: 0.0

1. Heat all ingredients in small saucepan over medium-low heat until melted and smooth, stirring constantly. Serve warm.

LIGHT TARTAR SAUCE

12 servings (about 1 tablespoon each)

- 2 cups fat-free mayonnaise
- 1/4 cup chopped onion
- 1/4 cup drained capers
- 1/4 cup chopped dill pickles
- 2 tablespoons minced parsley
- 1 tablespoon lemon juice
- 1 teaspoon sugar
- Dash red pepper sauce

Per Serving
Calories: 42
% Calories from fat: 1
Fat (gm): 0
Sat. fat (gm): 0
Cholesterol (mg): 0
Sodium (mg): 562
Protein (gm): 0.1
Carbohydrate (gm): 10.6

Exchanges
Milk: 0.0
Vegetable: 0.0
Fruit: 0.0
Bread: 0.5
Meat: 0.0
Fat: 0.0

1. Combine all ingredients.

ALFREDO SAUCE

6 servings (about 1/2 cup each)

- 3 tablespoons margarine
- 1/4 cup all-purpose flour
- 2 1/2 cups fat-free milk
- 1/4 cup (1 ounce) Parmesan cheese, freshly grated
- 1/8 teaspoon ground nutmeg
- 1/2 teaspoon salt
- 1/4 teaspoon black pepper

Per Serving
Calories: 125
% Calories from fat: 52
(25 with 2 ozs. pasta)
Fat (gm): 7.2
Sat. fat (gm): 2
Cholesterol (mg): 5
Sodium (mg): 374
Protein (gm): 5.8
Carbohydrate (gm): 9.2

Exchanges
Milk: 0.5
Vegetable: 0.0
Fruit: 0.0
Bread: 0.5
Meat: 0.0
Fat: 1.5

1. Melt margarine in medium saucepan; stir in flour. Cook over medium heat 1 minute, stirring constantly. Stir in milk; heat to boiling. Boil, stirring constantly, until thickened, 1 to 2 minutes.

2. Reduce heat to low and stir in cheese, nutmeg, salt, and pepper; cook 1 to 2 minutes.

JALAPEÑO CON QUESO SAUCE

8 servings (about 1/4 cup each)

Vegetable cooking spray
1 teaspoon finely chopped jalapeño chili
1 teaspoon ground cumin
1/2 teaspoon dried oregano leaves
8 ounces reduced-fat pasteurized processed cheese product, cubed
1/3-1/2 cup fat-free milk
1 1/4 cups (5 ounces) shredded fat-free Cheddar cheese

Per Serving
Calories: 92
% Calories from fat: 30
Fat (gm): 3.2
Sat. fat (gm): 2
Cholesterol (mg): 13.4
Sodium (mg): 562
Protein (gm): 12.2
Carbohydrate (gm): 4.4
Exchanges
Milk: 0.0
Vegetable: 0.0
Fruit: 0.0
Bread: 0.0
Meat: 2.0
Fat: 0.0

1. Spray medium saucepan with cooking spray; heat over medium heat until hot. Saute jalapeño chili until tender, about 2 minutes; stir in cumin and oregano.

2. Add processed cheese product; cook over low heat, stirring frequently, until melted. Stir in 1/3 cup milk and Cheddar cheese. Stir in additional milk if needed for desired consistency, cooking until hot through, 1 to 2 minutes.

WHITE CLAM SAUCE

8 servings (about 1/2 cup each)

4 cloves garlic, minced
2 tablespoons olive oil
1 bottle (8 ounces) clam juice
Juice of 1/2 lemon
1/2 cup dry white wine
1/2 tablespoon dried oregano leaves
2 tablespoons minced parsley
1/2 cup sliced mushrooms
2 basil leaves, coarsely chopped
3 cans (6 ounces each) minced clams, undrained
Salt and pepper, to taste

Per Serving
Calories: 140
% Calories from fat: 31 (18 with 2 ozs. pasta)
Fat (gm): 4.7
Sat. fat (gm): 0.6
Cholesterol (mg): 42.7
Sodium (mg): 110
Protein (gm): 16.9
Carbohydrate (gm): 4.4
Exchanges
Milk: 0.0
Vegetable: 0.0
Fruit: 0.0
Bread: 0.5
Meat: 2.0
Fat: 0.0

1. Saute garlic in oil in medium saucepan until golden brown, about 5 minutes. Add clam juice, lemon juice, wine, oregano, and parsley; heat to boiling. Reduce heat and simmer uncovered 20 minutes. Add mushrooms and simmer 5 minutes. Stir in basil and clams with liquor; simmer 5 minutes longer. Season to taste with salt and pepper.

WILD MUSHROOM SAUCE

8 servings (about 1/3 cup each)

Per Serving
Calories: 34
% Calories from fat: 5
Fat (gm): 0.2
Sat. fat (gm): 0
Cholesterol (mg): 0
Sodium (mg): 5
Protein (gm): 0.7
Carbohydrate (gm): 5.3

Exchanges
Milk: 0.0
Vegetable: 1.0
Fruit: 0.0
Bread: 0.0
Meat: 0.0
Fat: 0.0

Olive oil cooking spray
1/4 cup finely chopped shallots
2 cloves garlic, minced
2 cups chopped or sliced wild mushrooms (portobello, shiitake, cremini, etc.)
1/3 cup dry sherry, optional
2-3 tablespoons lemon juice
1/4-1/2 teaspoon dried thyme leaves
2 cups Vegetable Stock (see p. 48), *or* vegetable broth
2 tablespoons cornstarch
Salt and pepper, to taste

1. Spray medium saucepan with cooking spray; heat over medium heat until hot. Saute shallots and garlic until tender, 3 to 4 minutes. Stir in mushrooms; cook, covered, over medium-low heat until mushrooms are wilted, about 5 minutes. Stir in sherry, lemon juice, and thyme; heat to boiling. Reduce heat and simmer, uncovered, until mushrooms are tender and excess liquid is gone, about 5 minutes.

2. Mix stock and cornstarch; stir into saucepan and heat to boiling. Boil, stirring constantly, until thickened, about 1 minute Season to taste with salt and pepper.

MUSHROOM-WINE SAUCE

6 servings (about 1/2 cup each)

- Vegetable cooking spray
- 1 pound mushrooms, thinly sliced
- 1/4 cup chopped onion
- 1 clove garlic, minced
- 2 cups Chicken Stock (see p. 47), *or* fat-free chicken broth
- 1 tablespoon Italian seasoning
- 1 cup dry white wine
- 1 1/2 tablespoons cornstarch
- Salt and pepper, to taste

Per Serving
Calories: 71
% Calories from fat: 8
Fat (gm): 0.7
Sat. fat (gm): 0.1
Cholesterol (mg): 3.4
Sodium (mg): 9
Protein (gm): 2.9
Carbohydrate (gm): 7.1
Exchanges
Milk: 0.0
Vegetable: 1.0
Fruit: 0.0
Bread: 0.0
Meat: 0.0
Fat: 1.0

1. Spray medium saucepan with cooking spray; cook over medium heat until hot. Saute mushrooms, onion, garlic until tender, about 5 minutes. Add Chicken Stock and Italian seasoning and heat to boiling; reduce heat and simmer 10 minutes. Heat sauce to boiling; stir in combined wine and cornstarch, stirring until thickened, 1 to 2 minutes. Season to taste with salt and pepper.

JAMAICAN JERK SAUCE

8 servings (about 1/4 cup each)

- 1 large onion, cubed
- 1 whole garlic bulb, cloves blanched in boiling water and peeled
- 1/4 cup chopped pimiento
- 1/4 cup pickled jalapeño chilies
- 1/4 cup honey
- 1 tablespoon Worcestershire sauce
- 1 teaspoon dried thyme leaves
- 1 teaspoon ground cinnamon
- 1/2 teaspoon ground nutmeg
- 1/2 teaspoon black pepper
- 1/4 teaspoon cayenne pepper
- 1 teaspoon hot pepper sauce
- 2 tablespoons olive oil

Per Serving
Calories: 101
% Calories from fat: 31
Fat (gm): 3.7
Sat. fat (gm): 0.5
Cholesterol (mg): 0
Sodium (mg): 100
Protein (gm): 1.5
Carbohydrate (gm): 17.1
Exchanges
Milk: 0.0
Vegetable: 0.0
Fruit: 0.0
Bread: 1.0
Meat: 0.0
Fat: 0.5

1. Process all ingredients in food processor or blender until smooth.

ISLAND RUM-LIME SAUCE

6 servings (about 1/3 cup each)

- 2 cups Chicken Stock (see p. 47), *or* fat-free chicken broth
- 1/4 cup minced shallots
- 2 large cloves garlic, minced
- 1 tablespoon cornstarch
- 1/4 cup water
- 2 tablespoons light rum
- Juice of 1 lime
- 1/4 cup minced parsley
- Salt and pepper, to taste

Per Serving
Calories: 37
% Calories from fat: 9
Fat (gm): 0.4
Sat. fat (gm): 0.1
Cholesterol (mg): 3.4
Sodium (mg): 6.3
Protein (gm): 1.5
Carbohydrate (gm): 3.8

Exchanges
Milk: 0.0
Vegetable: 0.0
Fruit: 0.0
Bread: 0.5
Meat: 0.0
Fat: 0.0

1. Combine Chicken Stock, shallots, and garlic in medium saucepan; heat to boiling. Reduce heat and simmer 5 minutes. Stir in combined cornstarch and water, stirring until thickened. Add rum and boil 1 minute. Add lime juice and parsley. Season to taste with salt and pepper

LIGHT THAI PEANUT SAUCE

8 servings (1/4 cup each)

- 1 cup Chicken Stock (see p. 47), *or* fat-free chicken broth
- 3 tablespoons reduced-fat peanut butter
- 1 clove garlic, minced
- 1 cup shredded carrot
- 2 tablespoons rice wine vinegar, *or* other white vinegar
- 2 tablespoons sugar
- 1 tablespoon red pepper flakes

Per Serving
Calories: 61
% Calories from fat: 35
Fat (gm): 2.5
Sat. fat (gm): 0.5
Cholesterol (mg): 1.3
Sodium (mg): 10
Protein (gm): 2.4
Carbohydrate (gm): 7.8

Exchanges
Milk: 0.0
Vegetable: 0.0
Fruit: 0.0
Bread: 0.5
Meat: 0.0
Fat: 0.5

1. Combine all ingredients in small saucepan. Whisk over medium heat until smooth and hot.

SWEET-AND-SOUR SAUCE

8 servings (about 2 tablespoons each)

1 tablespoon cornstarch
1/3 cup chicken broth
1/3 cup red wine vinegar
2 tablespoons frozen pineapple juice concentrate
2 tablespoons chopped pimiento
1 tablespoon soy sauce
1/4 teaspoon garlic powder
1/4 teaspoon ground ginger
1 tablespoon sugar

Per Serving
Calories: 27
% Calories from fat: 5
Fat (gm): 0.2
Sat. fat (gm): 0
Cholesterol (mg): 0
Sodium (mg): 166
Protein (gm): 0.8
Carbohydrate (gm): 6.1
Exchanges
Milk: 0.0
Vegetable: 0.0
Fruit: 0.0
Bread: 0.5
Meat: 0.0
Fat: 0.0

1. Combine cornstarch and chicken broth in small saucepan. Heat to boiling; boil, stirring until thickened, 1 to 2 minutes. Stir in remaining ingredients. Cook over medium heat 1 to 2 minutes longer.

CLASSIC SPAGHETTI SAUCE

8 servings (about 1/2 cup each)

12 ounces ground turkey
1 cup chopped onion
1/2 cup chopped green bell pepper
1/4 cup chopped celery
2 cloves garlic, minced
2 cans (15 1/2 ounces each) diced tomatoes, undrained
1 can (6 ounces) tomato paste
1/3 cup water
2 tablespoons chopped parsley
1 teaspoon sugar
1 tablespoon chopped fresh basil leaves
1 teaspoon chopped fresh oregano leaves
1/2 teaspoon dried marjoram leaves
Salt and pepper, to taste

Per Serving
Calories: 109
% Calories from fat: 29 (15 with 2 ozs. pasta)
Fat (gm): 3.7
Sat. fat (gm): 0.9
Cholesterol (mg): 15.8
Sodium (mg): 376
Protein (gm): 8
Carbohydrate (gm): 12.7
Exchanges
Milk: 0.0
Vegetable: 2.5
Fruit: 0.0
Bread: 0.0
Meat: 1.0
Fat: 0.0

1. Cook ground turkey, onion, green pepper, celery, and garlic in large saucepan until meat is brown, about 10 minutes. Drain fat. Stir in remaining ingredients, except salt and pepper. Heat to boiling; reduce heat and simmer covered 30 minutes. Uncover, and simmer 10 to 15 minutes more or to desired consistency, stirring occasionally. Season to taste with salt and pepper.

MARINARA SAUCE

8 servings (about 1/2 cup each)

- 2 medium onions, chopped
- 6 cloves garlic, minced
- 2 tablespoons olive oil
- 2 cans (16 ounces each) Italian plum tomatoes, drained and chopped
- 1/2 cup dry white wine, *or* tomato juice
- 1/4 cup tomato paste
- 2 tablespoons fresh lemon juice
- 1/2 teaspoon salt
- 1/4 teaspoon black pepper

Per Serving
Calories: 85
% Calories from fat: 37
(11 with 2 ozs. pasta)
Fat (gm): 3.8
Sat. fat (gm): 0.5
Cholesterol (mg): 0
Sodium (mg): 325
Protein (gm): 1.9
Carbohydrate (gm): 10.2

Exchanges
Milk: 0.0
Vegetable: 2.0
Fruit: 0.0
Bread: 0.0
Meat: 0.0
Fat: 0.5

1. Saute onions and garlic in oil in large saucepan until tender, about 5 minutes. Stir in tomatoes, wine, and tomato paste; heat to boiling. Reduce heat and simmer, uncovered, until mixture is medium sauce consistency, about 20 minutes. Stir in lemon juice, salt, and pepper.

BASIC TOMATO-BASIL SAUCE

8 servings (about 1/2 cup each)

- 1 cup finely chopped onion
- 3 cloves garlic, minced
- 2 teaspoons olive oil
- 10 large fresh tomatoes, chopped, *or* 2 cans (28 ounces each) Italian plum tomatoes, undrained, chopped
- 1/4 cup chopped fresh, *or* 1-2 tablespoons dried, basil leaves
- 1 tablespoon chopped fresh, *or* 1 teaspoon dried, oregano leaves
- 1/4 teaspoon pepper

Per Serving
Calories: 60
% Calories from fat: 22
(11 with 2 ozs. pasta)
Fat (gm): 1.6
Sat. fat (gm): 0.2
Cholesterol (mg): 0
Sodium (mg): 325
Protein (gm): 2.2
Carbohydrate (gm): 10.9
Exchanges
Milk: 0.0
Vegetable: 2.0
Fruit: 0.0
Bread: 0.0
Meat: 0.0
Fat: 0.0

1. Saute onion and garlic in oil in large saucepan until tender, about 5 minutes. Stir in remaining ingredients; heat to boiling. Reduce heat and simmer, uncovered, until thickened, about 1 hour, stirring frequently.

ROMESCO SAUCE

8 servings (about 3 tablespoons each)

- 1 tomato, peeled, seeded, and chopped
- 1 small dried hot chili pepper, minced
- 3 cloves garlic, minced
- 3/4 cup dry white wine
- 2 tablespoons white wine vinegar
- 2 tablespoons dry sherry
- Salt and pepper, to taste

Per Serving
Calories: 26
% Calories from fat: 2
(7 with 2 ozs. pasta)
Fat (gm): 0.1
Sat. fat (gm): 0
Cholesterol (mg): 0
Sodium (mg): 3
Protein (gm): 0.3
Carbohydrate (gm): 1.8
Exchanges
Milk: 0.0
Vegetable: 0.0
Fruit: 0.0
Bread: 0.0
Meat: 0.0
Fat: 0.5

1. Process all ingredients, except salt and pepper, in food processor or blender until smooth; season to taste with salt and pepper.

MEDITERRANEAN TOMATO-CAPER SAUCE

4 servings (about 1/2 cup each)

2 cans (8 ounces each) reduced-sodium tomato sauce
2 teaspoons minced garlic
1 teaspoon dried oregano leaves
1 teaspoon ground cumin
1 teaspoon ground coriander
1 teaspoon paprika
Pinch ground cardamom
Pinch ground cinnamon
Pinch ground cloves
2 teaspoons lime juice
1/4 cup raisins
2-3 teaspoons drained capers
Salt and pepper, to taste

Per Serving
Calories: 83
% Calories from fat: 3
Fat (gm): 0.3
Sat. fat (gm): 0
Cholesterol (mg): 0
Sodium (mg): 88
Protein (gm): 2.7
Carbohydrate (gm): 18.3
Exchanges
Milk: 0.0
Vegetable: 2.0
Fruit: 0.5
Bread: 0.0
Meat: 0.0
Fat: 0.0

1. Combine all ingredients; refrigerate at least 2 hours for flavors to blend.

PIZZA SAUCE

4 servings (about 1/4 cup each)

Olive oil cooking spray
1 small onion, chopped
1/4 cup chopped green bell pepper
2 cloves garlic, minced
1 can (8 ounces) reduced-sodium tomato sauce
1/2 teaspoon dried basil leaves
1/4 teaspoon dried oregano leaves
Salt and pepper, to taste

Per Serving
Calories: 37
% Calories from fat: 2
Fat (gm): 0.1
Sat. fat (gm): 0
Cholesterol (mg): 0
Sodium (mg): 18
Protein (gm): 1.5
Carbohydrate (gm): 7.8
Exchanges
Milk: 0.0
Vegetable: 1.5
Fruit: 0.0
Bread: 0.0
Meat: 0.0
Fat: 0.0

1. Spray medium saucepan with cooking spray; heat over medium heat until hot. Saute onion, bell pepper, and garlic until tender, about 5 minutes.

2. Stir in tomato sauce and herbs; heat to boiling. Reduce heat and simmer, uncovered, until sauce thickens, about 5 minutes. Season to taste with salt and pepper.

POBLANO CHILI SAUCE

8 servings (about 1/4 cup each)

Vegetable cooking spray
2 medium tomatoes, chopped
1/2 medium poblano chili, seeds and veins discarded, chopped
1 small onion, chopped
2 cloves garlic, minced
1-2 tablespoons chili powder
Salt and pepper, to taste

Per Serving
Calories: 16
% Calories from fat: 14
Fat (gm): 0.3
Sat. fat (gm): 0
Cholesterol (mg): 0
Sodium (mg): 13
Protein (gm): 0.6
Carbohydrate (gm): 3.4

Exchanges
Milk: 0.0
Vegetable: 0.5
Fruit: 0.0
Bread: 0.0
Meat: 0.0
Fat: 0.0

1. Spray large skillet with cooking spray, heat over medium heat until hot. Cook tomatoes, poblano chili, onion, garlic, and chili powder until poblano chili and onion are very tender, 8 to 10 minutes.

2. Process mixture in food processor or blender until smooth; season to taste with salt and pepper.

GINGERED TOMATO RELISH

12 servings (about 2 tablespoons each)

1 1/2 cups chopped tomatoes
1/2 cup finely chopped zucchini
1/4 cup finely chopped carrot
1/4 cup finely chopped onion
1 tablespoon grated gingerroot
Salt and pepper, to taste

Per Serving
Calories: 9
% Calories from fat: 10
Fat (gm): 0.1
Sat. fat (gm): 0
Cholesterol (mg): 0
Sodium (mg): 4
Protein (gm): 0.4
Carbohydrate (gm): 2

Exchanges
Milk: 0.0
Vegetable: 0.0
Fruit: 0.0
Bread: 0.0
Meat: 0.0
Fat: 0.0

1. Combine all ingredients, except salt and pepper, in medium skillet. Cook, covered, over medium heat until tomatoes are soft and mixture is bubbly. Simmer, uncovered, until excess liquid is gone, about 10 minutes. Season to taste with salt and pepper. Serve warm.

TOMATO OLIVE SALSA

6 servings (about 1/3 cup each)

- 6 medium tomatoes, seeded, chopped
- 4 pitted black olives, sliced
- 2 tablespoons chopped red onion
- 2 tablespoons chopped fresh basil leaves
- 2 teaspoons chopped parsley
- 1 teaspoon dried oregano leaves
- 2-4 tablespoons lemon juice
- 2-4 tablespoons balsamic vinegar
- Salt and pepper, to taste

Per Serving
Calories: 51
% Calories from fat: 12
Fat (gm): 0.8
Sat. fat (gm): 0.1
Cholesterol (mg): 0
Sodium (mg): 39
Protein (gm): 1.2
Carbohydrate (gm): 9.7
Exchanges
Milk: 0.0
Vegetable: 2.0
Fruit: 0.0
Bread: 0.0
Meat: 0.0
Fat: 0.0

1. Combine tomatoes, olives, onion, and herbs in medium bowl; let stand at room temperature 30 minutes. Pour off any liquid that has accumulated; add lemon juice and vinegar. Season to taste with salt and pepper.

RED TOMATO SALSA

16 servings (about 2 tablespoons each)

- 2 large tomatoes, cut into wedges
- 1 small onion finely chopped
- 1 small poblano chili, veins and seeds discarded, chopped
- 1/4 jalepeño chili, seeds and veins discarded, chopped
- 1 clove garlic, minced
- 1/4 cup loosely packed cilantro, finely chopped
- Salt, to taste

Per Serving
Calories: 9
% Calories from fat: 10
Fat (gm): 0.1
Sat. fat (gm): 0
Cholesterol (mg): 0
Sodium (mg): 4
Protein (gm): 0.4
Carbohydrate (gm): 1.9
Exchanges
Milk: 0.0
Vegetable: 0.5
Fruit: 0.0
Bread: 0.0
Meat: 0.0
Fat: 0.0

1. Process all ingredients, except salt, in food processor or blender until finely chopped; season to taste with salt.

ZESTY COCKTAIL SAUCE

8 servings (about 2 tablespoons each)

- 3/4 cup low-sodium catsup
- 2 tablespoons prepared horseradish
- 2 tablespoons lemon juice
- 1/4 cup finely chopped celery
- 1 tablespoon chopped fresh, *or* 2 teaspoons dried, basil leaves
- 1 tablespoon minced parsley
- 1 teaspoon Worcestershire sauce
- Dash red pepper sauce

Per Serving
Calories: 5
% Calories from fat: 2
Fat (gm): 0
Sat. fat (gm): 0
Cholesterol (mg): 0
Sodium (mg): 61
Protein (gm): 0.1
Carbohydrate (gm): 1.2
Exchanges
Milk: 0.0
Vegetable: 0.0
Fruit: 0.0
Bread: 0.0
Meat: 0.0
Fat: 0.0

1. Combine all ingredients.

SUN-DRIED TOMATO PESTO

4 servings (about 2 tablespoons each)

- 1/2 cup sun-dried tomatoes (not in oil)
- 1/2 cup boiling water
- 1/2 cup packed basil leaves
- 2 cloves garlic
- 3 tablespoons olive oil
- 2 tablespoons grated fat-free Parmesan cheese
- Salt and pepper, to taste

Per Serving
Calories: 118
% Calories from fat: 75
(28 with 2 ozs. pasta)
Fat (gm): 10.4
Sat. fat (gm): 1.4
Cholesterol (mg): 0
Sodium (mg): 164
Protein (gm): 2.2
Carbohydrate (gm): 5.5
Exchanges
Milk: 0.0
Vegetable: 0.0
Fruit: 0.0
Bread: 0.5
Meat: 0.0
Fat: 2.0

1. Soak tomatoes in boiling water in bowl until softened, about 10 minutes. Drain, reserving liquid.
2. Process tomatoes, basil, garlic, oil, and cheese in food processor or blender, adding enough reserved liquid to make a smooth, spoonable paste. Season to taste with salt and pepper. Serve at room temperature.

MIXED HERB PESTO

4 servings (about 2 tablespoons each)

- 1/2 cup packed fresh, *or* 2 tablespoons dried, basil leaves
- 1/2 cup packed fresh parsley
- 1/4 cup packed fresh, *or* 2 tablespoons dried, oregano leaves
- 3 cloves garlic
- 2 tablespoons grated Parmesan cheese
- 1 ounce walnuts
- 2 tablespoons olive oil
- 2 teaspoons lemon juice
- 1/2 teaspoon salt
- 1/4 teaspoon pepper

Per Serving
Calories: 134
% Calories from fat: 77
(31 with 2 ozs. pasta)
Fat (gm): 12
Sat. fat (gm): 1.9
Cholesterol (mg): 2.4
Sodium (mg): 330
Protein (gm): 4
Carbohydrate (gm): 4.9
Exchanges
Milk: 0.0
Vegetable: 1.0
Fruit: 0.0
Bread: 0.0
Meat: 0.0
Fat: 2.5

1. Combine herbs, garlic, Parmesan cheese, and walnuts in food processor or blender. Process, adding oil and lemon juice gradually, until mixture is very finely chopped. Stir in salt and pepper. Serve at room temperature.

MICROWAVE CRANBERRY ORANGE SAUCE

16 servings (about 3 tablespoons each)

- 1 package (12 ounces) fresh cranberries
- 1/4 cup frozen orange juice concentrate
- 1 orange, unpeeled, cut into 8 pieces
- 2 tablespoons chopped walnuts

Per Serving
Calories: 27
% Calories from fat: 19
Fat (gm): 0.6
Sat. fat (gm): 0
Cholesterol (mg): 0
Sodium (mg): 0
Protein (gm): 0.5
Carbohydrate (gm): 5.5
Exchanges
Milk: 0.0
Vegetable: 0.0
Fruit: 0.5
Bread: 0.0
Meat: 0.0
Fat: 0.0

1. Combine cranberries and orange juice in 1-quart casserole or measure. Cover with vented plastic wrap, and microwave on High 5 minutes, or until cranberries are soft.

2. Process cranberries and orange in food processor until coarsely chopped. Pour into glass bowl; cool. Refrigerate until cold, about 1 hour. Sprinkle with chopped walnuts before serving.

FOURTEEN

Dessert Sauces

ORANGE YOGURT SAUCE

6 servings (about 3 tablespoons each)

- 1 cup plain low-fat yogurt
- 1 teaspoon grated orange rind
- 2 tablespoons brown sugar
- 1/2 teaspoon orange extract

Per Serving
Calories: 43
% Calories from fat: 12
Fat (gm): 0.6
Sat. fat (gm): 0.4
Cholesterol (mg): 2.3
Sodium (mg): 28
Protein (gm): 2
Carbohydrate (gm): 7.3
Exchanges
Milk: 0.5
Vegetable: 0.0
Fruit: 0.0
Bread: 0.0
Meat: 0.0
Fat: 0.0

1. Mix all ingredients in small bowl. Serve over fresh fruit.

STRAWBERRY SAUCE

10 servings (about 2 tablespoon each)

- 2 cups fresh, *or* frozen, thawed, strawberries
- 2 teaspoons cornstarch
- 2-4 tablespoons sugar

Per Serving
Calories: 13
% Calories from fat: 7
Fat (gm): 0.1
Sat. fat (gm): 0
Cholesterol (mg): 0
Sodium (mg): 0
Protein (gm): 0.2
Carbohydrate (gm): 3
Exchanges
Milk: 0.0
Vegetable: 0.0
Fruit: 0.0
Bread: 0.0
Meat: 0.0
Fat: 0.0

1. Process strawberries in blender or food processor until smooth. Combine berries, cornstarch, and sugar in small saucepan. Heat to boiling over medium heat, stirring constantly until thickened, 1 to 2 minutes. Cool; refrigerate until well chilled.

Note: Peaches, pineapple, cherries, blueberries, or raspberries, can be substituted for the strawberries.

HOT FUDGE SAUCE

10 servings (about 2 tablespoons each)

- 3/4 cup sugar
- 1/2 cup Dutch-process cocoa
- 1 can (5 ounces) evaporated fat-free milk
- 1/3 cup light corn syrup
- 4 tablespoons margarine
- 1 teaspoon vanilla extract

Per Serving
Calories: 156
% Calories from fat: 28
Fat (gm): 5
Sat. fat (gm): 0.9
Cholesterol (mg): 0.6
Sodium (mg): 85
Protein (gm): 2.1
Carbohydrate (gm): 26.9
Exchanges
Milk: 0.0
Vegetable: 0.0
Fruit: 0.0
Bread: 1.5
Meat: 0.0
Fat: 1.0

1. Combine sugar and cocoa in small saucepan; blend in evaporated fat-free milk and corn syrup. Cook over medium heat, stirring constantly, until mixture boils; boil and stir 1 minute. Remove from heat; stir in margarine and vanilla. Serve warm.

CRÈME ANGLAISE

8 servings (about 2 tablespoons each)

- 1 tablespoon cornstarch
- 2 teaspoons sugar
- 1 cup fat-free milk
- 1 egg yolk
- 1/2-3/4 teaspoon ground nutmeg

Per Serving
Calories: 26
% Calories from fat: 24
Fat (gm): 0.7
Sat. fat (gm): 0.2
Cholesterol (mg): 27.2
Sodium (mg): 17
Protein (gm): 1.4
Carbohydrate (gm): 3.5
Exchanges
Milk: 0.0
Vegetable: 0.0
Fruit: 0.0
Bread: 0.5
Meat: 0.0
Fat: 0.0

1. Mix cornstarch and sugar in small saucepan; stir in milk. Cook over medium heat until mixture boils and thickens, stirring constantly.

2. Stir about 1/2 cup milk mixture into egg yolk; stir egg yolk mixture into saucepan. Cook over low heat, stirring constantly, until thickened (mixture will coat back of spoon). Remove from heat; stir in nutmeg. Serve warm or cold.

BITTERSWEET CHOCOLATE SAUCE

12 servings (about 2 tablespoons each)

- 3/4 cup unsweetened cocoa
- 1/2 cup sugar
- 3/4 cup fat-free milk
- 2 tablespoons margarine
- 1 teaspoon vanilla
- 1/4-1/2 teaspoon ground cinnamon

Per Serving
Calories: 64
% Calories from fat: 27
Fat (gm): 1.9
Sat. fat (gm): 0.4
Cholesterol (mg): 0.5
Sodium (mg): 39
Protein (gm): 1.1
Carbohydrate (gm): 10.7
Exchanges
Milk: 0.0
Vegetable: 0.0
Fruit: 0.0
Bread: 1.0
Meat: 0.0
Fat: 0.0

1. Mix cocoa and sugar in small saucepan; stir in milk and add margarine. Heat over medium heat until boiling, stirring constantly. Reduce heat and simmer until sauce is smooth and slightly thickened, 3 to 4 minutes. Remove from heat; stir in vanilla and cinnamon. Serve warm or at room temperature.

CHOCOLATE SAUCE

8 servings (about 2 tablespoons each)

- 1/4 cup unsweetened cocoa
- 2 tablespoons sugar
- 1 tablespoon cornstarch
- 1/3 cup dark corn syrup
- 1/4 cup 2% reduced-fat milk
- 1 teaspoon margarine
- 2 teaspoons vanilla

Per Serving
Calories: 71
% Calories from fat: 8
Fat (gm): 0.6
Sat. fat (gm): 0.2
Cholesterol (mg): 0.7
Sodium (mg): 23
Protein (gm): 0.5
Carbohydrate (gm): 15.8
Exchanges
Milk: 0.0
Vegetable: 0.0
Fruit: 0.0
Bread: 1.0
Meat: 0.0
Fat: 0.0

1. Combine cocoa, sugar, and cornstarch in small saucepan. Stir in com syrup and milk until smooth. Cook over medium heat until mixture boils and thickens, stirring constantly. Remove from heat; stir in margarine and vanilla. Serve warm or at room temperature.

RICH CARAMEL SAUCE

12 servings (about 2 tablespoons each)

- 2 eggs, lightly beaten
- 1 cup packed light brown sugar
- 1 tablespoon flour
- 1/4 cup light corn syrup
- 1/4 cup 2% reduced-fat milk
- 1 teaspoon vanilla
- 4 tablespoons margarine, cut into pieces

Per Serving
Calories: 140
% Calories from fat: 29
Fat (gm): 4.7
Sat. fat (gm): 1.1
Cholesterol (mg): 35.7
Sodium (mg): 72.6
Protein (gm): 1.3
Carbohydrate (gm): 23.9

Exchanges
Milk: 0.0
Vegetable: 0.0
Fruit: 0.0
Bread: 1.5
Meat: 0.0
Fat: 1.0

1. Mix eggs, brown sugar, flour, corn syrup, milk, and vanilla until smooth in small saucepan. Add margarine and whisk over medium-low heat until brown sugar and margarine are melted; continue whisking over medium-high heat until mixture boils and thickens, 2 to 3 minutes. Serve warm or at room temperature.

Variations: **Honeyed Caramel Sauce**—Make recipe as above, substituting honey for the light corn syrup and adding a pinch of ground nutmeg.

Rum-Raisin Caramel Sauce—Make recipe as above, adding 1/2 cup raisins and 1 to 2 tablespoons rum or 1/2 to 1 teaspoon rum extract.

QUICK-AND-EASY CARAMEL SAUCE

12 servings (about 2 tablespoons each)

1 package (14 ounces) caramels
6 tablespoons 2% reduced-fat milk

Per Serving
Calories: 123
% Calories from fat: 7
Fat (gm): 1
Sat. fat (gm): 0.3
Cholesterol (mg): 0.6
Sodium (mg): 12
Protein (gm): 0.9
Carbohydrate (gm): 29.3

Exchanges
Milk: 0.0
Vegetable: 0.0
Fruit: 2.0
Bread: 0.0
Meat: 0.0
Fat: 0.0

1. Heat caramels and milk in medium saucepan, stirring over medium heat until melted.

RUM-RAISIN SAUCE

10 servings (about 2 tablespoons each)

1 cup plus 2 tablespoons water, divided
1/2 cup granulated sugar
1/2 cup packed light brown sugar
2-3 tablespoons margarine
Pinch ground cloves
1/2 cup dark raisins
1 tablespoon cornstarch
1 tablespoon rum, *or* 1 teaspoon rum extract

Per Serving
Calories: 128
% Calories from fat: 15
Fat (gm): 2.3
Sat. fat (gm): 0.5
Cholesterol (mg): 0
Sodium (mg): 32
Protein (gm): 0.3
Carbohydrate (gm): 27.2

Exchanges
Milk: 0.0
Vegetable: 0.0
Fruit: 0.0
Bread: 1.0
Meat: 0.0
Fat: 1.0

1. Heat 1 cup water, sugars, margarine, and cloves in medium saucepan, stirring until sugar is dissolved; boil, uncovered, until reduced to 1 cup. Add raisins and simmer 3 to 4 minutes. Combine remaining 2 tablespoons water and cornstarch until smooth. Add to saucepan and boil 1 minute; stir in rum.

WARM RUM SAUCE

8 servings (about 3 tablespoons each)

- 1/4 cup sugar
- 1 tablespoon cornstarch
- 1 1/4 cups fat-free milk
- 2 tablespoons rum, *or* 1 teaspoon rum extract
- 2 tablespoons margarine
- 1/2 teaspoon vanilla
- 1/8 teaspoon ground nutmeg

Per Serving
Calories: 76
% Calories from fat: 34
Fat (gm): 2.9
Sat. fat (gm): 0.6
Cholesterol (mg): 0.7
Sodium (mg): 53
Protein (gm): 1.3
Carbohydrate (gm): 9.2
Exchanges
Milk: 0.0
Vegetable: 0.0
Fruit: 0.0
Bread: 0.5
Meat: 0.0
Fat: 0.5

1. Mix sugar and cornstarch in small saucepan; stir in milk and rum. Cook over medium heat until mixture boils and thickens, stirring constantly. Remove from heat; stir in remaining ingredients. Serve warm.

HONEY SAUCE

8 servings (about 2 tablespoons each)

- 1/2 cup honey
- 1/2 cup apple juice
- 1 tablespoon cornstarch
- 2 tablespoons cold water
- 1 tablespoon margarine
- 2 teaspoons lemon juice
- 1/8 teaspoon ground mace

Per Serving
Calories: 88
% Calories from fat: 14
Fat (gm): 1.5
Sat. fat (gm): 0.3
Cholesterol (mg): 0
Sodium (mg): 18
Protein (gm): 0.1
Carbohydrate (gm): 20.2
Exchanges
Milk: 0.0
Vegetable: 0.0
Fruit: 1.5
Bread: 0.0
Meat: 0.0
Fat: 0.0

1. Heat honey and apple juice to boiling in small saucepan over medium heat. Mix cornstarch in cold water until smooth; stir into honey mixture. Boil, stirring constantly, until thickened. Stir in margarine, lemon juice, and mace. Serve warm or at room temperature.

FRESH GINGER SAUCE

8 servings (about 2 tablespoons each)

- 1 cup boiling water
- 2 tablespoons chopped fresh gingerroot
- 3 tablespoons honey
- 1-2 tablespoons margarine
- 2 teaspoons lemon juice

Per Serving
Calories: 38
% Calories from fat: 31
Fat (gm): 1.4
Sat. fat (gm): 0.3
Cholesterol (mg): 0
Sodium (mg): 17
Protein (gm): 0.1
Carbohydrate (gm): 6.8

Exchanges
Milk: 0.0
Vegetable: 0.0
Fruit: 0.0
Bread: 0.5
Meat: 0.0
Fat: 0.0

1. Pour boiling water over gingerroot and honey in small saucepan. Cover; let stand 30 minutes. Cook over medium heat until boiling; reduce heat and simmer 2 minutes. Strain; stir in margarine and lemon juice. Serve warm or cold.

TART LEMON SAUCE

12 servings (about 2 tablespoons each)

- 2 tablespoons margarine
- 2/3-1 cup sugar
- 1 cup lemon juice
- 2 eggs, slightly beaten

Per Serving
Calories: 77
% Calories from fat: 30
Fat (gm): 2.7
Sat. fat (gm): 0.6
Cholesterol (mg): 35.3
Sodium (mg): 33
Protein (gm): 1.1
Carbohydrate (gm): 13

Exchanges
Milk: 0.0
Vegetable: 0.0
Fruit: 0.0
Bread: 1.0
Meat: 0.0
Fat: 0.5

1. Melt margarine over low heat in small saucepan; stir in sugar and lemon juice. Cook over medium heat until sugar is dissolved.

2. Whisk about 1/2 cup of hot lemon mixture into eggs. Whisk egg mixture into saucepan; whisk constantly over low heat until mixture coats the back of a spoon, 2 to 3 minutes (do not boil). Serve warm or at room temperature.

BRANDIED CHERRY SAUCE

8 servings (about 2 tablespoons each)

- 2 tablespoons sugar
- 1 teaspoon cornstarch
- 1/4 teaspoon ground allspice
- 1 cup fresh, *or* frozen, thawed, pitted dark sweet cherries
- 1/2 cup water
- 1 tablespoon brandy, *or* 1/2 teaspoon brandy extract
- 1 tablespoon lemon juice

Per Serving
Calories: 32
% Calories from fat: 1
Fat (gm): 0
Sat. fat (gm): 0
Cholesterol (mg): 0
Sodium (mg): 0
Protein (gm): 0.2
Carbohydrate (gm): 7.3
Exchanges
Milk: 0.0
Vegetable: 0.0
Fruit: 0.5
Bread: 0.0
Meat: 0.0
Fat: 0.0

1. Mix sugar, cornstarch, and allspice in medium skillet or chafing dish. Stir in cherries, water, brandy, and lemon juice. Stir over medium heat until mixture boils and thickens; boil 1 minute, stirring constantly. Serve warm.

FESTIVE CRANBERRY SAUCE

12 servings (about 2 tablespoons each)

- 1/2 cup sugar
- 1 tablespoon cornstarch
- 1/4 teaspoon ground cinnamon
- 1 cup water
- 1/2 cup fresh, *or* frozen, thawed, cranberries

Per Serving
Calories: 37
% Calories from fat: 0
Fat (gm): 0
Sat. fat (gm): 0
Cholesterol (mg): 0
Sodium (mg): 0
Protein (gm): 0
Carbohydrate (gm): 9.6
Exchanges
Milk: 0.0
Vegetable: 0.0
Fruit: 0.5
Bread: 0.0
Meat: 0.0
Fat: 0.0

1. Combine sugar, cornstarch, and cinnamon in small saucepan. Stir in water and cranberries; heat to boiling. Cook stirring constantly, until thickened. Serve warm or cold.

RASPBERRY SAUCE

8 servings (about 2 tablespoons each)

- 1 pint fresh, *or* frozen, thawed, raspberries
- 1/4 cup sugar
- 1 teaspoon lemon juice

Per Serving
Calories: 39
% Calories from fat: 3
Fat (gm): 0.2
Sat. fat (gm): 0
Cholesterol (mg): 0
Sodium (mg): 0
Protein (gm): 0.3
Carbohydrate (gm): 9.9

Exchanges
Milk: 0.0
Vegetable: 0.0
Fruit: 0.5
Bread: 0.0
Meat: 0.0
Fat: 0.0

1. Process raspberries, sugar, and lemon juice in blender or food processor until smooth. Strain the puree; discard seeds.

FIFTEEN

Cakes, Cheesecakes, AND Cookies

GERMAN CHOCOLATE CAKE

16 servings

Per Serving
Calories: 368
% Calories from fat: 23
Fat (gm): 9.8
Sat. fat (gm): 3.3
Cholesterol (mg): 28.1
Sodium (mg): 265
Protein (gm): 6.2
Carbohydrate (gm): 66.5
Exchanges
Milk: 0.0
Vegetable: 0.0
Fruit: 0.0
Bread: 4.0
Meat: 0.0
Fat: 2.0

1 cup granulated sugar
3/4 cup packed light brown sugar
1/2 cup unsweetened applesauce
1 1/2 cups 1% low-fat milk
1 tablespoon lemon juice
4 ounces German sweet chocolate, melted
1 teaspoon vanilla
2 eggs
2 egg whites
2 cups all-purpose flour
1 teaspoon baking soda
1/2 teaspoon salt
Coconut Frosting (recipe follows)

1. Mix sugars and applesauce, milk, lemon juice, melted chocolate, and vanilla in large bowl. Beat in eggs and egg whites; mix in combined flour, baking soda, and salt.

2. Pour batter into 2 greased and floured 9-inch round cake pans. Bake at 350 degrees until cakes spring back when touched, about 25 minutes. Cool in pans on wire rack 10 minutes; remove from pans and cool completely.

3. Place 1 cake layer on serving plate; spread with 3/4 cup Coconut Frosting; top with second cake layer. Frost top and side of cake.

Coconut Frosting

makes about 2 1/2 cups

3/4 cup sugar
2 tablespoons plus 1 1/2 teaspoons cornstarch
5 tablespoons margarine
1/3 cup light corn syrup
1 1/4 cups evaporated fat-free milk
2 teaspoons vanilla
1/2 cup shredded coconut
1/2-3/4 cup chopped toasted pecans

1. Combine all ingredients, except coconut and pecans, in medium saucepan. Heat to boiling; stir in coconut and pecans. Cool until thick enough to spread, stirring occasionally.

LEMON PUDDING CAKE

8 servings

Per Serving
Calories: 208
% Calories from fat: 17
Fat (gm): 4.1
Sat. fat (gm): 1.1
Cholesterol (mg): 28.8
Sodium (mg): 114
Protein (gm): 4
Carbohydrate (gm): 39.9
Exchanges
Milk: 0.0
Vegetable: 0.0
Fruit: 0.0
Bread: 2.5
Meat: 0.0
Fat: 0.5

- 1 1/4 cups sugar, divided
- 1/2 cup all-purpose flour
- 1/8 teaspoon salt
- 1 cup 2% reduced-fat milk
- 1/3 cup lemon juice
- 2 tablespoons margarine, melted
- 1 egg
- 1 tablespoon grated lemon rind
- 3 egg whites
- 1/8 teaspoon cream of tartar

1. Combine 1 cup sugar, flour, and salt in large bowl. Combine milk, lemon juice, margarine, egg, and lemon rind; mix into dry ingredients.

2. Beat egg whites and cream of tartar to soft peaks in large bowl; beat to stiff peaks, adding remaining 1/4 cup sugar gradually. Fold egg whites into cake batter (batter will be slightly lumpy and thin).

3. Pour batter into greased 1 1/2-quart casserole or souffle dish. Place casserole in roasting pan on oven rack; add 1 to 2 inches boiling water. Bake at 350 degrees until cake is golden and springs back when touched, about 40 minutes. Cool on wire rack 15 minutes; serve warm.

OATMEAL CAKE

15 servings

Per Serving
Calories: 327
% Calories from fat: 28
Fat (gm): 10.6
Sat. fat (gm): 2
Cholesterol (mg): 28.6
Sodium (mg): 273
Protein (gm): 3.3
Carbohydrate (gm): 56.4
Exchanges
Milk: 0.0
Vegetable: 0.0
Fruit: 0.0
Bread: 4.0
Meat: 0.0
Fat: 1.5

1 cup quick-cooking oats
1 1/4 cups boiling water
6 tablespoons margarine
1 cup granulated sugar
1 cup packed light brown sugar
2 eggs
1 1/3 cups cake flour
1 teaspoon baking soda
1/2 teaspoon salt
1 teaspoon ground cinnamon
1/4 teaspoon ground nutmeg
Generous pinch ground cloves
Broiled Pecan Frosting (recipe follows)

1. Mix oats, boiling water, and margarine in large bowl, stirring until margarine is melted; let stand 15 to 20 minutes. Mix in sugars and eggs. Mix in combined remaining ingredients, except Broiled Pecan Frosting.

2. Pour batter into greased 13 x 9-inch baking pan. Bake at 350 degrees until toothpick inserted in center comes out clean, about 35 minutes. Cool on wire rack 10 to 15 minutes.

3. Make double the recipe for Broiled Pecan Frosting, except do not double pecans; spread evenly on cake. Broil 4 inches from heat source until mixture is bubbly and pecans browned, about 1 minute

Broiled Pecan Frosting

makes about 1 3/4 cup

1 cup packed light brown sugar
6 tablespoons flour
1 teaspoon ground cinnamon
6 tablespoons margarine
1/4 cup fat-free milk
1/3 cup coarsely chopped pecans

1. Heat all ingredients, except pecans, to boiling in small saucepan, stirring frequently; cook over medium heat 2 minutes, stirring constantly. Remove from heat; stir in pecans.

GLAZED BLUEBERRY CAKE

8 servings

Per Serving
Calories: 375
% Calories from fat: 31
Fat (gm): 12.9
Sat. fat (gm): 2.7
Cholesterol (mg): 53.3
Sodium (mg): 426
Protein (gm): 5.6
Carbohydrate (gm): 60.2

Exchanges
Milk: 0.0
Vegetable: 0.0
Fruit: 0.0
Bread: 4.0
Meat: 0.0
Fat: 2.0

1/2 cup margarine, softened
1 cup sugar
2 eggs
1/2 cup fat-free milk
1 teaspoon vanilla
2 cups all-purpose flour
2 teaspoons baking powder
Generous pinch ground nutmeg
1/2 teaspoon salt
3/4-1 cup fresh, *or* frozen, blueberries
Grated rind of 1 lemon
Lemon Glaze (recipe follows)

1. Beat margarine and sugar until blended in large bowl; beat in eggs, milk, and vanilla. Mix in combined flour, baking powder, nutmeg, and salt; fold in blueberries and lemon rind.

2. Pour batter into greased 8- or 9-inch square baking pan. Bake at 350 degrees until toothpick inserted in center comes out clean, 30 to 35 minutes. Cool on wire rack. Drizzle with Lemon Glaze.

Lemon Glaze

makes about 1/4 cup

1/2 cup powdered sugar
1-2 teaspoons finely grated lemon rind
3-4 teaspoons lemon juice

1. Mix powdered sugar, lemon rind, and enough lemon juice to make glaze consistency.

APPLESAUCE STREUSEL CAKE

9 servings

- 1/2 cup margarine, softened
- 3/4 cup packed light brown sugar
- 1 egg
- 3/4 cup applesauce
- 1 teaspoon vanilla
- 1 cup all-purpose flour
- 1/2 cup whole wheat flour
- 1/2 cup quick-cooking oats
- 2 teaspoons baking powder
- 1/2 teaspoon salt
- 1/2 teaspoon ground cinnamon
- 1/4 teaspoon baking soda
- 1/4 teaspoon ground cloves
- Crisp Streusel (recipe follows)

Per Serving
Calories: 348
% Calories from fat: 35
Fat (gm): 13.8
Sat. fat (gm): 2.8
Cholesterol (mg): 23.6
Sodium (mg): 441
Protein (gm): 4.3
Carbohydrate (gm): 53.3
Exchanges
Milk: 0.0
Vegetable: 0.0
Fruit: 0.0
Bread: 3.5
Meat: 0.0
Fat: 2.0

1. Beat margarine and sugar in large bowl until blended; beat in egg, applesauce, and vanilla. Mix in combined remaining ingredients, except Crisp Streusel, stirring until well blended.

2. Pour batter into greased 8- or 9-inch square baking pan. Sprinkle with Crisp Streusel. Bake at 350 degrees until toothpick inserted in center of cake comes out clean, 35 to 40 minutes. Cool on wire rack.

Crisp Streusel

makes about 3/4 cup

- 1/2 cup packed light brown sugar
- 2 tablespoons quick-cooking oats
- 2 tablespoons flour
- 2 tablespoons cold margarine, cut into pieces

1. Combine brown sugar, oats, and flour in small bowl; cut in margarine with pastry blender to form crumbly mixture.

MOIST GINGERBREAD WITH LEMON SAUCE

12 servings

- 1/2 cup margarine, softened
- 1/2 cup packed light brown sugar
- 1 egg
- 1 cup light molasses
- 1 cup boiling water
- 2 teaspoons baking soda
- 2 1/2 cups all-purpose flour
- 1/4 cup chopped crystallized ginger
- 1 tablespoon ground ginger
- 1 teaspoon ground cinnamon
- 1/2 teaspoon salt
- Tart Lemon Sauce (see p. 524)

Per Serving
Calories: 359
% Calories from fat: 26
Fat (gm): 10.6
Sat. fat (gm): 2.2
Cholesterol (mg): 35.3
Sodium (mg): 445
Protein (gm): 4
Carbohydrate (gm): 63.7
Exchanges
Milk: 0.0
Vegetable: 0.0
Fruit: 0.0
Bread: 4.0
Meat: 0.0
Fat: 1.5

1. Beat margarine and brown sugar until fluffy in large bowl; beat in egg. Mix molasses, boiling water, and baking soda; mix into margarine mixture. Mix in combined flour, crystallized ginger, spices, and salt.

2. Pour batter into greased and floured 13 x 9 -inch baking pan. Bake at 350 degrees until toothpick inserted in center comes out clean, 25 to 30 minutes. Cool in pan 20 minutes; remove from pan and cool 10 to 15 minutes. Serve warm with warm or chilled Tart Lemon Sauce.

LEMON POPPY SEED CAKE

12 servings

- 1 1/4 cups granulated sugar, divided
- 1/2 cup fat-free milk
- 1/3 cup vegetable oil
- 1/3 cup fat-free sour cream
- 1/3 cup unsweetened applesauce
- 2 egg yolks
- 1/2 teaspoon lemon extract
- 2 cups cake flour
- 1 teaspoon baking powder
- 1/4 teaspoon baking soda
- 1/2 teaspoon salt
- 2 egg whites
- 1/8 teaspoon cream of tartar
- 3 tablespoons plus 1 teaspoon poppy seeds, divided
- 1 tablespoon grated lemon rind
- Lemon Glaze (see pg. 531)

Per Serving
Calories: 260
% Calories from fat: 28
Fat (gm): 8.1
Sat. fat (gm): 1.2
Cholesterol (mg): 35.7
Sodium (mg): 186
Protein (gm): 3.8
Carbohydrate (gm): 43.7

Exchanges
Milk: 0.0
Vegetable: 0.0
Fruit: 0.0
Bread: 3.0
Meat: 0.0
Fat: 1.0

1. Mix 1 cup granulated sugar, milk, oil, sour cream, applesauce, egg yolks, and lemon extract in large bowl; mix in combined flour, baking powder, baking soda, and salt.

2. Beat egg whites and cream of tartar to soft peaks in medium bowl; beat to stiff peaks, adding remaining 1/4 cup sugar gradually. Fold egg whites, 3 tablespoons poppy seeds, and lemon rind into cake batter.

3. Pour batter into greased and floured 12-cup plain or fluted tube pan. Bake at 350 degrees until toothpick inserted in center comes out clean, about 45 minutes. Cool in pan on wire rack 10 minutes; remove from pan and cool completely.

4. Place cake on serving plate; drizzle with Lemon Glaze and sprinkle with remaining 1 teaspoon poppy seeds.

Variations: **Lemon-Blueberry Cake**—Make cake as above, substituting reduced-fat custard-style lemon yogurt for the sour cream and deleting poppy seeds; fold 1 to 1 1/2 cups fresh or frozen blueberries into cake batter. Bake and glaze as above.

Cranberry-Orange Cake—Coarsely chop 1 cup cranberries; mix with 1/4 cup of the sugar and let stand 10 minutes. Make cake as above, using 3/4 cup sugar, substituting reduced-fat custard-style orange yogurt for the sour cream, orange rind for the lemon rind, and omitting poppy seeds. Fold cranberry mixture into cake batter. Bake as above. Make Lemon Glaze, substituting orange juice for the lemon juice; glaze cake.

BANANA PECAN CAKE

12 servings

- 1 3/4 cups mashed ripe bananas (about 3 large)
- 2/3 cup packed light brown sugar
- 1/4 cup honey
- 1/4 cup margarine, melted
- 2 cups all-purpose flour
- 1 teaspoon baking powder
- 1 teaspoon baking soda
- 1/2 teaspoon salt
- Generous pinch ground nutmeg
- 1/3 cup chopped pecans
- Banana Glaze (recipe follows)

Per Serving
Calories: 250
% Calories from fat: 22
Fat (gm): 6.3
Sat. fat (gm): 1
Cholesterol (mg): 0
Sodium (mg): 293
Protein (gm): 3
Carbohydrate (gm): 47.2
Exchanges
Milk: 0.0
Vegetable: 0.0
Fruit: 0.0
Bread: 3.0
Meat: 0.0
Fat: 1.0

1. Beat banana, brown sugar, honey, and margarine in large bowl until well blended. Mix in combined flour, baking powder, baking soda, salt, and nutmeg; mix in pecans.

2. Spoon batter into greased 6-cup fluted tube pan. Bake at 350 degrees 50 to 55 minutes or until toothpick inserted in center comes out clean. Cool in pan on wire rack 10 minutes; remove from pan and cool completely. Drizzle with Banana Glaze.

Banana Glaze

makes about 1/4 cup

- 1/2 cup powdered sugar
- 1/4 teaspoon banana extract
- 3-4 teaspoons fat-free milk

1. Mix powdered sugar, banana extract, and enough milk to make glaze consistency.

CARROT CAKE WITH CREAM CHEESE FROSTING

16 servings

- 3 cups shredded carrots
- 1/2 cup raisins for baking
- 1 cup packed light brown sugar
- 1/3 cup vegetable oil
- 3 eggs
- 2 cups all-purpose flour
- 1 teaspoon baking powder
- 1 teaspoon baking soda
- 1 teaspoon ground cinnamon
- 1/4 teaspoon ground allspice
- 1/4 teaspoon ground nutmeg
- 1/4 teaspoon salt
- Cream Cheese Frosting (recipe follows)

Per Serving
Calories: 319
% Calories from fat: 23
Fat (gm): 8.1
Sat. fat (gm): 2.2
Cholesterol (mg): 44.7
Sodium (mg): 229
Protein (gm): 4.2
Carbohydrate (gm): 58.1

Exchanges
Milk: 0.0
Vegetable: 0.0
Fruit: 0.0
Bread: 3.5
Meat: 0.0
Fat: 1.5

1. Mix carrots, raisins, brown sugar, oil, and eggs in large bowl. Mix in combined remaining ingredients, except Cream Cheese Frosting.

2. Pour batter into 2 greased and floured 8-inch round cake pans. Bake at 350 degrees until toothpick inserted in cake comes out clean, 25 to 30 minutes. Cool in pans on wire rack 10 minutes; remove from pans and cool.

3. Place 1 cake layer on serving plate and frost. Top with remaining cake layer; frost top and side of cake.

Cream Cheese Frosting

makes about 2 1/2 cups

- 3/4 package (8-ounce size) reduced-fat cream cheese, softened
- 1 tablespoon margarine, softened
- 3 1/2-4 cups powdered sugar
- 1 teaspoon vanilla

1. Beat cream cheese and margarine in medium bowl until smooth; beat in powdered sugar and vanilla.

Variation: **Blueberry-Carrot Cake**—Make cake as above, deleting raisins; stir 3/4 to 1 cup fresh or frozen blueberries into cake batter. Bake in greased and floured 12-cup fluted cake pan until toothpick inserted in center comes out clean, 50 to 60 minutes. Cool on wire rack 10 minutes; remove from pan and cool. Beat 2 ounces fat-free sour cream with 1 cup powdered sugar; drizzle over cake.

BOSTON CREAM CAKE

12 servings

8 tablespoons margarine, softened
1 1/4 cups sugar
2 eggs
1 teaspoon vanilla
2 2/3 cups all-purpose flour
1 tablespoon baking powder
1/2 teaspoon salt
1 2/3 cups fat-free milk
Vanilla Cream Filling (recipe follows)
Chocolate Glaze (recipe follows)

Per Serving
Calories: 338
% Calories from fat: 24
Fat (gm): 9.1
Sat. fat (gm): 2
Cholesterol (mg): 54
Sodium (mg): 354
Protein (gm): 5.6
Carbohydrate (gm): 58.8
Exchanges
Milk: 0.0
Vegetable: 0.0
Fruit: 0.0
Bread: 4.0
Meat: 0.0
Fat: 1.0

1. Beat margarine, sugar, eggs, and vanilla until smooth in medium bowl. Mix in combined flour, baking powder, and salt alternately with milk beginning and ending with dry ingredients.

2. Pour batter into 2 greased and floured 8- or 9-inch round cake pans. Bake at 350 degrees until cake springs back when touched, about 40 minutes. Cool in pans on wire rack 10 minutes; remove from pans and cool to room temperature.

3. Place 1 cake layer on serving plate; spread with Vanilla Cream Filling. Top with second cake layer and spoon Chocolate Glaze over.

Vanilla Cream Filling

makes about 1 1/4 cups

- 1/4 cup sugar
- 2 tablespoons cornstarch
- 1 cup fat-free milk
- 1 egg, beaten
- 1/2 teaspoon vanilla

1. Mix sugar and cornstarch in saucepan; stir in milk. Heat over medium-high heat, stirring constantly, until mixture comes to a boil; boil, stirring constantly, until thickened.

2. Whisk about 1/2 of milk mixture into beaten egg in small bowl; whisk egg mixture back into saucepan. Cook over very low heat, whisking constantly, 30 to 60 seconds. Remove from heat; stir in vanilla and cool.

Chocolate Glaze

- 1 cup powdered sugar
- 2 tablespoons unsweetened cocoa
- 1/2 teaspoon vanilla
- 1-2 tablespoons fat-free milk

1. Combine powdered sugar and cocoa in small bowl; stir in vanilla and enough milk to make glaze consistency.

RED VELVET CAKE

16 servings

- 1 1/2 cups sugar
- 6 tablespoons vegetable shortening
- 2 eggs
- 1 teaspoon vanilla
- 2 bottles (1 ounce each) red food coloring
- 1/4 cup unsweetened cocoa
- 2 1/4 cups all-purpose flour
- 1 teaspoon baking soda
- 1/2 teaspoon salt
- 1 cup reduced-fat buttermilk
- 1 tablespoon white distilled vinegar
- Buttercream Frosting (recipe follows)

Per Serving
Calories: 361
% Calories from fat: 17
Fat (gm): 6.9
Sat. fat (gm): 1.7
Cholesterol (mg): 27.1
Sodium (mg): 207
Protein (gm): 3.4
Carbohydrate (gm): 71.8

Exchanges
Milk: 0.0
Vegetable: 0.0
Fruit: 0.0
Bread: 5.0
Meat: 0.0
Fat: 0.0

1. Beat sugar and shortening until well blended in large bowl. Add eggs and vanilla, blending well; beat in food coloring and cocoa until well blended. Mix in combined flour, baking soda, and salt alternately with combined buttermilk and vinegar.

2. Pour batter into 2 greased and floured 9-inch round cake pans. Bake at 350 degrees until toothpick inserted in center of cake comes out clean, 25 to 30 minutes. Cool in pans on wire rack 10 minutes; remove cakes from pans and cool completely.

3. Place 1 cake layer on serving plate; spread with generous 1/2 cup Buttercream Frosting. Top with remaining layer; frost cake.

Buttercream Frosting

makes about 3 cups

- 5 cups powdered sugar
- 2 tablespoons margarine, softened
- 1 teaspoon vanilla
- 3-4 tablespoons fat-free milk

1. Mix powdered sugar, margarine, vanilla, and enough milk to make spreading consistency.

EDDIE'S BANANA CAKE

16 servings

- 2 1/2 cups cake flour
- 1 2/3 cups sugar
- 1 1/4 teaspoons baking powder
- 1 1/4 teaspoons baking soda
- Pinch salt
- 1/2 cup vegetable shortening
- 2/3 cup reduced-fat buttermilk, divided
- 1 1/4 cups mashed ripe banana (1 large)
- 2 eggs
- 1/2 cup chopped nuts
- Brown Sugar Frosting (recipe follows)

Per Serving
Calories: 361
% Calories from fat: 26
Fat (gm): 10.6
Sat. fat (gm): 2.2
Cholesterol (mg): 26.9
Sodium (mg): 180
Protein (gm): 3.8
Carbohydrate (gm): 64.3

Exchanges
Milk: 0.0
Vegetable: 0.0
Fruit: 0.0
Bread: 4.0
Meat: 0.0
Fat: 1.5

1. Combine flour, sugar, baking powder, baking soda, and salt in large bowl. Add vegetable shortening, 1/3 cup buttermilk, and the banana; beat at medium speed 2 minutes. Add remaining buttermilk and eggs; beat at medium speed 2 minutes. Mix in nuts.

2. Pour batter into 2 greased and floured 9-inch round cake pans. Bake at 350 degrees until toothpick inserted in center comes out clean, about 35 minutes. Cool in pans on wire rack 10 minutes; remove from pans and cool.

3. Place 1 cake layer on serving plate; spread with 1/2 the Brown Sugar Frosting; top with second layer and spread top with remaining Brown Sugar Frosting.

Brown Sugar Frosting

makes about 1 1/2 cups

- 1 cup packed light brown sugar
- 1/4 cup fat-free milk
- 2 tablespoons margarine
- 1 1/2 cups powdered sugar
- Fat-free milk, optional

1. Heat brown sugar, milk, and margarine in medium saucepan until mixture is smooth; remove from heat. Mix in powdered sugar and milk if necessary, to make spreading consistency.

MARBLE POUND CAKE

12 servings

- 1 cup reduced-fat buttermilk
- 1 teaspoon vanilla
- 1/2 teaspoon baking soda
- 8 tablespoons margarine, room temperature
- 1/3 cup sugar
- 3 egg whites
- 2 cups cake flour
- 1/8 teaspoon salt
- 1 1/2 ounces semisweet chocolate, melted
- Chocolate Glaze (see p. 538)

Per Serving
Calories: 291
% Calories from fat: 27
Fat (gm): 9.1
Sat. fat (gm): 2.3
Cholesterol (mg): 0.8
Sodium (mg): 203
Protein (gm): 3.5
Carbohydrate (gm): 50
Exchanges
Milk: 0.0
Vegetable: 0.0
Fruit: 0.0
Bread: 3.0
Meat: 0.0
Fat: 1.5

1. Mix buttermilk vanilla, and baking soda; let stand 2 to 3 minutes. Beat margarine and sugar until fluffy in large bowl. Beat in egg whites one at a time, beating well after each addition. Mix in combined flour and salt alternately with buttermilk mixture, beginning and ending with flour mixture.

2. Reserve 2 cups batter; stir melted chocolate into remaining batter. Spoon batters alternately into greased and floured 9 x 5-inch loaf pan; swirl gently with knife.

3. Bake at 350 degrees until wooden pick inserted in center comes out clean, 60 to 70 minutes. Cool in pan on wire rack 10 minutes; remove from pan and cool completely.

4. Place cake on serving plate; drizzle with Chocolate Glaze.

Variation: **Lemon-Glazed Pound Cake**—Make cake, omitting chocolate and vanilla and adding 1 teaspoon lemon extract; bake as above. Heat 3/4 cup powdered sugar and 1/2 cup lemon juice to boiling in small saucepan, stirring until sugar is dissolved. Cool slightly. Pierce top of cake at 1-inch intervals with long-tined fork; spoon warm syrup over cake. Cool, remove from pan, then drizzle with Lemon Glaze (see p. 531).

PINEAPPLE UPSIDE-DOWN CAKE

8 to 10 servings

- 3 tablespoons light corn syrup
- 5 tablespoons margarine, softened, divided
- 2/3 cup packed light brown sugar
- 2-3 tablespoons chopped pecans
- 1 can (8 ounces) sliced pineapple in its own juice, drained, slices cut in halves
- 4 maraschino cherries, cut in halves
- 2/3 cup granulated sugar
- 1 egg
- 1/2 teaspoon pineapple extract, *or* vanilla
- 1 1/3 cups all-purpose flour
- 2 teaspoons baking powder
- 1/4 teaspoon salt
- 2/3 cup fat-free milk
- Light whipped topping, as garnish

Per Serving
Calories: 347
% Calories from fat: 23
Fat (gm): 9.1
Sat. fat (gm): 1.7
Cholesterol (mg): 27
Sodium (mg): 264
Protein (gm): 4
Carbohydrate (gm): 63.8

Exchanges
Milk: 0.0
Vegetable: 0.0
Fruit: 0.5
Bread: 3.5
Meat: 0.0
Fat: 1.5

1. Heat corn syrup and 1 tablespoon margarine until melted in small skillet. Stir in brown sugar and pecans and cook over medium heat until mixture is bubbly, 2 to 3 minutes. Pour topping mixture into ungreased 9-inch round cake pan; arrange pineapple slices and cherries on top.

2. Beat remaining 4 tablespoons margarine, granulated sugar, egg, and pineapple extract in medium bowl until smooth. Mix in combined flour, baking powder, and salt alternately with milk beginning and ending with dry ingredients. Pour batter over topping in pan.

3. Bake at 350 degrees until cake springs back when touched, about 40 minutes. Loosen side of cake with sharp knife and immediately invert onto serving plate. Serve warm with light whipped topping.

CLASSIC SPONGE CAKE

12 servings

- 3 egg yolks
- 1 cup sugar, divided
- 2 teaspoons vanilla
- 1/4 cup water
- 1 cup cake flour
- 1 teaspoon baking powder
- 1/4 teaspoon salt
- 5 egg whites
- 1/4 teaspoon cream of tartar

Per Serving
Calories: 122
% Calories from fat: 10
Fat (gm): 1.4
Sat. fat (gm): 0.4
Cholesterol (mg): 53.2
Sodium (mg): 114
Protein (gm): 2.9
Carbohydrate (gm): 24.3
Exchanges
Milk: 0.0
Vegetable: 0.0
Fruit: 0.0
Bread: 1.5
Meat: 0.0
Fat: 0.0

1. Beat egg yolks in large mixing bowl, gradually adding 3/4 cup sugar; beat at high speed until yolks are thick and lemon colored, about 5 minutes. Mix in vanilla and water, add combined flour, baking powder, and salt, beating on low speed just until blended.

2. With clean beaters and in separate large bowl, beat egg whites and cream of tartar to soft peaks. Beat to stiff peaks, gradually adding remaining 1/4 cup sugar. Stir 1/4 of the egg whites into batter; fold batter into remaining whites.

3. Pour batter into ungreased 12-cup tube pan. Bake at 350 degrees 35 minutes or until cake springs back when touched lightly. Invert pan onto funnel and cool to room temperature. Loosen side of cake with small metal spatula and remove from pan.

Tip: Cake can be baked in an ungreased 10-inch springform pan. Invert on wire rack or balance on 4 cans or custard cups to cool.

BASIC ANGEL FOOD CAKE

12 to 16 servings

- 12 egg whites
- 3/4 teaspoon cream of tartar
- 1 teaspoon lemon juice
- 1 teaspoon vanilla
- 1 1/2 cups sugar, divided
- 1 cup cake flour
- 1/2 teaspoon salt
- Vanilla Glaze (recipe follows)

Per Serving
Calories: 189
% Calories from fat: 0
Fat (gm): 0.1
Sat. fat (gm): 0
Cholesterol (mg): 0
Sodium (mg): 153
Protein (gm): 4.3
Carbohydrate (gm): 42.8
Exchanges
Milk: 0.0
Vegetable: 0.0
Fruit: 0.0
Bread: 2.5
Meat: 0.0
Fat: 0.0

1. Beat egg whites and cream of tartar to soft peaks in large bowl. Beat in lemon juice and vanilla; beat just to stiff peaks, adding 1/2 cup sugar gradually (do not overbeat). Sprinkle 1/2 cup sugar over egg whites and fold in. Combine remaining 1/2 cup sugar, flour, and salt; sift half the flour mixture over egg whites and fold in. Repeat with remaining flour mixture.

2. Pour batter into ungreased 12-cup tube pan. Bake until cake is golden and cracks look dry, about 40 minutes. Invert pan on funnel and cool completely. Loosen side of cake from pan with metal spatula and invert onto serving plate. Drizzle with Vanilla Glaze.

Vanilla Glaze

makes about 1/2 cup

- 1 cup powdered sugar
- 1 teaspoon vanilla
- 1-2 tablespoons fat-free milk

1. Mix powdered sugar, vanilla, and enough milk to make glaze consistency.

Variations: **Peppermint Angel Food Cake**—Make cake as above, folding in 1/3 cup crushed peppermint candy with last addition of flour. Drizzle with Vanilla Glaze, adding 1/4 teaspoon peppermint extract. Sprinkle cake with 2 tablespoons crushed peppermint candy.

Spiced Angel Food Cake—Make cake as above, folding in 1 1/2 teaspoons ground cinnamon, 1/2 teaspoon ground allspice, and 1/4 teaspoon ground nutmeg. Drizzle with Vanilla Glaze; sprinkle with cinnamon sugar and serve with sliced peaches.

BEST HOLIDAY FRUITCAKE

24 servings

Per Serving
Calories: 258
% Calories from fat: 23
Fat (gm): 6.9
Sat. fat (gm): 1.2
Cholesterol (mg): 26.5
Sodium (mg): 131
Protein (gm): 3.6
Carbohydrate (gm): 45.4
Exchanges
Milk: 0.0
Vegetable: 0.0
Fruit: 0.0
Bread: 3.0
Meat: 0.0
Fat: 1.0

- 2 cups all-purpose flour
- 1 teaspoon baking powder
- 1/2 teaspoon salt
- 1 teaspoon ground cinnamon
- 1 teaspoon ground allspice
- 1/2 teaspoon ground mace
- 1/2 teaspoon ground nutmeg
- 1/2 cup margarine, softened
- 3/4 cup packed light brown sugar
- 1/2 cup brandy, *or* apricot nectar
- 1/4 cup honey
- 1/4 cup apricot nectar, *or* orange juice
- 3 eggs
- 1 3/4 cups golden raisins
- 3/4 cup chopped apricots
- 3/4 cup chopped pitted dates
- 1 cup glaceed orange peel
- 1/2 cup halved glaceed cherries
- 1/2 cup glaceed pineapple chunks
- 3/4 cup walnut pieces

1. Combine all ingredients, except fruit and walnuts, in large bowl; mix on low speed until blended. Beat on high speed 3 minutes. Mix in fruits and nuts.

2. Spread batter evenly in greased 12-cup tube pan with removable bottom. Bake at 275 degrees until toothpick inserted in center comes out clean, 2 1/2 to 3 hours. Cover top of cake with aluminum foil during last hour of baking, if necessary to prevent overbrowning. Cool in pan on wire rack 10 minutes; remove from pan and cool.

3. Wrap cake in cheesecloth dampened with brandy; wrap in plastic bag or aluminum foil. Refrigerate at least 1 month and up to 1 year, dampening cheesecloth with brandy occasionally.

NEW YORK-STYLE CHEESECAKE

12 servings

Per Serving
Calories: 244
% Calories from fat: 31
Fat (gm): 8.5
Sat. fat (gm): 3.1
Cholesterol (mg): 46.5
Sodium (mg): 417
Protein (gm): 11.4
Carbohydrate (gm): 30.6
Exchanges
Milk: 0.0
Vegetable: 0.0
Fruit: 0.0
Bread: 2.0
Meat: 1.0
Fat: 1.5

Graham Cracker Crumb Crust (recipe follows)
3 packages (8 ounces each) fat-free cream cheese, softened
3/4 cup sugar
2 eggs
2 tablespoons cornstarch
1 teaspoon vanilla
1 cup reduced-fat sour cream

1. Make Graham Cracker Crumb Crust, pressing mixture evenly on bottom and 1/2 inch up side of 9-inch springform pan.

2. Beat cream cheese and sugar in large bowl until light and fluffy; beat in eggs, cornstarch, and vanilla. Add sour cream, mixing well.

3. Pour mixture into crust. Bake at 325 degrees until cheesecake is set but still slightly soft in the center, 45 to 50 minutes. Turn oven off; cool cheesecake in oven with door ajar 3 hours. Refrigerate 8 hours or overnight.

Graham Cracker Crumb Crust

one 8- or 9-inch crust

1 1/4 cups graham cracker crumbs
2 tablespoons sugar
3 tablespoons margarine, melted
1-2 tablespoons honey

1. Combine graham cracker crumbs, sugar and margarine in 8- or 9-inch pie pan; add enough honey for mixture to stick together. Pat mixture evenly on bottom and side of pan.

2. Bake at 350 degrees 8 to 10 minutes or until edge of crust is lightly browned. Cool on wire rack.

Variation: **Latte Cheesecake**—Make cheesecake as above, adding 1/3 cup espresso or double-strength coffee, 2 egg yolks, and 1/8 teaspoon ground nutmeg. Spread top of chilled cheesecake with 2 cups light whipped topping; sprinkle lightly with cinnamon and chocolate shavings.

RICOTTA CHEESECAKE

12 servings

Lemon Cookie Crumb Crust (recipe follows)
3 1/2 cups reduced-fat ricotta cheese
1/4 cup all-purpose flour
1/2 teaspoon salt
1 cup sugar
2 eggs
2 egg whites
1 tablespoon grated orange rind
1 tablespoon grated lemon rind
2 teaspoons vanilla
Ground nutmeg, as garnish

Per Serving
Calories: 253
% Calories from fat: 25
Fat (gm): 7.2
Sat. fat (gm): 2.5
Cholesterol (mg): 48.2
Sodium (mg): 261
Protein (gm): 12.7
Carbohydrate (gm): 34.7
Exchanges
Milk: 0.0
Vegetable: 0.0
Fruit: 0.0
Bread: 2.0
Meat: 1.0
Fat: 1.0

1. Make Lemon Cookie Crumb Crust, pressing mixture evenly on bottom and 1/2 inch up side of 10-inch springform pan.

2. Beat ricotta cheese, flour, and salt in large bowl until well blended. Beat in sugar, eggs, and egg whites; mix in orange rind, lemon rind, and vanilla.

3. Pour filling into crust. Bake at 350 degrees until filling is set, 1 to 1 1/4 hours. Cool on wire rack; refrigerate 8 hours or overnight. Sprinkle lightly with nutmeg before serving.

Lemon Cookie Crumb Crust

one 8- or 9-inch crust

1 1/2 cups lemon cookie crumbs (cookies with powdered sugar)
2 tablespoons sugar
2-3 tablespoons margarine, melted
2 tablespoons honey

1. Mix cookie crumbs, sugar, and margarine in bottom of 8- or 9-inch pie pan; mix in enough honey for mixture to stick together. Press evenly on bottom and side of pan.

2. Bake at 350 degrees 6 to 8 minutes. Cool on wire rack

WHITE CHOCOLATE CHEESECAKE

12 servings

Almond Crunch Crust (recipe follows)
2 packages (8 ounces each) fat-free cream cheese, softened
1 1/4 cups sugar
1 cup fat-free sour cream
3 eggs
1/4 cup lemon juice
1 tablespoon grated lemon rind
2 teaspoons vanilla extract
1/4 teaspoon ground nutmeg
Pinch salt
6 ounces white baking chocolate, melted

Per Serving
Calories: 266
% Calories from fat: 23
Fat (gm): 6.7
Sat. fat (gm): 3.8
Cholesterol (mg): 58.6
Sodium (mg): 266
Protein (gm): 9.8
Carbohydrate (gm): 40.7
Exchanges
Milk: 0.0
Vegetable: 0.0
Fruit: 0.0
Bread: 3.0
Meat: 0.0
Fat: 1.0

1. Make Almond Crunch Crust; sprinkle over bottom of greased 9-inch springform pan.

2. Beat cream cheese in large bowl until fluffy; beat in sugar, sour cream, eggs, lemon juice, lemon rind, vanilla, nutmeg, and salt. Mix in chocolate.

3. Pour batter into crust; bake at 325 degrees until cheesecake is almost set in the center, 1 to 1 1/4 hours. Cool on wire rack. Refrigerate 8 hours or overnight.

Almond Crunch Crust

makes about 1/3 cup

1/4 cup wheat-barley cereal (Grape-Nuts)
2 tablespoons sugar
2-3 tablespoons chopped almonds

1. Combine all ingredients in food processor or blender; process until finely ground.

CAPPUCCINO CHEESECAKE

12 servings

Mocha Crumb Crust (recipe follows)
2 cups 1% low-fat cottage cheese
2 eggs
2 egg whites
2 packages (8 ounces each) fat-free cream cheese softened
1 1/3 cups reduced-fat sour cream
1 1/4 cups sugar
1/3 cup all-purpose flour
1/2 teaspoon ground cinnamon
1/4 teaspoon ground nutmeg
1/4 teaspoon salt
3 tablespoons instant espresso powder
3 tablespoons warm water
Light whipped topping as garnish
Chocolate-covered coffee beans, as garnish

Per Serving
Calories: 310
% Calories from fat: 27
Fat (gm): 9.3
Sat. fat (gm): 3.7
Cholesterol (mg): 48.9
Sodium (mg): 531
Protein (gm): 15
Carbohydrate (gm): 41.7

Exchanges
Milk: 0.0
Vegetable: 0.0
Fruit: 0.0
Bread: 3.0
Meat: 0.0
Fat: 2.0

1. Make Mocha Crumb Crust, pressing mixture on bottom and 1 inch up side of 9-inch springform pan. Bake at 350 degree until set, about 8 minutes.

2. Process cottage cheese, eggs, and egg whites in food processor or blender until smooth. Beat cream cheese in large bowl until fluffy; beat in cottage cheese mixture, sour cream, sugar flour, spices, and salt. Dissolve espresso powder in warm water and add to cheese mixture.

3. Pour batter into crust. Bake at 300 degrees until cheesecake is almost set in the center, 60 to 70 minutes. Turn oven off; cool cheesecake in oven with door ajar, 1 hour. Cool on wire rack. Refrigerate 8 hours or overnight.

4. Garnish cheesecake with whipped topping and coffee beans.

Mocha Crumb Crust

makes one 9- or 10-inch crust

- 1 1/4 cups graham cracker crumbs
- 2 tablespoons sugar
- 2 tablespoons unsweetened cocoa
- 2 teaspoons instant espresso powder
- 1/2 teaspoon ground nutmeg
- 3 tablespoons margarine, melted
- 1-2 tablespoons honey

1. Combine all ingredients.

CHOCOLATE CHIP CHEESECAKE

16 servings

Per Serving
Calories: 340
% Calories from fat: 24
Fat (gm): 9.4
Sat. fat (gm): 5.1
Cholesterol (mg): 43.3
Sodium (mg): 373
Protein (gm): 11
Carbohydrate (gm): 56.1
Exchanges
Milk: 0.0
Vegetable: 0.0
Fruit: 0.0
Bread: 3.5
Meat: 0.0
Fat: 2.0

- Shortbread Crust (recipe follows)
- 2 cups 1% low-fat cottage cheese
- 2 eggs
- 1/4 cup fat-free milk
- 2 packages (8 ounces each) fat-free cream cheese, softened
- 1 cup granulated sugar
- 3/4 cup packed dark brown sugar
- 1 teaspoon vanilla extract
- 1/4 teaspoon salt
- 1 cup reduced-fat semisweet chocolate morsels
- 2 tablespoons chopped walnuts
- 3/4 cup chocolate-flavored syrup

1. Roll Shortbread Crust between two sheets of waxed paper to 1/8 inch thickness; cut into 11-inch circle. Reserve and refrigerate scraps. Ease pastry into 10-inch springform pan; press onto bottom and 1/2 inch up side of pan; pierce bottom of pastry with fork. Bake at 400 degrees until lightly browned, 8 to 10 minutes; cool on wire rack.

2. Process cottage cheese, eggs, and milk in food processor or blender until smooth. Beat cream cheese in large bowl until fluffy; beat in cottage cheese mixture, sugars, vanilla, and salt. Mix in chocolate morsels.

3. Roll pastry scraps on floured surface to 1/8 inch thickness; cut into 2-inch-wide strips. Press strips to inside of pan, covering side and sealing to bottom crust.

4. Pour batter into crust, sprinkle with walnuts. Bake at 350 degrees until cheesecake is almost set in the center, 50 to 60 minutes. Cool on wire rack. Refrigerate 8 hours or overnight. Serve with chocolate-flavored syrup.

Shortbread Crust

one 10- or 12-inch crust

- 1 1/3 cups all-purpose flour
- 1/2 cup powdered sugar
- Pinch salt
- 5 tablespoons cold margarine, cut into pieces
- 1 egg, lightly beaten
- 1 teaspoon vanilla

1. Combine flour, sugar, and salt in medium bowl. Cut in margarine until mixture resembles coarse crumbs. Mix in combined egg and vanilla with fork, stirring just until mixture forms a dough.

2. Form dough into a ball; flatten slightly and wrap in plastic wrap. Chill 1 hour or longer before using.

3. Roll and bake as recipe directs.

MARBLE MINT CHEESECAKE

12 servings

- Chocolate Cookie Crumb Crust (recipe follows)
- 1 teaspoon mint extract
- 1 package (8 ounces) fat-free cream cheese, softened
- 1/2 cup sugar
- 2 eggs
- 1 tablespoon green creme de menthe, *or* 1 teaspoon mint extract
- 1 cup fat-free sour cream

Per Serving
Calories: 331
% Calories from fat: 29
Fat (gm): 11.2
Sat. fat (gm): 6.2
Cholesterol (mg): 37
Sodium (mg): 307
Protein (gm): 7.1
Carbohydrate (gm): 54

Exchanges
Milk: 0.0
Vegetable: 0.0
Fruit: 0.0
Bread: 3.5
Meat: 0.0
Fat: 2.0

- 1 cup reduced-fat semisweet chocolate morsels
- 1/2 cup chocolate-flavored syrup
- 2-3 drops green food color
- 6 chocolate-covered thin mints, halved

1. Make Chocolate Cookie Crumb Crust, adding mint extract, and pressing evenly onto bottom and side of 9-inch pie pan. Bake as directed.

2. Beat cream cheese in large bowl until fluffy; beat in sugar, eggs, creme de menthe, and sour cream.

3. Melt chocolate morsels and chocolate syrup in small saucepan over medium heat, stirring constantly until smooth. Remove from heat and stir in 3/4 cup cheese mixture. Add green food color to remaining cheese mixture.

4. Alternately spoon chocolate and mint mixtures into crust; swirl with knife. Bake at 350 degrees until center is almost set, about 30 minutes. Cool on wire rack. Refrigerate 4 hours or overnight. Top with chocolate-covered thin mints.

Chocolate Cookie Crumb Crust

one 8- or 9-inch crust

- 1 1/4 cups chocolate cookie crumbs
- 2 tablespoons sugar
- 3 tablespoons margarine, melted
- 1-2 tablespoons honey

1. Mix cookie crumbs, sugar, and margarine in bottom of 8- or 9-inch pie pan; add enough honey for mixture to stick together. Press evenly on bottom and side of 8- or 9-inch pie pan.

2. Bake at 350 degrees 6 to 8 minutes. Cool on wire rack.

CHOCOLATE SWIRL CHEESECAKE

12 servings

Per Serving
Calories: 313
% Calories from fat: 29
Fat (gm): 10
Sat. fat (gm): 3.9
Cholesterol (mg): 49
Sodium (mg): 630
Protein (gm): 15.1
Carbohydrate (gm): 40.4
Exchanges
Milk: 0.0
Vegetable: 0.0
Fruit: 0.0
Bread: 2.5
Meat: 1.0
Fat: 1.5

Chocolate Cookie Crumb Crust (see pg. 551)
1 carton (16 ounces) 1% low-fat cottage cheese
2 packages (8 ounces each) fat-free cream cheese, softened
1 package (8 ounces) reduced-fat cream cheese, softened
1 1/4 cups sugar, divided
2 eggs
1 teaspoon vanilla
1/4 cup unsweetened cocoa
4 egg whites
1/4 teaspoon cream of tartar
Light whipped topping, as garnish
Chocolate curls, as garnish

1. Make Chocolate Cookie Crumb Crust, pressing mixture evenly onto bottom and 1/2 inch up side of 9-inch springform pan.

2. Process cottage cheese in food processor or blender until smooth. Beat cream cheese in large bowl until smooth; beat in cottage cheese, 1 cup sugar, eggs, and vanilla, blending well. Pour 1/2 of the mixture into medium bowl; stir in cocoa.

3. Using large clean bowl and beaters, beat egg whites and cream of tartar to soft peaks; beat to stiff peaks, adding remaining 1/4 cup sugar gradually. Mix 1/4 of the egg whites into cocoa mixture; fold remaining egg whites into plain cheese mixture.

4. Pour plain cheese mixture into crust; spoon large dollops of chocolate mixture over and swirl together with a knife. Bake at 325 degrees until almost set in the center, 40 to 50 minutes. Cool on wire rack. Refrigerate 8 hours or overnight.

5. Garnish slices with whipped topping and chocolate curls.

TURTLE CHEESECAKE

12 servings

Brownie Crust (recipe follows)
3/4 package (14-ounce size) caramels (about 35)
1/4 cup fat-free milk
2 packages (8 ounces each) fat-free cream cheese, softened
1/2 cup sugar
2 eggs
1/4 cup fat-free sour cream
Caramel Glaze (recipe follows)
1/4-1/2 cup pecan halves

Per Serving
Calories: 356
% Calories from fat: 22
Fat (gm): 9
Sat. fat (gm): 3.3
Cholesterol (mg): 56.2
Sodium (mg): 279
Protein (gm): 9.6
Carbohydrate (gm): 63.1

Exchanges
Milk: 0.0
Vegetable: 0.0
Fruit: 0.0
Bread: 4.0
Meat: 0.0
Fat: 1.5

1. Make Brownie Crust.

2. Heat caramels and milk in small saucepan over medium-low heat until melted, stirring occasionally. Pour caramel over Brownie Crust, spreading evenly. Refrigerate until caramel is cold, about 20 minutes.

3. Beat cream cheese and sugar in medium bowl until well blended. Beat in eggs, 1 at a time, beating well after each addition; mix in sour cream.

4. Pour batter over caramel. Place pan on cookie sheet and bake at 350 degrees 45 minutes or until center is almost set. Run sharp knife around side of pan to loosen cheesecake; cool on wire rack. Refrigerate 8 hours or overnight.

5. Remove side of pan; place cheesecake on serving plate. Pour Caramel Glaze over top of cheesecake; top with pecan halves.

Brownie Crust

makes one 9-inch crust

- 1/2 cup all-purpose flour
- 1/3 cup packed light brown sugar
- 1/3 cup reduced-fat semisweet chocolate morsels, melted
- 3 tablespoons margarine, melted
- 1 egg

1. Mix all ingredients in medium bowl until blended; spread evenly in bottom of greased 9-inch springform pan.

2. Bake at 350 degrees until firm to touch, 13 to 15 minutes; cool on wire rack.

Caramel Glaze

makes about 1 cup

- 1/2 package (14-ounce size) caramels (about 25 caramels)
- 1/3 cup fat-free milk

1. Heat caramels and milk in small saucepan over medium-low heat until melted, stirring occasionally. Let stand, stirring occasionally, until thickened enough to spread, 5 to 10 minutes.

Variations: **Triple-Chocolate Brownie Cheesecake**—Make cheesecake as above, omitting the caramels, milk, and Caramel Glaze and adding 1/4 cup unsweetened cocoa and 1/3 cup reduced-fat semisweet chocolate morsels to the filling. Bake as above.

Peanut Butter Cup Cheesecake—Make cheesecake as above, omitting caramels and milk, substituting brown sugar for the granulated sugar, and adding 3/4 cup reduced-fat peanut butter. Bake and chill as above. Omit Caramel Glaze; drizzle top of cheesecake with 1 ounce melted semisweet chocolate; garnish with halved peanut butter cup candies. Serve with Bittersweet Chocolate Sauce (see p. 520).

STRAWBERRY SPECTACULAR CHEESECAKE

14 servings

Graham Cracker Crumb Crust (see p. 545)
2 packages (8 ounces each) reduced-fat cream cheese, softened
2 packages(8 ounces each) fat-free cream cheese, softened
1 cup sugar, divided
2 tablespoons flour
1/2 teaspoon salt
2 egg yolks
1 tablespoon lemon juice
5 egg whites
1/2 teaspoon cream of tartar
2 pints small strawberries
1/2 cup currant jelly, melted

Per Serving
Calories: 301
% Calories from fat: 32
Fat (gm): 11
Sat. fat (gm): 5
Cholesterol (mg): 48.2
Sodium (mg): 508
Protein (gm): 10.5
Carbohydrate (gm): 40.3
Exchanges
Milk: 0.0
Vegetable: 0.0
Fruit: 0.5
Bread: 2.5
Meat: 0.0
Fat: 2.0

1. Make Graham Cracker Crumb Crust, using 10-inch springform pan.

2. Beat cream cheese until fluffy in large bowl; beat in 3/4 cup sugar, flour, and salt. Add egg yolks and lemon juice, beating well.

3. Using large, clean bowl and beaters, beat egg whites and cream of tartar to soft peaks; beat to stiff peaks, adding remaining 1/4 cup sugar gradually. Mix 1/4 of the egg whites into cheese mixture; fold cheese mixture into remaining egg whites.

4. Pour filling into crust. Bake at 300 degrees until center of cheesecake is almost set, 50 to 60 minutes. Turn oven off; cool cheesecake in oven 2 hours, with door ajar. Refrigerate 8 hours or overnight.

5. Remove side of pan; place cheesecake on serving plate. Arrange strawberries on cheesecake, pointed ends up. Melt jelly; brush or drizzle over strawberries.

Variation: **Glazed Plum Cheesecake**—Make cheesecake as above, omitting strawberries, currant jelly, and Step 5. Heat 3/4 cup orange juice, 1/2 cup apple jelly, and 1/4 cup packed light brown sugar to boiling in large skillet, stirring to dissolve sugar and jelly. Cut 6 to 8 plums into 1/2-inch slices and add to skillet. Reduce heat and simmer, covered, until plums are tender, 3 to 4 minutes. Remove plums and cool. Boil sugar mixture until thickened to a syrup consistency, 5 to 7 minutes. Arrange plums on cheesecake and drizzle with syrup.

LUSCIOUS LEMON CHEESECAKE

12 servings

Lemon Custard (recipe follows)
Sesame Crumb Crust (recipe follows)
2 packages (8 ounces each) fat-free cream cheese, softened
1 package (8 ounces) reduced-fat cream cheese, softened
1/2 cup sugar
1/2 cup fat-free sour cream
1/4 teaspoon salt
1 tablespoon grated lemon rind
Sesame seeds, as garnish

Per Serving
Calories: 272
% Calories from fat: 30
Fat (gm): 9
Sat. fat (gm): 3.4
Cholesterol (mg): 47.2
Sodium (mg): 498
Protein (gm): 11
Carbohydrate (gm): 36.2
Exchanges
Milk: 0.0
Vegetable: 0.0
Fruit: 0.0
Bread: 3.0
Meat: 0.0
Fat: 1.5

1. Make Lemon Custard and chill.

2. Make Sesame Crumb Crust, pressing mixture evenly on bottom and 1/2-inch up side of 10-inch springform pan. Bake at 350 degrees until browned, about 8 minutes.

3. Beat cream cheese until fluffy in large bowl; beat in sugar, sour cream, and salt. Beat in chilled Lemon Custard.

4. Spoon filling into crust, spreading evenly. Sprinkle with lemon rind and sesame seeds. Refrigerate until set, about 4 hours.

Lemon Custard

makes about 2/3 cup

- 1/2 cup sugar
- 2 tablespoons cornstarch
- 1/3 cup lemon juice
- 2 eggs
- 1 tablespoon, grated lemon rind

1. Mix sugar and cornstarch in small saucepan; whisk in lemon juice. Whisk over medium heat until mixture boils and thickens, about 1 minute.

2. Whisk about 1/2 the lemon mixture into eggs; whisk egg mixture into lemon mixture. Whisk in lemon rind. Cook over low heat, whisking constantly, 1 to 2 minutes. Cool; refrigerate until chilled, 1 to 2 hours.

Sesame Crumb Crust

makes one 9-inch crust

- 1 1/4 cups dry bread crumbs, *or* vanilla wafer crumbs
- 3-4 tablespoons toasted sesame seeds
- 2 tablespoons sugar
- 1/4 teaspoon ground cinnamon
- 3-4 tablespoons margarine, melted
- 1-2 tablespoons honey, *or* light corn syrup

1. Combine all ingredients, adding enough honey for ingredients to stick together.

Variation: **Daiquiri Cheesecake**—Make cheesecake as above, substituting lime rind and lime juice for the lemon rind and lemon juice in the filling and custard. Add 2 tablespoons light rum or 1 teaspoon rum extract to the custard before combining with eggs. Omit sesame seeds. Serve cheesecake with light whipped topping and garnish with lime slices.

RASPBERRY CHEESECAKE

14 servings

Lemon Cookie Crumb Crust (see p. 546)
2 cups fresh, *or* frozen, unsweetened raspberries
2 tablespoons sugar
2 packages (8 ounces each) fat-free cream cheese, softened
1 package (8 ounces) reduced-fat cream cheese, softened
1 can (14 ounces) low-fat sweetened condensed milk
3 eggs
1 teaspoon vanilla

Per Serving
Calories: 235
% Calories from fat: 27
Fat (gm): 7.3
Sat. fat (gm): 1.8
Cholesterol (mg): 57
Sodium (mg): 318
Protein (gm): 10.4
Carbohydrate (gm): 32.3

Exchanges
Milk: 0.0
Vegetable: 0.0
Fruit: 0.0
Bread: 2.0
Meat: 1.0
Fat: 1.0

1. Make Lemon Cookie Crumb Crust in 10-inch springform pan, pressing evenly onto bottom and 1/2 inch up side of pan. Bake as directed.

2. Combine raspberries and sugar in small bowl. Set aside. Beat cream cheese in large bowl until fluffy, beat in remaining ingredients until smooth. Gently fold in raspberry mixture.

3. Pour mixture into crust; bake at 350 degrees until center is almost set, about 45 minutes. Cool. Refrigerate 8 hours or overnight.

Variations: **Blueberry Cheesecake**—Make cheesecake as above, substituting blueberries for the raspberries, brown sugar for the granulated sugar, and orange extract for the vanilla. Add 1 tablespoon grated orange rind to the mixture.

Raspberry Chocolate Cheesecake—Substitute Chocolate Cookie Crumb Crust (see p. 551) for the crust in Step 1. Reduce amount of raspberries in Step 2 to 1 cup. Set aside. Divide cheese mixture into two bowls. Fold 4 ounces melted semisweet chocolate into one bowl. Pour into prepared crust. Fold raspberries into remaining cheese mixture; spoon over chocolate layer. Bake and cool as in Step 3. Serve with Chocolate Sauce or Raspberry Sauce (see pp. 520, 526).

ORANGE PUMPKIN CHEESECAKE

16 servings

Graham Cracker Crumb Crust (see p. 545)
1/3 cup ground pecans
2 teaspoons pumpkin pie spice, divided
1 package (16 ounces) 1% low-fat creamed cottage cheese
2 packages (8 ounces each) fat-free cream cheese, softened
1 package (8 ounces) reduced-fat cream cheese, softened
3/4 cup packed light brown sugar
2 tablespoons flour
1 can (16 ounces) pumpkin
2 eggs
2 teaspoons finely grated orange rind
1/4 teaspoon salt
4 egg whites
1/2 teaspoon cream of tartar
1/4 cup granulated sugar
Marmalade Sour Cream Topping (recipe follows)
1 medium orange, thinly sliced
1/4 cup orange marmalade, melted

Per Serving
Calories: 318
% Calories from fat: 28
Fat (gm): 10.1
Sat. fat (gm): 3.2
Cholesterol (mg): 36.7
Sodium (mg): 481
Protein (gm): 14.1
Carbohydrate (gm): 43.4

Exchanges
Milk: 0.0
Vegetable: 0.0
Fruit: 0.0
Bread: 3.0
Meat: 0.5
Fat: 1.5

1. Make Graham Cracker Crumb Crust, substituting 1/3 cup pecans for 1/3 cup of the crumbs, and adding 1/2 teaspoon pumpkin pie spice; press evenly on bottom and 1/2 inch up side of 10-inch springform pan.

2. Process cottage cheese in food processor or blender until smooth. Beat cream cheese until fluffy in large bowl; beat in cottage cheese, brown sugar, flour, pumpkin, eggs, orange rind, remaining 1 1/2 teaspoons pumpkin pie spice, and salt.

3. Using clean bowl and beaters, beat egg whites and cream of tartar to soft peaks in large bowl. Beat to stiff peaks, adding granulated sugar gradually. Mix about 1/4 of the egg whites into cream cheese mixture; fold cream cheese mixture into remaining egg whites.

4. Pour filling into crust. Bake at 300 degrees until almost set in the center, 1 to 1¼ hours. Turn oven off; cool cheesecake in oven 1 hour with door ajar.

5. Spread Marmalade Sour Cream Topping over top of cheesecake; bake at 350 degrees 10 minutes. Cool on wire rack, refrigerate 8 hours or overnight.

6. Remove side of pan and place cheesecake on serving plate. Arrange orange slices on top of cheesecake and brush with orange marmalade.

Marmalade Sour Cream Topping

makes about 2⅓ cups

- 2 cups fat-free sour cream
- ⅓ cup orange marmalade
- 2 generous pinches nutmeg

1. Combine all ingredients.

STRAWBERRY CREAM CHEESE SQUARES

9 servings

- 1½ cups coarsely crushed pretzels
- 2-3 tablespoons margarine, melted
- 2-3 tablespoons light corn syrup
- 1 package (8 ounces) fat-free cream cheese, softened
- ½ cup sugar
- 2 cups light whipped topping
- 2 cups boiling water
- 2 packages (3 ounces each) strawberry-flavored gelatin
- 2 packages (10 ounces each) frozen sweetened strawberries, partially thawed

Per Serving
Calories: 301
% Calories from fat: 15
Fat (gm): 5.3
Sat. fat (gm): 2.6
Cholesterol (mg): 2
Sodium (mg): 465
Protein (gm): 6.5
Carbohydrate (gm): 57.7

Exchanges
Milk: 0.0
Vegetable: 0.0
Fruit: 1.0
Bread: 2.5
Meat: 0.0
Fat: 1.0

1. Combine pretzels, margarine, and corn syrup; press mixture into bottom of greased 13 x 9-inch baking pan. Bake at 350 degrees until set, about 10 minutes. Cool on wire rack.

2. Beat cream cheese and sugar until smooth; fold in whipped topping. Pour mixture onto cooled crust. Refrigerate while preparing strawberry topping.

3. Pour boiling water over gelatin in large bowl; stir until dissolved. Add strawberries, stirring until thawed. Spoon strawberry mixture over cream cheese mixture. Refrigerate until set, about 4 hours.

CHOCOLATE CHIP COOKIES

5 dozen cookies (1 per serving)

- 8 tablespoons margarine, softened
- 1 cup packed light brown sugar
- 1/2 cup granulated sugar
- 1 egg
- 1 teaspoon vanilla
- 2 1/2 cups all-purpose flour
- 1/2 teaspoon baking soda
- 1/2 teaspoon salt
- 1/3 cup fat-free milk
- 1/2 package (12-ounce size) reduced-fat semisweet chocolate morsels

Per Serving
Calories: 66
% Calories from fat: 27
Fat (gm): 2
Sat. fat (gm): 0.7
Cholesterol (mg): 3.6
Sodium (mg): 70
Protein (gm): 0.8
Carbohydrate (gm): 11.2
Exchanges
Milk: 0.0
Vegetable: 0.0
Fruit: 0.0
Bread: 0.5
Meat: 0.0
Fat: 0.5

1. Beat margarine and sugars in medium bowl until fluffy; beat in egg and vanilla. Mix in combined flour, baking soda, and salt alternately with milk, beginning and ending with dry ingredients. Mix in chocolate morsels.

2. Drop cookies by tablespoonfuls onto greased cookie sheets. Bake at 375 degrees until browned, about 10 minutes. Cool on wire racks.

RAISIN OATMEAL COOKIES

2½ dozen cookies (1 per serving)

6 tablespoons margarine, softened
¼ cup fat-free sour cream
1 egg
1 teaspoon vanilla
1 cup packed light brown sugar
1½ cups quick-cooking oats
1 cup all-purpose flour
½ teaspoon baking soda
¼ teaspoon baking powder
1 teaspoon ground cinnamon
½ cup raisins for baking

Per Serving
Calories: 90
% Calories from fat: 27
Fat (gm): 2.7
Sat. fat (gm): 0.5
Cholesterol (mg): 7.1
Sodium (mg): 57
Protein (gm): 1.5
Carbohydrate (gm): 15.3
Exchanges
Milk: 0.0
Vegetable: 0.0
Fruit: 0.0
Bread: 1.0
Meat: 0.0
Fat: 0.5

1. Mix margarine, sour cream, egg, and vanilla in large bowl; beat in brown sugar. Mix in combined oats, flour, baking soda, baking powder, and cinnamon. Mix in raisins.

2. Drop dough onto greased cookie sheets, using 2 tablespoons for each cookie. Bake at 350 degrees until browned, 12 to 15 minutes. Cool on wire racks.

Variation: **Cherry Chocolate Chip Oatmeal Cookies**—Make cookies as above, omitting raisins, mixing ⅓ cup each dried cherries and reduced-fat semisweet chocolate morsels and ¼ cup chopped toasted almonds into the dough, and substituting almond extract for the vanilla.

FROSTED SUGAR COOKIES

6 dozen cookies (1 per serving)

10 tablespoons margarine, softened
2 tablespoons fat-free sour cream
1 egg
1 teaspoon lemon extract
1 cup powdered sugar
2 cups all-purpose flour
1 teaspoon baking powder
1/4 teaspoon salt
Sugar Frosting (recipe follows)
Ground cinnamon, as garnish

Per Serving
Calories: 48
% Calories from fat: 31
Fat (gm): 1.7
Sat. fat (gm): 0.3
Cholesterol (mg): 3
Sodium (mg): 45
Protein (gm): 0.5
Carbohydrate (gm): 7.7

Exchanges
Milk: 0.0
Vegetable: 0.0
Fruit: 0.0
Bread: 0.5
Meat: 0.0
Fat: 0.5

1. Beat margarine, sour cream, egg, and lemon extract in medium bowl until smooth; mix in sugar. Mix in combined flour, baking powder, and salt. Refrigerate dough 4 to 6 hours.

2. Roll dough on floured surface to 1/4 inch thickness. Cut cookies into decorative shapes with 2-inch cookie cutters. Bake at 375 degrees on greased cookie sheets until lightly browned, 8 to 10 minutes. Cool on wire racks.

3. Frost cookies with Sugar Frosting; sprinkle very lightly with cinnamon.

Sugar Frosting

makes about 3/4 cup

2 cups powdered sugar
1/2 teaspoon lemon extract, *or* vanilla
2-3 tablespoons fat-free milk

1. Mix powdered sugar, lemon extract, and enough milk to make spreadable consistency.

Variation: **Italian-Style Sugar Cookies**—Make cookie dough as above, substituting orange extract for the lemon extract, 1/2 cup yellow cornmeal for 1/2 cup of the flour, granulated sugar for the powdered sugar; substitute orange extract for the lemon extract in the Sugar Frosting. Garnish with pieces of glaceed orange rind, if desired.

GINGERSNAPPERS

4½ dozen cookies (1 per serving)

9 tablespoons margarine, softened
¾ cup packed light brown sugar
¼ cup light molasses
1 egg
2 cups all-purpose flour
1 teaspoon baking soda
1 teaspoon ground cinnamon
1 teaspoon ground ginger
½ teaspoon ground cloves
½ teaspoon dry mustard
¼ teaspoon ground black pepper
3 tablespoons granulated sugar

Per Serving
Calories: 54
% Calories from fat: 34
Fat (gm): 2
Sat. fat (gm): 0.4
Cholesterol (mg): 4
Sodium (mg): 49
Protein (gm): 0.6
Carbohydrate (gm): 8.3
Exchanges
Milk: 0.0
Vegetable: 0.0
Fruit: 0.0
Bread: 0.5
Meat: 0.0
Fat: 0.5

1. Beat margarine and brown sugar until fluffy in large bowl; mix in molasses and egg. Mix in combined flour, baking soda, spices, dry mustard, and pepper. Refrigerate, covered, 2 to 3 hours.

2. Measure granulated sugar into pie pan or shallow bowl. Drop dough by teaspoons into sugar and roll into balls (dough will be sticky). Place cookies on greased cookie sheets; flatten with fork or bottom of glass. Bake at 350 degrees until firm to touch, 8 to 10 minutes. Cool on wire racks.

CHOCOLATE CRINKLES

4½ dozen cookies (1 per serving)

8 tablespoons margarine, softened
1¼ cups packed light brown sugar
⅓ cup reduced-fat sour cream
1 egg
1-2 ounces semisweet baking chocolate, melted
1 teaspoon vanilla
1¾ cups all-purpose flour
¾ cup unsweetened cocoa
1 teaspoon baking soda

Per Serving
Calories: 60
% Calories from fat: 31
Fat (gm): 2.1
Sat. fat (gm): 0.6
Cholesterol (mg): 4.5
Sodium (mg): 49
Protein (gm): 0.8
Carbohydrate (gm): 9.8
Exchanges
Milk: 0.0
Vegetable: 0.0
Fruit: 0.0
Bread: 0.5
Meat: 0.0
Fat: 0.5

1 teaspoon ground cinnamon
1/4 cup granulated sugar

1. Beat margarine and brown sugar in large bowl until fluffy. Mix in sour cream, egg, chocolate, and vanilla. Mix in combined flour, cocoa, baking soda, and cinnamon. Refrigerate, covered, 2 to 3 hours.

2. Measure granulated sugar into pie pan or shallow bowl. Drop dough by tablespoons into sugar and roll into balls. (Dough will be soft.) Place cookies, on greased cookie sheets; flatten with fork or bottom of glass. Bake at 350 degrees until firm to touch, 10 to 12 minutes. Cool on wire racks.

JAM BUTTONS

4 dozen cookies (1 per serving)

8 tablespoons margarine, softened
1/2 cup sugar
1 egg
1 teaspoon vanilla
2 cups all-purpose flour
1/4 cup cornstarch
1/2 teaspoon baking powder
1/4 teaspoon baking soda
2 generous pinches ground nutmeg
1/4 teaspoon salt
1/2 cup jam (apricot, peach, strawberry, raspberry, etc.)
Powdered sugar, as garnish

Per Serving
Calories: 54
% Calories from fat: 33
Fat (gm): 2
Sat. fat (gm): 0.4
Cholesterol (mg): 4.4
Sodium (mg): 49
Protein (gm): 0.7
Carbohydrate (gm): 8.4
Exchanges
Milk: 0.0
Vegetable: 0.0
Fruit: 0.0
Bread: 0.5
Meat: 0.0
Fat: 0.5

1. Beat margarine and sugar in large bowl until blended; beat in egg and vanilla. Mix in combined remaining ingredients, except jam and powdered sugar. Refrigerate dough 3 to 4 hours (dough will be soft and easy to handle).

2. Roll dough into 48 balls and place 2 inches apart on greased cookie sheets. Make deep indentation in center of each cookie with thumb. Bake at 375 degrees until lightly browned, about 10 minutes. If indentations have puffed up, press down gently with spoon. Cool on wire racks. Fill center of each cookie with about 1/2 teaspoon jam. Sprinkle with powdered sugar before serving.

GLAZED CHOCOLATE SHORTBREAD SQUARES

5 dozen cookies (1 per serving)

- 1 1/2 cups all-purpose flour
- 1/4 cup unsweetened cocoa
- 2/3 cup sugar
- 1/4 teaspoon salt
- 8 tablespoons margarine, softened
- 1 egg
- 2 teaspoons vanilla
- Sugar Glaze (recipe follows)

Per Serving
Calories: 44
% Calories from fat: 33
Fat (gm): 1.6
Sat. fat (gm): 0.3
Cholesterol (mg): 3.6
Sodium (mg): 29
Protein (gm): 0.5
Carbohydrate (gm): 6.8

Exchanges
Milk: 0.0
Vegetable: 0.0
Fruit: 0.0
Bread: 0.5
Meat: 0.0
Fat: 0.0

1. Combine flour, cocoa, sugar, and salt in medium bowl; cut in margarine with pastry blender or 2 knives until mixture resembles coarse crumbs. Mix in egg and vanilla, stirring just enough to form a soft dough.

2. Place dough in bottom of greased jelly roll pan, 15 x 10 inches. Pat and spread dough, using fingers and small spatula, until bottom of pan is evenly covered. Pierce dough with tines of fork.

3. Bake at 350 degrees until firm to touch, 20 to 25 minutes. Cool on wire rack. Drizzle Sugar Glaze over shortbread and cut into squares while warm.

Sugar Glaze

makes about 1 cup

- 1 cup powdered sugar
- 1-2 tablespoons fat-free milk

1. Mix powdered sugar and enough milk to make glaze consistency.

CHOCOLATE FUDGE MERINGUES

2 dozen cookies (1 per serving)

3 egg whites
1/2 teaspoon cream of tartar
1/4 teaspoon salt
2 cups powdered sugar
1/2 cup unsweetened cocoa
1/2 package (6-ounce size) reduced-fat semisweet chocolate morsels, chopped

Per Serving
Calories: 58
% Calories from fat: 12
Fat (gm): 0.8
Sat. fat (gm): 0.8
Cholesterol (mg): 0
Sodium (mg): 34
Protein (gm): 0.7
Carbohydrate (gm): 12.8
Exchanges
Milk: 0.0
Vegetable: 0.0
Fruit: 0.0
Bread: 1.0
Meat: 0.0
Fat: 0.0

1. Beat egg whites, cream of tartar, and salt to soft peaks in medium bowl. Beat to stiff peaks, adding sugar gradually. Fold in cocoa; fold in chopped chocolate.

2. Drop mixture by tablespoons onto parchment or aluminum foil-lined cookie sheets. Bake at 300 degrees until cookies feel crisp when touched, 20 to 25 minutes. Cool on pans on wire racks.

FROSTED COCOA BROWNIES

25 brownies (1 per serving)

1 cup all-purpose flour
1 cup sugar
1/4 cup unsweetened cocoa
5 tablespoons margarine, melted
1/4 cup fat-free milk
1 egg
2 egg whites
1/4 cup honey
1 teaspoon vanilla
Sweet Cocoa Frosting (recipe follows)

Per Serving
Calories: 111
% Calories from fat: 24
Fat (gm): 3.1
Sat. fat (gm): 0.6
Cholesterol (mg): 8.6
Sodium (mg): 42
Protein (gm): 1.5
Carbohydrate (gm): 20.4
Exchanges
Milk: 0.0
Vegetable: 0.0
Fruit: 1.5
Bread: 0.0
Meat: 0.0
Fat: 0.5

1. Combine flour, sugar, and cocoa in medium bowl; add margarine, milk, egg, egg whites, honey, and vanilla, mixing until smooth. Pour batter into greased and floured 8-inch square baking pan.

2. Bake at 350 degrees until brownies spring back when touched, about 30 minutes. Cool in pan on wire rack. Spread with Sweet Cocoa Frosting.

Sweet Cocoa Frosting

makes about 1/2 cup

- 1 cup powdered sugar
- 2-3 tablespoons unsweetened cocoa
- 1 tablespoon margarine, softened
- 2-3 tablespoons fat-free milk

1. In small bowl, beat powdered sugar, cocoa, margarine, and enough milk to make spreading consistency.

Variation: **Cappuccino Brownies**—Make brownies as above, adding 1 to 2 tablespoons instant coffee crystals; omit Sweet Cocoa Frosting and make Cinnamon Cream Cheese Topping: Beat 8 ounces softened reduced-fat cream cheese, 3/4 cup powdered sugar, 1/2 teaspoon ground cinnamon, and 1/2 teaspoon vanilla; spread over cooled brownies. Drizzle with 1 ounce melted semisweet baking chocolate.

CARAMEL APPLE COOKIES

5 dozen cookies (1 per serving)

- 1/2 cup vegetable shortening
- 1 1/4 cups packed light brown sugar
- 1 egg
- 1/2 cup apple juice, divided
- 2 1/4 cups all-purpose flour
- 1 teaspoon baking soda
- 1/4 teaspoon salt
- 1 teaspoon ground cinnamon
- 1/4 teaspoon ground cloves
- 1 cup shredded, peeled apples
- 3/4 cup golden raisins

Per Serving
Calories: 81
% Calories from fat: 25
Fat (gm): 2.3
Sat. fat (gm): 0.5
Cholesterol (mg): 3.5
Sodium (mg): 39
Protein (gm): 0.8
Carbohydrate (gm): 14.5

Exchanges
Milk: 0.0
Vegetable: 0.0
Fruit: 0.0
Bread: 1.0
Meat: 0.0
Fat: 0.0

Caramel Frosting (recipe follows)
2 1/2-5 tablespoons finely chopped walnuts

1. Beat shortening and brown sugar in medium bowl until blended; beat in egg. Mix in 1/4 cup apple juice, combined flour, baking soda, salt, and spices; mix in remaining 1/4 cup apple juice, apples, and raisins.

2. Drop dough by teaspoons, 2 inches apart, onto greased cookie sheets. Bake at 350 degrees until browned, 10 to 12 minutes. Cool on wire racks. Spread with Caramel Frosting and sprinkle each cookie with 1/8 to 1/4 teaspoon walnuts.

Caramel Frosting

makes about 3/4 cup

2-3 tablespoons margarine, softened
1/3 cup packed light brown sugar
2 tablespoons water
1 1/2 cups powdered sugar
2-4 tablespoons fat-free milk

1. Heat margarine, brown sugar, and water over medium-high heat in saucepan, stirring until sugar dissolves. Remove from heat; beat in powdered sugar and enough milk to make spreadable consistency; use immediately. if frosting begins to harden, return to low heat and stir in more milk.

CAMPUS BARS

30 bars (1 per serving)

2 1/4 cups graham cracker crumbs
1 can (14 ounces) fat-free sweetened condensed milk
1/2 cup reduced-fat semisweet chocolate morsels
1/2 can (3 1/2-ounce size) flaked coconut
1/3 cup chopped walnuts
2 teaspoons vanilla
1/4 teaspoon salt

Per Serving
Calories: 125
% Calories from fat: 27
Fat (gm): 4
Sat. fat (gm): 1.8
Cholesterol (mg): 0
Sodium (mg): 74
Protein (gm): 2.5
Carbohydrate (gm): 20.9
Exchanges
Milk: 0.0
Vegetable: 0.0
Fruit: 0.0
Bread: 1.5
Meat: 0.0
Fat: 0.5

1. Mix all ingredients in bowl; press evenly in greased 11 x 7-inch baking pan. Bake at 350 degrees until set and browned, 20 to 30 minutes. Cool on wire rack.

MISSISSIPPI MUD BARS

2 dozen bars (1 per serving)

- 5 tablespoons margarine, softened
- 1/2 cup granulated sugar
- 1/2 cup packed light brown sugar
- 1 teaspoon vanilla
- 3 eggs
- 1 cup all-purpose flour
- 1/3 cup unsweetened cocoa
- 1/2 teaspoon baking powder
- 1/4 teaspoon salt
- 3 cups miniature marshmallows
- 1/3 cup chopped pecans
- 1/2 cup melted reduced-fat semisweet chocolate morsels

Per Serving
Calories: 140
% Calories from fat: 32
Fat (gm): 5.2
Sat. fat (gm): 1.9
Cholesterol (mg): 26.6
Sodium (mg): 81
Protein (gm): 1.9
Carbohydrate (gm): 22.9

Exchanges
Milk: 0.0
Vegetable: 0.0
Fruit: 0.0
Bread: 1.5
Meat: 0.0
Fat: 1.0

1. Beat margarine, sugars, and vanilla until blended; beat in eggs; 1 at a time. Mix in combined flour, cocoa, baking powder, and salt.

2. Pour batter into greased 13 x 9-inch baking pan. Bake at 325 degrees until toothpick inserted in center comes out clean, 18 to 20 minutes. Sprinkle top of cake with marshmallows and pecans; bake until marshmallows are lightly browned, 2 to 3 minutes. Cool on wire rack. Drizzle melted chocolate over marshmallows. Cut into bars.

APPLE CRANBERRY BARS

1½ dozen bars (1 per serving)

Per Serving
Calories: 137
% Calories from fat: 30
Fat (gm): 4.6
Sat. fat (gm): 1
Cholesterol (mg): 23.6
Sodium (mg): 126
Protein (gm): 2
Carbohydrate (gm): 22.2

Exchanges
Milk: 0.0
Vegetable: 0.0
Fruit: 0.0
Bread: 1.5
Meat: 0.0
Fat: 0.5

6 tablespoons margarine, softened
¾ cup packed light brown sugar
2 eggs
2 tablespoons honey
1 teaspoon vanilla
1 cup all-purpose flour
⅔ cup quick-cooking oats
¾ teaspoon baking powder
¼ teaspoon baking soda
¾ teaspoon ground allspice
¼ teaspoon salt
1 cup finely chopped peeled apple
½ cup chopped dried cranberries
Powdered sugar, as garnish

1. Beat margarine and brown sugar until well blended in large bowl; beat in eggs, honey, and vanilla. Mix in combined flour, oats, baking powder, baking soda, allspice, and salt. Mix in apple and cranberries.

2. Pour batter in greased 8- or 9-inch square baking pan. Bake at 350 degrees until a wooden pick inserted in center comes out clean, 35 to 40 minutes. Cool on wire rack; sprinkle with powdered sugar.

SIXTEEN

Pies and Pastries

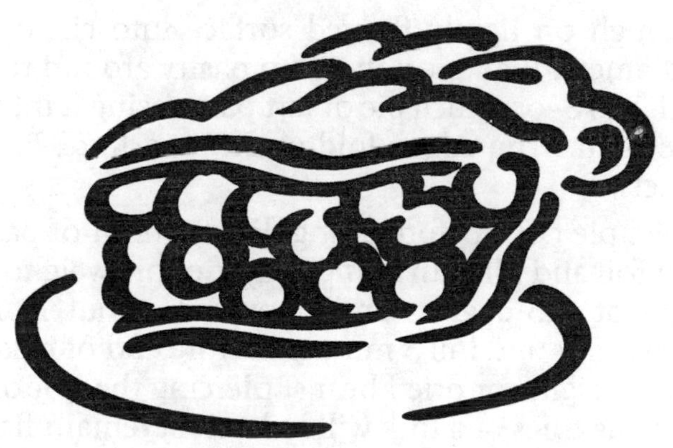

BASIC PIE CRUST

8 servings (one 8- or 9-inch crust)

- 1 1/4 cups all-purpose flour
- 2 tablespoons sugar
- 1/4 teaspoon salt
- 4-5 tablespoons cold margarine, *or* vegetable shortening
- 3-5 tablespoons ice water

Per Serving
Calories: 134
% Calories from fat: 39*
Fat (gm): 5.8
Sat. fat (gm): 1.1
Cholesterol (mg): 0
Sodium (mg): 140
Protein (gm): 2.1
Carbohydrate (gm): 18

Exchanges
Milk: 0.0
Vegetable: 0.0
Fruit: 0.0
Bread: 1.0
Meat: 0.0
Fat: 1.0

1. Combine flour, sugar, and salt in medium bowl. With pastry blender or 2 knives, cut in margarine until mixture resembles coarse crumbs. Sprinkle with water, 1 tablespoon at a time, mixing lightly with a fork after each addition until pastry just holds together.

2. Roll dough on lightly floured surface into circle 2 inches larger in diameter than pie pan. Wrap pastry around rolling pin and unroll into 8- or 9-inch pie or tart pan, easing it into bottom and side of pan. Trim edges, fold under, and flute. Bake as pie recipe directs.

Tip: To bake pie crust before filling, line bottom of pastry with aluminum foil and fill with a single layer of pie weights or dried beans. Bake at 425 degrees until browned, about 15 minutes, removing weights and foil 5 minutes before end of baking time. If not using weights or dried beans, piercing the bottom of the pastry with the tines of a fork will help crust remain flat.

*Percentage of calories from fat will decrease in servings of actual pie.

DOUBLE PIE CRUST

8 servings (one 8- or 9-inch double crust)

- 1 3/4 cups all-purpose flour
- 3 tablespoons sugar
- 1/2 teaspoon salt
- 5-6 tablespoons cold margarine, cut into pieces
- 5-7 tablespoons ice water

Per Serving
Calories: 181
% Calories from fat: 36*
Fat (gm): 7.3
Sat. fat (gm): 1.4
Cholesterol (mg): 0
Sodium (mg): 229
Protein (gm): 2.9
Carbohydrate (gm): 25.6

Exchanges
Milk: 0.0
Vegetable: 0.0
Fruit: 0.0
Bread: 1.5
Meat: 0.0
Fat: 1.5

1. Combine flour, sugar, and salt in medium bowl; cut in margarine with pastry blender until mixture resembles coarse crumbs. Add water, a tablespoon at a time, mixing with fork until dough forms.

2. Roll and bake as recipe directs.

*Percentage of calories from fat will decrease in servings of actual pie.

HAZELNUT PASTRY CRUST

8 servings (one 8- or 9-inch crust)

- 1/4 cup chopped hazelnuts, toasted
- 1 cup all-purpose flour
- 3 tablespoons sugar
- 1/2 teaspoon salt
- 3 tablespoons cold margarine, cut into pieces
- 4-5 tablespoons cold water

Per Serving
Calories: 143
% Calories from fat: 46*
Fat (gm): 7.4
Sat. fat (gm): 1
Cholesterol (mg): 0
Sodium (mg): 196
Protein (gm): 2.1
Carbohydrate (gm): 17.4

Exchanges
Milk: 0.0
Vegetable: 0.0
Fruit: 0.0
Bread: 1.0
Meat: 0.0
Fat: 1.5

1. Process nuts, flour, sugar, and salt in food processor until nuts are finely ground. Add margarine and process, using pulse technique, until the mixture resembles coarse crumbs. Sprinkle 4 tablespoons water over and process just until combined, adding additional water if needed.

2. Form dough into a ball and wrap in plastic wrap, flattening into a disk. Chill 1 hour or longer before using.

3. Roll and bake as recipe directs.

*Percentage of calories from fat will decrease in servings of actual pie.

CHOCOLATE COOKIE CRUMB CRUST

8 servings

1 1/4 cups chocolate cookie crumbs
2 tablespoons sugar
3 tablespoons margarine, melted
1-2 tablespoons honey

Per Serving
Calories: 158
% Calories from fat: 44*
Fat (gm): 8
Sat. fat (gm): 1.5
Cholesterol (mg): 0
Sodium (mg): 225
Protein (gm): 1.3
Carbohydrate (gm): 21.6
Exchanges
Milk: 0.0
Vegetable: 0.0
Fruit: 0.0
Bread: 1.5
Meat: 0.0
Fat: 1.0

1. Mix cookie crumbs, sugar, and margarine in bottom of 8- or 9-inch pie pan; add enough honey for mixture to stick together. Press evenly on bottom and side of 8- or 9-inch pie pan.

2. Bake at 350 degrees 6 to 8 minutes. Cool on wire rack.

Variation: **Chocolate Pecan Crumb Crust**—Make crust as above, decreasing margarine to 1 tablespoon, increasing honey to 3 tablespoons and adding 1/2 cup ground pecans.

*Percentage of calories from fat will decrease in servings of actual pie.

CREAM CHEESE TART CRUST

12 servings (1 large free-form crust, or 2, 9-inch crusts)

- 8 tablespoons margarine
- 1/4 package (8-ounce size) cream cheese
- 1/2 cup sugar
- 1 egg
- 1 teaspoon vanilla
- 2 1/4 cups all-purpose flour
- 1/4 teaspoon salt

Per Serving
Calories: 209
% Calories from fat: 42*
Fat (gm): 9.8
Sat. fat (gm): 2.7
Cholesterol (mg): 22.9
Sodium (mg): 157
Protein (gm): 3.4
Carbohydrate (gm): 26.6
Exchanges
Milk: 0.0
Vegetable: 0.0
Fruit. 0.0
Bread: 1.5
Meat: 0.0
Fat: 2.0

1. Beat margarine and cream cheese until smooth in large mixing bowl; add sugar, beating well. Add egg and vanilla and beat at high speed for 1 minute or until very smooth. Add combined flour and salt and mix just until blended.

2. Form dough into a ball; flatten slightly and wrap in plastic wrap. Refrigerate 2 hours or longer before using.

3. Roll and bake as recipe directs.

*Percentage of calories from fat will decrease in servings of actual pie.

UPSIDE-DOWN APPLE PIE

10 servings

- 2 tablespoons margarine
- 2 tablespoons corn syrup
- 2/3 cup packed light brown sugar
- 1/3 cup chopped pecans
- Double Pie Crust (see p. 575)
- 6 cups peeled, cored, sliced tart baking apples
- 3/4 cup granulated sugar
- 3 tablespoons flour

Per Serving
Calories: 369
% Calories from fat: 26
Fat (gm): 11.1
Sat. fat (gm): 1.9
Cholesterol (mg): 0
Sodium (mg): 222
Protein (gm): 3.2
Carbohydrate (gm): 67
Exchanges
Milk: 0.0
Vegetable: 0.0
Fruit: 2.0
Bread: 2.5
Meat: 0.0
Fat: 1.5

1 tablespoon lemon juice
1 teaspoon ground cinnamon
Pinch salt

1. Heat margarine, corn syrup, brown sugar, and pecans in small saucepan until sugar is melted; cool. Pour into bottom of deep-dish 9-inch pie pan.

2. Roll 2/3 of the Double Pie Crust on floured surface to form circle 2 inches larger than pan; ease pastry into pan, covering sugar mixture.

3. Toss apples with combined granulated sugar, flour, lemon juice, cinnamon, and salt in large bowl; arrange apples in pastry.

4. Roll remaining 1/3 Double Pie Crust to fit top of pie and place over apples. Trim edges of pastry to within 1/2 inch of pan; fold top pastry over bottom pastry and flute. Cut vents in top crust.

5. Bake pie at 425 degrees until apples are fork-tender and pastry browned, 40 to 50 minutes. Cover pastry with aluminum foil if becoming too brown. Cool on wire rack 5 minutes. Invert pie onto serving plate; cool.

POACHED PEAR TARTE TATIN

8 servings

7 pears, peeled, halved, cored
1/2 cup sugar
1/2 teaspoon ground cinnamon
2 1/2 cups dry red wine
Hazelnut Pastry Crust (see p. 575)

Per Serving
Calories: 330
% Calories from fat: 21
Fat (gm): 8
Sat. fat (gm): 1.1
Cholesterol (mg): 0
Sodium (mg): 196
Protein (gm): 2.8
Carbohydrate (gm): 53.3
Exchanges
Milk: 0.0
Vegetable: 0.0
Fruit: 1.0
Bread: 2.0
Meat: 0.0
Fat: 1.5

1. Arrange pears, cut sides up, in 12-inch stainless steel or nonstick skillet; sprinkle with combined sugar and cinnamon. Pour wine over pears. Heat to boiling; reduce heat and simmer, covered, just until pears are tender, 10 to 20 minutes, depending on ripeness of pears. Remove pears with slotted spoon; boil wine mixture until reduced to 1/2 cup.

2. Slice pears and arrange in 10-inch glass pie plate; pour wine mixture over.

3. Roll Hazelnut Pastry Crust between 2 sheets of waxed paper to 12-inch diameter. Place pastry over pears, folding in excess pastry and tucking in edges. Cut several vents in pastry.

4. Bake at 375 degrees until pastry is golden and crisp, about 40 minutes. Cool 5 minutes; invert onto serving plate.

Variation: **Custard Pear Tart**—Roll Hazelnut Pastry Crust as above, easing it into 10-inch tart pan. Line pastry with aluminum foil and fill with a single layer of pie weights or dried beans. Bake at 425 degrees until browned, about 15 minutes, removing weights and foil 5 minutes before end of baking time. Cool. Poach pears as above. Boil wine mixture until reduced to 1/3 cup. Fill pastry with Lemon Yogurt Pastry Cream (see p. 625); arrange sliced pears on top. Brush with reduced wine mixture to glaze. Sprinkle with 3 tablespoons toasted sliced almonds as garnish.

BEST CHERRY PIE

8 servings

- Double Pie Crust (see p. 575)
- 2 packages (16 ounces each) frozen unsweetened cherries, thawed, drained (about 4 cups)
- 1/2 teaspoon almond extract
- 3/4 cup plus 2 teaspoons sugar, divided
- 1/3 cup all-purpose flour
- 2 tablespoons cornstarch
- 1 teaspoon fat-free milk

Per Serving
Calories: 338
% Calories from fat: 21
Fat (gm): 7.9
Sat. fat (gm): 1.6
Cholesterol (mg): 0
Sodium (mg): 231
Protein (gm): 4.5
Carbohydrate (gm): 63.8
Exchanges
Milk: 0.0
Vegetable: 0.0
Fruit: 0.0
Bread: 1.0
Meat: 0.0
Fat: 3.5

1. Roll 2/3 of the Double Pie Crust on lightly floured surface to form circle 1 1/2 inches larger than inverted 8-inch pie pan. Ease pastry into pan.

2. Combine cherries and almond extract; toss with combined 3/4 cup sugar, flour, and cornstarch. Spoon fruit into pastry.

3. Roll remaining pastry into circle to fit top of pie and place over cherries; trim edges of pastry to within 1/2 inch of pan; fold top pastry over bottom pastry and flute. Cut vents in top pastry; brush with milk and sprinkle with remaining 2 teaspoons sugar.

4. Bake at 425 degrees 10 minutes; reduce heat to 375 degrees and bake until juices are bubbly and crust is golden, 45 to 50 minutes, covering edge of pie with aluminum foil if necessary to prevent excessive browning. Cool on wire rack.

Variation: **Coconut Streusel Cherry Pie**—Make Basic Pie Crust (see p. 574) in 8-inch pie pan. Prepare cherries as in Step 2 above. To make Coconut Streusel, combine 1/2 cup all-purpose flour, 1/2 cup packed light brown sugar, 1/3 cup quick-cooking oats, and 1/3 cup coconut. Cut in 3 tablespoons margarine until mixture resembles coarse crumbs. Sprinkle over cherries. Bake pie as in Step 4 above.

DOUBLE-CRUST BLUEBERRY PIE

8 servings

Double Pie Crust (see p. 575)
4 cups blueberries
1 cup sugar
1/3 cup all-purpose flour
2 teaspoons grated lemon rind
1 teaspoon cinnamon
1/2 teaspoon salt
2 teaspoons margarine

Per Serving
Calories: 347
% Calories from fat: 21
Fat (gm): 8.6
Sat. fat (gm): 1.7
Cholesterol (mg): 0
Sodium (mg): 390
Protein (gm): 4
Carbohydrate (gm): 65
Exchanges
Milk: 0.0
Vegetable: 0.0
Fruit: 1.0
Bread: 3.5
Meat: 0.0
Fat: 1.0

1. Roll 2/3 of the Double Pie Crust on lightly floured surface to form circle 1 1/2 inches larger than inverted 9-inch pie pan. Ease pastry into pan.

2. Combine blueberries, sugar, flour, lemon rind, cinnamon, and salt. Spoon fruit into pastry; dot with margarine.

3. Roll remaining pastry into circle to fit top of pie and place over blueberries. Trim edges of pastry to within 1/2 inch of pan; fold top pastry over bottom pastry and flute. Cut vents in top pastry.

4. Bake at 425 degrees 10 minutes; reduce heat to 375 degrees and bake until juices are bubbly and crust is golden, 40 to 50 minutes, covering edge of pie with aluminum foil if necessary to prevent excessive browning. Cool on wire rack.

Variations: **Black Grape Pie**—Substitute 5 cups seedless black or red grapes for blueberries. Decrease sugar to 2/3 cup, and substitute 3 tablespoons quick-cooking tapioca for the flour. Prepare fruit and bake pie as directed above.

Rhubarb Pie—Make pie as above, substituting 4 cups sliced rhubarb for blueberries. Increase sugar to 1 1/2 cups, and substitute orange rind for the lemon rind. Top with a lattice crust and bake as directed above.

Pineapple Rhubarb Pie—Make pie as above, substituting 3 cups sliced rhubarb and 1 cup crushed canned pineapple drained, for the blueberries. Increase sugar to 1 1/3 cups and substitute orange rind for the lemon rind; omit cinnamon.

SPICED SWEET POTATO PIE

8 servings

Basic Pie Crust (see p. 574)
1 1/2 cups mashed sweet potatoes, peeled, cooked
3/4 cup packed light brown sugar
1 egg
2 egg whites
1 1/2 cups fat-free milk
1 teaspoon ground cinnamon
1 teaspoon ground ginger
1/2 teaspoon ground mace
1/4 teaspoon salt
Light whipped topping, as garnish

Per Serving
Calories: 276
% Calories from fat: 21
Fat (gm): 6.6
Sat. fat (gm): 1.4
Cholesterol (mg): 27.3
Sodium (mg): 268
Protein (gm): 5.9
Carbohydrate (gm): 48.6

Exchanges
Milk: 0.0
Vegetable: 0.0
Fruit: 0.0
Bread: 3.0
Meat: 0.0
Fat: 1.0

1. Bake Basic Pie Crust according to recipe, using 9-inch pie pan. Cool on wire rack.

2. Beat sweet potatoes, brown sugar, egg, and egg whites in medium bowl until smooth. Mix in milk, spices, and salt. Pour into pie crust.

3. Bake at 350 degrees about 45 minutes or until sharp knife inserted near center comes out clean. Serve warm or at room temperature with whipped topping.

Variations: **Sweet Potato Brulée Tart**—Bake Basic Pie Crust in 10-inch tart pan. Complete recipe as above. Cool pie and chill 3 to 4 hours. Press 1/3 cup brown sugar through a strainer, forming an even layer on surface of cold pie. Cover edge of pie with strips of aluminum foil. Broil until sugar is melted and bubbly, 1 to 2 minutes.

Orange Sweet Potato Pie—Make pie as above, substituting fat-free evaporated milk for the milk and adding 1 tablespoon grated orange rind and 2 tablespoons orange liqueur or orange juice to filling. Mix whipped topping with 1 tablespoon orange liqueur, or 1/2 teaspoon orange extract, and 1 teaspoon grated orange rind.

CARAMEL PECAN PUMPKIN PIE

10 servings

Basic Pie Crust (see p. 574)
1/2 cup sugar
1 cup light corn syrup
2 tablespoons dark rum, *or* 1 teaspoon rum extract
1-2 tablespoons margarine
3 large eggs
3/4 cup canned pumpkin
1 teaspoon ground ginger
1/2 cup pecan halves, coarsely chopped

Per Serving
Calories: 320
% Calories from fat: 31
Fat (gm): 11.4
Sat. fat (gm): 1.9
Cholesterol (mg): 63.6
Sodium (mg): 184
Protein (gm): 4.4
Carbohydrate (gm): 51.5
Exchanges
Milk: 0.0
Vegetable: 0.0
Fruit: 0.0
Bread: 3.0
Meat: 0.0
Fat: 2.0

1. Make Basic Pie Crust, using 8-inch pie pan.

2. Cook sugar in heavy saucepan over low heat until melted and a deep caramel color, swirling pan or stirring occasionally with metal fork. Immediately stir in corn syrup, and stir until caramel dissolves. Add rum and margarine. Cool slightly.

3. Beat eggs, adding warm sugar mixture gradually. Mix in pumpkin, ginger, and pecans. Pour into pastry. Bake at 350 degrees until set, about 45 minutes. Cool on wire rack.

BLACK BOTTOM PIE

10 servings

- Chocolate Cookie Crumb Crust (see p. 576)
- 2 cups Lemon Yogurt Pastry Cream (double recipe) (see p. 625)
- 1 ounce unsweetened chocolate, melted
- 2 tablespoons unsweetened cocoa
- 4 teaspoons vanilla, divided
- 1 envelope unflavored gelatin
- 1/4 cup water
- 2 teaspoons meringue powder
- 2 tablespoons water
- 1/4 cup sugar
- 2 cups light whipped topping
- Grated semisweet chocolate, as garnish

Per Serving
Calories: 341
% Calories from fat: 33
Fat (gm): 12.6
Sat. fat (gm): 4.9
Cholesterol (mg): 88.9
Sodium (mg): 217
Protein (gm): 4.9
Carbohydrate (gm): 52.6

Exchanges
Milk: 0.0
Vegetable: 0.0
Fruit: 0.0
Bread: 3.5
Meat: 0.0
Fat: 2.0

1. Make Chocolate Cookie Crumb Crust, using 9-inch pie pan.

2. Make Lemon Yogurt Pastry Cream, doubling recipe. Mix 1 cup warm Lemon Yogurt Pastry Cream with melted chocolate, cocoa, and 2 teaspoons vanilla in small bowl. Spread evenly over crust. Refrigerate.

3. Sprinkle gelatin over water in small saucepan; let stand 3 to 4 minutes to soften. Cook over low heat, stirring, until dissolved; add to remaining Lemon Yogurt Pastry Cream. Refrigerate, stirring occasionally, until mixture mounds slightly when dropped from spoon.

4. Beat meringue powder with water until foamy; beat to stiff peaks, gradually adding sugar. Beat in remaining 2 teaspoons vanilla. Fold gelatin mixture into meringue. Pour over chocolate layer in crust. Refrigerate 2 to 3 hours. Top with whipped topping; sprinkle with grated chocolate.

Variation: **Banana Black Bottom Pie**—Make pie through Step 2. Slice 3 bananas over chocolate layer. Stir 1 tablespoon banana liqueur, *or* 1/2 teaspoon banana extract, into remaining Lemon Yogurt Pastry Cream. Complete pie as above; sprinkle with chopped pecans and shaved chocolate.

PEACHY PECAN PIE

10 servings

Basic Pie Crust (see p. 574)
2 eggs
2/3 cup sugar
2/3 cup corn syrup
1 teaspoon vanilla
1/2 teaspoon salt
1 package (10 ounces) frozen sliced peaches, thawed, well-drained, cut up
1/2 cup coarsely chopped pecans
10 tablespoons light whipped topping

Per Serving
Calories: 313
% Calories from fat: 28
Fat (gm): 10.2
Sat. fat (gm): 2
Cholesterol (mg): 42.4
Sodium (mg): 257
Protein (gm): 3.7
Carbohydrate (gm): 53.1
Exchanges
Milk: 0.0
Vegetable: 0.0
Fruit: 0.0
Bread: 3.0
Meat: 0.0
Fat: 2.0

1. Make Basic Pie Crust, using 9-inch pie pan.

2. Beat eggs, sugar, corn syrup, vanilla, and salt until well blended. Stir in peaches and pecans; pour into pastry.

3. Bake at 375 degrees until filling is set, 35 to 40 minutes. Cool on wire rack. Top each slice with 1 tablespoon of whipped topping.

PEACH-ALMOND STREUSEL PIE

10 servings

Basic Pie Crust (see p. 574)
5 cups sliced, peeled peaches
3/4 cup granulated sugar
3/4 cup packed dark brown sugar
1/4 cup all-purpose flour
1 teaspoon ground cinnamon
1/2 teaspoon ground nutmeg
1/4 teaspoon salt
2 tablespoons lemon juice
1 tablespoon grated orange rind
1 teaspoon almond extract
Almond Streusel (recipe follows)

Per Serving
Calories: 357
% Calories from fat: 21
Fat (gm): 8.2
Sat. fat (gm): 1.5
Cholesterol (mg): 0
Sodium (mg): 438
Protein (gm): 3.7
Carbohydrate (gm): 67.4
Exchanges
Milk: 0.0
Vegetable: 0.0
Fruit: 1.0
Bread: 3.0
Meat: 0.0
Fat: 1.5

1. Make Basic Pie Crust, using 9-inch pan.

2. Toss peaches with combined remaining ingredients, except Almond Streusel. Arrange fruit in pastry. Sprinkle with Almond Streusel.

3. Bake on baking sheet at 400 degrees 40 to 50 minutes until fruit is tender and bubbly and streusel browned. Cool on wire rack.

Almond Streusel

makes about 1 cup

- 1/4 cup all-purpose flour
- 1/4 cup packed dark brown sugar
- 1/4 cup quick-cooking oats
- 2 tablespoons cold margarine, cut into pieces
- 1/2 teaspoon almond extract
- 3 tablespoons sliced almonds

1. Combine flour, brown sugar, and oats. Cut in margarine until mixture resembles coarse crumbs; stir in almond extract and almonds.

LEMON SOUR CREAM PIE

8 servings

- Basic Pie Crust (see p. 574)
- 1 1/3 cups sugar, divided
- 3 tablespoons cornstarch
- Dash salt
- 1 cup fat-free milk
- 3 egg yolks, beaten
- 1-2 tablespoons margarine
- 1 teaspoon grated lemon rind
- 1/4 cup lemon juice
- 1 cup fat-free sour cream
- 3 egg whites
- 1/4 teaspoon cream of tartar

Per Serving
Calories: 364
% Calories from fat: 23
Fat (gm): 9.2
Sat. fat (gm): 2
Cholesterol (mg): 80
Sodium (mg): 221
Protein (gm): 7.6
Carbohydrate (gm): 62.6

Exchanges
Milk: 0.0
Vegetable: 0.0
Fruit: 0.0
Bread: 4.0
Meat: 0.0
Fat: 1.5

1. Bake Basic Pie Crust according to recipe, using 9-inch pie pan. Cool on wire rack.

2. Combine 1 cup sugar, cornstarch, and salt in medium saucepan; stir in milk. Heat to boiling; boil, whisking constantly until thickened, about 1 minute. Whisk about 1/2 cup of hot mixture into egg yolks; whisk egg mixture into saucepan. Cook over very low heat, whisking constantly, 1 to 2 minutes. Stir in margarine, lemon rind, and juice; cool 10 minutes. Stir in sour cream. Pour into pastry.

3. Using clean beaters and large bowl, beat egg whites until foamy; add cream of tartar and beat to soft peaks. Beat to stiff peaks, adding remaining 1/3 cup sugar gradually. Spread meringue over hot filling, sealing to edge of pastry. Bake at 400 degrees until meringue is browned, about 5 minutes. Cool on wire rack.

DRIED FRUIT TART

10 servings

Basic Pie Crust (see p. 574)
1 1/2 cups coarsely chopped mixed dried fruit
1/2 cup chopped dates
1/2 cup apricot nectar, *or* orange juice
1/4 cup packed light brown sugar
Cinnamon Streusel (recipe follows)
1 tablespoon cold margarine
1/3 cup chopped walnuts

Per Serving
Calories: 326
% Calories from fat: 28
Fat (gm): 10.7
Sat. fat (gm): 1.8
Cholesterol (mg): 0
Sodium (mg): 160
Protein (gm): 4
Carbohydrate (gm): 57.1
Exchanges
Milk: 0.0
Vegetable: 0.0
Fruit: 0.0
Bread: 3.5
Meat: 0.0
Fat: 2.0

1. Bake Basic Pie Crust according to recipe, using 9-inch tart pan. Cool on wire rack.

2. Heat mixed dried fruit, dates, apricot nectar, and brown sugar to boiling in medium saucepan; reduce heat and simmer, uncovered, 1 minute. Process in food processor until smooth. Cool completely, spread in bottom of crust.

3. Make Cinnamon Streusel, adding 1 tablespoon margarine and the walnuts. Sprinkle over the fruit.

4. Bake at 400 degrees until tart is bubbly and streusel browned, 20 to 25 minutes.

Cinnamon Streusel

makes about 3/4 cup

- 1/2 cup packed light brown sugar
- 2 tablespoons quick-cooking oats
- 2 tablespoons flour
- 1/4 teaspoon ground cinnamon
- 1/8 teaspoon ground nutmeg
- 2 tablespoons cold margarine, cut into pieces

1. Combine brown sugar, oats, flour, and spices in small bowl; cut in margarine with pastry blender to form crumbly mixture.

CREAM PUFFS

8 servings (1 large or 2 small puffs per serving)

- 1 cup fat-free milk
- 3 tablespoons margarine
- 1 cup all-purpose flour
- 1 tablespoon sugar
- 1/2 teaspoon salt
- 3 eggs
- 2 egg whites, *or* 1/4 cup no-cholesterol, real egg product

Per Serving
Calories: 144
% Calories from fat: 40*
Fat (gm): 6.3
Sat. fat (gm): 1.5
Cholesterol (mg): 80.1
Sodium (mg): 249
Protein (gm): 5.9
Carbohydrate (gm): 15.3
Exchanges
Milk: 0.0
Vegetable: 0.0
Fruit: 0.0
Bread: 1.0
Meat: 0.0
Fat: 1.5

1. Heat milk and margarine to boiling in medium saucepan. Add combined flour, sugar, and salt all at once, and stir over medium heat until mixture leaves side of pan and forms a ball, 1 to 2 minutes; remove from heat and allow to cool 5 minutes.

2. Beat in eggs and egg whites 1 at a time, beating until mixture is smooth after each addition. Drop dough by spoonfuls, or pipe with large pastry bag fitted with 1/2-inch plain tip, to form large or small cream puffs on parchment-lined or greased and floured cookie sheets. Gently smooth tops of cream puffs with pastry brush or fingers dipped in cold water.

3. Bake at 400 degrees 15 minutes for large cream puffs, 10 minutes for small cream puffs; reduce oven temperature to 325 degrees and bake until cream puffs are golden and crisp, 20 to 25 minutes for large cream puffs, 15 to 20 minutes for small cream puffs. Remove from oven; pierce side of each puff with sharp knife and cool on wire rack.

4. Cut top third off cream puffs and remove any soft dough from insides. Return to oven and bake at 325 degrees to dry insides, 3 or 4 minutes.

*Percentage of calories from fat will decrease in servings of actual puffs.

Variations and Fillings: **Profiteroles au Chocolat**—Make 8 Cream Puffs as above. Fill puffs with vanilla fat-free ice cream. Sprinkle with powdered sugar; serve with Chocolate Sauce (see p. 520).

Autumn Profiteroles—Make 8 Cream Puffs as above. Fill puffs with scoops of Pumpkin Spice Ice Cream (see p. 645); serve with Warm Rum Sauce (see p. 523).

Black Forest Cream Puffs—Make 8 Cream Puffs as above. Fill puffs with fat-free cherry ice cream. Serve with Brandied Cherry Sauce (see p. 525); garnish with light whipped topping and chocolate curls.

Cream Puffs Melba—Make 8 Cream Puffs as above. Fill each puff with Lemon Yogurt Pastry Cream (see p. 625) and 1/2 sliced small peach. Serve with Raspberry Sauce (see p. 526).

MOCHA ECLAIRS

8 servings

Cream Puffs (see pp. 587–588)
1 package (3 ounces) vanilla pudding and pie filling
1 1/2 cups fat-free milk
3 tablespoons coffee liqueur, *or* strong coffee
2 cups light whipped topping
Chocolate Eclair Glaze (recipe follows)

Per Serving
Calories: 366
% Calories from fat: 26
Fat (gm): 10.8
Sat. fat (gm): 4.8
Cholesterol (mg): 81.2
Sodium (mg): 462
Protein (gm): 8.6
Carbohydrate (gm): 55.9

Exchanges
Milk: 0.0
Vegetable: 0.0
Fruit: 0.0
Bread: 4.0
Meat: 0.0
Fat: 2.0

1. Make Cream Puff dough. Using a large pastry bag fitted with a 1/2-inch plain tip, pipe dough into 8 oval eclair shapes, about 3 1/2 inches long and 1 1/2 inches wide. Bake according to recipe.

2. Make pudding and pie filling according to package directions, using $1^1/_2$ cups milk. Stir in coffee liqueur; cover and refrigerate until chilled. Fold in whipped topping.

3. Fill eclairs with pudding mixture and frost with Chocolate Eclair Glaze.

Chocolate Eclair Glaze

makes about $^3/_4$ cup

- 2 ounces semisweet chocolate, chopped
- $^1/_4$ cup fat-free evaporated milk
- 1 teaspoon light corn syrup
- 1 cup powdered sugar
- $^1/_2$ teaspoon vanilla extract

1. Heat chocolate and evaporated milk in small saucepan over low heat until melted; remove from heat and stir in remaining ingredients until smooth. Use immediately.

Variations: **Banana Split Eclairs**—Make 8 eclairs as above. Make pudding, substituting banana liqueur or $^1/_2$ teaspoon banana extract for the coffee liqueur. Fill each eclair with pudding mixture and 4 to 6 slices banana; frost with glaze.

Rocky Road Eclairs—Make 8 eclairs as above. Substitute chocolate fudge pudding and pie filling for the vanilla pudding. Omit coffee liqueur and whipped topping. Fold $^1/_2$ cup mini-marshmallows and $^1/_2$ cup chopped dry roasted peanuts into pudding. Fill puffs with pudding mixture; frost with glaze.

BROWN SUGAR PECAN TARTS

12 servings (4 per serving)

- 1 egg
- 1 tablespoon fat-free milk
- 2 tablespoons margarine, melted
- $^1/_2$ teaspoon vanilla extract
- 1 cup packed light brown sugar
- $^1/_4$ cup chopped pecans
- Double Pie Crust (see p. 575)

Per Serving
Calories: 230
% Calories from fat: 34
Fat (gm): 8.8
Sat. fat (gm): 1.6
Cholesterol (mg): 17.7
Sodium (mg): 188
Protein (gm): 2.8
Carbohydrate (gm): 35.4

Exchanges
Milk: 0.0
Vegetable: 0.0
Fruit: 0.0
Bread: 2.5
Meat: 0.0
Fat: 1.0

1. Beat egg, milk margarine, vanilla, and brown sugar until smooth; stir in pecans.

2. Roll 1/2 the Double Pie Crust on floured surface to 1/8-inch thickness. Cut into rounds with 2 3/4-inch cutter; press each round into 1 3/4-inch mini-muffin pan. Repeat with remaining dough, re-rolling scraps if necessary. Chill 30 minutes.

3. Spoon 1 teaspoon filling into each tart shell. Bake at 400 degrees until golden brown, about 12 minutes. Cool in pans on wire rack 5 minutes; remove from pans and cool on wire rack.

APPLE TURNOVERS

12 servings

- 3 cups finely chopped, peeled cooking apples, divided
- 1 tablespoon margarine
- 1/4 cup apple cider
- 1 tablespoon lemon juice
- 1/4 cup packed light brown sugar
- 1/4 cup golden raisins
- 1/2 teaspoon ground cinnamon
- Pinch ground nutmeg
- Cream Cheese Tart Crust (see p. 577)
- 1 egg white, lightly beaten
- Brown Sugar Glaze (recipe follows)

Per Serving
Calories: 348
% Calories from fat: 28
Fat (gm): 10.9
Sat. fat (gm): 2.9
Cholesterol (mg): 22.9
Sodium (mg): 177
Protein (gm): 4
Carbohydrate (gm): 59.5

Exchanges
Milk: 0.0
Vegetable: 0.0
Fruit: 1.0
Bread: 3.0
Meat: 0.0
Fat: 1.5

1. Saute 2 cups apples in margarine in large skillet until lightly browned, about 5 minutes; add cider, lemon juice, brown sugar, raisins, cinnamon, and nutmeg, and cook until liquid has almost evaporated. Add remaining apples and refrigerate until chilled.

2. Roll Cream Cheese Tart Crust on lightly floured board into rectangle 16 x 12-inches; cut into 12, 4-inch squares. Spoon about 2 tablespoons apple mixture on half of each square. Fold pastry over to form triangles; seal edges with fork. Pierce tops.

3. Place turnovers on ungreased cookie sheet; brush with egg white. Bake at 400 degrees until golden brown, 15 to 20 minutes. Cool on wire rack. Drizzle with Brown Sugar Glaze.

Brown Sugar Glaze

makes about 1/4 cup

1 1/2 teaspoons margarine
1 tablespoon packed light brown sugar
1/2 cup powdered sugar
2 teaspoons hot water

1. Heat margarine and brown sugar in small saucepan until margarine is melted. Remove from heat and stir in powdered sugar and hot water; stir over medium-low heat until mixture is smooth, stirring constantly. Add a few drops more hot water if necessary to make glaze consistency.

BAKLAVA

9 servings

1 cup barley-wheat cereal (Grape-Nuts)
1/2 cup chopped walnuts
1/4 cup sugar
1 teaspoon ground cinnamon
3 tablespoons vegetable oil
2 egg whites, beaten
19 sheets frozen fillo, thawed
Butter-flavored vegetable cooking spray
Baklava Syrup (recipe follows)

Per Serving
Calories: 375
% Calories from fat: 26
Fat (gm): 11
Sat. fat (gm): 1.2
Cholesterol (mg): 0
Sodium (mg): 286
Protein (gm): 7
Carbohydrate (gm): 64.6
Exchanges
Milk: 0.0
Vegetable: 0.0
Fruit: 0.0
Bread: 4.0
Meat: 0.0
Fat: 2.0

1. Combine cereal, walnuts, sugar, and cinnamon. Beat oil and egg whites in small bowl until well blended.

2. Cut fillo into 38, 9-inch squares; cover with damp kitchen towel to prevent drying. Place 2 squares fillo in 9-inch square baking pan, brushing each lightly with oil mixture; sprinkle with 2 tablespoons cereal mixture. Repeat layering until all cereal mixture has been used. Continue layering remaining fillo, brushing each layer with oil mixture. Spray top with cooking spray. Carefully score through top layer with sharp knife into 3 x 3-inch serving pieces.

3. Bake at 350 degrees until golden, about 25 minutes. Cool to lukewarm.

4. Pour hot Baklava Syrup over baklava, allowing syrup to saturate layers. Let stand at room temperature 4 to 6 hours. Cut into pieces.

Baklava Syrup

makes about 1 cup

- 1 1/2 cups water
- 1/2 cup sugar
- 1/2 cup honey
- 2 sticks cinnamon
- 1 tablespoon lemon juice

1. Combine all ingredients in large saucepan; boil until syrup reaches 220 degrees on candy thermometer, about 20 minutes. Use immediately.

VIENNESE APPLE STRUDEL

8 servings

Per Serving
Calories: 283
% Calories from fat: 26
Fat (gm): 8.6
Sat. fat (gm): 1.1
Cholesterol (mg): 0
Sodium (mg): 158
Protein (gm): 3.7
Carbohydrate (gm): 49.4
Exchanges
Milk: 0.0
Vegetable: 0.0
Fruit: 1.0
Bread: 2.0
Meat: 0.0
Fat: 1.5

- 1/2 cup dry unseasoned bread crumbs
- 1 tablespoon margarine
- 1/2 cup apricot preserves
- 1 tablespoon brandy, *or* 1/2 teaspoon brandy extract
- 6 sheets frozen fillo, thawed
- 2 tablespoons vegetable oil
- 1 egg white, beaten
- 4 cups thinly sliced, peeled tart baking apples
- 1/3 cup packed light brown sugar
- 1/4 cup chopped walnuts
- 1/4 cup raisins
- 1 tablespoon grated lemon rind
- 1 teaspoon ground cinnamon
- Butter-flavored vegetable cooking spray

1. Cook bread crumbs in margarine in small skillet over medium heat until light brown, stirring frequently. Melt apricot preserves in small saucepan; add brandy.

2. Place 1 sheet fillo on counter (cover remaining fillo with damp kitchen towel to prevent drying); brush with combined oil and egg white. Top with second sheet fillo and brush with egg white mixture; repeat with remaining fillo and egg white mixture. Brush top of fillo with warm apricot mixture, sprinkle with toasted bread crumbs.

3. Mound combined remaining ingredients, except cooking spray, along one long edge of fillo. Fold over short edges of fillo and roll strudel from long edge. Place on greased baking sheet. Spray generously with cooling spray. Score strudel diagonally into serving pieces.

4. Bake at 350 degrees until apples are tender and strudel is golden, about 45 minutes; cool on wire rack.

PEAR FILLO TURNOVERS

9 servings

- 3 tablespoons dry unseasoned bread crumbs
- 3 tablespoons packed light brown sugar
- 1 1/2 cups finely chopped, peeled pears
- 1/3 cup dried cherries, *or* cranberries
- 1/4 cup chopped toasted pecans
- 1/4 cup granulated sugar
- 1/2 teaspoon ground cinnamon
- 1/2 teaspoon almond extract
- 9 sheets frozen fillo, thawed
- 2 tablespoons vegetable oil
- 2 egg whites, beaten
- Butter-flavored cooking spray

Per Serving
Calories: 199
% Calories from fat: 30
Fat (gm): 6.8
Sat. fat (gm): 0.8
Cholesterol (mg): 0
Sodium (mg): 126
Protein (gm): 3.3
Carbohydrate (gm): 32.8
Exchanges
Milk: 0.0
Vegetable: 0.0
Fruit: 1.0
Bread: 1.0
Meat: 0.0
Fat: 1.5

1. Combine bread crumbs and brown sugar in small bowl. Toss pears with cherries, pecans, granulated sugar, cinnamon, and almond extract.

2. Place 1 sheet fillo on counter (cover remaining fillo with damp kitchen towel to prevent drying); brush with combined oil and egg white. Top with 2 more sheets fillo, brushing each with egg white mixture. Sprinkle with about 2 tablespoons bread crumb mixture. Cut fillo stack lengthwise into three strips, each about 4 inches wide.

3. Spoon about 1/4 cup pear mixture about 4 inches from end of each fillo strip. Fold fillo over fruit, forming a triangle; continue folding back and fourth, as if folding a flag. Place turnover on greased cookie sheet; repeat with remaining fillo strips. Spray generously with cooking spray. Make 6 more turnovers using remaining ingredients.

4. Bake at 350 degrees until golden, about 15 minutes. Cool on wire rack.

Variation: **Cherry-Apple Fillo Turnovers**—Make recipe as above, substituting 1 1/2 cups pitted dark sweet cherries and 1 cup finely chopped tart apple for the pears, and omitting dried cherries and pecans.

SEVENTEEN

Desserts

AUTUMN FRUIT CRISP

6 servings

2 cups sliced fresh, *or* frozen, thawed, peaches
2 cups sliced, peeled Granny Smith, *or* other tart, baking apples
1/3 cup raisins
1/4 cup honey
1/2 teaspoon rum extract
Brown Sugar-Granola Streusel (recipe follows)

Per Serving
Calories: 287
% Calories from fat: 19
Fat (gm): 6.5
Sat. fat (gm): 1.3
Cholesterol (mg): 0
Sodium (mg): 142
Protein (gm): 2.8
Carbohydrate (gm): 57.9
Exchanges
Milk: 0.0
Vegetable: 0.0
Fruit: 2.0
Bread: 1.5
Meat: 0.0
Fat: 1.0

1. Combine peaches, apples, and raisins in 1 1/2-quart casserole; drizzle combined honey and rum extract over.
2. Sprinkle Brown Sugar-Granola Streusel over fruit.
3. Bake at 375 degrees until browned and bubbly, about 30 minutes.

Brown Sugar-Granola Streusel

makes about 1 1/4 cups

1/2 cup all-purpose flour
1/3 cup packed light brown sugar
1/2 teaspoon ground cinnamon
1/8 teaspoon salt
3 tablespoons cold margarine, cut into pieces
1/2 cup low-fat granola

1. Combine flour, brown sugar, cinnamon, and salt in small bowl; cut in margarine until pieces resemble coarse crumbs. Add granola and toss.

EASY PEACH CRISP

8 servings

6 cups sliced frozen, or canned, drained, peaches
1/4 cup sugar
Easy Crisp Topping (recipe follows)

Per Serving
Calories: 362
% Calories from fat: 17
Fat (gm): 7.2
Sat. fat (gm): 1.4
Cholesterol (mg): 0
Sodium (mg): 254
Protein (gm): 3.2
Carbohydrate (gm): 74.2
Exchanges
Milk: 0.0
Vegetable: 0.0
Fruit: 3.0
Bread: 2.0
Meat: 0.0
Fat: 1.0

1. Spoon peaches into 2-quart casserole; toss with sugar. Sprinkle Easy Crisp Topping over peaches. Bake at 350 degrees until cobbler is browned and bubbly, 35 to 45 minutes.

Easy Crisp Topping

makes about 1 1/4 cups

1 cup reduced-fat baking mix
1/2 cup quick-cooking oats
1/3 cup packed light brown sugar
1/2 teaspoon ground cinnamon
Generous pinch ground nutmeg
4 tablespoons cold margarine, cut into pieces

1. Combine all ingredients, except margarine, in medium bowl. Cut in margarine until mixture resembles coarse crumbs.

BLUEBERRY PEACH COBBLER

6 servings

- 2 pounds peaches, peeled, pitted, thickly sliced
- 2 cups blueberries
- 1 tablespoon lemon juice
- 1/2 cup plus 2 tablespoons sugar, divided
- 2 tablespoons cornstarch
- 1/2 teaspoon ground cinnamon
- Generous pinch ground nutmeg
- Sour Cream Cobbler Topping (recipe follows)
- Fat-free milk

Per Serving
Calories: 376
% Calories from fat: 14
Fat (gm): 6.2
Sat. fat (gm): 1.2
Cholesterol (mg): 0
Sodium (mg): 298
Protein (gm): 5.7
Carbohydrate (gm): 76.8
Exchanges
Milk: 0.0
Vegetable: 0.0
Fruit: 3.0
Bread: 2.0
Meat: 0.0
Fat: 1.0

1. Combine peaches and blueberries in 3-quart casserole; sprinkle with lemon juice. Toss with combined 1/2 cup sugar, cornstarch, and spices.

2. Place Sour Cream Cobbler Topping over casserole; cut several vents. Brush with milk and sprinkle with remaining 2 tablespoons sugar.

3. Bake at 375 degrees until toothpick inserted in cobbler topping comes out clean, 35 to 45 minutes.

Sour Cream Cobbler Topping

- 1 1/3 cups all-purpose flour
- 2 tablespoons sugar
- 3/4 teaspoon baking powder
- 1/4 teaspoon baking soda
- 1/4 teaspoon salt
- 3 tablespoons cold margarine, cut into pieces
- 1/2 cup fat-free sour cream
- 3-4 tablespoons water

1. Combine flour, sugar, baking powder, baking soda, and salt; cut in margarine until mixture resembles coarse crumbs. Whisk sour cream and water until smooth; add to flour mixture and mix to form dough. Knead several times until smooth on floured surface; let stand 5 minutes.

2. Roll dough on floured surface, or between sheets of waxed paper, into circle to fit top of casserole.

JAM-GLAZED PEACH AND PLUM KUCHEN

10 servings

- 2 3/4 cups all-purpose flour, divided
- 1/3 cup granulated sugar
- 1 package quick-rising dry yeast
- 1/2 teaspoon salt
- 1/2 cup hot water (115-120 degrees)
- 5 tablespoons margarine, melted
- 1 egg, beaten
- 1 1/2 cups sliced, peeled, pitted peaches
- 1 1/2 cups sliced, pitted plums
- 1/3 cup packed light brown sugar
- 1/4-1/3 cup peach spreadable fruit, warm
- Ground nutmeg, as garnish

Per Serving
Calories: 273
% Calories from fat: 21
Fat (gm): 6.5
Sat. fat (gm): 1.3
Cholesterol (mg): 21.2
Sodium (mg): 202
Protein (gm): 4.9
Carbohydrate (gm): 49.3

Exchanges
Milk: 0.0
Vegetable: 0.0
Fruit: 0.0
Bread: 3.0
Meat: 0.0
Fat: 1.0

1. Combine 2 cups flour, granulated sugar, yeast, and salt in large bowl; mix in hot water, margarine, and egg. Mix in enough remaining 3/4 cup flour to make smooth dough. Knead on floured surface until smooth, 4 to 5 minutes. Return to bowl and grease top of dough. Let stand, covered, in warm place until double in size, 30 to 45 minutes. Punch dough down.

2. Pat dough onto greased 12-inch pizza pan. Arrange fruit attractively on dough, pressing lightly into dough; sprinkle with brown sugar.

3. Bake at 400 degrees until dough is puffed and browned, 20 to 30 minutes, covering edge of dough with aluminum foil if becoming too brown. Cool on wire rack. Brush with spreadable fruit and sprinkle very lightly with nutmeg.

SPICED ORANGE SLICES

8 servings

Per Serving
Calories: 72
% Calories from fat: 1
Fat (gm): 0.1
Sat. fat (gm): 0
Cholesterol (mg): 0
Sodium (mg): 2
Protein (gm): 0.8
Carbohydrate (gm): 16.8
Exchanges
Milk: 0.0
Vegetable: 0.0
Fruit: 1.0
Bread: 0.0
Meat: 0.0
Fat: 0.0

1/3 cup orange juice
3 tablespoons packed light brown sugar
2-3 tablespoons orange-flavored liqueur
4 whole allspice
1 cinnamon stick
5 oranges, peeled, sliced
Mint springs, as garnish

1. Heat orange juice, brown sugar, orange liqueur, allspice, and cinnamon stick to boiling in small saucepan; pour over orange slices in glass serving bowl. Refrigerate, covered, 8 hours or overnight for flavors to blend. Garnish with mint.

BLUEBERRY-PEAR COMPOTE

6 servings

Per Serving
Calories: 344
% Calories from fat: 11
Fat (gm): 4.7
Sat. fat (gm): 0.8
Cholesterol (mg): 0
Sodium (mg): 81
Protein (gm): 2.5
Carbohydrate (gm): 77.9
Exchanges
Milk: 0.0
Vegetable: 0.0
Fruit: 5.0
Bread: 0.0
Meat: 0.0
Fat: 1.0

6 medium pears, peeled, cored
1 cup packed light brown sugar
2/3 cup water
2 tablespoons lemon juice
1 teaspoon grated lemon rind
2 tablespoons margarine
3 cups fresh, *or* frozen, blueberries
Cinnamon Sour Cream (recipe follows)

1. Stand pears in baking pan. Heat brown sugar, water, lemon juice and rind, and margarine in small saucepan to boiling; pour over pears.

2. Bake pears at 350 degrees, covered, until tender, basting occasionally, 45 to 60 minutes. Remove pears to serving dish. Boil basting mixture in medium saucepan until reduced to about 2/3 cup; add blueberries and heat to boiling. Spoon warm blueberry mixture around pears. Serve with Cinnamon Sour Cream.

Cinnamon Sour Cream

makes about 1/2 cup

- 1/2 cup fat-free sour cream
- 1 tablespoon light brown sugar
- 1/4 teaspoon ground cinnamon

1. Mix all ingredients.

FRESH BERRY RHUBARB

6 servings (about 3/4 cup each)

- 4 cups sliced rhubarb (about 1 pound)
- 1/2 cup sugar
- 1/2 cup water
- 1/4 teaspoon ground cinnamon
- 1 cup sliced strawberries
- 1 cup blueberries

Per Serving
Calories: 103
% Calories from fat: 3
Fat (gm): 0.3
Sat. fat (gm): 0.1
Cholesterol (mg): 0
Sodium (mg): 5.3
Protein (gm): 1
Carbohydrate (gm): 25.6

Exchanges
Milk: 0.0
Vegetable: 0.0
Fruit: 1.5
Bread: 0.0
Meat: 0.0
Fat: 0.0

1. Heat rhubarb, sugar, and water to boiling in small saucepan; reduce heat and simmer, uncovered, 10 minutes or until rhubarb is tender, stirring occasionally. Stir in cinnamon and cool; stir in strawberries and blueberries.

BAKED RHUBARB COMPOTE

6 servings

3 cups sliced (1 inch pieces) fresh, *or* frozen, rhubarb
1 large tart apple, peeled, sliced
1 orange, peeled, cut into 8 wedges
2/3 cup sugar
1/4 cup honey
3 tablespoons flour
Cinnamon Streusel (see p. 587)

Per Serving
Calories: 297
% Calories from fat: 12
Fat (gm): 4.2
Sat. fat (gm): 0.8
Cholesterol (mg): 0
Sodium (mg): 55
Protein (gm): 1.8
Carbohydrate (gm): 66.3
Exchanges
Milk: 0.0
Vegetable: 0.0
Fruit: 3.0
Bread: 1.5
Meat: 0.0
Fat: 0.5

1. Mix all ingredients, except Cinnamon Streusel, in 1 1/2-quart casserole; sprinkle with Cinnamon Streusel. Bake at 350 degrees until fruit is bubbly, about 45 minutes.

GINGERED RHUBARB

6 servings

1 1/2 pounds fresh, *or* frozen, rhubarb, cut into 1-inch pieces
1/4 cup fresh orange juice
1 tablespoon grated orange rind
2/3 cup sugar
1/4 cup chopped crystallized ginger, divided
Ground nutmeg, as garnish

Per Serving
Calories: 144
% Calories from fat: 2
Fat (gm): 0.3
Sat. fat (gm): 0
Cholesterol (mg): 0.1
Sodium (mg): 7
Protein (gm): 1.1
Carbohydrate (gm): 36.5
Exchanges
Milk: 0.0
Vegetable: 0.0
Fruit: 2.5
Bread: 0.0
Meat: 0.0
Fat: 0.0

1. Heat rhubarb, orange juice and rind, sugar, and 3 tablespoons crystallized ginger to boiling in medium saucepan. Reduce heat and simmer, covered, stirring often, until rhubarb is thick, 10 to 15 minutes. Cool; refrigerate, covered, until cold.

2. Serve rhubarb in bowls; sprinkle with remaining 1 tablespoon crystallized ginger and nutmeg.

PEACHES AND BLACKBERRIES WITH BLACKBERRY COULIS

4 servings

4 ripe medium peaches, peeled, halved
2 tablespoons Blackberry Coulis (recipe follows)
1 cup fresh, or frozen, thawed, black berries
Fat-free sour cream, as garnish
Honey, as garnish

Per Serving
Calories: 144
% Calories from fat: 2
Fat (gm): 0.5
Sat. fat (gm): 0
Cholesterol (mg): 0
Sodium (mg): 3
Protein (gm): 1.4
Carbohydrate (gm): 36.5
Exchanges
Milk: 0.0
Vegetable: 0.0
Fruit: 2.5
Bread: 0.0
Meat: 0.0
Fat: 0.0

1. Toss peaches with sugar and arrange in shallow serving bowls. Spoon Blackberry Coulis around peaches and sprinkle with blackberries; garnish with dollops of sour cream and drizzle lightly with honey.

Blackberry Coulis

makes about 1 1/2 cups

2 cups fresh, *or* frozen, thawed, blackberries, divided
1/2 cup water
2-3 tablespoons sugar
1-2 teaspoons lemon juice

1. Heat 1 cup blackberries and water to simmering in saucepan. Simmer, covered, until soft, about 5 minutes. Process mixture in food processor or blender until smooth; strain and discard seeds. Season to taste with sugar and lemon juice. Stir in remaining 1 cup blackberries.

STRAWBERRIES WITH BROWN SUGAR AND BALSAMIC VINEGAR

6 servings

4 cups halved *or* quartered strawberries
2-3 teaspoons balsamic vinegar
1/4 cup packed light brown sugar
1/8 teaspoon freshly ground black pepper
3/4 cup fat-free sour cream
1-2 tablespoons granulated sugar
2 teaspoons grated lemon rind

Per Serving
Calories: 110
% Calories from fat: 3
Fat (gm): 0.4
Sat. fat (gm): 0
Cholesterol (mg): 0
Sodium (mg): 30
Protein (gm): 2.6
Carbohydrate (gm): 24.6
Exchanges
Milk: 0.0
Vegetable: 0.0
Fruit: 2.0
Bread: 0.0
Meat: 0.0
Fat: 0.0

1. Sprinkle strawberries with balsamic vinegar, brown sugar, and pepper and toss; let stand 15 to 20 minutes.

2. Mix sour cream, granulated sugar, and lemon rind; serve with strawberries.

STRAWBERRIES WITH PEPPERCORNS

6 servings

1 quart strawberries
2 tablespoons raspberry, *or* balsamic, vinegar
1/2 teaspoon lime juice
2 teaspoons sugar
1-2 tablespoons drained green peppercorns

Per Serving
Calories: 39
% Calories from fat: 8
Fat (gm): 0.4
Sat. fat (gm): 0
Cholesterol (mg): 0
Sodium (mg): 1.5
Protein (gm): 0.7
Carbohydrate (gm): 9.4
Exchanges
Milk: 0.0
Vegetable: 0.0
Fruit: 0.5
Bread: 0.0
Meat: 0.0
Fat: 0.0

1. Cut strawberries into halves or quarters; spoon into serving bowl. Sprinkle combined remaining ingredients over strawberries and toss. Refrigerate 1 hour for flavors to blend.

STRAWBERRIES OLÉ

4 servings

4 cups halved strawberries
1/3 cup orange juice
2-3 tablespoons tequila
2-3 teaspoons lime juice
Freshly ground pepper, as garnish

Per Serving
Calories: 71
% Calories from fat: 6
Fat (gm): 0.6
Sat. fat (gm): 0
Cholesterol (mg): 0
Sodium (mg): 2
Protein (gm): 1.1
Carbohydrate (gm): 12.9
Exchanges
Milk: 0.0
Vegetable: 0.0
Fruit: 1.0
Bread: 0.0
Meat: 0.0
Fat: 0.0

1. Toss strawberries, orange juice, tequila, and lime juice in bowl; refrigerate 1 to 2 hours, stirring occasionally.
2. Spoon strawberry mixture into bowls; sprinkle lightly with pepper.
Variation: **Berry Buñuelos**—Spray 4 flour tortillas lightly on both sides with butter-flavored vegetable cooking spray; sprinkle tops lightly with sugar and cinnamon. Bake on cookie sheet at 375 degrees until browned and crisp, 5 to 8 minutes. Make recipe as above, omitting orange juice and pepper; do not refrigerate. Spoon strawberry mixture on tortillas; top with dollops of fat-free sour cream and sprinkle with sliced almonds.

PEACHES AND BLUEBERRIES WITH LIME CREAM SAUCE

6 servings

4 medium peaches, sliced
1 cup blueberries
Lime Cream Sauce (recipe follows)
Mint sprigs, as garnish

Per Serving
Calories: 119
% Calories from fat: 5
Fat (gm): 0.7
Sat. fat (gm): 0.4
Cholesterol (mg): 3
Sodium (mg): 208
Protein (gm): 6
Carbohydrate (gm): 23.6
Exchanges
Milk: 0.0
Vegetable: 0.0
Fruit: 2.0
Bread: 0.0
Meat: 0.0
Fat: 0.0

1. Arrange peaches and blueberries in bowls; spoon Lime Cream Sauce over and garnish with mint.

Lime Cream Sauce

makes about 1 1/4 cups

- 1 package (8 ounces) fat-free cream cheese, softened
- 1/3 cup sugar
- 2-3 tablespoons lime juice

1. Beat cream cheese until smooth; beat in sugar and lime juice.

HONEY-LIME MELON WEDGES

4 servings

- 3-4 tablespoons honey
- 1 small cantaloupe, *or* honeydew melon, cut into wedges
- 4 lime wedges
- Ground nutmeg, as garnish

Per Serving
Calories: 112
% Calories from fat: 3
Fat (gm): 0.5
Sat. fat (gm): 0
Cholesterol (mg): 0
Sodium (mg): 15
Protein (gm): 1.5
Carbohydrate (gm): 28.1
Exchanges
Milk: 0.0
Vegetable: 0.0
Fruit: 2.0
Bread: 0.0
Meat: 0.0
Fat: 0.0

1. Drizzle honey over melon; squeeze juice from lime wedges over and sprinkle lightly with nutmeg.

TROPICAL AMBROSIA

6 servings

1 large ripe pineapple
2 kiwis, peeled, sliced
1 cup cubed mango, *or* papaya
1 cup cubed cantaloupe, *or* honeydew melon
1 carton (6 ounces) custard-style low-fat lemon, *or* orange, yogurt
3/4 cup light whipped topping
2 tablespoons orange marmalade
Toasted coconut, as garnish
Macadamia nuts, *or* slivered almonds, as garnish
Mint sprigs, as garnish

Per Serving
Calories: 246
% Calories from fat: 7
Fat (gm): 2
Sat. fat (gm): 1.3
Cholesterol (mg): 1.9
Sodium (mg): 36
Protein (gm): 3.1
Carbohydrate (gm): 54.7

Exchanges
Milk: 0.0
Vegetable: 0.0
Fruit: 4.0
Bread: 0.0
Meat: 0.0
Fat: 0.0

1. Cut pineapple in half; remove fruit with grapefruit knife, keeping shells intact. Cut pineapple into cubes, discarding core. Mix pineapple and remaining fruit and spoon into pineapple halves.

2. Mix yogurt, light whipped topping, and marmalade. Spoon dollops of topping over fruit; pass remaining topping. Garnish with toasted coconut and macadamia nuts and mint.

CARAMEL APPLE SLICES

4 servings

- 2 large sweet, *or* tart, apples, unpeeled, cored
- 1/2 cup apple cider
- 1/4 cup packed light brown sugar
- Ground cinnamon, as garnish
- Ground nutmeg, as garnish

Per Serving
Calories: 104
% Calories from fat: 2
Fat (gm): 0.3
Sat. fat (gm): 0
Cholesterol (mg): 0
Sodium (mg): 5
Protein (gm): 0.1
Carbohydrate (gm): 24.1
Exchanges
Milk: 0.0
Vegetable: 0.0
Fruit: 1.5
Bread: 0.0
Meat: 0.0
Fat: 0.0

1. Cut apples into fourths; cut into scant 1/4-inch slices. Heat apples, cider, and brown sugar to boiling in medium skillet; reduce heat and simmer, uncovered, until apples are crisp-tender, 3 to 4 minutes. Remove apples to serving dish with slotted spoon.

2. Heat cider mixture to boiling; boil until mixture is reduced to a syrup consistency. Pour syrup over apples, and sprinkle very lightly with cinnamon and nutmeg.

BAKED STUFFED APPLES WITH CRÈME ANGLAISE

4 servings

- 4 large baking apples (Rome Beauty, McIntosh, Jonathan, *or* Granny Smith)
- 1/2 cup chopped mixed dried fruit
- 2-4 tablespoons chopped toasted pecans
- 3 tablespoons sugar
- 1/2 teaspoon ground cinnamon
- 1/8 teaspoon ground nutmeg
- 2-3 tablespoons cold margarine, cut into pieces
- Crème Anglaise (see p. 519)

Per Serving
Calories: 295
% Calories from fat: 29
Fat (gm): 10.2
Sat. fat (gm): 1.9
Cholesterol (mg): 54.4
Sodium (mg): 101
Protein (gm): 4
Carbohydrate (gm): 51.3
Exchanges
Milk: 0.0
Vegetable: 0.0
Fruit: 2.0
Bread: 1.5
Meat: 0.0
Fat: 1.5

1. Core apples, cutting to, but not through, bottoms; peel off 1 inch skin from tops. Stand apples in baking pan.

2. Combine dried fruit, pecans, sugar, spices, and margarine; fill apples with mixture. Bake at 350 degrees, loosely covered with aluminum foil, until apples are tender, about 45 minutes. Cool to room temperature.

3. Spoon Crème Anglaise around apples in shallow bowls.

Variation: **Meringue-Glazed Baked Apples**—Make recipe as above, omitting Crème Anglaise; bake 30 minutes. Beat 1 egg white to stiff peaks, gradually adding 1/4 cup sugar. Swirl meringue on top of apples; bake until apples are tender and meringue browned, about 20 minutes longer.

MIXED FRUIT KABOBS WITH RASPBERRY SAUCE

8 servings (2 kabobs per serving)

2 bananas
2 kiwi, peeled
2 peaches, unpeeled
2 pears, unpeeled
2 tablespoons margarine, melted
Raspberry Sauce (see p. 526)

Per Serving
Calories: 140
% Calories from fat: 21
Fat (gm): 3.5
Sat. fat (gm): 0.6
Cholesterol (mg): 0
Sodium (mg): 34
Protein (gm): 1.2
Carbohydrate (gm): 28.5

Exchanges
Milk: 0.0
Vegetable: 0.0
Fruit: 2.0
Bread: 0.0
Meat: 0.0
Fat: 0.5

1. Cut each piece of fruit into 8 equal pieces. Alternately thread fruit onto 16, 6-inch wooden or metal skewers.

2. Broil, 6 inches from heat source, 5 to 8 minutes or until bananas are golden, rotating kabobs occasionally and basting with margarine. Serve with Raspberry Sauce.

HONEY-BROILED PINEAPPLE SLICES

4 servings

1 medium pineapple, peeled, cored, and cut into eight 1/2-inch slices
3 tablespoons honey
2 tablespoons frozen orange juice concentrate
2 tablespoons minced fresh cilantro or mint

Per Serving
Calories: 143
% Calories from fat: 4
Fat (gm): 0.7
Sat. fat (gm): 0
Cholesterol (mg): 0
Sodium (mg): 3
Protein (gm): 0.8
Carbohydrate (gm): 36.5

Exchanges
Milk: 0.0
Vegetable: 0.0
Fruit: 2.5
Bread: 0.0
Meat: 0.0
Fat: 0.0

1. Arrange pineapple on broiler pan; brush with combined honey and orange juice concentrate. Broil 6 inches from heat source 3 minutes; turn and baste with honey mixture. Broil 2 to 3 minutes more or until golden. Sprinkle with cilantro.

BANANAS FOSTER

4 servings

1/4 cup packed light brown sugar
1 1/2 teaspoons cornstarch
1/2 cup water
1 tablespoon light rum, *or* 1/2 teaspoon rum extract
1 teaspoon vanilla
2 medium bananas, peeled, sliced
1/4 cup toasted pecan halves
1 1/3 cups low-fat vanilla frozen yogurt

Per Serving
Calories: 236
% Calories from fat: 20
Fat (gm): 5.5
Sat. fat (gm): 0.5
Cholesterol (mg): 0
Sodium (mg): 5
Protein (gm): 3.4
Carbohydrate (gm): 43

Exchanges
Milk: 0.0
Vegetable: 0.0
Fruit: 2.0
Bread: 1.0
Meat: 0.0
Fat: 1.0

1. Whisk brown sugar, cornstarch, and water in small saucepan; whisk over medium heat until mixture boils and thickens, 2 to 3 minutes. Reduce heat to low; stir in rum and vanilla.

2. Gently stir in bananas and simmer 1 to 2 minutes or until bananas are warm; stir in pecans. Serve warm over frozen yogurt.

SUGAR AND RUM PLANTAINS

4 servings

1 tablespoon margarine
2 large ripe plantains, peeled, diagonally cut into 1/4-inch slices
1/2 cup dark rum, *or* 1/2 cup water and 1 teaspoon rum extract
1/3 cup sugar
4 tablespoons fat free sour cream
Ground cinnamon, as garnish
1 tablespoon pine nuts, toasted

Per Serving
Calories: 295
% Calories from fat: 13
Fat (gm): 4.4
Sat. fat (gm): 0.9
Cholesterol (mg): 0
Sodium (mg): 50
Protein (gm): 2.8
Carbohydrate (gm): 48.6
Exchanges
Milk: 0.0
Vegetable: 0.0
Fruit: 3.0
Bread: 0.0
Meat: 0.0
Fat: 2.5

1. Melt margarine in large skillet; arrange plantains in skillet in single layer. Cook over medium to medium-high heat until plantains are browned, 2 to 3 minutes on each side. Arrange on serving plates.

2. Add rum and sugar to skillet; heat to boiling. Reduce heat and simmer, stirring constantly, until mixture is reduced to a thick syrup consistency. Drizzle syrup over plantains; top each serving with a dollop of sour cream. Sprinkle with cinnamon and pine nuts.

POACHED PEARS WITH BERRIES IN ROSEMARY SYRUP

4 servings

2 large pears, peeled, halved, cored
Rosemary Syrup (recipe follows)
1 cup raspberries
1 cup fresh, *or* frozen, thawed, blueberries
1 large orange, peeled, cut into segments
Mint sprigs, as garnish

Per Serving
Calories: 313
% Calories from fat: 3
Fat (gm): 1.1
Sat. fat (gm): 0.1
Cholesterol (mg): 0
Sodium (mg): 6
Protein (gm): 1.6
Carbohydrate (gm): 73.1
Exchanges
Milk: 0.0
Vegetable: 0.0
Fruit: 5.0
Bread: 0.0
Meat: 0.0
Fat: 0.5

1. Add pears to Rosemary Syrup in medium skillet; simmer, covered, until tender, about 10 minutes. Remove pears to shallow bowl; strain syrup over pears and cool. Refrigerate until chilled, 1 to 2 hours.

2. Arrange pears and remaining fruit in shallow serving bowls; spoon Rosemary Syrup over fruit. Garnish with mint.

Rosemary Syrup

makes about 1 cup

- 2/3 cup sugar
- 2/3 cup dry white wine
- 1 tablespoon balsamic vinegar
- 1 tablespoon dried rosemary leaves
- 1 bay leaf
- 1 teaspoon grated orange, *or* lemon, rind

1. Heat all ingredients to boiling in medium saucepan.

PEARS BELLE HÉLÈNE

6 servings

- 4 cups water
- 1/4 cup sugar
- 6 small pears, peeled with stems intact
- 1 1/2 cups low-fat frozen vanilla yogurt
- Bittersweet Chocolate Sauce (see p. 520)

Per Serving
Calories: 183
% Calories from fat: 5
Fat (gm): 1.1
Sat. fat (gm): 0
Cholesterol (mg): 0
Sodium (mg): 0
Protein (gm): 2.3
Carbohydrate (gm): 43.9

Exchanges
Milk: 0.0
Vegetable: 0.0
Fruit: 2.0
Bread: 1.0
Meat: 0.0
Fat: 0.0

1. Combine water and sugar in small saucepan; heat to boiling. Add pears; reduce heat to low and gently simmer, covered, 10 to 15 minutes or until pears are tender.

2. Cool pears in syrup; refrigerate until chilled, 1 to 2 hours. Drain.

3. To serve, flatten a scoop of yogurt in each of 6 dessert dishes. Place a pear on top and drizzle with Bittersweet Chocolate Sauce.

Variation: Pears Melba—Make recipe as above, substituting packed brown sugar for the granulated sugar, using 4 pears, omitting frozen yogurt, and substituting Raspberry Sauce (see p. 526) for the Bittersweet Chocolate Sauce.

SPICED PEACHES IN CHAMPAGNE

4 servings

- 4 cups champagne, *or* sparkling white wine, divided
- 1/4 cup sugar
- 1 cinnamon stick
- 8 whole cloves
- 4 whole allspice
- 1 star anise, *or* 1/2 teaspoon anise seed
- 4 small peaches, peeled, halved
- 2 envelopes unflavored gelatin
- Light whipped topping, as garnish
- Cinnamon sticks, as garnish

Per Serving
Calories: 258
% Calories from fat: 0
Fat (gm): 0.1
Sat. fat (gm): 0
Cholesterol (mg): 0
Sodium (mg): 9
Protein (gm): 1.3
Carbohydrate (gm): 31

Exchanges
Milk: 0.0
Vegetable: 0.0
Fruit: 2.0
Bread: 0.0
Meat: 0.0
Fat: 3.0

1. Heat 1 1/2 cups champagne, sugar, and spices to boiling in large skillet. Place peaches, cut sides down, in skillet and simmer, covered, until peaches are tender, about 5 minutes. Remove peaches; strain champagne mixture and discard spices.

2. Sprinkle gelatin over 1/2 cup champagne in small saucepan; let stand 3 to 4 minutes to soften. Cook over low heat, stirring until dissolved. Add gelatin mixture to champagne mixture in bowl; add remaining 2 cups champagne. Refrigerate until mixture is the consistency of unbeaten egg whites, about 45 minutes, stirring occasionally.

3. Press gelatin mixture through strainer, using rubber spatula, to create "champagne bubbles." Spoon 1/2 the mixture into 4 large champagne glasses; refrigerate until firm, but not set, about 30 minutes. Place peach halves in glasses and spoon remaining gelatin mixture over. Refrigerate until set, 2 to 3 hours. Garnish with dollops of light whipped topping and cinnamon sticks.

WINE-POACHED PLUMS

4 servings

- 2 cups white port wine, *or* dry sherry, *or* water
- 1/3-1/2 cup sugar
- 1 cinnamon stick
- 1 whole nutmeg
- 12 medium plums

Per Serving
Calories: 247
% Calories from fat: 4
Fat (gm): 1.2
Sat. fat (gm): 0.1
Cholesterol (mg): 0
Sodium (mg): 5
Protein (gm): 1.8
Carbohydrate (gm): 57.6
Exchanges
Milk: 0.0
Vegetable: 0.0
Fruit: 4.0
Bread: 0.0
Meat: 0.0
Fat: 0.0

1. Combine wine, sugar, cinnamon, and nutmeg in medium saucepan. Heat to boiling add plums, and reduce heat to low. Gently simmer plums, covered, 10 to 15 minutes or until tender. Remove plums to serving dish.

2. Heat poaching liquid to boiling; boil gently 12 to 15 minutes or until slightly thickened. Serve over plums.

Variations: **Pears in Cider Syrup**—Make recipe as above, substituting 1 cup apple cider for the white port wine and 4 peeled, halved small pears for the plums. Stir 1 to 2 tablespoons rum or 1/2 to 1 teaspoon rum extract into thickened poaching liquid; spoon around pears in serving dishes. Garnish pears with dollops of light whipped topping; sprinkle lightly with ground nutmeg and pomegranate seeds.

Ginger Poached Peaches with Mascarpone—Make recipe as above, substituting 1 cup peach nectar for the white port wine and 4 peeled, halved medium peaches for the plums; add 4 slices gingerroot to the peach nectar and omit sugar. Omit Step 2. Make 2/3 cup (1/2 recipe) Mock Mascarpone (see p. 624); beat with 2 tablespoons sugar until fluffy and fold in 2/3 cup light whipped topping. Spoon nectar mixture and peaches into serving dishes. Spoon mascarpone mixture into centers of peach halves and sprinkle with gingersnap crumbs.

BERRY BEST SHORTCAKE

8 servings

- 1/3 cup vegetable shortening
- 1 cup sugar
- 1 egg
- 1 teaspoon vanilla
- 2 cups all-purpose flour
- 2 teaspoons baking powder
- 1/4 teaspoon salt
- 3/4 cup fat-free milk
- 3 cups mixed berries *or* fruit
- Light whipped topping, as garnish

Per Serving
Calories: 320
% Calories from fat: 26
Fat (gm): 9.1
Sat. fat (gm): 2.3
Cholesterol (mg): 26.9
Sodium (mg): 216
Protein (gm): 5.2
Carbohydrate (gm): 54.4
Exchanges
Milk: 0.0
Vegetable: 0.0
Fruit: 1.0
Bread: 3.0
Meat: 0.0
Fat: 1.0

1. Beat shortening, sugar, egg, and vanilla in bowl until well blended. Mix in combined flour, baking powder, and salt alternately with milk beginning and ending with dry ingredients.

2. Spread batter in greased 11 x 7-inch baking dish; bake at 350 degrees until browned, about 25 minutes. Cool on wire rack 10 to 15 minutes.

3. Serve warm cake squares with berries and garnish with whipped topping.

STRAWBERRY-KIWI SHORTCAKE

8 servings

- 1 cup all-purpose flour
- 1 cup whole wheat flour
- 1/3 cup sugar
- 1 1/2 teaspoons baking powder
- 1/2 teaspoon baking soda
- 1/4 teaspoon salt
- 2/3 cup buttermilk
- 4 tablespoons margarine, melted
- 1 egg
- 2 egg whites

Per Serving
Calories: 39.1
% Calories from fat: 25
Fat (gm): 7.3
Sat. fat (gm): 1.5
Cholesterol (mg): 27.4
Sodium (mg): 319
Protein (gm): 6.5
Carbohydrate (gm): 39.1
Exchanges
Milk: 0.0
Vegetable: 0.0
Fruit: 1.0
Bread: 2.0
Meat: 0.0
Fat: 1.0

- 1 1/2 teaspoons vanilla
- 3 cups sliced strawberries
- 1 cup peeled, sliced, kiwi fruit

1. Combine flours, sugar, baking powder, baking soda, and salt in medium-size bowl. Mix buttermilk margarine, egg, egg whites, and vanilla in small bowl until smooth; stir into flour mixture, mixing only until dry ingredients are moistened.

2. With floured hands, lightly pat dough into lightly greased 8-inch round or square baking pan. Bake at 400 degrees 12 to 15 minutes or until toothpick inserted near center comes out clean. Cool on wire rack 10 minutes.

3. Slice cake into wedges or squares and top with strawberries and kiwi fruit.

Variation: **Raspberries with Pecan Shortcakes**—Make Steps 1 and 2 as above, substituting all-purpose flour for the whole wheat flour and adding 1/3 cup chopped pecans. Beat 2/3 package (8-ounce size) reduced-fat cream cheese with 1/4 cup sugar and 1 teaspoon vanilla until fluffy; mix in 2 cups light whipped topping. Cut warm cake in half horizontally; spread 1/2 the cream cheese mixture on bottom layer. Replace top layer, and spread with remaining cream cheese mixture; cut into wedges. Substitute 4 cups fresh raspberries for the strawberries and kiwi; spoon over shortcake wedges.

FRUIT BAKED IN PARCHMENT PACKETS

8 servings

- 2 cups peeled, sliced apples
- 1 1/2 cups peeled, sliced pears
- 1 cup raspberries
- 3 tablespoons brown sugar
- 1 teaspoon ground cinnamon
- 1/4 teaspoon ground nutmeg
- 3 teaspoons flour
- 3 tablespoons margarine, melted

Per Serving
Calories: 119
% Calories from fat: 33
Fat (gm): 4.7
Sat. fat (gm): 0.9
Cholesterol (mg): 0
Sodium (mg): 52
Protein (gm): 0.6
Carbohydrate (gm): 20.4

Exchanges
Milk: 0.0
Vegetable: 0.0
Fruit: 1.5
Bread: 0.0
Meat: 0.0
Fat: 0.5

1. Combine all ingredients, except margarine, in large bowl; gently toss.

2. Cut 8, 12-inch squares of parchment paper; fold each in half diagonally, making triangles. Open triangles and place on baking sheets; brush with margarine. Divide fruit mixture on papers and fold in half; fold edges inward twice to seal. Bake at 375 degrees 10 minutes.

3. Place packets on plates. To open, cut a 2-inch "X" in top of each packet with sharp knife.

FRUIT BAKED WITH MERINGUE PUFFS

4 servings

- 2 cups peeled, sliced peaches
- 1 pint raspberries
- 1/4 cup plus 3 tablespoons sugar, divided
- 3 egg whites
- 1/2 teaspoon vanilla
- 1/4 teaspoon ground nutmeg
- 2 tablespoons sliced almonds

Per Serving
Calories: 181
% Calories from fat: 11
Fat (gm): 2.3
Sat. fat (gm): 0.2
Cholesterol (mg): 0
Sodium (mg): 42
Protein (gm): 4.5
Carbohydrate (gm): 38.7

Exchanges
Milk: 0.0
Vegetable: 0.0
Fruit: 2.0
Bread: 0.0
Meat: 1.0
Fat: 0.0

1. Toss peaches and raspberries with 1/4 cup sugar; spoon into 4 custard cups and place in baking pan. Bake at 375 degrees 10 to 15 minutes or until hot through.

2. Beat egg whites to soft peaks in small bowl; beat to stiff peaks, adding remaining 3 tablespoons sugar gradually. Beat in vanilla and nutmeg. Spoon meringue over warm fruit mixture; sprinkle with almonds.

3. Bake until meringue is lightly browned, about 10 minutes. Serve immediately.

HONEYED BERRIES NESTLED IN FILLO

4 servings

4 sheets frozen, thawed, fillo pastry
Butter-flavored vegetable cooking spray
1 tablespoon sugar
1/4 teaspoon ground cinnamon
3 tablespoons honey
1 tablespoon lemon juice
1 cup small strawberries
1 cup blueberries
1 cup raspberries
Ground nutmeg, as garnish
Light whipped topping, as garnish

Per Serving
Calories: 165
% Calories from fat: 8
Fat (gm): 1.6
Sat. fat (gm): 0.2
Cholesterol (mg): 0
Sodium (mg): 95
Protein (gm): 2.2
Carbohydrate (gm): 37.8
Exchanges
Milk: 0.0
Vegetable: 0.0
Fruit: 1.5
Bread: 1.0
Meat: 0.0
Fat: 0.0

1. Stack fillo and fold lengthwise into quarters; cut into 1/2-inch strips with sharp knife or scissors. Unwind fillo strips and toss together in a greased 8-inch pie plate, shaping to form a large "nest." Spray fillo generously with cooking spray and sprinkle with combined sugar and cinnamon.

2. Bake at 400 degrees until golden, 10 to 12 minutes. Cool on wire rack, carefully remove to serving plate

3. Heat honey and lemon juice until warm. Fill fillo "nest" with combined berries and drizzle with honey mixture; sprinkle lightly with nutmeg. Garnish with light whipped topping.

APRICOT AND PEACH FILLO NESTS

6 servings

12 sheets frozen, thawed, fillo pastry
Butter-flavored vegetable cooking spray
1 1/2 pounds apricots, peeled, sliced
3/4 pound peaches, peeled, sliced
3 tablespoons packed light brown sugar
1/2 teaspoon ground cinnamon
1/4 teaspoon ground nutmeg
Mint sprigs, as garnish

Per Serving
Calories: 219
% Calories from fat: 11
Fat (gm): 2.8
Sat. fat (gm): 0.4
Cholesterol (mg): 0
Sodium (mg): 188
Protein (gm): 4.7
Carbohydrate (gm): 45.8
Exchanges
Milk: 0.0
Vegetable: 0.0
Fruit: 2.0
Bread: 1.0
Meat: 0.0
Fat: 0.5

1. Cut fillo, into 24, 8-inch squares. Spray 4 squares of fillo lightly with cooking spray; layer squares, turning each slightly so that corners are staggered. Carefully fit fillo into 8ounce custard cup, shaping edges to form "nest." Repeat with remaining fillo squares, lining a total of 6 custard cups. Arrange fruit in bottom of each "nest." Sprinkle combined brown sugar and spices evenly over fruit.

2. Place custard cups on cookie sheet and bake at 375 degrees until fillo is golden and fruit tender, about 15 minutes. Cool on wire rack; carefully remove "nests" from custard cups. Serve warm or room temperature, garnished with mint.

Variation: **Blackberry Strudel Cups**—Make recipe as above, substituting 1 pint blackberries or raspberries for the peaches, granulated sugar for the brown sugar, and omitting spices. Bake fillo "nests" without filling with fruit. Mix 1 cup light whipped topping and 1 carton (6 ounces) custard-style low-fat yogurt; mix in fruit and fill fillo "nests."

FRESH FRUIT WITH CHOCOLATE YOGURT CHEESE

4 servings

2 cups fat-free vanilla yogurt
2 tablespoons brown sugar
2 teaspoons unsweetened cocoa
2 pears, unpeeled, sliced
1/2 pint strawberries

Per Serving
Calories: 192
% Calories from fat: 2
Fat (gm): 0.5
Sat. fat (gm): 0
Cholesterol (mg): 0
Sodium (mg): 75
Protein (gm): 6.1
Carbohydrate (gm): 42.6

Exchanges
Milk: 0.5
Vegetable: 0.0
Fruit: 2.5
Bread: 0.0
Meat: 0.0
Fat: 0.0

1. Line a strainer with cheesecloth or a coffee filter and place over bowl; spoon yogurt into lined strainer and cover with plastic wrap. Refrigerate 12 hours or until yogurt is reduced to 1 cup in volume and is the consistency of softened cream cheese; discard liquid.

2. Transfer yogurt cheese to small bowl; mix in brown sugar and cocoa. Refrigerate 1 to 2 hours for flavors to blend. Serve with fruit.

EIGHTEEN

Puddings, Soufflés, AND Frozen Desserts

RICH CHOCOLATE PUDDING

4 servings

- 1/2 cup sugar
- 1/3 cup unsweetened cocoa
- 2 tablespoons cornstarch
- 1/8 teaspoon salt
- 2 cups 2% reduced-fat milk
- 2 egg yolks, slightly beaten
- 2 teaspoons vanilla

Per Serving
Calories: 219
% Calories from fat: 24
Fat (gm): 5.8
Sat. fat (gm): 2.3
Cholesterol (mg): 116
Sodium (mg): 133
Protein (gm): 7.3
Carbohydrate (gm): 34.4
Exchanges
Milk: 0.5
Vegetable: 0.0
Fruit: 1.5
Bread: 0.0
Meat: 0.5
Fat: 1.0

1. Mix sugar, cocoa, cornstarch, and salt in medium saucepan; stir in milk. Whisk over medium heat until mixture boils and thickens.

2. Whisk about 1/2 cup milk mixture into egg yolks; whisk egg yolk mixture back into saucepan. Whisk over medium heat 1 to 2 minutes. Stir in vanilla.

3. Spoon pudding into dessert bowls. Refrigerate, covered with plastic wrap, until chilled, 1 to 2 hours.

LEMON VELVET PUDDING

4 servings

- 1/2 cup sugar
- 2 tablespoons cornstarch
- 1/8 teaspoon salt
- 2 cups 2% reduced-fat milk
- 2 egg yolks, slightly beaten
- 2 tablespoons lemon juice
- 1 teaspoon lemon extract

Per Serving
Calories: 201
% Calories from fat: 22
Fat (gm): 4.9
Sat. fat (gm): 2.2
Cholesterol (mg): 116
Sodium (mg): 132
Protein (gm): 5.5
Carbohydrate (gm): 34.7
Exchanges
Milk: 0.5
Vegetable: 0.0
Fruit: 1.5
Bread: 0.0
Meat: 0.5
Fat: 1.0

1. Heat sugar, cornstarch, salt, and milk to boiling in medium saucepan, whisking constantly until thickened, about 1 minute.

2. Whisk about 1/2 cup milk mixture into egg yolks; whisk egg yolk mixture back into saucepan. Whisk in lemon juice and extract. Whisk over low heat 1 to 2 minutes.

3. Spoon pudding into dessert dishes. Refrigerate until chilled, 1 to 2 hours.

CARAMEL FLAN

8 servings

2/3 cup sugar, divided
4 cups fat-free milk
5 eggs, lightly beaten
2 teaspoons vanilla

Per Serving
Calories: 146
% Calories from fat: 21
Fat (gm): 3.4
Sat. fat (gm): 1.1
Cholesterol (mg): 135
Sodium (mg): 103
Protein (gm): 8.1
Carbohydrate (gm): 20.7
Exchanges
Milk: 0.5
Vegetable: 0.0
Fruit: 1.0
Bread: 0.0
Meat: 0.5
Fat: 0.5

1. Heat 1/3 cup sugar in small skillet over medium-high heat until sugar melts and turns golden, stirring occasionally (watch carefully as the sugar can burn easily!). Quickly pour syrup into bottom of 2-quart soufflé dish or casserole and tilt bottom to spread caramel. Set aside to cool.

2. Heat milk and remaining 1/3 cup sugar until steaming and just beginning to bubble at edges. Whisk into eggs; add vanilla. Strain into soufflé dish over caramel.

3. Place soufflé dish in roasting pan on middle oven rack. Cover soufflé dish with lid or aluminum foil. Pour 2 inches hot water into roasting pan. Bake at 350 degrees 1 hour or until sharp knife inserted halfway between center and edge of custard comes out clean. Remove soufflé dish from roasting pan and cool on wire rack. Refrigerate 8 hours or overnight.

4. To unmold, loosen edge of custard with sharp knife. Place rimmed serving dish over soufflé dish and invert.

Variation: **Pumpkin Flan**—Make flan as above, reducing milk to 2 cups, and mixing 1 cup canned pumpkin puree and 1 teaspoon cinnamon into milk mixture.

TIRAMISU

9 servings

$3^3/_4$ cups Mock Mascarpone (recipe follows)
$^1/_2$ cup sugar
2 tablespoons dark rum or 1 teaspoon rum extract
3 packages (3 ounces each) ladyfingers (36)
1 cup cold espresso or strong coffee
Chocolate shavings, as garnish

Per Serving
Calories: 309
% Calories from fat: 19
Fat (gm): 6.5
Sat. fat (gm): 3
Cholesterol (mg): 172.2
Sodium (mg): 493
Protein (gm): 16.9
Carbohydrate (gm): 43.4
Exchanges
Milk: 0.0
Vegetable: 0.0
Fruit: 0.0
Bread: 3.0
Meat: 2.0
Fat: 0.0

1. Mix Mock Mascarpone, sugar, and rum. Split ladyfingers in half lengthwise. Quickly dip cut sides of 18 ladyfinger halves into espresso and arrange, cut sides up, in bottom of 9-inch square glass baking dish; repeat with 18 more ladyfinger halves. Spread with half the mascarpone mixture. Repeat with remaining ladyfingers, espresso, and mascarpone mixture. Sprinkle with chocolate shavings.

2. Refrigerate, loosely covered, until chilled, 3 to 4 hours. Cut into squares to serve.

Mock Marscarpone

makes about $3^3/_4$ cups

3 packages (8 ounces each) fat-free cream cheese, softened
$^1/_2$ cup reduced-fat sour cream
$^1/_3$-$^1/_2$ cup 2% reduced-fat milk

1. Beat cream cheese until fluffy; mix in sour cream and enough milk to make desired consistency. Refrigerate several hours, or up to several days.

BERRY LEMON TRIFLE

10 servings

- Classic Sponge Cake (see p. 542)
- 3 tablespoons dry sherry
- 1/4 cup strawberry preserves
- 4 cups assorted fresh berries (sliced strawberries, blueberries, raspberries, etc.)
- Lemon Yogurt Pastry Cream (recipe follows)
- 1-1 1/2 cups light whipped topping
- Whole berries, as garnish

Per Serving
Calories: 279
% Calories from fat: 12
Fat (gm): 3.6
Sat. fat (gm): 1.8
Cholesterol (mg): 87.7
Sodium (mg): 169
Protein (gm): 6.1
Carbohydrate (gm): 54.5
Exchanges
Milk: 0.0
Vegetable: 0.0
Fruit: 1.0
Bread: 2.5
Meat: 0.0
Fat: 0.5

1. Bake Classic Sponge Cake in 13 x 9-inch pan; cool. Slice cake into 2 layers horizontally. Drizzle cut sides of cake layers with sherry; spread with preserves and cut into 1-inch cubes.

2. Place 1/2 of the cake cubes in 2-quart glass bowl; spoon 1/2 of the fruit and Lemon Yogurt Pastry Cream over cake. Repeat layering. Refrigerate until chilled, 2 to 3 hours.

3. Spread top of trifle with whipped topping; decorate with whole berries.

Lemon Yogurt Pastry Cream

makes about 2 1/4 cups

- 1/4 cup sugar
- 2 tablespoons cornstarch
- 1 cup fat-free milk
- 1 egg yolk, beaten
- 1/2 teaspoon vanilla
- 1 container (8 ounces) low-fat custard-style lemon yogurt

1. Combine sugar and cornstarch in small saucepan; whisk in milk. Whisk over medium-high heat until mixture boils and thickens, 2 to 3 minutes. Whisk 1/2 the milk mixture into egg yolk; whisk yolk mixture back into saucepan. Whisk over low heat 1 minute. Transfer to bowl; stir in vanilla. Cover surface of custard with plastic wrap. Cool; refrigerate until chilled, 1 to 2 hours. Stir in yogurt.

CREAMY RICE PUDDING

6 servings

- 3/4 cup uncooked rice
- 2 cups water
- 4 cups fat-free milk, divided
- 1/2 cup sugar
- 1/2 teaspoon salt
- 1 1/2 tablespoons cornstarch
- Ground cinnamon, as garnish

Per Serving
Calories: 214
% Calories from fat: 1
Fat (gm): 0.4
Sat. fat (gm): 0.2
Cholesterol (mg): 2.9
Sodium (mg): 279
Protein (gm): 7.2
Carbohydrate (gm): 44.9
Exchanges
Milk: 0.0
Vegetable: 0.0
Fruit: 0.0
Bread: 3.0
Meat: 0.0
Fat: 0.0

1. Heat rice and water in small saucepan over medium heat to boiling; reduce heat and simmer, uncovered, until rice is tender and water is absorbed, about 20 minutes. Reserve.

2. Heat 3 cups milk, sugar, and salt to boiling in medium saucepan. Stir in reserved rice and combined remaining 1 cup milk and cornstarch. Reduce heat and simmer, uncovered, stirring occasionally, until thick, about 20 minutes. Cool slightly; spoon into serving dishes or bowl. Sprinkle with cinnamon. Refrigerate, covered, until chilled.

Variations: **Apple Rice Pudding**—Make recipe as above, substituting brown sugar for the granulated sugar. Saute 1 cup coarsely chopped, unpeeled apple in 1 tablespoon margarine in large skillet until lightly browned. Stir apples and 1 teaspoon vanilla into rice pudding at the end of cooking time.

Almond Rice Pudding—Make recipe as above, simmering rice with 1 cinnamon stick, and reducing sugar to 1/4 cup. Stir 2/3 cup finely chopped toasted almonds, 2 teaspoons vanilla, and 1 teaspoon almond extract into pudding at the end of cooking time. Cool to room temperature; fold in 2 cups light whipped topping. Spoon into serving dishes and chill. Serve with Raspberry Sauce or Festive Cranberry Sauce (see pp. 526, 525).

BLUEBERRY BREAD PUDDING WITH TART LEMON SAUCE

8 servings

3 tablespoons margarine, softened
6 slices whole wheat bread
1 egg
2 egg whites
1/2 cup sugar
1/4 teaspoon salt
2 cups fat-free milk
1 teaspoon vanilla
1 cup fresh, *or* frozen, blueberries
Tart Lemon Sauce (see p. 524)

Per Serving
Calories: 295
% Calories from fat: 29
Fat (gm): 9.9
Sat. fat (gm): 2.2
Cholesterol (mg): 80.6
Sodium (mg): 325
Protein (gm): 7.4
Carbohydrate (gm): 46.5

Exchanges
Milk: 0.0
Vegetable: 0.0
Fruit: 0.0
Bread: 3.0
Meat: 0.0
Fat: 2.0

1. Spread margarine on one side of each slice of bread; cut into 2-inch squares and place in greased 9-inch baking dish or 1-quart casserole.

2. Combine egg, egg whites, sugar, and salt in medium bowl. Heat milk in small saucepan until just boiling; whisk milk into egg mixture. Stir in vanilla and blueberries; pour over bread cubes and toss.

3. Place baking dish in roasting pan on middle oven rack; pour 1 inch hot water into pan. Bake, uncovered, at 350 degrees 35 to 40 minutes or until knife inserted near center comes out clean. Serve warm or at room temperature with Tart Lemon Sauce.

Variations: **Rum-Raisin Bread Pudding**—Make recipe as above, substituting 1/3 cup raisins for the blueberries. Add 1 tablespoon grated orange rind, 1 tablespoon dark rum *or* 1 teaspoon rum extract, and 1 teaspoon ground cinnamon to the milk mixture. Serve with Warm Rum Sauce (see p. 523).

Dark Chocolate Bread Pudding—Make recipe as above, omitting blueberries, increasing sugar to 3/4 cup, and also melting 2 ounces unsweetened chocolate with milk in Step 2. Serve with Crème Anglaise or Bittersweet Chocolate Sauce (see pp. 519, 520).

Dried Cherry-Apricot Bread Pudding—Make recipe as above, substituting white bread for the whole wheat and omitting blueberries. Simmer 1/3 cup each sliced dried apricots and dried cherries in 1/2 cup orange juice until fruit is soft and juice absorbed; combine with milk mixture, spoon over bread cubes, and toss. Bake as above. Serve with Orange Sauce (see pp. 634–635).

Sourdough Bread Pudding with Caramelized Pears—Make Step 1 as above, substituting sourdough bread for the whole wheat bread and placing cubes in large bowl; omit blueberries. To make Caramelized Pears: Melt 2 tablespoons margarine in medium skillet; sprinkle with 1/2 cup sugar. Arrange 2 large, sliced pears evenly over sugar in skillet. Cook over medium-high heat until bubbly and browned, about 20 minutes. Arrange pears in bottom of casserole dish, scraping syrup over. Spoon bread mixture over pears and bake as above. Invert onto serving platter.

VANILLA DOLCE SOUFFLÉ

6 servings

1 tablespoon rum, *or* 1 teaspoon rum extract
1/4 cup finely chopped mixed candied fruit
1 vanilla bean (about 4 inches long)
1 cup fat-free milk
3 egg yolks
1/3 cup granulated sugar
2 tablespoons flour
6 egg whites
Pinch salt
2 tablespoons powdered sugar, divided

Per Serving
Calories: 153
% Calories from fat: 16
Fat (gm): 2.7
Sat. fat (gm): 0.8
Cholesterol (mg): 107.2
Sodium (mg): 80
Protein (gm): 6.6
Carbohydrate (gm): 24.2

Exchanges
Milk: 0.0
Vegetable: 0.0
Fruit: 0.0
Bread: 2.0
Meat: 0.0
Fat: 0.5

1. Grease a 1 1/2-quart soufflé dish; sprinkle lightly with sugar. Refrigerate dish.

2. Sprinkle rum over candied fruit; let stand 5 minutes. Split vanilla bean lengthwise; scrape seeds into milk in small saucepan. Heat over low heat until simmering.

3. Beat egg yolks and granulated sugar in small bowl until thick and lemon colored, about 5 minutes; stir in flour. Whisk half the warm milk into egg mixture; whisk mixture into saucepan. Whisk over medium heat until boiling and thickened. Stir in candied fruit mixture.

4. Beat egg whites and salt in large bowl until soft peaks form. Add 1 tablespoon powdered sugar, and continue beating to stiff peaks. Fold in egg yolk mixture. Spoon into prepared dish.

5. Bake at 400 degrees 20 minutes or until soufflé is golden brown. Sprinkle with remaining 1 tablespoon powdered sugar, and serve immediately.

Variations: **Ginger-Orange Soufflé**—Make recipe as above, omitting candied fruit, rum, and vanilla bean. Simmer milk with 2 tablespoons chopped fresh ginger, strain before adding to yolks. Stir 1/4 cup chopped crystallized ginger and 1 tablespoon grated orange rind into cooked egg yolk mixture in Step 3. Serve with Orange Sauce (see pp. 634–635).

Rum Raisin Soufflé—Make recipe as above, omitting vanilla bean, substituting 1/2 cup chopped golden raisins for the candied fruit, increasing rum to 1/4 cup *or* 1 to 2 teaspoons rum extract, and adding 1/8 teaspoon ground nutmeg. Serve with Rum-Raisin Sauce (see p. 522), substituting golden raisins for the dark raisins.

DOUBLE-CHOCOLATE SOUFFLÉ

8 servings

- 1/2 cup Prune Puree (recipe follows)
- 3 ounces semisweet chocolate, grated
- 2 tablespoons unsweetened cocoa
- 2 teaspoons instant espresso powder, *or* instant coffee granules
- 1 egg yolk
- 5 egg whites
- 1/4 cup granulated sugar
- 1 tablespoon powdered sugar
- White Chocolate Sauce (recipe follows)

Per Serving
Calories: 254
% Calories from fat: 25
Fat (gm): 7.6
Sat. fat (gm): 4.4
Cholesterol (mg): 28.7
Sodium (mg): 5.8
Protein (gm): 5.2
Carbohydrate (gm): 46

Exchanges
Milk: 0.0
Vegetable: 0.0
Fruit: 2.0
Bread: 1.0
Meat: 0.0
Fat: 1.5

1. Mix Prune Puree, chocolate, cocoa, espresso, and egg yolk until well blended.

2. Beat egg whites in large bowl to soft peaks; beat to stiff peaks, adding granulated sugar gradually. Fold 1/4 of the egg white mixture into chocolate mixture. Fold chocolate mixture into egg white mixture. Pour into 1 1/2-quart soufflé dish that has been lightly greased and sprinkled with sugar.

3. Place soufflé dish in square baking pan on middle shelf of oven. Pour 2 inches boiling water into pan. Bake at 350 degrees until puffed and set, about 55 minutes. Sprinkle with powdered sugar. Serve immediately with White Chocolate Sauce.

Prune Puree

makes about 1/2 cup

- 1/4 package (12 ounce-size) pitted prunes
- 1 1/2 tablespoons light corn syrup
- 3/4 teaspoon sugar
- 3 tablespoons water

1. Process all ingredients in food processor or blender until smooth.

White Chocolate Sauce

makes about 1 1/2 cup

- 2 tablespoons fat-free milk
- 3 ounces white chocolate, chopped
- 1 tablespoon coffee, *or* chocolate liqueur, optional

1. Heat milk over low heat in small saucepan to simmering; add white chocolate and whisk over very low heat until melted. Remove from heat; stir in coffee or liqueur, if using.

STRAWBERRY ANGEL SOUFFLÉ

6 servings

- 2 cups angel food cake crumbs
- 1 package (16 ounces) frozen strawberries in syrup, thawed, pureed, divided
- 1 tablespoon orange liqueur, *or* 1 teaspoon orange extract
- 5 egg whites
- 1/2 cup sugar

Per Serving
Calories: 245
% Calories from fat: 1
Fat (gm): 0.4
Sat. fat (gm): 0.1
Cholesterol (mg): 0
Sodium (mg): 298
Protein (gm): 5.3
Carbohydrate (gm): 56.8
Exchanges
Milk: 0.0
Vegetable: 0.0
Fruit: 2.0
Bread: 2.0
Meat: 0.0
Fat: 0.0

1. Combine cake crumbs, 1 1/2 cups strawberry puree, and orange liqueur in large bowl. Pour remaining 1/2 cup strawberry puree into bottom of 2-quart soufflé dish that has been greased and sprinkled with sugar.

2. Beat egg whites to stiff peaks in large bowl, adding sugar gradually; fold into cake mixture. Pour into soufflé dish. Bake at 350 degrees until puffed and set, about 35 minutes.

FRENCH MOCHA MOUSSE

6 servings

- 1 envelope unflavored gelatin
- 1/4 cup cold espresso, *or* strong coffee
- 1 cup sugar, divided
- 1/2 cup Dutch process cocoa
- 1 1/4 cups 1% low-fat milk
- 2 egg yolks, lightly beaten
- 4 ounces bittersweet chocolate, finely chopped
- 2 tablespoons coffee liqueur, *or* 2 teaspoons vanilla
- 2 egg whites
- 1/8 teaspoon cream of tartar
- Light whipped topping, as garnish
- Chocolate curls, as garnish

Per Serving
Calories: 318
% Calories from fat: 25
Fat (gm): 9.5
Sat. fat (gm): 5.2
Cholesterol (mg): 73
Sodium (mg): 55
Protein (gm): 6.8
Carbohydrate (gm): 53.3
Exchanges
Milk: 0.0
Vegetable: 0.0
Fruit: 0.0
Bread: 3.0
Meat: 0.0
Fat: 2.0

1. Sprinkle gelatin over espresso in medium saucepan; let stand 3 to 4 minutes. Heat over low heat until gelatin is dissolved, stirring constantly.

2. Mix 1/2 cup sugar and cocoa in medium saucepan; whisk in milk. Heat to boiling over medium-high heat; reduce heat and simmer briskly, whisking constantly, until thickened, 3 to 4 minutes. Whisk about 1/2 of the milk mixture into egg yolks; whisk yolk mixture into milk mixture in saucepan. Cook over low heat 1 to 2 minutes, whisking constantly. Remove from heat; add gelatin mixture, chocolate, and liqueur, whisking until chocolate is melted. Refrigerate until cool, but not set, about 20 minutes.

3. Beat egg whites, remaining 1/2 cup sugar, and cream of tartar until foamy in medium bowl; place bowl over pan of simmering water and beat at medium speed until temperature of egg whites reaches 160 degrees on candy thermometer. Remove from heat and beat at high speed until very thick and cool, about 5 minutes. Mix 1/4 of the egg white mixture into chocolate mixture; fold chocolate mixture into remaining egg white mixture. Pour into serving dishes or large glass bowl. Refrigerate until firm, about 4 hours. Serve with dollops of whipped topping and chocolate curls.

Variation: **Orange Pumpkin Mousse**—Make Step 1 of recipe, substituting 1/2 cup orange juice for the coffee. Make Step 2, substituting 3/4 cup brown sugar for the 1 cup granulated sugar, orange liqueur for the coffee liqueur, reducing milk to 3/4 cup, and omitting cocoa and bittersweet chocolate. Stir 1 can (16 ounces) pumpkin into custard mixture after removing from heat. Complete recipe as above.

STRAWBERRY RASPBERRY MOUSSE

8 servings (about 1 cup each)

- 3 envelopes unflavored gelatin
- 1/2 cup orange liqueur, *or* 1/2 cup water and 1/2 teaspoon orange extract
- 1 jar (7 ounces) marshmallow crème
- 1 package (14 ounces) frozen unsweetened raspberries, thawed
- 1 package (16 ounces) frozen unsweetened strawberries, thawed
- 4 cups light whipped topping
- Strawberries, *or* raspberries, as garnish
- Mint sprigs, as garnish

Per Serving
Calories: 255
% Calories from fat: 15
Fat (gm): 4.1
Sat. fat (gm): 4
Cholesterol (mg): 0
Sodium (mg): 20
Protein (gm): 1.1
Carbohydrate (gm): 45.4
Exchanges
Milk: 0.0
Vegetable: 0.0
Fruit: 3.0
Bread: 0.0
Meat: 0.0
Fat: 1.5

1. Sprinkle gelatin over liqueur in medium saucepan; let stand 3 to 4 minutes. Whisk over low heat until gelatin is dissolved. Add marshmallow crème, whisking over low heat until smooth. Remove from heat.

2. Process raspberries and strawberries in food processor or blender until smooth; strain and discard seeds. Stir pureed fruit into marshmallow mixture. Refrigerate, stirring occasionally, until mixture mounds slightly when dropped from spoon.

3. Fold whipped topping into fruit mixture. Spoon into stemmed serving dishes or serving bowl. Refrigerate until set, about 4 hours. Garnish each serving with berries and mint sprigs.

ORANGE BAVARIAN

6 servings

$^3/_4$ cup fresh orange juice
1 envelope unflavored gelatin
$^3/_4$ cup sugar, divided
1 tablespoon grated orange rind
2 eggs
2 cups light whipped topping
Orange Sauce (recipe follows)
Orange segments, as garnish

Per Serving
Calories: 311
% Calories from fat: 18
Fat (gm): 6.2
Sat. fat (gm): 3.7
Cholesterol (mg): 141.7
Sodium (mg): 28
Protein (gm): 3.7
Carbohydrate (gm): 59.7

Exchanges
Milk: 0.0
Vegetable: 0.0
Fruit: 2.0
Bread: 2.0
Meat: 0.0
Fat: 1.0

1. Heat orange juice, gelatin, 2 tablespoons sugar, and orange rind in small saucepan over medium heat, stirring constantly, until gelatin is dissolved.

2. Beat eggs and remaining 10 tablespoons sugar in medium bowl until light and fluffy. Whisk small amount of orange juice mixture into eggs; whisk egg mixture into saucepan. Stir constantly with a wooden spoon, over low heat, until mixture coats the back of spoon. Remove from heat; refrigerate until mixture mounds slightly when dropped from spoon.

3. Fold in whipped topping; spoon mixture into lightly oiled 1-quart ring mold. Refrigerate until set, about 4 hours. Unmold onto serving plate, serve with Orange Sauce and garnish with orange segments.

Orange Sauce

makes about 1$^1/_2$ cups

$^1/_2$ cup sugar
2 tablespoons cornstarch
1 cup orange juice
3 tablespoons lemon juice
2 tablespoons grated orange rind
2 egg yolks, beaten

1. Combine sugar and cornstarch in small saucepan; whisk in orange and lemon juices and orange rind. Whisk over medium-high heat until boiling and thickened, 2 to 3 minutes.

2. Whisk about 1/2 of the orange juice mixture into egg yolks; whisk yolk mixture into saucepan. Whisk over low heat 1 minute. Serve warm or at room temperature.

COFFEE CRÈME

8 servings

- 2 envelopes unflavored gelatin
- 2/3 cup sugar
- 1/4 teaspoon salt
- 1 cup water
- 1 quart fat-free coffee ice cream, softened
- 2 tablespoons lemon juice
- 1/4 cup dark rum, *or* 1 tablespoon rum extract
- Light whipped topping, as garnish
- Chocolate curls, as garnish

Per Serving
Calories: 178
% Calories from fat: 0
Fat (gm): 0
Sat. fat (gm): 0
Cholesterol (mg): 0
Sodium (mg): 147
Protein (gm): 4.2
Carbohydrate (gm): 38.6

Exchanges
Milk: 0.0
Vegetable: 0.0
Fruit: 0.0
Bread: 2.5
Meat: 0.0
Fat: 0.0

1. Mix gelatin, sugar, and salt in medium saucepan. Gradually stir in water. Whisk over medium heat until gelatin is dissolved; remove from heat.

2. Add ice cream, lemon juice, and rum, stirring until ice cream is melted. Pour into lightly oiled 5- or 6-cup mold. Refrigerate until set, about 6 hours.

3. Unmold onto serving plate; garnish with dollops of whipped topping and chocolate curls.

FRENCH VANILLA ICE CREAM

4 servings

- 2 egg yolks
- 1/3 cup sugar
- 1 tablespoon cornstarch
- 2 cups fat-free milk, divided
- 1 envelope (1.3 ounces) whipped topping mix
- 1 teaspoon vanilla

Per Serving
Calories: 208
% Calories from fat: 22
Fat (gm): 4.8
Sat. fat (gm): 2.9
Cholesterol (mg): 108.7
Sodium (mg): 67
Protein (gm): 5.6
Carbohydrate (gm): 32.9

Exchanges
Milk: 0.0
Vegetable: 0.0
Fruit: 0.0
Bread: 2.0
Meat: 0.0
Fat: 1.0

1. Whisk egg yolks, sugar, and cornstarch in small bowl until smooth; heat 1 cup milk to boiling in small saucepan. Whisk small amount of milk into egg yolk mixture; whisk yolk mixture into saucepan. Whisk mixture constantly over medium heat until boiling; pour into medium bowl. Refrigerate until chilled.

2. Beat whipped topping mix with remaining 1 cup milk until fluffy and thickened, about 5 minutes. Fold into chilled yolk mixture; stir in vanilla.

3. Freeze mixture in ice cream maker according to manufacturer's directions. Or pour mixture into 9-inch square baking dish and freeze until slushy, about 2 hours; spoon into bowl and beat until fluffy. Return to pan and freeze until firm, 6 hours or overnight.

Variations: **Grape-Nuts Ice Cream**—Make recipe as above, adding 1/3 cup Grape-Nuts cereal after adding vanilla.

Creamy Chocolate Ice Cream—Whisk 1 tablespoon unsweetened cocoa into the egg yolks, sugar, and cornstarch mixture in Step 1, and cook as above. Stir 1 ounce chopped semisweet chocolate into hot yolk mixture until melted; refrigerate until chilled. Complete recipe as above.

CARAMEL CHOCOLATE CHIP ICE CREAM SANDWICH

20 servings

- 2 packages (1 pound, 2 ounces each) reduced-fat refrigerated chocolate chip cookie dough
- 1/2 package (14-ounce size) caramels (about 25)
- 2 tablespoons fat-free milk
- 1 quart fat-free vanilla, *or* chocolate, ice cream, slightly softened
- Quick-and-Easy Caramel Sauce (see p. 522)

Per Serving
Calories: 372
% Calories from fat: 26
Fat (gm): 11.2
Sat. fat (gm): 3.8
Cholesterol (mg): 12.6
Sodium (mg): 145
Protein (gm): 4.6
Carbohydrate (gm): 65.6

Exchanges
Milk: 0.0
Vegetable: 0.0
Fruit: 0.0
Bread: 4.0
Meat: 0.0
Fat: 2.0

1. Line two 12-inch pizza pans with aluminum foil and grease lightly. Spread a package of cookie dough on each pan, spreading to edges. Bake at 325 degrees until browned, 17 to 20 minutes. Cool on wire racks. Invert cookies onto cookie sheets or pizza pans; peel off aluminum foil.

2. Heat caramels and milk in small saucepan over medium heat until melted, stirring constantly. Cool 2 to 3 minutes. Place 1 cookie, flat side up, on serving plate or pizza pan; pour caramel on cookie, spreading almost to the edge. Let stand, or refrigerate, until caramel is firm.

3. Spread ice cream evenly on flat side of second cookie; carefully invert caramel-covered cookie over ice cream. Freeze, covered with aluminum foil, until firm, 4 to 6 hours.

4. Invert ice cream sandwich onto serving plate, cut into wedges and serve with Quick-and-Easy Caramel Sauce.

COLOSSAL COOKIE SANDWICH

16 servings

Per Serving
Calories: 365
% Calories from fat: 30
Fat (gm): 12.3
Sat. fat (gm): 2.6
Cholesterol (mg): 28.4
Sodium (mg): 322
Protein (gm): 6.2
Carbohydrate (gm): 58.6
Exchanges
Milk: 0.0
Vegetable: 0.0
Fruit: 0.0
Bread: 4.0
Meat: 0.0
Fat: 2.0

10 tablespoons margarine, softened
1 1/4 cups packed light brown sugar
1/2 cup granulated sugar
2 eggs
2 teaspoons vanilla
1 3/4 cups all-purpose flour
1 1/4 cups quick-cooking oats
1 teaspoon baking powder
1/2 teaspoon baking soda
3/4 teaspoon salt
1/2 cup chopped pecans
1 1/2-2 quarts fat-free butter pecan ice cream, slightly softened
Light whipped topping, as garnish
24 fresh, *or* canned, peach slices

1. Beat margarine and sugars in large bowl until fluffy; beat in eggs and vanilla. Mix in combined flour, oats, baking powder, baking soda, and salt; mix in pecans.

2. Line 2, 12-inch pizza pans with aluminum foil and grease. Spread half the dough on each pan, using spatula or lightly floured fingertips.

3. Bake cookies at 350 degrees until browned, 12 to 15 minutes. Cool in pans on wire racks until firm enough to remove from pans, about 15 minutes. Using foil, slide cookies off pans; remove foil.

4. Place 1 cookie flat side up on serving plate or pizza pan; spread with ice cream and top with second cookie, flat side down. Freeze until firm, 4 to 6 hours.

5. Cut into wedges; garnish with whipped topping and peach slices.

ICE CREAM JELLY ROLL CAKE

8 servings

3 egg yolks
1/2 teaspoon vanilla
3/4 cup sugar, divided
3 egg whites
3/4 cup cake flour
1 teaspoon baking powder
1/4 teaspoon salt
1-1 1/2 quarts strawberry, *or* other flavor, fat-free ice cream, slightly softened
Powdered sugar, as garnish
Whole strawberries, as garnish

Per Serving
Calories: 229
% Calories from fat: 8
Fat (gm): 2
Sat. fat (gm): 0.6
Cholesterol (mg): 79.9
Sodium (mg): 197
Protein (gm): 7.2
Carbohydrate (gm): 47.2
Exchanges
Milk: 0.0
Vegetable: 0.0
Fruit: 0.0
Bread: 2.5
Meat: 0.0
Fat: 0.0

1. Grease jelly roll pan, 15 x 10 x 1-inch. Line bottom of pan with parchment paper; grease and flour parchment.

2. Beat egg yolks and vanilla in medium bowl until thick and lemon colored, 3 to 5 minutes. Gradually beat in 1/4 cup sugar, beating 2 minutes longer.

3. Using clean beaters and large bowl, beat egg whites to soft peaks; gradually beat in remaining 1/2 cup granulated sugar, beating to stiff, glossy peaks. Fold egg yolks into whites; sprinkle combined flour, baking powder, and salt over mixture and fold in. Spread batter evenly in prepared pan, using metal spatula.

4. Bake at 375 degrees until cake is golden and springs back when touched, 10 to 12 minutes. Immediately invert cake onto large kitchen towel sprinkled with powdered sugar; remove parchment. Roll cake up in towel, beginning at short end. Cool on wire rack 30 to 60 minutes.

5. Unroll cake; spread with ice cream. Reroll cake and freeze until ice cream is firm, 6 to 8 hours.

6. Trim ends from cake and place cake on serving plate. Sprinkle cake generously with powdered sugar and garnish with strawberries.

CARAMEL ICE CREAM PIE

10 servings

Graham Cracker Crumb Crust (see p. 545)
1 quart low-fat banana chocolate chip ice cream, slightly softened
1 large banana, sliced
Quick-and-Easy Caramel Sauce (see p. 522)

Per Serving
Calories: 361
% Calories from fat: 21
Fat (gm): 8.7
Sat. fat (gm): 2.5
Cholesterol (mg): 4.7
Sodium (mg): 163
Protein (gm): 4.6
Carbohydrate (gm): 69

Exchanges
Milk: 0.0
Vegetable: 0.0
Fruit: 0.0
Bread: 4.5
Meat: 0.0
Fat: 1.0

1. Make Graham Cracker Crumb Crust, using 9-inch pie pan.

2. Spoon ice cream into pie crust, spreading evenly; freeze until very hard, 8 hours or overnight.

3. Top with banana slices. Drizzle 1/3 cup Quick-and-Easy Caramel Sauce over pie; serve slices with remaining caramel sauce.

STRAWBERRY FREEZE

9 servings

2 packages (10-ounce size) frozen, thawed, sweetened strawberries
1 can (20 ounces) crushed pineapple in juice, undrained
1 can (11 ounces) reduced-fat, sweetened, condensed milk
1 container (9 ounces) light whipped topping

Per Serving
Calories: 275
% Calories from fat: 20
Fat (gm): 6.1
Sat. fat (gm): 3.9
Cholesterol (mg): 9.6
Sodium (mg): 47
Protein (gm): 3.3
Carbohydrate (gm): 52.1

Exchanges
Milk: 0.0
Vegetable: 0.0
Fruit: 4.0
Bread: 0.0
Meat: 0.0
Fat: 1.0

1. Stir together strawberries, pineapple and juice, and condensed milk until smooth. Fold in whipped topping. Pour into 13 x 9-inch baking pan. Freeze until firm, 4 to 6 hours. Remove from freezer 10 minutes before serving; cut into squares.

STRAWBERRY RHUBARB SORBET

8 servings

3 cups sliced fresh, *or* frozen, rhubarb (about 1 pound)
1 cup sugar
1/3 cup water
1 pint strawberries, hulled
2/3 cup orange juice
1 tablespoon grated orange rind

Per Serving
Calories: 129
% Calories from fat: 2
Fat (gm): 0.3
Sat. fat (gm): 0
Cholesterol (mg): 0
Sodium (mg): 3
Protein (gm): 0.8
Carbohydrate (gm): 32.3
Exchanges
Milk: 0.0
Vegetable: 0.0
Fruit: 2.0
Bread: 0.0
Meat: 0.0
Fat: 0.0

1. Combine rhubarb, sugar, and water in large saucepan; heat to boiling. Reduce heat and simmer, uncovered, until rhubarb is very tender, 10 to 15 minutes; cool.
2. Process rhubarb mixture, strawberries, orange juice, and rind in food processor or blender until smooth.
3. Freeze mixture in ice cream maker according to manufacturer's directions. Or pour mixture into 9-inch square baking dish and freeze until slushy, about 2 hours; spoon into bowl and beat until fluffy. Return to pan and freeze until firm, 6 hours or overnight.

LIME CHIFFON ICE

6 servings

1 cup sugar
3 1/2 cups water, divided
1/2 cup light corn syrup
1/8 teaspoon salt
1 envelope unflavored gelatin
3/4 cup lime juice
1 teaspoon grated lime rind
1 tablespoon meringue powder

Per Serving
Calories: 221
% Calories from fat: 0
Fat (gm): 0.1
Sat. fat (gm): 0
Cholesterol (mg): 0
Sodium (mg): 97
Protein (gm): 1.1
Carbohydrate (gm): 57.7
Exchanges
Milk: 0.0
Vegetable: 0.0
Fruit: 3.5
Bread: 0.0
Meat: 0.0
Fat: 0.0

1. Heat sugar, 3 cups water, corn syrup, and salt to boiling in large saucepan, stirring to dissolve sugar; boil uncovered 5 minutes. Sprinkle gelatin over 1/4 cup water; let stand to soften 2 to 3 minutes. Stir gelatin into sugar syrup and stir until dissolved. Add lime juice and rind; cool. Freeze, uncovered, in shallow bowl or baking pan until slushy, about 2 hours

2. Beat meringue powder and remaining 1/4 cup water to stiff peaks. Remove lime mixture from freezer and beat until smooth; fold in meringue mixture. Freeze mixture in ice cream maker according to manufacturer's directions. Or return mixture to bowl and freeze until slushy, about 2 hours; remove from freezer and beat until fluffy. Freeze until firm, 6 hours or overnight.

WATERMELON STRAWBERRY ICE

6 servings

- 2 cups cubed, seeded watermelon
- 2 cups sliced strawberries
- 1/2 cup sugar
- 2 tablespoons lemon juice
- 1 teaspoon balsamic vinegar, optional

Per Serving
Calories: 98
% Calories from fat: 3
Fat (gm): 0.4
Sat. fat (gm): 0
Cholesterol (mg): 0
Sodium (mg): 2
Protein (gm): 0.7
Carbohydrate (gm): 24.4

Exchanges
Milk: 0.0
Vegetable: 0.0
Fruit: 1.5
Bread: 0.0
Meat: 0.0
Fat: 0.0

1. Puree all ingredients in food processor or blender until smooth. Freeze mixture in ice cream maker according to manufacturer's directions. Or pour into 8-inch square baking dish and freeze until slushy, about 2 hours; spoon into bowl and beat until fluffy. Return to pan and freeze until firm, 6 hours or overnight.

PINEAPPLE CHAMPAGNE ICE

8 servings

1 envelope unflavored gelatin
$2^1/_2$ cups unsweetened pineapple juice
$^1/_2$ cup dry champagne, *or* sparkling wine
$^1/_4$ teaspoon ground nutmeg
8 slices fresh pineapple ($^1/_2$ inch thick)
Mint sprigs, as garnish

Per Serving
Calories: 66
% Calories from fat: 2
Fat (gm): 0.1
Sat. fat (gm): 0
Cholesterol (mg): 0
Sodium (mg): 2
Protein (gm): 1.8
Carbohydrate (gm): 57.6
Exchanges
Milk: 0.0
Vegetable: 0.0
Fruit: 1.0
Bread: 0.0
Meat: 0.0
Fat: 0.0

1. Sprinkle gelatin over pineapple juice in medium saucepan; let stand 2 to 3 minutes. Cook over low heat, stirring constantly, until gelatin is dissolved. Cool to room temperature. Stir in champagne and nutmeg.

2. Freeze mixture in ice cream maker according to manufacturer's directions. Or pour mixture into 9-inch square baking dish and freeze until slushy, about 2 hours; spoon into bowl and beat until fluffy. Return to pan and freeze until firm, 6 hours or overnight.

3. To serve, place pineapple slices on dessert plates. Top each with a scoop of Pineapple Champagne Ice. Garnish with mint.

LEMON ICE

8 servings

2 cups water
1 cup sugar
1 cup fresh lemon juice
$^1/_2$ cup grated lemon rind

Per Serving
Calories: 101
% Calories from fat: 0.0
Fat (gm): 0.0
Sat. fat (gm): 0.0
Cholesterol (mg): 0.0
Sodium (mg): 1.3
Protein (gm): 0.2
Carbohydrate (gm): 27.6
Exchanges
Milk: 0.0
Vegetable: 0.0
Fruit: 0.0
Bread: 1.5
Meat: 0.0
Fat: 0.0

1. Combine water and sugar in medium saucepan. Heat to boiling over medium-high heat, stirring until sugar is dissolved. Reduce heat and simmer, uncovered, 5 minutes. Remove from heat; cool to room temperature. Stir in lemon juice and lemon rind.

2. Freeze mixture in ice cream maker according to manufacturer's directions. Or pour into 8-inch square baking dish and freeze until slushy, about 2 hours; spoon into bowl and beat until fluffy. Return to pan and freeze until firm, 6 hours or overnight.

RASPBERRY CHEESECAKE SHERBET

16 servings

- 1 can (12 ounces) frozen raspberry-orange juice concentrate, thawed
- 1 quart reduced-fat buttermilk
- $1^{1}/_{2}$ cups sugar

Per Serving
Calories: 131
% Calories from fat: 3
Fat (gm): 0.6
Sat. fat (gm): 0.3
Cholesterol (mg): 2.1
Sodium (mg): 65
Protein (gm): 2.5
Carbohydrate (gm): 29.8

Exchanges
Milk: 0.0
Vegetable: 0.0
Fruit: 0.0
Bread: 2.0
Meat: 0.0
Fat: 0.0

1. Mix all ingredients until sugar dissolves. Freeze in ice cream maker according to manufacturer's directions. Or pour into 8-inch square baking dish and freeze until slushy, about 2 hours; spoon into bowl and beat until fluffy. Return to pan, and freeze until firm, 6 hours or overnight.

GINGER ORANGE ICE CREAM

8 servings

- 2 cartons (16 ounces each) fat-free sour cream
- 1 carton (8 ounces) fat-free orange yogurt
- 3/4 cup lightly packed light brown sugar
- 3 tablespoons honey
- 3 tablespoons minced crystallized ginger
- 2 teaspoons lemon juice
- 1/8 teaspoon salt
- Finely grated rind of 1 orange
- Pinch nutmeg

Per Serving
Calories: 266
% Calories from fat: 0
Fat (gm): 0
Sat. fat (gm): 0
Cholesterol (mg): 0
Sodium (mg): 150
Protein (gm): 8.3
Carbohydrate (gm): 57.2

Exchanges
Milk: 0.0
Vegetable: 0.0
Fruit: 0.0
Bread: 3.5
Meat: 0.0
Fat: 0.0

1. Process all ingredients in blender or food processor until smooth.

2. Freeze mixture in ice cream maker according to manufacturer's directions. Or pour mixture into 9-inch square baking dish and freeze until slushy, about 2 hours; spoon into bowl and beat until fluffy. Return to pan and freeze until firm, 6 hours or overnight.

Variation: **Pumpkin Spice Ice Cream**—Make recipe as above, reducing sour cream to 1 carton, omitting ginger, and adding 3/4 cup canned pumpkin, 1/4 cup chopped walnuts, 2 tablespoons dark rum or 1 teaspoon rum extract, and 1 teaspoon pumpkin pie spice to mixture before freezing. Mix all ingredients in large bowl; freeze as above.

NINETEEN

Memorable Menus

The 10 menus in this chapter have been designed for busy people like you, to take the guesswork out of the meal planning and cooking. The menus are perfect for family dining, casual entertaining, and festive occasions too.

Recipes for some of the menu items are not given because these are side dishes, breads, or desserts you already know how to make, can prepare according to package directions, or may purchase ready-made. Feel free to substitute a favorite recipe in any menu, or to look through other chapters in this book for more ideas.

Nutrional analyses have been given for each recipe as well as for the entire menu. For menu items without recipes, nutritional analyses were based on a per person serving of one-half cup side dish, one bread item with 1 teaspoon of margarine or butter, and one cookie.

Spring Fling

Herbed Cucumber Soup
Chicken Cordon Bleu
Asparagus with Lemon-Wine Sauce
Parslied Rice
French Bread
Sugared Lemon Squares

DO-AHEAD TIPS

1-2 Days in Advance
Make Cucumber Soup; refrigerate.

Early in the Day
Trim asparagus. Assemble Chicken Cordon Bleu; refrigerate. Make Sugared Lemon Squares.

40 Minutes Before Serving
Cook Chicken Cordon Bleu.

25 Minutes Before Serving
Cook rice. Make Lemon-Wine Sauce for asparagus.

10 Minutes Before Serving
Cook asparagus; spoon Lemon-Wine Sauce over.

Spring Fling
Herbed Cucumber Soup
Chicken Cordon Bleu
Asparagus with Lemon-Wine Sauce
Parslied Rice (1/2 cup)
French Bread (1 slice with 1 teaspoon margarine)
Sugared Lemon Squares

Per 1 Serving of Entire Menu
Calories: 666
% Calories from fat: 20
Fat (gm): 15.9
Sat. fat (gm): 2.9
Cholesterol (mg): 82.2
Sodium (mg): 934
Protein (gm): 49.9
Carbohydrate (gm): 83.5

Exchanges
Milk: 0.0
Vegetable: 3.0
Fruit: 0.0
Bread: 5.0
Meat: 4.0
Fat: 0.0

HERBED CUCUMBER SOUP

6 servings (about $1^1/_3$ cups each)

Per Serving
Calories: 79
% Calories from fat: 5
Fat (gm): 45
Sat. fat (gm): 0.1
Cholesterol (mg): 0
Sodium (mg): 67
Protein (gm): 4.7
Carbohydrate (gm): 14.6
Exchanges
Milk: 0.0
Vegetable: 0.0
Fruit: 0.0
Bread: 1.0
Meat: 0.0
Fat: 0.0

Vegetable cooking spray
1/2 cup chopped onion
6 medium cucumbers, peeled, seeded, chopped (about 3 pounds)
3 tablespoons flour
4 cups reduced-sodium fat-free chicken broth
1 teaspoon dried mint, *or* dill weed
1/2 cup fat-free half-and-half
Salt and white pepper, to taste
Paprika for garnish
6 thin slices cucumber

1. Spray large saucepan with cooking spray; heat over medium heat until hot. Saute onion until tender, 3 to 5 minutes. Add cucumbers and cook over medium heat 5 minutes. Stir in flour and cook 1 to 2 minutes longer.

2. Add broth to saucepan; heat to boiling. Reduce heat and simmer, covered, 10 minutes. Process soup in food processor or blender until smooth; stir in mint and half-and-half, season to taste with salt and pepper. Cool; refrigerate until chilled, 3 to 4 hours.

3. Pour soup into bowls; sprinkle lightly with paprika and top each with a cucumber slice.

CHICKEN CORDON BLEU

6 servings

6 boneless, skinless chicken breast halves (4 ounces each)
4 ounces sliced fat-free Swiss cheese
3 ounces lean smoked ham
Flour
2 egg whites, beaten
1/3 cup dry unseasoned bread crumbs
Vegetable cooking spray

Per Serving
Calories: 210
% Calories from fat: 18
Fat (gm): 3.9
Sat. fat (gm): 1.1
Cholesterol (mg): 73.2
Sodium (mg): 540
Protein (gm): 34.6
Carbohydrate (gm): 6.3

Exchanges
Milk: 0.0
Vegetable: 0.0
Fruit: 0.0
Bread: 0.0
Meat: 4.0
Fat: 0.0

1. Pound chicken breasts with flat side of meat mallet until very thin and even in thickness. Layer cheese and ham on chicken, cutting to fit. Roll up chicken and secure with toothpicks.

2. Coat chicken rolls lightly with flour; dip in egg and coat in bread crumbs. Spray rolls generously with cooking spray and cook in skillet over medium heat until browned on all sides, 8 to 10 minutes.

3. Bake chicken, uncovered, in baking pan until cooked through, about 30 minutes.

ASPARAGUS WITH LEMON-WINE SAUCE

6 servings

Butter-flavored vegetable cooking spray
1/4 cup minced shallots, *or* green onions (white parts)
1/2 cup dry white wine, *or* low-sodium vegetable broth
1 1/2 cups fat-free half-and-half, *or* fat-free milk
1/4 cup all-purpose flour
1 teaspoon dried thyme leaves
1 teaspoon dried marjoram leaves
1 tablespoon lemon juice

Per Serving
Calories: 100
% Calories from fat: 3
Fat (gm): 0.4
Sat. fat (gm): 0.1
Cholesterol (mg): 0
Sodium (mg): 73
Protein (gm): 5.3
Carbohydrate (gm): 15.1

Exchanges
Milk: 0.0
Vegetable: 3.0
Fruit: 0.0
Bread: 0.0
Meat: 0.0
Fat: 0.0

Salt and white pepper, to taste
1½ pounds asparagus spears, cooked until crisp-tender, warm

1. Spray small saucepan with cooking spray; heat over medium heat until hot. Cook shallots over medium to medium-low heat until tender but not browned, 2 to 3 minutes. Add wine and heat to boiling; reduce heat and simmer, uncovered, until wine is evaporated, 3 to 4 minutes.

2. Mix half-and-half, flour, and herbs; stir into saucepan and heat to boiling. Boil, whisking constantly, until sauce is thickened, about 1 minute. Stir in lemon juice; season to taste with salt and pepper.

3. Arrange asparagus in serving dish; spoon sauce over.

SUGARED LEMON SQUARES

25 servings (1 per serving)

¾ cup all-purpose flour
2 tablespoons margarine, room temperature
2 tablespoons low-fat sour cream
1 cup plus 2 tablespoons granulated sugar, divided
1 egg
2 egg whites
1 tablespoon grated lemon rind
3 tablespoons lemon juice
½ teaspoon baking powder
¼ teaspoon salt
Powdered sugar, for garnish

Per Serving
Calories: 72
% Calories from fat: 28
Fat (gm): 2.3
Sat. fat (gm): 0.6
Cholesterol (mg): 9
Sodium (mg): 57
Protein (gm): 0.9
Carbohydrate (gm): 12.2
Exchanges
Milk: 0.0
Vegetable: 0.0
Fruit: 0.0
Bread: 1.0
Meat: 0.0
Fat: 0.0

1. Mix flour, margarine, sour cream, and 2 tablespoons granulated sugar in small bowl to form soft dough. Press dough into bottom and ¼-inch up sides of 8-inch-square baking pan. Bake at 350 degrees until light brown, about 20 minutes; cool on wire rack.

2. Mix remaining 1 cup granulated sugar and remaining ingredients, except powdered sugar, in small bowl; pour over baked pastry. Bake until no indentation remains when touched in the center, 20 to 25 minutes. Cool on wire rack, cut into squares. Sprinkle lightly with powdered sugar before serving.

Autumn Harvest Menu

Ripe Tomato and Leek Soup
Rosemary Roast Pork Tenderloin
Baked Corn Pudding
Brussels Sprouts
Rye or Whole-Grain Bread
Pumpkin-Ginger Cake with Warm Rum Sauce

DO-AHEAD TIPS

1-2 Days in Advance

Make soup; refrigerate. Make Pumpkin-Ginger Cake and Rum Sauce.

Early in the Day

Prepare pork tenderloin for roasting; refrigerate in baking pan. Clean Brussels sprouts.

1 Hour Before Serving

Make Corn Pudding.

30 Minutes Before Serving

Roast the pork tenderloin. Cook Brussels sprouts. Reheat soup.

At Dessert Time

Heat Rum Sauce for cake.

Autumn Harvest Menu
Ripe Tomato and Leek Soup
Rosemary Roast Pork Tenderloin
Baked Corn Pudding
Brussels Sprouts (1/2 cup)
Rye or Whole-Grain Bread (1 slice with 1 teaspoon margarine)
Pumpkin-Ginger Cake with Warm Rum Sauce

Per 1 Serving of Entire Menu
Calories: 845
% Calories from fat: 26
Fat (gm): 24.9
Sat. fat (gm): 5.7
Cholesterol (mg): 147
Sodium (mg): 1095
Protein (gm): 45.9
Carbohydrate (gm): 111

Exchanges
Milk: 0.0
Vegetable: 2.0
Fruit: 0.0
Bread: 6.0
Meat: 4.0
Fat: 3.0

RIPE TOMATO AND LEEK SOUP

4 servings (about 1 cup each)

- 1 cup sliced leek (about 6 ounces)
- 2 cloves garlic, minced
- 1/2 teaspoons margarine, *or* olive oil
- 3 large tomatoes (about 1 1/4 pounds)
- 2 cups reduced-sodium fat-free chicken broth
- 1/2 teaspoon dried basil leaves
- Salt and white pepper, to taste
- 4 tablespoons fat-free sour cream, *or* plain yogurt
- Basil sprigs for garnish

Per Serving
Calories: 83
% Calories from fat: 19
Fat (gm): 1.9
Sat. fat (gm): 0.3
Cholesterol (mg): 0
Sodium (mg): 76.2
Protein (gm): 3.6
Carbohydrate (gm): 14
Exchanges
Milk: 0.0
Vegetable: 0.0
Fruit: 0.0
Bread: 1.0
Meat: 0.0
Fat: 0.0

1. Saute leek and garlic in margarine in large saucepan until tender, about 8 minutes. Add tomatoes, broth, and basil to saucepan; heat to boiling. Reduce heat and simmer, covered, 10 minutes.

2. Process soup in food processor or blender container until smooth; season to taste with salt and white pepper. Heat and serve soup warm, or refrigerate and serve chilled.

3. Pour soup into bowls; garnish each with a tablespoon of sour cream and basil sprigs.

ROSEMARY ROAST PORK TENDERLOIN

4 servings

- 1 pork tenderloin (about 16 ounces)
- 1 clove garlic, cut into 8 to 10 slivers
- Vegetable cooking spray
- 1 teaspoon dried rosemary leaves, crushed
- Salt and pepper, to taste

Per Serving
Calories: 139
% Calories from fat: 28
Fat (gm): 4
Sat. fat (gm): 1.4
Cholesterol (mg): 66
Sodium (mg): 47
Protein (gm): 23.5
Carbohydrate (gm): 0.4
Exchanges
Milk: 0.0
Vegetable: 0.0
Fruit: 0.0
Bread: 0.0
Meat: 3.0
Fat: 0.0

1. Cut small slits in pork and insert garlic slivers. Place pork in small roasting pan and spray lightly with cooking spray. Rub surface of pork with rosemary leaves. Sprinkle lightly with salt and pepper.

2. Roast pork at 425 degrees until meat thermometer inserted in center registers 160 degrees (slightly pink) or 170 degrees (well done), 20 to 30 minutes.

Note: Pork can be eaten slightly pink. It is safe to eat after the internal temperature has reached 140 degrees.

BAKED CORN PUDDING

4 servings

- Butter-flavored vegetable cooking spray
- 2 tablespoons plain, unseasoned bread crumbs
- 2 cups frozen, thawed whole kernel corn
- 1/2 cup fat-free half-and-half
- 1/2 cup fat-free sour cream
- 1 tablespoon margarine, melted
- 1 egg
- 2 egg whites
- 1/2 teaspoon baking powder
- 1/2 teaspoon dried savory leaves
- 1/4 teaspoon dried thyme leaves
- 1/2 teaspoon salt
- 1/8 teaspoon cayenne pepper
- 1/4 teaspoon black pepper

Per Serving
Calories: 172
% Calories from fat: 22
Fat (gm): 43
Sat. fat (gm): 1
Cholesterol (mg): 53.3
Sodium (mg): 466
Protein (gm): 9.2
Carbohydrate (gm): 25.9

Exchanges
Milk: 0.0
Vegetable: 0.0
Fruit: 0.0
Bread: 1.5
Meat: 1.0
Fat: 0.0

1. Spray 1-quart soufflé dish lightly with cooking spray; coat with bread crumbs.

2. Process remaining ingredients in blender or food processor until corn is coarsely chopped. Pour into soufflé dish. Bake at 350 degrees until puffed and set in the center, 45 to 50 minutes. Serve immediately.

PUMPKIN-GINGER CAKE WITH WARM RUM SAUCE

8 servings

- 1/2 cup canned pumpkin
- 1/2 cup packed light brown sugar
- 1/4 cup margarine, softened
- 1/4 cup light molasses
- 1 egg
- 1 1/2 cups all-purpose flour
- 1/2 teaspoon baking powder
- 1/2 teaspoon baking soda
- 1/2 teaspoon ground allspice
- 1/2 teaspoon ground cloves
- 1/2 teaspoon ground ginger
- Warm Rum Sauce (recipe follows)

Per Serving
Calories: 304
% Calories from fat: 28
Fat (gm): 9.5
Sat. fat (gm): 2
Cholesterol (mg): 27.3
Sodium (mg): 235
Protein (gm): 4.8
Carbohydrate (gm): 48.6

Exchanges
Milk: 0.0
Vegetable: 0.0
Fruit: 0.0
Bread: 3.0
Meat: 0.0
Fat: 2.0

1. Combine pumpkin, brown sugar, margarine, molasses, and egg in large mixer bowl; beat at medium speed until light and fluffy.

2. Combine flour, baking powder, baking soda, allspice, cloves, and ginger in medium bowl; add to pumpkin mixture. Blend at low speed until moistened. Pour batter into greased and floured 8-inch square baking pan.

3. Bake cake at 350 degrees until toothpick inserted in center comes out clean, 30 to 40 minutes. Cool in pan on wire rack 10 minutes; remove from pan. Cool completely on wire rack. Serve with Warm Rum Sauce.

Warm Rum Sauce

makes 1 1/2 cups

- 1/4 cup sugar
- 1 tablespoon cornstarch
- 1 1/4 cups fat-free milk
- 2 tablespoons rum, *or* 1/2 teaspoon rum extract
- 2 tablespoons margarine
- 1/2 teaspoon vanilla
- 1/8 teaspoon ground nutmeg

1. Mix sugar and cornstarch in small saucepan; stir in milk and rum. Cook over medium heat until mixture boils and thickens, stirring constantly.

2. Remove from heat; stir in margarine, vanilla, and nutmeg. Serve warm.

Friday Night Supper

Tuna Patties with Creamed Pea Sauce
Harvard Beets
Carrot-Raisin Salad
Warm Buns or Rolls
Rhubarb Crunch

DO-AHEAD TIPS

1 Day in Advance
Make Tuna Patties; do not cook. Refrigerate. Make Rhubarb Crunch.

Early in the Day
Cook and slice beets. Make Carrot-Raisin Salad.

20 Minutes Before Serving
Cook Tuna Patties and make Creamed Pea Sauce. Complete Harvard Beets.

Friday Night Super
Tuna Patties with Creamed Pea Sauce
Harvard Beets
Carrot-Raisin Salad
Warm Buns or Rolls (1 piece with 1 teaspoon margarine)
Rhubarb Crunch

Per 1 Serving of Entire Menu
Calories: 1052
% Calories from fat: 26
Fat (gm): 30.7
Sat. fat (gm): 5.6
Cholesterol (mg): 79.5
Sodium (mg): 1772
Protein (gm): 41.2
Carbohydrate (gm): 158

Exchanges
Milk: 0.0
Vegetable: 3.0
Fruit: 1.0
Bread: 8.0
Meat: 4.0
Fat: 3.0

TUNA PATTIES WITH CREAMED PEA SAUCE

4 servings

2 cans (6 1/8 ounces each) light tuna packed in spring water, drained
3/4 cup dry unseasoned bread crumbs, divided
1/4 cup finely chopped onion
1/4 cup finely chopped celery
2 tablespoons chopped red, *or* green, bell pepper
2-3 tablespoons fat-free mayonnaise
1-2 teaspoons Worcestershire sauce
Salt and cayenne pepper, to taste
1 egg
Vegetable cooking spray
Creamed Pea Sauce (recipe follows)

Per Serving
Calories: 325
% Calories from fat: 25
Fat (gm): 8.9
Sat. fat (gm): 2
Cholesterol (mg): 79.2
Sodium (mg): 726
Protein (gm): 30
Carbohydrate (gm): 28.6
Exchanges
Milk: 0.5
Vegetable: 1.0
Fruit: 0.0
Bread: 1.0
Meat: 3.5
Fat: 0.0

1. Combine tuna, 1/2 cup bread crumbs, onion, celery, bell pepper, mayonnaise, and Worcestershire sauce in medium bowl; season to taste with salt and cayenne pepper. Add egg, mixing until ingredients are well blended. Shape into 4 patties, generous 1/2 inch thick.

2. Spray large skillet with cooking spray; heat over medium heat until hot. Coat patties with remaining 1/4 cup bread crumbs; spray patties lightly with cooking spray. Cook over medium-low heat until browned, about 5 minutes on each side. Serve with Creamed Pea Sauce.

Creamed Pea Sauce

makes 1 cup

2 tablespoons margarine
2 tablespoons flour
1/2 cup fat-free milk
1/2 cup fat-free half-and-half, *or* fat-free milk
1/2 cup frozen, thawed peas
Salt and pepper, to taste

1. Melt margarine in small sauce an; stir in flour and cook, stirring constantly, over medium-low heat 1 minute. Whisk in milk and half-and-half; heat to boiling. Boil, whisking constantly, until thickened, about 1 minute.

2. Stir in peas; cook over low heat 2 to 3 minutes. Season to taste with salt and pepper. Serve hot.

HARVARD BEETS

4 servings

3 tablespoons sugar
1 1/2 tablespoons cornstarch
3/4 cup water
3-4 tablespoons cider vinegar
2 teaspoons margarine
Salt and white pepper, to taste
1 pound beets, cooked, sliced *or* julienned, warm

Per Serving
Calories: 94
% Calories from fat: 18
Fat (gm): 1.9
Sat. fat (gm): 0.4
Cholesterol (mg): 0
Sodium (mg): 70
Protein (gm): 1.1
Carbohydrate (gm): 19.3
Exchanges
Milk: 0.0
Vegetable: 2.0
Fruit: 0.0
Bread: 0.5
Meat: 0.0
Fat: 0.0

1. Mix sugar and cornstarch in small saucepan; whisk in water and vinegar. Heat to boiling, whisking constantly; boil, whisking constantly, until thickened, about 1 minute. Add margarine, whisking until melted. Season to taste with salt and white pepper.

2. Pour sauce over beets in serving bowl and toss gently.

CARROT-RAISIN SALAD

4 servings (about 1/2 cup each).

2 1/2 cups shredded carrots (3-4 large)
3/4 cup chopped celery
1/3 cup raisins
1/3 cup coarsely chopped walnuts
3/4 cup fat-free mayonnaise
1/2 teaspoon Dijon-style mustard
1-2 teaspoons sugar
1/8 teaspoon salt
Lettuce leaves

Per Serving
Calories: 173
% Calories from fat: 30
Fat (gm): 6.1
Sat. fat (gm): 0.5
Cholesterol (mg): 0
Sodium (mg): 690
Protein (gm): 3.9
Carbohydrate (gm): 28.8
Exchanges
Milk: 0.0
Vegetable: 3.0
Fruit: 0.75
Bread: 0.0
Meat: 0.0
Fat: 1.5

1. Combine carrots, celery, raisins, and walnuts in medium bowl; add remaining ingredients, except lettuce, stirring until blended. Serve on lettuce-lined salad plates.

RHUBARB CRUNCH

8 servings

- 1/2 cup all-purpose flour
- 1/2 cup whole wheat flour
- 3/4 cup packed light brown sugar
- 1/2 cup quick-cooking oats
- 1/4 cup bran, *or* quick-cooking oats
- 1 teaspoon ground cinnamon
- 5 tablespoons margarine, melted
- 1 pound fresh *or* frozen, thawed, rhubarb, cut into 1-inch pieces (8 cups)
- 1 cup granulated sugar
- 2 tablespoons cornstarch
- 1 cup water
- 1 teaspoon vanilla

Per Serving
Calories: 341
% Calories from fat: 10
Fat (gm): 7.9
Sat. fat (gm): 1.5
Cholesterol (mg): 0
Sodium (mg): 94
Protein (gm): 3.8
Carbohydrate (gm): 66.9

Exchanges
Milk: 0.0
Vegetable: 0.0
Fruit: 1.0
Bread: 3.0
Meat: 0.0
Fat: 1.5

1. Combine flours, brown sugar, oats, bran, and cinnamon in large bowl; stir in margarine to make a crumbly mixture. Press half the mixture evenly on bottom of 8-inch baking pan. Arrange rhubarb evenly over crust.

2. Combine granulated sugar and cornstarch in medium saucepan; add water and heat to boiling. Boil, stirring constantly, until thickened, about 1 minute. Stir in vanilla. Pour mixture over rhubarb.

3. Sprinkle remaining crumb mixture over rhubarb. Bake, uncovered, until bubbly around the edges, 45 to 55 minutes.

Country Chicken Dinner

Crisp Oven-Fried Chicken with Cream Gravy
Real Mashed Potatoes
Tiny Peas and Onions
Biscuits
Double-Crust Apple Pie

DO-AHEAD TIPS

1–2 Days in Advance
Make pie pastry and refrigerate.

Early in the Day
Peel potatoes; store in pan of water. Bake pie.

1 Hour Before Serving
Make Oven-Fried Chicken with Cream Gravy. Make Real Mashed Potatoes.

15 Minutes Before Serving
Make Tiny Peas and Onions. Bake biscuits.

Country Chicken Dinner
Crisp Oven-Fried Chicken with Cream Gravy
Real Mashed Potatoes
Tiny Peas and Onions
Biscuits (1 with 1 teaspoon margarine)
Double-Crust Apple Pie

Per 1 Serving of Entire Menu
Calories: 1041
% Calories from fat: 25
Fat (gm): 29.4
Sat. fat (gm): 6.7
Cholesterol (mg): 71.1
Sodium (mg): 1151
Protein (gm): 46.6
Carbohydrate (gm): 147.8

Exchanges
Milk: 0.0
Vegetable: 0.0
Fruit: 2.0
Bread: 8.0
Meat: 4.0
Fat: 3.0

CRISP OVEN-FRIED CHICKEN WITH CREAM GRAVY

6 servings

- 3 egg whites, *or* 1/2 cup real egg substitute
- 1/4 cup fat-free milk
- 6 skinless chicken breast halves (about 4 ounces each)
- 1/4 cup all-purpose flour
- 1 1/4 cups corn flakes, finely crushed
- 1/2 cup dry unseasoned bread crumbs
- Butter-flavored vegetable cooking spray
- Salt and pepper, to taste
- Cream Gravy (recipe follows)

Per Serving
Calories: 318
% Calories from fat: 21
Fat (gm): 7.4
Sat. fat (gm): 1.8
Cholesterol (mg): 70.6
Sodium (mg): 459
Protein (gm): 33.5
Carbohydrate (gm): 26.7

Exchanges
Milk: 0.0
Vegetable: 0.0
Fruit: 0.0
Bread: 1.0
Meat: 4.0
Fat: 0.0

1. Beat egg whites and milk until blended in shallow bowl. Coat chicken breasts with flour; dip into egg mixture and coat generously with combined corn flakes and bread crumbs.

2. Spray baking pan with cooking spray. Place chicken, meat sides up, in baking pan; spray generously with cooking spray and sprinkle lightly with salt and pepper. Bake at 350 degrees until chicken is browned and juices run clear, 45 to 60 minutes. Serve chicken with Cream Gravy.

Note: If desired, 1/2 teaspoon each dried rosemary and sage leaves and 1/4 teaspoon dried thyme leaves can be added to the corn flake mixture.

Cream Gravy

makes about 2 cups

- 2 tablespoons margarine
- 1/4 cup all-purpose flour
- 2 cups fat-free milk, *or* fat-free half-and-half
- 1-2 teaspoons chicken bouillon crystals
- 1/4 cup fat-free sour cream
- Salt and pepper, to taste

1. Melt margarine in medium saucepan; stir in flour and cook over medium-low heat 1 minute, stirring constantly. Whisk in milk and bouillon crystals; heat to boiling. Boil, stirring constantly, until thickened, about 1 minute.

2. Stir in sour cream and cook 1–2 minutes; season to taste with salt and pepper.

REAL MASHED POTATOES

6 servings (about 3/4 cup each)

- 2 pounds Idaho potatoes, peeled, quartered, cooked
- 1/2 cup fat-free sour cream
- 1/4 cup fat-free milk, hot
- 2 tablespoons margarine
- Salt and pepper, to taste

Per Serving
Calories: 165
% Calories from fat: 21
Fat (gm): 3.9
Sat. fat (gm): 0.8
Cholesterol (mg): 0.2
Sodium (mg): 70
Protein (gm): 4.1
Carbohydrate (gm): 29.6

Exchanges
Milk: 0.0
Vegetable: 0.0
Fruit: 0.0
Bread: 2.0
Meat: 0.0
Fat: 0.5

1. Mash potatoes, or beat until smooth in medium bowl, adding sour cream, milk, and margarine. Season to taste with salt and pepper.

Variations: **Garlic Mashed Potatoes**—Cook 10 peeled cloves of garlic with the potatoes. Follow recipe above, mashing garlic with potatoes.

Horseradish Mashed Potatoes—Make Real or Garlic Mashed Potatoes, beating in 2 teaspoons horseradish.

Potato Pancakes—Make any of the mashed potato recipes above; refrigerate until chilled. Mix in 2 egg whites *or* 1/4 cup real egg substitute, 4 chopped green onions and tops, and 1/4 cup fat-free grated Parmesan cheese (optional). Form mixture into 8 patties, using about 1/2 cup mixture for each. Coat patties in flour, dip in beaten egg white, and coat with plain dry bread crumbs. Cook over medium-high heat in lightly greased large skillet until browned, 3 to 5 minutes on each side.

TINY PEAS AND ONIONS

6 servings

1 package (10 ounces) frozen tiny peas
1/2 package (16-ounce size) frozen small whole onions
1/4 cup water
2-3 teaspoons margarine
1/4-1/2 teaspoon dried mint leaves
1/4-1/2 teaspoon dried dill weed
Salt and pepper, to taste

Per Serving
Calories: 63
% Calories from fat: 20
Fat (gm): 1.4
Sat. fat (gm): 0.3
Cholesterol (mg): 0
Sodium (mg): 57
Protein (gm): 2.5
Carbohydrate (gm): 10.4
Exchanges
Milk: 0.0
Vegetable: 0.0
Fruit: 0.0
Bread: 1.0
Meat: 0.0
Fat: 0.0

1. Heat peas, onions, and water to boiling in medium saucepan; reduce heat and simmer until vegetables are tender, 8 to 10 minutes. Drain. Add margarine and herbs to vegetables, stirring until margarine is melted. Season to taste with salt and pepper.

DOUBLE-CRUST APPLE PIE

10 servings

Basic Pie Crust, doubled to make 2 crusts (see p. 574)
8 cups peeled cored, sliced, tart baking apples
1 cup sugar
4-5 tablespoons all-purpose flour
3/4 teaspoon ground cinnamon
1/4 teaspoon ground nutmeg
1/8 teaspoon ground cloves
1/8 teaspoon salt
2 tablespoons margarine, cut into pieces, optional

Per Serving
Calories: 297
% Calories from fat: 19
Fat (gm): 6.3
Sat. fat (gm): 1.2
Cholesterol (mg): 0
Sodium (mg): 200
Protein (gm): 3.1
Carbohydrate (gm): 58.9
Exchanges
Milk: 0.0
Vegetable: 0.0
Fruit: 1.0
Bread: 3.5
Meat: 0.0
Fat: 1.5

1. Roll 2/3 of the pastry on floured surface into a circle 2 inches larger than inverted 9-inch pie pan; ease pastry into pan.

2. Toss apples with combined sugar, flour, spices, and salt in large bowl. Arrange apples in pastry and dot with margarine, if desired.

3. Roll remaining pastry to fit top of pie and place over apples. Trim edges of pastry to within 1/2 inch of pan; fold top pastry over bottom pastry and flute. Cut vents in top crust.

4. Bake pie at 425 degrees until apples are fork-tender and pastry browned, 40 to 50 minutes, covering pastry with aluminum foil if becoming too brown. Cool 10 to 15 minutes before cutting.

Family Favorites

Creamed Corn Soup
Salisbury Steaks with Mushroom Gravy
Twice-Baked Potatoes with Cheese
Steamed Green Beans
Multigrain Bread
Flourless Chocolate Cake

DO AHEAD TIPS

Several Days in Advance
Make Chocolate Cake; do not frost. Freeze.

1 Day in Advance
Thaw cake. Make Creamed Corn Soup; refrigerate. Assemble Twice-Baked Potatoes; refrigerate.

Early in the Day
Make Salisbury Steaks but do not cook; refrigerate. Clean green beans. Frost cake.

30 Minutes Before Serving
Bake Twice-Baked Potatoes. Cook Salisbury Steaks; make gravy. Cook green beans. Reheat soup.

Family Favorites
Creamed Corn Soup
Salisbury Steaks with Mushroom Gravy
Twice-Baked Potatoes with Cheese
Steamed Green Beans
Multigrain Bread
Flourless Chocolate Cake

Per 1 Serving of Entire Menu
Calories: 961
% Calories from fat: 21
Fat (gm): 22.6
Sat. fat (gm): 8.1
Cholesterol (mg): 103.4
Sodium (mg): 1248
Protein (gm): 52.4
Carbohydrate (gm): 148.7

Exchanges
Milk: 0.0
Vegetable: 2.0
Fruit: 0.0
Bread: 8.0
Meat: 5.0
Fat: 2.0

CREAMED CORN SOUP

4 servings (about $1^1/_2$ cups each)

Vegetable cooking spray
1/2 cup chopped onion
1 medium Idaho potato, peeled, cubed
2 cloves garlic, minced
1 can (15 1/2 ounces) whole kernel corn, drained
3 tablespoons all-purpose flour
1/2 teaspoon ground coriander
1/8 teaspoon cayenne pepper
3 1/2 cups vegetable, *or* chicken, broth
1 cup fat-free milk
2 medium tomatoes, chopped
Salt and pepper, to taste
Paprika for garnish

Per Serving
Calories: 144
% Calories from fat: 6
Fat (gm): 1
Sat. fat (gm): 0.2
Cholesterol (mg): 0.7
Sodium (mg): 313
Protein (gm): 5.2
Carbohydrate (gm): 31.2
Exchanges
Milk: 0.0
Vegetable: 0.0
Fruit: 0.0
Bread: 2.0
Meat: 0.0
Fat: 0.0

1. Spray a large saucepan with cooking spray; heat over medium heat until hot. Saute onion, potato, and garlic until onion is tender, about 5 minutes. Stir in corn, flour, coriander, and cayenne pepper; cook 1 to 2 minutes, stirring frequently. Stir in broth and heat to boiling; reduce heat and simmer, covered, until potato is tender, about 10 minutes.

2. Process mixture in food processor or blender until almost smooth; return to saucepan. Stir in milk and tomatoes; heat just to boiling. Reduce heat and simmer, uncovered, 5 minutes. Season to taste with salt and pepper. Serve soup in bowls; sprinkle with paprika.

SALISBURY STEAKS WITH MUSHROOM GRAVY

4 servings

1 pound ground beef eye of round steak, *or* 95% lean ground beef
2-4 tablespoons finely chopped onion
3 tablespoons water
1/2 teaspoon salt
1/4 teaspoon pepper
Vegetable cooking spray
Mushroom Gravy (recipe follows)

Per Serving
Calories: 184
% Calories from fat: 24
Fat (gm): 4.6
Sat. fat (gm): 1.7
Cholesterol (mg): 64
Sodium (mg): 341
Protein (gm): 28.7
Carbohydrate (gm): 5.2
Exchanges
Milk: 0.0
Vegetable: 0.0
Fruit: 0.0
Bread: 0.0
Meat: 3.0
Fat: 0.0

1. Mix ground beef, onion, water, salt, and pepper in medium bowl just until blended. Shape mixture into 4, 1-inch-thick oval patties.

2. Spray large skillet with cooking spray; heat over medium heat until hot. Cook patties until well done, 5 to 6 minutes per side. Serve with Mushroom Gravy.

Mushroom Gravy

makes about 1 1/4 cups

1 cup sliced mushrooms
1/4 cup finely chopped onion
1 1/2 tablespoons margarine
2 tablespoons flour
1 cup low-sodium beef broth
Salt and pepper, to taste

1. Saute mushrooms and onion in margarine in medium skillet until tender. Stir in flour; cook 1 to 2 minutes longer.

2. Add beef broth and heat to boiling; boil, stirring constantly, until thickened. Season to taste with salt and pepper.

TWICE-BAKED POTATOES WITH CHEESE

4 servings

2 large Idaho potatoes (8 ounces each)
1/4 cup fat-free sour cream
1/4 cup fat-free milk
3/4 cup (3 ounces) shredded low-fat sharp, *or* mild, Cheddar cheese, divided
Salt and pepper, to taste
Paprika for garnish

Per Serving
Calories: 177
% Calories from fat: 16
Fat (gm): 3.2
Sat. fat (gm): 1.6
Cholesterol (mg): 11.6
Sodium (mg): 314
Protein (gm): 8.4
Carbohydrate (gm): 29.2

Exchanges
Milk: 0.0
Vegetable: 0.0
Fruit: 0.0
Bread: 2.0
Meat: 0.5
Fat: 0.0

1. Pierce potatoes with a fork and bake at 400 degrees until tender, about 1 hour. Cut into halves; let cool enough to handle. Scoop out inside of potatoes, being careful to leave shells intact. Mash warm potatoes, or beat until smooth, in medium bowl, adding sour cream, milk, and 1/2 cup of cheese. Season to taste with salt and pepper.

2. Spoon potato mixture into potato shells; sprinkle with remaining 1/4 cup cheese and paprika. Bake at 400 degrees until hot through, 15 to 20 minutes.

FLOURLESS CHOCOLATE CAKE

8 servings

1/2 cup Dutch process cocoa
3/4 cup packed light brown sugar
3 tablespoons flour
2 teaspoons instant espresso coffee crystals
1/8 teaspoon salt
Pinch pepper
3/4 cup fat-free milk
1 teaspoon vanilla
2 ounces unsweetened, *or* bittersweet, chocolate, chopped

Per Serving
Calories: 335
% Calories from fat: 22
Fat (gm): 8.9
Sat. fat (gm): 3.6
Cholesterol (mg): 27.1
Sodium (mg): 107
Protein (gm): 6.3
Carbohydrate (gm): 66.1

Exchanges
Milk: 0.0
Vegetable: 0.0
Fruit: 0.0
Bread: 4.0
Meat: 0.0
Fat: 1.0

- 2 ounces semisweet chocolate, chopped
- 1 egg
- 3 egg whites
- 1/8 teaspoon cream of tartar
- 1/3 cup granulated sugar
- Rich Chocolate Frosting (recipe follows)

1. Combine cocoa, brown sugar, flour, coffee crystals, salt, and pepper in medium saucepan; gradually stir in milk and vanilla to make smooth mixture. Heat over medium heat, stirring frequently, until mixture is hot and sugar dissolved (do not boil).

2. Remove saucepan from heat; add chocolate, stirring until melted. Whisk about 1/2 cup chocolate mixture into egg; whisk egg mixture back into saucepan. Cool to room temperature.

3. Beat egg whites until foam in medium bowl; add cream of tartar and beat to soft peaks. Continue beating, adding sugar gradually, until stiff but not dry peaks form. Stir about 1/4 of the egg whites into cooled chocolate mixture; fold chocolate mixture into remaining egg whites.

4. Lightly grease bottom and sides of 9-inch cake pan; line pan with parchment paper. Pour batter into cake pan and place in large roasting pan on center oven rack; add 1 inch of hot water to roasting pan.

5. Bake cake at 350 degrees until just firm when lightly touched, 25 to 30 minutes (do not test with tooth pick as cake will still be soft in the center). Cool completely on wire rack; refrigerate, covered, 8 hours or overnight.

6. Loosen side of cake from pan with sharp knife. Remove from pan and place on serving plate. Frost with Rich Chocolate Frosting.

Rich Chocolate Frosting

makes about 3/4 cup

1-2 tablespoons margarine, softened
1 1/2 cups powdered sugar
1/4 cup Dutch process cocoa
1/2 teaspoon vanilla
3-4 tablespoons fat-free milk

1. Mix margarine, powdered sugar, cocoa, and vanilla with enough milk to make spreadable consistency.

Southwest Sojourn

Quesadillas
Black and White Bean Chili
Tossed Salad
Green Chili Cornbread
Pineapple Flan

DO AHEAD TIPS

Several Days in Advance
Make Chili.

1 Day in Advance
Make Flan and refrigerate; do not unmold. Thaw chili.

Early in the Day
Wash greens for salad. Make Quesadillas but do not cook; refrigerate. Make Green Chili Cornbread. Unmold Flan; refrigerate.

30 Minutes Before Serving
Heat Chili. Reheat cornbread. Make salad. Cook Quesadillas.

Southwest Sojourn
Quesadillas
Black and White Bean Chili
Tossed Salad (1 cup with 2 tablespoons fat-free Ranch dressing)
Green Chili Cornbread
Pineapple Flan

Per 1 Serving of Entire Menu
Calories: 979
% Calories from fat: 21
Fat (gm): 23.8
Sat. fat (gm): 7.3
Cholesterol (mg): 156.7
Sodium (mg): 2800
Protein (gm): 51.5
Carbohydrate (gm): 149.9

Exchanges
Milk: 0.0
Vegetable: 1.0
Fruit: 1.0
Bread: 8.0
Meat: 4.0
Fat: 2.0

QUESADILLAS

8 servings

Vegetable cooking spray
2 small poblano chilies, *or* green bell peppers, sliced
1 large onion, finely chopped
1½ teaspoons ground cumin
3 tablespoons finely chopped cilantro
1½ cups (6 ounces) shredded low-fat Cheddar cheese
8 flour tortillas
1 cup medium, *or* hot, salsa
8 tablespoons fat-free sour cream

Per Serving
Calories: 200
% Calories from fat: 25
Fat (gm): 5.7
Sat. fat (gm): 1.9
Cholesterol (mg): 11.4
Sodium (mg): 710
Protein (gm): 11
Carbohydrate (gm): 27
Exchanges
Milk: 0.0
Vegetable: 0.0
Fruit: 0.0
Bread: 2.5
Meat: 1.0
Fat: 1.0

1. Spray large skillet with cooking spray heat over medium heat until hot. Saute poblano chilies, onion, and cumin until vegetables are tender, 3 to 5 minutes; stir in cilantro.

2. Sprinkle cheese on half of each tortilla; spoon vegetable mixture over. Fold tortillas in half.

3. Spray large skillet with cooking spray; heat over medium heat until hot. Cook quesadillas over medium to medium-high heat until browned on the bottoms, 2 to 3 minutes. Spray tops of quesadillas with cooking spray; turn and cook until browned on the other side. Cut into wedges and serve warm with salsa and sour cream.

BLACK AND WHITE BEAN CHILI

8 servings (about $1\frac{1}{4}$ cups each)

- 1 pound lean ground beef
- Garlic-flavored vegetable cooking spray
- 2 cups chopped onions
- 1 cup chopped green bell pepper
- 1-2 medium jalapeño chilies, finely chopped
- 4 teaspoons minced garlic
- 1/2 cup sliced sun-dried tomatoes (not in oil)
- 4-6 tablespoons chili powder
- 1 tablespoon ground cumin
- 2 teaspoons dried oregano leaves
- 2 bay leaves
- 4 cans (16 ounces each) low-sodium whole tomatoes, undrained, coarsely chopped
- 2 cans ($15\frac{1}{2}$ ounces each) Great Northern beans, rinsed, drained
- 2 cans (15 ounces each) black beans, rinsed, drained
- Salt and pepper, to taste
- 1/2 cup finely chopped cilantro

Per Serving
Calories: 331
% Calories from fat: 21
Fat (gm): 8.7
Sat. fat (gm): 2.9
Cholesterol (mg): 35.2
Sodium (mg): 1004
Protein (gm): 27
Carbohydrate (gm): 44.9

Exchanges
Milk: 0.0
Vegetable: 1.0
Fruit: 0.0
Bread: 2.0
Meat: 3.0
Fat: 0.0

1. Brown ground beef in large saucepan; remove from pan and drain.

2. Spray large saucepan with cooking spray; heat over medium heat until hot. Saute onions, bell pepper, jalapeño chilies, and garlic until vegetables are tender, 8 to 10 minutes. Stir in sun-dried tomatoes and herbs; cook 1 to 2 minutes longer.

3. Stir in ground beef, tomatoes, and beans. Heat to boiling; reduce heat and simmer, covered, 30 minutes. Discard bay leaf; season to taste with salt and pepper. Stir in cilantro.

GREEN CHILI CORNBREAD

8 servings

Vegetable cooking spray
1/4 cup chopped red bell pepper
2 cloves garlic, minced
1/2 teaspoon cumin seeds, crushed
1 1/4 cups yellow cornmeal
1/4 cup all-purpose flour
2 teaspoons baking powder
1/2 teaspoon baking soda
1 teaspoon sugar
1/2 teaspoon salt
1 1/4 cups buttermilk
1/2 cup canned cream-style corn
1 egg
2 egg whites
3 1/2 tablespoons margarine, melted
1 can (4 ounces) chopped hot, *or* mild, green chilies, well drained

Per Serving
Calories: 207
% Calories from fat: 29
Fat (gm): 6.9
Sat. fat (gm): 1.5
Cholesterol (mg): 28
Sodium (mg): 632
Protein (gm): 6.3
Carbohydrate (gm): 31

Exchanges
Milk: 0.0
Vegetable: 0.0
Fruit: 0.0
Bread: 2.3
Meat: 0.0
Fat: 1.1

1. Spray small skillet with cooking spray; heat over medium heat until hot. Saute bell pepper, garlic, and cumin seeds until pepper is tender, 2 to 3 minutes.

2. Combine cornmeal, flour, baking powder, baking soda, sugar, and salt in large bowl. Add buttermilk, bell pepper mixture, and remaining ingredients; mix until smooth. Spread batter in greased 8-inch square baking pan.

3. Bake at 425 degrees until cornbread is golden, about 30 minutes. Cool in pan on wire rack.

PINEAPPLE FLAN

8 servings (about 2/3 cup each)

- 2/3 cup sugar divided
- 3 cups unsweetened pineapple juice
- 1 cup 2% reduced-fat milk
- 3 eggs
- 4 egg whites, *or* 1/2 cup real egg substitute
- Mint leaves, for garnish

Per Serving
Calories: 169
% Calories from fat: 13
Fat (gm): 2.5
Sat. fat (gm): 1
Cholesterol (mg): 82.1
Sodium (mg): 68
Protein (gm): 5.5
Carbohydrate (gm): 31.6
Exchanges
Milk: 0.0
Vegetable: 0.0
Fruit: 1.0
Bread: 1.0
Meat: 0.5
Fat: 0.0

1. Heat 1/3 cup sugar in small skillet over medium-high heat until sugar melts and turns golden, stirring occasionally (watch carefully, as the sugar can burn easily!). Quickly pour syrup into bottom of 2-quart soufflé dish or casserole and tilt dish to coat bottom completely. Cool.

2. Heat pineapple juice, milk, and remaining 1/3 cup sugar until steaming, and just beginning to bubble at the edges. Beat eggs and egg whites in medium bowl; whisk in hot juice mixture. Pour mixture through strainer into prepared soufflé dish.

3. Place dish in roasting pan on middle oven rack. Cover dish with aluminum foil or lid. Pour 2 inches hot water into roasting pan. Bake at 350 degrees until custard is just set in the center and a sharp knife inserted halfway between center and edge comes out clean, about 60 minutes. Remove dish from roasting pan; cool on wire rack. Refrigerate 8 hours or overnight.

4. To unmold, loosen edge of custard with sharp knife. Place rimmed serving plate over soufflé dish and invert. Garnish with mint leaves.

Weekend Dinner

Mock Chicken Legs
Warm Rice
Sauteed Squash with Snow Peas
Herbed Tomato Halves
French Bread
Praline Sundaes

DO AHEAD TIPS

Early in the Day
Trim and cut meats for Mock Chicken Legs. Assemble on skewers; refrigerate. Slice squash; clean snow peas. Make Herbed Tomato Halves but do not bake; refrigerate.

45 Minutes Before Serving
Cook Mock Chicken Legs. Cook Squash with Snow Peas. Bake Herbed Tomato Halves. Cook rice.

At Dessert Time
Make Praline Sundaes.

Weekend Dinner
Mock Chicken Legs
Warm Rice (1/2 cup)
Sauteed Squash with Snow Peas
Herbed Tomato Halves
French Bread (1 slice with 1 teaspoon margarine)
Praline Sundaes

Per 1 Serving of Entire Menu
Calories: 930
% Calories from fat: 19
Fat (gm): 20
Sat. fat (gm): 5.6
Cholesterol (mg): 111.6
Sodium (mg): 471
Protein (gm): 47.6
Carbohydrate (gm): 137.7

Exchanges
Milk: 0.0
Vegetable: 3.0
Fruit: 0.0
Bread: 8.0
Meat: 4.0
Fat: 1.5

MOCK CHICKEN LEGS

4 servings

Per Serving
Calories: 397
% Calories from fat: 20
Fat (gm): 8.7
Sat. fat (gm): 2.5
Cholesterol (mg): 66.6
Sodium (mg): 140
Protein (gm): 30.7
Carbohydrate (gm): 46.3
Exchanges
Milk: 0.5
Vegetable: 0.0
Fruit: 0.0
Bread: 2.5
Meat: 3.0
Fat: 0.0

12 ounces pork tenderloin, trimmed of visible fat
6 ounces beef sirloin steak, trimmed of visible fat
3 tablespoons all-purpose flour
Vegetable cooking spray
Water
Salt and pepper, to taste
1 1/2 cups Cream Gravy (recipe follows)
3 cups cooked rice, *or* no-yolk noodles, warm

1. Cut meats into 1-inch cubes; assemble on 4 skewers, alternating kinds of meat. Coat meat with flour, let stand at room temperature 15 minutes.

2. Spray medium skillet with cooking spray; heat over medium heat until hot. Cook kabobs over medium to medium-low heat until well browned on all sides, about 10 minutes.

3. Add 1/2 inch water to skillet; heat to boiling. Reduce heat and simmer, covered, until meat is fork tender, 15 to 20 minutes. Remove from skillet; season to taste with salt and pepper. Serve with Cream Gravy on rice or noodles.

Cream Gravy

makes about 2 cups

2 tablespoons margarine
1/4 cup all-purpose flour
2 cups fat-free milk, *or* fat-free half-and-half
1-2 teaspoons chicken bouillon crystals
1/4 cup fat-free sour cream
Salt and pepper, to taste

1. Melt margarine in medium saucepan; stir in flour and cook over medium-low heat 1 minute, stirring constantly. Whisk in milk and bouillon crystals; heat to boiling. Boil, stirring constantly, until thickened, about 1 minute.

2. Stir in sour cream and cook 1 to 2 minutes; season to taste with salt and pepper.

SAUTEED SQUASH WITH SNOW PEAS

4 servings

- Butter-flavored vegetable cooking spray
- 2 green onions and tops, sliced
- 2 cloves garlic, minced
- 2 medium yellow summer squash, sliced
- 2 ounces snow peas, strings trimmed
- 2 tablespoons finely chopped lovage, *or* parsley
- Salt and white pepper, to taste

Per Serving
Calories: 27
% Calories from fat: 10
Fat (gm): 0.3
Sat. fat (gm): 0.1
Cholesterol (mg): 0
Sodium (mg): 2
Protein (gm): 1.4
Carbohydrate (gm): 5.7
Exchanges
Milk: 0.0
Vegetable: 1.0
Fruit: 0.0
Bread: 0.0
Meat: 0.0
Fat: 0.0

1. Spray large skillet with cooking spray; heat over medium heat until hot. Saute green onions and garlic 2 to 3 minutes.

2. Add squash, snow peas, and lovage to skillet; spray with cooking spray and cook over medium heat until vegetables are crisp-tender, about 5 minutes. Season to taste with salt and pepper.

HERBED TOMATO HALVES

4 servings

- 4 medium tomatoes, halved
- 3 tablespoons fat-free grated Parmesan cheese
- 1 tablespoon dry unseasoned bread crumbs
- 1/2 teaspoon dried basil leaves
- 1/2 teaspoon dried marjoram leaves
- 1/2 teaspoon dried thyme leaves
- 1/8-1/4 teaspoon garlic powder
- 2-3 pinches pepper

Per Serving
Calories: 45
% Calories from fat: 9
Fat (gm): 0.5
Sat. fat (gm): 0.1
Cholesterol (mg): 0
Sodium (mg): 60
Protein (gm): 2.8
Carbohydrate (gm): 8.8
Exchanges
Milk: 0.0
Vegetable: 2.0
Fruit: 0.0
Bread: 0.0
Meat: 0.0
Fat: 0.0

1. Place tomatoes in baking pan. Combine remaining ingredients and sprinkle over tomatoes.

2. Bake at 375 degrees until tomatoes are hot and topping is browned, 15 to 20 minutes.

PRALINE SUNDAES

4 servings

- 1/4 cup packed light brown sugar
- 1 1/2 teaspoons cornstarch
- 1/2 cup water
- 1 tablespoon bourbon, *or* brandy, optional
- 1 teaspoon margarine
- 1/2 teaspoon vanilla
- 2 tablespoons chopped pecans
- 1 pint frozen low-fat vanilla yogurt

Per Serving
Calories: 256
% Calories from fat: 20
Fat (gm): 5.7
Sat. fat (gm): 1.9
Cholesterol (mg): 45
Sodium (mg): 72
Protein (gm): 8.3
Carbohydrate (gm): 41.1

Exchanges
Milk: 0.0
Vegetable: 0.0
Fruit: 0.0
Bread: 3.0
Meat: 0.0
Fat: 1.0

1. Mix sugar and cornstarch in small saucepan; stir in water. Heat to boiling over medium heat, stirring constantly until thickened, about 1 minute.

2. Stir in bourbon; cook 10 to 15 seconds. Remove from heat; stir in margarine, vanilla, and pecans. Serve warm over frozen yogurt.

Risotto Repast

Mushroom Bruschetta
Italian Sausage and Broccoli Risotto
Braised Whole Artichokes
Italian Bread
Spiced Orange Compote Biscotti

DO-AHEAD TIPS

1-2 Days in Advance

Make topping for Bruschetta and refrigerate. Make Biscotti (see Index for recipes).

Early in the Day

Make turkey mixture for risotto and steam broccoli; refrigerate. Make Spiced Orange Compote.

45 Minutes Before Serving

Complete risotto. Make Braised Artichokes. Assemble Bruschetta and broil.

Risotto Repast
Mushroom Bruschetta
Italian Sausage and Broccoli Risotto
Braised Whole Artichokes
Italian Bread (1 slice with 1 teaspoon margarine)
Spiced Orange Compote
Biscotti (1 piece)

Per 1 Serving of Entire Menu
Calories: 892
% Calories from fat: 25
Fat (gm): 25.3
Sat. fat (gm): 4.7
Cholesterol (mg): 22.8
Sodium (mg): 883
Protein (gm): 31
Carbohydrate (gm): 147

Exchanges
Milk: 0.0
Vegetable: 3.0
Fruit: 2.0
Bread: 7.0
Meat: 2.0
Fat: 2.0

MUSHROOM BRUSCHETTA

6 servings (2 each)

- Vegetable cooking spray
- 1/2 cup chopped yellow bell pepper
- 2 green onions and tops, thinly sliced
- 2 cloves garlic, minced
- 2 cups chopped portobello, shiitake, *or* white mushrooms
- 1 teaspoon dried basil leaves
- 2-3 tablespoons fat-free grated Parmesan cheese
- Salt and pepper, to taste
- Bruschetta (recipe follows)
- 1/4 cup (1 ounce) shredded low-fat mozzarella cheese

Per Serving
Calories: 136
% Calories from fat: 14
Fat (gm): 6.4
Sat. fat (gm): 0.6
Cholesterol (mg): 1.7
Sodium (mg): 275
Protein (gm): 6.4
Carbohydrate (gm): 22.8
Exchanges
Milk: 0.0
Vegetable: 0.0
Fruit: 0.0
Bread: 1.5
Meat: 0.0
Fat: 0.5

1. Spray medium skillet with cooking spray, heat over medium heat until hot. Saute bell pepper, onions, and garlic 2 to 3 minutes. Add mushrooms; cook, covered, over medium heat until wilted, about 5 minutes. Stir in basil and cook, uncovered, until mushrooms are tender and all liquid is gone, 8 to 10 minutes. Stir in Parmesan cheese; season to taste with salt and pepper.

2. Spoon mushroom mixture on Bruschetta and sprinkle with mozzarella cheese; broil until cheese is melted, 1 to 2 minutes. Serve warm.

Bruschetta

makes 12

- 1/2 loaf French bread (8 ounces)
- Olive oil cooking spray
- 1 clove garlic, cut in half

1. Cut bread into 12 slices; spray both sides of bread lightly with cooking spray. Broil on cookie sheet 4 inches from heat source until browned, 2 to 3 minutes on each side.

2. Rub top sides of bread slices with cut side of garlic.

ITALIAN SAUSAGE AND BROCCOLI RISOTTO

6 servings (about 1 1/2 cups each)

Homemade Italian Sausage (recipe follows)
1 small onion, chopped
2 cloves garlic, minced
1 1/2 cups arborio rice
1 1/2 quarts reduced-sodium fat-free chicken broth
2 cups broccoli florets, steamed
1/2 cup raisins
2 tablespoons grated Parmesan cheese, optional

Per Serving
Calories: 322
% Calories from fat: 16
Fat (gm): 5.6
Sat. fat (gm): 1.3
Cholesterol (mg): 21.1
Sodium (mg): 101
Protein (gm): 14.6
Carbohydrate (gm): 53.4
Exchanges
Milk: 0.0
Vegetable: 1.0
Fruit: 0.5
Bread: 2.5
Meat: 1.0
Fat: 0.5

1. Cook Homemade Italian Sausage in large saucepan until browned, crumbling coarsely with a fork; remove from saucepan, drain, and reserve. Add onion and garlic to saucepan; saute until tender, about 5 minutes. Stir in rice; cook over medium heat until rice is beginning to brown, 2 to 3 minutes, stirring frequently.

2. Heat chicken broth to boiling in medium saucepan; reduce heat to medium-low to keep broth hot. Add broth to rice mixture, 1/2 cup at a time, stirring constantly until broth is absorbed before adding another 1/2 cup. Continue process until rice is al dente, 20 to 25 minutes.

3. Add reserved Homemade Italian Sausage, broccoli, and raisins to risotto mixture during the last 10 minutes of cooking time. Serve in bowls; sprinkle with Parmesan cheese.

Homemade Italian Sausage

makes 12 ounces

12 ounces ground turkey
1 teaspoon fennel seeds, crushed
1 teaspoon dried sage leaves
1 teaspoon dried thyme leaves
1/2 teaspoon dried oregano leaves
1/4 teaspoon ground allspice
1/8 teaspoon ground mace
1/2 teaspoon salt, optional

1. Mix all ingredients; refrigerate, covered, several hours for flavors to blend.

BRAISED WHOLE ARTICHOKES

6 servings

- 6 medium artichokes
- Salt, to taste
- 3-6 teaspoons extra-virgin olive oil

Per Serving
Calories: 80
% Calories from fat: 24
Fat (gm): 2.4
Sat. fat (gm): 0.3
Cholesterol (mg): 0
Sodium (mg): 114
Protein (gm): 4.2
Carbohydrate (gm): 13.4

Exchanges
Milk: 0.0
Vegetable: 2.0
Fruit: 0.0
Bread: 0.0
Meat: 0.0
Fat: 0.5

1. Cut 1 inch from tops of artichokes and trim off stems. Place artichokes in medium saucepan and sprinkle lightly with salt; add 1 inch water. Heat to boiling; reduce heat and simmer, covered, until artichokes are tender (bottom leaves will pull out easily).

2. Remove artichokes from pan; discard any remaining water. Holding artichokes with a towel or hot pad, brush bottom of each with olive oil; return to saucepan. Cook, uncovered, over medium to medium-low heat until bottoms of artichokes are deeply browned, 10 to 15 minutes.

SPICED ORANGE COMPOTE

6 servings

- 5 oranges, peeled, sliced
- 1/3 cup orange juice
- 3 tablespoons packed light brown sugar
- 2-3 tablespoons orange-flavored liqueur, optional
- 4 whole allspice
- 1 cinnamon stick
- Mint sprigs, for garnish

Per Serving
Calories: 99
% Calories from fat: 1
Fat (gm): 0.1
Sat. fat (gm): 0
Cholesterol (mg): 0
Sodium (mg): 3
Protein (gm): 1.1
Carbohydrate (gm): 22.4

Exchanges
Milk: 0.0
Vegetable: 0.0
Fruit: 1.3
Bread: 0.0
Meat: 0.0
Fat: 0.0

1. Place orange slices in shallow glass bowl. Mix orange juice, brown sugar, orange liqueur, allspice, and cinnamon in small saucepan. Heat just to boiling; pour over orange slices. Refrigerate, covered, 8 hours or overnight for flavors to blend. Garnish with mint.

Elegant Evening

Steak Diane
Steamed New Potatoes
Mushrooms with Sour Cream
Warm Spinach Salad
Sourdough Bread
Raspberry-Glazed Blueberry Tart

DO-AHEAD TIPS

1 Day in Advance
Make and bake pie crust for the tart; store, covered, at room temperature.

Early in the Day
Clean spinach and assemble salad ingredients. Complete Raspberry-Glazed Blueberry Tart. Clean and slice mushrooms, discarding tough stems.

30 Minutes Before Serving
Make Mushrooms with Sour Cream. Make Steak Diane. Complete Spinach Salad. Steam potatoes.

Elegant Evening
Steak Diane
Steamed New Potatoes (1/2 cup)
Mushrooms with Sour Cream
Warm Spinach Salad
Sourdough Bread (1 slice with 1 teaspoon margarine)
Raspberry-Glazed Blueberry Tart

Per 1 Serving of Entire Menu
Calories: 725
% Calories from fat: 18
Fat (gm): 14.5
Sat. fat (gm): 3.8
Cholesterol (mg): 102
Sodium (mg): 780
Protein (gm): 40.2
Carbohydrate (gm): 72.7

Exchanges
Milk: 0.0
Vegetable: 4.0
Fruit: 1.0
Bread: 3.0
Meat: 4.0
Fat: 1.0

STEAK DIANE

4 servings

Vegetable cooking spray
4 beef eye of round steaks (4 ounces each), visible fat trimmed
Salt and pepper, to taste
1/3 cup brandy, *or* beef broth
14 cup fat-free sour cream
Finely chopped chives, *or* parsley, for garnish

Per Serving
Calories: 212
% Calories from fat: 20
Fat (gm): 4.5
Sat. fat (gm): 1.6
Cholesterol (mg): 64
Sodium (mg): 68
Protein (gm): 27.7
Carbohydrate (gm): 21.1
Exchanges
Milk: 0.0
Vegetable: 0.0
Fruit: 0.0
Bread: 0.0
Meat: 3.5
Fat: 0.0

1. Spray medium skillet with cooking spray; heat over medium to medium-high heat until hot. Add steaks to skillet and cook over medium heat to desired degree of doneness, 3 to 4 minutes on each side for medium. Season steaks lightly with salt and pepper; arrange on serving plates.
2. Add brandy, to skillet heat to boiling. Boil, scraping bottom of skillet to loosen cooked particles. Boil until reduced to about 2 tablespoons, 2 to 3 minutes; stir in sour cream and cook over low heat 1 to 2 minutes. Spoon sauce over steaks; sprinkle with chives.

MUSHROOMS WITH SOUR CREAM

4 servings

Butter-flavored vegetable cooking spray
12 ounces shiitake, *or* cremini, mushrooms, tough stems discarded, sliced
1/4 cup finely chopped onion
1 teaspoon minced garlic
1/4 cup dry white wine, *or* low-sodium vegetable broth
1/4 teaspoon dried thyme leaves
1/2 cup fat-free sour cream
Salt and cayenne pepper, to taste

Per Serving
Calories: 80
% Calories from fat: 2
Fat (gm): 0.2
Sat. fat (gm): 0.1
Cholesterol (mg): 0
Sodium (mg): 24
Protein (gm): 3.5
Carbohydrate (gm): 16.5
Exchanges
Milk: 0.0
Vegetable: 2.0
Fruit: 0.0
Bread: 0.5
Meat: 0.0
Fat: 0.0

1. Spray large skillet with cooking spray; heat over medium heat until hot. Add mushrooms, onion, and garlic to skillet; spray with cooking spray and saute 3 to 4 minutes.

2. Add wine and thyme to skillet, heat to boiling. Reduce heat and simmer, covered, until mushrooms are very tender, 8 to 10 minutes. Cook, uncovered, on low heat until mushrooms are dry and well browned, 20 to 25 minutes. Stir in sour cream; season to taste with salt and cayenne pepper.

WARM SPINACH SALAD

4 servings

- 1 package (10 ounces) salad spinach, rinsed, dried
- 4 green onions and tops, sliced
- 4 slices bacon, fried crisp, well drained, crumbled
- 2 hard-cooked eggs, chopped
- 1 cup fat-free bottled French, *or* sweet sour, salad dressing
- Salt and pepper, to taste

Per Serving
Calories: 95
% Calories from fat: 26
Fat (gm): 2.6
Sat. fat (gm): 0.8
Cholesterol (mg): 38.2
Sodium (mg): 418
Protein (gm): 3.4
Carbohydrate (gm): 12.6
Exchanges
Milk: 0.0
Vegetable: 1.0
Fruit: 0.0
Bread: 0.5
Meat: 0.0
Fat: 0.5

1. Combine spinach, onions, bacon, and eggs in salad bowl. Heat French dressing to boiling in small saucepan; immediately pour over salad and toss. Season to taste with salt and pepper.

RASPBERRY-GLAZED BLUEBERRY TART

8 servings

Basic Pie Crust (see p. 574)
1 tablespoon sugar
4 cups fresh blueberries
3/4 cup raspberry spreadable fruit
1 tablespoon raspberry-flavored liqueur, optional
2 teaspoons cornstarch
1/4 teaspoon ground cinnamon
1/4 teaspoon ground nutmeg

Per Serving
Calories: 169
% Calories from fat: 13
Fat (gm): 2.6
Sat. fat (gm): 0.4
Cholesterol (mg): 0
Sodium (mg): 70
Protein (gm): 2
Carbohydrate (gm): 13
Exchanges
Milk: 0.0
Vegetable: 0.0
Fruit: 1.0
Bread: 1.0
Meat: 0.0
Fat: 0.5

1. Prepare pie crust, adding 1 tablespoon sugar to recipe and using 9-inch tart pan. Line pastry with weights, and bake at 425 degrees until light brown, 10 to 12 minutes; remove weights and bake until golden, about 10 minutes longer. Cool on wire rack.

2. Arrange blueberries in cooled crust. Combine spreadable fruit, liqueur, cornstarch, cinnamon, and nutmeg in small saucepan. Heat to boiling, stirring constantly. Remove from heat and spoon over blueberries. Refrigerate tart until glaze is slightly firm, about 30 minutes.

Celebration Menu

Shrimp de Jonghe
Warm Rice
Herb-Crumbed Broccoli
Steamed Baby Carrots
Romaine Salad with Lemon-Garlic Dressing
Italian Bread
Lemon Meringue Cheesecake

DO-AHEAD TIPS

1 Day in Advance
Make cheesecake.

Early in the Day
Make croutons, clean lettuce, and make dressing for salad. Clean broccoli.

30 Minutes Before Serving
Make Shrimp de Jonghe. Cook rice. Make Herb-Crumbed Broccoli. Steam carrots. Complete salad.

Celbration Menu
Shrimp de Jonghe
Warm Rice (1/2 cup)
Herb-Crumbed Broccoli
Steamed Baby Carrots (1/2 cup)
Romaine Salad with Lemon-Garlic Dressing
Italian Bread (1 slice with 1 teaspoon margarine)
Lemon Meringue Cheesecake

Per 1 Serving of Entire Menu
Calories: 1169
% Calories from fat: 22
Fat (gm): 28.4
Sat. fat (gm): 5.3
Cholesterol (mg): 140
Sodium (mg): 1498
Protein (gm): 55.9
Carbohydrate (gm): 168

Exchanges
Milk: 0.0
Vegetable: 2.0
Fruit: 0.0
Bread: 9.0
Meat: 5.0
Fat: 2.0

SHRIMP DE JONGHE

4 servings

- 2 tablespoons finely chopped shallots, *or* onion
- 4 cloves garlic, minced
- 3 tablespoons margarine
- 2 tablespoons dry sherry, optional
- 1 tablespoon lemon juice
- 1/4 teaspoon dried marjoram leaves
- 1/4 teaspoon dried tarragon leaves
- Pinch ground nutmeg
- Pinch cayenne pepper
- 1 cup fresh white bread crumbs
- 1/4 cup finely chopped parsley
- Salt and pepper, to taste
- 1 pound shrimp, peeled, deveined

Per Serving
Calories: 370
% Calories from fat: 27
Fat (gm): 10.8
Sat. fat (gm): 2.1
Cholesterol (mg): 129.1
Sodium (mg): 287
Protein (gm): 22
Carbohydrate (gm): 42.8
Exchanges
Milk: 0.0
Vegetable: 1.0
Fruit: 0.0
Bread: 2.5
Meat: 2.0
Fat: 1.0

1. Saute shallots and garlic in margarine in medium skillet until tender, 2 to 3 minutes. Stir in sherry, lemon juice, marjoram, tarragon, nutmeg, and cayenne. Pour mixture over bread crumbs and parsley in bowl and toss. Season to taste with salt and pepper.

2. Arrange shrimp in single layer in shell dishes or 10 x 7inch baking dish; top with crumb mixture. Bake at 450 degrees until shrimp are cooked, about 10 minutes.

HERB-CRUMBED BROCCOLI

4 servings

- Butter-flavored vegetable cooking spray
- 2-4 tablespoons chopped pecans
- 1/4 cup dry unseasoned bread crumbs
- 1/2 teaspoon dried marjoram leaves
- 1/4 teaspoon dried chervil leaves
- 2 tablespoons finely chopped parsley
- 1 1/2 pounds broccoli, cut into florets and sliced stalks, cooked
- Salt and pepper, to taste

Per Serving
Calories: 92
% Calories from fat: 28
Fat (gm): 3.2
Sat. fat (gm): 0.3
Cholesterol (mg): 0
Sodium (mg): 96
Protein (gm): 5.6
Carbohydrate (gm): 13.1
Exchanges
Milk: 0.0
Vegetable: 2.4
Fruit: 0.0
Bread: 0.0
Meat: 0.0
Fat: 0.8

1. Spray small skillet with cooking spray; heat over medium heat until hot. Add pecans and spray with cooking spray; cook over medium heat until toasted, 2 to 3 minutes, stirring frequently. Add bread crumbs, marjoram, and chervil to skillet; cook until crumbs are toasted, 3 to 4 minutes, stirring frequently. Remove from heat and stir in parsley.

2. Season broccoli with salt and pepper to taste; arrange in serving bowl. Spoon crumb mixture over broccoli.

ROMAINE SALAD WITH LEMON-GARLIC DRESSING

4 servings

- 4 thick slices French, *or* Italian, bread
- 1 clove garlic, cut in half
- 6 cups torn Romaine lettuce
- 2 tablespoons lemon juice
- 2 tablespoons real egg substitute
- 1 tablespoon olive oil
- 1/2 teaspoon Worcestershire sauce
- 2 tablespoons grated fat-free Parmesan cheese
- 1/8 teaspoon dry mustard
- Dash red pepper sauce
- Freshly ground pepper, to taste

Per Serving
Calories: 127
% Calories from fat: 30
Fat (gm): 4.4
Sat. fat (gm): 0.6
Cholesterol (mg): 0
Sodium (mg): 200
Protein (gm): 5.3
Carbohydrate (gm): 17.1
Exchanges
Milk: 0.0
Vegetable: 1.0
Fruit: 0.0
Bread: 1.0
Meat: 0.0
Fat: 0.5

1. Rub both sides of bread slices with cut side of garlic; mince remaining garlic and reserve. Cut bread into 1/2- to 3/4-inch cubes. Bake on jelly roll pan at 425 degrees until toasted, about 5 minutes.

2. Place lettuce in salad bowl. Beat together lemon juice, reserved garlic, and remaining ingredients, except croutons and pepper. Pour dressing over lettuce and toss; season to taste with pepper. Add croutons and toss.

Note: As eating raw egg is not recommended, the recipe includes real egg substitute, which is pasteurized and safe to eat.

LEMON MERINGUE CHEESECAKE

8 servings

Basic Pie Crust (see p. 574)
- 3 packages (8 ounces each) fat-free cream cheese, softened
- 4 egg yolks
- 2/3 cup lemon juice
- 2 tablespoons flour
- 1 cup sugar
- 1/3 cup cornstarch
- 2/3 cup water
- 2 teaspoons grated lemon rind
- 4 egg whites
- 1/4 teaspoon cream of tartar
- 1/3 cup powdered sugar

Per Serving
Calories: 336
% Calories from fat: 13
Fat (gm): 4.9
Sat. fat (gm): 1.2
Cholesterol (mg): 121
Sodium (mg): 661
Protein (gm): 17.4
Carbohydrate (gm): 53.1
Exchanges
Milk: 0.0
Vegetable: 0.0
Fruit: 0.0
Bread: 3.8
Meat: 1.5
Fat: 0.0

1. Prepare pie crust, using 9-inch pie pan. Line pastry with weights and bake at 425 degrees until light brown, 10 to 12 minutes; remove weights and bake until golden, about 10 minutes longer. Cool on wire rack.

2. Beat cream cheese and egg yolks in medium bowl until smooth; beat in lemon juice and flour.

3. Mix sugar and cornstarch in medium saucepan; stir in lemon rind. Cook over medium heat, stirring constantly until mixture thickens and boils; boil 1 minute, stirring constantly. Remove from heat. Gradually stir in cheese mixture, mixing until completely blended. Pour hot mixture into prepared crust.

4. Beat egg whites and cream of tartar in large bowl until foamy. Gradually beat in powdered sugar, beating to stiff but not dry peaks. Spread meringue over top of pie, sealing it to edge of crust. Bake at 425 degrees until meringue is golden, about 10 minutes. Cool to room temperature on wire rack; refrigerate at least 4 hours before serving.

INDEX

P